Ted Shawn

Ted Shawn

His Life, Writings, and Dances

PAUL A. SCOLIERI

OXFORD
UNIVERSITY PRESS

OXFORD
UNIVERSITY PRESS

Oxford University Press is a department of the University of Oxford. It furthers
the University's objective of excellence in research, scholarship, and education
by publishing worldwide. Oxford is a registered trade mark of Oxford University
Press in the UK and certain other countries.

Published in the United States of America by Oxford University Press
198 Madison Avenue, New York, NY 10016, United States of America.

© Paul A. Scolieri 2020

Library of Congress Cataloging-in-Publication Data
Names: Scolieri, Paul A., author.
Title: Ted Shawn : his life, writings, and dances / Paul A. Scolieri.
Description: New York : Oxford University Press, [2019] |
Includes bibliographical references and index.
Identifiers: LCCN 2019002170 (print) | LCCN 2019018280 (ebook) |
ISBN 9780199331086 (updf) | ISBN 9780199331093 (epub) |
ISBN 9780190050580 (oso) | ISBN 9780199331062 (cloth : alk. paper)
Subjects: LCSH: Shawn, Ted, 1891–1972. | Dancers—United States—Biography. |
Choreographers—United States—Biography. | Modern dance—United States—History.
Classification: LCC GV1785.S5 (ebook) | LCC GV1785.S5 S46 2019 (print) | DDC 792.8092 [B]—dc23
LC record available at https://lccn.loc.gov/2019002170

1 3 5 7 9 8 6 4 2

Printed by Sheridan Books, Inc., United States of America

For my daughters—Valerie, Emilia, and Louisa.

Contents

List of Images

Acknowledgments

Ted Shawn was nothing if not gracious. Becoming America's foremost male dancer meant accepting favors from people across the spectrum of the theatrical world—from devoted students and supportive patrons, to compassionate critics and sympathetic stagehands—none of whom he ever forgot. Shawn was meticulous with paying debts, often conveying his gratitude in handwritten letters and autographed headshots or complimentary tickets and elaborate compliments. To repay big favors, he would gift crates of oranges or jars of honey shipped from his winter home in Eustis, Florida. In his later years, he sent his inner circle of fans, friends, and supporters personalized acknowledgments scribbled on the back of snapshots of himself in the nude with little more than a strategically placed bouquet of flowers from his garden. Far more inhibited than "Papa" Shawn, I will have to convey my gratitude in ways more modest though no less deeply felt.

Foremost, I thank Norton Owen, Director of Preservation at the Jacob's Pillow Dance Festival, the internationally renowned center that Ted Shawn founded in the Berkshire Hills in the 1930s. Simply put, this book would not exist without Norton. For over thirty years, he has scrupulously developed and maintained the archives, making research into the legacy of Ted Shawn and Jacob's Pillow possible. Since the moment I first considered writing this biography, Norton has unsparingly shared his expertise, guidance, and encouragement with me, and inspired me throughout the process through his own writings, exhibits (physical and virtual), programming, and lectures, that enliven dance history in imaginative and meaningful ways. For the benefit of his generosity and exuberance, I hereby convey my deepest thanks to Norton.

I also thank some very important people who shared with me their personal memories of Ted Shawn: Forrest Coggan, Jeannette Roosevelt, former Pillow faculty member Ann Hutchinson Guest, Shawn's publicist and friend Larry Humphries, and sisters Joanna ("Jo") Humphrey and Shirley Miller, who vividly conveyed their childhood memories attending some of the events described in this book, including the opening night of the Ted Shawn Theater in 1942, which their father architect Joseph Franz designed.

I must also acknowledge the kindness of Ella Baff and Pam Tatge, respectively, the former and current Artistic and Executive Directors of Jacob's Pillow, who have always treated me like a member of the Pillow family. I am also grateful for the many probing conversations I enjoyed at the Pillow—many at the picnic tables beside the boulder for which the "Jacob's Pillow" property is named. I must mention some of these inspiring interlocutors by name: Maura Keefe, Suzanne Carboneau, Nancy Wozny, Adam Weinert, and Patsy Gay.

One of Shawn's proudest decisions was to entrust his vast personal collection of letters, scrapbooks, photographs, motion pictures, and diaries to Genevieve "Gegi" Oswald, the founding curator of the Dance Collection or what is now the Jerome Robbins Dance Division of the New York Public Library, the world's largest and most comprehensive archive for dance research. I thank the visionary Gegi for her many enduring contributions to the field of dance, and more personally, for sharing with me her fond memories of Shawn and her excitement about my research.

Shawn would be delighted to know that his papers are in the exquisite care of the current staff at the Jerome Robbins Dance Division. For years of providing expert advice with uncommon collegiality and grace, I thank Curator Linda Murray, Tanisha Jones, Danielle Castronovo, Arlene Yu, Daisy Pommer, Alice Standin, Kathleen Leary, Cassie Mey, and Phil Karg. Thanks especially to Jennifer Eberhardt who provided endless assistance with accessing the materials as well as a translation that appears in this book!

I completed additional research at the Theatre Collection of the Houghton Library, Harvard University, where in 2011–12, I was awarded a Joan Nordell Fellowship. Some of this book's most vital lines of inquiry are based on research I conducted there. I am grateful for that extraordinary opportunity as well as for the special permission to reprint some of the gorgeous photographs from the John Lindquist Collection.

In 2014–15, I was awarded the Frederick Burkhardt Fellowship from the American Council of Learned Society, which enabled me to be in residence at the Library of Congress. I thank the staffs at the John W. Kluge Center, the Performing Arts Reading Room, and the Motion Picture and Television Reading Room for help with discovering new levels and directions for investigating Shawn's world.

I also conducted research at several other archives to which I am indebted: the Kinsey Institute for Sex Research at Indiana University; the National Portrait Gallery, Smithsonian Institution; the Archives and the

Celeste Bartos International Film Study Center at the Museum of Modern Art (MoMA); the Archives at Hampton University; the Beinecke Rare Book and Manuscript Library at Yale University, especially Susan Brady; the Carson Brierly Giffin Dance Library at the University of Denver; the Charles E. Young Research Library at UCLA, especially Genie Guerard, Manuscripts Curator; Julie Tarmy, Director of the Nahant Historical Society; the H. J. Lutcher Stark Center for Physical Culture and Sports, University of Texas at Austin, especially Cindy Slater; and Professor Tricia Henry Young who made it possible for me to inspect many original costumes and props in the Florida State University Killinger Collection.

For providing special permissions to reprint images and text in this book, I wish to recognize the generosity of Roy Freeman, Craig Highberger, and Camilla Titcomb.

I also wish to acknowledge some of the many colleagues who offered inspiration, support, and information: Ninotchka Bennahum, Karen Bradley, Helene Breazeale, Yvette Christiansë, Michelle Clayton, Pamela Cobrin, Lynne Conner, Joanna Dee Das, Julia Foulkes, Lynn Garafola, Kim F. Hall, Susan Jones, Deborah Jowitt, Jennie Kassanoff, Jonathan Ned Katz, Charles Kaufmann, Elizabeth Kendall, Rebekah Kowal, Matthew McKelway, Susan Manning, Lynn Matluck-Brooks, José Moya, Diane Roe, Mary Simonson, Jim Steichen, Robin Veder, Megan Wacha, and Bill Worthen. Here I also include my colleagues at Barnard College and Columbia University, as well as my many brilliant students, especially Rebecca Bass and Laura Quinton, who helped with researching various parts of this book.

Shawn wrote a memoir that he considered a major disappointment in large measure because he never found the right editor. I am fortunate to have had the thoughtful and steady guidance of Norm Hirschy, my editor at Oxford University Press, whom I thank profusely.

I thank all my family and friends, especially my parents for their unfailing support and Rita Tsividakis for her loving presence in my family's life. And finally, I thank Lavinel, who for the past twenty-five years has been my rock, *my* Pillow.

Abbreviations in Notes

BMP   Barton Mumaw Papers, c. 1930–60. *2004MT-66. Houghton Library, Harvard University.

DS   Denishawn Collection Scrapbooks: Clippings, Announcements, and Programs, vols. 1–34. *MGZRS. Jerome Robbins Dance Division, New York Public Library.

FHP   Fern Helscher Papers. (S) *MGZMD 191. Jerome Robbins Dance Division, New York Public Library.

JDC   John Dougherty Collection. *MGZMD 137. Jerome Robbins Dance Division, New York Public Library.

JEMC   Joseph E. Marks Collection relating to Ted Shawn and Jacob's Pillow, 1913–79. *2004MT-31. Harvard Theater Collection, Harvard University.

JLC   John Lindquist Collection, 1910–85. MS Thr 482. Harvard Theatre Collection, Houghton Library, Harvard University.

JPA   Jacob's Pillow Dance Festival Archives.

JPS   Jacob's Pillow Dance Festival Scrapbooks: Clippings, Programs, and Announcements. *MGZRS (Jacob's Pillow Dance Festival). Jerome Robbins Dance Division, New York Public Library.

JSP   Jane Sherman Papers, 1922–2004. (S)*MGZMD 193. Jerome Robbins Dance Division, New York Public Library.

KSDP   Katherine S. Dreier Papers/Société Anonyme Archive. YCAL MSS 101. Yale Collection of American Literature, Beinecke Rare Book and Manuscript Library, Yale University.

LPN   Lucien Price Notebooks and Correspondence, 1901–64. MS Am 2033. Houghton Library, Harvard University.

Newsletter   Ted Shawn's Annual Newsletters, 1945–71. Jacob's Pillow Dance Festival Archives.

OTONS   Ted Shawn. *One Thousand and One Night Stands*. Rev. ed. New York: Da Capo Press, 1979; originally published New York: Doubleday, 1960.

Reminiscences   *Reminiscences: From Childhood to the Dissolution of Denishawn.* Ted Shawn, interview by John Dougherty, January 11–30, 1969, sound recording and transcript. *MGZTL 4-69. Jerome Robbins Dance Division, New York Public Library.

RSD   Ruth St. Denis Papers. Collection 1031. UCLA Library Special Collections, Charles E. Young Research Library, UCLA.

RSDL   Ruth St. Denis Letters, c. 1914–59. (S) *MGZMC–Res. 32. Jerome
                Robbins Dance Division, New York Public Library.
RSDP   Ruth St. Denis Papers, c. 1915–58. (S) *MGZMD 6. Jerome Robbins
                Dance Division, New York Public Library.
TSBM   Ted Shawn Letters to Barton Mumaw 1940–71. (S) * MGZMD 126.
                Jerome Robbins Dance Division, New York Public Library.
TSC   Ted Shawn Collection. (S) *MGZMC-Res. 31. Jerome Robbins Dance
                Division, New York Public Library.
TSP   Ted Shawn Papers. (S)*MGZMD 133. Jerome Robbins Dance Division,
                New York Public Library.
TSPA   Ted Shawn Papers, Additions. (S) *MGZMD 419. Jerome Robbins
                Dance Division, New York Public Library.
UNPUB   Ted Shawn. Unpublished manuscript of Ted Shawn's Autobiography
                (*One Thousand and One Night Stands*). Jacob's Pillow Archives (Part I);
                Ted Shawn Collection [(S) *MGZMC-Res. 31; III, f. 613–622], Jerome
                Robbins Dance Division, New York Public Library, Parts II–X.

Chronology

1891   Edwin "Ted" Shawn is born (October 21)

1909   Is hospitalized with diphtheria

1912   Moves to Los Angeles

1913   Films *Dances of the Ages* for the Thomas A. Edison Company

1914   Marries Ruth St. Denis

1915   Opens First Denishawn School in Los Angeles

1917   Arrives at Camp Kearny

1920   Opens Ted Shawn Studio in Los Angeles (April 6)

1920   Publishes *Ruth St. Denis: Pioneer and Prophet*

1921   Concludes first solo tour at Apollo Theater in New York City (December 2)

1922   Opens Denishawn School at Chatsworth Hotel in New York City
       (February 1)

1922   Denishawn launches first Mayer Tour (October 2)

1923   Shawn travels through Spain and North Africa (April–June)

1925   Tours throughout Asia with Denishawn (August 1925–November 1926)

1926   Shawn publishes *The American Ballet*

1927   Denishawn performs four sold-out performances at Carnegie Hall
       (April 4–6)

1929   Publishes *Gods Who Dance*

1930   Shawn premieres in *Orpheus Dionysos* in Third German Dance Congress,
       Munich (June 22)

1933   Presents first all-male concert at Boston's Repertory Theatre (March 21)

1933   Launches first tour of Ted Shawn and His Men Dancers

1939   Final concert of Ted Shawn and His Men Dancers (May 7)

1942   Theater at Jacob's Pillow (later, Ted Shawn Theatre) built

1944   Publishes *How Beautiful upon the Mountain*

1946   Shawn takes sabbatical in Australia (March–August)

1946   Publishes *Dance We Must*

1947   Shawn returns to Jacob's Pillow

1954   Publishes *Every Little Movement*

1958   Shawn is knighted "Balletens Ridder" by His Majesty Frederick VIII of
        Denmark
1959   Publishes *Thirty-Three Years in American Dance*
1960   Publishes *One Thousand and One Night Stands*
1964   Celebrates his Golden Wedding Anniversary to Ruth St. Denis
1970   Is honored with *Dance Magazine* Award
1972   Ted Shawn dies in Florida (January 9)

Introduction: Firsts and Foremost

Ted Shawn (1891–1972) was the self-proclaimed "Father of American Dance," a title he repeatedly justified by enumerating his many accomplishments in the field as a series of "firsts." Foremost, Shawn was the first internationally prominent male interpretive dancer in the United States. Though there were professional male dancers in Shawn's day, he dedicated his life to creating the notion that an American man dancer could be a professional theatrical dance artist outside the world of ballet. Through his writing and choreography he dramatically transformed the principles, practices, and perceptions of dance from a popular entertainment into a theatrical art. In the process, he made dancing an acceptable profession for men. Between 1915 and 1930, along with his wife and dance partner, the international dance legend Ruth St. Denis (1879–1968), he founded and directed Denishawn, the first modern dance company and school in the United States. He stewarded the company's trailblazing domestic and international tours, including the first ever tour of an American dance company in Asia in 1925–26. Through Denishawn, he taught several generations of dancers and dance teachers who flocked to Denishawn schools in New York and Los Angeles or to one of its satellites across the United States. A few of his students went on to become legendary choreographers and performers in their own right, most notably his protégées Martha Graham, Jack Cole, Louise Brooks, Doris Humphrey, and Charles Weidman. Shawn also choreographed the first "all-dance film" for the Thomas Edison Company in 1913 as well as the first full-length modern dance in 1937. Between 1933 and 1940, he directed the first all-male dance company, Ted Shawn and His Men Dancers, which performed over 1,250 performances in 750 cities and four countries. The company was headquartered at Jacob's Pillow, a farm in the Berkshires of Massachusetts that Shawn transformed into an international dance festival and home of the first American theater dedicated to the presentation of dance. In 2003, the Jacob's Pillow Dance Festival was declared a National Historic Landmark, and in 2011, it became the first dance-presenting organization to receive a National Medal of the Arts. Shawn was also the first prominent American

Ted Shawn. Paul A. Scolieri, Oxford University Press (2020). © Paul A. Scolieri.
DOI: 10.1093/oso/9780199331062.001.0001

choreographer to publish widely on the subject of dance, writing nine books and hundreds of articles and editorials, all intent on establishing dance as an independent theatrical art.

Affectionately known as "Papa" Shawn to generations of dancers, he tried for many years and with great frustration to tell the story of his life's work in terms of its social and artistic value but struggled to move beyond reiterating his list of many "firsts." When asked about his greatest contribution to society, Shawn demurred that he lacked "sufficient perspective and detachment to talk impersonally about it."[1] Arguably, what made it difficult for Shawn to tell his story was that he was homosexual, a fact known only within his inner circle of friends and dancers. Unwilling to disturb the meticulously narrated account of his "paternal" exceptionalism, he remained closeted in most of his autobiographical narratives and instead scrupulously archived his journals, correspondence, programs, photographs, and motion pictures of his dances, anticipating that the full significance of his life, writing, and dances would reveal itself in time.

The major objective of this biography is to elucidate a hitherto untold story about the ways that Shawn's sexual identity informed his principles and practices of dance. Although Shawn was married to Ruth St. Denis, and remained so, at least on paper, for the rest his life, he had been aware of his homosexual desires since childhood. His struggle to understand his queerness drove him to pursue relationships with scientists and artists who around the turn of the twentieth century were leading a radical movement to depathologize homosexuality. Shawn was indelibly influenced by these male pioneers of the early gay rights movement, and conversely, their revolutionary ideas about sexuality were shaped by Shawn's choreography.

When Shawn was a young boy, he could never have fathomed that he would be a male dancer, a modern artist, or a homosexual, as none of these concepts had yet to exist. Shawn's life, writings, and dances reveal how these distinctly modern ideas intersect and were mutually constitutive. Making that case means telling Shawn's story anew, against the very version of his life's story that he had perfected throughout over a half-century in the public eye.

"My life is an open book!" Shawn claimed in a high-profile interview with popular sports writer O. B. Keeler.[2] That statement seemed true given the personal access Shawn generously provided anyone with a newspaper column. As it turns out, if his life story was an open book, it was always open only to the same page, which has kept his life, writings, and dances from receiving serious study. Throughout the Denishawn years, Shawn was frequently the

Figure 0.1. Ted Shawn in Practice Clothes, 1945–50. Photo by John Lindquist. Ted Shawn Collection. Courtesy of the Jerome Robbins Dance Division, New York Public Library.

subject of personality profiles and gossip columns in the newspapers, which often repeated three seemingly unrelated yet intersecting stories about his curious life as a dancer: his exceptional path from the ministry to the stage, his crusade to legitimate dancing as a respectable profession for men, and his physical transformation through dancing from a teenager temporarily stricken with paralysis to the ideal of American masculinity. All of these stories had an air of practical implausibility, but they were engrossing nonetheless and almost always accompanied by titillating images of Shawn in various states of undress.

Shawn had not seriously considered writing an autobiography until it became a professional and financial necessity. That time came following the dissolution of Denishawn, when he needed to establish his contributions to the emergence of the American art form of modern dance in order to ensure his next artistic venture, the formation of his Men Dancers company.

To that end, Shawn collaborated with artist and international art impresario Katherine S. Dreier (1877–1952), who along with Marcel Duchamp and Man Ray founded the influential collective Société Anonyme in 1920 in order to champion modern art in America. With an eye toward extending her reach from the gallery to the stage, in 1930, Dreier financed collaborations between Shawn and modern visual artists and lent her vast cultural and economic resources to support Shawn's first European solo tour in 1930. In 1933, she published *Shawn, the Dancer*, a book that was meant to help establish Shawn as a modern artist of international stature, much in the way Dreier had propelled the careers of visual artists, such as Duchamp, Alexander Archipenko, and Wassily Kandinsky. Modeled on art exhibition catalogs, the book includes portraits of Shawn wearing costumes from his most famous solo dances, as well as a catalog of his choreography until that time. Dreier's introductory essay legitimizes Shawn's stature as a serious artist and interpreter of American culture, though it hardly made the case to establish Shawn within international modern art circles, a position Shawn was ambivalent at best about occupying.

Around the same time as the publication of Dreier's book, Miss Emmy Oda Pohl, a physical education teacher in Mississippi and a devotee of Shawn's classes, wrote to him to propose writing his biography. Shawn considered the offer. He wrote to Lucien Price, a confidant in whom Shawn entrusted all literary matters and someone who had already written an influential article about Shawn's all-male dancing enterprise: "I feel a full-length biography now would indicate the termination of a career which I am in no mood to terminate; that if it is to be true and worthwhile, it would have to go into my personal life and emotional relationships, with resulting pain to myself and others concerned."[3] Still, Shawn sent the proposal to Price, tempting him to volunteer to write the biography himself. More than anyone else, Price shared Shawn's vision of dancing as a social experiment that could depathologize homosexuality, especially through ancient Greek philosophy to explain emerging ideas of modern sexuality. Price was one of the first authors of gay fiction in the United States. Shawn undoubtedly wanted someone with Price's sensibility writing about gay lives to handle Shawn's own biography. He baited Price with the prospect of writing his life story: "Can a woman do it anyway?"

Soliciting Price's interest most likely was an exercise in wishful thinking, as it would have been beyond the realm of possibility for Shawn to authorize a biography that revealed the ideas about homosexuality, freedom, and art that were at the center of his conversations and correspondence with Price. The truth would have been devastating to both his legacy and future. However, he experienced the same threat of exposure when he learned that St. Denis, his estranged wife, was working on her own autobiography. With justifiable concerns about her treatment of him and their marriage and the "irreparable damage" it could cause to his life and career, Shawn tried to control the content by various means. He appealed to her through humor ("I hear as how you are writing your autobiography! Is it a case of my having my suitcase packed for instant flight upon publication! That's just a joke—I know I am safe in your hands") and injunction ("I feel strongly as far as I am concerned, that my private life, loves and sexual experience is exclusively my affair—certainly the public has no right to it").[4]

St. Denis promised Shawn that she would give him the chance to review the final manuscript, though he received it the day before it was due to the publisher. He stayed awake until dawn to read it. He was relieved to learn that she honored his request for discretion about his private life, though she conveyed her ambivalence about her reticence: "How is it going to be possible for me to tell the spirit of this strange marriage so that it will not betray the depths and problems of Ted's life—which I am neither competent nor willing to attempt, this being my story and not his—nor unveil my perplexities and sins at the expense of his?"[5] Shawn was upset, however, that St. Denis insisted on revealing her own sexual and romantic peccadilloes for what they inferred about him. "It out Isadoras Isadora," he wrote, referring to the famous dancer Isadora Duncan's *succès de scandale*. In what appeared to be a conciliatory act, St. Denis promised Shawn she would publicly present him with the first inscribed copy at a press junket in New York City before one of his performances with his Men Dancers. That stunt never happened. Instead, Shawn happened upon St. Denis's *An Unfinished Life* (1939) in a bookstore window in Salina, Kansas, where he purchased his own copy.

Following the aftermath of St. Denis's compromising autobiography and the dissolution of his Men Dancers company, Shawn had to protect his otherwise sterling reputation, on which he based his personal and professional survival. Shawn had not only lost goodwill toward him based on his marriage to a beloved stage legend, but he was also losing his position in the dance world as one of its greatest ambassadors. The author of several books on dance, countless articles, editorials, and interviews, Shawn made himself available for any opportunity to talk about dance, dance fads, and dancers. A modern-day dance master, Shawn had a lecture for every topic—from religious dancing through the ages to techniques for dyeing costume fabric. However, Shawn's authority began to wane when in 1927, for the first time, three US newspapers appointed full-time dance critics: Mary Watkins at the *New York Herald Tribune*, John Martin at the *New York Times*, and Lucile Marsh at the *New York World*. This defining moment for American dance was arguably a direct result of Denishawn's historic appearance at Carnegie Hall in 1927, when it became the first dance company to sell out the concert hall for four consecutive performances. By 1940, however, he felt that the critics and other dancer writers were marginalizing his influence and presence, if not dismissing it altogether, in the histories of American modern dance that were taking shape.

In particular, Shawn was convinced that John Martin of the *New York Times* had wielded a "weapon of silence" against him by refusing to review his concerts. Despite Martin's avowed determination to build audiences for modern dance in America, he routinely dismissed Shawn, who reached more and more diverse audiences in the United States and abroad than the choreographers Martin tended to favor. Over the years, Shawn grew resentful over the way the platform and prestige of Martin's appointment at the *Times* eclipsed Shawn's own hard-won authority in the field.

Martin helped to galvanize an audience for modern dance through his reviews, his books, and his involvement in a series of influential lecture-demonstrations at the progressive New School for Social Research (1931–34). In 1933, he published his treatise *The Modern Dance* in which he defines dance modernism in relation to the classicism of ballet and the romanticism of Isadora Duncan. In Martin's conception of modern dance, St. Denis, an Orientalist accent of Romanticism, barely figures, and Shawn, not at all. In *America Dancing: The Background and Personalities of the Modern Dance* (1936), Martin mentions Shawn, but only as a foil to explain the iconoclasm of former Denishawn dancers Martha Graham, Charles Weidman, and Doris Humphrey—or "The Bennington Group," as Martin rebranded them. In 1936, to the detriment of his many other obligations, Shawn seized an opportunity to write a series of twenty-seven editorials for the *Boston Herald*. Published over the span of several months, Shawn raised critical points against Martin's theories of modernism and the accepted truths about the politics of modern dance. In an editorial about the still nascent dance criticism, Shawn laments the lack of "a rich background of dance knowledge or dance experience" among the two unnamed yet entirely well-known full-time dance critics. The unspoken contest for influence between these two closeted gay men made it so that Martin never acknowledged the modernist strains of Shawn's work.

Martin was not the only one to discredit or completely deny Shawn's place in dance history. About his exclusion from Lincoln Kirstein's *Dance, A Short History of Classic Theatrical Dancing* (1935), Shawn vented: "This is the fourth book now. John Martin's book (*Modern Dancing*) doesn't mention me at all—neither does that terrible Virginia Stewart book. The Elizabeth Selden book as you know speaks of Charles Weidman and Ted Shawn as pupils of Ruth St. Denis, and now this one which ignores the whole thing."[6] An oversight by someone with Kirstein's influence in the dance world was embarrassing. Kirstein was the director of American Ballet Caravan, one of the founders of the Harvard Society for Contemporary Art, and editor of the literary magazine *Hound & Horn*.

Shawn seized upon an opportunity for public recognition, ironically, one afforded by Kirstein. In October 1939, Kirstein established the Dance Archives in the new 53rd Street headquarters of the Museum of Modern Art (MoMA). Inspired by the Archives Internationale de la Danse founded by Swedish art collector Rolf de Maré, Kirstein conceived of the Dance Archives as an effort to bolster the reputation of dance as a serious art. He donated his own collection of books and prints to the archives. Other founding contributors were Gordon Craig, the late *Literary Digest* editor Fred King, and Helen Stewart, who donated her collection of Pavloviana. In its first year, the archive amassed 1,700 books (biographies, dictionaries, libretti), 3,000 photographs, 1,600 prints, 900 original drawings, clippings, sculpture, and a modest yet growing number of films. One of the standout items in the collection was a pair of men's shirt studs made of glass andenclosing tiny figures of Fanny Elssler with movable arms and legs.

At the request of Paul Magriel, a dance writer whom Kirstein enlisted to oversee the dance archives, Shawn agreed to donating his Denishawn memorabilia to the archives. Shawn understood the power that an institution like MoMA could bring to enshrining his legacy. More practically, Shawn was eager to find a home for his scrapbooks and photographs. In March 1940, the archives launched a small preview exhibit of its burgeoning collection, followed by a series of exhibitions at MoMA. From October 23 to November 19 that same year, it produced an exhibit featuring the Denishawn Collection as well as another recent acquisition, the Albert Davis Collection of minstrel memorabilia. The exhibit consisted of one long wall dedicated to old minstrel shows; skirt dancers, such as Lydia Thompson; "The Black Crook"; and early

George M. Cohan, ending with Loïe Fuller. An adjacent shorter wall was dedicated to Isadora Duncan. A third, longer wall was divided roughly equally between photos and memorabilia of St. Denis, Shawn, and Denishawn. There were a few images of Shawn's men's group, presumably included at Shawn's insistence. The fourth short wall highlighted Barbara Morgan photographs of Martha Graham, Doris Humphrey, and Charles Weidman.

Shawn wrote that the exhibit made St. Denis and him "feel like historical characters, long dead, to go around the walls of a museum and see ourselves hung as period pieces" and was taken by surprise that an entire wall would be dedicated to contemporary artists, most of whom were his former students.[7] Perhaps more upsetting to Shawn, in his review in the *New York Times*, Martin truncated the title of the exhibit from "American Dance and the Denishawns" to simply "American Dancing." He did not mention Shawn by name, though he referenced Denishawn in relation to the photos of Graham and Humphrey. Beyond misleading, Martin's omissions bordered on unethical.

Shawn had planned to convey his disappointment with the exhibit to Lincoln Kirstein at the opening night reception, but when the two men finally met for the first time, Kirstein immediately disarmed Shawn by profusely apologizing for the unintended slight. Kirstein even humored Shawn's criticism of his book *Dance* (1935), which Shawn faulted for excluding Shawn and St. Denis and failing to acknowledge their "inexpungable mark on the dance in America."[8] Humbly admitting to a limited knowledge of American dance, Kirstein promised to address the oversight in the book's second edition, which he did, though in a fashion that Shawn deemed both incomplete and insincere.

To further appease Shawn, Kirstein also published an essay about Denishawn and its influence on American dance for his journal *Dance Index*. He first commissioned dance critic and former Shawn acolyte Walter Terry to write the article but refused to publish it on account of its devotional tone. He then turned to music critic Baird Hastings who delivered the more sobering, though entirely flattering "The Denishawn Era (1914–1931)." In thirteen pages and a handful of photos, Hastings's essay delivers a brief account of the Denishawn enterprise, focusing on its importance to making dance an independent art in the United States and its undeniable influence on modern dance. Moreover, by departing from the official and somewhat isolationist Denishawn narrative about its origins and influences, Hastings raises some key points about Denishawn's significance to US dance through a series of comparisons to other artists and art movements. Foremost he situates Denishawn's "stylistic catholicism" among other artists of the era, including architects and visual artists Frank Lloyd Wright, Robert Henri, and Stanford White, as well as composers Arthur Foote and H. S. Gilbert. He favorably compares Denishawn to Diaghilev's Ballets Russes in terms of pioneering music for dance ("less organized and ambitious . . . though with more imagination") and places Shawn and Balanchine on the same choreographic plane: "Shawn believed in indigenous dances, Balanchine in American dancers." He even went as far as to credit St. Denis and Shawn for establishing an artistic lineage or a "sequence of creation" among "idiosyncratic followers," noting that the influence of the other recognized founders of modern dance, Isadora Duncan and Loïe Fuller, was more diffuse.[9]

Still, Shawn was displeased with the article and quick to point out several errors. It was published just weeks before the opening of the Ted Shawn Theatre at Jacob's Pillow on July 9, 1942, the first theater in the United States dedicated to presenting dance. With that honor came both a financial and artistic burden—and an increased pressure on Shawn to reestablish his personal and professional stature. To Shawn's further upset, just days after the premiere performance in the Ted Shawn Theatre, Martin highlighted the Kirstein journal in the *New York Times* and Hastings's article in particular, as one of the year's most significant events in dance: "If some of it is controversial, so much the better."[10]

Convinced that no one other than himself would or even could do justice to telling his story, Shawn decided to write an autobiography in 1942. He dedicated himself fully to the process, with mornings at the typewriter and frequent trips to the Dance Archives at MoMA to review his scrapbooks and memorabilia to jog his memory. Writing was a welcomed distraction from missing Barton Mumaw, the star of the Men Dancers company and his lover, who had been drafted into the army and was serving at Keesler Field in Biloxi, Mississippi. To concentrate on finishing a draft, Shawn spent the fall of 1944 at the retreat of his friend Bertha Damon in Alton, New Hampshire. Years later, Shawn admits that Damon, "a brilliant, erudite woman," was his first choice as an editor. He had known Damon since 1919 and she herself was the author of two bestsellers: *A Sense of Humus* and *Grandma Called It Carnal*. When Shawn first asked her to work with him on the book, she replied via a telegram that received censure from Western Union: "Prospect of literary midwifery most attractive. I will be with you." Shawn says Western Union flagged the message for its curious content. Ultimately, Shawn felt that working with Damon was not going to work out, as the two shared too much history, which made it difficult for them to tell his story for a general reader. Shawn left Damon's for his winter home in Eustis, Florida, to continue to write in seclusion.

In his inaugural newsletter to family and friends in 1944 Shawn announced the news about his autobiography, which he effectively made appear to be a decision to appease a relentless literary agent. He promised the book would be centered around the many amusing "anecdotes, adventures, and episodes" he encountered as America's first male dancer. By the time of his announcement, he had already written 250,000 words, covering his career only up to 1927. The following year, he proudly reported that by observing a rigorous schedule of writing, he had completed his manuscript on April 1, 1945. He jokingly called the 650,000-word manuscript "Gone with the Shawn." In his letters to Mumaw, he conveys a far more serious perspective on the process, noting that he was writing against the slow erasure of his legacy in dance.[11]

Shawn anticipated a fall 1945 publishing date, but it would take another fifteen years for the manuscript to become a book. The behemoth work scared off several confidants who promised to help shape it into a book. Following Damon, Price served as a ghostwriter. Then, in 1946, Walter Terry, the dance critic of the *New York Herald Tribune*, who had just returned from an army deployment in Egypt, promised to take on editorial duties. Terry delayed in making the manuscript his priority, so a year later, Shawn began to correspond with dance critic and arts patron Arthur Todd to gauge his interest in taking over the job. Todd cautiously considered the proposal, noting that he could attend to it only on weekends and proposed an exorbitant compensation rate of 75 percent of the royalties. Shawn refused the offer and left the manuscript in Terry's care. Shawn went as far as to encourage his legions of fans and correspondents to write Terry to pressure him into action. Terry held on to the manuscript for over five years without ever fulfilling his promise to edit it. (Decades later, Terry wrote a posthumous biography of Shawn.) Eventually, Terry relinquished the manuscript to Sally Jeter, another friend and former student of Shawn's, who drafted the first three chapters into something that could be circulated to prospective publishers by the end of summer in 1952. The remainder of the manuscript was then turned over to Gray Poole, the wife of Lynn Poole, the reputable press representative at Johns Hopkins University whom Shawn had known since he was a young aspiring dancer. A "top-flight" literary agent named Nanine Joseph took on the job of selling the book (now titled *Dance by the Mile*), made tough on account of Shawn's unrecognizable name, not to mention the lackluster sales surrounding the recently published Fred Astaire memoir. Finally, Joseph sold it to Doubleday, on the condition that the resulting book be about "a great human being and a fantastic personality" that would appeal to general readers ("and not only to dancers and cognoscenti, heaven forbid!"). Poole's task to edit the manuscript into a trade book was monumental, especially as she had to constantly balance Shawn's wishes to develop it as a "memoir" with Doubleday's insistence that she edit it as an "autobiography" (a term Shawn said was "poison"). Shawn did not want to feel obligated to tell the story of his life that autobiography implies nor divulge information that an autobiography requires.

One Thousand and One Night Stands was finally published on October 21, 1960, Shawn's sixty-ninth birthday. Shawn called the twenty-year process to write and publish his autobiography a "sad story" and the final result one of his life's biggest disappointments. He partially blamed the book's failure on the revolving cast of editors and the marketing plan that sold it as an autobiography rather than a "memoir." Ultimately, however, he blamed himself. He felt that the book was compromised by his inability, or at least unwillingness, to be completely truthful about his homosexuality. Shawn indicates as much in a brief disclaimer in the final paragraphs of his extensive draft, acknowledging his many omissions, as well as his disinclination "to discuss inner, psychological matters much more deeply than I have." He conceded: "Perhaps during my lifetime it will be impossible for me to be completely honest and free about many deeply vital phases of my life."[12] Determined to protect his legacy as the "Father of American Dance," he deleted parts of his manuscript, mostly concerning his relationships with men, including a remarkable section of his correspondence with Lucien Price and his wartime letters with his lover Barton Mumaw. When the book was declared "out of print," the publisher burned all remaining copies in stock without even offering Shawn an opportunity to buy them at remainder rates. The thought that copies of his memoir were burned seared his ego. To make up for his upset with *One Thousand and One Night Stands*, Shawn sought opportunities to be more open about his inner life and the social significance of his work. In the summer of 1962, just two years after the publication of his memoir, Shawn wrote to Lucien Price with the idea of publishing their correspondence. A reputable writer at the *Boston Globe* and one of the first US writers to publish gay fiction, Price was still in the midst of unparalleled literary success with his book *Dialogues of Alfred North Whitehead* (1954), a series of interviews with the influential Cambridge philosopher. Shawn thought he and Price could attain similar success by publishing a collection of their correspondence during the seven years of Shawn's Men Dancers company, 1933–1940, of which Price was an honorary member for his unqualified support of the venture from its inception to dissolution. Shawn and Price were convinced that readers would be interested in a chronicle of the great social experiment that was the first and only all-male dance company. They also hoped that their reflections on homosexuality and the arts would reach a gay readership. Shawn proudly claimed that their letters read like "a Platonic dialog about the creative force of homosexuality in the twentieth century."[13] The correspondence was part of Shawn's unedited manuscript, but it was ultimately omitted, along with any other mention of Lucien Price.

In 1963, Shawn invited Price to the Pillow for a long weekend to edit the letters together, with the intent of publishing them in a book called *Seven Magic Years*. Shawn enlisted one of his students, Joseph Marks, to work on the project. Each day Marks read aloud the letters to Shawn. Shawn admitted to welling up with tears while rereading them. "I hope to see this whole correspondence in print while I am still alive!" Unfortunately, Price died in 1964 before the project was ever realized, though they each were deeply moved by the time reflecting on how their genuine friendship allowed them to influence each other's art.

Around the same time, two women earned their doctorates with dissertations about Shawn. Christena Schlundt, a graduate student at the University of California at Los Angeles wrote two extensive chronologies that document the repertory, performance dates, venues, and casts of the major tours during the Denishawn and Men Dancers eras. Betty Poindexter, a graduate student at Texas Women's University (1963), wrote a dissertation on Shawn's career, which he facilitated and closely supervised. These were major contributions to collecting and synthesizing important information about Shawn's professional life, though neither was an appropriate outlet for the story of Shawn's life that he felt he had yet to convey—a story that he increasingly felt burdened to share.

Throughout the 1950s and 1960s, Shawn closely watched as cultural and social views on homosexuality began to change. Foremost, he tracked the impact of the Kinsey Report, to which he had contributed his own sexual history. He followed the career of Lucien Price and his completion of his cycle of fiction novels *All Souls* throughout the 1950s, becoming the most ambitious literary enterprise in gay fiction to date. Through Price, Shawn met Gore

Vidal and followed his work, as well as the 1950 English translation of André Gide's *Corydon*, the Socratic dialogs on homosexuality.

Shawn watched the infamous television broadcast of the 1967 CBS documentary "The Homosexuals" with Mike Wallace. He also keenly followed the career of Rudolf Nureyev and his defection to the West. He saw Nureyev perform with the Chicago Opera Ballet at the Brooklyn Academy of Music in New York. He was disappointed with his actual performance, certain that the hype made it impossible for Nureyev to thrill, but Shawn still watched as Nureyev became an international celebrity with a lifestyle that Shawn must have envied. He followed trends in gay magazines, in tourist books, and in the theater. Shawn wrote to his gay friends about the 1968 play *Boys in the Band*. In the summer of 1969, he read eyewitness reports from a friend who attended the Stonewall Riots and Matachine Society meetings. That same year, he read an article titled "The New Homosexuality" in *Esquire* magazine, an issue to which he contributed an essay, about an entirely unrelated topic, that made him feel "as old fashioned as a lace valentine."[14] Shawn wanted to lay claim to the contribution of his life's work to the rapidly evolving gay liberation movement around him, though he lacked the language and distance to be able to articulate it. Certain that his life's work contributed momentum to these radical movements around him, he once again felt inspired to tell his story. Shawn was determined to conduct an extensive oral history that would complement and emend his "sad" autobiography, a project that in Shawn's mind he could pursue once St. Denis had died.

When St. Denis passed in the summer of 1968, Shawn flew to Los Angeles against the suggestion of doctors and loved ones, who felt the physical and emotional toll would be too much for him, as his emphysema had increasingly made it difficult for him to breathe. It would have been an impossible experience for him were it not for the assistance of John Ellwood Dougherty, a dance critic and educator who had made his professional dance debut with Denishawn in 1929. Dougherty went on to attend the University of Pennsylvania in 1934 and later earned a master's degree in English, on which basis St. Denis, with whom he maintained a relationship, asked him to work with her on her autobiography *An Unfinished Life*. In 1964, he became her personal secretary and manager. Dougherty took exquisite care of "Papa" during his trip to Los Angeles to attend St. Denis's funeral. The two men bonded over their shared loss. Before boarding his return flight, Shawn invited Dougherty to come to his winter home in Eustis, Florida, to conduct interviews with him, just as Dougherty had for St. Denis. Shawn had hoped the interviews would produce fodder for "ten sequels" to *One Thousand One Night Stands*.[15]

Dougherty arrived at Shawn's Eustis home on January 6, 1969. He stayed in the guest cottage Shawn referred to as the "Pout House," where they planned to meet for a series of daily interview sessions until March with the goal of documenting a deeper and more transparent account of Shawn's life and work.[16] Some of the interview questions were drafted by Genevieve "Gegi" Oswald, the founding curator of the Dance Collection at the New York Public Library, who encouraged Shawn to embark on this oral history. To avoid the pitfalls of his first effort at autobiography, Shawn sought a method other than isolating himself to pour memories into a typewriter. Instead, he adopted a process similar to that of his favorite autobiographer, Mark Twain, by extemporaneously recounting anecdotes prompted by personal objects, photos, and books in his archives. His approach to retelling his life story was also informed by the nineteenth-century movement theorist François Delsarte, whose principle of triunity—that meaning emerges in the correspondences between body, mind, and spirit—undergirded Shawn's life-long philosophy of dance education and choreography. When reminiscing about the defining moments and relationships of his life, Shawn paid special attention to the ways his physical, mental, and emotional experiences shaped each other. To facilitate this inquiry, he drew upon his training as a theology student and devised a chart of three columns, an organizational schema he adapted from ancient manuscripts of the Bible that were similarly organized by three columns, each dedicated the Latin, Greek, or Aramaic translation of scripture. Fortunately, he abandoned the idea of employing such a scholastic approach in favor of creating conditions that would allow him the freedom to divulge aspects of his sexual history, just as he had once done to Kinsey scientists. By combining the influences of Twain, Delsarte, the Bible, and Kinsey, Shawn hoped finally to tell his exceptional American story about dance, religion, and sexuality.

During the first few days, Shawn reminisced about his childhood and adolescence, periods of time that he glossed over in *One Thousand and One Night Stands*. While scrutinizing the snapshots, letters, and clippings from his personal papers, Shawn pieced together the defining people, events, and experiences of his life. When talking about his family, his tape-recorded voice sometimes swells with nostalgia; at other times it tightens with sadness, especially when recounting the tragic deaths of both his parents and his older brother. The impact of their deaths registers not only in Shawn's explorations of his search for belonging but also in the accounts of his practical survival. Work is a constant theme in Shawn and Dougherty's conversation, as Shawn was obligated to take on jobs, sometimes several at a time, to help his family make ends meet. Echoing the "rags-to-riches" refrain of a Horatio Alger character, Shawn insisted that he never felt sorry for himself. The skills and confidence he developed through work influenced his ideas about dance as much as anything else, including his early sexual memories.

Shawn's recollections about family and work are braided in these interviews with a hitherto untold account of his sexual awakening. For all of Shawn's onstage exhibitionism, his sexual memories are relatively modest in detail though suggest how his evolving ideas about sex shaped his desire to dance. Shawn spent his career disavowing the presumed homosexuality of the male dancer, yet in his conversations with Dougherty he reflects on how his desire to dance was driven not only by an obsession with male beauty but also by a search for a lost fraternity with his older brother Arnold, who had died when Shawn was just a boy. Shawn often avowed that his "artistic birth" took place the night he first saw Ruth St. Denis perform in 1911. However, his conversations with Dougherty suggest an artistic gestation that was more intimately linked to his formative experiences with family, work, sex, and dance.

The following week's reminiscences center around his relationship to Ruth St. Denis, their sex life, and a hitherto fictionalized account of his 1922 meeting with pioneering eugenicist and sexologist Havelock Ellis in London. Shawn was first aware of Ellis through his groundbreaking six-volume *Studies in the Psychology of Sex* (1897–1910). One of those volumes is *Sexual Inversion* (1897), the first English-language medical textbook on the topic of homosexuality. Written in collaboration with the poet, travel writer, and literary critic and "aesthetic, philosophical Hellenist" J. A. Symonds, *Sexual Inversion* posited that "inversion" is an instinct or "congenital element" as opposed to "acquired"—a critical distinction to the depathologization and decriminalization of homosexuality.[17] Indeed, Ellis's medical explanations for homosexuality were adopted by campaigners for homosexual rights.[18]

Widely deemed obscene, *Sexual Inversion* was banned in most sectors in the United States and abroad. However, Shawn had special access to a copy owned by the Denver Public Library, where Shawn worked. He noticed the book only because its entry in the card catalog had a special symbol to indicate that access to it was restricted on account of its sexual content, which only increased Shawn's determination to read the book, which he did, along with all the other volumes in the library's collection that were restricted for sexual content. Every night for several months Shawn spent three hours reading cutting-edge research in the emerging field of sexology, thus acquiring the "rawest possible picture" of sexuality and sexual difference, as well as progressive ideas about homosexuality, marriage, and the "art of love."[19] Understanding Shawn's sustained engagement with Ellis and other writers such as Edward Carpenter and Walt Whitman offers a new lens through which to view the relationship between Shawn and St. Denis, particularly their commitment to create a modern marriage that, like their choreography, was not limited to heteronormative imperatives.

In addition to co-authoring *Sexual Inversion*, which influenced Shawn's formative ideas about sexuality, Ellis wrote "The Philosophy of Dancing," an article published by the *Atlantic Monthly* in 1914 that later formed the basis of Ellis's book *The Dance of Life* (1923), his most successful publication in the United States. In this article, Ellis argues that dancing and architecture are the two "primary and essential arts."[20] Enraptured by Ellis's serious philosophical inquiry into dance, Shawn became obsessed with Ellis, the scientist who liberated his thinking on matters that most interested him: sexuality and dance. Over the years of their association and correspondence, Shawn refers to Ellis as "St. Havelock," the "Saint of Sex," and "one of the greatest messiahs," and speaks of Ellis's article "The Philosophy of Dancing" as "the dancer's bible."[21]

From the interview with Dougherty, we learn that when Shawn and St. Denis met with Ellis, their conversation was less about high-minded matters of art, an impression that both Shawn and St. Denis conveyed in subsequent years, and more about practical concerns about their troubled marriage—Shawn's homosexuality, St. Denis's infidelities, and their childlessness. Ellis was an ideal person with whom to address these concerns, since he was also in an unconventional and childless marriage. Ellis famously lived apart from his wife Edith, who lived with her female lover. Shawn's candor about his visit with Ellis adjusts the perspective on their marriage from professional mirage to a radical experiment in modern love.

Two weeks into the interview sessions, Shawn addressed the topic of Martha Graham, whose fame and influence had far surpassed his own. He reminisced about her arrival at the Denishawn school in 1916 and their work together on vaudeville tours in the post–World War I years. All told, Shawn clocked more hours on stage with Graham than with any other female dancing partner, including St. Denis. He enumerated the reasons for his frustration with her, her disloyalty to him when she accepted a teaching job that had previously been his own, her flaunting her affair with Denishawn accompanist Louis Horst, thus tarnishing the reputation of the Denishawn brand, and so on. Above all, he could not tolerate the arrows she flung at his choreography. On this topic, Shawn broadens his complaint to include Humphrey and Weidman. More than forty years after he recorded the interview, it is easy to hear that Shawn was still unnerved by the way these three had diminished his life's work as inane play with garlands and veils.

"Before I blow a fuse, I will take a moment's pause," he told Dougherty.

That statement is the last sentence in the transcript. That night, Shawn suffered an embolism, forcing him to discontinue the oral history project with Dougherty but in no way deterring him to seek a way to emend his life's story. Throughout the following years, Shawn reached out to Walter Terry who at the time was writing a posthumous biography of St. Denis and who had already secured a publishing contract for Shawn's. Shawn wanted Terry to visit him in Eustis so he could relay personal details that he dared not commit to a tape recording. Shawn unsuccessfully tried to bait him with "fresh meat" in his imported gay porn magazines.[22]

In 1976, four years after Shawn's death, Terry published his biography *Ted Shawn: Father of American Dance*, which largely makes the case to recognize Shawn as the "Father of American Dance," a designation that Shawn himself proposed close to forty years earlier. In a letter dated January 30, 1938, Shawn berated Terry for a review that celebrated Ruth St. Denis's influence on modern dance yet ignored Shawn's role as the "father of modern dance." Shawn urged Terry to "straighten out" that oversight.[23] Terry did just that in many subsequent reviews for a variety of newspapers, and again in his posthumous biography. Shawn would have been utterly delighted by the title of Terry's biography, less so by some of the unflattering perspectives Terry shares within it.

The biography's preface introduces Shawn as a "New Prometheus"—a modern forethinker. Terry claims to have arrived at the comparison only after "months of self-search and research," though he may have just as easily lifted the idea directly from W. Raymond McClure's biographical tribute to Lucien Price, *Prometheus: A Memoir of Lucien Price* (1965). Terry upholds Shawn as a Titan, though one ultimately bound "by his flaws and inadequacies of a less than perfect dancer's body, less than faultless artistic taste, less than creative genius." [24] Although Terry had the benefit of Shawn's unedited autobiography in his possession for more than twenty-five years, Terry chose instead to paint a condescending and perhaps even retaliatory portrait of Shawn with the interpretation of a psychoanalyst and former Shawn student, Gerry Franklin, who arrived at the idea that St. Denis was "a mother substitute"—a pathologizing explanation that overlooks some of the more compelling questions about the radical artistic and sexual relationship between Shawn and St. Denis.[25]

To be fair, Terry never claimed to have written an unbiased account— or even a reliable one. He took a decidedly anti-intellectual approach to Shawn: "The indexing, appendixing, footnoting scholar does not believe in magic. I could not possibly footnote him. That is a task he left for pedants and scholars."[26] Turning a critical eye away from the massive task before him, Terry overlooked Shawn's vast literary output, his relationships with major figures (Ellis, Price, Kinsey, Dreier, among them), and gives only a passing glance to Shawn's choreography. Though Terry somewhat downplays Shawn's sexuality, no doubt in deference to Shawn's own secrecy about the topic, he does go on the record about it ("He himself, obviously, was bisexual"[27]) and even makes a few cautious remarks about an unnamed male lover who came between St. Denis and Shawn. However, Terry never endeavored to understand Shawn's ideas about sexuality or the way they figured into the way he understood himself and the world.

Describing Terry's effort as "a definitive biography, a masterful evocation of the very being of Ted Shawn," John Dougherty opined, "It seems likely that no future writer will surpass it."[28] Barton Mumaw was not as convinced. He wrote to Jane Sherman, a former Denishawn dancer and author of several books on Denishawn, about Terry's biographies of Shawn and St. Denis: "I don't think Walter really did it for either of them. He has not done the job that needs to be done although he has certainly managed to make a living off Denishawn for all these many years."[29]

Sherman encouraged Mumaw to write his own book about Shawn. Mumaw ultimately decided against it after making a cursory review of Shawn's papers and calculated the emotional cost of revisiting their relationship. He also considered completing *The Seven Magic Years*, the edited volume of letters between Shawn and Price, but after a discussion with an attorney, decided against that idea also. Additionally, he thought too few people would be interested in reading about the accomplishments and obstacles of a touring company, apparently unaware of the deeper significance of the correspondence.

Instead, with Sherman's guidance, Mumaw embarked on writing *Barton Mumaw, Dancer: From Denishawn to Jacob's Pillow and Beyond* (1986). A sensitive but modest reflection on his career that focuses on his relationship with Shawn, the memoir sold about 880 copies in four years. Written during the height of the AIDS pandemic in the United States and the intensified stigma against homosexuality, a topic that infiltrates their letters to one another throughout the process, Sherman and Mumaw went back and forth weighing the risks of being open about Shawn's homosexuality, going as far as to seek legal counsel about possible defamation claims. Sherman sent Mumaw clippings about libel suits and legal definitions of what constitutes a "public figure," trying to determine what they could reasonably reveal without threat of backlash from anyone with a claim to Shawn's life, including the brother of John Christian, Shawn's lover from the latter thirty years of his life. Even Mumaw's lover after Shawn, Marvin Morgenstern, is identified only as "M." in the first edition of the book.

In spring 1983, Mumaw learned from a local book dealer about a book auction at Shawn's Eustis home. Under the impression that most personal items and mementos were already removed, he went anyway to find over 350 people ahead of him on line to register. Mumaw eyed a lot of Denishawn and Men Dancers costumes but was unable to compete with another bidder, Pam Killinger, who recognized the historical value of the costumes and purchased them for $850.[30] When the estate lawyers learned that Mumaw was at the auction, they handed him boxes that Shawn had labeled and set aside for him. Two of those boxes contained the wartime correspondence between him and Shawn. Shawn had included a redacted version of these letters in his unedited manuscript, though they never made it into the final version of his memoir.

Mumaw and Sherman maintained their correspondence until Mumaw's death in 2001, keeping each other abreast of projects, concerts, and publications related to the Denishawn legacy. There was a noticeable uptick in correspondence between them in 1991, most of which concerned their reactions to the recent publication of Agnes de Mille's biography *Martha: The Life and Work of Martha Graham* and Martha Graham's autobiography *Blood Memory*. Both Sherman and Mumaw were disappointed in de Mille's near caricature of Shawn. By all accounts, Shawn's bad behavior did not require exaggeration, but de Mille's treatment often lacks empathy and imagination (to say nothing of accuracy). De Mille had known Shawn since she was a child, as Shawn was friendly with her uncle the great filmmaker Cecil

B. DeMille. She freely admitted her respect for Shawn. She even wrote to him just months before his death to announce her contract with Doubleday to write Graham's biography. She took the opportunity to thank Shawn for his support throughout her career, especially at its beginning. In a draft of her book, she goes as far as to say that she counts herself among those "who owe their careers to his generosity and belief" and describes him as "kind and helpful" and a "discerning and courageous impresario."[31] Apparently, in the intervening years between signing the book contract and publishing the biography, de Mille adopted her subject's attitude toward Shawn.

Indeed, *Blood Memory*, an autobiography attributed to Martha Graham, contains brief yet demeaning references that take aim at Shawn's artistic integrity. In one instance she remarks: "Miss Ruth was a goddess when she danced. Ted was a dancer dressed as a god."[32] The barb starkly contrasts with a sentiment she once expressed in a letter to him: "In my heart you are a god." De Mille similarly discredited Shawn's artistic integrity by calling his technique "distortion."

However justified or sincere Graham's thoughts were on Shawn's life on stage, her damaging statement about Shawn's personal life wreaks of hypocrisy, retaliation, and homophobia. Recalling Shawn's process for recruiting men dancers, she wrote: "They had to send nude pictures of themselves, and God knows what else, which came from all different areas of the country. I thought it was rather horrible. I'd never seen anything like it before in Santa Barbara."[33] There's little doubt that Shawn had volatile romantic escapades with young men during the time he was performing with Graham. It is conceivable, too, that Shawn solicited and received nude photographs of men, though that is hardly grounds for Graham's vitriol concerning Shawn's moral or ethical integrity, especially considering that Graham herself had posed nude for photographers and was having a sexual affair with the married Louis Horst during the period of time in question. Her feigned incredulity reads more like homophobia than moral high ground. De Mille, too, limns a moral universe of extremes in which sexuality is always repudiated. She wrote: "Miss Ruth was a devout Christian Scientist. Ted was an avid hedonist and deep-rooted homosexual."[34] De Mille's understanding of their relationship fails to imagine Shawn's own relation to Christian Science and St. Denis's own hedonism or her homosexuality for that matter.

In her letters to Mumaw, Sherman dismisses Graham's homophobic aspersions, claiming that she herself had never experienced anything Graham describes in Shawn's professional dealings. Admittedly, Sherman best knew Shawn at a different period of his life, when most of his time was spent with St. Denis. However, she and Mumaw exchanged thoughts about the great extent to which Shawn policed his personal life in order to do his creative work. During his Men Dancers years, he had to carefully choreograph his personal life so as to ensure that his homosexuality—and his sexual relationship with Mumaw in particular—did not threaten to unravel his reputation and life's work.

For over a century, the story of Shawn's personal and artistic life has been hampered, denied, repudiated, or otherwise shaped by homophobia. Inasmuch as Shawn was subjected to personal and institutional forms of discrimination, by remaining closeted to protect his own artistic and entrepreneurial enterprise, he himself became a proponent and perhaps even an architect of modern homophobia. In the press, he asserted his version of American masculinity against the likes of the flamboyant expressive dancer Paul Swan and Russian ballet star Vaslav Nijinsky, even though on stage, he imitated some of their most successful roles and styles, barely veiling his own queerness with a muscular physique and well-rehearsed hypermasculinity. Preoccupied with any threat to the idealization of white masculinity, Shawn often extolled the value of the male dancer as hyper-masculine and in the process denigrated male effeminacy, often drawing directly from the rhetoric of various social and religious movements—eugenics, social Darwinism, and muscular Christianity.

For example, in 1938, Shawn sat for a radio interview with balletomane Irving Deakin in which the two men decry the "prejudice against the male dancer" even as they all but repudiate queerness and femininity, lamenting that "the American credo still clung tenaciously to the belief that a male dancer was but another variant of Dorian Gray." Deakin tries to assure his listeners that Shawn is a "native son" then lisps that he is "no St. Petersburg prancer in disguise." Deakin's own homophobia radiates through every thought and anecdote, including his admission that the cracks in his office walls were lined with autographed photos of male dancers, including the object of his "boyhood hero-worship" who became his father-in-law, the ballet star Adolph Bolm.[35]

The narrative around Shawn and St. Denis has largely been dominated by writers determined to protect the secret of Shawn's homosexuality out of an admirable yet somewhat misplaced sense of respect. For example, even years after the death of both St. Denis and Shawn, one writer published an article about the couple's "breakup" based on her examination of St. Denis's personal diaries, which had only recently become accessible at the University of California-Los Angeles (UCLA).[36] Even when confronted with St. Denis's explicit references to Shawn's homosexuality (not to mention St. Denis's own anxieties about her own nonconforming heterosexuality), the writer ultimately published an article that featured diary excerpts focusing on St. Denis's periodic desire to restore their marriage, without ever mentioning the cause for their separation to begin with. For some, it is hard to accept that the "mother" and "father" of American modern dance were queer.

More recent dance scholarship has exposed the queer roots of American modern dance, creating a space to reconsider the received narratives about the dance past.[37] The major objective of this biography is to elucidate a hitherto untold story about the ways that Shawn's ideas about homosexuality informed his principles and practices of dance. For example, one of Shawn's most meaningful relationships was with Havelock Ellis, the British scientist and sex reformer who co-wrote the first English language book about homosexuality. Shawn often told a story that when he was a theology student at the University of Denver he pored over Ellis's multivolume *Studies in the Psychology of Sex* and vowed to one day meet the so-called Saint of Sex. In 1914, Ellis wrote an essay about dance in the *Atlantic Monthly* titled "The Philosophy of Dancing" that examined the art of dance through eugenics—"the art of race betterment." The article fascinated Shawn and prompted him to write Ellis, initiating a correspondence that lasted several years. In 1922, while abroad on tour, Shawn finally met Ellis at his London home. Through Ellis, Shawn gained a deep and prolonged exposure to eugenics, from which Shawn derived a framework and language to legitimize his emerging brand of theatrical dancing. For Shawn, eugenics and dancing were both methods for reproducing ideal bodies.

During the same tour, Shawn met British poet Edward Carpenter, an experience Shawn later described as "the most tremendous human contact" he ever had. Carpenter wrote *Homogenic Love* (1894), a book that gave Shawn the language to name his own same-sex desire for the first time in a 1920 letter to St. Denis. In 1922, following one of Shawn's performances in London, he and Carpenter met. Shawn was moved by Carpenter's confident defense of homosexuality, as well as by Carpenter's willingness to share his intimate knowledge about Walt Whitman, who inspired many of Shawn's dances.

Shawn's friendship with Lucien Price, the *Boston Globe* editor whose influential writings about art, society, and philosophy earned him the title "Mentor to New England" was also pivotal. It was with Price's encouragement that

Shawn made the radical decision to form an all-male dance company. Price advised Shawn about almost every aspect of his company—from casting decisions and music selection to handling the press. It is also clear that Price even devised the scenarios for some of Shawn's most important choreographies. Price mentored Shawn in the codes of gay history, culture, and literature, all of which made their way into Shawn's choreography. Conversely, characters based on Shawn's dancers populated Price's novels. Price also maintained personal correspondence with almost all of the Men Dancers. He often counseled them on matters concerning literature, he advised them on resolving conflicts with Shawn, and in at least once instance, he wrote coded love letters to one of Shawn's dancers with whom he had a sexual relationship. Price also left behind journals with many entries dedicated to his trips up to the farm when the Men Dancers were creating and rehearsing. These journals are filled with detailed descriptions of his experiences in the studio, his private conversations with Shawn, the natural beauty of the Pillow itself. Rest assured, there are also endless descriptions of the dancers' beauty, their glistening bodies, their eyes, their feet, their hair, the way they dance, eat, bathe, labor, and his favorite activity: reading to them on the studio porch at noon as they rested naked in the sun.

In 1946, pioneer of American "sexology" Alfred Kinsey initiated contact with Shawn to explore his fascination with the relationship between male dancers and homosexuality. Since the early 1940s, Kinsey had collected nude photographs of famous ballet and modern dancers by George Platt Lynes. Having heard about Shawn's company, Kinsey requested nude photos of Shawn's men dancers. Shawn hesitated at first but ultimately complied once he understood the radical implications of Kinsey's research for gay men. In fact, Shawn eventually participated in groundbreaking sexual interviews that led to the historic Kinsey Report. Telling his sexual story to Kinsey's team of scientists was an empowering experience, all the more so when he saw the impact of the report on American society.

Homophobia, including and especially Shawn's own, is not the only factor that has led to a critical apathy surrounding his life and legacy. Perhaps more significant than the conflicting attitudes toward Shawn's sexuality are the pernicious racial and ethnic stereotypes that pervade his dances and writings. From early dramatic solos depicting dancing primitives to his later full-scale dance-dramas that reenact ceremonies and rituals from all corners of the globe, Shawn's repertory trafficked in "exotic" myths, sets, costumes, and music. Though cultural appropriation (if not outright theft) was the hallmark of the vaudeville milieu of Shawn's day, his reasons for and approaches to conjuring ethnographic reality on the stage cannot be justified by historical relativism. Of course, Shawn was a man of his times, but he was undoubtedly aware of the potentially negative implications of representing national, religious, and cultural traditions. This much is clear from his initial decision against performing his own versions of "Oriental" dances when Denishawn toured Japan in 1925. That Shawn was concerned with offending Japanese sensibilities reveals the degree to which he recognized the politics surrounding ethnic and racial representation, to say nothing of his fear of being considered an imposter. Such an accusation would have led to serious economic repercussions, given that he had built his brand on the promise of authenticity.

In Japan and elsewhere throughout the Denishawn's groundbreaking tour of Asia in 1925–26, Shawn paid dancing masters in China, India, Malaysia, Sri Lanka, and elsewhere for lessons in traditional local dances which he later adapted for the American stage. To Shawn, the economic transaction implied a blessing (if not an outright "license") to perform authorized versions of the dances he had learned. In essence, Shawn viewed his adaptations as a result of trade secrets shared between dancing masters and not an infringement on cultural property.

However, in at least one instance, Shawn's "borrowing" of cultural dances bordered on exploitation. His dance-drama *Feather of the Dawn* (1923) featured several dances inspired by indigenous Hopi rituals, including a dance of the sacred katchinas or spirits, a ceremony that Native American communities had prohibited tourists from photographing in an effort to maintain its sacred significance. In restaging a katchinas dance, Shawn actively sought to capitalize on the ban by providing a live-action reenactment of the ceremony, despite the prohibitions against such representation of the sacred ceremony, of which Shawn was certainly aware. Shawn's pursuit of ethnic, national, and racial dances was surely economic. A businessman foremost, his treatment of all manner of "foreign" dances was in line with how he sought to capitalize on all theatrical trends. For example, in 1923, Shawn traveled Spain and North Africa to study dances in order to gain a competitive edge on the spate of successful Spanish dance troupes that had recently toured the United States and the Hollywood film industry's latest obsession with bejeweled dancing girls of the Sahara Desert. During that trip he revealed a disturbing insensitivity to the abject social and economic conditions of the dancers he met, especially the women of the Ouled Naïl, the Saharan tribe whose exotic dress, dance, and nomadic lifestyle had captured the imagination of Romantic artists and writers. Shawn made an arduous journey throughout the Algerian desert to pursue these women, often paying to experience private performances and to study their dances. All the while, he remained unfazed by the conditions of poverty, sexual abuse, and social ostracism they faced or the risk he visited upon them by requesting they perform dances banned by the French colonial government. The resulting dances Shawn created based on his experience with them perpetuated a romantic fantasy of the dancing desert girls that belied their reality. Shawn was determined to convince the world about the dignity of dancing, sometimes to the point of dismissing the indignities faced by dancers throughout the world.

In addition to their box office value, the religious, national, and otherwise cultural dances Shawn drew upon served a crucial artistic purpose: they provided scenarios that justified his presence as a male dancer on stage. In the hyper-masculine dances of a Spanish matador, the sacred whirling of a Mevlevi dervish, or the martial maneuvers of a Japanese warrior, Shawn legitimized his presence as a man dancer on stage. For a brief yet defining moment at the height of the Denishawn enterprise, Shawn began to justify his racial and ethnic embodiments by drawing upon the discourse of eugenics. Convinced that choreography was a means to achieve the eugenic goal of "race betterment," he reasoned that that his idealized white male body had the capacity to perfect the non-European, non-Christian dances he performed. Though Shawn's experiment with the science of eugenics was both brief and relatively superficial, Shawn recognized the inherent racism in his writings and dances, a realization that likely accounts for his determination to meaningfully include ethnic and foreign dancers in every concert he ever produced in later years at Jacob's Pillow, as if to reverse the negative impact of his dances and writings about ethnic dance on the field and his legacy.

From the outset of his career, Shawn was conscious of his legacy. "Like Tutankaman, I'm a historic figure," he once wrote. With that awareness, he meticulously collected, organized, and preserved choreographic notes, letters, photographs, press clippings, and other ephemera. From relatively early in his career, he dedicated his morning hours to business and personal correspondence, most written on a portable typewriter that he would take with him on tour. Thus, he left behind a remarkably legible archive that includes carbon copies of his own letters that would otherwise be lost to time. A bibliophile, Shawn wrote books, collected them, shared them, and reviewed them. Thus, he seized the opportunity to move his papers from the Dance

Archive at MoMA to the Dance Collection of the New York Public Library in 1950. He supplemented his papers with materials dating back to St. Denis's first matinee performance in 1902: 8,000 photographs, 70,000 clippings and programs, and more than 300 letters. The collection expanded again in 1966–67, when Shawn donated an additional 1,900 letters, scrapbooks, and most significantly, over 100 reels of motion pictures from the Denishawn and Men's Dancers eras. Later he added a collection of 150 reels of film from the Jacob's Pillow Dance Festival archive—an astounding range of ballet, modern, folk, and international dance performances from the festival, including those in which he performed. Later came diaries and personal effects, some of which have only recently been made accessible. Also came hundreds (if not thousands) of other letters in the Ted Shawn Papers. As recently as 2016, additional Shawn materials were processed at the New York Public Library, most donated by the estate of John Christian, Shawn's lover at the time of his death as well as his designated successor at the Pillow.[38]

Throughout these massive collections of materials, Shawn left clues— scribbled in margins, on the backs of photographs, in transcripts—for both himself and for future biographers to decipher. These clues sometimes appear explicitly, as when in his journal he often makes references to sources for additional information on a topic. (See letters with so-and-so for details about a so-and-so event, crisis, or dance.) He refers to some of his correspondence with his closest friends as "diary-letters"—journal entries he sent to friends with the proviso that they be returned so he could compile them into a more durable chronicle. He also suggested organization for a biography, people to interview, and topics for follow-up studies. He managed his papers with a certain expectation that there would be many books written about him. In fact, he left his future biographers suggestions for book topics—one on Denishawn, one about Jacob's Pillow, and another about his lifelong interest in nudity, as well as a book called *Names I Have Dropped* about all of the artists and nobility he encountered. He also proposed a book on the dancers with whom he had shared a special connection, such as African American choreographer Alvin Ailey, Danish ballet star Erik Bruhn, Russian prima ballerina Alexandra Danilova, and Mexican American choreographer José Limón. At the time Shawn completed the draft of his manuscript in the mid-1940s, he left his future biographers a list of eight names and contact information for interview subjects that he felt necessary to get a "three-dimensional portrait" of him should he die. The list includes his lovers St. Denis and Mumaw, his closest friends Terry and Price, his loyal assistants and managers Margerie

Lyon and Fern Helscher, and his stepmother Mrs. Mabel C. Shawn. Topping the list of contacts is Lillian, or Mrs. Eugene R. Cox, whom Shawn described as the "greatest friend of my life, spiritual guide, and teacher since 1914."[39]

In addition to the personal papers, Shawn also left behind a significant literary output. Dance critic Margaret Lloyd affectionately called him "the writingest of dancers," an appellation Shawn would include in many of his biographies. Beyond his memoir, *One Thousand and One Night Stands* (1960), he wrote a high-end photo-essay book dedicated to the career and legacy of his wife, *Ruth St. Denis: Pioneer & Prophet; Being a History of Her Cycle of Oriental Dances* (1920); a treatise on dance as a theatrical art, *The American Ballet* (1926); a collection of his ethnographic and travel accounts of dances from around the word, *Gods Who Dance* (1929); a self-published booklet about the story of the Jacob's Pillow Dance Festival, *How Beautiful upon the Mountain* (1944); a collection of lectures he delivered at the Peabody Institute, *Dance We Must* (1946); a book about the movement principles of François Delsarte, *Every Little Movement* (1954); and a highly subjective essay on the main currents in American Dance, *Thirty-Three Years in American Dance, 1927–1959* (1959). His books are just a small share of his overall bibliography, which includes countless editorials, articles, and program notes that he wrote for a range of trade publications, including his own short-lived publishing venture the *Denishawn Magazine*.

One of the most curious aspects about the millions of words Shawn wrote in his lifetime is the relatively insignificant number dedicated to describing his experience as a dancer and choreographer. Fortunately, he left choreographic scenarios, music scores, notations, costumes, and set designs that give us a sense of the lived experience of his dances. Most especially, Shawn had the extraordinary foresight to film most of the dances he created over his lifetime. These form a collection of silent 16mm films that is arguably the earliest and most extensive motion-picture archive of any individual choreographer's repertory. As if the films were not enough of a boon to dance history, in the 1950s, Shawn watched all the films while tape-recording his play-by-play commentary on them, shedding additional light on his choreographic process and sharing insight into his thoughts about dances that he had performed but had not seen in years, if not decades.

It is now possible, over a century after Shawn began his career, to see how his life, writings, and dances were influenced not only by evolving scientific thinking about the body promulgated by sexology and eugenics but also by the health and fitness industry, especially by way of Shawn's professional relationships with figures like "Mr. America" Bernarr Macfadden, a pioneer of the physical culture magazine industry, and Joseph Pilates, who originated his own system for physical development and rehabilitation. Shawn also held an interest in Christian Science, the American religious movement founded by Mary Baker Eddy in the nineteenth century with the publication of her book *Science and Health with Key to the Scriptures* (1875). Also known as Divine Science, Christian Science offered Shawn and St. Denis a set of metaphysical principles with which to understand relationships between the mind and the body, between the divine and material worlds. They in turn freely adapted Christian Science for their own means. As Christian Scientist historian Stephen Gottschalk has contended, "Christian Science made its deepest appeal not so much to sick bodies as to troubled souls."[40] Shawn and St. Denis used the language and principles of Christian Science in their tormented letters to one another, grasping for a way to understand their deep emotional and artistic connection to each other against and alongside their sexual indifference. In some measure, they adapted the Christian Science principle of "separate spheres" or the belief that the ideal human was composed of male and female attributes into a private meditation on queerness. Whereas St. Denis remained committed to many Christian Science teachings throughout her adult life, though she was never accepted as an official member of the church, Shawn tended to come back to the teachings only during moments of crisis. During his travels abroad and during both wars, he tended to practice lessons and perform ablutions most regularly. In Christian Science Shawn discovered a theory of choreography, wherein dancing became a demonstration of the Divine's encounter with the material world. Of course, Christian Science's distinctly American origins and character coincided perfectly with his artistic sensibility: an American dance needed an American religion.

Between 1933 and 1940, Ted Shawn and His Men Dancers toured theaters, colleges, and gymnasiums throughout the depression-era United States with a repertory of dances that dramatized Shawn's contention that dancing shared an affinity with revered spheres of physical activity, such as the military, religion, labor, and sports. The all-man company rode a wave of interest piqued by Muscular Christianity, a Progressive era social movement that emphasized the links between patriotism, athleticism and religiosity. In the United States, Muscular Christianity promised to rescue "Christian manliness" from the emasculating and enervating effects of modern living. The doctrine undergird the foundation of the Young Men's Christian Association (Y.M.C.A.), perhaps most especially a branch in Springfield, Massachusetts,

that later became Springfield College, which by 1930, had become a preem-
inent center for training physical educators and not coincidentally, where
Shawn's all-male troupe took shape.

Though a man of introspection, Shawn was also a self-styled Rough
Rider. Simply put, he was addicted to adventure and exploration. There is
no other way to explain his commitment to the emotional, financial, and
physical precarity of tours throughout the country and beyond for over
twenty years. His adventurous spirit was honed in the many masculine
spaces he occupied during his formative years: a worker's camp, the ministry, the fraternity, and the military, not to mention brotherhoods of all
stripes from the Dance Masters Association to the mysterious and infamous Bohemian Club. He went to great lengths to "discover" dances in remote corners of the globe. This "modern" man flew in a single-engine plane
in the Sahara, traveled horseback up the Himalayas, and twice crossed a
crocodile infested swamp to see what he called "primitive dance." Most
often he had to rely on local guides and informants to find such dances. Few
spoke English and those who could were never quite sure they understood
him correctly, as it seemed implausible that anyone would have an interest
in seeing dances that were largely ignored by the locals. He was one of the
few dancers who traveled extensively internationally—to Cuba, Australia,
Africa, and all throughout Europe and the Far East. His obsession with
"primitive" dancing was not purely an intellectual or artistic curiosity, but
was also a religious one, and based on his extensive experiences traveling
abroad he perpetuated the idea that in primitive societies, men danced to
express the sacred whereas women danced the profane. He widely disseminated this patronizing view of dance history to defend, even elevate, his decision to become a professional dancer as a moral imperative to revitalize
dance as a sacred rite from its anemic state in the secular worlds of entertainment and amusement.

In a career that spanned more than fifty years, Ted Shawn brought to the
American stage nearly every archetype of masculinity. His specialized in re-
ligious figures, such as ancient Greek gods and priests, biblical prophets and
kings, the Hindu god Siva, and once even "Atomo," the god of nuclear energy.
(See Figures 3.10, 6.11, and Insert Figure 6.12.) His most beloved role was St.
Francis, the embodiment of Christian asceticism. (See Figure 4.13.)

In his repertory of "ethnic" dances, he portrayed both cowboys and various
types of "Indians" (Osage-Pawnee, Toltec, Hopi, Zuni), Spanish bullfighters,
a Muslim dervish, and a Japanese rickshaw coolie. He also depicted nearly

every conceivable variety of martial artist—a Japanese spear warrior, a Spanish conquistador, an American doughboy. (See Figures 2.20 and 3.4.)

He had a fondness for embodying fictional figures from literature, poetry, and philosophy, such as the Divine Idiot from Plato's "Allegory of the Cave" and characters inspired by Walt Whitman's poetry. On rare occasion, he played nonfictional figures from history such as emperors Napoleon and Montezuma, and American abolitionist John Brown.

At various points in his career, and under specific conditions, he even played women, such as a dual Lady/Demon character in his adaptation of a Chinese opera as well as an "Oriental sissy" in a college fraternity play. (See Figures 1.7 and 3.11.)

Shawn also played abstractions, whether the physical embodiment of music from Bach to Negro spirituals and kinetic expressions of visual art from Renaissance sculpture to the modern paintings of Katherine S. Dreier and Alexander Archipenko.

He once even played himself, a forty-nine-year-old choreographer prepared to say farewell to his company of men dancers. It was the last role that he performed with his all-male company. Shawn also sought to perform a role that had eluded him his entire career, perhaps the one role for which he was most suited: Johnny Appleseed. In the months following the final performance of Ted Shawn and His Men Dancers, he reached out to Stephen Vincent Benét, the American writer whom Shawn considered the "American Aeschylus" and author of the epic poem *John Brown's Body* (1928) upon which Shawn based one of his most successful solos. Shawn persuaded him to consider writing a scenario for a two-hour dance based on the myth of Appleseed, but plans were delayed and then Benét prematurely died before the two ever began work on the project.

John "Johnny Appleseed" Chapman (1774–1845) was a semi-mythic American pioneer who traveled from Massachusetts to the Midwest sowing orchards on untamed swaths of prairie to sell to settlers. The "spitters" that Chapman's orchards yielded were not necessarily edible, but they were ideal for making hard cider and applejack, thus earning him the designation "American Dionysius." Shawn, too, was often called the "American Dionysius," which might account for his fascination with the Johnny Appleseed legend, a model of American entrepreneurialism that Shawn wanted to emulate.

Within a few years and miles of Johnny Appleseed's death in Indiana on March 22, 1845, the Von Schauns came to the United Stated to escape political upheaval in Germany. They sowed their own seeds, which ultimately produced a grandson named Ted Shawn, who would travel along Appleseed's trail in reverse, originating in the Midwest where he was raised and making a circuitous route back to Massachusetts, along the way sowing the seeds of bacchanalia though dance rather than drink.

1

The Making of Personality

Fraternities, 1891–1912

Ted Shawn's paternal grandparents, the von Schauns, were among the thousands who fled Germany in 1848, resettling in the United States to escape the absolute power of the Otto von Bismarck regime. The von Schauns established their growing family in Carlisle, Indiana. The youngest of their thirteen children was Elmer Ellsworth, born in 1861. By the time Elmer had turned five, both of his parents had died of tuberculosis, as had many of his siblings. Thus, he was left in the care of the family's next-door neighbors, the Arnolds, who legally adopted him. Elmer studied a few years in a small red schoolhouse but left without receiving a grade-school diploma. At twenty-one, he changed his name to E. E. Shawn and entered the burgeoning communications field, eventually working for Norborne Mordecai Booth, who owned and operated the first telegraph and telephone companies in Indiana and Kentucky. In fact, it was the voice of Booth's daughter Mary that was first transmitted across state lines via telephone. Years later E. E. Shawn met and married Mary, Ted Shawn's mother. (See Figures 1.1 and 1.2.)

Mary, or "Minnie," had a very different childhood experience from that of her husband. She was raised in a large, tight-knit family that could be traced back for ten generations. The Booths were of Danish ancestry with ties to British nobility at the time of William the Conqueror. In the 1690s, Mary Shawn's great-great-great-grandfather moved to Virginia. Purportedly, the King of England granted him a parcel of land in Kentucky, the site of the family's 3,000-acre farm called the Bend. Legend has it that in addition to several military heroes, the family counted the renowned nineteenth-century actor Edwin Booth and the infamous actor-assassin John Wilkes as kin.

Born in Louisville, Kentucky, Mary spent long periods of time at the Bend with her large and talented family. Like her siblings, she was an accomplished musician. She was also a champion horseback rider. Standing at 5'10", she was the mightiest "Minnie" one could ever know. Her family described her as

Ted Shawn. Paul A. Scolieri, Oxford University Press (2020). © Paul A. Scolieri.
DOI: 10.1093/oso/9780199331062.001.0001

Mlinnie B. Shawn,

Figure 1.1. Mary "Minnie" B. Shawn. Joseph E. Marks Collection. Courtesy of Houghton Library, Harvard University.

both an "Amazon" and an "empress."[1] She was also exceptionally bright and as a young adult became a high school principal.

E. E. Shawn and Mary married in 1884 and moved to Kansas City, Missouri. E. E. Shawn became a writer and editor for the Associated Press and soon after for the *Kansas Star*. He also published fictional works in literary magazines such as *McClure's* and *Century*. In 1888, the couple welcomed their first son, Arnold, named in honor of E. E. Shawn's adopted family. Five years later, on October 21, 1891, they welcomed their second son, Edwin Myers Shawn, named for the doctor who delivered him but who was better known as "Ted." (See Figure 1.3.) Ted Shawn had many fond memories of his early childhood. In fact, he could not recall a single moment of strife among the "very happy, very close foursome."[2] Even when his mother spanked him, she did so in the "justest manner possible."[3]

The Shawns enjoyed an upper-middle-class existence. They employed an Irish cleaning lady and "two negro cooks," one of whom had a boy Shawn's age named Irwin. Shawn once described his relationship to Irwin as "blood

Figure 1.2. Elmer Elsworth Shawn. Walter Terry Papers. Courtesy of the Jerome Robbins Dance Division, New York Public Library.

brothers," though he makes no other mention of him.[4] Because of his father's position at the *Kansas Star*, the Shawns regularly received free tickets to the theater, often for the best seats in the house. Thus, Shawn, from a very early age, was exposed to a broad range of stage entertainments—from Ibsen plays and Wagner operas to vaudeville acts and music concerts. Mary, accustomed to the excitement of a large family, performed and directed plays at the local school and church, casting her second son in several children's roles. She also hosted visiting musicians and performers at their home. Shawn entertained family guests, too, transforming the family's back parlor into a stage. Arnold acted as a stage manager, operating the sliding parlor doors as if they were theater curtains to reveal his brother in a dramatic pose, then closing them. Young Ted would change costumes, strike another pose, and so on. (See Figure 1.4.)

When he was five, Shawn announced to his family his plans for the future: "Most of the week, I'll be an actor but on Sunday and Wednesday nights, I'll be a preacher."[5] His interest in becoming a minister was sparked by his

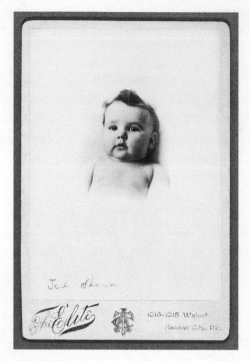

Figure 1.3. Edwin "Ted" Shawn at six months. Courtesy of Houghton Library, Harvard University.

family's regular attendance at the Second Presbyterian Church. Though active members of the church, his parents "took their religion easy."[6] They were never "that sort of cramped, mean, pinched, ascetic Christians."[7] Thus, young Shawn's desire to become both a minister and a performer did not seem contradictory to them. In fact, his parents encouraged his theatrical ambitions by giving him piano and voice lessons, though he showed little talent for either. He also took dance lessons. At the age of six, Shawn attended a local dance school where he studied ballroom dances, such as the waltz, two-step, and the schottische, as well as folk dances such as the Virginia reel. The school did not provide serious dance training but instead taught deportment to the city's "better people" and hosted formals where youngsters could rehearse the ritual of social etiquette.

Shawn recalled an episode when he dressed as a character in the *Little Colonel*, a series of children's illustrated books by Annie Fellows Johnston, a native of Evansville and a close friend of Shawn's mother. He received autographed copies of each book in the series. For a party one day, he dressed

Figure 1.4. Ted Shawn, four years old, and brother Arnold, eight years old. Joseph E. Marks Collection. Courtesy of Houghton Library, Harvard University.

as a stiff-collared officer. His mother begged Shawn to change into a more comfortable costume, but he refused, understanding that pleasing an audience often required a quotient of pain: "No, mama, anything to be pretty."[8] It was a lesson he carried with him for the rest of his life.

Although young Shawn enjoyed the spotlight in the security of his family home, he was otherwise introverted and liked to read in solitude, preferably in his bedroom or in a field of sweet clover blossoms. He entered elementary school already able to read and write. He estimated that he had read over 5,000 books by the time he was fifteen years old.

His older brother Arnold took responsibility for making sure Shawn remained social by inviting him to tag along with Arnold's friends. When necessary, Arnold protected his bookish younger brother from the taunts of his football teammates—and Shawn worshipped him in return: "He was my idol and my god, so loving, so kind, so beautiful in character and so beautiful in body. Arnold was everything that I was not!"[9] By age sixteen, Arnold was a lean, six-foot-tall athlete with an aquiline nose and a head of bronze curls.

One of Shawn's most vivid memories of his brother was seeing a tumbling act in a vaudeville show which they recreated the next day in Arnold's bedroom:

> We were both of us stark naked, and he of course was the stronger and bigger one, I was the smaller one—and he'd get me up, and I'd be holding his hands and shaking. Then he'd make me put the soles of my feet on the soles of his feet, and try to stand up. Of course the minute I'd let go of his hands I slipped and came down, landing on his solar plexus, or anything. He never was cross, he never got impatient, he never scolded me for being so dumb. He just went patiently on, feeling that somehow, maybe, by some miracle, he could make a junior acrobat out of me.[10]

In recounting this childhood memory, Shawn tapped into the root of his obsession with nudity, beauty, and fraternity—the distinctive trait of his later men's dances. For Shawn, cavorting naked with his older brother was an expression of intimacy, wholesomeness, and brotherly love, confirmed by the fact that his father watched the brothers perform their routine without expressing the slightest bit of judgment or shame. Arnold indeed influenced his younger brother to become an acrobat of sorts and perhaps one of the most successful vaudevillians, a fact that would have made him proud had he lived beyond the age of sixteen.

In June 1902, a massive flood wiped out a section of Kansas City known as The Bottoms. The weather cut off the city's water supply, electricity, and streetcars. Hundreds of houses were swallowed up and sent whirling in the floodwater, taking untold numbers of lives with them. One of Arnold's friends owned a motorboat, so the two young men went out on an unsuccessful rescue mission. In the following days, Arnold began to have excruciating pain in his forehead right above his eye. Dr. Myers came to visit Arnold and diagnosed him with neuralgia, a nerve disorder. He prescribed calomel and quinine, but Arnold's pain kept worsening. He was taken to the hospital, which still had no electricity or running water. In those inhospitable conditions, Arnold was finally diagnosed with cerebral meningitis and underwent several operations to remove some of the gangrenous bone from his forehead. He barely survived the surgery and within days died while screaming in agony.

Following Arnold's death, the family realized that his condition was not precipitated by his rescue mission as they had assumed but instead was the result of a traumatic head injury he had suffered at home when he tripped while walking across a room to close a window his mother had left open. Minnie blamed herself for her son's accident and subsequent death and entered a devastating spiral of physical and mental deterioration. Shawn recollected: "After [Arnold] died it was as if someone had laid an axe to my mother's taproot. You could see the top withering."[11] And wither she did.

Following Arnold's death, Shawn and Mary went to the Bend with the hope that being surrounded by her extended family might diminish her despair. Shawn did his part to lift her spirits.

"Mama, you have *me*. You still have me!" Shawn reminded his inconsolable mother. Her pain was too encompassing to acknowledge his affection, leaving him with "that feeling of not actually being rejected, but not worth living for."[12]

When they returned home to Kansas City, Mary developed an unspecified abdominal condition for which she needed an operation and from which she developed septicemia. On March 15, 1903, almost eight months after Arnold's death, Mary Shawn died. Shawn described losing his mother and brother as a "trauma, long buried" which he thought was the source of any malevolent impulses he experienced later in life.[13] He was convinced that his mother's death was a direct result of her depression, forever lowering his threshold for tolerating indulgence in emotional pain—his own or anyone else's.

Shawn's father sent him back to the Bend the summer following his mother's death. However, instead of healing his emotional wounds, his time there created new ones. One day Shawn followed his older cousins to the Ohio River for a swim. At the time, Shawn did not know how to swim, so he just splashed around in the shallow part of the river. He saw one of his cousins in the river's depths begin to choke and get carried off by the current. Two older cousins went in after her, but they, too, became caught in the river's force. Crying hysterically, Shawn and his younger cousin Lucy ran along the riverbank, trying to keep their focus on their cousins' rapidly drifting bodies. Shawn and Lucy were eventually rescued by boats about a mile downstream. His three other cousins were not as fortunate. Shawn watched as authorities retrieved one of their bodies from the river. Days later the other two bodies were found. Shawn attended three funerals in one week.

When Shawn returned to Kansas City, he and his father moved from one boarding house to the next. Eventually, his father married a young woman from the neighborhood named Mabel Cook. Shawn knew Mabel well, as she used to babysit him and his brother whenever his parents spent a night on the town. Shawn had great affection for Mabel, though he resented his father for remarrying so soon after his mother's death.

That fall, Shawn enrolled in the country's first Manual Training High School, becoming the youngest student ever admitted to high school in Missouri. During Shawn's junior year, his father accepted a position with the *Rocky Mountain News* and *Denver Times*, so he and Mabel moved to Denver, leaving Shawn behind in Kansas City to finish the school year. Shawn moved in with Mr. and Mrs. Ibs, a young couple from the neighborhood. He kept to himself most of that year, immersing himself in books and magazines and nurturing his morbid fascination with news reports about the 1906 San Francisco earthquake. He managed to hold on to a few friendships. Arnold's friends adopted Shawn into their circle of upper classmen, though mostly as a mascot in deference to Arnold's memory. His one peer was Wesley Wynan Stout, a classmate with whom he would bicycle to school each day. Years later Stout became editor-in-chief of the *Saturday Evening Post*. In that capacity, Stout betrayed his friendship with Shawn by putting the kibosh on a *Post* writer's pitch to profile Shawn as a rising dance star in the magazine.

The pubescent Shawn had interests beyond books. He recalled becoming "strongly sexed" and necking with girls, though never going so far as to "break the rules." He also remembered being attracted to beauty both male and female, a feeling he described in hindsight as "completely bisexual." He developed an obsession with a magazine advertisement that featured a college athlete in a turtleneck sweater and a dinky cap. The ad was illustrated by J. C. Leyendecker (1874–1951), "The Master of the Magazine Cover," whose drawings of all-American sailors, athletes, and top-hatted gentlemen appeared on the covers of many magazines, including those that published the writings of Shawn's father. The masculinity of these images lay behind some of the earliest and most successful advertising campaigns for companies such as Arrow Shirt, Jockey Underwear, and Gillette. Many of Leyendecker's men were based on the illustrator's lover, the model Charles Beach, yet the illustrations betray that intimacy. Leyendecker's men either stare off into the distance or engage in physical activity, seemingly oblivious to the stares attracted by their beauty, constituting a choreography of the gaze that Shawn would later employ in his dances for men.

And Shawn did stare. In fact, he cut the illustration of the college athlete from the magazine and kept it framed on his desk. He reckoned that his fixation with the image must have been a symptom of "incipient homosexual tendencies."[14] Yet it is plausible that the image also stirred feelings of mourning

Figure 1.5a. Arnold Shawn at sixteen years old. Joseph E. Marks Collection. Courtesy of Houghton Library, Harvard University.

Figure 1.5b. Illustration by J. C. Leyendecker on *Collier's* magazine, October 16, 1909.

for his brother Arnold, who at that time would have been a college athlete himself. For Shawn, the framed Leyendecker image was an object of desire as well as a symbol of loss that transformed his desk into both a peep-show and a shrine. (See Figures 1.5a and 1.5b.)

At the end of the school year, Shawn moved to Denver to live with his father and Mabel. This was not the happy household of Shawn's childhood. Shawn was sensitive to the lack of affection between his father and stepmother. He speculated that Mabel was frigid and did not sexually satisfy his father. Moreover, he resented Mabel's forcing his father to lecture him about the perils of masturbation. The age difference between his father and Mabel did not help matters, nor did his father's intermittent health problems, which put economic and emotional strains on the household. Shawn searched for ways to escape the forced intimacy of their small house.

The Shawn home was cater-corner to the Grace Methodist Church, led by the Reverend Dr. Christian Ficthorne Reisner (1872–1940), a minister with a theatrical bent that Shawn knew from Kansas City. Shawn described Reisner's Sunday evening service as a "cross between a refined concert and a vaudeville show."[15] Reisner delivered sermons in a Scottish accent and invited whistlers, guitarists, and Negro spiritual singers to the altar, which he once covered with snow carted in by rail from the Great Divide for a Christmas service.[16] Reisner invited Shawn into his church, though Shawn initially doubted whether he was worthy. He told the minister, "Dr. Reisner, it is part of the Methodist doctrine that three cardinal sins are dancing, card playing, and theater-going, and I don't think they are. I've danced all my life. I've gone to the theater every week of my life, and my parents, brother and I played cards at home, and I don't think any of these are wrong." Reisner responded, "If you can kneel and pray to Jesus, and rise up from your knees and go to a dance with a clear conscience, then it's all right for you."[17]

Reisner shepherded Shawn into his flock and guided the lost sheep to becoming a minister himself. Reisner secured for Shawn the Evans Scholarship to the University of Denver by appealing to Miss Anne Evans, a member of his congregation and the daughter of one of the university's founders. In 1907, Shawn enrolled at University of Denver Preparatory School to complete his pre-theology studies before entering the university proper.

Shawn began the university prep school that fall, though he had to drop out when an unspecified rheumatic disorder kept his father from working. Shawn had to contribute to the family income and thus took on a variety of jobs during high school and later in college that not only instilled in him a matchless work ethic but also trained him in skills that paid professional dividends once he became an artist and businessman.

One of Shawn's first jobs was as a shop assistant in the art department of the Dow Art company store. During his ten-hour shifts at $5 per week, he swept floors and stocked shelves while learning to frame paintings, cut glass, and create shadow boxes, all skills that came in handy years later when he oversaw the production of his concert programs and posters. He worked alongside a man named Mr. Gates, "a very elegant gentleman" whom Shawn in hindsight characterized as "an old queen."[18] One day, Gates took Shawn to help with the delivery of an expensive oil painting. Without warning, Gates led Shawn down to Market Street, Denver's notorious red-light district and past a row of cathouses displaying the likes of "Polish Minnie," "Irish Maureen," and "Swedish Anna." They made their way to an elegant brothel at the street's end. Shawn watched as the prostitutes prepared themselves for their evening visitors, then suffered the embarrassment of being called an "unplucked chicken." Unfazed, Mr. Gates hung the painting on the wall according to the Madam's directions. It was by no means a typical young man's visit to a brothel, but it was Shawn's.

In 1908, the summer before his freshman year at the University of Denver, Shawn found a job at a sawmill located in the Rocky Mountains. The job required staying in a bunkhouse for several weeks at a time and performing hard labor for ten hours a day at $2.50 per day. At the time, Shawn was fifteen years old—"soft in body and with the skin of a girl." He was in no condition to meet the physical demands of the job, but he decided to go nonetheless. His stepmother Mabel reluctantly escorted him to the train station. "Well, you'll be back soon," Mabel said, with a combination of doubt and concern. Shawn thrived on defying people's expectations of him, especially when he felt he was being patronized. He was determined to stick it out at the sawmill, even if it meant returning home in a coffin or so he insisted.

The first few weeks Shawn was miserable. The verminous bunkhouse he shared with eighty lumberjacks was a far cry from the comforts of the Bend. The work was even less tolerable. He was assigned to the gang saw, which spewed large planks of lumber that he would have to wrestle and load onto trucks. It was grueling work, though he took some pleasure in the knowledge that his body was hardening as a result. At the advice of an old Irish logger, Shawn refused to wear leather cuffs to protect his wrists. Although the pain and swelling made him cry himself to sleep, he was consoled by the realization that he had strengthened his otherwise limp wrists.

Eventually, life at the mill began to improve, especially after Shawn met Stanley, a boy his age and the son of a prominent Denver minister. The two became fast friends. They moved out of the bunkhouse and began to board together in the tent of a family that had recently arrived at the mill. Mr. Gillette was the mill's new engineer. His son Paul worked as an oiler; his daughter waitressed and washed dishes at the mill's commissary. Mrs. Gillette maintained the tent.

Shawn regularly joined the Gillettes for dinner followed by sing-alongs around the campfire. For the first time in years, he felt as if he belonged to a family. The Gillettes were captains of the Salvation Army, and Shawn appreciated their religious inclination, though he initially could not fathom the circumstances that brought this otherwise upstanding family to perform hard labor in a lumber camp. He learned that they were working to raise money to fund an appeal for their eldest son, Chester, who was in New York serving a sentence for the 1906 murder of his pregnant girlfriend, Grace Brown. As if unwilling to lose yet another older brother, Shawn closely followed Chester's trial in the newspapers and was saddened to learn that he was sentenced to electrocution two years later. Chester Gillette's harrowing tale was loosely chronicled in Theodor Dreiser's 1925 novel *An American Tragedy*.

Before heading back to Denver at the end of the summer, Stanley and Shawn hiked to "Devil's Thumb," a huge monolith in the Rockies that nobody, it was said, had ever reached from its eastern slope. They reached it and slept there without incident. Inspired by their adventure, the pair made another trek, this time to the Berthoud Pass across the Great Divide. The journey introduced Shawn to the pleasure of exploring uncharted territory, which explains his willingness to travel countless miles as a performer in the years ahead. They then trailed to Longmont where they returned by train to Denver.

Thanks to the Reverend Reisner, Shawn entered the University of Denver in September 1908. At the time, the university was led by Chancellor Henry Augustus Buchtel (1847–1924), an ordained Methodist minister and former missionary. Buchtel accepted the post of chancellor in 1900, and in 1907, he was elected governor of Colorado, a position he held until 1909. Shawn began to attend church services seven times a week, in part to demonstrate to Buchtel and Reisner his dedication to becoming a minister. Shawn took great comfort in the fact that Buchtel recognized his seriousness and thought highly of him. He told Dougherty, "I was the fair-haired boy. He just adored me and I thought that I was, you know, the cat's pajamas."[19]

During his first three years at the University of Denver, Shawn studied English, Greek, Latin, history, mathematics, theology, and physics.[20] He began a course in French, one of several unsuccessful attempts to learn the language. Shawn developed many relationships during his college years, some more enduring than others. He joined the fraternity Gamma Sigma Tau and formed an "inseparable trio" with fraternity brothers Hugh Kellog and Harold Hickey. Although Shawn sensed that the three shared a physical attraction, "there was nothing ever overt" between them. Shawn tried to keep in touch with his fraternity brothers in the ensuing decades and made it a point to plan reunions whenever he toured the Denver area. However, the friendships proved hard to maintain. Hugh became a lawyer and Paul, a doctor. They shared little common ground with America's "Father of Dance."

By contrast, Shawn established lifelong friendships with two women during his college years. One was Ida Kruze MacFarlane, an English instructor who later edited Shawn's dispatches from the Orient, which became his book *Gods Who Dance*. During his freshman year, Shawn also met Allene Seaman, a senior in his Greek class. They devised a divide-and-conquer approach to homework and swapped translations during their daily streetcar rides to the campus. After dealing with homework, she schooled Shawn in lessons about art, philosophy, and politics. About Seaman and her influence, Shawn said: "She was a liberal mind, free, progressive, and opened up many vistas to me, expanding my thinking, and liberated me from many of the bonds of scholastic theology."[21]

In particular, Seaman exposed Shawn to the Arts and Crafts movement, which extolled the virtues of craftsmanship in an era of industrialization. The Arts and Crafts movement began in England during the second half of the nineteenth century and spread to the United States largely through the writings of its most celebrated American exponent, Elbert Hubbard. Once a leading figure in the burgeoning mail-order business, Hubbard gave up his career to become a writer. In 1895, he founded Roycroft, a printing press and arts colony in East Aurora, New York. Hubbard self-published his writings in his literary magazine the *Philistine: A Periodical of Protest*. Initially, Hubbard's essays championed the "craftsman ideals" of simplicity, harmony, and authenticity by distilling the transcendentalist ideas of Thoreau, Emerson, and Whitman. However, his essays came eventually to reflect a broader critique of religion, government, military, and industry. Roycroft fast became the center of a countercultural bohemian movement.

A Hubbard devotee, Seaman spent her holidays and summers in East Aurora, where she planned to move following graduation. Shawn listened carefully to her as she read essays from the *Philistine* and took careful note of Hubbard's model of the artist-scholar-entrepreneur, which he would later emulate. Shawn remained close to Allene Seaman who accompanied him on his 1930–31 solo tours of Europe after the collapse of the Denishawn company.

Shawn immersed himself in the social, moral, and intellectual world of the University of Denver, yet maintained a critical eye. For instance, one summer he took a job at a general store in Estes Park, Colorado, a resort for Denver's elite. He was intrigued by the store's owner, Elizabeth M. A. Foote, a follower of Christian Science, the American religious movement based on the teachings of Mary Baker Eddy that had gained momentum in the late nineteenth century. Foote used to invite Shawn to her ranch for long talks. Her walls were covered with Christian Science maxims. Shawn recalled one placard that read: "There is no life, truth, intelligence, nor substance in matter." He asked Foote about the significance of this. She hesitatingly explained the idea of metaphysics, careful neither to confuse nor upset Shawn, as she knew he was preparing to become a Methodist minister.

Shawn welcomed her challenge: "Miss Foote, I cannot preach anything that I can't defend!"[22]

That fall, Shawn told Reisner about his conversations with Foote. Reisner called her a "wicked woman." He attempted to keep Shawn on the steep and narrow path, but Shawn occasionally wandered. For example, social dancing was prohibited at the University of Denver, so when his fraternity decided to hold a social, Shawn craftily worded the invitation to avoid censure: "You're invited to come play folk games with us to music on a slick floor." At a Halloween party held at the Grace Methodist Church, Reisner caught Shawn entertaining friends with a dance while singing Bessie McCoy Davis's popular "The Yama-Yama Man." Reisner cast a glare at Shawn that stopped his song mid-verse.[23]

During the school year, Shawn helped to make ends meet by delivering newspapers for the *Denver Post*. On Saturday evenings, he earned an extra dollar by delivering an early edition to the VIPs on the "free list"—politicians, city officials, and distinguished businessmen. The list also included the manager of the Pantages Theater. After delivering the paper backstage, Shawn would sneak into the theater to watch one or two acts. Of the many vaudeville performers he had seen, he specifically recalled John Lind (1877–1940), a Swedish female impersonator who performed pastiches of signature dances of celebrated female artists, such as Loïe Fuller's butterfly dances, Isadora Duncan's interpretive dances, and Carmencita's Spanish dances. In 1902, Lind set off on a tour of the United States. Shawn saw his revue titled *?Lind?* in which he performed *The Five Senses*, a dance that shared a nearly identical scenario to Ruth St. Denis's *Radha: The Mystic Dance of the Five Senses* (c. 1905)—the dance that had catapulted her to international renown. Like St. Denis's *Radha*, Lind's *Senses* was a suite of dances, each inspired by one of the five human senses. Shawn was captivated by Lind's beauty and dancing ability. In effect, Shawn's first introduction to St. Denis's choreography and stage persona was through an illusion conjured by the body and theatrics of a Swedish man. (See Figure 1.6.)

Inasmuch as Shawn credited his newspaper route for revitalizing his passion for the theater, he also blamed it for precipitating one of the most harrowing experiences of his life. In the fall of 1909, during his junior year, Shawn contracted diphtheria, a contagious respiratory infection. Shawn believed he contracted the illness while walking through a snowstorm to deliver his papers. The next day he was rushed to the Steele Hospital for contagious diseases and diagnosed. A doctor overdosed Shawn with 32,000 units of antitoxin, which left him paralyzed from the hips down.

Figure 1.6. John Lind in *The Five Senses*. Reproduced with permission of the Blekinge Museum, Karlskrona, Sweden.

Shawn was quarantined for over three months and immobilized, unable even to move his head from his pillow. The lymph nodes in his neck had swollen to the size of grapefruits, so he was fed a liquid diet through a feeding tube. He occasionally saw doctors and nurses, but neither his father nor Mabel visited. As a result of his isolation, and quite possibly his medication, he entered into what he described as a spiritual awakening that somehow allowed him to distinguish between his own authentic ideas and desires and those instilled in him by others. His spiritual awakening was accompanied by an arduous physical rehabilitation to regain his balance, coordination, and strength. At first, he was able only to wiggle his toes, but through sheer determination was soon able to bend his ankles and knees. Soon, he started to stand and eventually take a few steps, albeit using his hospital bed as a crutch.

Shawn left the hospital convinced that he no longer wanted to be a minister and needed to find a new path. Instead of returning home, he boarded with family friends, the Munns, taking with him not a single personal effect. Acting on Hubbard's interpretation of Emersonian self-reliance, Shawn surrounded himself only with things that he himself had made.

He had missed too much of his junior year to return to the university, so he enrolled in the Barnes Commercial School, which was owned by members of the Grace Methodist Church. He commuted with his then-girlfriend, a neighbor named Winifred Boynton. Winifred owned a Detroit Electric, an early battery-operated automobile. She drove him to school and helped him negotiate the ramps and stairs around campus, as he still was not yet fully mobile.

After completing the course, Shawn found a job as the private secretary to Jesse M. Wheelock, a general agent for the Northwestern Mutual Life Company, the third largest insurance agency in the country. Wheelock quickly recognized Shawn's organizational skills and offered him a raise to stay on at the agency rather than return to college. Shawn had no interest in pursuing a career in the insurance business, but he accepted the offer because the job afforded him the financial means to nurture his interest in theater.

Throughout 1910–11, Shawn regularly attended the theater in Denver where he was exposed to multiple forms of new dance, albeit some in derivative forms. He saw a number of young female performers who imitated the natural "interpretive" dancing of Isadora Duncan (1877–1927), a San Francisco native who had gained international notoriety as a soloist who rejected the conventions of nineteenth-century ballet. As with Hubbard in the field of arts and crafts, Duncan transformed the field of dance with American transcendentalist ideas about harmonizing the mind, body, and soul. Duncan's ideas about dance resonated with Shawn, but her many imitators did not satisfy Shawn's appetite for narrative and spectacle whetted by the work of the Russian choreographer Michel Fokine (1880–1942).

In 1909, Fokine began to create a repertory of dances for Serge Diaghilev's Ballets Russes, a company that wed dance to contemporary literature, painting, and music in new and exciting ways. Influenced by Duncan's "primitive, plain, natural" movement, Fokine developed a "liberating aesthetic" that eschewed "the imperative of virtuosity and the conventions supporting it."[24] Collaborating with Diaghilev's artists and composers, Fokine created dramatic works, many based on exotic themes, such as *Schéhérazade*, a one-act ballet inspired by *A Thousand and One Nights*, and the Egyptian-inspired *Cléopâtre* (1909).

A fine dancer himself, Fokine also reintroduced the male dancer to Western European audiences, especially the most celebrated star of the Ballets Russes, Vaslav Nijinsky (1889–1950). At the time, there was no established tradition for theatrical male dancers on the American stage outside of the ballet, nor was there an equivalent to Fokine's ballets. However, by 1909, Ballets Russes dancers began to appear in New York and soon after to tour the United States. Promoters tried to acclimate US audiences to this radically new art form by advertising it as "visual opera."[25] Shawn was first introduced to Fokine's choreography in November 1910 when he attended a performance by the erstwhile star of the Ballets Russes Anna Pavlova (1881–1931). According to local press, Pavlova arrived in Denver with her own company in trains especially built to accommodate the company's seventy dancers and musicians, massive sets, and a Russian library that converted into a chapel. Pavlova's program featured her signature solo *The Dying Swan* (1907), choreographed by Fokine himself. The rest of the eclectic program included an abridged version of the Romantic ballet *Giselle* and a divertissement of Hungarian and Russian character dances. The show also included "pirated" versions of other Fokine dances staged by Pavlova's dance partner Mikhail Mordkin, who like Pavlova, had danced with the Ballets Russes in 1909. Next to Nijinsky, Mordkin was the most celebrated male ballet dancer of the time. For the Pavlova tour, he was responsible for "arranging" choreography, which in effect meant staging Fokine's work without the choreographer's authorization. Shawn saw Mordkin's "arrangement" of the "Bacchanal," a purloined section of Fokine's *Cléopâtre*. The US tour was doubtlessly built as a vehicle for Pavlova, but Mordkin also received critical praise as a dancer, especially for his "Bow and Arrow" dance adapted from Fokine's *Prince Igor*. In this dance, Mordkin leaped across the stage while shooting arrows into the wings.

The following fall, Shawn once again encountered the genius of Fokine, this time through Theodore Kosloff's unauthorized stagings of several Fokine ballets. A former Bolshoi dancer, Kosloff had appeared in the inaugural Ballets Russes performances in Paris and replaced a typhoid-stricken Nijinsky late in the season.[26] Based on his glowing reviews, producer Morris Gest engaged Kosloff to stage "pirated" versions of Fokine's *Schéhérazade*,

Cléopâtre, and *Les Sylphides* to star Gertrude Hoffman, a dancer and chore-ographer said to be the highest paid American stage performer at the time. Following a brief season at the Winter Garden in New York in 1911, Kosloff joined Hoffman on a national tour, which gave vaudeville audiences a more complete impression of Fokine's choreography.

Apart from the cross-dressing John Lind, Mordkin and Kosloff were the first serious male dancers that Shawn had ever seen. Their impact was deep and sustained, as they demonstrated that the male dancer could be mascu-line yet beautiful, noble yet expressive, classical yet exotic. The dances and dancers of Diaghilev's Ballets Russes left a perceptible influence on Shawn's later Denishawn dances, although Shawn denied such influence and later came to reject it outright.

Instead, he attributed his "artistic birth" to the American dancer Ruth St. Denis, whom he first saw perform at the Broadway Theater in Denver in March 1911.[27] St. Denis was midway through her third tour of the pro-gram of Oriental dances that had made her an international star in 1906. She had performed her program of "divine dances" in the world's greatest opera houses and concert theaters; in less than a year's time, she would take the very same program on the vaudeville circuit. Shawn saw St. Denis perform *Radha*, a version of which he had previously seen performed by Lind. However, it was St. Denis's *Incense* that most captivated him. In this brief work, St. Denis emerges from a cloud of smoke that emanates from an incense burner she holds before her. She walks toward her audience, places the incense bowl at the foot of the stage, and begins to sway as if intoxicated by its perfume. Then, as if transformed into a burning ember, she begins to smolder and glow with arms rippling like a trail of smoke. Her dancing was simultaneously an in-vocation, a meditation, and a purification that embodied what Duncan's imitators and the Russian dancers lacked—a devotion to the divine.

For Shawn, the prospect of returning to the university became increasingly less appealing. Though he remained in touch with his fraternity brothers, he increasingly began to socialize with a group of friends associated with Denver's amateur theater. Forming something of a poets' society, they met in a local park dressed in white blazers, sat upon gay-colored blankets, and paddled in the central fountain to Sousa marches and Strauss waltzes. Shawn even wrote a creed for the group:

> Dare to be a Daniel!
> Originality is a cardinal virtue.

Receive new ideas gladly.
Equal these ideas with your own efforts.
Quickly grasp progressive thought.
Use your every faculty ungrudgingly.
Arrive while others are still planning to arrive.[28]

"It was all such an idyllic world," Shawn recalled. "Everything was so se-cure." Through his association with these new friends, Shawn made his stage debut in bit parts in the spring of 1911. In May, he received a pos-itive notice for his performance in the parlor farce *A Box of Monkeys* by Grace Livingston Furniss (c. 1899).[29] Shawn played the supporting role of Chauncey Oglethorpe, a British nobleman and business partner to Edward Ralston, the American owner of a gold mine. In a hilarious scene, Edward teaches the socially and physically awkward Chauncey the art of seduction. Edward wraps an afghan around his waist to assume the role of "the perfect lady" and coaches Chauncey's clumsy attempts to woo him, though they be-come seduced by their own charms. They grasp each other's hands, embrace, and eventually kiss. Chauncey then begs Edward to show him how to "back" his female partner without tearing her dress to ribbons. Edward complies, and the unlikely couple performs a turn of the bowery waltz, a vaudeville routine lampooning two inebriated last-callers.

Shawn had not yet fully regained his physical coordination, which might have contributed to his slapstick success. Nevertheless, his bowery waltz was a highlight of the show, at least according to one *Denver Post* critic who made a point to mention that Shawn "caused the audience much merriment" in an otherwise lukewarm review. The uncredited critic turned out to be a highly regarded dancer and teacher Hazel Wallack. A tall, beautiful, and aloof eighteen-year-old, Wallack achieved a level of notoriety as a "barefoot dancer" in New York. She studied under Malvina Cavalazzi and Maria Bonfanti of *Black Crook* fame and was a member of the Metropolitan Opera Ballet, where she was discovered by an impresario who touted her as the next Isadora Duncan or Maud Allan, then sent her out on the vaudeville circuit.[30] Wallack's career was cut short when her mother, her reluctant chaperone on tour, threat-ened to kill herself unless they returned home to Denver. Wallack complied, giving up a promising career as a serious artist to perform alongside her ama-teur students so that she could reimburse her grandmother for the money she had borrowed for their return trip home. She also started writing reviews of local theater productions as a way to build her reputation.[31]

When Shawn later discovered that Wallack wrote the flattering notice, he wanted to thank her personally for it, so he approached her one night as she was leaving a Woman's Club. Wallack immediately sized up Shawn, noticing that he was taller than all of the local boys she had been auditioning to be her partner in the fledgling ballet company she was forming. She told Shawn about her ballet class and prodded him to attend—if he had the "guts." He showed up to Wallack's class the very next day.

Shawn was immediately taken with ballet. He began to wake up in the early morning so as to spend an hour in the studio practicing at the barre before heading to work at the insurance office. Then in the late afternoons he took half-hour private lessons. According to Shawn, he funded his new addiction by taking a part-time job at the Denver Public Library. Wallack remembered differently, suggesting that Shawn, eighteen, made "an arrangement" for lessons with Wallack's mother, forty-two, by becoming her lover. Thinking she could use Shawn to help build her company and school, Wallack tolerated her mother's public displays of affection toward Shawn. ("Just motherly kisses," Wallack's mother protested). Plus, Wallack figured her mother needed the distraction from the recent dissolution of her marriage, which her mother blamed entirely on her absence from home while tending to her daughter's career. Wallack was a professional for whom teaching dance and performing was a means for survival, whereas Shawn was a passionate amateur for whom learning ballet and performing character roles were a means of personal exploration. Fittingly, the month following his first ballet lesson, Shawn appeared in *The Man Who Lied to Himself*, a play that lightheartedly deals with a man's struggle to choose a profession, a theme that must have resonated with him, given that he was seeking temporary refuge from the ministry in the theater.[32]

Shawn's acting skills sufficiently impressed his fraternity brothers, that they enlisted him to produce a fraternity fundraiser. He wrote and performed in a two-act play called *The Female of the Species*, a farce about the women's suffrage movement.[33] The play centers on a college suffragette named Phyllis whose intense involvement in the women's suffrage movement stirs so much ire among her colleagues and professors that they conspire to teach her a lesson that would force her to step down from her soap box. Phyllis's sorority sisters sneak into the chemistry lab and concoct a sleeping potion that they then administer to her. As she sleeps, her sorority sisters and fraternity brothers transform the dormitories into a futuristic world ruled by women. When she awakens from her drug-induced sleep, she walks through the dorm. In one room she finds her sorority sisters presiding over a meeting of the local government. In another, she finds her fraternity brothers enjoying an afternoon tea, all dressed in "ruffled trousers, laced waists, ear-rings, vanity bags." A very mincing, "sissy" man sings with all the affectations of a high school girl. Another man then dances an "Oriental dance of effeminate style." Phyllis becomes particularly distressed when she sees her sisters making unwanted sexual advances on men. Phyllis cannot bear the horror she witnesses, so she rushes off to the college's dean of women, who at first willingly participates in the charade but eventually reveals to Phyllis the terrible trick that her peers had played on her. Relieved, Phyllis renounces feminism and promises to work against the women's movement.

Shawn's fraternity performed *The Female of the Species* on February 2, 1912, at a woman's club. To ensure that the play struck the right tone, he sent a draft of the script to Allene Seaman, his most trusted source for matters regarding social reform. By that time she had moved to the Roycroft colony to work alongside Hubbard. She vetted the script without "a single criticism."[34] That said, Shawn was less concerned about the play's message about the women's suffrage movement than he was interested in creating a role for himself that would allow him to repeat the success he garnered with his comic turn in *A Box of Monkeys*. In *The Female of the Species*, Shawn made his debut solo performance as a dancer as the "Oriental sissy," a role that allowed him to integrate the physical comedy of Chauncey Oglethorpe, the exotic masculinity of Theodor Kosloff's slave in *Schéhérazade,* and John Lind's cross-dressed lampoon of Maud Allan's Salome. (See Figure 1.7.)

Shawn continued his ballet lessons with Wallack, though quickly realized that he was too tall and too old to become a classical dancer but ideally suited as a ballroom dance partner. Wallack started to coach Shawn in ballroom dances. In a matter of weeks, he was sufficiently prepared to make his debut alongside Wallack at a charity event hosted by students at the University of Denver and attended by Denver high society, including Shawn's fraternity brothers. A day before the event, a newspaper article ran showcasing photographs of Shawn and Wallack in various poses from the illicit French "La Danse d'amour," framing the dance's "naughty thrills and whirls" as an affront to Chancellor H. A. Buchtel's ban on dancing at the Methodist university.[35] At the ball, Shawn in white tie and tails and Wallack in a fuchsia gown took the floor. During the dance, Wallack's skirt split. The accidental exposure of her stocking-clad leg was enough to bristle the audience, especially Shawn's fraternity brothers. (See Figure 1.8.)

Figure 1.7. Ted Shawn as the "Oriental Sissy" in *Female of the Species* (1912). Ted Shawn Collection. Courtesy of the Jerome Robbins Dance Division, New York Public Library.

Claud Kellog, who had helped Shawn find work at the sawmill, was incensed by the display and by Shawn's pursuit of dancing more generally. He took Shawn into a private room and scolded him like a Dutch uncle: "Ted, but *men* don't dance." Shawn tried to justify his interest in dance as an enlightened art form. He told Claud about Mordkin and Kosloff, but his explanations fell on deaf ears. "Oh, but those are Russians! No nice, clean young man would expose his naked body on stage cavorting around and so on," Kellog rejoined.[36]

Word of Shawn's dancing made its way to Chancellor Buchtel, who wrote a letter to Shawn expressing his regret that Shawn was no longer officially a student at the University of Denver so that he could have the pleasure of expelling him for having performed such an "obscene dance" with Wallack.[37] Any lingering interest Shawn might have had in the ministry was now meaningless, as Buchtel had effectively excommunicated him from the university. The Reverend Reisner had departed for New York and thus could not help to reconcile the matter had Shawn wanted a reconciliation. How confusing it must have been for Shawn to receive such a stern reprimand for dancing with a woman at a charity ball yet receive rave reviews for dancing as an Oriental

Figure 1.8. Ted Shawn and Hazel Wallack, his first dance teacher and partner, in *A French Love Waltz* (1911). Hazel Wallack Papers. Courtesy of the Jerome Robbins Dance Division, New York Public Library.

sissy in *Female of the Species* or with a man in *A Box of Monkeys* less than a year earlier.

In an effort to adjust perspectives on their public display, Shawn proposed marriage to Wallack. He dimly recalled becoming "loosely engaged" by giving her a ring "or something." Wallack recalled that there was never a ring ("Poor Ted would never have had enough money to buy a diamond ring!"). Instead, Shawn gave her a rolled piece of paper with an inscribed poem, proposal, and opinion: "men and women should be virgins at the time of marriage."[38] Curiously, this was not Shawn's first marriage proposal linked to a traumatizing stage incident. During his senior year of high school, Shawn gave a ring to Esther Rawlins, a professional singer who convinced him to sing as part of his school's graduation exercises. He took her advice and performed to devastating result. It was the last time Shawn ever sang in public. Rawlins returned the ring.[39] Wallack, on the other hand, never accepted Shawn's proposal, though she did not refuse it outright, perhaps to prolong the pleasure she received from her mother's jealous rage over the proposal. Though Wallack and Shawn spent a great deal of time in each other's arms in the studio, outside of the studio, she kept him at arm's length. Decades later, she insisted that she never once kissed him, leaving matters of physical intimacy to her mother. Increasingly, she tried to avoid him altogether, seemingly to dodge his aggressive pursuit of an affirmative response to his marriage proposal. In fact, Wallack claims to have devised an elaborate plan to avoid Shawn (or as she put it: "I saw a way to get rid of him"). She planted the seed in his mind that they and her mother ought to vacation in California and convinced him to head west first to secure a place for them to stay. Wallack's plan was to flee to New York in the meantime. Shawn described their incompatibility in aesthetic terms: Wallack was devoted to classical ballet, whereas he found himself searching for "untried paths of the dance."[40] Indeed, Shawn was ready to take almost any path that led him away from the constraining parochialism of Denver. From his perch in the "MileHigh" city, Shawn had a broad yet diffuse perspective of the world—a perspective that was sharpened by the incisiveness of one book.

While working at the Denver Public Library, Shawn had come across a special collection of books marked "loaned only with special permission of the librarian." Naturally, the "locked-up literature" piqued his curiosity, so one by one he stealthily removed the volumes from the shelf and read them. Among the seven volumes in the revolutionary *Studies in the Psychology of Sex* by the British physician Havelock Ellis, was *Sexual Inversion* (1897), the first English-language medical book about "inversion," a nineteenth-century term for "homosexuality."[41] Based on extensive case studies, Ellis argues against the Victorian perspective that homosexuality is either a mental illness or a congenital abnormality. He extends his scientific opinion into a social and legal argument by condemning the criminalization of homosexuality. He believes that laws regulating decency and sodomy unjustly target homosexuals and interfere with their ability to live otherwise productive and satisfying lives.

To mitigate the perception of sexual inversion as vice, crime, or disease, Ellis emphasizes his belief that homosexuals have a proclivity for artistic excellence. To demonstrate this point, he includes a social history of famous homosexual artists and inverts of belles lettres: Da Vinci, Michelangelo, Erasmus, Christopher Marlowe, to name a few. (Shakespeare only "narrowly escapes inclusion in the list of distinguished inverts.")[42]

For his controversial reappraisal of homosexuality, Ellis was taken to a London court and charged with obscenity. As a result, his subsequent *Studies* were available only in the United States, and even there restricted to medical professionals until 1935. Thus, by reading the book, Shawn joined an elite group of scientists and scholars who were aware of cutting-edge ideas about modern sexuality that the general scientific community would not encounter for years to come.

Sexual Inversion is not necessarily addressed to homosexuals and is hardly a guide to sexual self-actualization. While the book might have explained, if not validated, Shawn's sense about the relationship between homosexuality and art, it also conveyed a cautionary tale about homosexual persecution. If, as Shawn claims, he carefully pored over all seven volumes of *Studies*, then he learned that homosexuality was universal yet universally repudiated. Shawn never claimed that reading the book was a liberating experience. In all likelihood, the opposite was true. The book almost certainly instilled in Shawn an acute hypersensitivity to his own "inverted" behaviors. That is to say, even though Ellis systematically dismantles taboos about homosexuality, he reaffirms certain stereotypes about homosexual bodies and behaviors— an aversion to science, preference for green clothing, large penises, and love of applause—stereotypes that Shawn learned to manipulate both on and off the stage.

A few years later Ellis would take up the subject of dancing and sexuality in his essay "The Philosophy of Dancing," published in the *Atlantic Monthly* in 1914. This essay was later revised and expanded in *The Dance of Life* (1923), Ellis's most widely read book in the United States. Ellis's idea that dancing was the natural expression of human sexuality provided Shawn with a philosophical basis on which to legitimate his approach to theatrical dance. He met Ellis in London, and Ellis wrote the introduction to one of Shawn's most controversial books, *The American Ballet* (1926). Eventually, Shawn would publicly and persistently claim Ellis as "his god." Shawn's pantheon of fraternal idols grew over time, but Ellis was perhaps the most significant, second only to his brother Arnold.

However, in the Denver Public Library that spring of 1912, Shawn could hardly fathom how Ellis's revolutionary ideas about homosexuality could help direct him as a man and artist. He was financially independent, divorced from the church, and seriously studying dance. Shawn had finally established a measure of equilibrium in both body and mind, though that balance would soon be tested by the sudden death of his father.

Sometime after Shawn was hired by Northwestern Mutual, he convinced his employer to send his father on the road to sell insurance. In March 1912, an old telegrapher friend of his father's called Shawn with news that he had found his father immobilized and speechless in a hotel room. His father apparently had suffered a stroke. It turned out that the underlying cause of E. E. Shawn's ongoing health problems was a brain tumor, and on March 20, 1912, E. E. Shawn died at his home in Denver at the age of fifty-one.[43] The following month, Shawn's grandfather, Norborne Mordecai Booth, the man who had brought his parents together, died as well. His passing made Shawn, then twenty-one years old, the sole survivor of his immediate family, a position that brought him an equal amount of freedom and distress in the years to come.

Shawn's childhood and adolescence is a study in resiliency and imagination. Despite the numerous traumas, illnesses, and conflicts he had to confront, he managed to maintain the most self-affirming concomitants of youth, especially the confidence he developed while performing his dance routines for his family in the parlor of their Kansas City home. By the time he reached adulthood, Shawn had encountered cross-dressers and lumberjacks, fraternity brothers and feminists, a theatrical man of the cloth and a wayward Christian Scientist, the governor of Colorado and stars of the Ballets Russes. Always impressionable, Shawn allowed these charismatic people to lead, challenge, and guide him. However, in the wake of his father's death, his youthful flights of fancy were grounded and transformed into muscular determination. It was time to leave Denver to recover the beauty, love, and unconditional protection he had experienced dancing naked with his brother Arnold.

Old World Dancing Masters in a Modern World, 1912–1914

In the summer of 1912, Ted Shawn and his father's widow Mabel went to Los Angeles for a two-week vacation. At the time, Los Angeles had just begun to experience the symptoms of the "modern dance" craze. Although ragtime music had permeated private homes, taverns, and concert stages since the 1890s, it was now increasingly heard in the dance halls and theaters of San Francisco, Memphis, Chicago, New York, and Kansas City. In 1911, Irving Berlin's "Alexander's Ragtime Band," the composer's first hit, became wildly popular, along with its associated dance, the Turkey Trot. In October 1910, the internationally renowned exhibition dancer and teacher Maurice Mouvet returned to New York to unleash his "brutal" Apache dance on

American ballrooms. The following year, he famously performed the dance with Florence Walton in a Florenz Ziegfeld production. By the summer of 1912, the American dancing couple Irene and Vernon Castle had created an international buzz with their performances of American ragtime dances at the Café de Paris. By the time Shawn arrived in Los Angeles, the city was ripe for ragtime.

When Shawn realized the opportunities for a young male dancer in the fast-developing city of Los Angeles, he impulsively decided to stay. It had become clear that Denver was no place for a man to pursue a career as a dancer. He wired his resignation to Mr. Wheeler at the Northwestern Mutual Life Company and within three days had landed a job in the auditor's division of the Los Angeles City Water Department. He began as a temporary replacement, but passed his civil servant's exam and worked there for nearly two years. Now gainfully employed, he began to scour newspaper advertisements for local dance studios where he could study the ballroom dances of the day. He soon realized, however, that he knew as much as the local teachers, so he rented a studio by the hour and began to teach his own dance classes. Shawn kept a very busy schedule of working, teaching, and performing. He learned to be very efficient at juggling many odd jobs. With the permission of his supervisor at the water company, he took fifteen-minute lunch breaks (just enough time to down his chocolate and raw egg malted) so that he could leave the office at 4:15 to teach.

He also entered the fray of exhibition ballroom dancing. His partner was Norma Gould, a young dancer who performed "Greek" and "Oriental" dances in the style of Isadora Duncan and Maud Allan. Shawn recalled one of her more popular dances to Antonín Dvořák's "Humoresque," which she performed in a pink crêpe de Chine dress, pink tights, and pink ballet slippers. He began to perform with Gould for the Elks, the Masons, and women's clubs. The pair also began to teach and perform in hotel ballrooms. Shawn claimed they were the first to offer "Tango Teas" at the posh Angelus Hotel, and later, at the Alexandria Hotel, where they entertained after-theater crowds with their exhibition dances.[44] As his relationship with Gould grew into a romance, Shawn found himself telephoning Denver once again, this time to rescind his unanswered marriage proposal to Hazel Wallack, who was relieved.

As Shawn pursued a career as a "modern" dancer, he continued to choreograph theatrical "art" dances. For this reason, he and Gould made a good pair. She was just as comfortable performing the Bunny Hug as she was embodying a Greek maenad. Gould had an established clientele of students, mostly children, and Shawn soon recruited a group of thirty adolescent students with whom he began to create "experimental choreographies."[45]

He also explored prospects in the burgeoning film industry. When Shawn arrived in Los Angeles, only one feature film had been produced in the city—D. W. Griffith's *In Old California* (1910). The silent film industry was another "stage" that Shawn hoped to fill with dancing. Shawn wrote several screenplays involving dance as a vehicle for his own stardom. For example, he wrote a screenplay entitled *Diana and Endymion* about a shepherd who falls asleep in the woods, envisions the goddess Diana, then pursues her through a choreographed hunt. *When the World Was Young: A Classic Dance Pantomime* is a version of the Mallarmé poem "L'Après-midi d'un Faune" set in the American workplace.[46] The screenplay centers on a young lawyer named Walter Shaw and his stenographer Allene King (no doubt a nod to Allene Seaman, Shawn's closest Denver friend). As Walter dictates a letter to Allene, he notices a book on her desk entitled *Myths of Ancient Greece*. To convey his shared passion for mythology, he shows her a portfolio of drawings he keeps in his desk. The two linger over a drawing of a faun and nymph as the film cross-fades, transforming the office into a forest and Shaw and Allene into those mythological characters. As they dance, the faun ventures a kiss, but before their lips meet, the film fades back to Shawn's office, where the lawyer and the stenographer are locked in embrace. Shawn also wrote a screenplay based on *The Female of the Species*, the farce he had written for a fraternity fundraiser in Denver.

Each of Shawn's extant film scripts include a dream sequence where dancing temporarily suspends the narrative action. The one exception was a scenario for *Dances of the Ages*, which Shawn conceived as "an all-dance film" that endeavored to transport viewers through time and place with short divertissements from the caveman's fire dance to contemporary rag dances. It was the only scenario that was actually ever produced. The Thomas A. Edison Company agreed to make the film, though unbeknownst to Shawn at the time, modified his original treatment by situating his choreographic scenario within a larger plot about the modern dance craze. According to Shawn, "The theme was—well, I must say they gussied it up a bit with sort of an opening and closing. The idea *they* added was that an Old Time ballet master with white mustachios and beard was starving to death in an attic, because all of the kids wanted to Bunny Hug and the Turkey Trot, and the Grizzly Bear, and Texas Tommy and so on."[47] Shawn filmed *Dances* during a two-week vacation from the Water Department. He and Norma along with a cast of their student dancers shuttled back and forth between Los Angeles and the Edison studios in Long Beach.

In the film's opening scene, we meet the Old World dancing master, Professor Ottoheim, ambling about his neglected apartment. He wears a fez, indicating his membership in a society of dancing masters. His landlady knocks at the door, demanding that he pay his overdue rent and utilities. He pleads for an extension and shows her a newspaper ad he has placed to attract new students. After threatening to evict him, she leaves. The Dancing Master briefly composes himself before he is startled by another knock at the door. This time it is "a modern young miss" who has come in response to his ad for dancing lessons. Thrilled, the Dancing Master launches into a spirited demonstration of ballet port de bras, fouettés, and cabrioles. The young lady balks at his display, preferring instead to study the "modern dances" of the day. She immediately leaves, and the despondent Dancing Master sits at his desk, puffs on his pipe, and nods off into "a distorted dream."

The film cuts to a parlor where Professor Ottoheim and nine other dancing masters, all dressed in tuxedos and holding beer steins, consort around a banquet table. Though they have gathered to "protest against modern methods of dancing," they are first treated to a performance of the Dancing Master's troupe of "tiny dancers" who magically appear on the banquet table before them. The Dancing Master announces: "Gentlemen, let me introduce you to my two little dancers who will take you down through the ages." What follows is Shawn's original concept of a suite of dances, with each dance introduced by title screens that situate it in time and space.

The first screen reads "Stone Age: Prehistoric Dance of Primitive Man." We then see two "miniaturized" dancers (Shawn and Gould) projected on the banquet table. They stand before a cave entrance. She kneels before a mound of dirt as he thumps around a fire pit, struggling to hold his body erect as he performs a fire dance. The next scene takes us to Egypt in the year 1200 B.C. with the "Dance of the Priest Ra." With two women crawling at his side, Shawn emerges from a secret door of the Great Pyramid. He snakes his away around three columns, then bends backward and spins with arms in a hieroglyphic design. (See Figure 1.9.)

Next we are transported to Greece in the fifth century B.C., through an interpretation of a bacchanal. Led by Shawn and Gould, young maidens spin and skip with Dionysian abandon as they display their flower garlands. Next

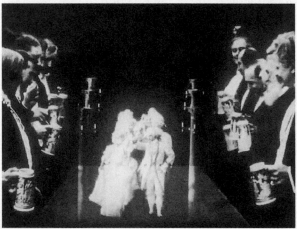

Figure 1.9. Scenes from *Dances of the Ages* (1913): "Egypt 1200 B.C. Dance of the Priest of Ra" (*top*); "England 1760. The Minuet" (*center*); and "America 1898. The Cakewalk" (*bottom*). Courtesy of the Jerome Robbins Dance Division, New York Public Library.

we enter a third-century Chinese court where Shawn, in turban and bodice, dances before a group of courtesans. With arms crossed before him, he deliberately steps and poses to demonstrate his balance, symmetry, and control. The next dance leaps across a thousand years to an eighteenth-century English ballroom, where five couples perform the minuet. Illuminated by candelabra and wearing powdered wigs, the dancers perform the figures and *reverences* of the courtly dance. The following section represents a French commedia dell'arte troupe in 1850. Shawn, as Pierrot, and Gould, as Columbine, lead the troupe in an exuberant display of lifts, jumps, and kicks as they throw confetti and steamers. The penultimate dance brings the Dancing Master closer to home: "America 1898: The Cakewalk." Men with top hats and canes link arms with women, strutting their way through the prize line of the minstrel-era dance. The dancing masters line up beside the table and imitate their moves.

The film culminates with the "modern" ragtime dances of 1913. The couples hold each other in a close embrace and sway from side to side in an outdoor dance space lined with lanterns. The Dancing Master becomes furious at the apparent delight his fellow masters take in the rag, which turns his dream into a nightmare. He awakens. Disgusted by the sight of the "modern" dance (much as the final film would disgust Shawn), the Dancing Master shakes his fist, resolved to fight against the popularity of ragtime, but his determination is fleeting. His landlady returns to his apartment, this time to deliver an envelope that contains a letter from the father of his two remaining students notifying him that his daughters wish to learn modern dancing and as such will find a new dancing master.

The Dancing Master gives up the fight: "I suppose I must keep up with the times!" he reasons, as he reaches for his desk chair, gives it a bunny hug, and trots around his apartment.

Ironically, the Edison company's "Dancing Master" plot dramatized Shawn's own professional predicament. As with Professor Ottoheim, Shawn's dedication to theatrical dancing was diverted by his involvement in the Los Angeles ballroom dance scene (and the film industry, for that matter). Shawn came to resent the Edison Company. Although he later made several attempts at having his choreography commercially filmed, he pursued those ventures on his own terms.

The Edison Company was a leading force in the development and commercialization of film in the late nineteenth and early twentieth centuries. Edison himself never directed a film. Instead, he coordinated a team of directors and scientists to develop and market technology and produce content. Dance was an early subject in the company's foray into motion pictures. Between 1894 and 1896 it produced several twenty-second, single-shot novel films of performers at the Black Maria, a tarpaper shack studio at Edison's West Orange Laboratory. Between 1894 and 1897, the company made multiple films of Annabelle Whitford's Serpentine and Butterfly dances. In 1894, they shot Buffalo Bill Cody's Wild West Show, capturing its interpretation of the Sioux Ghost Dance. Additionally, the Edison company filmed "ethnic" and novelty acts, such as the Imperial Japanese Dancers, the Spanish dancer Carmencita, and Fatima, Muscle Dancer.

In 1894, the company opened Edison Kinetoscope Parlors on Broadway in New York City. In that year it earned $89,000 in profits (approximately $21 million in today's currency). The rapid commercialization of the kinetoscope (and the vitascope in 1896) required new content. A dance film had to offer audiences something different from what they could enjoy on stage in order to maintain its commercial viability. By the 1900s, the Edison company began producing "trick" films, a term given to novelty films that featured special effects, such as stop motion or multiple exposures. The technology allowed people and objects on screen magically to appear and disappear or, as in the case of *Dances of the Ages*, to change scale.

By the 1910s, serial films with longer sequences of actions, with outdoor shots, special effects, and more complex plots and emotional expressivity began to appear. The Edison company turned its attention to filming spectacles, such as historical reconstructions, famous attractions such as Coney Island by night, trick films and fantasies, cops and robbers movies. Thus, even by 1913 standards, *Dances of the Ages* was a very rudimentary film. Its biggest technical failure is the disconcerting asynchronicity between the reactions of the dancing masters and the "tiny dancers." This is most evident when the dancing masters swing and sway as if to a march or a polka as Shawn performs the lyrical gestures of the Egyptian Sun God. It is also evident when the masters point or stare at points in space where no dance action is taking place.

Dances of the Ages was released on May 26, 1913.[48] Shawn went to see it in the movie theater and was utterly shocked by how the Edison Company literally and figuratively diminished his high-minded scenario and choreography with a series of editing tricks. Shawn's vision was to create a spectacle that would transport viewers to other worlds by saturating the screen with sets, costumes, props, and dances. Instead, the Edison company miniaturized his grand vision (and perhaps most upsetting to Shawn, his six-foot stature).

Dances of the Ages imitated film techniques popularized by the French filmmaker George Méliès, "The Wizard of Cinema," who used miniaturized dancers in "trick" films. The Edison-Shawn collaboration was a cinematographic failure compared to two of Méliès's most successful films, both about dancing. "*La Danseuse microscopique*" (literally, "The Microscopic Dancer") was filmed in 1902 and released in the United States under the title "The Dancing Midget." The film depicts a tiny ballerina who "hatches" from a giant egg, then dances on a tabletop for a magician and his assistant. Then, with the stroke of the magician's wand (and the magic of the jump cut), the tiny dancer becomes a life-sized woman. Enamored of his creation, the magician walks off arm in arm with his "tiny dancer." The second dancing film is "*Le Cake-Walk Infernal*" (1903). Filmed on an actual stage, the film depicts a minstrel show in hell. A couple in blackface leads a walkaround of chorus girls amid flames of fire and demon acrobats. They then circle a giant cake (the "prize" for the best strutters in a cakewalk contest), upon which the Devil magically appears. As he dances on top of the cake, his legs and arms are magically detached from his body, though his limbs continue to move in time with the music. In the film's final scene, the stage is flooded with cakewalkers, wearing only their undergarments, who high-step, kick, and strut with lascivious abandon. The devil returns and with a single gesture, engulfs all the cakewalkers into a plume of smoke.

Unlike the Edison Company, which took its cinematic cues from Méliès's experiments, Shawn drew inspiration from Ballets Russes style theatrical spectacles. Shawn told Dougherty that he had based his choreography on books, newsreels, and lessons from folk dancers in the Los Angeles area. Nevertheless, there is an undeniable link between *Dances of the Ages* and the Gertrude Hoffmann ballets that Shawn had seen in Denver the year before, though Shawn never acknowledged the influence. For example, the "Oriental" and "Egyptian" sections of *Dances* bear a striking resemblance to the pirated versions of Michel Fokine's *Schéhérazade* and *Cléopâtre* that featured Theodore Kosloff. There is also a visual and thematic similarity between Shawn's "Carnival," set in 1850s France, and Fokine's one-act ballet *Carnaval* (1910), set in France a decade earlier. Moreover, while Shawn might have based the choreography for his bacchanal on Gould's repertory of Duncanesque dances, he could just as easily have been inspired by Anna

Pavlova and Mikhail Mordkin's version of the dance, which he had also seen in Denver.

Although *Dances of the Ages* was an unsuccessful imitation of both the "magic" of Méliès and the virtuosity of Russian dancers, Shawn's choreography was original and inventive on at least one front: its evolutionary scenario. That is, Shawn's scenario for *Dances of the Ages* was pirated not only from the stages of the new art dance but also from the pages of encyclopedias, manuals, and treatises about "modern" dancing published at the turn of the century. Most of these studies espoused a stadial theory of culture, "the view that human history was developing in stages, progressing generally from the savage to the barbaric to the civilized to the enlightened."[49]

Two of the most influential contemporary books about the relationship between "primitive" and "modern" dances were James Frazer's *The Golden Bough* (1890) and Lilly Grove's *Dancing: A Handbook of the Terpsichorean Arts in Diverse Places and Times, Savage and Civilized* (1895).[50] They both arrive at the similar conclusion that "primitive" or "savage" dance is worthy of philosophical and historical inquiry and exerted a deep influence on modern principles and practices of dancing. With his theory of "primitive magic," a distinguishing characteristic of primitive dance, Frazer especially argued that vestiges of magical thought continued to pervade modern dancing.[51]

Although Shawn never mentioned having read any of these specific writers, he made an oblique reference to consulting "books about dance" to develop the scenario for *Dances of the Ages*, which in fact rests upon and "cinemizes" their ideas about dance history.[52] While progressive scholars were exploring the role of dance in human evolution and as an important aspect of human intellectual and cultural history, anti-dance religious leaders and social reformers argued with growing virulence that dancing threatened human devolution. *Dances of the Ages* indirectly engages with this anti-dance movement, which had begun to shape public policy regarding dance halls and targeted the dancing master as someone who leased American virtue for commercial gain.

In fact, Professor Ottoheim might well have been modeled on the infamous "Ex-Dancing Master" Thomas A. Faulkner, the former proprietor of the Los Angeles Dancing Academy. Faulkner began to dance at the age of twelve and spent most of his early life working in dancing parlors and academies. He became a dance teacher, a champion of fancy and round dancing on the Pacific Coast, and "the author of many of the round dances which are the popular fads of the day."[53] He owned a dancing academy located at Hill and

Sixth Streets in Los Angeles, where he hosted social dances for the local elite. At the time, he also served as the president of the Pacific Coast chapter of the Dancing Masters' Association, a national organization of dance teachers and dance hall owners.

As with the dancing masters in *Dances of the Ages*, the members of the Dancing Masters' Association struggled with balancing their commercial, artistic, and social aspirations. The national organization gathered in cities throughout the United States to discuss these matters and to develop best practices to protect themselves from prohibitions imposed by local governments and religious leaders. The Dancing Masters' Association also frequently met with another fraternity of dance instructors, the International Association of Masters of Dancing. The rivalry between these two organizations made headlines in local papers wherever they convened and thus drew public attention to the embattled state of dancing in American society.

Faulkner's conversion from dancing master to anti-dance crusader occurred after the 1890 death of his sister, which he partially blamed on the dangers of the dance hall. Within months of his sister's death, he gave up dancing and closed his academy so as to turn his attention to warning the public of the dangers of modern dancing. In that pursuit, he wrote two anti-dance treatises: *From the Ball-room to Hell* (1892) and *The Lure of the Dance* (1916). In the first, he outlines his perception of the dangers of dancing in the following way: "It is a startling fact, but a fact nevertheless, that two-thirds of the girls who are ruined fall through the influence of dancing. Mark my words, I know this to be true. Let me give you two reasons why it is so." The first reason he cites is that no woman "can perform the waltz without being improperly aroused, to greater or lesser degree." When in the close embrace of a man, she cannot help but think "though unconsciously" about "sowing seed which will one day ripen." Faulkner warns that when a man wishes to marry "he chooses for a wife a woman who has not been fondled and embraced by every dancing man in town." His second reason has to do with the "fiends" or "professional seducers" who frequent dance halls, deploying their good looks, speaking skills, and elegant moves to lure young girls into the world of the brothel.

Faulkner's ideas were repeated and elaborated by various other anti-dance crusaders. For example, *Immorality of Modern Dances* (1904) is an edited volume that contains a variety of theological sermons, pseudo-psychological portraits of dancers, and testimony from different denominations of Christian clergy members about the moral indifference brought about by dancing.[54] *From Dance Hall to White Slavery* (1912) by H. W. Lytle and John Dillon was a religious screed against jazz dancing. Instead of preaching and testifying about the immorality of dancing, the authors offer a series of cautionary tales about young women, most of them immigrants, who are sucked into Chicago's vortex of dance halls and theaters. Each chapter chronicles how a young woman's obsession with dance hall culture leads her into poverty, disease, and death.[55]

The tensions among the dance adversaries, the contentious dancing masters, and the emerging cadre of dance scholars converge in *Dances of the Ages*, placing Shawn at the center of debates in which he had neither a clear investment nor allegiance. Shawn became disenchanted with the prospects for building his career in Los Angeles, where he was able to stay gainfully employed but not artistically satisfied. All this would soon change.

In the months following the filming of *Dances of the Ages*, Shawn came across a glossy magazine that featured an excerpt from *The Making of Personality* by the celebrated Canadian poet Bliss Carman. Shawn found a copy of the book and read it cover to cover, entranced by its central idea that "the human body in every tissue and movement is but the living simulacrum of the mind and soul that pervade it."[56] In Carman's text he found not only a validation of movement as an expression of personhood as a fine art, but also an ideal means of harmonizing spirit, mind, and body. In Carman he found a dancing master who understood how the dancing could be simultaneously religious, artistic, and modern, unlike those dancing masters who penned books putting faith and science, religious ritual and art at odds with one another.

Carman's formative interest in dance and movement developed from his professional and personal relationship with his literary collaborator, Richard Hovey, whose wife, Henrietta Hovey, was a leading American proponent of Delsartism, a popular turn-of-the-century training system for physical and vocal expression that both Isadora Duncan and Ruth St. Denis had studied. After his initial exposure to Delsartism through Hovey, Carman studied with Mary Perry King, who soon became the poet's muse, mentor, lover, and patron. Together they wrote *The Making of Personality* (though King received no credit) in order to disseminate the school's philosophy. A treatise on the pursuit of a modern "art of living," the book appropriated the central tenet of Delsartism that movement could be a means of "harmonizing" the physical, social, and spiritual. Indeed, Carman and King taught their own version of Delsarte principles and exercises under the name "uni-trinianism" at their school, the Uni-Trinian School of Personal Harmonizing and Self-Development in New Canaan, Connecticut.[57]

Before dedicating himself to "Uni-Trinianism," Carman was known for his efforts to make poetry an acceptable pastime for American men. Through his association with the Visionary, a homosocial poetry society based at Harvard, Carman was part of a movement that challenged the public perception that only effeminate men read and wrote poetry. No doubt Carman's ideas about "poetry for men" inspired Shawn, an aspiring male dancer, to write to Carman soliciting his advice. To convey his seriousness and presumably, his artistic temperament, Shawn sent along photographs of himself in dramatic poses. (See Figure 1.10.) These included shots from a photo session in his stage costumes and another in his bathing suit taken on the beach at Ocean Park in Santa Monica. Carman responded to Shawn, commending the "confidence and skill" he displays in the photographs, though he bluntly shared a discouraging thought: "I am not very sanguine about dancing for men as a profession" unless the man first went to Europe to establish

Figure 1.10. Ted Shawn at Ocean Park in Santa Monica, California, 1912. Ted Shawn Papers, Additions. Courtesy of the Jerome Robbins Dance Division, New York Public Library.

"prestige" as a dancer.[58] Following this bleak appraisal, he summoned Shawn to his school, declaring that the only one he knew who could instill in Shawn the "scientific principles of good motion and help you lay a sound foundation for future development" is Mrs. King. Shawn took his advice and began planning a trip east.

Decades later, Shawn confirmed that his decision was as much motivated by his desire to expand both his sexual and artistic horizons. During this time, he had begun to socialize with a group of people he later realized were "leaning towards the homosexual." Shawn distinctly recalled that these friends tried to arrange a sexual liaison between himself and an attractive young man named Arthur, the son of French woman and a Spanish man. Shawn loved Arthur's accent. One night after a party, the two shared a room. Shawn recalled that he and Arthur were too shy to pursue anything beyond a "little mutual fumbling."[59]

With his salary from the Water Department and earnings from *Dances of the Ages*, Shawn saved $3,000, enough for him to make a comfortable "pilgrimage" to attend the Uni-Trinian School of Personal Harmonizing and Self-Development, the "mecca of New Canaan."[60] At 4:15 P.M. on December 31, 1913, Shawn finished his last day of work at the Los Angeles Water Department and headed to the train station. Rather than pay for a transcontinental fare, he took part in a program offered by the Santa Fe Railroad that paid the round-trip fare of talent acts that performed for passengers and employees at designated stops along the way. He convinced Norma Gould and two of his own dancers, Otis Williams and Adelaide Munn, to participate. He also took along a dramatic soprano and a pianist. Together they formed the "Shawn-Gould Company of Interpretive Dancers." On January 2, 1914, Shawn performed his "first one-night stand" and went on to perform in nineteen different cities across the country, where fellow passengers were treated to the company's interpretations of Greek and Oriental dances, folk dances such as Hungarian czardas and Mexican jotas, as well as "modern" dances such as the tango and the maxixe.[61]

The troupe finally arrived in New York City at 6 A.M. on or around January 23, 1914. In zero-degree weather, they took a bus ride along Fifth Avenue and up Riverside Drive. At the Martinique Hotel, they feasted on an exotic meal of guinea hen served under a glass dome. At nightfall, they boarded a train to New Canaan. One can only wonder what the twenty-one-year-old Shawn was thinking on that first tour east. During his time in Los Angeles and his subsequent travels across the country, he was exposed to competing ideas about the state of American dancing, ideas that he would spend the rest of his life and career negotiating in order to delineate his own vision of American dance. He had gained the assurance that he could prosper in the commercial world of dance as a teacher, choreographer, and performer. Even if *Dances of the Ages* was not an altogether successful artistic venture, it was a lucrative one that gave him the confidence to pursue his conviction that dancing could be both a commercial and artistic enterprise, if not in film, then in other arenas, where he could control and protect his artistic vision. Shawn's evolutionary vision of dance history in *Dances of the Ages* suggests that he immediately embraced the impulse of amateur historians and proto-anthropologists of the era who brought into relief the broad significance of dancing as a trans-historical and transcultural phenomenon. The recognition they brought to the idea that dancing was a meaningful aspect of social evolution appealed to Shawn's deep respect for history. Conversely, Shawn drew upon the rhetoric of the anti-dance movement to become one of the most unlikely and outspoken critics of ragtime and jazz dancing, which enjoyed a popularity that largely eclipsed that of the fledgling theatrical dance movement with which he identified. In the writings of Carman and King, he discovered an approach to dancing as a theatrical art that could possibly reconcile the competing scientific and religious perspectives on dance. Moreover, Carman's "poetry for men" inspired Shawn to pursue a "dance for men." With these thoughts in mind, Shawn arrived at the train station in New Canaan, determined to lead American dance into the future.

Carman and King awaited Shawn and Gould at the station and drove them to the boarding house. He spent $150 to enroll in a fifteen-session elementary course in eukinetics, which he completed in under two weeks.[62] Shawn was inspired by Mrs. King's high-minded ideals about art and the spirit. However, he became disillusioned by her lowly assessment of Shawn's professional prospects: "What are you going to do? You are too big for a classic dancer, you started to dance ten or more years too late to ever acquire a technique to make you a ballet dancer. You are mildly good looking, but you'd never stop a bus on Fifth Avenue! Just what do you think you can do?"[63] King then suggested that he and Gould pursue roles in vaudeville. Shawn retorted that he had hardly traveled 3,000 miles and spent all of his savings in training to perform the role of an Irish policeman in a vaudeville show. Shawn knew it was time to leave Carman, King, and their "mecca." Years later,

Shawn admitted that he remained cordial with Mrs. King as an excuse to rub her nose in his success by periodically sending her clippings that highlighted his many professional feats.

With a diploma in hand and a disappointing experience behind them, Shawn and Norma Gould left for New York. Shawn immediately began to study every variety of dance: ballroom, Italian ballet, and Spanish dancing especially. He even took classes in pantomime from someone who had recently studied with the Austro-German director Max Reinhardt. Shawn and Gould began to perform, once at the MacDowell Club, an outpost of the MacDowell Colony, an artist retreat established in 1907 in Peterborough, New Hampshire. The program featured Lydia Lopokova, former ballerina with Diaghilev's Ballets Russes, and Edmund Makalif (née McAuliffe) who billed himself as "the first American *premier danseur.*" Shawn and Gould held their own even alongside these international stars, and, as a result, Shawn was able to recruit private students. He rented a studio by the hour in the Van Dyck Building on Eighth Avenue, where decades later Joseph Pilates would build his studio.

A ballroom dancer named Marianne Moeller came to Shawn one Friday afternoon in desperate need of three solo dances for a cabaret performance that coming Monday. Over the course of the rehearsal, Moeller casually mentioned that she had been at a party with the legendary Ruth St. Denis the night prior. Shawn was stunned with amazement. Given the extraordinary help he was providing her, he figured Moeller owed it to him to make an introduction to St. Denis, so Moeller went to the Divine Dancer and explained Shawn's admiration and willingness to pay for private instruction. Of all the styles he had learned, he had never studied Oriental dance. Within days, St. Denis's brother Buzz came to meet Shawn on behalf of his famous sister to approve moving forward with any personal audience. Moreover, what Shawn did not know was that St. Denis had just recently unsuccessfully auditioned several men to perform modern dance interludes on her upcoming concert tour program, though found all of them "superficial in attitude and so inadequate in their dancing."[64] Curiously, Bliss Carman made a similar criticism of Ruth St. Denis in *The Making of Personality*. Though he dutifully praised St. Denis and Isadora Duncan for raising dancing to a fine art "in an almost deserted field," Carman contends she had "a good deal to learn about the meanings of motions and the making of magic." As a child, St. Denis studied Delsarte from her mother, though her dancing evolved in a way that was less concerned with expression of meaning than with the power of experience.

According to Carman, "She has the cleverness which arouses interest and makes one admire, but not the touch of rapture which would carry one away, as all competent art should."[65] Concerned that her capacity to arouse interest and admiration was no longer sufficient, St. Denis needed a new direction for her upcoming tour. A few days later, she sent a handwritten letter to Shawn summoning him to join her for tea at her Manhattan apartment.

2

An Interesting Experiment in Eugenics

Strange Marriage, 1914

Shawn arrived at St. Denis's 89th Street apartment near Riverside Drive in Manhattan with the expectation that the international dance star would give him a private lesson in Oriental dancing. As he waited for someone to answer the door, he thought back to a conversation with Laura Sawyer, one of St. Denis's former dancers, who performed in his *Dances of the Ages* film. Sawyer told Shawn a well-kept secret—that offstage, St. Denis had a head of prematurely white hair, a fact that belied her status as an exotic stage beauty. Shawn braced himself for the possibility that he might not recognize the star should she happen to answer her own door. She did not. Instead, a servant welcomed Shawn and led him into a sitting room where he waited for St. Denis to appear. When Shawn heard heavy footfalls nearing him, he assumed it was another servant approaching, but around the corner appeared Ruth St. Denis herself. "Barefoot, she walks like Helen of Troy; in high heels, Helen of Troy, New York," Shawn thought.[1] From head to foot, St. Denis was all illusion.

Ruth Dennis was the daughter of Ruth Emma Hull, "a freethinker and a feminist" and the second woman to graduate from medical school at the University of Michigan, and Thomas Laban Dennis, a veteran of the Civil War and a machinist.[2] She was raised on the family's farm in Somerville alongside her father's son from a previous marriage and her parents' youngest son whom they named "Brother." Though the farm was in relative physical isolation, young Ruth was exposed to a world of ideas from contact with the many bohemian travelers who came through the farm's boarding house. Through her mother, she was introduced to "diverse cultural influences of Methodism, utopian socialism, Swedenborgianism, phrenology, and mesmerism." Mother Dennis also introduced her daughter to Delsarte technique and had her study ballroom and skirt dancing with local teachers.

By age fifteen, the young New Jersey farm girl had begun traveling to New York City to perform acrobatic routines and skirt dances on vaudeville and variety stages. Within five years, she was contracted as a "bit player" by

Ted Shawn. Paul A. Scolieri, Oxford University Press (2020). © Paul A. Scolieri.
DOI: 10.1093/oso/9780199331062.001.0001

theater impresario David Belasco, who "canonized" the young Ruth Dennis as "Ruth St. Denis." With his acting company, she performed throughout the United States and Europe for over five years, all within the watchful eye of Mother Dennis who traveled with her daughter as chaperone and stage manager. In 1904, she had yet another transformation, this one initiated by an experience in a drugstore in Buffalo, New York, where she saw an image of the Egyptian goddess Isis in a cigarette advertisement. Throughout her life, St. Denis repeatedly told the anecdote of how this image inspired her to create her own goddess dances. Her vision came to fruition on January 28, 1906, when she performed a program of solo "Oriental" dances of her own creation at the Hudson Theater in New York—the first ever program of solo dances by a single artist on a Broadway stage. Her success begat a string of sold out performances on concert stages and high-profile appearances at society functions. Her sensuous, mystical dances catapulted her to international recognition allowing her to perform extensively stateside and abroad, and once even for King Edward VII.

St. Denis's streak of successes came to a sudden halt in the spring of 1912, when her major financial supporter, the Broadway producer and theater owner Henry B. Harris, died on April 15, in the sinking of the Titanic, dashing her "hopes for a highbrow career, her financial security, her most valued professional friend."[3] Eventually, Harris's estate pulled its financial backing, unwilling to add to the $30,000 debt that her previous tour, *Egypta*, had accrued. She was left stranded. Through her new manager Harry Bell, she finally contracted a vaudeville tour in the South. However, she needed to diversify her program for audiences less inclined to sit through a program of solo Orientalist dances, so she recruited Brother (appearing as René St. Denis) and Miss Alice Martin to perform ballroom dances. Still, St. Denis needed a distinctive edge to her program. Enter Ted Shawn.

When St. Denis set her eyes on Shawn, he struck her as sad and defenseless. Years later she clarified the perception, noting that she immediately sensed an insecurity related to his homosexuality, or as she put it, she felt that he was burdened by "all of the great problems and desires and perplexities of his own nature that were yet to come."[4] After sharing a few pleasantries, the two delved into an engrossing conversation. Shawn was vibrating with St. Denis's interest in him, his life in the ministry, and especially his bold decision to leave the church to pursue a life in dance. She had never before met a man who shared her devotion to both dance and the divine. Plus, he was young and had beautiful eyes. She invited him to stay for tea, then dinner. It became increasingly evident to Shawn that he would never receive that dance lesson. He called Norma Gould to ask her to cover his evening class so he could spend more time with St. Denis, which he did until midnight, then left with the promise that he would return the next day to demonstrate his dances.

When he returned, Shawn gave her a poem he had written in the style of the Sufi mystic Omar Khayyám. It was called "Adolescent." St. Denis found it morose, yet cried, moved by Shawn's earnestness. Finally, he performed his *Dagger Dance*, in which he played a young Aztec warrior valiantly resisting his capture that would certainly lead to sacrifice. The dance must have confirmed St. Denis's initial feeling about this young man, who devised a dance that would allow him to display his physical struggle for survival against the invisible yet certain forces of religion and tradition.

Days after Shawn's audition, St. Denis talked over the possibility of inviting Shawn to join her next tour with Brother, who served his sister's career in various capacities over her long career: stage manager, photographer, performer. At her sister's request, Brother met with Shawn to offer him the opportunity to join her upcoming tour as her dancing partner. It struck Shawn as odd that the renowned St. Denis would invite a newbie dancer to share the stage with her. He learned, however, that St. Denis had an ulterior motive. She now wanted to add Shawn's *Dagger Dance* to the lineup. When he initially refused out of a sense of obligation to Norma Gould, they extended an offer to Gould as well to join the tour and perform their "modern dances." They offered Shawn $40 per week, which actually amounted to less than what he was earning as a teacher once he factored in the cost of hotels, meals, and laundry for which he would be responsible on tour. Still, he figured, the prestige of the position was worth the sacrifice. Shawn went back to his apartment in the West Forties to tell Gould about the offer. She was surprised, but for a different reason. Gould was expecting a marriage proposal, not a touring contract. She begrudgingly agreed to go on tour, but just a few days before taking to the road, she had "a complete nervous breakdown" and headed back to California.[5]

Shawn spent the next few days training a dancing partner to replace Gould. Hilda Beyer was a former member of St. Denis's *Egypta* cast. She was a young beauty, not a trained dancer. "Blond and Swedish" is how St. Denis described her. One critic gushed that she was "considered by sculptors the most perfect formed girl in America and selected to pose for the statuary decorations for the Panama exposition, also for the country home of John

D. Rockefeller." Shawn worked around the clock to teach her Gould's roles. One of the first reviews of their performance remarked, "How magnificently Miss Hilda Beyer danced, ably supported by Mr. Ted Shawn." Shawn found the critic's observation ironic: "He didn't know how ably supported, because I was still talking out of the corner of my mouth, 'Come here, go there, one-two, get into it kid!'"[6]

The tour was scheduled to open on April 13, 1914, in Paducah, Kentucky, the first time St. Denis and Shawn ever shared a stage. For decades to come, they would rehearse the story of how they fell in love in Paducah. Despite St. Denis's promise to Shawn to share billing, top billing went to St. Denis, who was "assisted by Hilda Beyer and Ted Shawn." The program also included Miss Evan B. Fontaine, a Chicago society girl who had studied with "the best dancing masters of Petrograd and Paris," society and ballroom dancing partners Norwood and Mitchell, and Mlle. Psychema (aka Desiree Lubovska, née Winniefred Foote), who with her brother formed a ballroom dance team in Los Angeles. "Discovered" by St. Denis, Lubovska spent a season with her on the Orpheum Circuit as a leading dancer before she joined the tour of the Southeast performing Shawn's *Danse Egyptienne*.

Most reviewers paid respect to St. Denis, noting her storied past from Passing Shows to the world stages with Belasco, or played to the shock of her being an American who captured the essence of the exotic. They also recognized that her "classical" dances were of a bygone era and that her assistants were the future of dance. A critic in Indiana noted that no one "went wild over her" and her "classical" dances. "The few say it's art—and the others acquiesce and they try to make themselves believe it." Another Hoosier flat out claimed that Shawn and Beyer's routine was the cleverest. It might have been the comparisons to the younger dancers and the descriptions of her as "something of a Cubist" who created "bizarre effects" on stage that led St. Denis to experiment with her well-defined stage image by considering dancing a pretty duet with Shawn. For the remainder of the tour, they worked together to create the dance, the first of many collaborations.[7]

One Sunday evening after a rehearsal in Norfolk, Virginia, Shawn and St. Denis enjoyed a romantic dinner at a dining room on the top floor of a posh hotel. After their meal, they stepped out onto the terrace to continue their conversation about dancing together. Moved by his infatuation with his new artistic collaborator, Shawn spontaneously proposed marriage to her. She did not accept the proposal. St. Denis had never intended on becoming someone's wife, and even if she had been tempted by Shawn's spontaneous gesture, she knew that she would first need to get her mother's blessing, which would not be easily won. Instead, they enjoyed the remaining weeks of the tour creating dances and plotting an impossible future together.

The tour concluded with a two-week engagement at Ravinia Park in Chicago. At the popular amusement park and music festival, St. Denis premiered a new solo, *The Peacock: A Legend of India*, in which she portrays a vain Indian princess whose soul is condemned to life as a peacock that haunts the courtyard of her former palace, which involved St. Denis preening and manipulating a bejeweled train to her costume's dress to convey the majesty of a peacock's tail. Shawn and St. Denis also premiered their first artistic collaboration, *Arabic Suite* (later called *Ourieda, A Romance of a Desert Dancing Girl*).[8] Set in North Africa, the dance evoked the heat and mystery of two lovers in the desert. It introduced what would become one of the couple's signature moves—Shawn loosely embraces St. Denis from behind and in profile, they walk across the stage, reaching toward a visible yet distant oasis. (See Figure 2.1.) One critic noted that the most successful part of the pantomime was when the dancers were silhouetted against the backdrop of the moonlit desert and the sound of the insistent orchestra was replaced by a Victrola—"surely the most effective use to which that instrument has been put on stage."[9] Based on the review of the dance, and the concert program that contained advertisements for both Schmelzer's Victrola and Victor Dance Records, it seems likely that this first St. Denis-Shawn collaboration was largely created to demonstrate how modern technologies of the Victrola and phonograph could be used to create the experience of the theater at home. It certainly was not the last time they employed their art for commercial means.

St. Denis left Ravinia to join her mother on the shores of Marblehead, Massachusetts. Shawn stayed in Ravinia but wrote to her daily to report on his successful performances. Addressing her as "My T-Ruth," his letters expressed his devotion to her and her art, along with scenarios for new dances that they could perform as husband and wife. He pressured her for a response to his marriage proposal by casually mentioning how Chicago socialites promised to raise funds to send him to Russia to study at the Imperial School. Addressing him as "Eager Boy," she politely declined his proposals by blaming her reluctance to accept his proposal on her mother's disapproval. But Shawn persisted, prompting St. Denis to write Shawn a twenty-six-page letter that spelled out her marital expectations.[10] Using the language of the

Figure 2.1. Ruth St. Denis and Ted Shawn in their first duet, *Ourieda, A Romance of a Desert Dancing Girl* (1914). Denishawn Collection. Courtesy of the Jerome Robbins Dance Division, New York Public Library.

"Divine Science" (she had testified before Marblehead's Christian Science congregation the night prior), as well as through a meandering discussion of Walt Whitman and D. H. Lawrence's book *Rainbow*, published in 1915 and prosecuted on grounds of obscenity for its explicit treatment of sexual desire, she elucidated her anxieties about entering a "new and other state of marriage." St. Denis asks for "an all around living, progressing, experimenting partnership—in which sex in its particular sphere is a part but not the whole—this is my sense of love + loyalty + fidelity—first of all a friend, then a lover."

From the outset of their relationship, St. Denis demonstrated a disarming transparency and empathy in regard to all matters sexual. To her mind, "an experimenting partnership" had to endure trials of all kinds, including sexual ones. In the letter she mentions her remorse for her violent reaction when Shawn confided in her about a sexual episode he experienced with "Frank Something":

> An experience had come to you, that you were not responsible for, you did not start it, you did not make it, yet because . . . the general thought of the world on any sex attraction—you felt uncomfortable, you had no real desire to deceive me, you came to me, and I did the usual thing, I reacted violently in pride and fear! It was a long time before I could crawl out from under the universal epidemic—I knelt down under it—like I did with the flu— nothing to be proud of—something to destroy and come up from, into the sunshine.[11]

When they reunited in New York, Shawn rented a boarding room at St. Denis's house. As expected, Mother Dennis expressed her disapproval of Shawn's presence and the threat he posed to the life and career of her daughter. Shawn was not familiar with the dynamics of parental manipulation, so he confronted her forthrightly, during a six-hour showdown. Mother Dennis ultimately determined that Shawn was no serious threat to St. Denis's image as a chaste goddess, a carefully controlled illusion that she herself helped to develop in distinction to Isadora Duncan.

On August 13, 1914, Edwin Myers Shawn married Ruth St. Denis.

"That statistical statement, while quite true, is completely misleading in its simplicity," wrote Shawn in his memoir.[12] He recalled that there were "cloak and dagger overtones" to the entire marriage. Though she agreed to marry Shawn, the institution of marriage upset St. Denis's sense of herself as an independent "free woman." Thus, she refused to play the part of a blushing bride. Instead, she put on a wrinkled serge suit and a cheap straw hat, then followed Shawn to city hall for a marriage license "to get this thing over with," as St. Denis trivialized their union. With marriage license in hand, they went uptown to Aeolian Hall, a concert hall built in 1912 for the piano manufacturing company, where a retired minister turned Christian Scientist named Dr. W. F. Ottarson solemnized the intimate ceremony. Brother St. Denis and his newlywed wife Emily served as witnesses. St. Denis refused a wedding ring and insisted on striking the word "obey" from their vows. After the ceremony, the newlyweds went home to break the news to Mother Dennis but could not find her anywhere. They went looking for her and eventually found her down the block by the Sailors and Soldiers Monument on Riverside Drive. St. Denis recalled, "The defeated, hopeless gesture of her body told me more than any words that she accepted our marriage as the end of her long devotion to my career."[13]

St. Denis insisted that Shawn keep their marriage a secret. There were professional reasons for the secrecy. St. Denis's appeal as a mysterious and exotic beauty was based in part on concealing the realities of the conditions by which she lived and labored. There were also profoundly personal ones. Through she had a reputation for being seen on the town with powerful men in cities across the globe, the thirty-five-year-old St. Denis was a virgin. By her own admission, her fear of pregnancy and motherhood kept her from developing romantic intimacy. Years later, St. Denis would affirm as much in a letter to Shawn: "Some day you will realize that I appreciated your virginity so much—that I married you for it!"[14] For the first few months of the marriage, their union was never announced, never celebrated, never consummated. Indeed, St. Denis admitted that theirs was a "strange marriage."[15]

Instead of a romantic honeymoon, the pair embarked on a grueling seven-month tour of one-night stands starting in Saratoga Springs and heading westward to San Francisco. The program featured some of St. Denis's most famous dances alongside "a mix of Oriental, Greek, Classic and Modern dances." The reviews of the program were favorable. Audiences clamored to see St. Denis's *Radha: The Mystic Dance of the Five Senses*, alongside more modern fare of ballroom dances and burlesque-style routines, such as the *Ta-Toa: A Chinese Minuet* performed by Brother (once again as René St. Denis) and Evan-Burrows Fontaine.

Though news of their marriage had not yet leaked to the press, early notices raised excited curiosity about Shawn's presence on the tour, forcing questions about his identity. He quickly became called the "American Mordkin," though Shawn rebuked the association with the Russian ballet star. He began to get favorable notices for his dancing if not his physical presence: "Mr. Shawn dances not with very much of what used to be called steps but with a grace and suggestion of physical force that commands admiration." Another reviewer went as far as to say that he "was even as great as Miss Denis, when one considers his remarkable physique, and his usual gift of grace. He occupied the stage even more than the real star and his earnest support was of great value to Ruth St. Denis."[16]

Shawn seized the attention to launch what would become his lifelong defense of the male dancer. In early interviews on the topic, Shawn concentrated on the argument that dancing is "a manly sport."[17] Some writers ran with the relatively novel comparison between dance and athletics based on physicality and strength, whereas others fixated on the comparison between dancing and another type of competition: beauty contests. In the early months of the tour, a few writers playfully if not sardonically speculated on the outcome of Shawn's participation in a hypothetical male beauty contest. "No Contest Here" wrote one reporter in Akron, declaring Shawn "The Most Beautiful Man in the World."

The issue with the title was that it already had been associated with "Greek dancer" Paul Swan, a figure with whom both Shawn and St. Denis were very familiar. In February 1913, Swan appeared as a Greek slave on stage with St. Denis before 400 guests at an Egyptian pageant hosted by Louis C. Tiffany. Shawn had gone to see Swan perform his version of *Dying Swan* and *Narcissus* in New York City just months earlier. Shawn claimed to have been revolted by the performance and began to model his own stage persona against Swan's. In practice, however, there were striking similarities between their stage acts as well as their personal backgrounds. Both were raised Methodists in the Midwest. As a result, reporters could barely tell them apart, some never realizing that Shawn and Swan were actually two different people, inconceivable as it was for there to be two interpretative male dancers on the scene. One writer offered a foolproof way to distinguish between them by noting that whereas Swan's pink complexion made him look feminine, Shawn's greasepaint gave him "a healthy sunburn hue," making him appear masculine, perhaps even ethnic.[18]

Shawn revolted against the comparison, especially when the association with Swan's unapologetic display of male beauty placed Shawn's masculinity in question. For instance, in the real estate section of a New York newspaper ran an advertisement for a "beautiful gentleman's home to let," a living option described as perfect for men such as Paul Swan, Ted Shawn, or female impersonators Julian Eltinge or Martelle. Curiously absent from this list was the famous Russian dancer Vaslav Nijinsky, who also was referred to as the "Most Beautiful Man in the World" and about whom a book had recently been published in the United States.[19] Inasmuch as Shawn's beauty placed him in the company of effeminate men and female impersonators, he resisted, gladly accepting "World's Most Handsome Man" as a conciliatory title.

For Shawn, the burden of being hailed as "beautiful" was that it drew attention away from his dancing and heightened the scrutiny of his physique. One reporter went to great lengths to emasculate Shawn through an infantilizing description of his body: "Ted's limbs are delicate, smooth and rounded. His arms are childlike, his features ethereal in their chiselment and his hair one of those thick, crinkly masses that you want to crop off and put in a football. There are no knobs of honest toil about his figure and he altogether looks like a fellow just good enough to put on a cat's hide and pose before crowds of sensual society dames in the name of Art."[20] The perception that Shawn's brand of physical beauty was of interest to "society dames" was astute, especially given that during this time, Shawn was the subject of a sketch by society portraitist John Singer Sargent (1856–1925). (See Figure 2.2.) In the portrait, Shawn is depicted lounging naked but for a draped cloth, gaze averted, with

Figure 2.2. Portrait of Ted Shawn (c. 1915) by John Singer Sargent. Courtesy of the National Portrait Gallery, Smithsonian Institution.

palm primed at his groin. Sargent summoned the very narcissistic homoe-
roticism against which the writer railed, prompting him to suggest that instead of a male beauty contest what was needed was a "male homely contest"
for "men working with the very devil for seven children and a wife." St. Denis
rose to Shawn's defense against depictions of him as an aesthete or man of
leisure, once telling a reporter, "My husband and myself are nauseated by this
newspaper talk that he is a pretty man. Pretty nothing—he's a manly man.
Big, brawny and full of the old Nick. Please correct the foolish rumor that Ted
is a human doll with pink lips and chic complexion."[21]

These queries opened up topics about the nature of art, beauty, and
masculinity—often quite literally. "When Is Art Art?" asked the *Chicago
Herald*, prompted by a public uproar surrounding the display of photographs
depicting a scantily clad Shawn and Beyer in the windows of an Evanston,
Illinois, photographer's studio. The incident required the involvement of the
commissioner of public safety to mediate the impassioned debates among
reporters and local leaders about the line between art and "indecency."[22]

When the publicity surrounding Shawn's beauty showed no signs of stopping, St. Denis violated her own vow of secrecy by letting it slip to a reporter
that she had married "the world's most beautiful man."[23] St. Denis denied
that her admission was a self-interested ploy to siphon Shawn's newfound celebrity. Her innocence was plausible, given that just days before the interview
the newlyweds finally had consummated their summer marriage on Shawn's
October 22 birthday. Shawn said it was St. Denis's birthday present to him.[24]
Both were virgins at the time.

A blind item in a St. Louis newspaper on October 30 announced their
union: "St. Denis Married."[25] In the following days the news about the
dancing couple's "secret marriage" was reported in local papers across the
country. Within a month's time, the short news item developed into complete features on the couple, now characterizing their marriage as "an interesting experiment in eugenics." On November 22, 1914, the *Washington
Post* announced the marriage between Shawn and St. Denis in a satirical article entitled "Students of Eugenics Closely Watching this Marriage: Union
of the Splendidly Developed Dancer Ruth St. Denis and Edwin Shawn, 'the
Handsomest Man in America,' May Produce Results of Great Value to the
Science of Race Betterment." (See Figure 2.3.) The writer mocked the couple's
"eugenic charms" and speculated that the medical community will scrutinize
these "perfect specimens of humanity" given their great promise to produce
a "eugenic baby" and to "improve our poor, deformed race." Shawn and St.

Denis left themselves vulnerable to the writer's sendup by relaying anecdotes about their physical and artistic exceptionality. St. Denis, the established world-famous dancer, is portrayed as a beauty with strength that would "prostrate an ordinary man" yet is "remarkably qualified to be the progenitor of a more beautiful race." St. Denis explained that she decided to marry Shawn because she "could not bear to think of leaving him alone with those nymphs," referring to the young female dancers who always surrounded him on and off stage. Shawn's unquestionable beauty forced the writer to speculate whether a eugenicist would approve of him as an "ideal of manhood." Shawn apparently misled the reporter into thinking that he "never had a serious illness in his whole life, and that every organ is in perfect condition,"

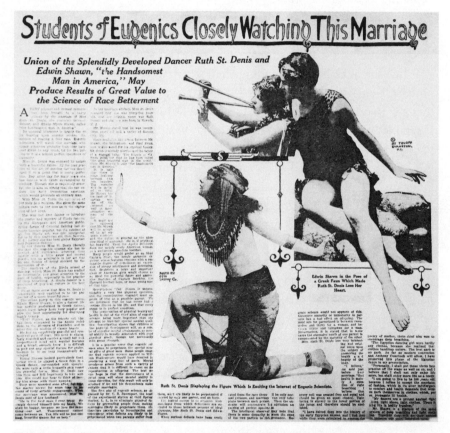

Figure 2.3. "An Interesting Experiment in Eugenics," *Washington Post*, November 22, 1914. Denishawn Scrapbook, vol. 4. Courtesy of the Jerome Robbins Dance Division, New York Public Library.

when, in fact, during his junior year of college, he was hospitalized with temporary paralysis from the waist down, a reaction to medicine he was prescribed for diphtheria. Ultimately, the writer's exaggerated descriptions of the couple's superiority dramatize the "unusual" nature of their union, especially their twelve-year age difference and unconventional profession as dancers. "Eugenic science would not approve of this," quips the writer, who also mentions the inexplicable gap in time between the couple's August wedding and its November announcement, pointing to a potential crack in the veneer of their eugenic luster.

Eugenics—a nineteenth-century neologism derived from the Greek, meaning "wellborn" or "good breeding"—was a "pseudoscience" or "an epiphenomenon of a number of sciences, which all intersected at the claim that it was possible to consciously guide human evolution" toward a physical, intellectual, and moral ideal through selective breeding.[26] By the 1920s, the United States had become a "eugenical world."[27] From the courtroom to the cinema, the scientific laboratory to the museum, eugenics permeated nearly every sphere of American culture, spreading its promise of "race betterment" and anxiety about American degeneracy. This eugenic creed would form the basis of Shawn's own conviction that dancing was "the supreme method for becoming identified with cosmic forces and through that identity being able to shape those forces towards the benefits of one's own tribe and self."[28] For Shawn, eugenics and dancing were affined "methods" for (re)producing ideal bodies.

The term "eugenics" was coined by Sir Francis Galton, a British scientist who developed the theories of evolution and natural selection made famous by his cousin Charles Darwin. By taking a statistical approach to the study of heredity, Galton inspired a social movement aimed at improving the genetic gene pool (what he referred to as "germ plasm") through "selective breeding."[29] This end was most often sought through two means: "positive eugenics," which promoted higher rates of fertility among the most socially and physically able members of society, and "negative eugenics," which sought to improve the gene pool through the restriction, segregation, or elimination of undesirable traits of the "unfit," including the "feeble-minded," insane, poor, and terminally ill. Rarely applied neutrally, these measures carried out a broad range of policies that cut across the ideological and political spectrum. Eugenics influenced a host of progressive reforms, including the development of sex education, the legalization of birth control, labor reform, and women's suffrage. However, eugenic theories also advanced discriminatory attitudes and policies based on race, ethnicity, class, and sex. For instance, it provided a "scientific" rationale for sterilization programs and anti-immigration policies. The most extreme manifestation of negative eugenics was the Nazi Party's "Final Solution," a program that justified involuntary sterilization and euthanasia of the mentally retarded and terminally ill, and, subsequently, the systematic extermination of Jews, blacks, and homosexuals in order to promote the "Master" Aryan race. As its genocidal implications became painfully clear in the aftermath of the Holocaust, the international eugenics movement lost its momentum.

In the United States, the eugenics movement gained momentum at the turn of the century through the establishment of scholarly organizations and research institutes. Three of the most influential centers of eugenics research, publishing, and teaching were the American Breeders' Association, which was founded in 1903 and published *American Breeders Magazine* (later, the *Journal of Heredity*); the Eugenics Record Office, which opened in 1919 in Cold Spring Harbor, New York; and the American Eugenics Society, which formed in 1922 in New Haven, Connecticut, and counted among its members J. P. Morgan, Miss E. B. Scripps, and Dr. John Harvey Kellogg, who delivered the welcoming address to the First National Conference on Race Betterment in January 1914.[30] With financial support from philanthropic organizations such as the Carnegie Institute, eugenics research was conducted at leading universities, including Yale, Harvard, Columbia, and Stanford.[31] Eugenics also found an influential spokesman in former US president Theodore Roosevelt, whose 1914 article "Twisted Eugenics" warned against the threats of "race deterioration."[32] Ideas about "race betterment" were disseminated to the American masses by "combining entertainment with art and education with recreation" via "better baby" contests and hygiene exhibitions at public fairgrounds.[33] For example, the Eugenics Record Office trained young eugenicists to perform field studies and gather information for the institute's degeneracy studies. In 1913, one of its first tasks was to write a play titled *Acquired or Inherited?*, a "eugenical comedy in four acts."[34] In 1913, Wisconsin was the first of thirty-five states that eventually adopted eugenic marriage legislation. States began to require that couples earn marriage certificates based on successful completion of medical exams, which often included tests for sexually transmitted diseases.[35] It was in this context of marriage reform that Shawn and St. Denis wed.

Despite the public fascination with eugenics, especially in the year leading to their marriage, Shawn and St. Denis initially rejected their eugenic status in an interview with the *San Francisco Bulletin*. "Eugenics was not our motive when we married. Was it, Ted?" St. Denis led." Shawn nodded in agreement, then added: "Of course, if it turns out that way we would be delighted."[36] Though they understood their union in terms of religion and not science, they eventually welcomed the association with eugenics if it meant helping the public to better understand their art. The burden of their eugenic promise infiltrated the way they understood their unconventional relationship as well. Writing to Shawn, St. Denis described how their life would lead them to create a type of eugenic art that brought faith and science together:

> I go back not naturally to your first long letter about your tragically starved state—sensationally and emotionally and I agree to its right to be satisfied—you are so constituted that it throws your whole being out of harmony—when your need for joy in sensation is denied—it may be that it is the urge of unborn children crying to be born—that gives us this longing for delight—it doubtless is—yet it is equally plain to me that we are endowed with the capacity to born other children—other forms of creation = art + science and labors of all kinds—and that or these we need also the joy of conception.[37]

Almost immediately following the spate of articles declaring their marriage an "interesting experiment in eugenics," St. Denis and Shawn began adopting the language of eugenics to promote their artistic vision, namely, that dancing was a means toward attaining social and physical health. This much reflected in the title of an article St. Denis and Shawn published in *Mercury*: "Dancing Real Factor in Developing Strong and Virile Race of Men."

Following the tour, Shawn and St. Denis set out to establish a school in Los Angeles so that they could fulfill their eugenic promise—or as St. Denis wrote so "that parentage which it was our destiny to achieve began to gestate." "The School" invaded most of their underlying thoughts as they completed the tour. As with all matters in their "experimenting relationship" they had to negotiate all the details of their personal and professional lives, including the name of this venture. To bolster ticket sales in each city, St. Denis was routinely roped into various marketing gimmicks. In Houston, Texas, for example, she was asked to auction bales of cotton, the proceeds from which were to be donated to a local charity. In Portland, Oregon, a theater manager organized a competition to rename *The St. Denis Mazurka*, a dance that meant to capture the excitement generated from the popular *Pavlova Mazurka*. (See Figure 2.4.) Reportedly, over 300 Portlandians submitted an entry. The selection committee (including two local dancing teachers) selected the offering of a young girl named Miss Margaret Ayer who suggested the title *Denishawn Rose Mazurka*. If her innovative contraction of the artists' last names were not enough, her reference to "The Rose" City, an emblem of Portland, tipped the scale in her favor.

Figure 2.4. Ted Shawn and Ruth St. Denis in *St. Denis Mazurka* (1915). Photograph by Hartsook. Denishawn Collection. Courtesy of the Jerome Robbins Dance Division, New York Public Library.

Long gone from Portland, St. Denis and Shawn received word of the winning title in San Francisco during the final days of the first tour. The "Denishawn" name came just as they were plotting to settle on the West Coast with a school. It was an ideal name for the school, though St. Denis insisted on a qualification: "Ruth St. Denis School of the Dance and Its Related Arts." Indeed, nearly nine months from their wedding night, the Denishawn School opened its doors.

Birth of a Dancing Nation, 1915–1917

The Denishawn School was established in the spring of 1915 at the Parkinson Estate, a craft house that sat high above the intersection of Sixth and St. Paul Streets in Los Angeles. The house accommodated a few residential students, but the first cohort of Denishawn students were local young women, mostly former students of Shawn's, who paid the $1 daily rate, which covered class, lunch, and a lecture. All activities took place within the walled-in grounds of terraced lawns and eucalyptus trees. A 40' x 80' dancing platform with a gabled roof was erected to serve as an outdoor studio; this turned out to be a far better alternative than the original idea, which was to conduct class on the lawn. (See Figure 2.5.) The house also had a small pool, where students cooled off after hours of dancing under the intense summer sun, and a spacious living room for private lessons in the afternoon for those with professional ambitions. In brochures and interviews, Shawn and St. Denis boasted that the property was ideally situated in relative isolation but a short walk to the shopping district; like the dances they created there, Denishawn house was idyllic yet never too far from the commercial path.

Shawn launched a recruiting campaign directed at dance teachers and exhibition dancers. He printed brochures about the school's philosophy and curriculum, promising that within two lessons students would master the *St. Denis Mazurka*, "the Shawn step," the barcarolle, and the Hawaiian hesitation. He also advertised private lessons for children at $5 per hour, as well as $1 open classes in the late afternoon "for mothers and Club Women" and another for "business women and older school girls." Evening options included a class for "young women who are employed during the day" and an evening men's class. The brochure also advertised Shawn's services as a talent agent to place dancing acts in vaudeville. The school hosted its first Friday night supper dance on March 28, hosted by a roster of patronesses followed

Figure 2.5. Tented dancing platform at the Denishawn School, 600 St. Paul Street, Los Angeles, California. 1916. Photograph by Putnam and Valentine. Courtesy of the Jerome Robbins Dance Division, New York Public Library.

by a full day of classes the next day. Shawn hired a capable secretary he had known from his days at the water department to help market the school and collect tuition in a cigar box.

Shawn was the main instructor. Each morning for an hour and a half to two hours he led students in stretching and breathing exercises, a ballet barre, lessons derived from Delsarte and Duncan, national and folk dances, and sometimes unspecified "experimental exercises." Shawn also lectured to aspiring young artists about dance as a profession and art. St. Denis would join for the last hour to teach an Oriental dance or a "silent dance" (what she called dancing with percussion only). Shawn was proud of the curricular inclusivity: "This was the summer of 1915, and practically every important principle of movement was in use at Denishawn that summer, a curriculum that the 'modern' German school claimed to have discovered and first promulgated five to ten years later."

For publicity purposes, Shawn lured cameramen to the property with the promise of capturing his young students prancing about in bathing suits.

He often repeated the rumor that there was a heavy uptick in rental fees for the apartments in the building that faced the Denishawn property. Those peeping Toms, as well as the entire Denishawn enterprise, were lampooned in a large cartoon published in the *Los Angeles Record*. (See Figure 2.6.) The sendup depicts Denishawn students as society matrons in search of their missing figures or blushing maidens anxious to acquire a few athletic

Figure 2.6. "Men are barred from this Modern Garden of Eden." Satirical cartoon of the Denishawn School. *L.A. Record*, May 29, 1915. Denishawn Scrapbook, vol. 3. Courtesy of the Jerome Robbins Dance Division, New York Public Library.

curves while their husbands crowd on the neighboring rooftops, desperate to find out what their wives and daughters were doing in the "Adamless," "modern" garden of Eden. Drawn from the point of view of a spy who was crouched just beyond the estate walls, the cartoon also points out the hypocrisy that Denishawn's "back-to-nature beauty dancing" was accompanied by the modern technology of the Victrola. The press struggled to understand Denishawn and its pretenses—or more nearly, its boldness to blur the lines between the stage and real life. It might be said that the Denishawn student's most rigorous training was in imagination and audacity. That is not to say that looking exotic and natural was only a matter of the mind. Maintaining one's appearance also required tremendous talent and resources. Perhaps the best example of the Denishawn dissonance is symbolized by its most distinctive resident, a peacock that Shawn had given to St. Denis as a first wedding anniversary gift. (She gifted Shawn an opal wedding ring, a family heirloom.) Though meant to convey a luxurious exoticism, the peacock was a costly pet, requiring Shawn to spend several days building a cage large enough to contain it. (At first he did not believe that peacocks could fly.) Later that summer, the peacock escaped, forcing Shawn to scale rooftops over a mile from the Denishawn house. Having failed to catch the peacock, he entrusted a twelve-year-old boy with capturing the bird, for which Shawn paid him a dollar.

It is possible to get a glimpse of what those peering neighbors might have seen thanks to an extant three-minute film of Denishawn from the summer of 1916.[38] The film leads the viewer onto the grounds, following a group of well-dressed guests, quite likely the patrons of one of the famous supper dances. It then cuts to a scene of young Denishawn students filing in from the dressing room, each pausing before a turbaned servant to disrobe and hand him her kimono. The film also captures a rare instance of St. Denis leading a class, demonstrating a gesture of the arms, as well as Shawn teaching a private lesson to a young girl on pointe. Emphasizing the school's scholarly aspirations, Shawn sits on the porch with an oversized French costume book. Adding a sense of the glamour and mystery, St. Denis pulls a peacock feather from a vase, while embracing her very own live peacock. The film then captures students cooling off in the pool, a scenario that evokes Mack Sennett's bathing beauties, which came to the screen in 1915. Although Sennett's bathing queens were part of his slapstick antics, mostly of lower- and middle-class girls, the Denishawn girl was a socialite or starlet. In the final moment of the film, the Denishawns prepare for an afternoon tea, in respectable formal clothes.

Inasmuch as Shawn promoted Denishawn as a locus of social activity and public interest, it was foremost a center for making serious art and learning. He and St. Denis continued to create work together, though he became increasingly frustrated with how she would turn rehearsals into performances, inviting so many people into the studio that there would be hardly any space to dance. Their effort to create a serious arts school was not entirely lost on the press. By July, the *Los Angeles Herald* pronounced the Denishawn School "An Institution of National Importance" noting that the school was the nation's only to rival Duncan's small school outside Paris, the Dalcroze school in Dresden, and the Bolshoi in Moscow. Of course, there already existed several influential dance schools in the United States, though no "great" ones in the estimation of the writer who claimed Denishawn as a tourist destination: "To have been to Los Angeles and not to have visited Denishawn, is not to have seen Los Angeles."

Denishawn was not the only "institution of national importance" gaining notoriety in Los Angeles. A banner year for both the art of dance and film, 1915 saw the establishment of America's first school dedicated to the development of a national dance, as well as the release of D. W. Griffith's epic silent film *Birth of a Nation*, starring Denishawn student Lillian Gish. Film producers and directors took notice of Denishawn. From its very first year as a school it established itself as a go-to place for aspiring motion picture stars to study the art of physical expression. D. W. Griffith, who knew Shawn from his tango tea days at the Angelus Hotel, sent over a group of girls to Denishawn twice a week for dance and movement instruction. Among the aspiring starlets were the two co-stars of his film *Lilly and the Rose*, Lillian Gish and Roszika Dolly (of the Dolly Sisters), for whom Shawn created dances for the film. Though Shawn never devoted himself to choreographing for motion pictures, in the ensuing years he would coach dancers, help to create routines for incidental scenes, and even serve as choreographer for several popular and experimental film projects.

As the first summer session at Denishawn in Los Angeles came to a close, Shawn and St. Denis began to concentrate on their upcoming tour arranged by Harry W. Bell. They subleased the Denishawn house to Lillian and Dorothy Gish's mother who used the space in the early mornings and late evenings for the young ingénues to practice their lessons. (The Denishawn house made a perfect hideaway for Mother Gish to keep her daughters' careers in film a secret from the rest of the family.) The tour launched at the Mason Opera House in Los Angeles and concluded at the Hudson Theater in New York, where on January 28, 1906, St. Denis had made history as the first dancer to present a program of solo dances on a Broadway stage. A decade later, St. Denis appeared with Shawn and the first lineup of "Denishawn Dancers," a select group of eight young women, including Margaret Loomis, the daughter of the owner of the Angelus Hotel in Los Angeles; Carol Dempster, who later became a star in D. W. Griffith's *Broken Blossoms*; and Florence Andrews, who rechristened herself Florence O'Denishawn when she joined the Ziegfeld Follies. An accomplished ballerina, Sadie Vanderhoff, joined Denishawn in spring 1915 after St. Denis and Shawn saw her perform at a charity ball at the St. Francis Hotel. She studied that first summer at Denishawn and performed as Vanda Hoff, later becoming the main fixture in Brother St. Denis's vaudeville dance-drama *The Dancing Girl of Delhi*, and after that, the bride to Paul Whiteman, "Broadway's monarch of jazz." Claire Niles, a boyish brunette, performed a baseball dance and later appeared in the "Ruth St. Denis Concert Dancers." Yvonne Sinnard, married but restless, and Chula Mongon were the only two not to go on to "individual fame." Another key member joined the company along the tour: accompanist Louis Horst. Shawn and St. Denis met the pianist in San Francisco and immediately recognized that he would be an asset to the company. He started as accompanist and within the year was elevated to musical director. In some measure, Horst provided the foundation the company sorely needed when Brother Denis left the company to study engineering at Columbia University. Though he would later come back into the Denishawn fold, he left the company in fine standing. Based on the success of their Hudson Theater appearance, Brother was able to book the company on a fifty-six-week vaudeville tour starting in the spring of 1916 with time off to run the Denishawn School again that summer. Their Hudson Theater concert was a huge success, attracting Meyerfeld of the Orpheum Circuit to come see for himself. He eventually booked them in the Palace Theatre in New York, "the Ultimate Mecca," where no other performer apart from Sarah Bernhardt had booked a second week. The Denishawn concerts turned away 5,000 people.

The Denishawn vaudeville tour on the Keith circuit coincided with the first US tour of Diaghilev's Ballets Russes, the avant-garde ballet company. Escaping war-torn Europe, the Ballets Russes set out to bring its modernist dance, music, and art to seventeen American cities. *The Dramatic Mirror* suspected that Keith's plan was to have Denishawn trail the path of the Ballets Russes. The intense media attention that gave Shawn the opportunity to distinguish Denishawn from the European counterpart in nationalist terms, even as it resembled and aspired to some of the most distinguishing aesthetic innovations of the Ballets Russes. As the specter of the war gripped the country and in the presence of the foreign artistic behemoth that was Diaghilev, Denishawn was rebranded as a distinctly American enterprise in the pages of national magazines. As US involvement in the war seemed inevitable, Denishawn's nationalist appeal made it possible for the company to resonate with a diverse and wide range of audiences.

Within a span of fifteen months, Shawn's dancing enterprise leaped from the society pages to the features section of diverse and influential publications with national circulations. Perhaps the most surprising of places was the most visible: Shawn and St. Denis landed on the pages of *National Geographic* in April 1916, the month the United States entered the war—in a special photoessay called "The Land of the Best," a celebration of the country's "scenic grandeur and unsurpassed natural resources." The special issue meant to recalibrate the focus on overseas destinations within travel literature and guide books by inspiring readers to marvel at America's own "hallowed and historic spots." To that end, the issue featured stunning black and white photos of landmark sites (a snowy Capitol Hill, the Brooklyn Bridge, Old Faithful) as well as a panoply of American "types" (the near-extinct cowboy, a Hopi basket maker, a medicine man). At the heart of this photo-essay was a section of color autochromes, the first to appear in *National Geographic*, including two featuring Shawn and St. Denis in poses from their dance *The Garden of Kama*, a dance they had created the year prior. (See Insert Figures 2.7 and 2.8.) The dance took its title and inspiration from a popular 1901 collection of love poems purported to be English translations of Indian and Persian verse, when in fact they were the eroticized lyrics of English poet Adela Florence Nicolson published under a male pseudonym, Laurence Hope, and with the exoticizing drawings by British illustrator Byam Shaw. The book, and the Denishawn dance it inspired, rode the wave of interest created by Richard Francis Burton's English translations of *Arabian Nights* and the *Kama Sutra*. However, that interest does not explain the confounding presence of St. Denis and Shawn in full Orientalist costume in the mythical garden of Indian mythology, nor how their dance fits into a nationalist vision of American life. The Garden of Kama is not quite Yosemite.

Whereas *National Geographic* established Denishawn's place on the American landscape, the April 17, 1917, issue of *Vogue* increased its glamour quotient with a feature on the school directed at young socialites who aspired to a life on the stage.[39] "The Education of the Dancer," attributed to Ruth St.

Denis, celebrated the school's approach to training dancers using the "individuality system," wherein the teacher builds training around each student's physical and kinesthetic strengths and personality, all determined in a "diagnostic lesson" during which a "prescription" is issued for artistic development. Focused on the individual's "original inclination" rather than imitating another, this no-approach approach is described by St. Denis as distinctly American and thus preferable to any imposed foreign system. "The system of training at 'Denishawn' is, paradoxically, to have no system." Individuality was essential not only to Denishawn's artistic mission, but also its marketing strategy, as Shawn sought to attract aspiring performers in need of unique routines to make it in vaudeville. Artistic differentiation was the building block of a career in dance. Though it heralded an inclusive curriculum, Denishawn was not nearly as focused on teaching its students to dance as in teaching them to be dancers.

The *Vogue* article also features photographs and brief accounts of Denishawn's success stories, focusing on the most dramatic transformations made by the Denishawn method. Chief among them was Ada Forman, who arrived at Denishawn "not a tremendously promising young lady," but her training made her suitable for a paying public—and a star in the Marigold Follies in Chicago with Javanese dances created for her by Shawn. Forman is appropriately pictured performing *The Vogue Dance*. In addition to courting charity ball and pageant darlings, Shawn vigorously recruited aspiring film actresses to Denishawn, including Margaret Loomis, who attended both summers of the school. The article explains how, thanks to the Denishawn method, Loomis began to land leading roles with Lasky Studios, giving her access to work she wouldn't otherwise have ever encountered and thus saving her from becoming "morbidly introspective," a hazard of her family's wealth.

As Denishawn gained notoriety, Shawn, too, emerged from behind the veils of St. Denis. He appeared on the cover of two popular magazines, each featuring articles about his vision for dancing for men. The trade magazine the *New York Dramatic Mirror* featured Shawn as the Egyptian god Osiris on its May 6, 1916, cover. (See Figure 2.9.) The following week the same publication ran his "A Defense of the Male Dancer" in which he espoused dance as a "life of work and a science" as opposed to leisure and art, thus positioning himself in contradistinction to the famous Russian ballet star Vaslav Nijinsky who was soon to embark on a fifty city tour of the United States. With one stone, Shawn took aim at both Nijinsky and the European audiences that celebrated him: "[Nijinsky] represents the decadent, the freakish, the feverish.

In Paris, before the war, only the unusual could interest the sex-tired, blasé city. So Nijinsky conquered."[40] Shawn lays down the proverbial gauntlet against the Russian dance star's sexual ambiguity by declaring that "American demands masculinity more than art." Shawn's critiques of Nijinsky would escalate over the years especially when Nijinsky encroached on Shawn's territory of American dance. During his tour of the United States, for example, Nijinsky went to the press with his ideas for creating an American ballet with American set designs and themes based on the writings of Edgar Allan Poe. Shawn retorted by calling Nijinsky "a wild orchid on a rotting log."[41] Nijinsky was not Shawn's only target. He increasingly set out to diminish the artistry of women performers as well, such as Gertrude Hoffman ("Never an artist, always an imitator"), Maud Allan ("not a creative artist"), Anna Pavlova, and Adeline Genée ("not creative or original"). In a curious departure from the glowing strains in which he had previously discussed Isadora Duncan, Shawn leveled a serious criticism against the great dancer, a criticism so pernicious that the article's author would dare not repeat Shawn's explanation for how "she failed as a dancer." Another writer less concerned about slander published Shawn's claim that "Isadora gave us style but no great dances."

As Shawn tried to muscle his way into the tight circle of international dance elites, he also began to display his physique in the pages of proto-muscle and fitness magazines. Shawn appeared on the cover of the July 1917 issue of *Physical Culture*, a magazine created by Bernarr Macfadden, a self-branded "kinesitherapist" or "teacher of higher physical culture" who trains in "the use of movements in the cure of disease." The unofficial magazine of the eugenics movement, *Physical Culture* published its first issue in March 1899 and grew to sell close to 50 million copies between the two world wars. MacFadden's publication empire grew and to this day is the publisher of record for *Dance Magazine*.

For the cover, Shawn posed regally, barefoot and bare-chested, in a pair of floral bikini briefs and a red cape. (See Figure 2.10.) The accompanying article "Dancing for Men" offers a pithy yet questionable history of dance that chastises the European court for feminizing dance. To counter that history, Shawn extols the virtues of the ancient all-male Pyrrhic dance and includes a sidebar of exercises along with twenty-four bars of music—an excerpt from the *Denishawn Schottische*—so that a man could perform the routine at home to achieve Shawn's physique. Shawn even suggests that soldiers would benefit from dance training, a comment that, like the magazine's "War Bread for America" coverline, signals the ongoing war crisis. It was a telling comment,

Figure 2.9. Ted Shawn on the cover of the *Dramatic Mirror*, May 6, 1916. Photograph by Ira L. Hill.

Figure 2.10. Ted Shawn on the cover of *Physical Culture*, July 1917.

seeing that Shawn himself would enlist within months of the magazine's publication.

When Denishawn completed its first vaudeville tour and returned to Los Angeles in summer 1916, it was ready for its second summer school session. Students from across the country were successfully recruited via features and ads in *Harper's* and *Vogue*. Among the new students was a twenty-two-year-old Martha Graham. Horst recalled accompanying her first lesson with St. Denis. Private lessons with St. Denis cost $50 and included two complete dances lessons as well as costume designs.

Shawn recalled saying to Graham, "'You have no money for private lessons, but I am so interested. I still believe that we can do something with this. I want to do this on my own. I will work with you, give you all the time I can. I'm interested in seeing what we can bring out of this.' So we did work together. It came along."[42]

Other new personalities at the school that summer included a young sculptor named Allan Clark. A student at the Art Institute of Chicago, Clark wanted to specialize in moving figures. Shawn convinced him that if he wanted to specialize in dancers, he would need to learn to dance himself, so Clark left school for Los Angeles. The two became close friends. At some point, Shawn and Allan Clark spent a few days at "The Honeysuckle Court" at Laguna Cliffs. Clark's sculpture of Shawn was one of Shawn's prized possessions.

The highlight of the 1916 season was the historic appearance of Shawn and St. Denis in a pageant at the Greek Theatre at the University of California at Berkeley, to an audience of 10,000 to 12,000 people. A gift from publishing magnate William Randolph Hearst, the Greek Theatre had presented theatrical stars like Sarah Bernhardt and Maude Adams, but never before had the venue hosted a dance performance. A Berkeley English professor named William Dallam Armes encouraged the University Trustees to extend an invitation to Ruth St. Denis, which they did. St. Denis was not unfamiliar with the pageant circuit, herself appearing in a famous pageant for Louis C. Tiffany in New York City. As one reporter put it: "America is masque-mad and pageant crazy." Pageantry in the early 1900 focused on "process over product" to address unique local community goals. Shawn's pageants were spectacles but refused the reformist ideology embedded in contemporary pageantry. For this occasion, Shawn and St. Denis created a hybrid performance they called a "dance-pageant."

It was an arduous three-week undertaking. In addition to composing, teaching, and rehearsing the dances, Shawn had to oversee the sets and costumes, many of which he created himself. Plus, he had to manage a cast of forty performers from Los Angeles and over a hundred more extras from the student body of the university. On top of all that, Shawn underwent massive dental work right before the dance-pageant and was in excruciating pain.

To court the attention of newspaper photographers, Shawn held fully costumed "rehearsals" in public venues throughout the Los Angeles area. He rehearsed the Egyptian section on the beach, transforming the Pacific Ocean into the banks of the Nile. The group practiced their Indian nautch dances on the Sierras standing in for the Himalayas. And they reviewed Greek dances on the San Gabriel Mountains, with Mount Lowe standing in for Mount Olympus. For this particular rehearsal, they were sponsored by the Hupp Motor Company, whose popular automobile conspicuously shows up in all the press photographs, including a provocatively anachronistic juxtaposition of Denishawn dancers processing as if in an ancient frieze in the background of a photo of the modern Hupmobile. (See Figure 2.11.)

Figure 2.11. Denishawn Dancers in Automobile Feature. *Los Angeles Examiner*, June 17, 1917. Denishawn Scrapbook, vol. 2. Jerome Robbins Dance Division, New York Public Library.

A Dance-Pageant of Egypt, Greece, and India (or *The Life and After-life of Greece, India, and Egypt*) premiered at the Greek Theatre on the evening of July 29, 1916. By framing the dance-pageant as a representation of both life and the afterlife in three great ancient civilizations (on the Styx, Nile, and Ganges), Shawn and St. Denis opened up possibilities to move between ethnographic realism and spirited mythic exploration, as well as to present dance as an expression of both social science and religion. (See Insert Figure 2.12.) The pageant opened with a duet by St. Denis and Shawn called *Tillers of the Soil*, a noble depiction of physical labor exerted by a couple who plow and sow their land. One critic noted: "The labor is glorified as to take on new meaning." It was a solemn and restrained way to open a program that would celebrate the highly eccentric customs and rites of the ancient world.

The Greek section included all manner of ancient dance—veil dances, urn dances, a Pyrrhic dance, and a bacchanal. It even featured a compressed dramatization of the Orpheus and Eurydice myth featuring Shawn, Margaret Loomis, and three children, set to music by Massenet and Ada de Lachau and arranged by Louis Horst. *Pyrrhic Dance* was for all-men dancers, including Arthur Buruel, with whom Shawn had a sexual tryst when he had lived in Los Angeles. One critic noted that this dance for men received the greatest response, triggering an encore, which Shawn modestly denied.

In the Indian section of the pageant, Shawn performed the role of a hunter slain by his enemies, then, set to the sounds of Wagnerian Fire Music, cremated on a funeral pyre with St. Denis coming on to perform *suttee*, the custom of a widow immolating herself on the pyre. Then, a snake charmer (played by Edward Kuster) played a flute, inciting six young women to emerge from baskets and perform a writhing and slithering dance. One critic highlighted the importance of the all-men dances in the Hindu and Greek sections, noting this as a valuable contribution (and perhaps more sophisticated as it required a level of imagination): "If women are going to vote, why under the sun should men not dance?"[43]

The dance-pageant was an unqualified success for Shawn, who enjoyed his largest audiences to date, not only in Berkeley but in encore productions in San Diego on the following Saturday evening (August 5) and before 4,000 people at the original Shrine Auditorium in Los Angeles (September 15)—a "Farewell to LA" performance before they headed off on a thirty-six-week tour.[44] It generated enough interest and was enough of a society event to fill seats in theaters across America with audiences eager to catch a glimpse into the world of pageants that was once reserved for the likes of Tiffany and

Hearst. The dance-pageant was also an artistic coup in that it required both St. Denis and Shawn to venture beyond creating solo and partner dances into choreographing for groups. The many short ensemble dances they composed for the dance-pageant provided content for Denishawn programs for years to come. Moreover, the experience of performing to the accompaniment of a forty-piece orchestra opened the door for Denishawn to enter the world of orchestral music (even though the musicians who performed for the dance-pageant were displeased by having to perform for dancers.)

The wholesome Denishawn image displayed in the pages of newspapers and magazines was a welcomed relief from the relentless headlines reporting devastating war activity throughout Europe. Denishawn saw its enrollment swell, requiring Shawn to find a new home for its operations. On June 11, 1917, the second Denishawn School opened its doors for its third summer program, this time in a residence of three connected multi-story buildings at 616 S. Alvarado Street facing Westlake Park (now MacArthur Park). (See Figure 2.13.) The new school boasted larger dormitories, several rehearsal floors, and a theater, the first-ever dedicated to dance. A tented dancing platform placed over a tennis court served as the open-air Denishawn Dance

Figure 2.13. Second Denishawn School, Westlake Park, Los Angeles, Summer 1918.

Theater, which seated 400 people. The inaugural performance series in the new theater attracted socialites and celebrities, which led to coverage of their attendance in the *Hollywood Inquirer*. The first was a benefit for the Red Cross.

The curriculum, program, and faculty were also expanded to match Shawn's grander vision for the school. The twelve-week semester cost $500 and included private lessons with St. Denis, room and board, lectures, and craft arts (set design, costume design, prop design) under the supervision of a master craftsman as well as visiting sculptors, photographers, and painters of note. The school offered a special course in Synthetic Stagecraft taught by Maxwell Armfield (husband of the novelist Constance Smedley). Henrietta Hovey, an exponent of the Delsarte method, also joined the faculty to teach "the motion and science of gesture." Hovey had seen Shawn perform in Los Angeles and approached him backstage to both compliment and scold: "Young man there was once you walked across the stage like a God—as for the rest of what you did—rot!" Shawn began to take private lessons with her and quickly realized the many similarities between the principles and exercises she taught under the rubric of Delsarte and the "Uni-Trinianism" of Mary Perry King and Bliss Carman. This was not a coincidence; Shawn learned that King was a former pupil of Hovey's. The lessons in Delsarte method transformed Shawn's approach to choreography, offering him a theory for harmonizing mind and body. Also on the roster was Miss Marion Kappes, who had received her training from the Dalcroze Institute in Hellerau and studied Eurhythmics, a highly physical approach to music training, with Émile Jaques-Dalcroze himself. The Denishawn brochure listed supporters and other pupils of the Dalcroze method, among them Mark Twain and William Butler Yeats.

The brochure boasted the acquisition of motion pictures of "real native dancing" from Burton Holmes (1870–1958), the "World's Most Famous Traveler." Famous for "bringing the world home," Holmes made excursions into the exotic, unknown, and hard-to-reach corners of the world, later incorporating his hand-painted photographs on glass slides and motion pictures of his travels into lecture presentations he called "travelogues." Many of Holmes's motion pictures are the first ever taken in certain countries, several including examples of dance. Shawn purchased some of those films with dances from Malaysia, Korea, Java, Spain, and beyond. Holmes's films signaled an important distinction between Denishawn and other schools, or at least it made that impression upon young dancers, including new student

Doris Humphrey. In fact, in her autobiography Humphrey notes that the brochure announcing the Holmes films was one of the reasons she decided to study at Denishawn.

At the outset of the summer of 1917, the plan was for the Denishawn School to run a thirty-six-week course starting in September and continue with its performance series, while the company would embark on a thirty-week tour starting in October. Despite the success of the summer program and the great exposure from the press, the war negatively impacted their touring prospects. St. Denis implausibly announced to the press her intention to take a hiatus from performing to focus on the development of the school, a clear signal that there was no work. The suggestion that St. Denis would choose teaching over performing was so incredible that rumors spread that she might be pregnant.

"I am not going to be a Mother!" St. Denis protested, then defended her right to take a break from the stage."[45] To affirm her devotion to the school, she disclosed her campaign to raise $500,000 to purchase a twenty-acre property to form an artist's colony with an amphitheater and swimming pool. Whatever her intentions were for making these public proclamations about her life and career, St. Denis was privately hoping for a way out of the business. In her diaries she expressed that she wanted Shawn to finish his college degree, while she minded the school.

Drills and Demonstrations, 1917–1918

In October 1916, Shawn went public with an idea for composing a dance liturgy, by which he meant performing a full church service entirely in movement. To the local papers, he likened the idea to the popular "rousing tent services" conducted by Billy Sunday "the baseball evangelist." The most popular proponent of Muscular Christianity in the United States, Sunday, like Shawn, had suffered from childhood frailty and had rebuilt his body as an athlete for Christ.[46] Shawn spoke of the idea as a way for him to heed his original calling to be a minister. A dance liturgy would also nicely balance a Denishawn program, tempering St. Denis's Buddhist and Hindu dances with a sobering dose of Christianity. He contextualized the concept of a dancing service by explaining that dancing was part of the Christian liturgy until the dawn of asceticism in the Middle Ages or Dark Ages when beauty and pleasure were condemned, then elaborated a larger vision for reestablishing the church liturgy, complete with a photo of himself in a religious vestment with arms open.

By the fall of 1917, this idea had evolved and with meager prospects for touring, Shawn took advantage of the lull in his schedule to deliver a "devotional dance service." By this time, his idea had begun to focus on a liturgy that demonstrated ideas of Christian Science. In fact, the press surrounding his dance liturgy briefly touched on the news that he and St. Denis had joined the Christian Scientists because of its emphasis on happiness. Shawn's liturgy offered "reverent, suitable movements to express all of the subtle relations between man and Maker" and required a fully responsive congregation in "vital expressive motion" rather than the usual perfunctory involvement of congregations.

The liturgy premiered on September 18, 1917, at the Scottish Rite Auditorium in San Francisco, to an audience of 300 women and a sprinkling of men, by one reporter's estimation. The performance started with an "invocation" from the Reverend Henry Frank, leader of the First Interdenominational Church, who received criticism for his support of the event. The choreography mimicked a complete service: an opening prayer, the twenty-third psalm, a hymn, the Doxology, the Gloria, a sermon, and a benediction. The Reverend Frank came in at intervals to explain the program, though a skeptical attendee thought the prayer seemed addressed to Delsarte rather than to the Lord. Most of Shawn's movement was pantomimic: breaking free from shackles (which inspired humorous comparisons with Houdini), walking in the desert, and listening to a choir of invisible angels.

News of Shawn's unorthodox liturgy made front-page news in San Francisco in an article about local clergymen's opinion of religious dancing (or at least dancing in church) as a "new method of worship." Apparently, a reporter asked the clergymen if they would attend the liturgy. Most responded with indifference, though a few vehemently opposed the idea, calling it a "sacrilege" that threatened to turn "a church into a dancehall." Another prepared to sermonize against it, using Shawn's performance as an occasion to emphasize that dancing might be a sign of worldliness but not godliness. The press even solicited a response from the Reverend Dr. Christian F. Reisner, the theatrically inclined minister from Denver who initially inspired Shawn to join the clergy. Reisner responded ambivalently, calling Shawn a "dreamer" who was "mistaken about the relationship between dancing and church."

Shawn returned to his idea of a dance liturgy several times throughout his career. When he performed parts of the liturgy in his theatrical program in 1921, he received even greater praise, with critics clamoring that audiences were held "spellbound by the dignity and exaltation of the service." With greater praise came fiercer criticism from both the clergy and the press. The performance even drew an informal protest at the First Methodist and Congregational churches in Riverside, California, which led to a resolution to ban all "sacrilegious entertainment." At least one of the congregants, how- ever, came to Shawn's defense by writing a letter to the editor of the local newspaper to point out that the Doxology, Psalms, and Gloria have been represented in music and art literature, and thus asked "why not dance?"[47] In time, Shawn effectively transformed the negative press, protests, and bans into grounds for his artistic martyrdom: "You know the man who translated the Bible into the English language was unceremoniously burned at the stake, so under the circumstances, I feel lucky that I wasn't tarred and feathered at least."[48]

Throughout the fall of 1917, Shawn volunteered as a Four-Minute Man, part of an effort established by President Woodrow Wilson to deliver brief pro-war messages to the public. He also participated in benefit performances that raised thousands of dollars for the Red Cross. Several were performed at Camp Kearny, a mobilization and training camp near San Diego, one of the thirty-two new military bases created in 1917, the same year that the Selective Service Act was implemented, another sign of the size the military would need to achieve in order to win the war overseas. Shawn, twenty-six, real- ized he would eventually be drafted from the stage to one of the camps. He weighed the possible benefits of enlisting versus getting drafted, namely, the possibility that he would be able to get transferred to the unit of his choosing, preferably the nearby Kearny, which would make it possible for him to re- main close to Denishawn operations. In December 1917, he enlisted and petitioned the general to be stationed at Kearny in the ambulance corp with which he had become familiar. He wrote: "I pictured myself, I guess, a sort of male Florence Nightingale, putting the cool hand on the fevered brow— a He-angel of mercy."[49] Shawn was all too eager to enlist in a "constructive rather than destructive" branch of the army. Plus, he genuinely liked the men at Kearny and looked forward to the possibility of living alongside them.

Always pragmatic, before heading to Camp Kearny Shawn took out an in- surance policy for St. Denis and an additional government insurance policy for $10,000, which would have left her $35,000 in case of his death. He also

quickened his pace on completing a manuscript that became *Pioneer &*
Prophet, a two-volume book dedicated to the art and career of Ruth St. Denis.
The idea for the book originated in 1915 when he found bundles of clippings
in St. Denis's home on 89th Street in New York, which he immediately organized into scrapbooks. He acted on the idea upon the publication of Arnold
Genthe's *The Book of the Dance* (1920), which featured the photographer's
portraits of dancers with "modern dance tendencies," including St. Denis, as
well as Isadora Duncan, Maud Allan, Loïe Fuller, and Anna Pavlova. *Pioneer*
& Prophet was a labor of love. It was also an insurance policy of sorts, as
Shawn was counting on its proceeds to support his wife should he not return
from war.

His concern for St. Denis's welfare intensified when on December 4, 1917,
St. Denis's seventy-year-old father Thomas Dennis died. A Civil War veteran,
he was buried at Soldier's Home. During the week of her father's death, St.
Denis gave birth to a new idea while watching Isadora Duncan dance at the
Shubert Theater on December 7, 1918, in Los Angeles. She coined the term
"music visualization"—a type of dance she would later define as "the scientific translation into bodily action of rhythmic, melodic and harmonic structure of a musical composition, without intention in any way to 'interpret'
or reveal any hidden meaning apprehended by the dancer."[50] Shawn, too,
began to experiment with composing dances wherein the movement faith-
fully followed the musical dynamics. He wrote to St. Denis about his progress
on creating a music visualization piece to a Bach "Two-Part Invention" and
the Denishawn students' excitement for it. He admitted that during working
hours, he missed Louis Horst more than St. Denis. He had to postpone his
work on the music visualizations until after the war. In the meantime, he prepared the school for his eventual absence; he planned for it to run through
the year at a profit, with Shawn teaching whenever possible to give students
their money's worth.

Before he left for Kearny, Shawn indulged in leisurely lunches planning future projects with Arthur Buruel and Allan Clark and swimming lessons with
surfer Vance Veith. He also began to search for a new house where he and
St. Denis could nest after the war.

The night before he left for Kearny, the faculty and staff at the school threw
him a farewell party. "I didn't know I was so loved as tonight," he wrote to St.
Denis.[51] Unwilling to sit idle as Shawn began military training, St. Denis decided to join the war effort by launching a vaudeville tour to raise money for
the Liberty bonds.

On February 1, 1918, Shawn arrived at the 158th Ambulance Company, 115th Sanitary Train at Camp Kearny near San Diego. The press had a field day reporting that the "Most Handsome Man" who had become famous performing ancient martial dances from far off places was now wearing fatigues for the United States while his wife hit the road to raise money. The press exaggerated the circumstances with headlines such as "Ruth St. Denis Dances Husband's Composition, While He Fights." Of course, St. Denis did not actually perform any of Shawn's dances on that tour (or any tour for that matter) nor did Shawn ever "fight" or even see a battlefield.

Shawn and St. Denis maintained a near-daily correspondence during his time at Kearny; these letters convey his relative easy adaptation to military life, much of which he genuinely enjoyed. He was proud to realize that he was able to match if not exceed many of the other soldiers in terms of physical strength and endurance when performing military drills, pouring concrete, or carrying sacks of potatoes. He found pleasure even in marching in line formation for over two hours in the oppressive heat and in full uniform. Shawn took it as a lesson in choreography: "The ultimate aim of this training is a body which responds immediately to the orders of the brain and handles itself with the least waste and jar under all circumstances." He also enjoyed the camaraderie and fraternity he found with other soldiers, even with a twenty-two-year-old illiterate bohemian man who called himself "Nigger Jensen." Shawn tried to justify his unlikely new friendship by explaining how Jensen was "a real person—with a real solid, substantial, character and a most likable personality and he has been good to me."[52] He assured St. Denis that his developing friendship with Jensen would not be a repeat of his relationship with "Frank Somebody" that turned sexual: "It is not a 'Frank' case at all. Divine Love always has met and always will meet. Perhaps the right real man friend will come in Jensen." Jensen would go on to become an important person to Shawn, someone who years later would perform in one of his most successful vaudeville ventures. By every measure, Shawn seemed to be thriving. He bragged: "Everyone here seems ecstatic over me in uniform—say I look marvelous, ten years younger—well rested beyond belief. This whole thing has been a blessed demonstration."

By "demonstration," Shawn was referring to his war experience using a favorite term of Christian Science founder Mary Baker Eddy to indicate a human act or expression that affirms belief in Divine Love. Shawn's letters to St. Denis were full of language and principles of Christian Science—or what they referred to as "CS." They were even written on stationery from the

Christian Science Camp Welfare Room, a beautiful space on the main street in San Diego that he had discovered during his first week at Camp Kearny.

Shawn was initially exposed to Christian Science years earlier from a woman he met in the worker's camp in Colorado. When he arrived in New York from California, before his marriage to St. Denis, he sought out more instruction from Lillian Cox, a once highly regarded member of the CS organization who had since relinquished her post as Second Reader at the Fifth Church. A strong, individual, progressive soul, Cox left the organization when she divorced her first husband Charles Charter, an unorthodox decision for a woman of her time. She eventually remarried, this time to Eugene R. Cox, chairman of the Publication Committee for the Christian Science Church, but remained a force of CS outside the fray. Shawn had met Cox before he married St. Denis, and she fast became his spiritual guide and teacher and remained so for many years. He consulted Cox a year earlier when he suggested a break from his Methodist upbringing to create a complete ballet based on the principles of Christian Science (CS). Cox helped Shawn use CS to guide his artistic vision.

For Shawn and St. Denis, the CS language of Spirit, Divine, Truth was a vehicle for expressing their love. He even addressed his wife as "My T-Ruth." They applied the CS belief that thought and prayer could correct the physical, sensual, material existence and desire to understand their interpersonal relationship and to give religious significance to their sexual attraction or lack thereof. CS offered a practical means to becoming more in the likeness of God. It emphasized a technique for becoming more godly, "a system of self-help domestic healing or as a religion of private contemplation."[53] For St. Denis, CS founder Eddy was a powerful feminist role model, especially as she privileged women's experience as a form of spiritual knowledge over the law of man. CS was a system that valued the creative power of thought and meditation over indoctrination, a "technique" that affined with Denishawn's own individuality system.

Before too long, Shawn had introduced CS to several soldiers. And at their request, he started to lead lessons, first with four and then six per week. When Jensen suffered from a very bad stomach ulcer that the doctor in the base could not readily heal, Shawn performed a faith healing and cured him. News of Shawn's healing powers brought more followers to help him to build a CS reading room at Kearny despite the deep antagonism from military brass. St. Denis sent him a copy of "First Church and Miscellany" for the library.

Woven throughout their exchanges about their shared devotion to divine concerns of Spirit and Truth were knotty threads concerning matters of flesh and sex. Shawn told St. Denis that the sexual frustration he experienced in the marriage was somehow resolved by the "primal manliness" of military life:

> I am going to speak of something <u>inside</u> which I am sure will interest you. You know how constantly my mind has been filled with sex in the past—sometimes to a torturing degree. Well, in the past three weeks I have thought less and felt less in this direction than any similar three weeks in over ten years. This is no emasculation but open air, hard work, a full brain, and a total lack of aesthetic surroundings.[54]

Less than a month later, he wrote St. Denis with an altogether different portrait of military life. Specifically, he described to her a traumatic dream he had involving other soldiers subjecting him to sexual images from which he needed St. Denis's protection:

> A fellow showed me some rotten, dirty pictures—the vilest things I have ever seen—beyond my powers of imagination. I felt like someone had thrown much all over my ideals of body, sex and all things sacred and beautiful. I wanted you to pick me up and wash me clean—but I had to do it myself—so I did.
> This herding together of these thousands of men is an unnatural condition and things [abhorrent] are bound to develop under these circumstances so it behooves me to stand guard at portals of thought.[55]

Shawn's upsetting dream—about a man forcing him to witness disturbing sexual images that shattered his sense of self—came at a time when he had rekindled his relationship with Frank "Something"—a man with whom he had had an affair years earlier. Frank "Something" was Frank Losee, a movie actor Shawn had met when he first moved to Los Angeles from Denver. He reconnected with Lossee when he returned to Los Angeles, despite St. Denis's skepticism about Shawn's inviting him back into his life—now theirs. She especially was upset by the idea that Shawn invited Lossee to board at Denishawn, sympathetic to the fact that his mother was terminally ill. Shawn ruminated on the irony that Lossee would be living at their marriage home, especially given that Shawn's affair with Frank was the cause of one of their first marital woes: "Truly this is a queer world."[56]

St. Denis did not tolerate the confession well. She wrote directly to Lossee, diagnosing his spiritual problems and detailing CS healing lessons she suggested he perform. To Shawn, she wrote hurtful responses about her desire to be independent from him both artistically and romantically. Her frankness tortured Shawn. Her explicit talk of her other romantic interests, her disparaging tirades against the institution of marriage, her flippantly entertaining the thought of bearing children were crushing to Shawn and she knew it. She shouldered her own guilt for finding herself in a failing marriage. St. Denis seemed to need the space to prove to herself that she could survive on her own, especially without her recently deceased father, her married brother, or even Belasco. With Shawn at Kearny, she now had the opportunity to take the risk. To the public eye, they were an ideal American couple—St. Denis was using her art to raise money for the war effort, Shawn at the army base protecting the freedom they enjoyed as artists. Within months, they were unraveling, jealous over the return of Shawn's male lover and St. Denis's return to her status of solo performer. Shawn knew the only way to salvage the marriage—and Denishawn—was to be in St. Denis's physical presence, to use his charm to persuade her to stay, though he had no idea when that time would come.

Shawn was given special weekend leave from Camp Kearny to perform at benefit performances. In his first three months alone he performed at eight Red Cross benefits that raised over $15,000. This service generated tremendous goodwill from Kearny brass that translated into granting Shawn permission to leave the base to attend to other professional projects. Even as early as a month into his time at Kearny he was off to Busch Gardens in Pasadena, to choreograph a dance for a film titled *Wild Youth* (1918), a period piece based on a novel by Sir Gilbert Parker. Shawn created a number of "allegorical scenes" to dramatize the novel's plot about the marital woes between a young wife and the older man she was forced to marry. Shawn was especially well suited for the task, given his own May–December marriage, and created group dances meant to convey to freedom and frivolity of youth. He later incorporated photo stills of his dancers frolicking in a glade with garlands into an advertisement for motion picture trade magazines, alerting producers that "no high class film production is complete without the Denishawn dancers" and promising the ability to deliver "dances correct as to country, period, and costumes."

"There is only one place in the United States where one can get a perfectly trained dancer and that is at Denishawn," said silent film actress Theda Bara, the star of *Cleopatra* (1917).[57] She might have come to that understanding by working alongside Denishawn dancers on the making of the film, one of many cast with Denishawn dancers.[58] Part of Denishawn's reputation as a starlet factory was based on the persistent falsehood that St. Denis and Shawn choreographed or were otherwise associated with D. W. Griffith's silent film *Intolerance* (1916). Though the film involves many Orientalist dancing scenes and thousands of dancers, neither St. Denis nor Shawn was part of the production.[59]

Within a month's time as a private in the army, Shawn formed a Christian Science reading group, created a dance for a motion picture, and reconnected with a former lover, all the while proving he was officer material. His captain recruited him for a training program for physical educators. Shawn was flattered and immediately agreed to take the examination, which he passed. For this specialized training, he was sent to the Fourth Officers' Training School. For the first time in a long while, Shawn felt out of his league—"an aesthetic nut" training alongside "hard boiled types" like sergeants, pugilists, rough guys generally. He started a rigorous ten-day program of exercises and drills. During a race he trampled over a fallen trainee, skinned his knee, and tore his pants, which reminded him of his "Old Dagger Dance days!"

St. Denis was impressed with his promotion. By June 1918, she had finished her tour and was back in Los Angeles, spending time with the Denishawn students she felt she had abandoned. In time, she even came around to understanding Shawn's determination with all matters related to Denishawn: "I had again such a clear sense today that what you are doing is making it possible for us to have our being + life + harmony—every hour of peaceful activity in dance is paid for, now—by your sweat and loneliness and drudgery—and that service—dear—cannot be lost."[60]

Later that month, St. Denis and Margaret Loomis joined Shawn to perform a benefit performance for the Red Cross at the Knights of Columbus Building near Camp Kearny. Shawn created buzz for the benefit by releasing to the press a letter he had sent to the US Secretary of War that outlined a proposal for integrating dance technique into military training for combat soldiers. In the letter, Shawn offered his expertise as dancer and soldier to implement the proposal, one that would modernize military training. Of course, Shawn's point was that dance training could instill efficient principles of motion such as coordination, agility, and strength. He clarified that he was not advocating that "American soldiers should fox-trot to Germany's capital or waltz with Hindenburg at his famous line in north France."[61] However, the press had a field day with Shawn's disarming idea, publishing photos of him in costume as a Greek warrior (complete with saber, shield, and Trojan helmet) alongside bombastic headlines such as "Terpsichore More Deadly Than Mars" and "Ted Shawn Would Lick Germans with Rhythm."

Later that summer, St. Denis came to Kearny to headline a benefit performance, the first of several visits she made to entertain the troops. (See Figure 2.14.) The concert was attended by 5,000 officers and civilian men, the largest audience ever assembled at the base. One reporter claimed that the hall was so full that some eager spectators took to the roof to watch the stage through a skylight. On opening night, the dancing couple delivered rousing patriotic speeches for which they were enthusiastically applauded.

For three nights later that fall (October 28–30, 1918), St. Denis performed specifically for the 32nd Infantry, the unit to which Shawn had been yet again promoted, leaving behind his "Florence Nightingale" ambulatory unit for an artillery unit. The concert featured St. Denis and her dancers. Miss Mary

Figure 2.14. Ruth St. Denis and Ted Shawn near Camp Kearny, 1918. Photograph by Harold A. Taylor. Denishawn Collection. Courtesy of the Jerome Robbins Dance Division, New York Public Library.

Caldwell performed a military takeoff called "On Parade." At some point in her routine, an excited soldier stood on his seat to get a better view of the stage. When another soldier shouted "Get down!" Miss Caldwell dropped to the floor as if she had been shot. Shawn very much wanted to perform in uniform with his wife for his fellow soldiers. Unfortunately, an active quarantine policy against the threat of Spanish flu restricted Shawn from getting within ten feet of St. Denis, but they performed nonetheless, mirroring each other's moves on opposite sides of the stage. One writer was impressed by the military precision with which Shawn maintained distance yet accuracy.

Shawn was discharged within weeks of Armistice Day, November 11, 1918, making it possible for him to attend the closing program of the Denishawn School. To mark the special occasion, he premiered a new duet with Doris Humphrey titled *Cupid and Psyche*, which dramatized the revenge that Cupid, the winged son of Venus, sought to inflict on Psyche for surpassing his mother's beauty. Leveraging his new military status, he credited himself as "Choreographer Lieut. Ted Shawn."

After closing the school, Shawn traveled to Detroit to meet St. Denis's tour. On the morning of her performance, he invited the press to a rehearsal he conducted in uniform with St. Denis's company. The *Detroit News* wrote that "Lieut. Adonis Drills Nymphs," running an interview with Shawn in which he uses his military status to further his cause for men in dance: "You know, the hardest work in the army is child's play when compared to dancing. In our athletic activities I have seen 200 men panting and exhausted after dancing around in a circle twice."[62]

Shawn tried to convince St. Denis to stay with the school by telling her of his plans to rebuild Denishawn. St. Denis once again insisted that she wanted no part of the school or company. Accepting defeat, Shawn returned to Los Angeles to confront the aftermath of both the war and Denishawn. He gave up the lease on two of the three buildings that made up the Westlake Denishawn School. Though the school had not been fully operational during the war, he hoped to run one more summer session. Instead, Shawn had to dismantle Denishawn: "I felt warlike killing my own child."[63]

Afternoon of a Shawn, 1918–1922

Just weeks before Armistice Day and his discharge from the army, Ted Shawn took a special leave from Camp Kearny to appear in the silent feature film

Don't Change Your Husband (1919) directed by Cecil B. DeMille. The film stars Gloria Swanson in her first featured role, as Leila Porter, a forlorn wife whose vibrant imagination helps her to cope with the ennui of married life. In one of her many escapist daydreams, Leila conjures herself as a woodland nymph who is chased by a faun played by Shawn, who is near naked save a few strategically placed vines. (See Figure 2.15.) The faun sidles beside the nymph near a stream, then seduces her by plucking a bunch of grapes from a nearby vine, and squeezing its juice into her mouth before kissing her for a full twenty-eight cranks of the camera. As the mythical creatures lose themselves in their passionate kiss, the scene cross-fades to the reality of an upper-class drawing room where Leila awakens to the unwanted advances of her husband. DeMille claimed that he had created the role of the faun specifically for Shawn, no doubt as a vehicle to showcase his exceptional looks and physique. Little could DeMille have known how well suited Shawn actually was to play a sexual misfit who relentlessly pursues an otherwise disinterested wife.

Figure 2.15. Ted Shawn in "Vision of Love" sequence from Cecil B. De Mille's film, *Don't Change Your Husband* (1918). Denishawn Collection. Jerome Robbins Dance Division, New York Public Library.

About the time of the film's release, a music critic conveyed his resentment for having to cover one of Shawn's live stage performances. Dumbfounded by Shawn's spectacle of physical beauty and emotional expressivity, the music critic wondered why "a man, the pink and hairless brother to the ape insists on going naked to his raptures."[64] He might as well have been writing about Shawn's melodramatic turn as a faun. Indeed, the writer titled the review "Afternoon of a Shawn," a disparaging reference to Russian ballet dancer Nijinsky's controversial *L'Après-midi d'un Faune* (1912), which shares a premise similar to the one in Shawn's scene in the DeMille film. In the Nijinsky ballet, a faun awakens on a boulder somewhere deep within the woods, then pursues a nymph, who escapes, but leaves behind her scarf, with which he attempts to sexually gratify himself. Of course, these are not the same fauns. Whereas Nijinsky's faun discovers a narcissistic, homoerotic resolution to his drama, Shawn's faun complies with the heteronormative logic of the romantic comedy. The difference matters little to the self-described "sober and baldheaded music critic" who mocks both displays of male sexual desire. In fact, the review's jab at the trope of the faun in modern theater receives its filmic expression in Charlie Chaplin's short film *Sunnyside*, also from 1919, wherein the great physical comedian lampoons Nijinsky's faun. In Chaplin's care, the faun is reimagined as a tramp who is thrust into motion when he accidentally sits on a heavily thorned cactus, which propels him to unintentionally chase a chorus of tunic-frocked maenads across a dewy glen. One hardly needs to know about Nijinsky's radical choreography of male sexual pleasure to appreciate the humor in the film. However, less apparent is how these scenarios limn related yet opposing views on dance, masculinity, and sexuality in the post-war years. Ted Shawn found himself negotiating the space between the stylized abstraction of Nijinsky and the populist pantomime of Chaplin.

"Afternoon of a Shawn" is perhaps the best way to describe the period of time between Shawn's discharge from the army in late 1918, a time when it appears that Denishawn had run its course, and 1922, when Denishawn regroups and embarks on its unprecedented years of critical and commercial success. Shawn described the four-year period as "a great rebirth" that brought forth his "richest period of creation and achievement." During this time "America's Most Handsome Man" was artistically prolific and created some of his most significant solo dances, as well as his most successful vaudeville acts. He also emerged as a leading man in a string of plays, benefit performances, pageants, and exhibitions that brought him closer to the type and quality of artistic dancing he was yet determined to create.[65] It was also a period of Shawn's sexual exploration with men. For most of this time, he was estranged from St. Denis, who no longer would share her limelight with him, choosing instead to tour with a small ensemble of dancers and to distance herself from Shawn and the Denishawn machine. Though Shawn would make appearances with ensembles billed as the "Denishawn Dancers," the celebrated company that had formed before the war no longer existed. The economic and professional obstacles of the post-war years were exhausting but nothing near as harrowing as the personal trial between him and St. Denis. Shawn said he spent most of the period of the armistice and years following barely surviving St. Denis's "streak of sadism." "It was hell, unadulterated ghastly suffering such as I've never known."[66]

When Shawn returned to Los Angeles from his crushing visit with St. Denis in Detroit in December 1918, he was determined to change her mind about pursuing a professional and personal life without him. He leased two of the three buildings on the Westlake property, retaining a small building with a studio to create work and teach private lessons. He also kept a skeleton staff to teach a "special Red Cross" class that offered students instruction in two complete dances with the designs for the costumes to participate in benefit performances. He also invited Martha Graham, who had been teaching children's classes, to teach an adult class in the studio. The invitation was something of a quid pro quo, as Shawn once again needed a new dance partner to explore possibilities to rebuild his career and was very aware how Graham's talent and determination could help him in that pursuit.

In an attempt to save his marriage to St. Denis and their Denishawn company, he set up a home to which she could retire from her "farewell to vaudeville" tour. He leased a house belonging to Edwina Hamilton, the former Denishawn School manager. It was a modest ranch in Eagle Rock City near Pasadena, California, with none of the glamour of the Denishawn house with its roaming peacocks and pools, but Shawn exercised his mind-over-matter Christian Scientist sensibility and rechristened the bungalow "Tedruth." Whereas Denishawn was a symbol of the couple's business partnership and artistic aspiration, Tedruth was a personal retreat, a "charming simple country home" for private reflection and a place to store their growing collection of dance prints, music scores, books, and sets and costumes. Awaiting his wife's return, Shawn remodeled the home. He even erected a wooden fence and platform between two enormous pepper trees for creating and rehearsing new Denishawn dances, or so he had hoped.

Their chance for a professional and personal reunion came even before they moved into Tedruth. They were presented with an irresistible offer to perform once again at the Greek Theatre at the University of Berkeley. This time, St. Denis was cast in the leading role in *Miriam, Sister of Moses*, a biblical play written especially for her by her long-time friend Constance Smedley with an original score by Berkeley music professor E. G. Strickland. Conceived as a "synthetic drama," the production was an experiment in integrating drama with movement, color, and sets. In her first speaking role since her David Belasco days, St. Denis was tasked with uniting her dancing with a dramatic script to retell the biblical story of the exodus of the Israelites from Egypt through the experiences and emotions of Miriam, misunderstood sibling of Moses. Shawn was initially engaged to create the group choreography for the play and later assumed the role of Moses to replace the actor who was originally cast but unexpectedly quit. The pageant brought St. Denis and Shawn together on stage for the first time in two years, at the site of their successful 1916 pageant at that—all the makings for a successful personal and professional renewal.[67]

To accommodate the summer rehearsals in Berkeley, Shawn arranged for him and St. Denis to live in a guest house at Wildwood, the Piedmont estate of Mrs. Frank C. Havens, recent widow of the real estate developer and patriarch of one of the founding families of Shelter Island. Shawn also rented out the garage with the intent of offering a six-week dance course. Though he advertised the classes without using the Denishawn name, he announced that registered students would automatically be cast in the Miriam production, and thus share a stage with St. Denis and himself. Though there was still buzz in the air from the previous Berkeley pageant, Shawn did not expect the high level of interest generated by the advertisement to perform in a Bible drama. Over a hundred young women registered for the class, most of whom were young socialites willing to give up their summer social calendars for the Denishawn experience. In advance of the play's opening, Shawn and St. Denis did some of their best publicity work. With strong enrollment, Shawn found himself with extra money, enough to buy a second-hand Packard limousine and hire a chauffeur to drive him and St. Denis between home and the theater. The drive was so rocky between Piedmont and Berkeley that St. Denis was routinely ill. She wondered, to the press, whether the symptoms suggested morning sickness. The chauffeured drive and its resulting pregnancy scare were part of a larger effort to intensify interest in Denishawn in the Bay area. As local newspapers were running ads for the pageant, they began to leak stories to reporters about St. Denis's refusal to appear in films, claiming that she had been besieged with offers for the past five years, one from Fox for $10,000 to appear in just one scene! These reports, of course were meant to ramp up tickets sales to see the legend on stage, where she exclusively performed. To underscore the value of St. Denis's physical body, early that summer reports circulated that she had insured her fingers and toes for $1 million, though there is no proof that such a policy ever existed.

Shawn further fueled their public relations machine by promising reporters that the biblical drama would feature a chorus of dancers performing the popular shimmy. Headlines ran with the shocking and blasphemous claims that "Miriam Ballet Girls Do Shivery Dance" or "Naughty Dance in Biblical Play." In the fine print, however, Shawn stridently shared his opinion that the ragtime dance is "disgusting and disgraceful when danced in a ballroom," but was choreographically justified in the play's dramatization of the Golden Calf scene, where utter licentiousness is supposed to be expressed through dance.[68] Thus Shawn found a way to exploit the popularity of the shimmy without moral consequence.

If the promise of a chorus of shimmying sisters of Miriam was not enough to attract a sizable audience, Shawn also carefully staged photos of him and his troupe of bathing-suit clad socialites splashing about in a pool in the style of Mack Sennett's bathing beauties. In 1915, the comic actor and film producer Sennett organized a bevy of beauties to perform antics wearing risqué modern bathing suits in silent film shorts. The "Beauties" also appeared in magazine pinups, a favorite of the army doughboys, and spawned several knockoffs. Shawn, not one to pass up the opportunity to exploit a fad, invited local papers to cover his daily trips to the beach with his dancers in tow to proclaim that dancing and swimming were good for one's health. These various publicity ploys worked: an estimated 7,000 people attended each of their performances on August 1 and 2, 1919. (See Figure 2.16.)

Critics applauded St. Denis's interpretation of Miriam as a rousing if not subversive spiritual prophet and leader. Shawn, too, received mostly positive notices, though he did not think highly of his own performance. "I made a very bad Moses. I was supposed to be 80 years old, and I didn't walk or move that way, even with all the whiskers in the world on my chin."[69] The scale of the amphitheater and its theatrical trappings did not suit Shawn's expressive talents. He recalled the failed highpoint of his performance when he, as Moses, had to scale an iron staircase to a platform high above the stage from which he had to hurl the Tablets of the Law inscribed with the Ten

Figure 2.16. Ted Shawn and His Dancing Beauties, featuring Pauline Lawrence (*left*) and Eugenia Vandeveer (*right*). Photographs by McCullagh (July 1919). Denishawn Scrapbook, vol. 2. Courtesy of the Jerome Robbins Dance Division, New York Public Library.

Commandments. When he released them to the stage, they bounced. The audience was forgiving. St. Denis, less so, unleashed criticisms that "at no time did he rise to dramatic brilliance" and that Shawn was hampered by "a little too much hand and foot work."[70] He at least came away from the experience content with his choreographic effort, which was roundly praised.

After the play closed, Shawn and St. Denis retreated to their bungalow Tedruth. As summer turned to fall, the couple nested, rehearsing a life of domesticity as they independently pursued separate careers. However, on November 8, Tedruth burned to the ground. Shawn suffered minor burns and scrapes from his attempt to save items from the burning house. He was devastated over the loss of his growing library of dance books, orchestrations, and costumes as well as original photographs, paintings, and sculptures from the early years of his career. He especially mourned the loss of a sculpture of him in "Death of Adonis," which crushed under the heat of the fire. His dance library was valuable for a variety of personal reasons, but most of all, it was the basis upon which he promised film companies dance recreations "correct as to country, period, and costume." Shawn estimated they lost $50,000 in property for which they recovered only $7,500 from insurance. For St. Denis, the fire symbolized the end of their domestic life. They moved back into the city, to a property on Sixth Street called "The Compound," adjacent to the former Denishawn School.

Shawn's creative work stalled in the aftermath of this personal setback. He was reduced to create buzz for a concert at a nearby ostrich farm, where the troupe performed a new novelty dance called the *Feather Dance*, wearing costumes made entirely of ostrich feathers.

Before the proverbial ashes of Tedruth settled, Shawn opened yet another dance school on April 6, 1920. This time, he entered a six-year lease for an irresistible price on a property on Grand Street in Los Angeles, where he opened the Ted Shawn Studio. Though the school was an independent venture, the sign hanging between the building's columns and the school's new letterhead indicated it was under the auspices of "Denishawn Dance Productions." The neoclassical building was "gruesome, and depressing" but had a studio of 5,600 square feet with a stage at one end and a balcony at another. Shawn commissioned artist Edward Buk Ulreich to restore the dilapidated building's glamour with designer furniture, light fixtures, and a frieze in the auditorium. Ulreich decorated one hall with black carpet and black lacquered walls.

Shawn lived in the building's third floor apartment. In the studio, he created and rehearsed new vaudeville acts to fulfill an arrangement he entered with legendary producer Alexander Pantages, who commissioned Shawn to create headlining acts for his circuit of theaters, the largest in the country at the time. Shawn gladly accepted the commission, proud to give work to Denishawn dancers who were left jobless because of St. Denis's refusal to tour with the company. Moreover, with his vaudeville earnings, he planned to finance a solo concert tour and further his career as America's foremost male dance artist.

Vaudeville turned out to be one of his only options at the time. Shawn's high art ambitions were somewhat thwarted by fierce new competitors in the post-war theatrical market: former Denishawn students and company members, many of whom leveraged their association with the popular troupe to establish their own solo careers. Just as St. Denis and Shawn recounted their own origin story, so too did each Denishawn dancer fabricate fantastic explanations for their transformation from ordinary American girls into artistes. St. Denis continually recounted an anecdote about sitting at a drugstore counter in Buffalo, New York, when she saw an image of the goddess Isis on a poster for Egyptian Deities cigarettes, which divinely inspired her to perform Oriental dances. Shawn had two related backstories he told in alternation, depending on the circumstance, to explain his most unusual decision to become a professional male dancer. The first story centered on dance as a physical practice, emphasizing how through studying dance, he transformed himself from a young man afflicted with paralysis to a cover model for physical and health magazines. The other was a vocation story, about his calling to leave divinity school to pursue his spiritual path through dancing, using his practice to restore the lost art of movement to the Christian service and simultaneously bring faith to the art of dance.

Among the former Denishawners on the circuit was Miss Beth Becker, who was once rendered frail and sickly from a cyclone accident in her hometown of Omaha, Nebraska, but whose health was fully restored at Denishawn thanks to a combination of physical movement, the proximity to the seashore, and time spent in a bathing suit. Margaret Severn appeared in a "mask" routine in the Greenwich Village Follies in 1919. When asked how she conceived of her unique dance, she modestly answered, "It just happened" when one day she visited the studio of W. T. Benda, the New York–based Polish illustrator and designer whose masks summoned her. Although the masks were sold for $2,000 each, she determined that they were a good value, seeing that wearing them meant "You don't have to makeup at all."[71] Then there was Margaret Loomis, the wealthy socialite daughter of the Loomis hotel empire, who was still living with her wealthy parents even after touring with Denishawn and a few rounds on the pageant circuit. She adapted her art for the domestic sphere with a cooking class titled "The Application of the Art of Dancing to Housework." Though Loomis was a talented dancer, she most likely knew nothing about housework.[72]

If the broad strokes of the former Denishawn dancers' career stories seemed familiar, so too were the dance routines they performed. Over the years, Shawn taught the same dances to hundreds of students in various cities across the country. As these routines made their way into reviews and pageants, he had to retroactively devise policies to govern the right for students to use his dances and the Denishawn affiliation in their publicity and advertisements. Similar to the circumstances that yielded the name "Denishawn," Shawn held a contest for the best proposal to "brand" former students in a way that allowed for individuality but clearly linked them to Denishawn.[73] The most successful case of a student assuming a stage name that reflected the Denishawn pedigree was Florence O'Denishawn (née Florence Andrews), one of the students in the first cohort at the Denishawn School. According to Shawn, he gave her the stage name "Florence of

Denishawn" along with a series of dances and costumes after she had performed with the company for two years. Another account suggests that Florence did not want her family name in the program, likely in deference to her father, a prominent Los Angeles businessman. However, the name "Florence of Denishawn" was changed to "Florence O'Denishawn" in a program by an incredulous printer. However attributed and printed, the name stuck, and Florence went on to a successful career. Known as the "Pavlova of America," she danced in some of the most prominent musical reviews of the day, including three Broadway editions of *Hitchy-Koo* with music by Cole Porter and Jerome Kern, the opening company of the *Music Box Review*, and the *Ziegfeld Follies of 1921*.

In addition to protecting the equity of the Denishawn brand, Shawn found himself increasingly defending the originality and authorship of his own choreography. During the Denishawn run at the New York Palace in 1916, one *Variety* writer observed a similarity between a dance choreographed by Shawn and performed by Lubowska and a dance performed months prior by Ada Forman, a member of the first Denishawn cohort, both set to "March Indienne" by Adolphe Sellenick. A convincing litigator, Shawn explained that he had been previously accused of stealing this dance and so attempted to set the record straight with a history of the dance, pointing to its presence in the *Dances of the Ages* film as irrefutable evidence of his authorship. If that were not enough, he explained that the dance from the film was subsequently restaged as *Zuleika* on Norma Gould in Los Angeles, then again as a *Danse Egyptienne* for Evan Burrows Fontaine during the first 1914 transcontinental tour, and then finally for Lubowska (then known by the name "Psychema"), who had told reporters that she created the dance at the actual tombs in Egypt. Shawn explained that he recostumed and retooled the very same dance into a Javanese number especially for Ada Forman.[74]

The complaint was tried again in the pages of *Variety* magazine where Forman published a letter to protest Shawn's allegation that he had taught her the dance "step by step." She instead explains how the dance was part of her repertory from her pre-Denishawn days in Chicago, though admits that under the guidance and suggestion of St. Denis and Shawn, she changed some steps, the music, and costume.[75] Though her damages seemed negligible, Fontaine apparently suffered greatly from Shawn's public "attack" and thus recruited Brother St. Denis to serve as an expert witness. By this point, Brother had bitterly distanced himself from the Denishawn enterprise and took the opportunity to express his resentment for his sister's unhappiness toward Shawn. Brother submitted a brief yet damaging letter to support Fontaine's claim concerning "the originality of the greater part of her Egyptian dance." Ultimately, Shawn was not necessarily accused of "stealing" choreography so much as he was of lacking artistic originality, a common charge on the vaudeville circuit but a grievous violation of Denishawn's artistic code.

Shawn and St. Denis also found themselves in court to protect their own interests against other dance school competitors. St. Denis served as star witness in a trial against so-called dancing master Ivan de Marcel who was brought up on false advertising charges by the Portland Ad club for using photos of other masters in his ads. On May 8, 1918, before a packed courtroom, filled mostly with Denishawn students, many dressed in stage costumes, St. Denis convincingly testified that Marcel had plagiarized her writings in his publicity materials. The jury found Marcel guilty, though the judge was lenient in terms of sentencing, given the lax laws around plagiarism and the otherwise "flamboyant practices of the theatrical world."[76]

The post-war show business landscape was a minefield that was difficult to maneuver, even for a trained soldier like Shawn. His first effort as a work-for-hire vaudeville choreographer was a three-act dance drama inspired by a minor character from the *Arabian Nights*. Though Shawn insisted the idea was inspired by his childhood fascination with Orientalist folk tales, he likely took his cue from Michel Fokine's 1912 ballet *Schéhérazade*, which US audiences came to know when the Ballets Russes toured in 1915–16 with Léonide Massine (who replaced the recently terminated Nijinsky) in the starring role. Shawn created a three-act drama (involving four different elaborate sets!) about a peripheral character named Julnar, "The Seaborn." Taking liberties with the narrative, Shawn devised a scenario involving an earthly prince who travels to the ocean's depths to woo Julnar, a plot that is elucidated in words by the narrator Scheherazade. The reviews were uniformly enthusiastic though predominantly about the exquisite set designs by Maxwell Armfield. The major sets included "The Bronze Palace," where Scheherazade perched on a divan, narrating the story to an invisible shah; "The Bottom of the Sea," where the earthly prince encounters sea creatures such as a shark and an octopus lurking in the cavernous abyss; and "The Slave Market," where the hero finds Julnar amid a chorus of odalisques. With its cast of seventeen, *Julnar of the Sea* premiered in Los Angeles on November 3, 1919, with Lillian Powell in the leading role, earning $75 a week when most dancers were paid $35. The production then enjoyed a successful run of

1,250 performances and earning an impressive $1,600 a week for over a year on the road with Louis Horst serving as accompanist and company manager. (See Figure 2.17.)

The other major act Shawn created for Pantages was *Xochitl*, a dance-drama based on a Toltec legend about the origin of *pulque*, the indigenous alcoholic libation created from fermented juice of the maguey plant. The drama centers on the beautiful Toltec maiden Xochitl, whose farmer father discovers the secret of brewing pulque. In the first scene, she watches her father as he stumbles about intoxicated for the first time, a discovery he decides must be shared with the Emperor Tepancaltzin. In the second scene, the maiden and her father present a gourd filled with pulque to the enthroned emperor. After imbibing the strange elixir, the emperor asks Xochitl to dance for him, and she obliges. (Shawn was planning a Salome ballet in the months before creating Xochitl, which might account for this familiar scenario of a young woman dancing before a ruler.) The emperor then, as Shawn delicately

Figure 2.17. *Julnar of the Sea* (1919) with Miles Smith as the Prince. Photograph by Putnam and Valentine. Denishawn Collection. Courtesy of the Jerome Robbins Dance Division, New York Public Library.

phrased it, proceeds "to pursue the innocent." Taken back into the throne room, Xochitl frantically cries as she attempts to protect her virginity. To defend his daughter, Xochitl's father attempts to stab Tepancaltzin, but Xochitl intercedes and rescues the emperor from her father's impassioned attack.

More "art" than an "act," *Xochitl* was a favorite on the Pantages circuit. Its theme of intoxication resonated with audiences, given that the 1919 Volstead Act prohibiting alcohol consumption had only recently gone into effect. Newspaper reporters loved the connection, calling it a "home brew" ballet.[77] *Xochitl* was the most involved and perhaps most successful collaboration of Shawn's career up until that point and arguably beyond. To create the work, he commissioned two noted artists. Composer Homer Grunn, best known for his interpretations of Southwest Native American music, composed the score. Mexican visual artist Francisco Cornejo created the daring sets and costumes ("a la Léon Bakst" noted one critic, linking the production to the designer of Fokine's *Schéhérazade*).[78] Cornejo arguably devised the scenario as well, though Shawn never conceded as much. Instead, Shawn claimed that he drew inspiration for *Xochitl* from American historian William Hickling Prescott's epic history *Conquest of Mexico* (1843). When discussing his inspiration for *Xochitl*, Shawn repeatedly mentioned a stirring visit to the library at the University of Texas, Austin, where he had a personal tour of its extensive collection of Aztec artifacts. However, that visit took place on November 7, 1921, well after the premiere of the dance-drama.[79]

Xochitl remained active in the Denishawn repertory for five years, and as such, saw many different dancers cast in the leading role, including Louise Brooks at one point. Shawn created the dance as a star vehicle for Martha Graham, a role that would eventually serve as her ticket out of Denishawn. Shawn wrote glowingly about Graham, who not only was teaching in earnest at his new school but also contributing on every front, most especially by racking up positive reviews in the press. He wrote to St. Denis with a loving description of how Graham passed time on the train resewing the sequins on Cornejo's elaborate headdress, drawing the attention of all the other passengers.[80] The official preview of *Xochitl* was in Graham's adopted hometown of Santa Barbara, California. She took advantage of the opportunity to distance herself from Shawn, as well as establish a tone for discussing her standards as an artist: "So far the only value of my work—if it has art value—is absolute sincerity. I would not do anything that I could not feel. A dance must dominate me completely until I lose sense of anything else. Later what I may do may be called art, but not yet."[81]

German music critic and scholar Bruno David Ussher gave *Xochitl* serious consideration in a music journal. He recognized the dance as "one of the best presentations . . . by the disciple Ted Shawn."[82] To develop his analysis, he visited one of Shawn's classes, offering a rare perspective into Shawn's approach to training. Ussher encouraged Shawn to reflect on Francis Bacon's essay "On Beauty" and its central premise that "the principal part of beauty is in decent motion." He criticized Shawn's use of musical accompaniment as "mechanical" and "primitive" and thus undermining the purported goal of Shawn's technique to increase expressivity. He encouraged Shawn to refine his use of musical phrasing in his training.

The opening of the Ted Shawn Studio and the success of his independent vaudeville dances highlighted the obvious separation between Shawn and St. Denis, though they occasionally appeared together for special events and concerts. St. Denis pursued her own solo career, pouring her energies into a chamber dance group she toured with and a handsome actor named Craig Ward with whom she performed poetry and song. She did not miss an opportunity to write Shawn about the budding romance between her and Ward, which incensed Shawn, if not for his professional jealousy that St. Denis shared a stage with someone other than himself then for the skepticism Ward's presence cast on the validity of their marriage and Shawn's sexuality by extension. Indeed, rumors began to swirl about their impending divorce.[83] They deftly deflected these rumors on the occasion of their sixth wedding anniversary by renewing their vows before a crowd of reporters and photographers. Shawn reminded the press that he and St. Denis had entered into their marriage on a trial basis, intending to renew their vows every five years, pending their individual happiness. He also defended their living arrangement by stating that as artists, he and St. Denis maintained separate studios for professional reasons. (Shawn rehearsed at his Los Angeles studio and St. Denis in the dome of a nearby hotel more appropriate for her chamber group). Shawn insisted that they came together on weekends as man and wife. To convince the skeptical crowd, Shawn asked the press corps "Does this look like a divorce?" before planting a prolonged kiss on his wife in front of a battery of still and motion cameras, not unlike his famous on-screen moment with Gloria Swanson.

"Cut!" shouted one cameraman in the crowd, concerned, perhaps that the prolonged kiss violated the rules imposed by the Board of Censorship. More likely, he was calling attention to the very self-conscious theatricality of this staged public display of affection. Their marriage renewal was perfectly timed to coincide with the publication of *Ruth St. Denis, Pioneer and Prophet, Being a History of Her Oriental Dances* (1920), a beautiful two-volume book with photographs of St. Denis in her most celebrated roles and brief contextualizing essays written by Shawn. A private press printed 350 copies, of which Shawn could secure advance sales for only a hundred. The publicity event took place just weeks before the passage of the Nineteenth Amendment on August 18, 1920. St. Denis never felt more out of step with the suffrage movement than when she partook in this duplicitous charade as Shawn's personal goddess, especially as accounts of his sexual escapades with other men circulated within the Denishawn circle.

It was during the time that Shawn was creating *Xochitl* that he had developed a romantic relationship with Robert "Bob" Gorham who played the role of the emperor. Graham and Horst both bristled at Shawn's infatuation with Gorham, which distracted him from work in the studio. Moreover, Brayton "Nigger" Jensen, Shawn's former tent mate at Camp Kearny, was a member of the *Xochitl* cast, resulting in what Shawn described as "a queer series of affairs."[84] Horst recalled some of the sexual high jinks that ensued when the show was on the road, describing how one of Shawn's lovers "kidnapped" another of his "boyfriends" in the cast, who left the touring troupe and forced Shawn to find a substitute male dancer. A young dancer named Charles Weidman was sent out to fill the spot.

On New Year's Eve, Shawn wrote to St. Denis to recap his professional and personal highs and lows of 1920. It is a painfully candid letter in which he confirms his struggles to understand his own sexuality: "The fact which stands out above all things is the experience I have had in my emotional sex-love nature. I am afraid this is still unclassified to me—partaking of both good and bad—and will have to be taken up later."[85] He goes on to address his infidelities, not only with Gorham but also with Arthur Buruel, the man with whom Shawn had an affair when he first moved to Los Angeles.

> The year opened wrong. As the year began I was with Bob and Arthur. Arthur was very unhappy . . . and my underlying motives were wrong and I was held conscious of this. The whole lie of my being of a homogenic sex nature—like a boil—was gathering all of its pus (foreign matter which had no real place in the clean body of my love life)—sorely into a head. Another boil once before began to gather—but was driven back into the blood only gathering to come to a head in this experience with Bob.[86]

Here Shawn denies his "homogenic" sex nature, using British poet and social activist Edward Carpenter's preferred term for "homosexuality." He then
describes a biological process through which his body had cleansed itself of
his homosexuality, figured as a boil. To ensure his body's "purification" of any
homogenic sex desire, Shawn also sought spiritual cleansing. He explains to
St. Denis how he had been deeply engaged in Havelock Ellis's writings about
St. Francis, especially his ideas about ascetism, which enabled him to recognize his reliance on the "strongly sensuous," be it with food, beauty, or sex.
Following the example of St. Francis, Shawn pursued a path of "abstinence
from gratification."[87] He expressed contrition to St. Denis: "Surely I have
been going through a great rebirth. But evidently the end is not yet. All of
the self I have let go of my art consciousness is only a part. The purification of
my sex life in relationship to my wanderings is only a part."[88] In exchange for
her forgiveness, he offered himself: "You know you can enjoy me physically
to the utmost whenever it strikes your fancy—and the whole world approves
it." Indeed, Shawn focused intensively on his work in an attempt to avoid the
confusion and distraction of his homosexuality. He also spent some nights
awake until dawn writing to St. Denis, declaring his devotion to her and their
marriage in penitential tones.

Shawn was aware of the correlation between his sexual confusion and his
choreographic clarity. In fact, that year he was acknowledged as an artist
of importance by one of the most elite and powerful fraternities in the nation: the Bohemian Club, the exclusive all-male club that hosts an annual
midsummer retreat on its 2,700 acre grove of majestic redwood trees on the
northern outskirts of San Francisco. Founded in 1872, the Bohemian Club's
charter members included artists, poets, actors, and newspaper men, but by
1920 the membership grew to attract the most powerful and influential men
in finance, politics, and business.

Shawn was a welcomed addition to the Grove, as the ten-day encampment
centered around theatrical entertainment and esoteric rituals. Shawn served
as "Director of Dance" for the annual Grove play, the main stage production
for which Bohemian Club members always serve as playwright, composer,
and performers, often *en travestie*. In that role, Shawn created and performed
in dances for a play by Charles Caldwell Dobie titled *Ilyu of Murom* based on
tales of Little Russia.[89] For this production Shawn created several numbers
including a "Russian Peasant" ensemble dance and a "Demon-Bird Dance"
in which he performed a featured role. Shawn posed in one of the signature

poses from the dance for sculptor Joseph ("Jo") Mora (1876–1947) who was among the artists at camp that year. (See Figure 2.18.)

Shawn was enraptured by the opportunity to choreograph for the main stage at the camp, with its many leveled platforms nestled between trees and with natural paths serving as its "wings." Framed by a backdrop of rolling hills, the natural setting was a model for the performance spaces Shawn would later establish at Jacob's Pillow. In addition to his performance duties as Director of Dance, Shawn entertained the campers during the day, catering to the camp's culture of myth and fantasy. An existing film from the encampment captures some of Shawn's activity at the Grove.[90] One clip shows him participating in a campfire throwing back drinks, a favorite pastime at the retreat, then combing back the hair of one of his drinking buddies. In another clip, he is fully costumed for *Invocation to the Thunderbird*, a solo dance he created years prior but premiered at the "High Jinks" performance at the Grove's Field Circle. Wearing only a feather war bonnet, a beaded belt, and moccasins, Shawn emerges from a hollowed cavity in the trunk of a mighty

Figure 2.18. Ted Shawn as "Demon Bird" from the play *Ilya of Murom*, Bohemian Club, 1920. Denishawn Collection. Courtesy of the Jerome Robbins Dance Division, New York Public Library.

Redwood, then slowly raises his arms in salutation to the sun. In yet another clip, he dashes from the grove to the river, darting his head from side to side as if on the lookout for stray arrows. (See Figure 2.19.)

Shawn served as Bohemian Grove's Director of Dance for the following two summers. It proved to be a good training ground for his work with all-male casts later in his career, especially as he had to shepherd untrained bankers, insurance salesmen, and politicians, most of them inebriated, into

Figure 2.19. Ted Shawn in *Invocation to the Thunderbird* at Bohemian Grove, 1920. Ted Shawn Papers, Additions. Courtesy of the Jerome Robbins Dance Division, New York Public Library.

dresses (for those taking on the women's roles) and Hungarian folk dance formations. For one scene that called for a flight of angels, Shawn had to squeeze the soft flesh of middle-aged captains of industry into harnesses with wings.

He also continued his association with Bohemian Grove playwright Charles Caldwell Dobie that following winter, when he appeared once again as Moses alongside St. Denis, this time in a play called *Ramati, Seed of the Lotus*, an "Egyptian play" that Dobie wrote for St. Denis based on one of her favorite childhood novels, *Idyll of the White Lotus*.[91] Shawn had the opportunity to redeem his interpretation of Moses, this time as a suitor to St. Denis's Ramati, a young Egyptian girl. It was also an opportunity for Shawn to reconnect with St. Denis and prove his fidelity to her. Following their brief reunion in *Ramati*, Shawn joined St. Denis that next summer at her *thés dansants*—social events at leading resort hotels on the Pacific, which attracted well-heeled audiences from Los Angeles, Pasadena, and San Diego. Billed as the "highest salaried dancer," St. Denis appeared under the sponsorship of piano manufacturers Wm. Knabe & Co. The performances were an artistic departure for her, an experiment synthesizing the "trinity" of word, music, and movement in the ancient mode. She performed these events with poet Craig Ward who served a narrator of sorts. Of course, she also presented her Oriental dances for good measure. Shawn performed his solos, including a new dance called *Le Contrabandier*, an image of which accompanied an article extolling masculine grace in an issue of *Physical Culture* magazine.[92] Drama critic and art connoisseur John D. Barry gave a serious review of the performance. Far from dismissing the experimental performance as indulgent confections for the society audiences, he praised their unique stage instincts—St. Denis's capacity for impersonation and Shawn's to "underact."[93]

Shawn also joined St. Denis in her vaudeville act at Hoyt's in Long Beach, making it the first time the couple had shared a vaudeville stage in over two years, since Shawn had been enlisted in the army. St. Denis announced it as her final week in vaudeville, thus making it a record breaker in Long Beach theatricals. Another review declared that the reunion "put Long Beach on the theatrical map." The brief reunion rekindled the personal and professional light between them, so much so that they began to swap sentimental letters where they once again address each other by their pet names. St. Denis agreed to return to teaching at Denishawn and admitted to taking an interest, even pleasure, in the school and supporting Shawn in his effort to make it successful: "This is the best time I have ever had in the school," she insisted.[94]

The truce was short-lived, as Shawn wanted to turn the brief reunion into a Denishawn encore. One night Shawn called St. Denis in the wee hours of the night for a rare discussion of their emotional life—a "bubbling up" he called it.[95] A discussion of sex and monogamy sent their summer high into a downward spiral. He asked her to end her relationship with Ward. St. Denis responded with "cruel and ruthless" letters that pulled harder than ever at their strained bonds of marriage.[96] Decades later Shawn remarked how the tone of their letters reflected their "arrested development" both emotionally and sexually.[97] As if to get revenge for Shawn's own homosexual transgression the year prior, St. Denis sent detailed letters of her sexual wanderings. The path toward a regrouping of Denishawn was once again dashed, a circumstance that proved to be both a blessing and a curse, as it prompted Shawn to take a leap of faith into his own solo career.

Earlier that year in 1921, Shawn met Harry Hall, a tall handsome man who proclaimed himself to be both an impresario and a Christian Scientist. He convinced Shawn of his interest in him as a person and artist and offered to fulfill Shawn's goal of mounting a solo concert tour. Not since before the war had Shawn had theatrical representation. For the prior two years in vaudeville, Shawn had negotiated all the deals himself with Pantages and was justifiably nervous about putting his career in someone else's hands, but he eventually succumbed to handing over the control. Hall appeared capable, immediately putting together a route list for the 1921–22 season and advertising the tour widely in places such as *Musical America*.[98]

Billed as "American Man Dancer," Shawn initiated his solo tour in September 1921 in Los Angeles. It was not so much a "solo" tour as it was a tour without St. Denis or Denishawn. Moreover, it featured several small ensemble dances, including a pared down version of *Xochitl*, starring Shawn as the emperor and Charles Weidman as the father. The program showcased his versatility as a choreographer and performer. On the program he included his "interpretative" dances, which he had just started to call "music visualizations," accompanied by an Ampico player piano onstage. He also included his religious dances, Spanish dances, solo dances, and group dances. The range was not lost on the reviewers, nor was Martha Graham's star presence.

Spear Dance Japonesque (1919) was one of his most popular dances on the program. (See Figure 2.20.) Based loosely on the traditional dance-dramas of Japan, the solo depicts a samurai warrior in the throes of battle with an invisible enemy. When the warrior falters, he pulls a tourniquet from his waistband and a fan, then whirls his spear. Though Shawn claimed the dance was inspired by the sibling sword duel from St. Denis's Japanese-inspired *O-Mika,* in all likelihood it was also influenced by Japanese choreographer Michio Itō, particularly his *noh*-style *Sword Dance,* presented in New York in 1918.[99] Itō's *Sword Dance* shared the program alongside his adaptations of noh plays, such as the Ezra Pound and Ernest Fenollosa translation of *Tamura* at the Neighborhood Playhouse, both in 1918 and 1921. Shawn might have been inspired by Itō's modernist adaptations of traditional dance-dramas. As Shawn clarified to reporters, his dance was an "Occidental adaptation": "I evolved my *Japonesque*—not Japanese—but *Japonesque* because it has taken the essence and the spirit of the Japanese dance while making it a less blood curdling affair."[100] Shawn said that before the war, he bought at auction an antique six-foot spear with curved blade, which he used to study for an entire season with Anzai, whom he identifies as the "ballet master of the Royal

Figure 2.20. Ted Shawn in *Spear Dance Japonesque* (1919). Photograph by Arthur Kales. Denishawn Collection. Courtesy of the Jerome Robbins Dance Division, New York Public Library.

Opera House of Tokyo" and thus "the greatest authority on Japanese dance." Following his discharge from the army, Shawn choreographed the dance based on the training he had received from Anzai. For the music, Louis Horst made a special arrangement of British composer Granville Bantock's "Songs of Japan." Shawn performed the dance throughout his entire performing days, including his final appearances on stage and screen.

Another feature on the program was Shawn's *Invocation to the Thunderbird*, which was set to John Philip Sousa's brassy and propulsive "The Red Man." Depicting a native medicine man, Shawn scatters cornmeal while moving along a series of pathways that trace the silhouette of a thunderbird, the symbol of the rain god. The dance ends with the exultation of pouring rain. On his knees, facing away from the audience, Shawn hinges backwards, shoulders to floor, his body splayed to the audience. Shawn choreographed the dance in 1917 at the request of a student who wanted a fiercer dance than Shawn's other Native American dances, though Shawn did not perform it regularly until Bohemian Grove. He strategically narrated the story of the dance's origins, careful to avoid the appearance that he stole the idea from Michel Fokine, whose own *Thunderbird* had its New York premiere as part of the Dillingham revue *Get Together* at the New York Hippodrome on September 3, 1921. Based on an Aztec legend, Fokine's *Thunderbird* is more akin to his popular *Firebird* than Shawn's ethnographic dance, yet Shawn was concerned about the appearance of plagiarism and how it might impact his New York performance, especially as Shawn had borrowed heavily from scenarios of ballets that Fokine had created for the Ballets Russes, including the Arabian Nights themed *Julnar of the Sea*. Shawn also choreographed a quartet to Chopin's fiery "Revolutionary Etude" (op. 10, no. 2). A music visualization, the dance featured him and Graham moving in correspondence to the chaotic melody embodying the "red reign of terror of the French revolt" while Dorothea Bowen and Betty May, covered in swaths of red chiffon, symbolized the "hectic kinematics" of blood and flame.[101]

Critics praised Shawn's range more than his performance in any individual dance, so much so that reviews expressed fascination with the mechanics of his performance itself—about rationale of programming, the logistics of makeup and costumes, the selection of music. One reporter wrote: "It is difficult to credit the truth that the barbaric Emperor of ancient Mexico could be personated by the same dancer who had done the divine in the Church service."[102]

Shawn also performed his Christian dance liturgy on the road. When the tour brought him to Shreveport, he picked up the morning edition to check on any advance press and advertising. He came across a letter to the editor written by the local ministerial association condemning Shawn's performance of his church service. The letter implores the chief of police and mayor to enjoin his performance and threatened "tarring and feathering the dancer if he dared to put his church service number on."[103] One Baptist minister, "in keeping with the peaceful teachings of the Gentle Nazarene," Shawn noted ironically, threatened harm with his army of "a thousand men who will spring up and tear that opera house to the ground if he tries to do that Church service."[104] More than 150 members of the ministerial association descended on city hall to protest Shawn's caricature of the Protestant Bible. Shawn explained his ordeal at a lunch in his honor hosted by the family of Ruth Estes, a former Denishawn student. She cautioned Shawn about the threats to his safety, describing lynchings as "the favorite out of door sport of the native Lousianian."

Shawn went to the theater surrounded by the entire Shreveport police force, about thirty in total, which gave him some measure of confidence to go through with the performance. He resigned himself to the possibility that there might be violence, which he hoped to avoid, but if not, reasoned he would at least have strong standing to sue the city for over $100,000. Shawn's finances were at an all-time low and he was acutely aware of the breadlines as he traveled across poverty-stricken, post-war America: "The country is in a worse panic and financial depression than any time for over 20 years." More valuable than any court settlement, the news of his potential lawsuit "would break into the front page of every newspaper in America, which would be worth approximately $1,000,000" in free advertising.

The matinees were poorly attended, but the mayor and other local officials showed up and warmly responded to the service, visiting Shawn backstage to convey their embarrassment at the religious fanaticism. Following the final evening performance, Shawn and company rushed to the train and boarded for a grueling four-hour trip in the upper berths. The adrenaline of the Shreveport fiasco waned, and soon came an unavoidable slump. To make matters worse, the tour had gone bust, an inevitable consequence of mismanagement. Harry Hall turned out to have entered a series of illegitimate contracts with local managers, leaving Shawn and company stranded on the road.

Shawn desperately wired his Aunt Kate to ask for a loan of $2,000 to cover his debts and the company's transportation to New York where he was determined to produce his solo concert. She obliged. It was a favor that Shawn never forgot and credited all his subsequent successes to her generosity. To bolster box office on the road, Hall advertised that the tour would end with a "dance concert" at the Metropolitan Opera House. However, Shawn soon learned that Hall never secured the date at the venue, thus jeopardizing his ability to produce his solo concert in New York, the heart of the market for theatrical and concert bookings. Shawn knew he needed to present his concert there if he were to take his career beyond the vaudeville and pageant circuits. Committed to presenting his solo concert program in the city, he scrambled to rent the Apollo Theater for a Saturday matinee on December 2, 1921.

Shawn was anxious about this gamble and hoped to receive a sign of support from his wife, but the big day arrived without a word from her. He wrote to St. Denis from his dressing room at the fifteen-minute call for his first solo appearance before a New York audience since 1917: "I am dressed made up and ready to go on. . . . I want you to know my last thoughts are for you—and that I feel your loving Spirit brooding over me. I had hoped for a wire from you but none has come."[105]

Shawn was genuinely surprised that the matinee attracted a standing room only audience, even without papering the house. (*Musical Courier* described the turnout as a "good sized audience.")[106] Shawn was similarly taken off guard by the greatest applause of his whole life and "a real ovation" that prompted encores for nearly every dance on the program and seven bows for his *Spear Dance Japonesque*. He was so moved by the reception, in New York of all places, that he struggled to compose himself enough to reset the piano roll on the player piano to accompany his encore, so he called Horst on stage to play live.

After the performance, more than thirty former Denishawn students came backstage to greet him. The photographer Arnold Genthe, whose discriminating eye always vexed Shawn, had only praise to lavish on his performance, especially for *Gnossienne* (1919), a solo set to the music of Erik Satie that conjures an ancient Minoan priest performing rituals in honor of the Snake-Goddess. Genthe called the dance "a genuine contribution." Paul Swan, too, came to Shawn's dressing room. Though the lives and reputations of these two dancers were intimately linked, they had never before met. Shawn was aloof toward Swan, likely because he knew it would be a liability to be associated with the outlandish Swan, with his black velvet jacket, stage makeup, and bleached hair. Shawn had little sympathy for Swan, who continued to perform in a Carnegie Hall studio for "a ghoulish few" who largely attended to ridicule him. Shawn focused his attention instead on the string of potential agents and managers who came backstage, including representatives from the UBO (United Booking Office) as well as the Shubert and Ziegfeld organizations. The Shubert representative pitched the idea of building a midnight show around Shawn's concert as a permanent production at the Century Roof, a glassed-in theater overlooking Central Park.

The most consequential of his visitors came at intermission. Producer Daniel Mayer, the "Great Orchestrator," was one of the leading musical impresarios in all of Europe. He had made a name for himself managing artists such as pianist and composer Ignacy Jan Paderewski and ballet star Anna Pavlova. The stealthy Mayer was eager to add Shawn to his roster, so at intermission, even before seeing the second act invited him to a meeting at his office the following afternoon. It was the precise opportunity he had hoped to create by gambling on the solo tour and the Apollo Theater performance. He went to Mayer's office the next day and signed a contract on the spot for a fall concert tour. Mayer initially offered Shawn $1,000 a week for six weeks, less 20 percent of gross receipts. Shawn's share had to cover all other expenses: advertising, print, press-agent, postage, telegrams, production costs, and salaries. It was a decent deal, but Mayer dangled a second, more lucrative offer before Shawn involving a three-and-a-half year contract on the condition that he convince Ruth St. Denis to join the bill.

Without initially mentioning Mayer's offer, Shawn repeatedly reached out to an unresponsive St. Denis: "No letter from you for three days, and no wire for my matinee yesterday, and no answer to my wire telling of success."[107] He eventually did receive a congratulatory response from St. Denis on his return to the New York stage and for finally becoming an "art dancer." Shawn eventually came forward with the complete Mayer proposition and suggested that she travel east to meet face to face with him and Mayer in Greensburg, Pennsylvania, to discuss logistics and test the waters with a trial concert. St. Denis opened negotiations on this professional venture with a personal proposal: an open marriage. In a letter to him, she justified her desire for an open marriage on the basis "that harmony can only be between [them] in a basis of honesty and freedom . . . each of [them] feeling reasonably satisfied that his own soul is his own and not another's."[108]

Shawn neither accepted nor refused St. Denis's proposal for an open marriage. Instead, he tried other ways to seduce her into the arrangement. First
he wrote her a letter in which he mourns the loss of his youthful, queer self
and suggests that she accept the "new man" that he has become, a man that
has resurrected from his dead queer body:

> Life is a constant dying—a constant dying to make room for other things
> to be born. And last night, as I lay awake all night after sending my hyster-
> ical wire to you, something more died in me—more of the boy who was
> Teddy—making room for this strange new man who is being born. He
> was a lovely boy this Teddy, and I loved him very dearly, and so of course
> I grieve every time he dies—and when he is completely dead I shall be very
> sorry indeed, although no doubt much better equipped for the battle of life
> without his impulsiveness, his passion, and his sentimentality.[109]

A few days later he tried to dispel any of her concerns about his homosexuality in more explicit terms: "I have not had so much as a flicker of romantic
interest in any other person, male or female, since I left you and I have no expectation of having in the near future."[110] While trying to convince her that
he has reformed, he blamed her for not fulfilling her wifely duties, leaving
him to contend with unresolved sexual desire: "I am sex hungry for you in a
bitter and terrible way. . . . It has gotten so that I walk the floor hours at night
like a fever for the very abstract desire of Woman. I cannot see my own naked
body in a mirror without inflaming my sex instinct, and nude pictures in art
magazines are like a knife thrust in a wound."[111] He tells her how he goes to
bed at night with a Christian Science pamphlet that he hopes would "kill"
his sex desire.[112] His "date" with the Christian Science pamphlet is interrupted by noisy neighbors who were "singing their own version of the Song
of Solomon." Shawn swears he could hear "flesh entering flesh."

"I have given you my youth, my virginity, the one great love of my life," he
wrote, hoping to manipulate her into believing that the only defense against
his homogenic nature was for St. Denis to join him on tour. St. Denis knew
she had little chance of refusing Shawn in person, so instead she offered the
flimsiest of excuses: "I am ready neither in mind nor clothes."[113] Though he
recognized they were both in debt, he argued they have borrowed money for
lesser things and thus sent her a paid ticket and $200 to unburden her finan-
cial concern. He also appealed to her ego: "I think you are the greatest artist
the dance has ever known. I am willing to appear with you, even if I were not

billed at all." Finally, he appealed to her more material desires, emphasizing that the tour would likely mean they would "clean up $50,000" each.

It is hard to know which line of appeal cinched the deal, but St. Denis finally agreed to meet in Greensburg, Pennsylvania, to test out a program and iron out the logistics with Mayer. They met on February 24, 1922, the first time the couple had seen each other in months, and performed eight consecutive nights to great ovation. The chemistry was apparently excellent offstage as well, as the ensuing letters between them reflect a renegotiation of their sex lives: "Today I don't know where sex comes in at all! I'm just chuckling as I remember some things—a not long ago bridal room (for us anyway) at the Blackstone! But today if you please I have the feeling of a child or a sage! The fact of the matter is the more perfect our sex life the less noise it makes!"[114]

They agreed to a preliminary tour of the South that April, a tour in London in June, and another of the United States in the fall. In her autobiography St. Denis remorsefully reflected: "Why, after all my rebellions and resentments against the school and joint performances, I leaped to the idea of a long-term contract under Mayer is difficult to analyze."[115]

They signed a contract with Mayer to appear under the billing "Ruth St. Denis, Ted Shawn, and their Denishawn Dancers" for three and a half years. For the first time since before the war, Denishawn was back again. Shawn wasted no time to act on the news. He rechristened the Ted Shawn Studio in Los Angeles as Denishawn and welcomed back St. Denis to the faculty. In typical fashion, they rushed into plans well beyond their resources and readiness. They explored a real estate agreement with developer and future US senator Ed Fletcher to establish a Denishawn School on his Grossmont estate in San Diego. He was especially eager to support their idea for an America Synchronic Ballet, a national dance school with students from each state in the union. Fletcher promised to help finance the school, so long as they could come up with the initial $25,000 for the building plans and construction. Unfortunately, they did not even have the $200 to hire an architect to do the initial land survey.

Mayer and Fletcher were not the only ones interested in investing in Denishawn. Miss Mabel Beardsley, a successful manager of society balls, charity benefits, and private parties, presented Shawn an irresistible offer to establish a branch of the Denishawn School in New York. A well-heeled woman with purple highlighted hair, Beardsley agreed to manage his teaching enterprise, taking charge of advertising, organizing, and managing the school. The offer required no expense on his part, though Beardsley withheld $300 per month for subleasing an apartment to him at the Hotel Beaux Arts (8 West 40th Street), facing Bryant Park, from which he taught the occasional private lesson. They eventually found a permanent headquarters for the Denishawn School, a penthouse and studio at the Chatsworth Hotel at 72nd Street near Riverside Park. *Vogue* announced the school's debut twelve-week course, which began on February 1, 1922. The first day of class was covered by the press, which ran one of the only images of Martha Graham in Shawn's class, though she was a fellow faculty member at the time.[116] (See Figure 2.21.)

Most of Shawn's days in New York were spent with Horst and Graham. They ate meals, attended performances, and created dances together. Shawn was surprised by how his relationship with Horst had developed during the tour. Writing to St. Denis, he remarked: "Louis's spirit on this trip is the finest I have ever known him. He is younger and sweeter in his nature than I could have imagined. He has been splendid to me, and says that I have won his complete admiration and respect for the way I have acted under these

Figure 2.21. "Ted Shawn Opens Dancing School Here for Busy Bookkeepers and Tired Typists," with Ted Shawn and Martha Graham (*front right*).
Denishawn Scrapbook, vol. 9. Courtesy of the Jerome Robbins Dance Division, New York Public Library.

repeatedly difficult situations. He has a very sweet friendship with Martha that is absolutely respectful and harmless."[117]

Shawn relied on them to successfully run the school and did whatever he could to keep them gainfully employed. He leveraged Mrs. Beardsley's connections to get him and Graham hired at the Gold Room of the Hotel de Beaux Arts for $200 a week. Shawn was impressed with the offer. Over lunch at a restaurant close to the school, Shawn later proposed the idea that Graham work with department store managers to give a recreational dance class to clerks and salesgirls. Graham outright refused, declaring that she was an artist and found his proposition degrading. Shawn was dumbfounded, unable to reason how she could refuse him while he was supporting both of them. According to Shawn's account of the ensuing fallout, "Her royal highness stood up from the lunch counter and screamed 'You can't talk to me that way.' She grabbed the whole white tablecloth, pulled it off onto the floor, silver, glassware and all, and ran screaming out of the restaurant. And of course poor fat waddly Louis merely got up and ran after her, and left me there with the irate proprietor and the customers looking." Shawn followed them to the cab and told them he never wanted to see them again. But the next morning, according to Shawn, Graham showed up at his penthouse door at the Chatsworth, dropped to her knees and started crawling across the floor. " 'Oh, Ted can you ever forgive me? I'm so mortified. I'm so ashamed of myself. Can you ever have the heart to forgive me and take me back into your love—I owe so much to you' and so on and so on." Shawn responded: "Oh, for God's sake get up and dry your tears and we'll start again fresh."[118]

And start again they did, with an innovative project that brought Shawn back to his early experiments with film. He was hired to work on the first "music film," the brainchild of Broadway theater owner Hugo Riesenfeld, the former music director at major film theaters in New York City. The innovation of the "music film" was to synchronize onscreen action with live musical accompaniment. This was achieved by displaying the head and arms of a musical conductor within the field of the screen, thus allowing live musicians to follow the baton of the pantomimic director permanently wedded to the action. The father of a dancer, Risenfeld figured the best way to demonstrate his innovation was through dance, thus he filmed twelve music-films in Prizma Color featuring Shawn's choreography and dancers.[119] The dances included *Danse Arabe, Valse Ballet, Bubble Dance*, and *Egyptian Dance.* Over the course of twelve weeks in spring 1922, the films played at several New York theaters, such as the Rivoli, Rialto, and Criterion. A critic in the

New York Times counted them "among the year's most significant and satisfying works."[120]

In the midst of opening the New York school and preparing for the Mayer
tour, Shawn developed another vaudeville act, *Javanese Ballet of Masks* for a
week's run at the Grauman Theater in Los Angeles. He also focused on his
dancing by taking private lessons with Spanish dance master Manuel Otero
at Unity Hall. He also spent a good deal of downtime networking within
New York's artistic and social circles. By day, he modeled for sculptor Allan
Clark. By night, he escorted friends to the theater and parties, and other
cultural events, including an exhibition at various art clubs throughout
New York City that featured a life-sized portrait of him by Max Wieczorek.[121]
He also went several times to see the vaudeville-style Broadway production
of *Shuffle Along*. He regularly attended the Metropolitan Opera to see and
be seen with his friend the opera diva Amelita Galli-Curci. Shawn met the
coloratura soprano in 1915 and had remained in touch ever since. He occasionally accompanied her and her husband to dinner. He also appeared
on stage at the Metropolitan Opera, as a member of a "farewell committee"
convened to honor Anna Pavlova on the occasion of her farewell US tour. On
April 25, 1922, at an intermission of Pavlova's appearance in *Giselle*, the committee of prominent patrons and artists joined the great ballerina on stage to
present her with a silver cup. St. Denis purportedly knelt down and kissed
the Russian dancer's hand, while delivering the following message: "We will
never see anything in her line so perfect as Pavlova." Embarrassed by the display, Pavlova yanked St. Denis up to her feet.[122]

Despite the considerable professional opportunities he created for himself, Shawn was still dealing with overwhelming feelings he described as
"depression." Some days he reserved for traveling out to Great Neck, Long
Island, to seek Lillian Cox's spiritual counsel. Cox had recently given him
a copy of the *Bhagavadgita*, which he took with him everywhere, reading it
with hopes of instilling the "kill out the attachment" philosophy. His upset
worsened as he and St. Denis began to rehearse for their London engagement. As they prepared to reunite their professional lives, they hoped to resolve the seemingly irreconcilable differences in their personal relationship.
With the opportunity to travel to London, they made arrangements to seek
the counsel of the one man whose experience with dance and the pressures of
an unconventional and childless marriage rivaled their own: Havelock Ellis,
the great "Saint of Sex" and one of the most outspoken proponents of the eugenics movement.

Unconscious Eugenics, 1922

In the scientific world, Havelock Ellis was best known for his pioneering role in "sexology," the science of sexuality. With J. A. Symonds, Ellis wrote the first English-language medical book on the topic of homosexuality, *Sexual Inversion* (1897), which posited that "inversion" is an instinct or "congenital element" as opposed to one that is "acquired"—a critical distinction to the depathologization of homosexuality.[123] Ellis's ideas for sexual reform were influenced by the eugenics movement. He corresponded directly with its leading proponents, including its founding figure, Galton, with whom he actively participated in devising strategies to shape public opinion that would eventually lead to legislative reform.[124] For example, in 1906, Ellis declared St. Valentine the "patron saint of sexual selection" so as to convey the impression that "eugenics had an eminently respectable, romantic, and importantly national past."[125]

Ellis's eugenic ideas extended beyond "selective breeding" into the domain of "social hygiene," or the methodical application of scientific principles to reform the spheres of sexuality, education, and labor. In his book *The Task of Social Hygiene* (1912), he famously argues that "it is the task of this hygiene not only to make sewers, but to re-make love, and to do both in the same spirit of human fellowship, to ensure finer individual development and a larger social organization."[126] For Ellis, "re-making love" included advocating women's suffrage, birth control, and sexual education. It also meant challenging the prevailing Victorian view that dance was a form of moral degeneracy and instead promoting dance as a eugenic means toward sexual and religious fitness.

Shawn and St. Denis initially became aware of Ellis through his article "The Philosophy of Dancing," which was published by *Atlantic Monthly* in 1914. The article formed the basis of Ellis's book *The Dance of Life* (1923), his most successful publication in the United States, in which he argues that dancing and architecture are the two "primary and essential arts." Ellis's ideas about dance were meant to expand a parochial Victorian view of dance as sexually illicit and culturally degrading. In fact, for Ellis, dancing is the "supreme symbol" of sex and religion.[127] For example, he explains that the human impulse to dance activates during the "process of courtship," wherein the males compete not only with other males in a contest of sexual selection but also with females whose "imagination" they must capture.

For Ellis, dancing is an unconscious reenactment of a choreographed battle for individual and racial survival. The "strenuous school of erotic dancing" teaches humans the skills of sexual discrimination. Just as dancing reenacts a primal scene of sexual conquest, so, too, does it propagate religious beliefs by representing sacred myths. Inasmuch as religious dancing reenacts "divine drama[s]," Ellis maintains that dancing is a sign of a religion's fitness.[128]

In an article about Ellis's *Dance of Life*, Judith Alter points out that choreographers and writers uncritically embraced his broad and unconditional validation of dance as an art form. She observes the influence that Ellis had on John Martin, Walter Sorell, and Roderick Lange, among others. She also mentions that Shawn had an "admiration" for Ellis, which is an understatement at best.[129] Shawn completely idolized Ellis with a devotion he often expressed in religious terms. In the inaugural issue of *Denishawn Magazine*, Shawn refers to Ellis as "St. Havelock," the "Saint of Sex," and "one of the greatest messiahs" and to Ellis's article "The Philosophy of Dancing" as "the dancer's bible." Shawn even described the experience of meeting Ellis "as holy as the Last Supper" and likened his contact with Ellis to touching "the hem of the garment of Jesus."[130]

In 1922, St. Denis and Shawn were completing a four-week engagement at the London Coliseum. Shawn received rave reviews for his performances, which catapulted him out from St. Denis's limelight and made him an internationally acclaimed dancer. Shawn considered the London performances a great artistic and professional achievement, even though the success was somewhat eclipsed by his sadness and jealousy over St. Denis's public liaisons with other men. Shawn was tortured by St. Denis's search for "'romance' in all directions" and commiserated with Martha Graham, who was similarly heartbroken. Graham was in love with Louis Horst, the Denishawn musical director, who not only refused to divorce his wife but also brought her along with the company to London. Shawn recalled walking with Graham near the theater and thinking: "Here we are in London, the Strand, Fleet Street, Piccadilly Circus, Westminster and it doesn't mean anymore to us than if we were in Coffeyville, Kansas or Kankakee, Illinois. We were just two miserable souls and we couldn't have cared less about being in London, and for the first time too."[131]

It was during this trip that St. Denis and Shawn separately met with Ellis at his home in the London suburbs. Shawn recorded the date of the meeting in his diary: Tuesday, June 3, 1922, at 11A.M. St. Denis had visited Ellis a day earlier, which minimally suggests the highly personal nature of their talks. In their respective autobiographies, St. Denis and Shawn describe these meetings as philosophical salons on the topic of dance. In reality, they were more like marriage-counseling sessions. In fact, months before these meetings, Ellis mailed Shawn a paper on the topic of "childless marriage," which strongly suggests that St. Denis and Shawn had already begun to communicate with Ellis about their marital problems.[132] In a 1969 interview, Shawn exposed additional details about his meeting with Ellis, explaining that he had hoped to meet Ellis above all other Brits, including King George, and that he had imagined the meeting would be like "a charming garden party." It was quite the contrary.

> Well it was a memorable meeting. I went out to his strange bleak, suburban apartment. I don't know what I expected, but this noble head, snow white hair, long patriarchal white beard, and sort of very rough, smelly tweeds. Tweeds always seem damp when they're thick. He sat back in a chair, sort of concave, hands folded, and this strange, high-pitched little voice that I was totally unprepared for. But if I ever came into the presence of a saint! This man, to me, rates as one of the greatest messiahs, one of the avatars. I was— with him, every moment, I was aware that I was in the presence of divinity itself. It was a thrilling, ennobling experience.[133]

Despite the unexpected sterility of the surroundings, Shawn opened up to Ellis: "Since he was the great saint of sex, and had preached on the beauty and rightness of sex, the art of love—how marvelous, how ecstatic, how right, how wonderful it can be—I began to pour out my heart, the agonies and sufferings that I was going through."[134] Shawn must have felt confident talking with Ellis about the state of his marriage, particularly the great shame and embarrassment he felt owing to St. Denis's affairs. Ellis would have been an ideal person to address Shawn's concerns, since he was also in an unconventional and childless marriage. Ellis's biographers tell us that he was impotent. Moreover, like Shawn and St. Denis, Ellis and his wife Edith lived apart for long periods of time, as she preferred the company of her lesbian lover.

As the foremost medical authority on the topic of sexual inversion (a nineteenth-century term for "homosexuality") and the husband of a lesbian, Ellis was, in some measure, the ideal person to counsel Shawn, who confided in Ellis about his homosexuality. Moreover, Shawn might have confided in Ellis about his suspicion that St. Denis was herself a lesbian.[135] However, Ellis's response to Shawn's "agonies and sufferings" was not as sympathetic as Shawn might have expected from his "Saint of Sex." Ellis replied: "Well I have always maintained that two artists should never marry." Consequently, Shawn asked Ellis whether he should consider divorcing St. Denis, to which Ellis gave the following contradictory advice: "Once a marriage has been made, it becomes a thing itself. It is a living entity, and . . . once you have created that entity you've created something that if you tried to kill it, it would be like murder. This is now your karma. You work it out."[136]

Shawn was not entirely persuaded by Ellis's advice to remain married to St. Denis—a decision that would have kept him from ever realizing his eugenic promise. In fact, Shawn questioned the reliability of this advice when he met another of his idols just a few days after meeting with Ellis. At Ellis's insistence, the British philosopher and poet Edward Carpenter (1844–1929) attended a matinee performance of the Denishawn company at the London Coliseum. Shawn and St. Denis had written in glowing terms about Carpenter and his collection of poems *Towards Democracy* (1883–1902). Shawn likened him to Walt Whitman, especially for his bold declarations of sexual freedom. Comparing Carpenter to Whitman was not entirely coincidental, as Shawn might have known that the two literary giants had once been lovers. In fact, Carpenter wrote *Homogenic Love* (1894), whose neologistic title gave Shawn the language to identify his own same-sex desire. "The Little Green Book" about homosexuality circulated in private. Assisted by a younger man, the frail eighty-year-old Carpenter met Shawn backstage after the performance. They dined together, and, according to Shawn, "a beautiful rapport was established."[137]

During their meal, Shawn asked Carpenter about the integrity of Ellis's marriage to Edith, to which Carpenter cryptically responded: "Edith Ellis believed that if society would totally and completely recognize and accept homosexuality as simply one form that is right and normal in the way of a sex expression, give it such complete acceptance that it is never even questioned or thought about as anything but the ordinary experience of life, she believed that this would release enormous stores of creative energy for the benefit of mankind." After a pause he said very simply, "And so do I." Shawn described Carpenter's response as an "epic making statement" that validated his own sexual views: "Of course it was so sweet, so tender, so utterly simple for him to say." Shawn went on to call his meeting with Carpenter "the most tremendous human contact I ever had."[138]

Notwithstanding Shawn's proclivity to exaggerate, his time in London was a life-defining experience, both professionally and personally. That said, he left London with conflicting advice about the state of his marriage and his desire to procreate from, of all people, an impotent eugenicist and a homosexual poet. Evidently, Ellis regretted the advice he had given Shawn. A month after their meeting, Ellis wrote to Shawn, empathizing with Shawn's "complicated situation."[139] Ellis rescinded his advice to stay married to St. Denis and instead encouraged Shawn to "be true to his own nature or else suffer the difficulty in attaining harmony between one's own ideals and the facts of life one is up against."

Though Ellis encouraged Shawn to accept his homosexuality "as right and normal," Shawn remained married to St. Denis, at least on paper.[140] He could not easily "murder" his marriage for reasons that were as much financial and artistic as romantic; yet remaining married to St. Denis also meant that he needed to find an alternate way to leave a legacy befitting "the handsomest man in America." If he was not going to fulfill his eugenic promise as a husband and father, then he would fulfill it through his art.

3

Tales of a Terpsichorean Traveler

A Dancing Geography Lesson,
October 1922–April 1923

On October 2, 1922, in Lewiston, Pennsylvania, Denishawn launched its maiden tour under the management of Daniel Mayer. Within the following six months, the company performed 180 concerts in almost as many days. This tour allowed the company to travel extensively to cities and small towns predominantly on the eastern seaboard but with legs in the South, the Midwest, and the West. The tour was the start of a three-year association with Mayer during which Shawn made some crucial professional strides that impacted the emerging field of modern dance in the United States. Unlike the company's vaudeville appearances, this first Mayer tour allowed Denishawn to present full programs of dances in concert halls and established music series, thus reaching an entirely new audience of opera and symphony aficionados. The tour was unquestionably a success, but the new audiences and greater critical attention forced Shawn to shake his well-trained instinct to dazzle with spectacle in order to fulfill Denishawn's purported mission of presenting dancing as a serious independent and modern art.

The tour had impressive advance sales owing to an advertising campaign that focused on Ruth St. Denis's return to the concert stage after a five-year hiatus. Another serendipitous event fueled the tour's success: within the first weeks, the tours of Denishawn and Isadora Duncan converged in New York City. Neither Denishawn nor Duncan had appeared in New York for over five years. With Denishawn at the Selwyn Theater, performing with an augmented orchestra under the direction of Louis Horst, and Duncan at Carnegie Hall, touring for the first time in years with her recently betrothed husband, poet Alexander Yesenin, New Yorkers had the opportunity to see Duncan, St. Denis, Shawn, Graham, Doris Humphrey, Charles Weidman, and Denishawn newcomer Louise Brooks on stage in a single weekend. The positive buzz helped boost ticket sales for both tours.

Ted Shawn. Paul A. Scolieri, Oxford University Press (2020). © Paul A. Scolieri.
DOI: 10.1093/oso/9780199331062.001.0001

In other cities, the Denishawn tour trailed Duncan's, which often worked to Denishawn's advantage as it received praise for its relative wholesomeness in the wake of Duncan's abstraction and seriousness: "No 'vitsky's' or foreign sounding endings" in the Denishawn dancers' names. However, Duncan's tour was sometimes a liability for Denishawn. A women's committee in Louisville, Kentucky, threatened to censor an upcoming Denishawn concert on account of the "indecent anatomical display" at a recent Duncan concert, a display that escalated into the "The Isadora Duncan Affair."[1] This was still the period before the establishment of dance criticism and since society columnists, sportswriters, and music critics who often covered the emerging dance scene were generally disinclined to offer aesthetic evaluation, they often fabricated news based on an artist's personality. In this instance, reporters filled newspaper pages with allegations about a professional rivalry between St. Denis and Duncan. Up until that point St. Denis and Shawn had always spoken in glowing terms about Duncan, whom they considered a kindred revolutionary. Fully ensconced in the cult of "Isadoration," they were unwilling to take the bait put before them by reporters seeking a disparaging comment about her.[2] That said, they were also unwilling to give up the press, so they said the right amount of nothing to score a headline without offending: "Ruth St. Denis Refuses to Give Her Opinion of Isadora Duncan." Once when Shawn was pressed to speak about Duncan, he gave a deceptively ambiguous statement: "Why, eh. I couldn't put all I think of that woman in an encyclopedia."[3]

In addition to leveraging the Duncan tour to Denishawn's advantage, Shawn and St. Denis successfully aligned themselves with Anna Pavlova who was also making her final rounds on her farewell tour of the United States, preparing to head to Asia where she would blaze a path that Denishawn would follow in the years to come. St. Denis and Pavlova were involved in a mutually beneficial campaign of kindness in the press. When Pavlova arrived in the United States earlier that year for her farewell tour, she greeted the press surrounded by her young American fans at the Alexandria Hotel, the same site where Shawn launched his career as a dance teacher. Pavlova told reporters, "I find the American women very beautiful and very gorgeously attired, but they all look alike! If only they would dress to express their own personalities how much more delightful they would be!"[4] Careful not to alienate her American fans, she qualified the statement by blaming the American retail industry for offering so little variation in women's wear, whereas in Paris "artistes and modistes" compete to outdo one another to

dress their clients. Pavlova implored American women to launch a dress reform movement and suggested that Ruth St. Denis lead the charge owing to
her great individual style.

St. Denis returned the compliment by representing a cohort of American
artists and patrons at the Metropolitan Opera that year to celebrate Pavlova's
tour. St. Denis also took Pavlova's cue and led a crusade (in the press only) to
modernize American women's fashion, putting her own spin on the Russian
ballerina's criticism of the fashion industry. In a spate of newspaper articles,
St. Denis urged women's colleges to appoint a Chair of Dressing: "The purpose in establishing a chair in good dressing would not be so that women
would give more thought to clothes, but so they might give less."[5]

St. Denis's strategically inflammatory comments embroiled Denishawn
within the 1920s dress reform debates spurred by flappers who challenged
conventional standards of behavior and dress. In fact, in Louisville, the company was programmed in a performance series called "Fashions and Dances
of 1923," which also included Duncan and Irene Castle. St. Denis came out
against the flappers, encouraging young women instead to seek their own
personal style ("a defiance of fashion's edict") and find an appropriate balance between the corset and the jazz age. Like her dancing, St. Denis's fashion
sense embodied a freedom of expression tailored to the values of traditional
femininity.

The sartorial debates served Denishawn well. At the outset of the tour,
Shawn and St. Denis entered a reciprocal sponsorship deal with the
Robinson Silk Company. Shawn and St. Denis used press interviews to emphasize the importance of silks to their modern choreography and allowed
Robinson to use the Denishawn name to advertise its fabrics in *Women's
Wear Daily*. During interviews, Shawn and St. Denis made it a point to
mention *The Wind*, a dance involving a huge swath of rose-colored Indian
silk, which gave "the most fascinating illusion of the vagaries of the air,
from gentle zephyrs to wild hurricanes." They were very effective spokes-
people, generating numerous reviews that noted their costumes and use of
fabric, extolling how Denishawn dancers could "make draperies dance and
talk."[6]

Denishawn also harnessed the popularity with the "Egyptian style" in dress
inspired by British archaeologist Howard Carter's 1922 discovery of King
Tutankhamun's tomb. King Tut hats, blouses, and furnishings had become de
rigueur at society pageants and balls where Denishawn was commissioned to
perform its Egyptian dances.[7] (See Figure 3.1.)

Figure 3.1. Ruth St. Denis and Ted Shawn performing a scene from *Egyptian Suite* on the Thames Embankment near Cleopatra's Needle in London, 1922. Photograph by Worldwide Studios. Denishawn Collection. Courtesy of the Jerome Robbins Dance Division, New York Public Library.

The Denishawn program was routinely applauded for the quality of the sets, costumes, and overall production. Unfortunately, many audiences did not get to experience the Denishawn effect as some venues could not accommodate all of the sets and lights. That, however, did not deter audiences—or producers, for that matter—from attending. Regardless of venue size, audience reception was overwhelming and consistently positive throughout the tour. Producer James A. Bortz telegrammed Mayer immediately after seeing a Denishawn concert at Carnegie Music Hall in Pittsburgh, in order to book the company again for the following year. The *Musical Courier* reported that in Chicago nearly the entire program was repeated by encore.[8] When Denishawn appeared in Boston they attracted the largest-ever audiences to the Boston Opera House in its thirteen-year history, setting a new box-office record for a dance attraction. In Manchester, New Hampshire, more than 1,500 people braved a storm to attend a Denishawn performance.

Shawn and St. Denis seized the opportunity afforded by the good press and solid ticket sales to recruit new students. On the road, they convinced audiences that studying dance was not only for aspiring performers but also a worthy pursuit for shopkeepers, secretaries, bookkeepers, and salesgirls. Shawn worked the science and health angle, arguing that dance is an ideal means of self-moderation: "I have observed in our eight years at the school that thin girls grow fat and fat girls grow thin, because dancing normalizes."[9] Just before the tour Shawn had met with Bernarr Macfadden, the founder and publisher of *Physical Culture* magazine. Shawn tried to encourage him to publish a magazine geared for dancers, an idea that eventually evolved into *Dance Lovers Magazine*. In the meantime, Shawn agreed to write an article titled "Dancing Cures Nerves" for *Physical Culture*, which appeared as the tour was winding its way across the country. The spread featured Shawn posing nearly naked, displaying his body as the ultimate specimen of balance, harmony, and regulation. Drawing on the writing of Havelock Ellis, Shawn claims that "normal, robust, healthy life is always rhythmic. Nervous people, it is well known, are jerky, spasmodic and unrhythmic." Having asserted this pathological distinction between the normal and the nervous, Shawn explains how dancing involves the free expressive use of the body, thus providing the ideal means of embodying music and thus synchronizing the rhythms between body and mind. He goes as far as to suggest that expressive dancing could root out mental disturbances and nervous disorders such as nervousness, hysteria, melancholy caused by "inhibitions," "complexes," and "repressed desires." Indeed, Shawn describe expressive dancing as a cure for sexual pathology, since by dancing one develops a healthy sense of one's body thus healing sexual disorders. The rest of the brief essay went further to correlate the relationship between a healthy body and repression: "The unexpressed person is a dangerous person, to himself and to others. Life is a force, and force without an outlet . . . is dammed up until a catastrophe occurs in the explosive breaking forth. The Freudian theory also claims that most things that are wrong with us are due to the pent up forces of sex."[10]

Although it is highly unlikely that Shawn believed (or even wrote) all of the ideas presented in this particular article, it is nonetheless relevant that his body was presented as the symbol of functional expressivity months after he heeded Ellis's advice to repress his own sexual leanings in order to maintain his marriage to St. Denis.

The tour made Shawn a star in his own right, with many critics focusing as much on his personality, performance, and physique as they did on St. Denis's marquis status. One interviewer lingered on every detail of his clothing, body, and face:

> Everyone was enchanted with Ted Shawn's appearances. He wore a black frock coat, and black trousers, a pearl grey vest, beautiful grey silk tie, black patent leather shoes and pearl grey spats. His pearl grey velour hat was on the back seat at the rear of the room. His only affection of jewelry was a little finger ring which the author of this talk forgot to examine at close range. He is very tall and very handsome, with dark meditative eyes, and interesting alert face, and long dark hair, which he wears combed straight back from his bow. His voice is clear and melodious, and arresting. His diction is perfect, his language flowing, his choice of words, excellent.[11]

With all the bluster and press about dress reform, "dancing" draperies, weight-loss regimens, Freudian repression, and box office records, it must have been hard for many to appreciate Denishawn's aesthetic contributions during this period. Even if the Denishawn stage seemed to take pleasure in excess, in the studio and in the press Shawn and St. Denis espoused the idea that dancing balances the forces of mind and body. Moreover, it was during this tour that the term "Music Visualization" began to appear on Denishawn programs.[12] Music visualization was an approach to choreography that sought correspondence between movement and musical structure, melody, and rhythm. St. Denis once gave a narrower definition, stating that visualization was "the scientific translation into bodily action of the rhythmic, melodic and harmonic structure of a musical composition, without intention to in any way 'interpret' or reveal any hidden meaning apprehended by the dancer."[13] Defining movement visualization as a "science" rather than an "art" was a way to distinguish their approach from the "interpretive" one associated with Isadora Duncan, though both St. Denis and Shawn openly acknowledged that their idea for musical visualization came to them while watching Duncan perform in Los Angeles. Louis Horst claimed that visualization was his idea.[14] One of Shawn's first music visualization pieces was *Gnossienne*, which he started before leaving for Camp Kearny. Set to the experimental music composition of the same name by Erik Satie, the short solo features a priest of ancient Crete performing the sacred rites before an altar of the snake goddess. Following the narrative implied by the title (a term invented by Satie to describe an experimental composition lacking time signatures or bar divisions), the music and dance were deeply connected in their sparseness. As if he were a bas-relief sculpture come to life, Shawn moved in rigid two-dimensionality and on demi-pointe throughout the dance, employing two distinctive characteristics of Nijinsky's movement style in *L'Après-midi d'un faun*. Shawn's costume, too, was sparse; he performed bare chested with a pair of shorts with an archaic design and rolled tubes at his waist and arms. By and large, such music visualizations were the hit of the Denishawn concerts, though one critic noted that this approach could rob some music lovers who "prefer the elusive and eerie phantoms of their own imagination magically conjured but the master touch of a musician at his instrument."[15]

Gnossienne could have just as easily fit within another category of dances on the program: "national dances," which referred to Denishawn's interpretations of primitive dance. Savvy reviewers questioned the logic of the term "national dances": "hard to imagine modern Egyptians claiming as 'national' dance figures and postures of which are copied from friezes in the time of the Pharaohs."[16] Semantics aside, the reviewer said the dances were "extremely convincing" at least on an emotional level. They engendered "the feeling of authenticity," even if it sometimes bordered on a "geography lesson."

Of course, Denishawn had its detractors as well. Some were simply unwilling to even consider dancing a theatrical art, chiding that "One must go see the dance in an exalted mood. It is art. Everybody says so."[17] But the opinions that mattered most belonged to the music critics for trade magazines, such as *Musical Courier* and *Musical America*, who uniformly praised Denishawn in artistic terms.[18] In fact, in the final stretches of the first Mayer tour, Shawn and St. Denis found themselves on the cover of *Musical Courier* listed as "Premier American Dancers." The accompanying article succinctly elevated Denishawn into its own orbit, with the bold assertion that "the American public seems to have awakened to the fact that in these truly great artists we have native dancers who are achieving all the glamor and brilliance of production and ethic that we have formerly associated only with the Russians."[19]

Shawn and St. Denis recognized the money-making potential of leveraging their newfound status as American dance pioneers and steering Denishawn toward the evolving and increasingly experimental intersection of dance and music. They pandered to new audiences who were attune to musical trends by promising that the next year's repertory would feature music exclusively by American composers. They whetted the appetites of *Musical Courier* readers with a proposal to commission composers to create works specifically for dancers, just as one would for a violin or a voice. They dropped names like Homer Grunn (who composed the music for *Xochitl*) and Mischa Levitzki, a naturalized Russian, whose "Waltz in A major" was performed in Carnegie Hall and became vogue among piano students everywhere—at the same time that St. Denis danced to it on stages across America. Shawn also announced his plan to collaborate with American composer Charles Wakefield Cadman, whose music accompanied Shawn's *Invocation to the Thunderbird* among other dances and whom he had met in London a year prior to inviting him to write music for a new dance-drama based on Hopi Indians. Eventually, that dance became *Feather of the Dawn* (1923). In a somewhat surprising move, Shawn and St. Denis also named two women composers as desirable collaborators: Carrie Jacobs Bond and Mana-Zucca.

Shawn was determined to maximize the awesome opportunity of his new celebrity and simultaneously exceed the high expectations (from audiences and critics alike) for Denishawn's next tour. He decided that the best way to deliver on the promise of America's foremost dance company was to look abroad.

Castles in Spain, April–May 1923

"Do you remember when we used to dream of castles in Spain—and the land of your heart's desire?" asked Martha Graham in a farewell letter of sorts.[20] On the surface, the letter was Graham's way of wishing Shawn a bon voyage as he set off for a month-long excursion to Spain and North Africa, yet beneath, it was Graham's adieu to Shawn and the Denishawn enterprise altogether. Toward the end of the first Mayer tour, Graham announced that she would end her seven-year association with Shawn and the company. In her letter to him, she pays him an unqualified expression of respect and gratitude that Shawn had always felt she owed him. In conciliatory strains, she begs him: "Don't say I've flown the nest. Denishawn—in all—is my religion. What it is built upon is what I believe. It has made me immortal but I can't seem to say anything—It's like saying 'I love you' to the person who means most to you in the world." Indeed, she expresses her love for Shawn four times in the five small sheets of stationery on which she composed her letter: "Oh, Teddie, we do love you so much. . . . Always I love you—and believe and know you to be a great person and artist—I can't even dance apart from you—in my heart."

Unquestionably, Graham's departure created a drag on Denishawn's forward momentum. Shawn had shared the stage with Graham more than any other dancer, including his wife. However, Shawn appreciated Graham's financial reasons for taking the opportunity to join the Greenwich Village Follies, the downtown revue that featured upscale musical, dance, and comedy sketch acts, rivaling the more popular and enduring Ziegfeld Follies. After all, Shawn helped her to secure the job and even choreographed dances for her to perform that first year. Doing so was a way to extend his brand. Shawn also knew the emotional toll that Graham's proximity to the married Louis Horst had taken on her.

Following the successful Daniel Mayer Tour (October 1922–April 1923), Shawn found himself with $1,800 and a narrow window of opportunity to travel. And so, four days following the final performance in Montclair, New Jersey, Shawn set off on a trip to Spain in pursuit of perfecting and deepening his expertise in Spanish dancing. He also planned an expedition through North Africa in pursuit of the Ouled Naïls, the nomadic tribe of bejeweled dancing girls that had captured the imagination of Romantic artists and writers.

The trip was prompted by the fanatical responses to Shawn's Spanish dances in the final stretches of the Mayer tour. On the program was *Spanish Suite* (1921) which included *Danza Espagnol* (choreographed by Shawn for St. Denis), *Tango* (a solo by and for Shawn), and *La Malagueña y el Torero* or *The Young Girl from Malaga and the Bull Fighter*) (a duet for Shawn and Graham and later, St. Denis). (See Figure 3.2.) One reviewer noted that at a performance at Town Hall in New York, audiences commanded Shawn to perform more than a dozen encores. Interest in Spanish music and dance among US audiences had grown since the turn of the century, when the famous La Carmencita (1868–1913) appeared at Niblo's Garden in 1894, a performance that was immortalized in a film by the Thomas A. Edison Company. During the 1917–18 theatrical season, a troupe of Spanish dancers led by "the world's greatest Spanish dancer," L'Argentina (1890–1936), made

Figure 3.2. Ted Shawn with Martha Graham in *Malaguena* (1921).
Photography by Arthur Kales. Denishawn Collection. Courtesy of the Jerome
Robbins Dance Division, New York Public Library.

several critically acclaimed appearances in New York. Hailed as "the best musical comedy Broadway ever harbored," the review *Land of Joy* brought in unprecedented box office numbers. People flocked to hear the music by Joaquín
Valverde and see the eleven dances.[21] The appearance influenced writer and
photographer Carl Van Vechten to dedicate a chapter on Spanish dance
revues titled "Land of Joy" in his book *Music of Spain* (1918). Van Vechten
swore by its addictiveness: "It is as intoxicating as vodka as insidious as co-
caine, and it is likely to become a habit like these stimulants."[22] In the book,
Van Vechten asks: "What have we been thinking all these years in accepting
the imitation and ignoring the actuality I don't know."[23] It was van Vechten
who recommended that Shawn study with Manuel Otero, a former member
of the *Land of Joy* review, from whom Shawn had learned a traditional dance
that he later performed for decades. One writer mentions that one evening
Shawn performed an encore called *Land of Joy*, also to a score by Granados,

though the writer did not think highly of Shawn's effort, at least not compared to the original troupe: "It was, however, not done at all as the native Spanish dancers did it here several years ago."[24]

Always with one eye on the Russians, Shawn must have seen reviews or images of Diaghilev's 1921 Ballets Russes production of *Cuadro Flamenco* that featured traditional Andalusian dances set to music arranged by Manuel de Falla and with sets and costumes designed by Pablo Picasso. Performed by Spanish dancers led by Maria Dalbaïcin, it premiered on May 17, 1921, at the Théâtre de la Gaîté-Lyrique in Paris.[25] Upon his return from Spain, Shawn created his own *Cuadro Flamenco*, though he took a very different approach, centering the dance around a matador, inspired by a transformative experience in Barcelona seeing a bullfight for the first time. Shawn's *Cuadro Flamenco* attempted to capture romance, drama, and authenticity, unlike the Ballets Russes version, which juxtaposed traditional dances (there was no choreographic credit in the program) against Picasso's modernist backdrop depicting a distorted theater hall, box seats, and an art gallery.

Shawn was not only dreaming of castles in Spain. He was reading everything about the country's culture, including Havelock Ellis's *Soul of Spain* (1908), especially its chapter on Spanish dancing, which Ellis contends "is something more than an amusement in Spain. It is part of that solemn ritual which enters into the whole life of the people. It expresses their very spirit."[26] In the *jota* dance he finds "a combat" between the sexes, a kernel of thought that he would later develop into his eugenic theory of dancing. Ellis lamented the veritable lack of scholarly writing about Spanish dance, inciting Shawn to fill the gap with his own personal account of its meaning.

Shawn left for Spain aboard the RMS *Berengaria* on April 25, 1923. The *New York Sun* covered his departure, complete with a photo of him planting a farewell kiss on a visibly reluctant St. Denis. Shawn dedicated a chapter in his own autobiography to a condensed account of his two-month trip, focusing on the characters he encountered abroad—from nameless café dancers, to the world-famous Burton Holmes and his wife. His account of Spain and North Africa later made its way into his book *Gods Who Dance*. The chapter is largely based on the daily letters he wrote to St. Denis, which he titled "The Tales of Teddy the Terpsichorean Traveler," extended journal entries about the performances and lessons he experienced and the practicalities of traveling, as well as an exhaustive list of props, costumes, and designs he had purchased for future dances. These were all punctuated with expressions of devotion, fidelity, and longing for St. Denis's presence. In most of the letters he seems genuinely happy. He was certainly at his thinnest, a fact he mentions several times.

Shawn brought with him a photo of St. Denis in her role as Chinese goddess Kuan Yin framed in a blue and silver leather frame, which he sometimes enshrined on his bedside table or positioned in her honor at an empty chair at a dining table. Several times throughout the trip, he introduced himself as St. Denis's husband and presented the photograph to establish his identity and legitimacy as an artist.

Arthur Buruel accompanied Shawn to Spain as a travel companion and interpreter. Buruel was the young man with whom Shawn had a sexual tryst when he first moved to Los Angeles, and later he was a dancer in Shawn's all-male *Pyrrhic Dance* presented at the Berkeley Pageant. For the transatlantic crossing, they were joined by Daniel "Father" Mayer, who was heading back to London for the summer to reclaim his management business that had been confiscated during the war. Shawn and Mayer enjoyed each other's company. Plus, Mayer got a kick out of Shawn's minor celebrity and enjoyed the special treatment they received on board as a result. Mayer encouraged the ship's purser to arrange it so Shawn could perform for the passengers at the evening concert. Though he feigned resistance, Shawn eventually pulled together a costume and danced a tango to "Dance de la Banana." Calling themselves the "Three Musketeers," Shawn, Mayer, and Buruel enjoyed long nights of conversation, massages, and nude swimming. Shawn mentioned Buruel's modesty: "He is shy about public nudity. Need I say, I am not! I need not!"[27]

The *Berengaria* arrived at its destination of Cherbourg, France, in record time. From there, Shawn and Buruel made a side trip to Paris. Shawn had visited the City of Lights during the company's London tour just a few months earlier. As with that brief excursion, he made the surprising realization that he felt ambivalent toward the city, even though he had studied French and considered himself a Francophile. He feared committing "sacrilege" by admitting that he did not "just love" Paris, though realized he needed time to experience its rhythms and was frustrated to feel like a tourist anywhere. He sensed a bitterness beneath the museums, civic pageantry, and even the nightlife. Thinking the Paris arts scene might help salvage his perception of the city, he went to see the latest revue of choreographer and performer Polaire Harry Pilcer, which boasted a version of *l'Apres-midi d'un faune* that turned out to feature a few nymphs prancing about in silver gowns and satin white heels.

From Paris, he traveled to Fort Bou on the Spanish border, then to Barcelona, taking in glimpses of scenic port cities along the Mediterranean. He was somewhat disappointed by how mundane everyone appeared, noting that one man wore the very same hat he was wearing. The police, on the other hand, wore garish uniforms that Shawn thought rather looked like costumes for a musical. Shawn's theatrical frame of reference was so entrenched that everything he experienced either reminded him of a dance or inspired one.

Shawn's first real engagement with authentic Spanish culture came at a musical review in Barcelona. He was transfixed by the three-hour show, especially the amateurish charms of the young dancers, who performed *coplas* in cheap imitations of Paris fashions, and, to his utter shock, without any makeup. The main attraction was Carolina La Riva who came on stage in what Shawn described as "Velasquez Infanta style," working the castanets in a manner that nearly made him lose his senses. The number was a ghastly dance she had learned from a correspondence class in "Russian-Ballet-Oriental" dancing, apparently in an effort to diversify her program. Buruel slipped down to the orchestra to speak with the conductor about a piece of music. He learned that the conductor Joaquin Savall was the music director at the school where La Riva studied and made arrangements to take a class there the following day.

The rest of the evening Shawn spent wandering around the hundreds of cabarets in Barcelona. Just a few hours before sunrise, he came upon a club where "real gypsies" performed. Shawn was taken by the intensity of the crowd, the weightiness of the *zapateo* and the guitar, which he considered "a new instrument in these men's hands." The next day he visited Antoni Gaudí's unfinished Sagrada Familia cathedral en route to his dancing lesson at Savall's school. At the school, he walked up five flights of stairs to the top floor studio—"Denishawnish" he described it—as he saw a level of activity among the young girls working on their steps. He was introduced to a young and good-looking teacher named Perfecto Perez. With Buruel's translations and Perez's articulate physical demonstrations, Shawn quickly learned a series of sequences on a 10x12-foot platform. Perez was impressed with Shawn's ability to grasp the dance, a complicated rhythmic dance called the *farruca*.

Shawn was so impressed with Perez's teaching and his own progress that he postponed his trip to Madrid to spend more time studying with him. Classes bled into long dinners and late-night conversations with Perez, whom Shawn had begun to affectionately call "my *maestro de baile*." Shawn found Perez "altogether a very desirable person," and, for whatever reason, receiving validation from a teacher was meaningful to him. In Perez, he found someone truly sympathetic and someone he looked up to not because of reputation but for his skill. "Furthermore," he explained to St. Denis, "he has a nice figure, is young and a good dancer." Shawn took comfort in Perez's confidence in Shawn, who would regularly pat him on the shoulder and assure: "Calma, calma!" He discussed with Perez the possibility of coming to the United States to teach at Denishawn and to perform in vaudeville. Shawn asked Perez to teach him a few duets that he could perform with St. Denis. He proudly learned an entire dance from the Triana district of Seville, as well as some basic rhythms on the castanets. In addition to learning these ready-to-perform dances, Shawn met with Savall to listen to his original compositions that he had transposed to solo piano. Shawn bought them for five pesetas (about eighty cents) each.

He wrote to St. Denis about the new dances he planned to teach her: "You must get queer vibrations sometimes—the call I sent out is so poignant and so strong. Oh, dearest heart, I am so happy in our love. Life is expanding and is radiant because of you, and the unity which has come to us."[28]

Hard as it was to leave Perez and Barcelona, Shawn made his way to Madrid for a relatively brief stay before heading to Seville. Shawn found the capital beautiful but stressful as there were few opportunities to immerse himself in dancing culture. The shopping and culture hardly impressed him either: "Most of the stuff is imported and stupid." He went to see *Nino de Oro,* a *zarzuela* set in the caves of Granada. Inspired by the play, Shawn was immediately convinced that he needed to create a dance-drama based on the theme of a gypsy wedding. Later that evening at a club, Shawn had the opportunity to learn about gypsy culture more intimately when a local guide propositioned him with a private show and sex with a group of *gitanas.* Shawn remonstrated the guide, who could not understand his desire to see women dance for any reason beyond foreplay.

Shawn attended the *academia de baile* of Otero, which was owned by the uncle of Manuel Otero with whom Shawn had studied in New York. He booked classes with another of Otero's nephews for his remaining five days in Seville, arriving early every day to watch the young women arrive to class wearing all black, fringed shawls, and mantillas, escorted by their maids and dueñas. He was impressed by how they greeted their teacher with a kiss on the cheek as a sign of respect and thought about implementing the tradition at Denishawn.

The next day when he arrived at Otero's *academia* he ran into Troy Kinney and his wife Margaret, artists and authors of a broad history of dance titled *The Dance: Its Place in Art and Life* (1914). They had just arrived in Seville. They watched Shawn's lesson, then joined him for lunch. Shawn used the opportunity to expose the ardent balletomanes to some "good Denishawn propaganda." He explained how he encouraged all his students to read their book, which he considered excellent, despite its obsession with ballet. But Kinney was more interested in Russians and had not even seen the latest Denishawn tour. The year following this meeting, the Kinneys published a second edition of their book, including a new chapter on dance between 1914 and 1924, which also makes no mention of Denishawn. In response, Shawn published an eight-column review of the book in *Denishawn Magazine* that drew out the Kinneys' "fundamentalism," and in so doing, eviscerated much of the book's authority, especially as it pertains to Oriental dancing.[29]

From Seville, Shawn wrote to St. Denis to mention a twenty-four-hour stomach "disaffection" but not even that slowed him down, for as he explained, it kept him from having to stop for lunch and thus allowed him to maximize his time touring the museums, shopping for shawls, embroideries, and vests.[30]

He frequented a café at the Puerta de Jerez, situated within view of the royal tobacco factory (Real Fabrica de Tabacos) made famous by the opera *Carmen* whose title character worked there as a *cigarerra*. (Incidentally, Georges Bizet, the composer, was a nephew of influential movement theorist François Delsarte, a connection that would have been meaningful to Shawn.) Shawn watched as older workers left the building, each with a flower in her hair. He wrote: "What a wonderful thing imagination is—to have envisioned Carmen among this bunch."

After several weeks in Spain, Shawn embarked on the second leg of his trip: a tour through the Sahara in pursuit of the Ouled Naïl. It proved difficult for Shawn to leave the security of mainland Europe. He had not received any letters from St. Denis in weeks and thus was uncertain whether she had been receiving his. He was counting on those letters reaching the United States so there would be some indication of his whereabouts should he go missing. It was a legitimate concern, seeing that his next destination was Algeria and he no longer had a translator nor an itinerary. All he had was the cash in his pocket and an inexplicable need to come face to face with the dancing girls of the Sahara.

"Sheiking" in the Desert, May–June 1923

As Shawn prepared for his arrival in Algeria, he wrote to St. Denis: "I have been your ragged camel-boy lover whom you have stolen out of the city to meet you on the sand dunes—perhaps I will return to you really your Sheik."[31] His conjuration of a sexualized desert narrative was likely incited by the exceedingly popular 1921 silent film *The Sheik*, which starred Rudolph Valentino in the titular role and established the actor as Hollywood's first male sex symbol. Like Shawn's seemingly coy proposition to St. Denis, the film's plot centers around sexual desire fueled by a choreography of racial impersonation. Set in the desert oasis city of Biskra, Algeria, but filmed on various locations throughout California, the film features several scenes representing the mysterious dancing girls of the Ouled Naïl—or at least a veil-swirling approximation thereof. The first scene of a dancing girl comes at the precise moment in the film's plot when the heroine, a "cultured English girl" traveling solo in the desert, decides to borrow a dancer's costume in order to infiltrate a casino harem. Her impersonation succeeds so well that an Arab gambler at the casino selects her as his prize bride. She is quickly revealed as an impostor, setting her into a dizzying array of plot twists that result in her falling captive to a powerful sheik with whom she falls in love, a feeling she eventually confesses to her captor, though not before she learns that the sheik is not Arab at all but the adopted son of a British man and a Spanish woman.

The Sheik influenced a whole wave of desert romance films, such as *A Son of the Sahara* and *The Arab*, both of which were shot on location in Algeria in 1924 and featured scenes with Ouled Naïl dancers. These films were created to satisfy an American fascination with Oriental dancing that was sparked by the veil dancers featured in the "Streets of Cairo" exhibit at the Chicago World's Fair in 1893. Just days before Shawn's transatlantic crossing, the *Chicago Daily Tribune* ran a feature story about travel in Algeria, including encounters with the women of the Ouled Naïl. The travel writer was disappointed with the moves of the "Delilahs of the Desert," claiming that the dancers who performed at the Chicago World's Fair and the Chicago Columbia Exhibition "shook a lot more life into the dances." The dance of the real Ouled Naïl, while "soothing and restful is somewhat too decorous to bring out the SRO signs. Many visitors to American county fairs have traveled less and seen better."[32]

It was precisely this box office demand for authentic desert dancing that informed Shawn's relentless search for the actual Ouled Naïl, a two-week journey that took him 1,500 miles into the northern Sahara via hired car, mail plane, barouche, and mule-drawn cart. He was determined to return home with an authentic version to bring to the stage, to satisfy an appetite whetted by Valentino. He was not interested in the commercialized versions of belly dancing that filled the tourist theaters of coastal Mediterranean cities, the hip-gyrating spectacles of European musical revues, nor the fair-ground sideshows back home in the States. Instead, he wanted to see the desert courtesans for himself, to affirm a vision of them that he had carried with him for over a decade. Shawn first became aware of the Ouled Naïl via a photo-essay in the January 1914 issue of *National Geographic*. "Here and Now in North Africa" featured over a dozen exquisite yet romanticized photographic portraits of young women identified as "the dancing girls of the Ouled Naïl Tribe," though they are barely mentioned in the essay proper. Their identity and place within Algerian social circles are relegated to a single photo caption: "A tribe of desert-Arabs living in Algeria, whose girls resort to the cities to earn money by dancing. As they appear unveiled and bedecked in jewels, they are outside the pale of respectable women. The gold pieces which form their headdress make up their dowry when they return to their tribe to get married." One photo depicts two women with meticulously painted eyebrows and glistening lips embracing each other. Another photo captures a young girl in repose, "dreaming of the day when she will have accumulated enough in coins and jewels to return to the tents of her tribe a heavily dowered bride." Several photographs suggest the "turning, twisting, and undulating" of their dances.[33] Longing to experience an unmediated encounter with this source of beauty and drama that he could exploit for the stage, Shawn journeyed into the heart of the Sahara. That his experience with dancing Arab women might also transform him into a sexually desirable "sheik" in the process was a possibility he would not refuse.

After deboarding the ship from Spain, Shawn and Buruel made a brief stop at the hotel, then ventured to see the sites of Algiers. They climbed to the top of a hill to visit the Museum of Antiquities. Shawn was captivated by the extensive collection of Roman and Islamic artifacts, and even more entranced by the physical beauty of the people he encountered as he wandered through the *kasbah* filled with women in veils and men in white burnooses, turbans, and fezzes. "The natives are every bit as picturesque as I dreamed they would be." He was struck by the beautiful "heifer" eyes of the officers and porters ("no matter how dirty, how otherwise scrawny and miserable") and even the beggars ("so picturesque are their rags in color and line").

As with his time in Spain, Shawn saw everything through the prism of theater or fiction: "I felt as if I were a character in a play or like Jurgen, had been given the power to enter into the realms of literature and mythology." That said, he was not unaware of the political reality that shaped Algerian resistance or ambivalence to the presence of Western tourists such as himself: "They look right through you, as if you were not even there. They seem to say 'We have been conquered before, but always with patience and time the white man has vanished, and the land becomes ours exclusively again. So now, why even pay attention to these puny, pale interlopers—before long they will be gone again, but we are here from the beginning of Time to end.' " Shawn, however, saw himself outside the forces of colonialism, assured that his sympathetic gaze as a dancer and his sincere pursuit of "authentic" Arab culture somehow excluded him from the political and sexual economies that drove intercultural exchanges, the tourist industry around the Ouled Naïl most especially. Shawn held that dancers belonged to a culture of their own that transcended the strictures of nation, race, and religion.

Whereas Shawn saw physical beauty everywhere during his days in Algiers, he failed to find a single example of dancing that satisfied the impossible expectations conjured by the photographs in *National Geographic*. Even the infamous "la Reina de las danza" who starred at the Salon Novedades only turned out a lackluster display of castanets. Convinced that he needed to get out of the city and into the desert to find authentic dancing, he embarked on an eight-day trip from Algiers to Bou-Saada, an oasis town and major center of the Ouled Naïl. Accompanied by an Irish guide named O'Kelly, Shawn traveled through the Sahara, passing Bedouin tribes beside their camel-hair tents ("I must have one of those tents! What a perfect thing for a stage setting!") and a town of mud homes ("It was like being in a book! I can't feel the reality of it all!") Finally, in Bou-Saada, he checked into a hotel where the guests included a garrison of handsome French officers and their chic wives, most sporting tennis apparel.

After dinner, he set out to a nearby house where he was told a dancer lived. He knocked at the door and she answered. At last, he laid eyes on a real Ouled Naïl, though his first impression of this elusive stranger only reminded him of home: "I felt sure I was at Denishawn the costume was so familiar in all its details. But had I been at home I would have jumped on her, for it was not up to our standard! She was really rather cheaply got together compared with the picture of Ouleds I have seen." Inside the room were two musicians, another woman, and a young barefooted girl about six years old. Shawn took a

seat at one end of a deep room and drank Arab coffee as they prepared an im-
promptu performance for him. The dancing ultimately disappointed Shawn,
too, as it consisted only of three basic movements (possibly only two and a
half)—an arm gesture, a step, and a postural shift.

The principal dancer went behind a curtain, only to reemerge nearly
naked but for a headdress. She was eighteen years old but Shawn figured she
could have been any age with a body as thin and muscular as hers and a face
"as hard and dry as the desert." She danced a wearisome routine, "a professional selling of a body. It was in no way alluring, nor was there any attempt
to make it so," Shawn groused. Turned off by the dancer, he focused instead
on the young girl who shadowed the dancer's movements, imitating the
dancer's steps while holding an English walking stick in her two hands above
her head. Shawn did not explain his reasons for finding the younger girl's imitation more compelling than the "authentic" Ouled Naïl's performance. In
all likelihood the young girl's playful variation shifted the locus of attention
away from the sexual exchange the dancing invited, thus relieving him from
the unwanted sexual gaze he could not reciprocate. Despite the unequivocally "professional" aspect of the performance, Shawn wondered "It's wonderful, but is it Art?" thus imposing a Western burden on the dance that the
Ouled Naïl neither claimed nor desired.

His distaste for the transactional quality of the experience did not deter
him from approaching the dancer after the performance to make an offer on
her bracelets with "evil looking spikes." He learned these spikes were designed
to defend against unwanted advances from men in the coffee houses. Shawn
struck a deal to buy them right off the dancer's arms. "I wanted to have
something from the first Ouled Naïl I had ever seen dance." Even though he
propositioned her for the bracelet, he ultimately blamed her for the mean-
inglessness of the exchange: "Probably she sells them to every tourist."

Shawn pervasively denied the fact that nearly all of his experiences of
dance in Africa were enmeshed in sexual economies. This was especially
true of his visit to a brothel in the major trade city of Setif, the next stop on
his journey. A local guide brought him to a brothel knowing there would be
Arab and Berber dancing. For the price of one franc, he gained entrance to
a room full of more than 100 men watching women swirl and pose to the
sound of a small orchestra and the distinctive wailing sound of a musette.
Shawn paid very close attention to the design and color of the dresses, more
so than the actual dancing. One dancer got worked up, inspiring someone to
pull out a one franc note which she clenched between her teeth then stealthily

deposited on a tray near the musicians. Shawn noted that another dancer, the prettiest and best by his estimation, performed a "nautch turn" and a "grape-vine" step, though he came to realize that there was no intrinsic meaning behind the choreography; the dancing was simply a way of attracting the attention of men in the crowd. He observed how men and women paired off and went upstairs without uttering a single word to each other. Shawn made no mention of his visit to a brothel in his *Gods Who Dance* book, except to say that he visited Bou-Saada and saw dances that resembled a *chassé*, a French term for a chasing step. It was a telling association.

He left Bou-Saada on a five-hour drive to the desert city of Biskra, home to an actual Rue des Ouled Naïl (or Street of the Ouled Naïl). Surely, he thought this would be his best shot to see authentic Ouled Naïl dances, yet it was off-season and with few tourists in town, most women retreated to their homes farther south. Nonetheless, he stayed to watch a performance at a local café, where he saw a performer with what he considered the most refined "sense of choreography" that he had seen in Algeria. Whereas most of the dancing girls he had previously witnessed would abruptly stop whenever they were tired or distracted, this dancer displayed an attention to musicality and phrasing, holding each pose until the last note of the music, even while carrying a saber or balancing a pitcher of water on her head. Shawn was impressed by the dancer's "greater rhythmic feeling" during the abdominal rippling "danse du ventre." This dancer, ironically, was actually a man performing a woman's dance, affording him a certain luxury if not obligation to focus his attention on the enactment of femininity rather than (or not only) on the business of sex.

In Bou-Saada Shawn met a local guide who promised to put together a varied program of Arab dances for Shawn within twenty-four hours. The following evening Shawn followed the guide to a tiny room above one of the buildings on the Rue des Ouled, only to find a "fat harlot." Shawn's patience wore thin. He threw a tantrum until the guide offered to compensate with a trip to see an actual dervish at a hut on the edge of town, off the beaten path of French colonial authorities who had prohibited the ritual. When they arrived, waiting for them was a "cast of five": a tom-tom player, a flutist, a sad priest with mystic eyes, a mangy dervish, and his attendant. The dervish began to shake to the sound of the drumming, then knelt before his attendant and snuffed something from a little box, which the guide promised was only tobacco. The dervish then took what appeared to be a hatpin and began to pierce himself right through his cheek without shedding a single drop of blood. He followed this trick by yanking coals directly from a brazier with his bare hands, then licking them until white plumes of smoke were visible. The dervish then stripped down to his trousers and grabbed two bundles of straw, which he set on fire. The flames lit up his bare torso as he danced around. When the straw burnt out, the dervish knelt close to Shawn, who became visibly unnerved by the dervish's physical proximity to him and by the fear of what physical boundary he might next cross. The dervish exposed the crook of his elbow to Shawn, then bit into his bicep only to pull his face away revealing rhythmic spurts of blood gushing from his vein. The dervish then placed his mouth over his gushing arm, held it there a while, then pulled his face away again, this time to reveal perfectly smooth, unwounded skin. The trick left not a trace of blood, but rendered the dervish moaning and quivering. His attendant provided him comfort by covering him with a burnoose but, as Shawn described, "he was no sooner covered than he sprang up and went around kissing each one of the other black men very emotionally—and I fully expected to be kissed myself—but he only shook hands with me, thank God!" The dramatic intensity of the display and the anticipation of a kiss from a man were resolved in the most perfunctory way—a handshake and a cash payment, the equivalent of $1.65 in American dollars.

"I am sick about not finding the real Ouled Naïl here," he confided to St. Denis. However, the intense and rare experience of the dervish in Biskra convinced him he was getting closer to an encounter with authentic Arabic dance for which he had come to Algeria. The next day he pursued a plan to get to Touggourt, the permanent residence of the Ouled Naïl tribe. His options for traveling to the far reaches of the desert were limited to a weekly train (that had left the day prior) or a camel caravan (that would have taken eight days, far more time than remained before his ship was to set sail for Europe). He decided on a $40 passenger seat on a mail plane, allowing him to make the round trip in one day. It was Shawn's first ever flight. The plane's pilot, Captain Perrier, spoke no English but promised to pass along Shawn's request to meet dancers, as best he understood the message in translation from O'Kelly, Shawn's Irish guide.

On the ground in Touggourt, Shawn made it to a hotel where a hotelier helped to select from the hundreds of women who responded to Perrier's call for dancers at fifteen cents a dance. Shawn was amazed at the women's physical beauty, "even by our American Ziegfeld standards," though he was appalled at Perrier's approach to casting, which mostly involved pinching their breasts, as if he were "picking cantaloupes." Accompanied by a native officer, Shawn and Perrier went into the quarter where the chosen women lived and watched as they began to dress in their finery. Through Perrier, he asked about the diadem he remembered seeing in the special issue of *National Geographic*, only to learn that those were worn only by the Ouled Riches, the wealthy women who were able to live in the northern cities and to "buy" a husband for the purposes of procreation. Shawn led the women to the rooftop where there was enough light to take photos of them with his Graflex camera. The girls obliged despite the oppressive afternoon heat. They performed their routines with Shawn stopping them whenever he saw a pose he wanted to capture. That process made them laugh, so much so that they could barely get through their dances. Their giddiness might have been a response to Shawn, who was visibly wracked with pressure to capture so much in so little time. Quite possibly they were nervous about Shawn's apparent upset that they had put on men's heavy socks to protect their feet from the sun-baked desert roof, thus marring his photographic efforts. Despite the many obstacles and distances in his way, Shawn eventually got his photos of actual dancing girls of the Ouled Naïl, three of which were published in *Gods Who Dance*, though none of them suggest dancing nor in any way resemble the exquisite photographs he had seen in the pages of *National Geographic* that initially inspired his journey.

Shawn left by foot at three o'clock in the afternoon as he had missed the mule cart that was to take him back to the plane and the only automobile in Touggourt was in disrepair. Once he finally was airborne, he scribbled a letter to St. Denis: "I have told you I love you under a lot of circumstances and I must add this one to it: We are very high and I see villages and oases below me—we are returning to Biskra." (See Figure 3.3.)

The next day in Biskra, he went to Chateau Landon to visit its famous lush garden that inspired the popular 1905 novel *The Garden of Allah* by British author Robert S. Hichens and, thereafter, the popular Hollywood hotel, which at the time was owned by Russian actress and dancer Alla Nazimova. Shawn wrote that the setting was a "dream place—it calls out for lovers to inhabit it." He spent the morning there taking photographs of a beautiful seventeen-year-old Arab boy named Mami Abraham, whom he described as "full of all the guile and sin of which an Arab is capable." Mami worked for the Royal Hotel. He asked Shawn to take him back to America to serve as his garçon. "He would be diverting," Shawn admitted in a letter to St. Denis, suggesting at least that he had considered the proposition. Shawn eventually declined the offer. Mami asked if Shawn wanted to watch him smoke hashish

Figure 3.3. Ted Shawn in Biskra, Algeria, 1923. Denishawn Collection. Courtesy of the Jerome Robbins Dance Division, New York Public Library.

instead. He declined that offer, too, then asked Mami to promise him that he would never again smoke it either.

From Biskra, Shawn headed to Constantine, a city perched on a plateau high above the desert. In a scene reminiscent of *The Sheik* film, he attended a command performance of an Ouled Riche who made a fortune dancing in the Biskra casino, affording her the luxury to live in an extravagant home in Constantine during off season. "Almost a real beauty," the large woman wore a velvet dress threaded with gold and lace gloves that exposed some of her skin, which was covered with elaborate henna tattoos. To music played by her own musicians, she performed four different dances including a "muscle dance" (a type of torso rippling number) and a dance with handkerchiefs. Shawn thought hers were the finest versions of the Ouled Naïl dances he had yet to see. What Shawn valued above her physicality was her approach to dancing. "She danced as a dancer, and not as a woman displaying her body for sale (or rent) which spoils everything for me."

Shawn was lucky to have obtained an invitation to see the Ouled Riche perform in her home, seeing that it was illegal for women to dance in public at the time. He also went to a café to see young men perform these dances in women's clothes. He was astonished to see a ten-year-old boy dart across the room while sustaining "his rear end in a continual lateral vibration that had the speed of an electric buzzer, almost a blur." At yet another place he saw four old men with white robes, white turbans, and long white beards chanting and dancing together with tremendous grace and dignity. "I could have wept with the beauty of it," Shawn wrote.

Shawn caught a train from Constantine to Tunis. Serendipitously, Burton Holmes, the "Father of the Travelogue," and his wife boarded at one of the subsequent stations, joining Shawn in his otherwise empty compartment. Shawn had contacted Holmes years earlier to acquire films of dances Holmes had recorded on his tours throughout the world. The films played an important role in the development of the Denishawn dance curriculum. Denishawn also would often follow Holmes's events in various circuits, often performing at the same venues on consecutive nights. In some respect, the Denishawn concerts were the "live action" counterpart of Holmes's travelogues in their attempt to "bring the world home" for local audiences through romanticized forays into remote cultures. The "Father of the Travelogue" and the "Father of American Dance" talked for hours aboard this train in northern Africa. Shawn's vision of world dance had been filtered through the lens of Holmes's camera. Now, Shawn had the opportunity to see these traditions alongside Holmes with his own camera in hand. No doubt Holmes welcomed Shawn's company as well for his expertise in interpreting and evaluating the dances Holmes filmed though never quite fully understood. They spent the next four days touring Tunisia together.

Their first outing was deeply upsetting to Shawn. The Tunisian guide brought him and the Holmeses to a private Moorish home to see some local music and dance. Shawn expressed outrage over the dancers—two raggedly dressed women who seemed never to have danced before. Shawn was embarrassed to appear unable to procure a decent local dancer and to have been taken for a tourist in front of Holmes, an assumption that did not bother Holmes at all. The guide appeased Shawn with some impressive sights and experiences, including a visit to an outlawed Aissaoua ceremony. He also escorted the curious Americans to an old *fondouk* or camel stable, where under a starry sky they saw a woman perform a dance with *crotales*. It was a subtle dance that paired beautifully with the aroma emanating from clusters of jasmine that men had tucked in their turbans. They spent their remaining days visiting the holy Islamic city of Kairouan, sitting at cafés watching street performers and snake charmers. They also went to the *souks* to purchase all manner of apparel and accessories to outfit a cast for a dance Shawn would create about the Aissaoua—red leather boots, fezzes with tassels, jewelry, and gandourahs (loose sleeved gowns).

The Holmeses crossed the Mediterranean with Shawn on a boat ride from Tunisia to Palermo, where Arthur Buruel joined them. Shawn took a certain pleasure in seeing Holmes, arguably the world's most experienced traveler, blunder with tickets, get "gipped," and in general get stranded in new locales. "It relieved my conscience about myself." But soon they went their separate ways.

Though Shawn traveled to Spain and Algeria seeking artistic inspiration, it was his sweeping tour of Italy that provided the most creative invigoration. Following a trip to Pompeii and Naples, Shawn and Buruel headed north to Rome to take in all the major sites. At the Vatican Museum, Shawn basked in the male beauty of his "favorite boy" in the Sistine Chapel, wept over a sculpture of Greek warriors, and endured the "suffering pleasure" of a Pyrrhic bas-relief. At the Galleria dell'Accademia in Florence, Shawn "worshipped" Michelangelo's David for over an hour. These confrontations with male beauty made him contemplate his own burden as a dance artist: "My work is to express virile perfection in movement, and that is some job." More pragmatically, it renewed Shawn's long-standing desire to create a sculptural dance that evoked the "unattainable perfection" of the male form. Buruel assured Shawn that the timing was right, since his body was looking "so thin and lovely . . . really better looking than ever." Indeed, upon his return stateside, Shawn would begin creating a sculpture dance *Death of Adonis* that captured the form and feeling of the male beauty he experienced in Italy.

After Rome, Shawn made a detour to Florence to spend time at Villa Braggiotti, the estate of the wealthy Boston family whose daughters Berthe and Francesca both studied at Denishawn and later opened the most influential Denishawn franchise school in Boston. Though a brief respite, Shawn had a wonderful experience dancing in the lovely music hall at Villa Braggiotti, a castle whose walls were adorned with bas-relief sculptures of Bach, Beethoven, and Mozart. His host summoned Shawn to dance as Papa Braggiotti improvised at the piano and a family friend, a lawyer and poet named Leon Francisco Orvieto, read his verse. Shawn obliged his small audience of friends, and found himself dancing with an intensity and freedom he had not experienced in quite some time.

From Florence, Shawn headed to Paris, where he saw as much dancing as he could fit into a weekend. He started with a review recommended by Burton Holmes that turned out to be "a dull dish of smut." He also went to the Théâtre des Champs-Élysées to see the Ballet Suédois, the avant-garde Swedish ballet company founded by the wealthy impresario Rolf de Maré. Shawn was unimpressed with the concert, especially *Le Boit de Joujoux*, a dance about "the old mouldy idea of a toy store coming to life." He took in a performance of the Dolly Sisters, impressed by the "brilliant costuming and complete nakedness." He also attended a program of the Ballets Russes at the Gaîté Lyric. He had already seen *Prince Igor*, but new to him were *Chout* ("hideous grotesques") and *Parade* ("an insult to human intelligence"). However, *Les Noces* ("a really great creation") made Shawn recognize the genius of Bronislava Nijinska, the sister of Vaslav Nijinsky and the company's star both as a performer and choreographer. "I must take my hat off to her, for she has done a big thing. She has beaten us to the combination of choral singing as an accompaniment to dance."

The extravagant production values of the dances he saw in Paris overwhelmed Shawn—the size of the theaters, the live orchestras, the stunning sets and costumes. This final leg in the two-month journey of Teddy, the Terpsichorean Traveler, caused him to lament: "Oh, why wasn't I made with a fatal beauty, so that I could sell my virtue for a high price!?"

If nothing else, his was a shockingly apathetic statement to have made, revealing his inability to recognize the relatively high levels of privilege, access, and power that made it possible for him to travel and study, to say nothing of the apathy it conveyed toward the women of the Ouled Naïl, whose romanticized image he relentlessly pursued yet whose economic and social reality within a cruel sexual and tourist economy he was neither willing nor able to fully acknowledge. When arriving in Africa, Shawn blithely expressed a desire to become a sheik, or at least a version of the mysterious, sexualized Arab that was emerging in early Hollywood cinema. By the end of his two-month transcontinental odyssey, however, Shawn instead mused that he ought to be more like a dancing girl of the Ouled Naïl and trade sexual desirability into social and economic power. Notwithstanding his direct view into the precarious existence of the dancers he met, Shawn focused on his own insecurities about his place within the world of art.

Shawn and Buruel flew from Paris to London where they reunited with fellow "musketeer" Daniel Mayer. One of their few nights on the town ended at the venerable Pagani's restaurant where Shawn signed his autograph on a wall covered with those of other theatrical celebrities such as Sarah Bernhardt, Jean Genet, and Nijinsky. He followed Mayer to his hometown of Bexhill, where Mayer had been mayor before the war, then set sail for New York on the SS *Aquitania*, landing on June 28, just in time to translate his experiences of his terpsichorean travels into dances for the upcoming program of his highly anticipated second Daniel Mayer tour.

A Dance King and His Empire,
July 1923–August 1925

Ted Shawn returned to New York from his trip to Spain and North Africa on June 28, 1923, prepared to deliver on his great promise to Daniel Mayer to create a touring program of dances set exclusively to music by American composers. He rehearsed the remainder of the summer in a painfully small studio at 327 West 28th Street in New York City, having been forced to give up his Carnegie Hall studio lease. He also expanded. As he had done the previous summer, before Denishawn set out on tour, Shawn spent a few weeks at Mariarden, an outdoor stage and summer theater school founded by Mrs. Marie Glass Buress Currier, a former actress and wife of wealthy Boston businessman Guy Currier. Mrs. Currier purchased a 150-acre farm in Peterborough, New Hampshire, at auction to serve as her summer playground for the arts, complete with a school for drama and what was possibly the first outdoor theater in the United States. Currier met Shawn through Denishawn costume designer Grace Ripley and promptly invited him to serve as "Director of Dancing" for the summer dance course and even went as far as to advertise Mariarden as "the Eastern Denishawn."[34]

That summer, while Shawn was still abroad, St. Denis started teaching and working on her dance *Cupid and Psyche* (1923). Upon his return they both alternated teaching duties at Mariarden and New York Denishawn. Inspired by his time in Italy worshipping the Renaissance sculptures of male nudes, that summer at Mariarden Shawn created one of his most famous solos, *Death of Adonis*. Shawn conceived of the dance as a "living statue" routine set to Benjamin Godard's "Adagio Pathetique." Shawn performed the dance nearly naked save for a fig leaf, with his body covered in white makeup meant to give the illusion that he was made of marble. While standing on a plinth, Shawn moved through a sequence of poses evoking the god of beauty as he is awakened, hunted, and ultimately killed by a wild boar.

When Shawn announced his intent to premiere the dance at Mariarden, Mr. Currier asked that he reconsider to avoid protests from locals who thought the dance was immoral, chief among them, the Mariarden cook. Shawn accepted a compromise to present the dance to an invited audience of Peterborough's most cultured and liberal. Shawn encountered resistance to performing *Death of Adonis* elsewhere, though never complied with requests to remove the solo from his program and sometimes even threatened to cancel a show instead. Shawn found a way to make the protests work to his advantage, promptly writing an article about the virtue of nudity in art for *Theater Magazine*. Accompanied by a series of suggestive photographs of Shawn as Adonis, the article ran with the misleading title "Is Nudity Salacious?" that Shawn swore he did not author. In the article he mentions an interview he gave in 1917 wherein he predicted that within ten years he would be able to perform nude on the stage. Echoing the popular logic of physical culture, he repeated the troubling equation of one's personality with physicality: "that beautiful qualities of person and character tend to manifest themselves in beauty of body." It was as if Shawn believed that the display of his physical perfection in *Death of Adonis* could offer moral redemption for his homosexuality and childlessness: "To see the body of one who is healthy, strong, symmetrical and of noble proportion is to experience a sense of divine revelation, and one is moved to something akin to exaltation."[35]

Death of Adonis turned out to be one of the most popular dances on the second Mayer tour (1923–24), which opened at Nixon's Apollo in Atlantic City in mid-October. Another widely admired production was Shawn's *Feather of the Dawn* (1923), a thirty-minute dance-drama about a "a day in the life" of a Hopi Village driven by the drama of a marriage proposal between an Indian youth (performed by Shawn) and the chief's daughter (performed by Louise Brooks). The plot sets into motion dances of corn maidens, hunters, and basket weavers, as well as the famous ceremonial dance of the *katchina* or Hopi spirits. Set to an original commissioned score by Charles Wakefield

Cadman, the dances were performed on different levels of the set's two-story adobe dwelling.[36] To complement the elaborate set, designer Earle Franke created costumes of masks, mantas, and moccasins all based on images at the Smithsonian Institution and procured authentic stage props, including strings of red peppers, rattles, turquoise jewelry, and baskets. (See Figure 3.4.)

Shawn's praise for the way Franke achieved authenticity with the production's visual design is interesting given that Shawn uncharacteristically

Figure 3.4. Ted Shawn and Louise Brooks in *Feather of the Dawn* (1923). Photography by White Studio. Courtesy of the Jerome Robbins Dance Division, New York Public Library.

emphasized that his choreography was not a "literal reproduction" of the ceremonial dances but an "adaptation" based on his experience seeing them
himself at Hopi pueblos in Arizona and New Mexico.[37] He even went as far
as to offer a disclaimer about his own featured turn in the "Eagle Dance,"
which many critics enthusiastically hailed as the masculine equivalent to
Pavlova's *Dying Swan*. About his own portrayal, Shawn wrote in more meas-
ured tones: "There is no living white man today (and that includes all of the
greatest of the Russian Ballet, as well as American dancers, including myself)
who, after spending a year studying this dance, would be able to reproduce
it."[38] He emphasized that his role as an artist was to interpret, unlike that of
"the scholar and museum field worker" whose task was to reproduce. Shawn's
heightened awareness around issues of authenticity concerning his choreographic approach to *Feather* indicates that Shawn was aware that since 1913,
the Walpi pueblo had infamously banned tourists from photographing the
ceremonial dances to maintain the sacred aspect of the rituals.[39] His meas-
ured claim that his effort was an "adaptation" was meant to circumvent a possible backlash for his clear violation of the spirit of the prohibition (although
the ban was on photographing and not necessarily reenacting the dances)
while also trying to capture the intense fascination with Hopi dances that had
made them such a tourist attraction to begin with.

Once again, the company had terrific box office draw, selling out
performances sometimes a month in advance. However much theater producers wanted to add dates, there was never room in the schedule to accommodate this, nor was the production nimble. The ambition of (and perhaps
competition between) St. Denis and Shawn backfired as the tour was weighed
down by the scale of the sets. Stage handlers had to take down the entire Hopi
Village for Shawn's *Feather of the Dawn* and erect a Babylonian temple for
St Denis's *Ishtar*. The wait between dances infuriated audiences. Despite the
huge box office success, Shawn ended the tour $30,000 in debt (and double
that by the time they went back on stage for the 1924–25 tour) because of
high production costs.

In the summer of 1924, Shawn and St. Denis returned to Mariarden to
perform, but "Eastern Denishawn" was no longer. Instead, Currier invited
Martha Graham, fresh off her first year with the Greenwich Village Follies,
to teach in place of Shawn. In turn, Shawn confronted Graham on the questionable ethical and professional grounds on which she had accepted the
teaching position, pointing out that he had never charged her for her instruction and that she would be teaching proprietary Denishawn material.

Graham rebuffed: "Then I will make up material of my own." She did. And thus Shawn gave himself partial credit for instigating Graham's revolutionary movement invention.

In fall 1924, Denishawn embarked on its third Daniel Mayer tour with what Shawn called an "economy production" because they scaled back considerably from the large dance-dramas of the previous two years.[40] They went on the road with a more modestly sized company of twenty-five dancers and a more streamlined set. Shawn premiered *Vision of Aissaoua: An Algerian Dance Drama*, based on the dances he encountered during his trip to Africa. When Shawn was in Biskra, dancing among the Aissaoua was prohibited by French colonial authorities. Shawn made good use of this fact when promoting the dance, garnering headlines about his performance of an outlawed dance. When Burton Holmes saw the dance at the Brooklyn Academy of Music, he slipped $5 into Shawn's hand backstage in the dressing room, making good on a bet that Shawn would never be able to translate the dances they had seen together into a theatrical work.

Since their school suffered financially whenever they were on the road, Shawn and St. Denis decided to close the school for the 1924–25 touring season. Though a wise business decision, the school reminded Shawn and St. Denis about the artistic ambition of the Denishawn enterprise. Without the school, the endless routine of traveling, performing, and courting the press wore thin, especially the third time out on the road for Mayer. Audiences noticed an apathy in St. Denis's performance or what Shawn called a "hangdog manner" on stage. The company could not profitably move forward in such condition.

In January 1925, Shawn received an exceptional offer for Denishawn that would spare them from the grind of touring. Months earlier, Mayer had introduced Shawn to Asway Strok, a Russian impresario who had launched several successful tours of musicians and opera singers throughout Asia. Strok presented Shawn with a contract for Denishawn to tour the Far East for six months. Shawn immediately recognized the significance of the invitation: theirs would be the first-ever tour of the "Orient" by an American modern dance company, a distinction he wanted to claim, especially on the heels of Anna Pavlova's successful Asian tour in 1922–23. They accepted the offer, which meant severing ties with Mayer, except for the percentage they would owe him from ticket sales on the upcoming overseas tour.

In the final week of the tour, Horst went into Shawn's room at the Allentown Hotel to explain that he would be leaving Denishawn to study composition.

Shawn offered Horst whatever he wanted to reverse his decision but to no avail. "And that was the beginning of the end of Denishawn," St. Denis wrote in her diary.

By 1925, Ted Shawn's rapidly expanding dance empire had never been more lucrative or diverse. One of his former university fraternity brothers took note of his success and hailed him as "Ted Shawn—A Dance King."[41] At the center of Shawn's entrepreneurial pursuits were the two main branches of the Denishawn School of Dancing and Its Related Arts. The Los Angeles branch was under the direction of Hazel Kranz, though St. Denis would occasionally appear to endow the students with her presence and inspiration. The school had only recently skirted charges for operating without a license. An easily remedied administrative offense, the charge was resolved with a one-page application, though the press managed to criminalize Shawn and St. Denis for the transgression in the dailies. Following that embarrassing incident, Shawn put the reins of the school in the hands of his stepmother Mabel Shawn.

In addition to the Denishawn "headquarters" in Los Angeles and New York, Shawn established a network of affiliate schools across the country that were led by former students or current Denishawn dancers. The artistic and fiduciary relationship between these "branches" varied from school to school and over time. Some operated as franchises with structured agreements whereas others functioned as associations that mutually benefited the local schools and Denishawn, either by serving as a feeder school to one of the main branches or by hosting master classes with Shawn and St. Denis when they came through town on tour. The most successful was Berthe and Francesca Braggiotti's Boston branch, which opened in 1924.[42] Shawn and St. Denis had at least two separate yearly agreements in 1922 and 1923 (possibly more) with Alice Mills to run a branch in Wichita, Kansas. The contracts stipulated that Mills should consider herself an employee of Denishawn, taking all artistic and administrative cues from headquarters and teaching only Denishawn exercises and dances. The rates for classes and private lessons were fixed with 25 percent of net profits going to Denishawn. The first agreement also had Mills paying Denishawn 25 percent of any ticket sales from her personal performances, apparently in exchange for "the exclusive right, license and privilege" to conduct a school and use the Denishawn name in advertising it and her performances. The agreement also made a provision for incentivizing the franchiser with tuition remission from normal courses at the main Denishawn schools if the net profits exceeded $500 per year.[43]

Florence Colebrook Powers, a former ballroom dancer who studied with Vernon Castle, led a branch in Rochester, assisted by Miss Olive Mayer, a star pupil from the Boston branch and a graduate of the Denishawn teachers' course. There was also a San Francisco branch led by Betty Horst, which was little more than a summer camp at the new Golden Bough Theater in Carmel-by-the-Sea. In 1930, Lester Shafer and Marian Chace, a married couple who had danced with Denishawn on the Ziegfeld tour, opened an "authentic" and "authorized" branch of the Denishawn School of Dancing in Chevy Chase, Maryland.[44] Other Denishawn affiliate directors included Enza Hanlon in Minneapolis, Estelle Dennis and Carol Lynn in Baltimore, Ernestine Day in Kansas, Edith James in Dallas, and Lillian Granzow in Detroit.[45]

Denishawn also generated revenue from partnerships with nonaffiliate dance schools through a variety of mail-order services. Shawn licensed his dances to private schools, provided that the teacher first study with him at one of the main schools or during special intensive workshops geared for teachers, which were usually held during the summer. Shawn partnered with Ampico Records to produce phonographs and piano rolls to accompany the dance classes and performances. He also had a provisional yet unfulfilled deal with Eastman Kodak to create a library of 16mm teaching films that would allow him to teach dancing remotely in local schools.

To complement the sale of choreographic notes, phonographs, and piano rolls for Denishawn dances, Shawn created and sold posters with photographs of him in poses from a given dance, sequenced to serve as a visual aide-mémoire to the students and teachers who purchased them. (See Figure 3.5.)

To solidify and market this array of services, Shawn had the idea of publishing Denishawn Magazine. A "house organ" for the Denishawn empire, the quarterly magazine was geared toward the brand's growing population of students, teachers, and audiences, especially former students and teachers— and devoted to the art of dance. Before the first issue even hit the press, the magazine had 800 subscribers and went on to sell over 20,000 single copies in theater lobbies during the upcoming tour. The launch issue was bundled with the company's recent souvenir program, which Shawn began to print with the 1923–24 tour.

The front and back covers of the magazine prominently featured the Denishawn logo, created by artist Rose O'Neill. (See Insert Figure 3.6.). The Orientalist yin-yang design at the center of the cover was meant to capture the harmony or balance between action and reaction, the basic elements of the

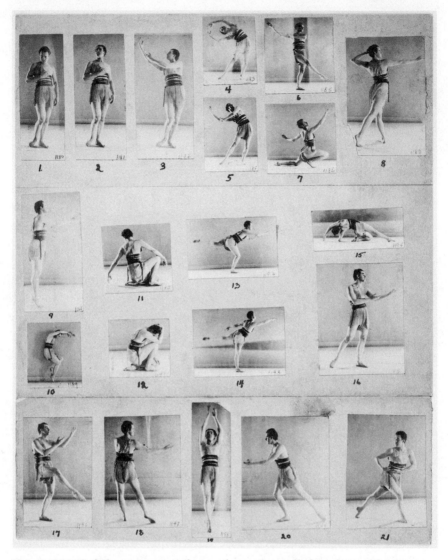

Figure 3.5. Ted Shawn in poses from a dance class called *Sculpture Plastique* (1916). Denishawn Collection. Courtesy of the Jerome Robbins Dance Division, New York Public Library.

divine mind—a fairly explicit reference to Christian Science. The embryonic design, invoking the figures of a naked man and woman (perhaps Shawn and St. Denis themselves) in fetal position, also emphasizes the eugenic balance and perfection (and related sexual imperative) at the core of the Denishawn brand. Indeed, the logo was the figural representation of the Denishawn credo that the company represented "the embryo" of a real American ballet.[46]

As he was developing a publishing arm of the Denishawn empire, Shawn took cues from Elbert Hubbard's mail-order empire. In 1899, Hubbard published his popular essay "A Message to Garcia" in the *Philistine*, which went on to sell 40 million copies, eclipsing sales figures of all other publications that year, save the Bible and the dictionary. He also made profitable appearances on the vaudeville circuit lecturing on topics ranging from business to social reform.[47] Though Hubbard wanted to ensure that Roycroft's handmade books, furniture, and leather goods were accessible to all, they were very expensive to produce and thus affordable only to the wealthy. Allene Seaman, Shawn's childhood friend who first introduced him to Hubbard, arranged for *Denishawn Magazine* to be published by Roycroft, which explains its similarity in design and appearance with the famous *The Roycrofters* publication.

In addition to its production values and visual branding, Roycroft offered Shawn a model for an artistic community. Hubbard's progressive ideas about the role of the artist in American society inspired Shawn to conceive of a union of professional independent dancers that could collectively bargain with exploitative booking agents and theater owners. Two tours with Mayer, professional as they were, brought into relief the inequity between the for-hire dancers and the union musicians and stagehands who enjoyed better salaries, working conditions, transportation, and lodging. In fact, the musicians generally earned more than any of the dancers, including Shawn and St. Denis. One of the greatest hardships for Shawn and St. Denis was enduring their second-class status in the theatrical world. Stagehands at local theaters were often abusive to them, even more so than audiences, critics, and bookers. In fact, Shawn exhausted a great deal of his time and energy building and managing relationships with stagehands, knowing they were most directly responsible for the quality of his performances. He spent a vast amount of uncompensated labor trying to avoid technical mishaps of both the accidental and intentional variety: ruined cues, misplaced props, loud talking, or construction behind the scenes during a performance .

To address these conditions, Shawn took a cue from professional actors, who in 1923 organized Actors' Equity and achieved a union contract (although only 80 percent of the performers in any given production were required to be members). In the inaugural issue of *Denishawn Magazine*, Shawn introduced his idea for the Denishawn Guild of American Dancers and Their Related Artists, with the purpose of organizing American dance artists into a collective "with a unity of ideals and purposes, [ready to] meet the world with a solid front in order that the art of the dance may receive its rightful response."

Though the dancers' union was never realized in this form, Shawn and St. Denis continued to follow Hubbard's lead by pursuing the creation of their own artist colony where all Denishawn activities could prosper. They called this business plan "A Greater Denishawn." The plan was to concentrate their artistic and entrepreneurial pursuits in New York City, thus relinquishing the Denishawn school in Los Angeles. It was a plan they would pursue in earnest upon their return from the Orient, which at the time they expected to be about six months away.

With the intense swirl of activity involved in completing the last Mayer tour and preparing the programs for the Far East tour (with a new musical director at that!) Shawn had nearly neglected his contractual obligation with Henry Holt & Co. to write a book on dance. He had not even begun to write when he stepped aboard a Pullman car in New York on a cross-country trip to Seattle where he was to meet the company for his trans-Pacific crossing to Japan. By the time he arrived in Seattle, he had dictated five chapters of a treatise for American dance, to lay the ideological groundwork upon which he would justify his vision for a "A Greater Denishawn." By the time he reached Seattle, he had finished the first five chapters. The rest he completed aboard the ship to Japan.

The American Ballet is Shawn's treatise on American theatrical and social dancing and a call to reform attitudes towards American dancers. In the foreword, he introduces his vision for American dance as if it were a birth announcement for a eugenic baby. He proclaims that "the long period of pregnancy is nearly at an end—the new birth is imminent." This "American" dance would be conceived by "spiritual seed" and nurtured in the "cradle" of America for it to develop from a "strange and red-faced" newborn "without teeth [or] hair" into a "healthy baby." However, within the book's opening pages, it becomes clear that Shawn did not necessarily want to give birth to a new dance, technique, or style so much as he wanted to revive the dances of his Anglo-Saxon forebears—the Virginia Reel, the March and Circle, and the Boston Fancy. To justify his vision, Shawn selectively and sometimes erroneously draws upon Havelock Ellis's key passage about the "unconscious eugenics" at play in the dance of sexual selection, the idea that dancing holds a crucial biological function in sexual selection and thus "the higher development of the race." Interestingly, and perhaps even unconsciously, Shawn mistakenly attributes this passage to the ancient Greek philosopher Lucian (c. 120), and not to Ellis.[48]

Ellis would have likely appreciated the oversight. Ellis reluctantly wrote the introduction to *The American Ballet*, a quid pro quo for Shawn's having published an article titled "The Dancer's Bible," a paean to "St. Havelock" in *Denishawn Magazine*. Decades later, Shawn revealed that he was commissioned to write the article by the Houghton-Mifflin Publishing Company in advance of the distribution of Ellis's book in the United States. In exchange, Ellis agreed to write the introduction to Shawn's book, though he by no means reciprocated Shawn's adulation. Overall, Ellis condescendingly refers to Shawn's writing as a form of "eloquent pleading" and distances himself from Shawn's book in several other ways. Ellis renounces his own newfound status as the "prophet" of dance, as he had neither "practical connection with the ballet nor any scientific knowledge of dancing." He then dissociates himself from Shawn's central claims, which Ellis explicitly acknowledges "may be discounted." In some measure, his ambivalent introduction undermines Shawn's use of eugenics to clarify his vision for an American dance. Ellis was clearly uncomfortable with Shawn's liberal application of his scientific ideas about eugenics to dance.[49]

Shawn envisions the future of American dance as a "democratic" art that would "encompass all forms." However, throughout the book, he interpellates his presumed Anglo-Saxon reader through a series of expressions that invoke a shared racial past. He refers to "a new social dance of *our own*," a return to the "American country dances of the time of *our grandmothers*," and to the threatened "tradition of *our Anglo-Saxon forefathers*."[50] Elsewhere, he describes this new dance as a spiritual bequest to "America's Elect." The power of this dance, he promises, will restore the nation to a state "that was conceived by men who wrote the Constitution," many of them slaveholders.[51]

To his readers, Shawn poses the rhetorical question: "What is the fine thing, what is the deep and abiding and permanent thing which we have to express through the medium of dance?" He ultimately determines that "this fine thing" is Anglo-Saxon folk dances and European court dances, though he also recognizes some "fine" qualities in the dances of "local color," such as those of the "two alien races of the red man and the black man." Based on his conviction that Native Americans are "the most sensitive and advanced souls of the entire white race" albeit "deteriorated," he insists that their dances are "worthy of our study" as they reflect the "high order" and "ethical nobility" of the race. Shawn claims that "Negro" dances could be another source of "great profit" for the "art dance of America," though not without certain caveats, which he bases on a series of convoluted pseudoscientific claims about the negro's physical, emotional, and spiritual development. For instance, Shawn envisioned that there could one day be a "negro ballet," provided that "native" dances went through a process wherein they would become "refined." Moreover, he concedes that the "inexhaustible inventiveness" of some jazz dances, such as tap dancing, the Charleston, and the "shimmy" were distinctive and impressive.

Shawn's views on jazz were contradictory. Though he acknowledges the artistic value of jazz, he characterizes jazz as a type of "poison and putrefaction" and decries white America's obsession with it as a "public astigmatism." In fact, the topic of jazz brings Shawn's anxiety about racial dysgenia into full relief. He writes: "When one sees a white person do these [jazz] dances, it is disgusting, because the negro mental and emotional conditions cannot be translated into the white man." Here he echoes the racist diatribe against jazz in modern dance pioneer Isadora Duncan's 1927 autobiography. Both Duncan and Shawn claimed to have been moved by the democratic poems of Walt Whitman, yet they similarly dismissed jazz dance and music as expressions of the "primitive savage."[52] Shawn intensifies Duncan's dismissal on evolutionary grounds. He calls jazz an "absolute retrogression" and, quoting Daniel Gregory Mason, the "doggerel of music." In lectures at civic organizations and high schools, Shawn espoused the same racist diatribe: "Persons fond of jazz are in an infantile state of mind, either temporarily or permanently."[53]

Taking this notion to its eugenic conclusion, Shawn proposes that American dance be cleansed of jazz's infectious presence: "Jazz is the scum of the great boiling that is now going on, and the scum will be cleared off and the clear fluid underneath will be revealed." By "great boiling," Shawn obviously refers to—and reverses—the process of ethnic integration made famous by Israel Zangwill's *The Melting Pot* (1908)—"the biggest Broadway hit—ever."[54] Indeed, Shawn suggests a type of choreographic segregation; jazz could be a "fine thing" as long as it is performed by "Negros" and not by whites. Drawing upon a common rhetorical device from eugenic discourse, Shawn appeals to his readers' racial panic and threatens them with a metaphorical racial annihilation:

> Do we want to accept the dictum of the hectic Broadwayite, the denizen of the cabaret, the habitué of the slums, the negro from the dives of southern

cities, and the inhabitants off the Barbary Coast of San Francisco as our last word in the way of social dancing? Do you think that the low interpretation of these people is capable of making a dance form which will express you? Do you think that the mental and moral conditions of those people will produce a type of social dancing which will be an expression of your personality? I think you will all agree in the negative. Then what are we going to do about it? Apparently if we go to a place where there is dancing, we have only one alternative—to stand still or to dance what everyone else is dancing.[55]

Shawn's ultimatum is backed by two equally disturbing threats—to "stand still" or to "dance what everyone else is dancing"—both of which lead to the paralysis, annihilation, or disappearance of the white race. This threat is posed not only from the jazzy Negroes of the South but also from those on the "Barbary Coast," the poor ("the habitué of the slums"), and the "hectic Broadwayite," an oblique reference to Jews. Elsewhere, Shawn references the threat of "the moron." This was not a generic aspersion but a specific reference within eugenic discourse to the "feeble-minded" and "mentally retarded" as anomalies to the eugenic ideal.

In the last chapter of *The American Ballet*, Shawn describes his "dream" for a dance school that would be a breeding ground for eugenic dancers. He envisioned a campus of sixty to a hundred children "chosen in regard to parentage which would indicate artistic leanings, physical health and beauty, character and intelligence." However, the curriculum would cover the "universality of the dance," including dance forms of Spain, Japan, and East India. Students would be exposed to "the great foreign dancers of the world"; yet his own "American" dance company would include only "American born and American trained dancers, dancing to music by American composers, with scenery and costumes designed by American artists, and under the direction and management of American business men of great vision."[56]

Shawn's central premise in *The American Ballet* is unmistakably similar to that of an article written by Ballets Russes star Adolph Bolm titled "The Future of the Dance in America" that was published two years earlier in the arts journal *Shadowland*.[57] Read in a certain light, Bolm's article is a blueprint for Shawn's *The American Ballet* inasmuch as it covers identical topics, albeit from opposing perspectives. Both men deal with the future of American dance, best methods for dance training, the impact of ballroom and national dances in relation to concert dance, and the threat of jazz, all in pseudoscientific tones of eugenics. Written from the point of view of an outsider who had worked in the United States for the better part of a decade, the Russian-born Bolm advocates a return to "the original expression of the dance instinct in the people. Let us take up again the mazurka, the polka, the waltz, and other forms derived from these." Like Shawn, Bolm considered ballroom dances "positively immoral," though not necessarily on aesthetic grounds, but for how they represent "a corruption, a degeneration of the self-expression of the extraordinary and tragic race—the Negro." For Bolm, black dance represented a great hope for the future of American dance, not only for its significance to social dance forms but also for its influence on modernism, an impression he developed from his experience watching black dancers at revival meetings. He writes: "I have seen their genuine native dances, and was sincerely surprised, touched and inspired by the passionate spontaneity, the pathetic tragedy, the humility, the ecstasy, the abandon, the imagination, and even the genius they reveal in both dance and song. Their contribution to this branch of modern art is, in its day, just as remarkable as anything the white race has done." Bolm's condescending compassion notwithstanding, he identifies black dance as the greatest hope for—rather than threat to—American dance. For Bolm, the true threat to a vital national dance was the "average American home," which he notes "is by no means an art center." He especially laments the lack of musical literacy among American youth and thus advocates the formation of neighborhood clubs to offer instruction to "re-learn these old and delightful forms" sensitive to the fact that dance instruction is expensive and thus limited to those with economic means and social access. Inasmuch as Bolm made a significant portion of his income as a ballet teacher, his suggestion to create public dance schools was a benevolent gesture, more so than Shawn's solution to teach American ballet through an elitist national school. This is to say, Shawn's vision for an American dance school appropriates and commercializes Bolm's idea for a dance school in pursuit of developing a national art. At least this is true on paper. In practice, over his career Shawn taught a wider variety of dances to a more diverse range of students than Bolm ever did.

It is fair to say that some of the most virulent strains of racist and eugenic logic that ran through Shawn's vision for American dance remained on the page and never made it to the stage or even the classroom. Despite the influence of eugenics on Shawn's writings, he did not create "eugenic art," certainly not compared with the standards established in the visual arts, literature, and drama. That said, Shawn at least once conceived of a spectacle of human degeneracy and a cautionary tale of American dysgenia. This much we know from a typewritten outline and first scenario for a three-act dance unsurprisingly titled "An American Ballet."[58] Although the dance was never produced, the scenario reveals the extent to which Shawn imagined adapting eugenic thought from the page to the stage. As outlined, the dance is loosely based on Whitman's *Leaves of Grass* and dramatizes the central idea of Shawn's *The American Ballet* book—namely, that dance is an ideal means toward producing a "more perfect race."[59] It makes that case by dramatizing the history of America from its primordial beginnings to what Shawn perceived as its modern state of racial and ethnic dysgenia, a condition created by the combined forces of immigration, industrialization, commercialism, and jazz. In all likelihood, Shawn conceived of the dance while writing *The American Ballet*, though possibly earlier. He must have written the scenario after 1924, since he annotated it with the Doubleday edition of *Leaves of Grass* published that year.

As written, the first act begins with St. Denis as the "Spirit of the Sea," whose movements represent the expansiveness of the earth, the glory of the mountains, and the beauty of the landscape.[60] Shawn, as "Man," discovers the "Spirit of the Sea" and plants himself into the earth. In a scene that recalls both Ellis's "dance of life" and the Garden of Eden, the "Sea" and "Man" experience a "sexual awakening," which leads to the "peopling of a new Continent."

The second act, the "Dance History of America," comprises a sequence of nine sections of dances by "American types": Native Americans, pioneers, colonial laborers (blacksmiths, harvesters, woodsmen), lumberjacks, cowboys, and Negroes. This section also features a dance called "The Love of Comrades," a variation on a line from the "Calamus" poems of Whitman's *Leaves of Grass* : "the manly love of comrades."[61] Though Shawn redacted the reference to homosexuality, in his scenario for a "pageant" of "American types" he stipulated that the dance should be performed by men—"virile and wholesome—but with a romantic theme."

Having established the formation and population of America, in the third act, Shawn dramatizes the threats to its destruction by choreographing the "melting pot," the metaphorical symbol of American ethnic integration. In Shawn's care, the "melting pot" is more of a meltdown. Not surprisingly, he sets this meltdown in New York City, which he had repeatedly described as a type of modern-day cesspool: "New York . . . is a city of the world and not a city of America. . . . It has a huge foreign population which intends to remain foreign; therefore, if we are to understand what the message of America is, we cannot expect to find anything but a small portion of it in New York."[62] Shawn's vision of New York could not have less in common with Whitman's, especially given the latter's valorization of the city's ethnic and class diversity, succinctly expressed by the following lines in *Leaves of Grass*:

> Superb-faced Manhattan!
> Comrade Americanos!—to us, then, at last, the Orient comes.
> To us, my city.[63]

In a revealing gesture, Shawn casts St. Denis as "New York," the symbol of impurity, promiscuity, and danger. At first, she sits enthroned, a symbol of wealth and power, but soon begins to stir the pot of immigrants who pour into her city. These "immigrants from all [over] the World" perform "episodic dances of Europe: Spain, Italy, Hungary, Russia; Africa: Savage and Negro; Asia: East Indian, Japanese, Chinese, etc." Shawn's melting pot is a chaotic, dangerous "maelstrom," wherein "crowds of immigrants are all sucked into a whirlpool of American City People" yet "emerge just long enough to establish identity and then are sucked back." The intensity of the melting pot transforms them into an unidentifiable mob of impurity. They emerge as dehumanized levers, wheels, and cogs of a machine that manufactures "cheap masked figures" or the "Spirit of Jazz." In Shawn's view, both technology and jazz represented modernity's dehumanizing effects on man.

To restore their lost humanity, Shawn appears as the "Artist Soul of America"—a messianic figure who heals the world of its dysgenia through art. Shawn's outline emphasizes that the "Artist Soul" character represents the "art consciousness of America" who has come to protect American purity from the threats of "commerce, jazz, sensuality, and greed." To guide the nation, the "Artist Soul" takes to the city streets wielding a torch, which Shawn says, is like a "flame in Liberty's Torch" with the power to "heal the Mob and surmount them." However, in the "Notes to the Composer" that he includes in the scenario, Shawn explains this same scene in slightly different terms, emphasizing the "beauty" and perfection of the "Artist Soul" who triumphs over the dysgenic mass:

> Then comes the artist soul of America who sees the tops of the great buildings like some golden dream city—signifying the beauty that may and shall emerge from America's beginnings. He starts for his goal but is met by the forces of the commercial business world, by cheap jazzy pleasure

seekers, by sensual desires, by other obstacles. Hurled back he searches within and finds his inner light, which turning on the crowd reveals to each of them his perfect self and they acclaim him—Messiah. He mounts until he stands on the torch of Liberty, and radiating light, the Artist Soul becomes itself the flame of Liberty's Torch.[64]

In this final moment of "An American Ballet," Shawn stages an Armageddon, using his own body as a weapon against the threats of annihilation posed by the degenerate masses. Abiding by the admonition that he levels at his readers in *The American Ballet*, Shawn offers his body as an exemplar of racial, ethnic, and moral perfection: "We must in all our activities be a torch to the world, and in the dance most of all."[65] He describes this form of physical display as a "battle," invoking the proto-eugenic language of Darwin's "battle of the fittest," and paradoxically, as a type of eugenic beauty pageant. Shawn's victory is won through physical display rather than physical conquest. Indeed, his victory is inherited rather than earned. This much is conveyed by the "Artist Soul's" "torch," the unmistakable symbol of human heredity. Upon "searching within," the prophet figure learns that he is the bearer of "radiant light," a curious healing substance that links him to "America's beginning," not unlike the mysterious germ plasm in the science of eugenics, the hidden store of genetic material that is carried forward from one generation to the next as if in a eugenic relay race. Of course, Shawn's "torch" also evokes the Statue of Liberty's welcoming beacon, although in his hands, the "flame of Liberty's Torch" is used to repel rather than attract foreign bodies and to spotlight his own physical perfection. After all, throughout *The American Ballet*, he laments the attention that jazz takes from the Denishawn brand of theatrical dancing. Here his battle with the "dark charms" of greed, sensuality, and jazz are not necessarily with the forces themselves but with the attention they draw away from his practice of an emerging "art" dance.

The final "battle" scene in "An American Ballet" resolves when the "Artist Soul" "heals" the forces of evil embodied by immigrants, pleasure-seekers, and jazz freaks. Essentially, Shawn's torch-wielding dance enacts a purification rite—a metaphorical ethnic cleansing. In turn, the masses recognize him as the "Messiah." In the final scene, Shawn's eugenic fervor converges with his deep belief in dance's healing power, a belief based on his experience recovering from diphtheria during his adolescence. Shawn's fundamental belief in the sacred healing power of dance, combined with his adoption of eugenic ideas about ethnicity and sex, informs the final moment in the dance, wherein his beautiful, white, Christian body overcomes the forces of unfitness in an attempt to restore purity to the national body.

However, it is important to note that Shawn's spectacular racial triumph transpires only in relation to a silent sexual victory. Twice when describing his "battle" with the forces of "Commerce, Jazz, Sensuality, and Greed," Shawn cryptically alludes to "other obstacles" (in the notes) or "etc." (in the outline). Presumably, sexual puritanism counts among these un-named forces at contest for America's soul. In *The American Ballet*, Shawn expresses his disapproval of the American obsession with partner dancing between men and women, which he goes so far as to say is "degenerate" and an obstacle to the creation of art. He writes: "The wooing and courtship theme in life has its place, and a very important place, but it should not absorb all of our life. We would not get any business done, and we would not produce any works of art."[66] His criticism partially explains how "An American Ballet" clears the stage of heterosexual courtship in order for new sexual desires to emerge. Within the dance's narrative of human evolu-tion there is a distinctive development of sexual relations: the dance begins with the mating of "Man" and the "Spirit of the Sea," progresses toward a dance among "comrades," and concludes with the solo performance of a demigod-like figure who transcends sexuality. Indeed, the dance charts a sexual evolution that reflects Shawn's own narrative of sexual discovery—his eugenic pairing with St. Denis, his relationships with "comrades" such as Havelock Ellis and poet Edward Carpenter, and later, his vow of purity. Thus, Shawn stages himself as the "flame in Liberty's Torch" not necessarily to shadow his glaring sexual "unfitness" (his childlessness, his adulterous marriage, his homosexuality) but perhaps to spotlight how through his identification as an artist—and as the "Father of American Dance"—he believed he had transcended it.

The irony of Shawn's isolationist fantasy for the future of American dance was that his own immediate future involved a tour of Asia that would last over a year during which time he would immerse himself in the very for-eign dance cultures he identified as a threat to American exceptionalism. His experience performing for audiences abroad and studying with masters of stage, court, and temple traditions throughout Asia only intensified his in-terest in staging "authentic" adaptations of foreign dances, much the way he had with dances he learned on his trip to Spain and North Africa just two years prior.

America's Unofficial Ambassadors,
August 1925–November 1926

On August 7, 1925, Ted Shawn, Ruth St. Denis, and the Denishawn company boarded the SS *President Jefferson* to travel from Seattle to Yokohama, Japan, where they began what was scheduled to be a twenty-four-week tour of the Far East, the first ever by an American dance company. (See Figure 3.7.). In the early mornings, Shawn found time to finish *The American Ballet*, the book manuscript he had hurriedly drafted on the train from New York to Seattle. In their autobiographies, Jane Sherman and Doris Humphrey, then young Denishawn dancers, recall playing and dancing while aboard the ship.

Figure 3.7. Ted Shawn and Ruth St. Denis (*front*) with Denishawn Company on the SS *President Jefferson*, August 7, 1925. *Left to right*: Clifford Vaughan (pianist), Pauline Lawrence, George Steares, Ernestine Day, June Rhodes, Grace Borroughs, Edith James, Brother St. Denis, Geordie Graham, Doris Humphrey, Mary Howry, Jane Sherman, Ara Martin, and Anne Douglas. Ruth St. Denis and Ted Shawn in foreground. Courtesy of the Jerome Robbins Dance Division, New York Public Library.

St. Denis remembers lounging on the ship's deck while "Papa" Shawn recited verses of Walt Whitman to the Denishawn company and crew.

In the unedited manuscript of his autobiography, Shawn wrote extensively about the Denishawn Tour of the Far East—or what he referred to as "The Orient Tour." He includes descriptions of the major tourist attractions he visited, the performers and dance traditions he encountered, his fascination and frustration with travel, and some anecdotes connected to the dances he created for Denishawn while there. He also kept two journals that meticulously account for his dispersal of salaries, his personal and company expenses, and contact information of the many people he met abroad. Miraculously, he used down time on vertigo-inducing boat trips and eye-bouncing trains, plus late nights in poorly lit hotels to write more than a dozen articles about the dances he had seen and studied. He then sent these dispatches back to the United States, where they were published in *The Dance* magazine (later, *Dance Magazine*). Upon his return stateside, Shawn compiled these articles, along with additional chapters on his travels to Spain and Africa, into *Gods Who Dance* (1929), a book that reversed the isolationist ideas that Shawn had been developing in *The American Ballet* and "An American Ballet" in the weeks leading up to the Orient Tour. Neither *Gods Who Dance* nor his diaries reveal much about his inner world as he traversed foreign lands. The frantic pace of his travels kept him from his regular correspondence through which he otherwise chronicled his life. Moreover, his most favored correspondent, Ruth St. Denis, was at his side throughout the entire odyssey.

St. Denis, however, kept a personal journal throughout the tour. So, too, did her brother, Brother St. Dennis, who traveled with the company and manned a motion picture camera to record the company on location and, more important, to document dances for reference in future choreographic projects. Clifford Vaughan, the musician who replaced Louis Horst at the piano (though not his advisory role in Denishawn), kept programs, photos, and travel brochures.[67] One of the most remarkable accounts of this tour comes from Jane Sherman. At seventeen years old, Sherman was the youngest member of the company. She published an edited version of her journal and letters in *Soaring: The Diary and Letters of a Denishawn Dancer in the Far East* (1975). Doris Humphrey, too, shared her experiences in letters she sent home to her father.

The tour was a defining moment for all involved, Shawn especially. Foremost, it was an opportunity for him to establish himself as a leading artist on the global stage. Indeed, one of his chief supporters in Japan, the

influential writer Baron Ishimoto, introduced Japanese audiences and critics
to Shawn and the company as "America's Unofficial Ambassadors."

Shawn took seriously his unofficial role as a diplomat for American dance
when dealing with an impressive network of colonial officials, missionaries,
émigré socialites, scholars, royalty, and captains of industry that helped
Shawn to gain unprecedented access to dance performances and leading
dance figures. Shawn established these connections through friends as well
as through former students with influential families. Patriarchal views ran
deep in both the diplomatic and theatrical circles Shawn encountered, which
afforded him a level of respect and recognition as a businessperson, an entrepreneur, and a performer that he rarely felt in the United States and that
often placed him on equal footing with St. Denis, sometimes to her degrada-
tion. His theatricalizations of gender were somehow more familiar to Asian
audiences, especially in Japan and China, where female impersonation was
recognized as part of classical traditions. Shawn reveled in the recognition
and played the part of the accidental diplomat, appearing everywhere in his
custom-tailored white suits with jade buttons and green tie.

Shawn quickly learned that his encounters with "native" dancers would
be mediated by his hosts. He had disabused himself of the notion that he
could experience unadulterated or pure encounters with foreign dancers, but
that did not keep him from taking every possible opportunity to break away
from the company whenever possible to seek out the dance traditions he had
read about in preparation for the trip. He intended to use his extensive network to gain access to performances of many classical and folk dances so
that he could study and restage them for Denishawn's future tours. In this
regard, he took his cue from Anna Pavlova's successful tour of the Orient
in 1922–23, from which she developed "Oriental Impressions," a program
of divertissements based on the ballet star's meetings with leading dancers,
actors, painters, and musicians she visited throughout Asia. From them, she
acquired not only technical details but also the costumes, music, and musical
instruments to accompany her dances.[68] During the fifteen months Shawn
ultimately spent abroad, in addition to handling all company business, including nearly all the travel and lodging arrangements, as well as leisure activities for the company, he also managed to complete several articles and to
create and rehearse a number of new dances based on his study of traditional
arts throughout the continent. He accomplished this all while contending
with tropical heat, a new accompanist and an orchestra of Russian-speaking
musicians, and his ongoing personal conflicts with St. Denis and her brother.

The company's first stop was a two-month tour in Japan, an experience that shattered Shawn's preconceived notion of "the Orient" as a portal to the past. The company arrived in Yokohama to a flood of press photographers, then were whisked away via electric train to Tokyo where more fanfare and press awaited. Shawn was beside himself with the level of interest in their arrival. They opened their twenty-five-performance run at the Imperial Theater to a sold-out crowd. In Shawn's estimation, 95 percent of the audience was Japanese; the remainder were US and British foreigners and diplomats, several of whom Shawn would meet throughout his time in Tokyo, at tea ceremonies, formal interviews, backstage meet-and-greets, and lectures. Prince Kuniomio, second son of the emperor, also attended a performance. With a perception of "modern" dancing fueled by American musical films, Japanese audiences had not anticipated the reverence and spirituality of Denishawn's repertory, qualities that resonated with traditional dance-drama forms like *kabuki*. Indeed, the poster announcing the Denishawn company outside the Imperial Theater depicted Shawn and St. Denis in the *ukiyo-e* or "floating world" style of drawing, associated with Edo era kabuki and entertainment, literally and figuratively incorporating them into the visual language of the Japanese theater. (See Figure 3.8.) Several writers claimed that Japanese audiences favored Denishawn to Anna Pavlova, who in 1921 toured Japan with her modern ballet dances, which Japanese audiences found "alien" and lacking in spirituality.[69] Shawn closely monitored audiences from backstage, though he had difficulty gauging the intensity of audience response owing to the Japanese custom of applauding with cupped hands. To avoid negative reception to Denishawn, Shawn carefully programmed the concerts without potentially upsetting Orientalist content, including his *Spear Dance Japonesque* (1919), one of his most popular dances back home.

The day following their first performance (September 21), Shawn and St. Denis began morning lessons with Matsumoto Koshiro, Japan's greatest kabuki actor-dancer, and Madame Fujima, who led the Fujima School of Dance. They would continue with a lesson every morning for their month-long stay in Tokyo. Shawn filmed one of his lessons and a scaled-down performance, demonstrating his use of fans and swords. Shawn focused on learning sections of *Momiji-Gari* (Search for autumn leaves), a Meiji-era kabuki play that was running matinees at the Kabukiza Theatre, the traditional kabuki theater, which allowed Shawn to see the play before his own evening curtain time at the Imperial. The performance fascinated him and he attended the show several times to figure out how to adapt it for Denishawn.

Figure 3.8. Illustration of Ruth St. Denis and Ted Shawn on poster for Imperial Theater (Tokyo, Japan), 1925. ("Denishawn Ballet: Western Dance, Various types, [accompanied by] members of the western instrumental group.") Clifford Vaughan Papers, Huntington Library.

He also met with other leading kabuki stars, such as Onoe Baikŏ and Onoe Kikugorŏ VI, both masters of the *onangata* or female kabuki roles tradition-ally performed by men. The company also toured the music department of the Imperial household located on the palace grounds, where they saw ancient instruments and costumes connected to Bugaku, an ancient impe-rial dance-drama tradition, and viewed an ancient book with plates of the exquisite costumes. The wife of a music department official made a hand-painted copy of the book, which she presented to Shawn upon his return to Japan more than a year later. Shawn and St. Denis continued to receive the royal treatment, quite literally, when they had tea with Prince Tokugawa, the last of the Shogunate, during a break in the performance of the traditional noh performance.

Shawn was astonished by the depth of care the traditional arts received in Japan, from the theater staff to the royal family. A powerful sense of hu-mility washed over him when one evening Koshiro entertained Shawn in his dressing room before a performance at the Imperial Theater. Shawn was mesmerized by the beautifully appointed dressing room, which was nothing like the makeshift arrangements Denishawn tolerated. When time came for makeup, a private dresser entered and in hushed tones invited Koshiro to take his seat and then applied beautiful watercolors to his face from a lacquer box—nothing like the greasepaint from tubes of Max Factor that Denishawn slapped on.

For all of its rich history, Japan was a nation in cultural and physical transition. The damage from the 1923 Tokyo-Yokohama earthquake was in plain sight, with temporary wooden offices erected on foundations of demolished buildings standing beside modern office towers. Shawn ex-perienced the tension between the traditional and modern everywhere in Japan, perhaps most strongly when he made a pilgrimage to the Shinto shrines in Kamakura and Nikko. There he saw ancient dances, once performed by shrine maidens, while he was in the company of one of the most modern and progressive women in Japan, the Baroness Ishimoto (Shidzue Kat), a strong supporter of the eugenics movement and an advo-cate for birth control and reproductive rights. Three years earlier she had escorted Margaret Sanger, the women's activist who coined the term "birth control," through the same sites.[70]

After several weeks at the Imperial Theater in Tokyo, the company toured the provinces and spent ten days performing in the Takarazuka Opera House. Takarazuka was a popular tourist destination, home not only to a

mineral springs resort that drew audiences from Kobe and Osaka but also
to the beloved performance troupe of young women that mounted Western
musicals. The performance complex was composed of three theaters, owned
by the company that owned the railroad. Shawn was surprised to learn that
the new theater was more technically advanced than any in the United States.
Backstage was a "city in miniature."

In Kyoto, they attended the farewell performance of legendary geisha
master Haruko Katayama at the Theater of the Geisha. A "national treasure,"
Katayama had established the "Miyako Odori" or "Spring Dance Festival"
wherein she presented her hundred young geishas to audiences of locals
and tourists. To observe her eighty-eighth birthday, Katayama danced in
public for the last time. Before an audience of devoted fans, she performed
a twenty-minute solo, which she finished by kneeling with her back to the
audience and bending over backward until her head touched the floor between her feet. About Katayama's display, St. Denis wrote the following in her
journal: "She moves now with tremendous power. That this ancient geisha
is still flourishing after a life well spent in gaiety is a source of consternation
to the missionaries." St. Denis, then forty-seven years old, admired the way
the younger geishas fluttered about Katayama with "reverence for this aged
but remarkable dancer." Witnessing the women celebrate their sisterhood,
St. Denis arrived at the conclusion that "this theater was a feminist theater
long before we Western women took to cutting our hair." Although St. Denis
might have misinterpreted the significance of the Spring Festival (it started
as a tourist production in 1873) and the powerful display of Katayama (who
at eighty-eight, was indeed old, but not exactly "ancient"), she left the Temple
of the Geisha convinced that an aging American dancer such as herself could
lead a "feminist theater," and she spent the remainder of her life in pursuit
of establishing an arts center dedicated to feminist performance. As such,
the world's most famous "Oriental dancer" left her with the deep conviction
that Asian dance and spirituality celebrated the feminine more fully than the
West ever had.[71]

After visiting twelve cities in eight weeks in Japan—and just days after
Shawn's thirty-fourth birthday—Denishawn made a two-day crossing from
Japan to the Chinese port city of Dalian (or what Shawn knew as Dairen, the
"Paris of Asia"). There Shawn began to write his dispatches for *The Dance*
magazine. From Dalian, they were to travel via train to their first stop in
Tianjin, but rail travel proved dangerous as there was significant civil un-
rest related to the ongoing Chinese Revolution (1925–27). Denishawn's

tour of China came under the shadow of the death of the founding father of the modern republic Sun Yat-sen, who died in Beijing on March 12, 1925. Having heard reports of rail tracks blown away by protesters, the company traveled instead by boat to Tianjin. In fact, all subsequent travel plans between cities—Beijing, Shanghai, Hong Kong—were made with military precision based on the latest news so as to avoid any armed conflict.

Shawn thought Tianjin would be sufficiently remote to allow him to experience full immersion in Chinese culture. To his great disappointment, the local Rotary Club met him upon arrival with an invitation to a luncheon, which he reluctantly accepted. He also agreed to meet with the Women's Club, the American Board Mission, and a Theosophical Society. Through his encounters with the predominantly American and British members of these organizations, Shawn began to notice how colonials and expatriates throughout Asia recreated home abroad and tried to insulate themselves from the world that Shawn himself was so desperate to penetrate. They also discouraged him from venturing into the real China. He was isolated from locals in the theater as well. During Denishawn's nine days at the Empire Theater in Tianjin, audiences were predominantly American with some British, French, and Russians, the inverse of the audience composition in Japan. The young Denishawn dancers did not mind the brief reminder of Western civilization, as they cavorted with the vice-consuls of the American consulate—"our Consulate boys," as the young Jane Sherman referred to them—who kept them busy with sightseeing excursions, fancy formal dinners, and dancing. Sherman learned that she would make "an ideal wife for a diplomat."[72] Dancer George Steares once told Sherman that Shawn was jealous that she kept in contact with one of those handsome diplomats throughout the trip. During the tour, for every young American or British man the dancers met whose attention they sought, there was an officer or magistrate who made unwanted advances, often during what Shawn called "command appearances"—social events that dancers were obligated to attend as ambassadors of the Denishawn envoy.

The company moved from Tianjin to Beijing, where Shawn was hosted by the director of the Beijing Society of Fine Art, Mary Ferguson. She was also the sister-in-law of the Braggiotti sisters who ran a Denishawn school in Boston and the daughter of Mr. John Ferguson, a man who went to China as a Methodist missionary then became a professor and collector of Chinese art, and later a trusted advisor to the emperor. Ferguson introduced Shawn to US ambassadors and officials who hosted him in their lavish homes and escorted him and St. Denis on shopping trips. They perused the theatrical costumes on Jade Street, purchasing headdresses and feathers. The hosts guided them to tourist sites as well, such as the Forbidden City and the Temple of Heaven, a visit that inspired one of St. Denis's signature solos *White Jade*, her paean to Kuan Yin, the goddess of mercy at the Altar of Heaven. Mary Ferguson also facilitated Shawn's introduction to Mei Lanfang (1894–1961), China's most revered stage performer and star of the Beijing Opera. Lanfang attended Denishawn's opening night in Beijing, seated in the first box at the Pavilion Theater (November 8). St. Denis performed her *Waltz* to Brahms "unwigged," allowing her naturally white hair to flow, which added a measure of "emotional maturity." Lanfang considered St. Denis's performance "without a doubt one of the most beautiful things ever seen."[73]

Shawn was unable to see Lanfang perform live in a full production, as it was off-season for the Beijing Opera. However, the following evening, after Denishawn's program, Lanfang took the stage along with his company and performed scenes from its repertory. Shawn and St. Denis saw the performance from the house, still dressed in their costumes—Shawn in a North African burnous, St. Denis in an East Indian sari.

The following day, Lanfang joined Shawn and the company for lunch in Denishawn's honor at a private home, giving the two men of the stage an opportunity to talk at length. The conversation focused on dance in China, or a version of Chinese dance history that centered on Mei Lanfang as its savior or at least as a "single and isolated example of an artist in China" or "a tender shoot from a dead trunk."[74] The two men—both symbols of national arts—might have also talked about their recent performances in Japan, seeing that both Lanfang and Shawn had groundbreaking appearances there within a year of each other, both at the Imperial Theater. Lanfang was the first Chinese actor in modern times able to perform abroad. Whatever the topic of conversation, the intimate encounter with the otherwise reclusive Lanfang allowed Shawn to affirm that "in private life, while slender and sensitive, Mei Lanfang is not in the slightest degree effeminate." He presented a costume to St. Denis and gave Shawn a set of photos of Lanfang in every one of his roles. Shawn was proud to think that he had achieved a level of success that would allow him sit face to face with an artist of Lanfang's renown, but immediately following their meeting, Shawn learned that Lanfang earned the equivalent of $20,000 in gold a month, an exorbitant figure that humbled Shawn, but also led him to believe that a male dancer could achieve similar earning power in the United States.

The rest of the time in Beijing, Shawn enjoyed luncheons, teas, and cocktail parties at diplomats' homes, where on several occasions the festivities were interrupted by the sound of nearby artillery fire. The fighting had come so close to the capital city at that time that the company had to cancel its plans to visit the Great Wall. In fact, because of the ongoing violence, Denishawn delayed its departure from Beijing, then hurriedly left on receiving a frantic message from the local producer to "get out quick"; the company then traveled via boat on the Yellow Sea to avoid destroyed roads and rail track. They arrived at 7 P.M. in Shanghai, leaving them about two hours to get to the hotel and then set up at the Olympic Theater for a 9:15 P.M. curtain. Remarkably, they unloaded and delivered the costumes and sets for a 10 P.M. curtain, with Shawn stalling audiences with lectures about the history of dance. It was the first of thirteen sold-out evenings.

Shanghai was a city with a bustling nightlife, one that Shawn jokingly said made Paris look like a sleepy Midwestern town. Its countless nightclubs and cabarets hosted floor shows with full Russian ballets, catering to the city's 25,000 Russian refugees. Shawn went to the theater with a lady-in-waiting, took tiffin with consular officials, and enjoyed a day at the Cercle Sportif, one of the most lavish clubhouses in the world. Among the Russian émigrés living in Shanghai was the tour's producer, Asway Strok. A violinist who came to Shanghai to flee the Bolsheviks, Strok also organized Denishawn's orchestra of "white Russian" musicians (including a cellist and a flutist) that accompanied the company throughout. Strok managed Pavlova's tour, as well as the tour of a soprano from the Metropolitan Opera. Though his business brokered in high culture, he himself was quite unrefined. Shawn described him as "a lonesome soul" who was short and fat with interest only "in women, money, champagne in that order." Though Shawn claimed to be forever indebted to Strok for the opportunity of the tour, he had an increasing number of reasons for resenting him. Strok misled Shawn about many facets about the tour, chief among them its duration and the quality of the venues and travel conditions. Though contractually obligated to buy first-class accommodations for the entire company, he honored this commitment only for Shawn and St. Denis. He also disregarded his obligation to travel with the company to be the interface with local theaters and press. Instead, he left the company for long stretches of time, sometimes without any communication at all. When Strok's letters did arrive, they sometimes included notifications of salary cuts. Unprofessionalism aside, Strok's personal demeanor was abhorrent. According to Shawn, Strok systematically propositioned each of the young female Denishawn dancers, a situation made worse by the fact that Strok's own daughters traveled with the company on certain legs of the tour and befriended the dancers. Strok most aggressively pursued Doris Humphrey, whom he promised, in exchange for sex, to depose St. Denis and install her as the company's star.[75]

Strok stayed behind in Shanghai as the company left for a brief stop in Hong Kong. Shawn often tried to discuss with St. Denis his new plans for "A Greater Denishawn," yet whenever the topic of conversation turned to business, the "emotional battle" between them resumed. To avoid those flareups, they bonded over their shared obsession with shopping. During any downtime before performances or between trains, they scoured markets and shopping districts for souvenirs or anything they thought they could incorporate into a dance: amber, jade, lace, lacquer, glass, snuff bottles, mandarin coats, shawls, and untold hundreds of cheap fans—enough to supply each dancer with two a performance for an entire tour. They were hopeless at bargaining, too afraid to offend local artisans or worse, to reveal their ignorance about the many unfamiliar objects they coveted. They often found themselves spending hours trying to figure out just exactly how merchants were able to sell them items for which they had neither need nor use, all at prices they could never afford. Soon they learned to ask their guides to do their bargaining. They had amassed so many crates of souvenirs that Shawn had to arrange for periodic shipments back to the United States. The obsession with acquiring such unique and exotic objects reached a feverish pitch, if not when St. Denis purchased a white cockatoo named Dada, then when Brother Dennis bought a monkey. Their best investments were the elaborate theatrical costumes they purchased in nearly every country they visited. Dressed in these costumes, Shawn and St. Denis spent days staging elaborate photographs on location at iconic tourist destinations—the Palace of the Sultan in Jahore, the Taj Mahal, and the ruins of Jubbulpore. Upon their return home, the costumes made their way into future Denishawn productions and the photographs filled the pages of Denishawn souvenir books, advertisements, and magazines.

On December 7, they sailed into the harbor of Singapore, perhaps Shawn's most highly anticipated destination. Shawn was titillated by the city's reputation for danger. However, he found its colonial reality daunting—"the dullest crowd of English colonials who were determined to be more British than at home."[76] Shawn was equally fazed by the audiences, which were large but unresponsive or worst, inappropriately "ginny and noisy."

At sunrise on December 20, the company arrived via boat in Yangon, Myanmar (what Shawn knew as Rangoon, Burma), to the spectacular sight of the early morning sun illuminating the golden spire of the Shwe Dagon Pagoda. They opened their two-week stay there on Christmas Eve. Shawn scurried around the city to find a plant that faintly resembled a Christmas tree and made it the centerpiece at the company's dinner table. He also sent off his 200-plus Christmas cards back to the United States, as well as a Malay necklace he purchased as a Christmas present for Martha Graham.

Once again Shawn benefited immeasurably from his connections—this time an American friend from California who had married Maung Paw Tun, president of the Legislative Council, a recently formed Burmese governing body. It was through this connection that Shawn met U Po Sein, the greatest living Burmese dancer. The fifty-four-year-old idol hosted St. Denis and Shawn in his home. At the time they met, Po Sein was observing a period of mourning for one of his wives, though he broke his retreat from the public to attend the Denishawn performances at the Excelsior Theater. He also

Figure 3.9. Ruth St. Denis and Ted Shawn in Singapore, December 1925. Denishawn Collection. Courtesy of the Jerome Robbins Dance Division, New York Public Library.

gave private lessons to Shawn and taught the company a *pwe*, a traditional Burmese ritual dance, for an undisclosed fee. Based on these lessons, St. Denis and Humphrey created a dance called *Burmese Yein Pwe*. Captivated by St. Denis, Po Sein also ordered his costume makers to create costumes for the Denishawn company to wear in their version of the dance.

Four months into the tour, Shawn adopted a new tactic for programming concerts while on tour in Asia. Whereas he had decided against presenting Denishawn's repertory of "Oriental" dances, Strok urged him to test the waters by programming St. Denis's celebrated interpretations of nautch dances, the devotional dances performed by *devadasis* or Hindu temple maidens, to audiences in Yangon. Audiences responded wildly, inciting a change of heart about the programming that forever changed the course of the tour, especially in India, their next stop.

The company spent four months in India, criss-crossing the subcontinent to deliver more than 100 performances in over fifteen cities. For most of that time, Shawn and St. Denis sought out authentic nautch dancers. For Shawn, "nautch" had always been a "magical" word that meant "romance" and "conjured up palaces of Rajahs, perfume and incense laden air, long sensuous nights, dark-eyed and dazzling dancers, who wove spells by the complicated rhythmic patterns of sound created by their ankle bells."[77] It was, after all, a nautch dance that St. Denis had performed when Shawn first saw her dance in Denver, Colorado, in 1911. Upon arrival in Calcutta, they asked their hosts and locals to arrange meetings with nautch dancers, though they quickly learned that "nautch" dancing was a far more complex tradition and practice than they had understood. In colonial India, the term "nautch" was not only associated with the divine *devadasi* but also with street performers and courtesans.

The day after arriving in Calcutta, the company opened a seventeen-day run at the Empire Theater, which true to its name, was a temporary home to the British Royal Opera Company as well as a range of musical and dance acts from the British Empire and Russia. On the opening night, St. Denis performed her *Black and Gold Sari* and *Nautch*. The colonial newspapers were impressed with St. Denis's performance and praised her beauty and her use of veils, though they remained entirely silent on the cultural significance of an American woman performing a devotional Hindu dance. The Nobel Prize–winning poet and philosopher Sir Rabindranath Tagore (1861–1941) attended the following evening. Shawn's first ever gift to St. Denis had been a copy of Tagore's poems *The Gardener*, presented to her on the night they first shared the stage in Paducah, Kentucky. They were reasonably anxious to learn whether his opinion of their dancing would match the esteem they held for his poetry. Moved by St. Denis's nautch dances, he allegedly claimed that "Miss Denis has revealed to India of today that dancing can be restored to the plane of ancient days by lifting it from the mud of the modern nautch."[78] Tagore invited St. Denis to stay in India to teach dancing at his university and "to inspire the youth as dance had fallen centuries back, into the hands of the illiterates and moral outcasts."[79] This invitation, extended by someone of such high standing, formed the basis of one of the most pervasive anecdotes surrounding Denishawn's Orient Tour—that St. Denis inspired a renaissance of nautch dancing in India, a claim that has been refuted on several fronts for a variety of reasons.[80] Among general elites, especially those less familiar with the complex history of nautch dancing, St. Denis might have made a convincing case that she was the unlikely exponent of this dance tradition. Alternatively, the enthusiasm for her nautch dances might have been an expression of colonial resistance among Indian nationals, a possibility raised by Jane Sherman years after the tour. She wondered: "Perhaps the anti-British, pro-Independence 'natives' were besides themselves with joy at the sight of 'white' women so demeaning themselves? The truth probably lay somewhere between the peak of admiration and the pit of scorn."[81]

At the end of their run in Calcutta, the American consulate organized an invitation from a wealthy Muslim merchant to attend a party where there would be nautch dancing. Per Shawn's request, the event was planned for the afternoon before the company's evening performance. One of the dancers was Bachwa Jan, who was introduced as "the most famous dancer in India." According to Shawn, she was "a stringy old pullet about 60-years-old . . . emaciated but spritely." For over an hour, she demonstrated various styles of *kathak*, a rhythmic form of dancing from north India. Shawn marveled at the way the movement of her eyebrows punctuated her explosive footwork. Another dancer, Malka Jan, was middle-aged, plump, and "beautiful in a sort of Theda Bara way." She wore a sari but was otherwise a model of Victorian elegance. With crimped gray hair and a dog collar of seed pearls, she would have looked completely at home at a Boston Symphony matinee. She also declined to dance barefoot, but wore men's socks all the time. However, she also wore twenty pounds of ankle bells, and with these did the most amazing feats. Bachwa and Malka Jan attended the Denishawn performance at the Empire, though we know nothing of their impression of St. Denis's version of nautch dancing. Shawn and St. Denis were advised that they would have better luck seeing authentic nautch dancing in the North. At a bazaar in the northern province of Quetta (then a part of "British India," now Pakistan), they encountered and even filmed nautch dancers whose ability to turn astonished them. These dancers were actually young boys dressed as women, continuing a tradition of men performing female roles when the women were outlawed from performing publicly.

As Shawn sought out nautch dancers while in India, he also was determined to create a Hindu-inspired dance that would correspond with the religiosity and theatricality of St. Denis's nautch. For this, he set out to compose a dance based on the Hindu myth of the "dance of bliss" (tandava) through which Siva, the god of creation, preservation, and destruction brought the world into existence. Havelock Ellis wrote about the "supreme religious importance" of Siva's cosmic dance. Ellis's valorization of this dance inspired Shawn to actively pursue learning the dance. To that end, Shawn hired a guide named Boshi Sen who helped him with his research into Siva, using his connections within the Vedanta Society, exponents of orthodox Hindu philosophy. Boshi introduced Shawn to Rama Krishna, a Vedanta swami in Allahabad Math, who instructed him to think of Siva in metaphysical terms:

> When you see the birds flying in rhythmic circles, that is Siva; when you see the leaves of the trees swaying beautifully in the breeze, that is Siva; you see the surf breaking in measured cadences on the shore, that is Siva; when children dance spontaneously at play, that is Siva dancing; when the flames on the burning ghat dance as they consume the corpse, that also is Siva dancing.[82]

Shawn shared with Boshi his doubt that he could create a compelling theatrical work from such sacred forces. Boshi advised Shawn, "Make your body an instrument and remove your petty self from it, and Siva will use your body to dance through it. . . . Siva will be dancing through you." Just as Shawn collected information and steps for the dance across various cities and from different perspectives, so too did he design the dance's costume and set. He created the costume from many intricate pieces that he gathered along his travels. In his diary, he kept a list of its various parts and prices: bells from Calcutta, girdles and anklets from Lahore, an "hour-glass drum" made of two human skulls from Darjeeling, pendants and rings from Bombay, and $200 of virgin silver from the bazaar at Cawnpore. Shawn discovered a foundry and metal shop that agreed to create a life-sized prabhamandala, the symbolic ring of flames that surround Siva in the bronze statues that depict him in the form of Nataraja (the "Lord of the Dance"). Shawn's commissioned piece tested the artisan's skills, as the frame had to be designed so it could be disassembled for transport. He also had the shop design and make him a Siva crown, similar to a bishop's miter, adorned with iconography from iconic Siva sculptures: cassia leaves, flowing hair, snakes, a crescent moon, and the head of the Hindu river goddess.

During his final days in Madras, Shawn visited Mahabalipuram ("The Seven Pagodas"), the eighth-century seaside temples dedicated to Dancing Siva. It was a blistering hot day, so much so that Shawn could not pose with the metal prabhamandala as he had planned, for the heat made the metal too hot to touch. Instead, he assumed various poses associated with the "Lord of the Dance" in temple courtyards and archways. (See Figure 3.10.)

For the dance's score, Shawn commissioned Lily Strickland, an American composer whose work he had already used. Strickland had been living in India for more than ten years because of her husband's shipping business, so Shawn took the opportunity to meet with her to make decisions about the piano accompaniment. The three sections of the piano score provide the overall structure of the dance. The choreography begins with Shawn standing within the prabhamandala in the iconic Siva pose of one leg bent, lifted, and crossing the standing leg. His left arm makes the *gaja hasta* (or "elephant trunk") gesture; his right arm forms the *abhaya mudra* which means "fear not." He shakes the *damaru* drum to represent the cosmic rhythm that created life. In the second section, he steps down from the platform and performs a sequence of shape-shifting postures and gestures associated with Siva in visual iconography, demonstrating the ideal of preservation. The final section, a demonstration of destruction, is a rhythmically vibrant dance wherein Shawn attempts to perform footwork, likely inspired by the *tatkaar* or rhythmic footwork of kathak dancing but in no way recognizable as such. For effect, he ignited incense on the floor of the platform to create smoke, invoking Siva's favorite dancing place, the burning *ghats* of the Ganges, the site for ceremonial cremations.

The resulting dance, *The Cosmic Dance of Siva*, combined aspects of two of the most successful dances in the Denishawn repertory. A "living-statue" dance, it borrowed the conceit of Shawn's most popular solo, *Death of Adonis*. It also took several choreographic cues from St. Denis's *Incense*, if not for its pious air, then for its actual use of incense onstage to create smoke, as well as St. Denis's signature gesture of billowing arms. Shawn reluctantly premiered

Figure 3.10. Ted Shawn at Mahabalipuram ("Seven Pagodas") in India, posing in costume for *Cosmic Dance of Siva* (1926). Courtesy of Jacob's Pillow Dance Festival Archives.

The Cosmic Dance of Siva in Manila. The audience included five high-ranking American military officers who accompanied Mary Hay Caldwell, a former Denishawn student and daughter of Brigadier General Caldwell, commander of the US Fortress Caldwell in the Philippines. It was the first opportunity Shawn had to run the dance with music, costume, and set. He also experimented with applying dark body makeup to give his body the distinctive patina typical of Siva bronze statues. However, the heat and humidity made it impossible for the makeup to set, and so he instead looked like a piece of melting chocolate. The audience was bewildered by Shawn's dance, especially the military officers who were under the impression that they were going to see a dance about the Queen of Sheba.

When not performing or conducting research on nautch dancers and the lord of the dance, Shawn saw a wide variety of dance. The company performed for royalty, the Nizam of Hyderabad, a princely state of India. One of the wealthiest men in the world, the Nizam owned the diamond mines in Golconda. Given his wealth, Shawn was shocked to learn that the royals also earned and kept money off the sale of tickets to their performance. The Bishop of Calcutta advised Shawn to visit the Chotanagur district of Western Bengal to see various ethnic Hindu and Muslim dances and rituals in Central India. During a week's break from performance, Shawn and Doris Humphrey took a treacherous excursion via train and automobile approximately 6,000 feet above sea level to the Mount Everest Hotel, a palatial resort that rests on the slopes of the Himalayas in Darjeeling. Through Boshi, Shawn made contact with General Laden La, a native Tibetan whom the British colonial administration deputized to oversee border patrol. He effectively determined which foreigners had access to the city. The general escorted Shawn via horseback to the Bhutia Monastery, a Buddhist compound set on a remote hill with a magnificent view of the Himalayas. He personally gave Shawn a tour of the building, then offered running commentary to the series of dances that were performed in his honor in its courtyard. Shawn saw several "devil dances"—a derogative term European colonists used to refer to the animistic dances that lamas or Buddhist monks performed. He also saw lamas perform masked dance-dramas about myths and supernatural forces. The general explained to Shawn that the lamas had performed the dances since A.D. 899 in strict accordance with the meticulous descriptions contained within the scriptures housed in the monastery's library.

When Shawn returned to the Mount Everest Hotel, the manager offered to arrange a special performance by a troupe of devil dancers who had recently performed at the British Empire Exhibit at Wembley in 1924 and the Exposition des Arts Decoratifs in Paris in 1925. The troupe came and performed on the hotel's tennis courts a series of traditional masked pantomimes, some with acrobatic "stunts," some of which Shawn thought he recognized from US vaudeville and musical comedy stages. Shawn never mentioned (and possibly never knew) that the troupe of devil dancers he saw was embroiled in a diplomatic controversy between Tibet and the United Kingdom known as "The Affair of the Dancing Lamas." The troupe's performance at the British Expedition was part of a publicity campaign for the film

The Epic of Everest (1924), a documentary about a failed British expedition to reach the summit of Mount Everest, yet nonetheless led to unwanted tourism at the sacred Tibetan site.[83]

On May 12, 1926, the company departed India for a brief yet inspiring visit to Colombo, Sri Lanka (then, Ceylon), which for Shawn was "a dancer's paradise." Along with the company's two male dancers, Weidman and Steares, Shawn studied Kandyan healing dances (also known as "Devil Dances"), which he later integrated into *Primitive Rhythms* (1936) for his Men Dancers.[84] The company then returned to Singapore for an unexpected though not entirely unwelcome break from the tour. Though a financial setback, it was the first substantive respite since they had arrived in Asia about nine months earlier. During the layoff in Singapore, Shawn used the Victoria Theater to rehearse new works for the upcoming tour based on the dances they had studied in the Far East. These works would be the centerpiece of a program for Denishawn's return to the United States.

It was also during the layoff week in Singapore, on June 30, 1926, to be exact, that Shawn received his author's copy of *The American Ballet*, the book he had written just before the tour of Asia began. He had not given the manuscript a single thought since, but when it arrived, he locked himself into his hotel room to read it cover to cover, especially the introduction by Havelock Ellis, which he had not read before receiving it in print. Shawn was pleased with Ellis's comments, though it is hard to imagine why, lukewarm as they were. About his own writing, Shawn admitted that he had barely recognized it as his own, making him concerned whether the dengue fever he had contracted caused some memory loss. The disconcerting feeling he had toward his own writing more likely was estrangement from the xenophobic undertones in the book after having traveled throughout Asia for nine months. Although he does not outright disavow the book's isolationist ideals, the fact that he was in the process of rehearsing a Chinese opera, Kandyan medicine dances, and the dance of Siva minimally suggests that the fervor with which he had repudiated all dances other than those from Europe had since subsided. Indeed, anyone following Shawn's writings closely might have been confused by the contradictory ideas about dance that he presents in *The American Ballet*, which was published in 1926, and those in his commissioned dispatches from various locations abroad that concurrently appeared in *The Dance* magazine. It would have been difficult for readers to reconcile Shawn's lengthy descriptions of Asian dances and detailed accounts of his search for authentic nautch dances—not to mention the photographs of him proudly wearing traditional Asian costumes, such as the one of him in a Chinese garden in full Beijing Opera regalia, that accompanied the magazine articles—with the nationalist assertions in *The American Ballet*, such as the following: "We need never to borrow material from any nation, for we are full to abundance with undeveloped ideas and themes."[85]

On July 16, 1926, the company sailed for Java, where they spent more than a month. Under the sponsorship of Kunstkring, a members-only art society, Denishawn performed a slew of one-night stands within the organization's network of clubhouses throughout the island nation, each with a small theater that exclusively served its members. The Kunstkring officials extended Shawn and the company an invitation to join Dutch officials at the Palace of the Sultan. On Sunday, August 8, 1926, they were escorted into Kraton, the enclosed royal city within the city of Jakarta, then proceeded to the golden dance pavilion where a traditional dance-drama was already under way. Shawn could barely pull his attention away from the action for a formal introduction to the Sultan, who personally greeted each member of the company.

Seeing Javanese Court dancers at the royal palace was a highlight of Shawn's time abroad, rivaled only by a related experience he had the following month in Cambodia. An American diplomat in Saigon was able to secure an invitation for Shawn to attend a performance at the Royal Palace in Phnom Penh, Cambodia, to attend the birthday celebration of King Sisowath, a staunch patron of the arts. St. Denis, Humphrey, Weidman, and Geordie Graham, Martha's younger sister, joined Shawn for a treacherous six-hour car drive that involved four river crossings that required locals to carry the car on poles. They arrived early at the palace, eager to secure front row seats in the Hall of Dance, the open-air dance pavilion on the palace grounds. Shawn described the performance he saw there as "one of the most enchanting" he had ever seen. In the process of trying to write about the highly stylized movement of the ancient Khmer dances—the exquisite and deliberate gestures, the hypnotic rhythms, the sense of floating and flying—he came to a broader realization about dance. As he watched the dances, likely trying to imagine how he might recreate a version of them for Denishawn, he arrived at the conclusion that "we never could duplicate or recreate this dance art exactly. . . . In the study of the dances of every nation and race of the world, I am never concerned with imitation, but with the surprising secret source of their charm and beauty, that I, too, may tap that source, and let the divine essence flow through me, perhaps in new forms, to the world."[86]

They made the return trip just in time to catch their ship to Hong Kong, which the company would call home base during their short ventures into Manila and Saigon. The pace began to wear on Shawn. What was meant to be a six-month tour had now stretched well over a year, and the final dates in Japan were still two months in the future. The stress of travel was made all the more difficult by managing the extreme conditions they experienced, from sitting in royal pavilions in Cambodia to performing in the neglected, bat-infested Manila Grand Opera House, for example. Overall, there was little to no interest in Denishawn among the Filipinos. Strok insisted they present Spanish dances on every program with hopes they might resonate with some of the colonial Spanish-style folk dance.

However, in the Philippines, Shawn had the rare opportunity to have lunch at the Malacañan Palace with Leonard Wood, the US Army governor and governor-general of the Philippines. The invitation was arranged by Lillian Cox's nephew, Major Burton Read. General Wood was widely deplored by the Filipinos, mostly for his negative assessment of the nation's readiness for independence. Wood outlined his views against self-determination in the Wood-Forbes Report, which contained the findings of a commission charged by newly elected US president Warren Harding. In the mountainous city of Baguio, Wood arranged for Shawn a command performance of dances from a range of indigenous groups—Baguio, Ifugaos, Apavaos, Igorots, and Bontocs. Guided by an American military translator, Shawn spent the morning watching a range of ceremonial head-hunting, wedding, and court-ship dances. In perhaps the most uncanny moment of Shawn's time in the Far East, later that evening, the entire performance was repeated for colonial administrators in front of a bonfire on a country club golf course. At night, under the influence of alcohol and in the glare of the fire, the indigenous performers took on another level of intensity, literally illuminating the fear and terror with which Wood had depicted the lands.

Shawn remained ingratiated to Wood for this extraordinary and unique opportunity, not to mention swayed by Wood's personal charm. The combi-nation of the two led to Shawn's complete defense of the Wood report in his own article about dance in the Philippines that was published in the February 1927 edition of *The Dance* magazine. Foremost, the title of Shawn's article, "Dancing on the Isles of Fear," was a reference to Wood's controversial book *The Isles of Fear: The Truth about the Philippines* (1925) by American writer Katherine Mayo, which not only defended Wood and US imperialism, but also rationalized measures to thwart independence movements. Shawn was complicit in American imperialism abroad inasmuch as his writing conveys a negative view of colonial subjects and a condescending and threatening portrayal of the "noble primitives" (Shawn's term) through dance.

As Shawn prepared for the final stretch of the tour, he increasingly felt anxious about the future of Denishawn. He was homesick, too, especially when he received a letter with the sad news that his maternal grandmother had died. He had last visited Grandmother Booth a few years earlier. He wistfully remembered that she had played "We Met by Chance" on the piano, telling Shawn that it was the tune with which she had won his grandfather's heart. She was the last living member of his bloodline.

Shawn grew disillusioned throughout the remainder of the tour, suffering from what he called "mental indigestion," especially as the company embarked on its return trip to Japan. He had shed any pretense that he could immerse himself in another culture. A number of incidents in the final weeks of the tour signaled to Shawn that the company might have overstayed their welcome, too. In Nagasaki, local police forced Shawn to remove a bit performed by George Steares in a new work based on Chinese theater, *General Wu's Farewell to His Wife*. The objectionable action involved Steares, in the role of a property man, eating from a lacquer bowl with chopsticks and reading a newspaper offstage whenever he was not busy with action on stage. Locals found the imitation of their manner of eating insulting. The police were once again called to the theater in Kobe, when Shawn assaulted a stagehand that he was convinced tried to sabotage his performance with the wrong music and curtain cues. Shawn also admitted to getting enraged with Strok in Japan over his continued attempts to bilk them out of their guaranteed box office revenue during the final weeks of the tour. Shawn thought his outburst established a boundary with Strok that he never again crossed and even assumed his rage possibly finally earned him Strok's respect.

Mental indigestion and police interventions aside, Shawn managed to make good use of the final stretch abroad by getting various new works he created in the Far East before an audience, testing them out before the company returned home with its promised program of new Oriental dances. In Japan, he refined his adaptation of *Momiji-Gari* under Koshiro's expert eye. Shawn created a condensed version of the fifty-minute drama as a vehicle for him to play the related dual roles of a Demon and Lady Sarashina. (See Figure 3.11.) The company performed the work in traditional costume, wigs, and makeup. Shawn showed Koshiro the improvements he had made to the dance-drama, including a trick he learned from street performers in Kandy

Figure 3.11. Ted Shawn as Lady Sarashina in *Momiji-Gari* (1926). Ted Shawn
Collection. Courtesy of the Jerome Robbins Dance Division, New York Public
Library.

who used a bamboo device that made it appear that one could blow smoke.
Shawn paid the performer for his secret and employed the trick in one of the
play's fight scenes.

Shawn was pleased with the positive responses to his adaptations of Asian
dance-dramas from local audiences and especially from some of the local
masters. However, he began to doubt whether Japanese artists had truly understood the Denishawn aesthetic once he was confronted with the influence
Denishawn had made on the Japanese stage. In Japan, Shawn and St. Denis
were escorted to see "modern" dance, but what they found were "lousy"
Denishawn imitations with themes, steps, and costumes lifted entirely from
Denishawn concerts presented there the year before. Doris Humphrey
recalled her shock when she saw postcards of a Japanese woman performing
her "Hoop Dance" in a loose-fitting dress instead of her skin-tight leotard.[87]
Shawn expressed his "amazement and disgust" at a rendition of his "Death of

Adonis," a solo dance dedicated to the god of beauty. The Japanese imitation was performed by two short men accompanied by a flashy ensemble beneath a huge mirrored ball. He likened the whole effort to Rube Goldberg cartoons depicting outlandish contraptions and elaborate processes that perform the most basic functions.

Shawn was further confounded by the Japanese impression of Denishawn when he and St. Denis were presented with traditional clay "Hakata" dolls that ressembled them in costume for *Hopi Indian Eagle Dance* and *Black and Gold Sari*, respectively. When Shawn and St. Denis first visited Hakata over a year earlier, they posed for local artists, never imagining that those sketches would be rendered into actual Hakata dolls, coveted ones at that. At first, Shawn did not know what to make of "the 'imitativeness' (worst, the outright stealing)" of his dances and likeness by Japanese artists.[88] He even went as far as to raise the issue of copyright and royalties, which was ironic, given that he had just spent the past fifteen months learning local traditional dances and planned to adapt and stage them in US commercial theaters. Perhaps he thought the nominal fees he paid to all of the respected stewards of dance that he encountered gave him license to restage the dances as he saw fit. However, Shawn came to the conclusion that Denishawn dances were just one of the many American products and goods that were meticulously copied by Japanese artisans and entrepreneurs. Ultimately, he claims he was "impressed" that his dances and likeness were commoditized like the American razor blades, chocolate bars, and canned goods he saw in shop windows, all with an uncanny resemblance to the American originals.

The tour, however, left a more enduring impact than the dances and commodities. About the Denishawn "Orient Tour," Baron Ishimoto warned: "Whenever a historian tries to write a book on the relations of the U.S. and Japan, he cannot ignore the coming of the Denishawn dancers in 1925 to Japan because by their appearance on the stage of Tokyo the Japanese attitude toward America in respect to art has been completely changed."[89] Though the test of time has proven that the tour might not have transformed international relations, it certainly made a profound impact on Denishawn— and Shawn's relationship with St. Denis, who came to recognize that the young man she married a decade earlier had become an accomplished artist in his own right: "He is easily the greatest man dancer in the world today," she wrote in her journal. "No one realizes he is strong in personality more [than] I do—He is a rare and forceful personality capable of great singleness of purpose . . . and an artist of fine concepts. This shows in his dancing—which is beautifully balanced—his character or his personality dances are not in my opinion while excellent as good as his lyric or his plastiques. . . . His natural equipment of bodily structure and temperament are perfect instruments for his vision of beauty."[90]

After nearly fifteen months abroad and nineteen days at sea, "America's Unofficial Ambassadors" disembarked in San Francisco on December 1, 1926. Shawn returned stateside counting on positive press about the tour—and the many new dances it generated—to refresh the Denishawn brand and its mission, and in turn, to help attract new audiences and students. While in Asia, Shawn had also been plotting an ambitious plan for establishing an arts colony outside Manhattan called "Greater Denishawn." Despite the great physical and emotional toll the tour exacted on St. Denis, she entertained Shawn's vision for expansion, persuaded as always by his passion and perseverance.

4

America's Greatest Male Dancer

A Greater Denishawn,
December 1926–October 1929

In May 1926, while the Denishawn Company was still on tour in Asia and over six months away from returning stateside, it was announced that Denishawn would return to the American stage under the new management of Arthur Judson (1881–1975), "the most powerful music manager of the time and arguably in all of American music history."[1] "The Great Orchestrator," Judson was the mastermind who had booked Denishawn in the Lewisohn Stadium concert series the summer before the company left for Asia, making Ted Shawn and Ruth St. Denis among the most recognizable names on the influential promoter's roster of dancers, pianists, violinists, and singers. The company arrived in San Francisco on December 1, 1926, leaving them just a few days to rehearse before opening in Los Angeles at the Philharmonic. The programs were filled with new dances inspired from the "Oriental" tour, such as *Momiji-Gari, White Jade, Sinhalese Devil Dance, General Wu's Farewell to His Wife, Javanese Court Dance*, and *Danse Cambodienne*, as well as a section of dances titled "Gleanings from Buddha Fields" and some sacred dances, such as the *Burmese Yein Pwe* and Shawn's *Cosmic Dance of Siva*. Though the tour was an immediate critical success, Shawn was displeased with his involvement with Judson or lack thereof. Shawn had met the infamous promoter only a handful of times, and that in part was the problem. Judson made agreements to theater owners that Shawn could not keep, especially ridiculously low box office shares. Given the critical success the company achieved, Shawn felt he no longer needed to stand for Judson's lies, secret deals, and belittling treatment, so Denishawn's first tour under Judson's management was its last.

The Judson tour did not include any dates in New York City, so Shawn self-produced a concert at Carnegie Hall at the tour's end. Between April 4 and April 6, 1927, Denishawn gave four sold-out performances that proved to be a historic success, not only for Denishawn but also for the field of dance at

Ted Shawn. Paul A. Scolieri, Oxford University Press (2020). © Paul A. Scolieri.
DOI: 10.1093/oso/9780199331062.001.0001

large, as it was the first time a dance company had sold out a major venue for four consecutive performances, winning rave notices in the process. St. Denis called it the "peak of the whole Denishawn organization."[2] Mary Watkins of the *New York Herald Tribune* called the program "the best in New York this season." Watkins also credited Shawn's maturity as a performer, favorably comparing him with St. Denis: "Mr. Shawn's talents are perhaps more versatile than his wife's, and he is equally charming as a toreador or gay Hussar."[3] The *New York Times* ran a review that praised the high quality of the production and the inventiveness of Clifford Vaughan's musical adaptations of Asian music for the "series of gorgeous pantomimes, miniature dramas, and divertissements inspired by the native dances of Japan, China, India, and Java."[4]

Denishawn's successful Carnegie Hall performances prompted Edith Isaacs, the influential editor of *Theater Arts Magazine*, to write a petition to her editorial counterparts at major newspapers to hire dedicated and expert critics to cover an art form that had at last proven itself deserving.[5] According to Shawn, the performance and petition led directly to the appointment of two dance critics at major newspapers: Mary Watkins (wife of music critic Edward Cushing) at the *New York Herald Tribune* and, a few weeks later, John Martin at the *New York Times*. Of course, Shawn was upset that Walter Terry was not offered the *Times* post and thus tried to delegitimize Martin's appointment by claiming that Olin Downes, the *Times* music editor who was reluctantly charged with making the hire, selected Martin based solely on the recommendation of a friend of his. Shawn also justifiably questioned Martin's credentials for the post, noting that at the time of his appointment, Martin "had been associated with the Boleslavsky Laboratory Theatre as sort of a secretary and had himself taught some 'elocution' but whose entire knowledge of dance had been a few lessons in tap!"[6]

Amid what was arguably the most successful series of performances of Shawn's career, and an overwhelmingly positive reception from New York audiences and critics, St. Denis swept in to take credit. During the bows after the final performance, St. Denis spontaneously delivered a curtain speech to the Carnegie Hall audience to expound on Denishawn and in the process represented the company and school as her own, without sharing any credit with Shawn. Despite her endless complaints against touring and running the school, when the opportunity came, she took complete credit for the company's success, devastating Shawn in the process. She later admitted that her action was an "unpardonable mistake."[7]

Despite his personal upset with St. Denis, Shawn had every intention of leveraging the string of successes since the company's return from Asia to reclaim the momentum they had lost in the States with respect to both the company and the school. For once he had the means to reinvest in both, for the Carnegie Hall performances grossed $23,000 at the box office.

Following the successful year of touring, culminating in the Carnegie Hall performances, Shawn faced a period of summer downtime. With the intent of establishing his own summer camp, he scouted a possible location at a "rest home" for artists, writers, musicians, and dancers on the Saugatuck River in Westport, Connecticut. The owner, a native Hawaiian named Nell Alexander, ran the property like the missionary camp on which she had been raised. Shawn was utterly charmed by Alexander's personality and the novelty of eating her home-cooked Hawaiian food on the lanai of the camp's main house on the bank of the river. Shawn purchased an acre of Alexander's property to build a studio. The deed was placed in his name only, making it the first financial venture without St. Denis since they were married. Shawn did not immediately build his studio, though he contracted an architect to design a Japanese pavilion complete with *shoji* (sliding door panels) for three sides of the building, *tatami* (thick, oblong matting to cover the floors in the rooms), and wood lanterns.

The Westport studio was one facet of his vision for rebuilding the Denishawn empire. Throughout the tour of Asia, Shawn had continuous conversations with St. Denis about building what he called a "Greater Denishawn," a colony for dance artists that would fulfill the plan for dance in America as articulated in the final chapter of *The American Ballet*. At various points throughout the trip, St. Denis was tempted by Shawn's vision, perhaps because it promised some future stability amid the constant chaos of the tour. On their return to the United States, he had to convince her with financial logic rather than artistic aspiration. He explained to her his plan for building a combination school and dormitory on two property lots that St. Denis and her brother had purchased years earlier during an auction of the Van Cortlandt estate in the Bronx. Investing in the development of this property, as well as purchasing adjoining lots, would essentially cost the same amount as renting a studio, an apartment, and a storage space. Plus, they would own the property outright in eleven years. Shawn's financial advisors agreed that this was a sound idea, at least on paper.

Greater Denishawn was to include dance studios, a dormitory, a museum, a library, storage, costume shop, art and set design studio, and a printing press. Additionally, it would serve as headquarters for the dance guild, which he proposed in his book *The American Ballet*. The property was pastoral, surrounded by trees and enclosed by a patio with a natural rock garden, though still easily accessible by a half-hour and 5-cent car fare to either the west or east side of Manhattan. To protect the main house's exquisite view of the Van Cortland reservoir, Shawn purchased adjacent lots where new buildings were certain to be built.

To help finance the extraordinary plan for Greater Denishawn, Shawn plotted his first fundraising campaign. In a draft of a development proposal, he estimated they needed $2 million to see Greater Denishawn come to fruition—$1 million to build a theater and $1 million in endowment.[8] He wrote personal letters to potential patrons. He and St. Denis also agreed to pay June Hamilton $100 per week in "propaganda expense money," essentially employing her as the first development officer for a dance company. In that role, Hamilton was to advertise and garner press for Greater Denishawn "with a religious urgency." One fundraising scheme they developed was to identify a donor from each of the fifty states to underwrite a scholarship for a student from each respective state to attend Greater Denishawn.

All signs seemed to indicate to Shawn that the timing was right to pursue his vision for a Greater Denishawn. While waiting to reap the rewards of his development plan, another source of funding presented itself in the form of an invitation to join a touring company of the Ziegfeld Follies, the renowned theatrical revue based in New York City. A "small-time" revue producer George Wintz had recently purchased the rights to produce a "tab-show" or a pared down version of the Ziegfeld Follies for touring purposes.[9] Whereas the Ziegfeld girl had become a New York City institution, the wholesome Denishawn dancer had more box office appeal with audiences in smaller cities. They were the perfect addition to Wintz's eclectic roster of performers.

Wintz successfully recruited St. Denis and Shawn with a handsome salary of $3,500 (approximately $50,000 in today's currency) per week for thirty-eight weeks, plus travel and lodging. This rate had to cover the $55–$100 per week salaries of the small ensemble of Denishawn dancers, though Shawn did not have to forfeit the usual 20 percent booker commission. They each were to perform two solos, as well as appear in an ensemble work. St. Denis's serene *White Jade* and Shawn's fiery *Cosmic Dance of Siva* were programmed in an evening that glorified the American Girl, alongside toe dancers, black bottom dancers, contortionists, and naked girls posing on the back of an elephant in a Ben Ali Haggin tableau. With no space on the program for featured soloists, Shawn convinced Doris Humphrey and Charles Weidman to stay in New York to teach. Shawn also encouraged them to use the school's studios and accompanists to develop their own choreography.

Shawn and St. Denis set off with the Follies just days after Isadora Duncan had died in a fatal car accident on September 17, 1927. Shawn collected and saved Duncan's death notices in the Denishawn scrapbook, as if her untimely demise were somehow intimately linked to the company's story. It might have seemed to Shawn that the coinciding of Duncan's death and Denishawn's return to the commercial stage signaled an end to the great experiment in expressive art dancing or perhaps that Duncan's death revitalized his commitment to a Greater Denishawn, especially given the company's new standing in the dance world now without its most celebrated forerunner.

St. Denis and Shawn's lofty visions for a Greater Denishawn were buoyed by the time and money afforded by the Ziegfeld Follies tour. Liberated from the burden of supervising every aspect of a touring theatrical production, Shawn began to enjoy a new lifestyle as an entertainer. Though he and St. Denis claimed that they only drew "living expenses" while on the road, with all other income going to pay off their tremendous mortgages on a new Denishawn House, those expenses funded a lavish lifestyle. They dined at fine restaurants with Wintz and his wife Nyla, a comic singer who was also in the show. Shawn enrolled in correspondence classes in French and psychology at the University of Wisconsin to stave off the monotonous chatter of chorus girls on Pullman train rides. He hired a "colored valet" named Douglas, whom Shawn had met in Birmingham, Alabama, at the start of the tour. Douglas helped to keep the appearance that Shawn lived a life of luxury, managing what Shawn called his "brown out" period wherein all his clothes were dyed a sepia brown so as not to look dirty when Shawn's stage makeup would inevitably rub off on them. His post-show baths in a corrugated iron tub with Sayman's vegetable wonder soap did not always remove the make-up. He especially wanted to protect the custom summer suits of Biltmore homespun wool that he had ordered. Douglas never missed a night of watching Shawn on stage and became a trusted critic of his performances. Regrettably, Shawn never mentioned the quality or kind of feedback Douglas gave him.

Less than a month into the Follies tour, Shawn and St. Denis were on a train when they met Jimmy Holmes, the owner of the swanky Breakers Hotel in Corpus Christi, Texas, their next tour stop. The hotelier invited the couple to a suite at the hotel for rest and relaxation between their matinee and evening performance that day. Neither Shawn nor St. Denis could refuse the invitation, if not for the chance to indulge in a bit of luxury, then for the opportunity to get better acquainted with Holmes's younger friend who was accompanying him, "a tall, finely built young man with irregular features, but with great charm, whose name was Fred Beckman."[10] Beckman offered to escort Shawn and St. Denis to the hotel and they both jumped at the chance. On the drive out to the Breakers, Beckman told them all about himself, that he was twenty-nine (he was actually thirty-one), that he had attended the University of Wisconsin and later Princeton, then worked in the US Consulate in Paris, and was once attached to the American Embassy in London.[11]

It was a beautiful day, so Shawn and St. Denis went directly to the hotel room, changed into bathing suits and headed to the beach where Beckman awaited them. He was talking with a young woman who, even before introducing herself, grabbed Shawn's attention: "I can stand on my head—can you?" Without waiting for an answer, she demonstrated a flawless headstand. Her name was Fern Helscher, and given Shawn's fondness for people willing to please him, the two became fast friends from that moment on. In the years ahead Helscher would also professionally serve him as press agent, booker, business manager. It might have been Helscher who snapped a photo of Beckman flanked by Shawn and St. Denis in her Ziegfeld Follies bathing suit. It is a prescient photo, with Beckman getting between the couple and nearly edging St. Denis out of the picture. (See Figure 4.1.)

Decades later, Shawn freely admitted his impression of Beckman: "Now, if I am frank and honest. I became absolutely infatuated with him, and by this I mean it was a strong, overwhelming sexual attraction."[12] The problem, of course, was that St. Denis had the same response to Beckman, and Shawn knew it: "Ruth and I both in the slang phrase of the day asked 'Where have you been all my life' and took him to our hearts."[13] They also took him into Denishawn. Calling Beckman "the answer to our prayers," Shawn convinced St. Denis to offer him a position as company manager, absorbing Margerie Lyon's duties while she was in Europe scouting bookings for St. Denis's tour. Shawn also wanted Beckman as a personal business representative to oversee his interests beyond Denishawn, such as his post-Ziegfeld tour activity and the Westport studio. St. Denis agreed and Shawn wrote to Beckman inviting him to join them for four days during their stay in Little Rock the first week of December to iron out the details. St. Denis also wrote her own letter of

Figure 4.1. Ruth St. Denis (*left*), Fred Beckman (*center*), and Ted Shawn (*right*) at the Breakers Hotel in Corpus Christi, Texas, 1927. Ted Shawn Papers, Additions. Courtesy of the Jerome Robbins Dance Division, New York Public Library.

invitation to Beckman, an exceptionally rare letter with no typographical or grammatical errors and none of the misspellings that impede meaning in most of St. Denis's correspondence. Quite possibly, Shawn typed it for her so that it would make a good impression. The letter curiously reads as if St. Denis were playing matchmaker between Shawn and Beckman:

> I am so glad that (whether we work together or not) avenues of communication been you and Ted have opened up, that perhaps you may, anyway, play together! Teddy needs play so badly. He has borne a great responsibility, really beyond his years, yet few persons ever reach his inner life, ever play with him (mostly we don't have time) which, being interpreted means to so act upon him as to release both the fun and beauty that waits to be released in his nature.[14]

Whether it was Shawn's invitation to work or St. Denis's invitation to play, Beckman agreed to meet them in Little Rock, and though it appeared the three clearly enjoyed one other's company and shared excitement about the future of Greater Denishawn, Beckman did not yet formally accept the job. In her journal, St. Denis began to question Beckman's intentions, as well as mourn what seemed to be the inevitable loss of her Teddy "Bumpkins" to him. She was in an awkward state, in love with Beckman yet wondering if he was good enough for Shawn:

> Fred? His influence on our lives and art?
> Is there a real inner core—to all his charm and intelligence?
> Will this be for Ted's real growth or real new vision
> of himself—his powers—his splendid career.
> held up to him by Fred's affection + illusion
> or will it peter out into heartache for T—?
>
> This element that Fred seems
> To draw out of him is that element
> Which ever my deepest love can't
> Supply—I have always known this—
> Is meant "right" I know to T sincerely wants
> This too. Just very the "rainbow" beautiful + strong
> Will it lead to strength + faith—will it be
> a bridge over which each of them can go
> + find pasture?[15]

Over the Christmas break, St. Denis and Shawn went to see the completely built and furnished Denishawn House. (See Figure 4.2.) They marveled at their accomplishment: "Every brick a one-night stand," St. Denis famously calculated. However proud, they owed close to $30,000 in mortgage payments, and so went back to work. Their hopes for Denishawn seem to intensify as they rang in the New Year learning about the death of Loïe Fuller on January 1, 1928. Within a space of six months, the dance world lost two of its greatest stars, leaving St. Denis as the only surviving member of a triumvirate of pioneers in American dance. Next stop was Havana, Cuba.

Beckman met Shawn and St. Denis in Havana, where the Follies appeared before sold-out crowds at the National Theater. Shawn was disappointed by the "favorable but dumb" critics, as well as for not listening to his instinct that the tango and Spanish numbers would not go

Figure 4.2. A Greater Denishawn: Denishawn House in Van Cortlandt Park, New York, 1928. Ted Shawn Papers, Additions. Courtesy of the Jerome Robbins Dance Division, New York Public Library.

over well in Havana. He was right. Still, he went to see authentic Cuban rhumba dancing, which he dismissed as "choreographed sex" but nonetheless folded into his own repertory, along with the designs for the rumbero's iconic shirt with ruffled sleeves. He was pleased, however, with one reporter who made a provocative association between one of Shawn's dances and a scandalous Parisian revue that had recently visited the island: "The Bataclan from Paris had introduced naked women to Havana and *Allégresse* had introduced naked men, thus balancing the city's morals."[16] Choreographed specifically for the Judson tour, *Allégresse* was a cabaret version of Nijinsky's *L'Après-midi d'un faune*, even down to the two-dimensional frieze-like posing on demi-pointe. The dance featured Ernestine Day in a risqué leopard print fleshing that revealed her spectacular body and Shawn equally exposed, in a g-string and a cape draped on his elbows. A chorus of six girls costumed in extremely transparent violet pleated chiffon and wigs of an archaic Greek design first danced friezelike. Shawn entered, preceded by one boy, then another, each costumed in the briefest of g-strings. Two boys each carried a wine jug on their shoulders, but Shawn carried above his head a basket, six feet in diameter, overflowing with white, yellow, and orange flowers. (See Figure 4.3.)

Figure 4.3. Ted Shawn in costume for *Allégresse* (1926). Photograph by Mortenson, 1928. Denishawn Collection. Courtesy of the Jerome Robbins Dance Division, New York Public Library.

Photographs of Shawn in costume for *Allégresse* suggest a certain pleasure in the exhibitionism the dance allowed, a pleasure that also invited a Cuban critic to make an association between Shawn and a Parisian showgirl. One night after a performance he reveled in a description of a costume malfunction: "My *Allégresse* trunks break and my reputation literally hung by a thread!"[17] The increased display of his body during the Follies tour made him more conscious of his physique. He was particularly concerned with how he looked in his Shiva costume, especially with unsightly bulges that would form against his metallic trunks. He might have also been self-conscious now that he was intermittently sharing a hotel room with the younger Beckman. To manage his "disposition to fat," he began to alternate between a three-day orange juice fast and an egg and tomato diet.

Before leaving Havana, Beckman decided to serve as Shawn's business representative, a position he would hold for the next three years. He traveled with Shawn to Miami Beach to stay at the winter home of Shawn's Aunt Kate, and then to West Palm Beach where Beckman's father and relatives were visiting. Shawn sensed tension between Beckman and his father. He learned that Mr. Beckman's disappointment in his son stemmed from his son's relatively unstable professional life, which was due to the debts Beckman had incurred during his college years. Shawn went to lengths to give Beckman's father a picture of his son as industrious and disciplined in his new role as business representative.

Beckman lived up to Shawn's expectations. He left the tour for New York as home base to oversee some of Shawn's ongoing projects, including the construction of the Westport studio and Denishawn House, as well as the publication of his book *Gods Who Dance*, which was contracted with Dutton. Shawn marveled at how effortlessly Beckman made social connections and used his savoir faire to advance Shawn's professional agenda. Beckman could make things happen, like procure tickets for VIPs to sold-out shows, and talk about Shawn's vision to everyone from governors to fraternity brothers. One of Beckman's biggest coups for Shawn was brokering one of his long-standing pet projects, a dance-drama based on *Jurgen, A Comedy of Justice* by James Branch Cabell. He even arranged for Shawn to meet the author at his home in Richmond, Virginia. Upon hearing Shawn's plans to adapt his play, Cabell claimed, "Really, Shawn knows more about *Jurgen* than I do!"

The Ziegfeld Follies tour ended earlier than Shawn had anticipated, wreaking havoc on the Denishawn budget. Though they were no longer earning their salaries, they had to pay the cast (a total of $1,000) as well as carry the full salaries of Pearl Wheeler, Beckman, and Margerie Lyon. After the tour, Shawn, Beckman, and St. Denis drove to "The Bend," Shawn's family farm in Indiana to which he had not returned since he was a child and had witnessed the deaths of his three cousins. Most of the property had been destroyed by time and the elements, but Shawn found a four-poster bed that once belonged to his great-grandmother, grandmother, and mother. He asked to keep it and had it shipped to Denishawn House. Years later it would find a home in the farmhouse at Jacob's Pillow.

On July 9, 1928, Denishawn classes began at the Westport studio and in two different New York locations, at Denishawn House and downtown at the Carnegie Hall Studios. It was a very different Denishawn, however, in that Humphrey and Weidman had officially left the company that spring. As much as Shawn tried to incentivize both to stay, he could not offer the independence both artists desired. In her autobiography, Humphrey claimed that she left Denishawn in response to Shawn's alleged decision to implement a new policy that restricted enrolment of Jewish students into the company and school to 10 percent. It was the first time that Humphrey had heard "either director express a racial prejudice."[18] Shawn and St. Denis did in fact draft a new constitution for Greater Denishawn; however, it did not mention such a quota. Humphrey and Weidman established their own classes, taking many Denishawn students along with them. As with Martha Graham, who took over Shawn's teaching at Mariarden, Shawn felt betrayed by their decision to break with Denishawn. Shawn was convinced that Elsa Findlay, a Dalcroze teacher and one of Martin's friends, was jealous of Shawn and thus encouraged Humphrey and Weidman to turn against him. He began to use the word "enemy" to describe his former Denishawn students, especially those in the graces of John Martin.

Shawn had high hopes for his first summer at Westport. It was the beginning of a productive relationship between him and Mary Campbell, a pianist at the Braggiotti branch of Denishawn, who traveled to Westport to accompany a special program of Japanese dances Shawn presented to enliven the artistic climate. He even invited John Martin to attend, offering him a place to stay and a homemade meal. The hospitality came off as bribery to Martin, who came, but to Shawn's dismay did not write about his program.

Lacking the serious critical attention he enjoyed while on the Ziegfeld Tour, Shawn resorted to one of his publicity stunts from his early Denishawn days. To commemorate the couple's fourteenth wedding anniversary, Shawn purchased St. Denis a suite of jewels that French Emperor Napoleon had designed and given to Empress Josephine, who in turn had given them to a lady-in-waiting. The couple reimagined their duet *Valse Directoire* into *Josephine and Hippolyte* as a vehicle to display the jewels. Interestingly the new scenario was based on a historical love triangle between Napoleon, his empress, and her lover Hippolyte. The empress ultimately did not believe the emperor could deliver the power and prestige befitting an empress and instead wanted a lover—even if a commoner, as was the case. It was a revealing scenario, considering that St. Denis's journal entries at the time convey a sense of domestic bliss she experienced in the company of Beckman. She described an afternoon when Beckman had accompanied her to go shopping for a new dress and how she had pretended the entire time that Beckman was her young husband. In another entry she recalls walking in the Hollywood hills and seeing a thatched roof house. She uncontrollably sighed "Oh, Fred!" wondering if she would ever be the little woman, with a little house and a husband. Dancing the role of Josephine was the perfect vehicle for her to express her desire for two lovers: "an artistic husband and a civil husband."[19]

Shawn noticed St. Denis and Beckman were spending more time together, or in his words, she began to "work on him," leading him to wonder: "Would Fred also fall for that dynamic charm, and fall from his clear allegiance to me and his strong faith in me?"[20] Even as Beckman supported Shawn's professional ventures, perhaps more so than anyone had previously, Beckman undermined his emotional stability by refusing to acknowledge his feelings toward Shawn. Shawn lamented: "I know in his own way he is devoted to me—but if he would only say so just once in a while!"[21] Moreover, Beckman's desire to impress St. Denis often incited tension between her and Shawn. In one of their long conversations, Beckman bloviated to St. Denis about her professional rivalry with Shawn, an opinion she later repeated verbatim to Shawn in a letter: "Darling if you would ever face the fact that your destiny in life is to serve me and my career and be my subordinate you might find some happiness in life. Because this is truly your destiny, this is the only thing that you are meant to do."

Shawn retorted, "Well, Darling, I just don't see it that way."[22]

St. Denis realized that Beckman had irrevocably changed the power dynamic of their marriage, whereby Shawn would accept his subordination to her. She sensed that in Beckman's presence, Shawn was somehow a new man: "He is thin and he does now reflect more manly qualities than in all the years I was with him."[23] In fact, St. Denis seems to have understood the tacit relationship between Shawn and Beckman better than they themselves understood it. In a compassionate yet confrontational letter to Beckman that she drafted, though possibly never sent, St. Denis explicitly acknowledged his sexuality (or as she put it: "the fact of your life that you are homosexual or bisexual") and the apparent romantic chemistry between him and Shawn.[24] In an uncharacteristic gesture of selflessness, she even came close to giving the men she most loved permission to love each other:

> If Teddy does find his chief stimulus to strength, progress and self-reliance in his love for man rather than woman (and I am not for a moment negating the fact that he has had and at times needs the spiritual help of women such as Lillian and I hope he will always let me be to him) but if his real joy and harmonious relationship of both desire and work is really with men and he has at last become convinced that this would always have been had I not cut across the progress of his life with the need of my love then he must in all

honesty and fairness so take his <u>stand</u>. There is much understanding in the world of today. He need not feel that his life will be made difficult because his love life is not the regular biologic life of the world.[25]

Though she leaves unexplained how she expected Shawn to "take his stand," she seems to suggest that he make a public disclosure of his sexuality along the lines of "coming out." In all likelihood, she imagined an arrangement similar to that of Havelock and Edith Ellis, who broke away from the design of traditional marriage. Indeed, St. Denis goes as far as to warn Shawn that living under the false pretenses of heterosexuality was no longer an option lest he "pay the full penalty of denying [his] birthright," curiously figuring homosexuality not as a moral transgression but somehow, as a social entitlement, perhaps in hopes that Shawn's "stand" would free her to be with one of her love interests.

Whether she actually relayed her admonitions or only expressed them in the draft of the letter she kept tucked in her journals, St. Denis seems to have envisioned a more queer, more liberating relationship for Shawn or Beckman than either man seemed willing or able to envision for himself. Confronting Shawn and Beckman about their unspoken homosexuality led St. Denis to confront her own. In her journal, she observed how she has been the object of queer affection ("All men attracted to me have been bisexual or homosexual").[26] She then wondered if she herself was a homosexual or if allowing herself to be the object of desire–not only for homosexual men, but also for her assistant and dresser Pearl Wheeler—was itself a form of homosexuality:

> Some questions after all these years that I have to ask myself is what kind of sex enjoyment do I really want—do I really want because of some element in myself—the curiosity (perhaps) more in the hunt of the homosexual— am I homosexual myself—should I really aspire to be content with the hunt of another woman—is this really coming to it—or do I want the more masculine but still homosexual pleasure—in some manner which I can't even imagine.[27]

Years later, Shawn speculated about St Denis's lesbian attraction to Wheeler: "Between you and me, privately, it was apparent to me that it was inherently Lesbian, although so far as I know there was no overt expression of this. When there was any real question of choice, she belonged to Ruth body and soul—as maid, companion, general errand girl, as well as costumer, wardrobe mistress, costume designer, dancer—anything Miss R needed, Pearl tried to be that."[28]

Though sympathetic to Shawn's struggle to come to terms with his sexuality, St. Denis's own sexual desires ultimately took priority. One afternoon Shawn was in Beckman's apartment while he was away. He noticed a long letter that St. Denis had written to him and wondered: "What was she writing a long fat letter to him about?" Without hesitation, he read it. He immediately recognized the devotional tone from thousands of romantic letters she had written to him. She called Beckman her god, her ideal. She expressed how she looked forward to the day when she could call herself "Mrs. Fred Beckman," declaring that Shawn was never a real husband, but a little boy that she had mothered. St. Denis said that she had gone through the legal ceremony with her fingers crossed, and never considered herself married or bound by it in any way. Shawn was humiliated and unable to contain his anger, so he confronted both St. Denis and Beckman together, an event St. Denis would later describe as the "final denouement." Though she showed exceptional discretion in her book when discussing this "one awful night in Denishawn House" she also made it clear: "Ted had no more wish to wound me than I had to wound him."[29]

On an evening when they reportedly had met Mrs. Calvin Coolidge (who had just ended her run as US First Lady the week before) after a performance at Smith College, they toyed with the idea of a complete separation.[30] Shawn wrote, "Now that I have loosed you and let you go, you were never truly so 'my own.' "[31] Just as they mythologized their eugenic marriage, transforming their union into a basis for an entire artistic revolution, so, too, did Shawn make the dissolution of their marriage a reflection of their art: "Meet me daily in the Upper Air, my lovely and Beloved Siddha—there is nothing lost but the dross which would have kept us down."[32] It seemed Shawn even considered the idea of integrating Beckman into their marriage:

I feel that true love between us three would be a state of all three giving without demanding, withholding or prohibiting. But I am at work in the center—not the circumference on this. I have truly loosed you and let you go—there are no prohibitions in my heart regarding you—nor do I withhold anything I have to give you, either. But for years I have conceived of our relationship in a somewhat conventional mold—marriage. It took me long years to get this foolish idea beaten out of me. Now I know there is an impregnable relationship between us. I don't know its name or whether it can ever be named. Whatever you do, I shall not love you less—nor with-hold any expression of that love I can genuinely feel and give. I do feel desire for you and now I feel it for many others for I have opened my need to the Universe to see if a greater answer than I could ever dream of is not wanting to come to me. But I too am not physically fulfilling my desire for I want not a lesser fulfillment—but a greater.[33]

St. Denis fled to California, largely to escape the emotional turmoil. Reneging on her commitment to the Denishawn School, she began work on a play called *Light of Asia* in Hamden. She arranged and supervised a ballet for twelve but did not dance in it herself. The getaway also allowed her to spend time with her elderly mother, a meaningful way to pass the days given the upsetting news from Wheeler that she had no prospects for a tour in Europe.

Beckman stayed with Shawn, though made it patently clear that theirs was strictly a business relationship. They would meet only during busi-ness hours—no affection, no sex. Under the new terms of their relation-ship, Shawn grew frustrated with many of Beckman's ways that he had once found charming—his long-distance phone calls to friends in far away places, his endless chit-chat about the chic parties he would frequent. Shawn real-ized the impossibility of having a monogamous romantic relationship with Beckman: "His friends, and by friends, I mean the people he slept with, ranged from famous Broadway producers and their wives, sleeping with both of them at the same time, and these titled people of England who knew him would drift in, Texas millionaires that he had met somewhere."[34]

The debacle with Beckman seriously upended the plans for a Greater Denishawn. On account of their personal strife, for the first time since 1922, there was no plan for Denishawn to tour in the 1928–29 season, save for a few dates. Shawn secured a few performances in late fall with a scaled down en-semble, seeing that Humphrey and Weidman were now on their own. In fact, in September of that year, Humphrey and Weidman presented their own concert, accompanied by Louis Horst.

On April 15, 1929, Shawn performed a solo concert at Carnegie Hall, his first major appearance without St. Denis as a headliner. He was justifiably anxious about audience turnout and the critical response, especially in such a high-stakes setting. About his decision to produce a solo concert at this juncture of his career, he said: "I was so up against the final and ultimate wall, the jumping-off place, that I figured if I lost on this gamble—I really wasn't a suicide type—but I was still a good stenographer, shorthand, typewriting—I could be a good business secretary. My plan was to figure out a town big enough where I was not really well known . . . maybe particularly a town that had no particularly active dancing school. . . . I could surely find a job . . . as a private secretary. . . . I would just vanish."[35]

Ultimately, his professional concerns did not eclipse his personal confidence. Thanks to his orange juice diet, he was a lean 162 pounds and still tanned from a New Year's vacation in Jamaica that he had taken with Beckman, a mutually agreed upon respite from their newly established business-only relationship. Beckman served as stage manager for the Carnegie concert but limited his conversations with Shawn to production and press matters. Shawn threw down the proverbial gauntlet, deciding that if the concert were not a success that he would change his name, move to the Midwest, and become a stenographer. The ante on his success was raised higher yet by a *New York Times* article published a few months earlier by John Martin on the topic of dancing as "a man's art." Martin profiled three standouts from the new generation of men dancers—Charles Weidman and theater dancers Blake Scott and Jacques Cartier—whose careers "triumphed over old opposition." While recognizing the extraordinary talent of these dancers, Martin laments the absence of an apprentice system where such men might have benefited from the experience of masters, entirely disregarding that Shawn mentored Weidman for several years in his school and company. In conclusion, Martin acknowledged that Shawn "made a market for himself" and in the process "gained recognition for dancing as a career for men with grit and determination if not with his talent and vision."[36]

Shawn was gratified that Martin covered his 1929 solo concert with previews and an actual review. Martin offered a slew of praises about Shawn's technique and physicality—his strength ("dashing and alive"), endurance ("physical reserve . . . superb"), and style ("incisive and clean").[37] However, when concerning Shawn as a choreographer, Martin was rarely ever sincere or forthcoming. In fact, throughout the review, Martin seems determined to brand Shawn "an out-and-out romanticist," if only to then publish a follow-up article in two weeks that sounded the death knell to romanticism: "An Era Ends: Increased Opposition to Romantic Domination." In the article, Martin makes a critical distinction between romanticism and modernism in dance: "Where the dancer of the romantic school reacts to certain emotional stimuli and expects to get his effect from an audience by a sympathetic reaction, the modern dancer creates these emotional stimuli in terms of concrete form which he presents directly to his audience. He is himself the esthetic agent instead of being a semi-passive intermediary between the agent and the audience." Put another way, the difference is "to create instead of to interpret . . . an appeal to intelligence instead of merely to the emotions." The distinction was observed by other dance critics. Writing about Shawn's concert for the *Herald Tribune*, Mary F. Watkins noted, "Keen intelligence, objective vision, and a highly developed talent for observation and reproduction mark his performance, rather than vividness of imagination and his method is that flawless compound of fire and vigor and control which denote the first class artists the world over."[38]

These distinctions were made by analyzing Shawn's solo concert at Carnegie Hall against and alongside several new modern dances presented within a month's time of the concert, especially works by Shawn's protégés, including a concert by Martha Graham accompanied by Louis Horst and the premiere of Doris Humphrey's *Life of the Bee* at the Guild Theater. Martin praised Humphrey's dance as her most successful choreographic effort to date and "a major contribution to the meager repertoire of modern dance."[39] Upon further reflection, two weeks after the premiere, he goes further to say that "few dancers have a gift for composition which ranks with hers" and notes Humphrey's exceptional ability to choreograph for an ensemble. Martin similarly praises Graham for "a triumphant debut of her dance group in a recital."[40]

Shawn was less concerned about the critics' philosophical musings on "modernism" than he was about his ability to pull plausibly positive quotes from their reviews to include in his marketing materials, such as brochures and souvenir programs. This is not to say that Shawn was not interested in the debates about aesthetics, but his New York City appearances at Carnegie Hall and Lewisohn Stadium were foremost an investment he made to strengthen the Denishawn brand. As with most Denishawn productions in New York, Shawn's solo concert made no money, but production expenses were an investment in Shawn's artistic credentials, not to mention his visibility in the theatrical world. The Carnegie Hall concert was well attended: "Everyone who has any interest in the art of dance was there," Watkins declared. He also predictably received standing ovations and performed encores of his Spanish dances, which "brought down the house, as usual."

Perhaps because of the clear critical feedback on his solo concert, Shawn's new works for Denishawn's third appearance at the Lewisohn Stadium that August were decidedly more ambitious and experimental than ever. He presented a new work called *Fingal's Cave*, inspired by the legendary sea

cave on the Scottish island of Staffa, which has inspired many forms of literary and artistic expression. Shawn's dance was performed to live accompaniment of Felix Mendelssohn's overture "The Hebrides" (later known as
"Fingalshöhle"), op. 26, inspired by the composer's excursion to the cave in
1829. Shawn's visualization of the score focused on the romance between a
young couple set into motion by mythical sea creatures and nymphs, who
kept the cavernous stage of Lewisohn Stadium in perpetual motion with billowing waves of fabric, swirling skirts, and cascading ribbons.

After securing the rights from author James Branch Cabell, Shawn created a dance based on the satiric novel *Jurgen: A Comedy of Justice* (1919).
When Shawn first read the novel upon its publication, he cautioned his
students from reading it because of its obscene passages and sexual tone, but
he had since come to view Cabell's use of myth to provide commentary on
contemporary American life as inspiration. He described it as "a great allegory of Self-Indulgence," a topic that resonated with Shawn. He set the piece
to a two-piano version of composer Deems Taylor's musical interpretation
of the novel, a one-movement "tone-poem" about twenty-five minutes in
length, which had premiered in 1925 by Walter Damrosch and the New York
Symphony but never performed since.[41]

Pacific 231 (1929) was a dance for fourteen men, performed to the orchestral work of the same name by Arthur Honegger, that captured the intensity of the steam locomotive, introduced in 1923. Music critic Charles
D. Isaacson of the *New York Telegraph* was disappointed by the lack of precision in the group works, expecting more drill and formation of a Roxy,
Ziegfeld, or Dillingham.[42]

With these ambitious collaborations with composers, writers, and
filmmakers, Shawn was attempting to maximize the opportunity of working
with live musical accompaniment as well as to create works to music that
would appeal to Lewisohn's audiences of music aficionados. His efforts did
not impress Martin who merely repeated the claim that "interpretive dancing
is nowadays popular art, and a new radicalism has arisen to threaten it."[43]
Martin did not even mention *Jurgen* and in fact suggested that he had left the
concert before it was even performed.

Following Lewisohn, Shawn sent out a group of dancers led by Ernestine
Day under the Denishawn name for local appearances. He had to find
work for his dancers or risk losing them to other projects along with all the
time and energy he gave to placing them in Denishawn repertory. His own
prospects for work were bleak. Despite its signed agreement with Shawn and

St. Denis, the Follies management went out on tour with flamenco dancer "La Argentina" (Antonia Mercé) in 1929-30 instead of Denishawn. Shawn decided against pursuing legal action so as to avoid the risk of damaging his reputation in the field. This meant Shawn and St. Denis were out of work and in need of income outside of the school to meet mortgage payments. They agreed to a tour booked by Edward Lowrey (the predecessor to Daniel Mayer who had since died) and performed as a duet so as to avoid the overhead of a traveling company. And so, as in the beginning days of Denishawn, Shawn and St. Denis set out on tour with just four musicians and repertory of mostly solos, a suite of duets, and the bejeweled *Josephine and Hippolyte*.

To make the tour work, Shawn and St. Denis had to recalibrate their relationship. He wrote to St. Denis to convince her that their relationship was strained not by anger but by love and thus suggested another way of relating to one another: "It's just Roofie and Teddy—not husband and wife—not jealous lovers—not antagonistic artistic egos—not any cut + dried, labeled, pigeonholed relationship—but you and me—ever growing, ever fluid."[44] In his letters, Shawn finally expressed an independence and confidence that St. Denis had always tried to awaken in him, either by encouragement or threat: "I am a man—an adult, strong man—and that manhood is yours forever. Whatever else I am—and I am many things—these need not concern you—my real strength and perseverance are yours."[45] As was the case throughout much of their relationship, sex was the resolution to their personal and professional conflicts: "We still found complete and perfect physical communion—that never failed us, and many times when our minds had met in a deadlock, we resolved our differences, at least temporarily by going to bed together."[46]

They set out in mid-October 1929. On Saturday, October 26, two nights after "Black Thursday," when the signs of an impending stock market crash were beginning to show, they performed at the Greenbrier, a luxury resort in the Allegheny Mountains of West Virginia. Shawn vividly recalled the bustling activity of the audience in the ballroom that evening, if only because it was a stark contrast to the eerie silence that came over the resort the following morning, when practically all of its well-heeled members fled to the city to consult with their brokers and braced themselves for the financial disaster that lay ahead.

The crash on *Wall Street* came two days later on "Black Tuesday," changing the course of American history, including the spending habits that put even a modest operation like Denishawn into a huge debt, one from which it would never recover. Though the financial crisis did not immediately impact their previously scheduled dates for the duets tour, Shawn and St. Denis understood quite well what it would mean for the future of Denishawn, or lack thereof.

Shawn determined that the only way he would weather the coming storm would be to find a benefactor. Even in the most prosperous times in the United States, Shawn was always on the brink of insolvency. Fortunately for him, during the months leading up to the crash he had nurtured a relationship with the great modern artist and philanthropist Katherine S. Dreier who offered an escape from the grind of touring, the perpetual financial despair of Denishawn, and the rejection from the New York moderns. Shawn was only too eager to accept this offer, though it meant he would need to deny his well-exercised romantic reflex and fully embrace "modernism."

American Prometheus, 1929–1931

Ted Shawn ushered in 1929 with a three-week vacation in Jamaica with Fred Beckman. Never before had he taken such a long break purely for relaxation. Settled in a secluded fishing village on the island's north shore, he enjoyed nude sunbathing, swimming, and sleeping, without a single thought of choreography or scheduling. He even relieved himself of the burden to keep up his correspondence, except for a Christmas message to Ruth St. Denis. In the letter, he describes how he and Beckman spent Christmas Eve drinking cheap Jamaican champagne, taking a two-hour horse and carriage ride through town, and watching "the natives making whoopee." He assures her that they had not "marred their relationship" and are respecting each other's time and space, as well as promises that he is thinking of her. He even flatters her by saying he is performing her stunt of "walking upstairs backwards— but I am moving and it is up!"[47]

Among the small bundle of books he brought on the trip was *Western Art and the New Era* (1923) by Katherine S. Dreier, the influential artist, curator, patron, and crusader devoted to the internationalization of modern art. Shawn had corresponded with Dreier months earlier when she invited the Denishawn dancers to tea following the company's successful string of performances at the Brooklyn Academy of Music. Shawn enthusiastically accepted the invitation to speak with the influential Dreier about the "way the world of art is going and should go."[48] Shawn understood the potential value of her support. An accomplished artist, Dreier displayed two of her own oil paintings—*The Avenue, Holland* (c. 1911–12) and *The Blue Bowl* (1911)—in the groundbreaking 69th Regiment Armory Show in 1913, the first major exhibition of modern art in the United States and perhaps the most influential art exhibition ever mounted outside Europe. In 1920, along with artists Marcel Duchamp and Man Ray, she had founded the Société Anonyme, an organization dedicated to presenting modern art while educating the US public about this new genre. She wrote *Personal Recollections of Vincent Van Gogh*, "the first book on the artist in the English language and one of the first books published in America on the modern art movement."[49] Over the years she introduced many international artists to the American art scene and, most notably, curated the introductory solo shows for Alexander Archipenko (1921) and Wassily Kandinsky (1923).

Aboard the ship home from Jamaica, Shawn wrote to Dreier about her book's tremendous impact on him. Excited by her willingness to talk with him about his future projects, he obsequiously declared: "I feel as if my whole life were a preparation—an apprenticeship. I feel a mighty song foaming in me." Upon his return to New York, Shawn met with Dreier to present his ideas for three new dances along with sketches for their design, including plans for a work based on the Prometheus myth. He performed for her some of his choreographic sketches. They hit it off immediately, bonded by their shared missionary zeal for the arts, the nationalist undertones of their aesthetics, and their theosophy—that art is a moral matter. Moreover, Dreier felt a connection to Shawn over their shared history of physical lameness, which for both came during young adulthood—for him at seventeen, for her at eighteen. Dreier's lasted throughout her life. Shortly following their meeting, Dreier wrote to Shawn with an offer to finance the construction of the set (though not its design) for his Prometheus dance with funds from the Société Anonyme coffers. Grateful, Shawn accepted her choreographic advice but not her money, at least not immediately, though he offered a convoluted explanation as to how he would repay her should he ever need to borrow funds in the future. Within a month, Dreier had donated several hundred dollars toward the construction of a set for another of Shawn's new works. This donation came with a suggestion for the carpenter, as well as some choreographic feedback. "Personally what I felt needed most attention was the final pose or gesture, which at present is too conventional," she wrote to him. She suggested that "the study of your hands" also needed more attention: "At present they do not form the best silhouettes. They must be the culmination of the line."[50] Here she wanted Shawn to keep "unity" or "oneness" in mind to make sure there was continuity between the choreographic line and the set.

Their talk about Prometheus was an introduction to an important chapter in Shawn's life, one that would test his professional standing in the international arena. In their correspondence they would share updates about their respective art worlds and spiritual journeys, including many references to Dr. Pedro P. Pequeño, "the spiritual healer/movement coach."[51]

On January 3, 1930, Dreier held a tea at the Brooklyn Museum in honor of St. Denis and Shawn. By introducing them into her circle of modern artists, she hoped to widen her influence by bridging the visual and performing arts in the vein of Serge Diaghilev of the Ballets Russes and Rolf de Maré of the *Ballet suédois* (Swedish Ballet). So intense was her interest in recruiting Shawn into her stable of artists that in a modernist baptism of sorts, she renamed him "Rolf": "He has outlived the name Ted," she rationalized.[52] Shawn indulged her, often signing his letters to her in the diminutive "Rolfie." However, there was nothing diminutive about Dreier's vision for Shawn's future: "As Rolf you become master of your fate which is your destiny."[53] Indeed, in Shawn, Dreier saw not only the future of American modernism but also a modern spiritualism. In her analysis of Dreier's painting *The Psychological Abstract Portrait of Ted Shawn* (1929), art historian Robin Veder convincingly decodes the theosophic symbolism embedded in Dreier's use of line, shape, and color to reveal Dreier's conviction that Shawn was "one of the priests of theosophy's forthcoming race."[54] (See Insert Figure 4.4.) Indeed, one of Dreier's main interests in Shawn was how his dancing uniquely manifested a benevolent spiritual force, a power Shawn referred to as the "white magic of the dance." He wrote an entire essay on the topic in which he quotes author Ivan Narodny, who declared that "Dance is the only art which retains its ancient metaphysical power."[55] For Dreier, Shawn's "white magic" expressed "the now and its needs," forming a bridge between the aesthetic and the spiritual, especially in masculinist terms that Dreier favored.[56]

Soon after Dreier hosted St. Denis and Shawn for tea, she sent Shawn a check for $1,300 to underwrite his trip to Germany where he would introduce his brand of American dance as a solo artist. This was the first time the Société had supported a dance artist. Dreier also gave him $500 to cover Mary Campbell's travel and salary to accompany him. Shawn sailed to Hamburg on the SS *America* on February 13, 1930, a day later than originally planned owing to an explosion of a German luxury passenger liner the *Muenchen*. He traveled with Katherine S. Dreier and her sister Mary

E. Dreier, the prominent social reformer, who planned to visit relatives. Shawn was flattered by the fifty people who came to see him off, and his well-appointed stateroom filled with baskets of fruit, presents, and dozens of bon voyage telegrams, including one from Mei Lanfang. Aboard the ship, Shawn indulged in sleep and food and practiced his German with Dreier. He also performed his flamenco dance for the passengers at the ship's party.

Beckman went ahead of Shawn to arrange bookings and joined them when they landed in Plymouth, UK. Shawn was excited to see him, Dreier not as much. By this point, Dreier was outwardly upset about Beckman's indiscriminate use of letters of introduction that she had provided for him to present on Shawn's behalf to cultural leaders, theater owners, and art brokers. She grew wary of Beckman having any professional or artistic role in Shawn's life, apart from that of "a playmate."[57]

All three of them landed in Hamburg on February 24 and then traveled to Berlin, which served as home base for Shawn's time abroad. With only three weeks to rehearse before the premiere of *Prometheus*, Shawn and Beckman were able to find the perfect excuse for a quick escape from the Dreiers. They took a train to Cologne to oversee the design of the rock for the Prometheus set, which was under the supervision of Hans Strohbach, art director of the Cologne Opera. It turned out to be something of a special getaway. Late at night, they checked into a hotel room with a balcony overlooking the cathedral. That morning Shawn was mesmerized by the view of sunlight coming from behind its spires. The next evening, Shawn was treated to another light show inside the cathedral, as Strohbach took Beckman and Shawn to experience his design for the new modern lighting system that had just been installed in the cathedral. They sat alone in the cathedral for an hour as Strohbach experimented with his switchboard and the Dom-vicar played the organ.

As with his trip to Spain, Shawn was disappointed by the cosmopolitanism of the cities, which kept him from seeing people in folk or traditional dress, with one major exception. Shawn saw two tall, good-looking young men walking down the street in white trousers with flared, black velvet coats, wide brimmed black hats, and in one ear only, each had a large, filigreed silver earring. Strohbach explained that they were members of the carpenter and mason union called *zimmerleute*, which kept a tradition of traveling from one town to another singing and dancing folk songs and dances.[58] Strohbach took Shawn and Beckman to a small bar where these zimmerleute convened, giving Shawn a chance to meet and talk with them, hear them sing their songs, and buy them many a "boot full of beer," literally a life-sized glass boot filled with beer. It was precisely the type of folk fraternization Shawn craved.

Upon his return to Berlin, Shawn focused on his upcoming performances at the Bachsaal, the prestigious concert hall. With less than two weeks until opening night, he had to arrange for a costumer and a pianist. He also had to find rehearsal space, for which he went to the Wigman-Schule in Berlin (a branch of the Dresden school where Mary Wigman herself taught). He watched a class there and then met the school director, Margarete Wallmann, a founding member of a union for progressive dancers (*Deutsche Tanzgeneinschaft*). (See Figure 4.5.) Not yet twenty-six-years-old, Wallmann was an influential figure in the German dance scene, though her performing career was prematurely cut short by a hip injury. Before working with Wigman, she was herself a successful touring solo dancer as a teenager, performing mostly ballet. Only later in her career (at age seventeen) did Wallmann see Wigman perform, an experience that led her to commit to Wigman's radical approach to dance. She eventually joined Wigman's troupe, which included Gret Palucca and Harald Kreutzberg. Shawn was deeply flattered that Wallmann considered the Denishawn School to be "the greatest and only serious school in America" and that "all the worthwhile dancers in America" were its pupils.[59] Shawn invited her to watch him rehearse and was deeply moved by the "rare and beautiful way" she responded to his work.

Between rehearsals, Dreier vied for Shawn's attention, wanting to introduce him to her network of German artists. They traveled to Dusseldorf to meet painters Heinrich Campendonk and Ivo Pannaggi. Shawn was impressed with neither. About Campendonk's work he wrote: "His paintings were the kind of 'modern' painting that I do not care for—a grim looking cow, wandering through a black night scene, with now and then the four of hearts floating through space." In Munich, Dreier introduced him to Frau Hofrat Hanfstaeng, the American-born matriarch of an influential family in the arts and publishing. Her son Edgar was married to the famous mezzo-soprano Zdenka Fassbender, for whom Richard Strauss wrote the roles of Elektra and Rosenkavalier. Her son Ernst "Putzi" later became intimate with Hitler. Dreier had Nazi sympathies, too.[60]

Dreier also took Shawn to see Gret Palucca, the first "genuine" modern dancer. A former student of Wigman's, Palucca was by 1930 the director of her own dance school in Berlin and later performed in the dance ceremony of the 1936 Berlin Olympic games. On seeing her perform, Shawn wrote: "It felt as if a mule had kicked me in the solar plexus!" This was a

Figure 4.5. Margarete Wallmann and Ted Shawn at the Wigman School (Berlin, 1930). Ted Shawn Papers, Additions. Courtesy of the Jerome Robbins Dance Division, New York Public Library.

telling expression, describing Palucca's movement as negatively targeting what Isadora Duncan described as the body's site of liberation. Shawn found Palucca masculine and dynamic with great acrobatic control, but her style was diametrically opposed to what he was trying to achieve in dance. He characterized her dancing as a type of desecration for which he harbored "a deep instinctive hate." Yet again, Shawn and Dreier clashed over artistic sensibility.

The only positive introduction Dreier made to Shawn during the trip was Exzellenz von Kaulbach, the widow of Wilhelm von Kaulbach, Germany's greatest portrait painter, who twenty-five years earlier had painted Ruth St. Denis performing both her *Nautch* and *Incense* dances. A nobleman, Exzellenz von Kaulbach explained to Shawn that Ruth St. Denis was the only person from "the world of the theatre" that he ever deigned to host in his home. Shawn was touched to find that St. Denis's memory was alive all over Germany. Wherever he went, Germans showed him picture postcards of St. Denis that they had bought twenty-five years before and still cherished. He wrote to assure her that she continued to have a fan base in Germany.[61]

Shawn made his solo debut in Bachsaal, Berlin, on March 15. The sold-out audience included Dreier, Palucca, and Wallmann as well as the *tanztheater* founder Kurt Jooss, plus other composers, professors, and writers. Pearl Wheeler, "on leave" from her position as Denishawn company costume designer, was serendipitously in Berlin chaperoning an aspiring debutante named Eugenia Vandeveer, one of Shawn's former students from Grand Avenue. The two-hour program included a mix of his Spanish, Native American, and Greek dances, plus the premiere of *Prometheus Bound*.

The Bachsaal was not an ideal space to present dance, with its oblong house incorporating a balcony running along both sides and the rear. Only after a heated argument with the theater administration was Shawn permitted to drape a black curtain over the organ pipes at the back of the stage. Despite the production limitations, audiences generously received his *Invocation to the Thunderbird* and *Spear Dance Japonesque*. He counted three bows and an encore for each dance. His flamenco dances went over even better—five bows and three encores.

The audience response to *Prometheus Bound* was also surprising, though for an entirely different reason. A study in limitation, the dance portrays the Titan forerunner in a state of eternal torture for the benefit of mankind—a theme that increasingly informed his dances. In this variation, a near naked Shawn as Prometheus is shackled by the right wrist to a massive promontory, where each night an eagle tears out his liver, and each day it regrows. Tethered to the newly constructed set—financially underwritten by Dreier— Shawn strikes out against the eagle, writhes in pain, and tries in vain to escape his interminable fate. (See Figure 4.6.)

At the premiere, the dance was met with protestations from members of the audience during the performance. Shawn described the scene to St. Denis:

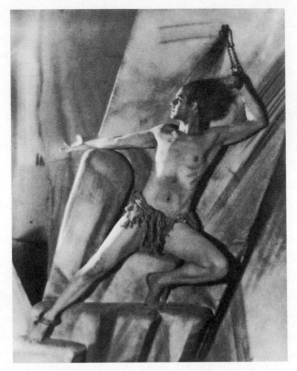

Figure 4.6. Ted Shawn in *Prometheus Bound* (1929). Photo by Ralph Hawkins. Denishawn Collection. Courtesy of the Jerome Robbins Dance Division, New York Public Library.

I thought the police would have to intervene. The audience broke into two camps, one side hissing and whistling, and the other side calling "Bravo" and applauding wildly. It seems that the "absolute dance" has ruled that anything in the nature of scenery is <u>out</u>, and especially on a concert stage. The reverberations have been coming in ever since—the critics with very few exception tore it limb from limb and nearly everybody has struck at it. Two people down stairs during the Grosse Pause which followed it were so nasty and loud in their dirty remarks that they were asked to leave and as they were being escorted out the whole audience rose and cheered and yelled things at them such as "You don't belong here, get out, you shouldn't have come anyway." Several other pointed arguments almost reached fist fights.[62]

In the immediate aftermath of the performance, Shawn described the protest in artistic terms, namely, a German distaste for Shawn's version of modernism. He explained: "'Absolute dance' is the one and only way to dance (according to modern Germany). You can have no scenery or props, no costume that means anything at all, and no gesture that has any dramatic or emotional significance."[63] Later and elsewhere, he explained that there were political motives behind the disturbance and that the protestors were "a group of Nazis, [that] even then exhibited an anti-American disturbance [and] were put out by the police."[64] "As a matter of fact," he wrote, "the National Party sent a group of young long haired intelligentsia to my concert to make a disturbance."[65] He characterized their outrage as a form of anti-Americanism stemming from the signing of the Young Plan in 1929, though Shawn never explains why he thought "Nazis" would target *Prometheus Bound* rather than the other dances on the program that evening.

Dreier tried to spread news of Shawn's success to America, likening the upheaval to the riots against the Ballets Russes at the 1913 premiere of Nijinsky's *Rite of Spring*. "It resembled more a political meeting than a dance recital," she wrote to her sister Mary, who had since returned home.[66] "The excitement at the performance itself was so great that—two people had to be ejected. This came as such an unexpected surprise to Shawn that it rather upset him because of his fatigue. The audience was the most brilliant which generally only attend operas—hardly an American."[67]

The demonstrations did not impede Shawn from completing his performance as Prometheus. After the dance, he composed himself and returned to the stage for *Gnossienne* (1919), which calmed the audience. The ritualistic *Bull God* (1930) did not go over so well, and later met with critical disapproval. *Siva* went over extremely well with Shawn taking about five bows in character. "I put on my shantung robe, the house lights were turned on, and for thirty minutes by the clock I kept going out for bows, hundreds having left their seats and crowded around the stage. Many people came back stage."[68]

After the premiere, Dreier hosted a supper for eighty VIPs at the posh Adlon Hotel. Frau Luise Wolff, Berlin's greatest patron of music, signed her name along with fifteen other eminent guests to a cable to St. Denis, penned by the editor of the influential newspaper the *Berliner Tageblatt*: "Shawn's debut, great success. Berlin does not stop applauding."

Shawn needed a break from the intensity of the Berlin performance, so he and Beckman took a "cheap little hotel at Potsdam for the weekend" to catch up on sleep, walk through the parks of the Sans Souci, take boat rides, and play cards.[69] He came to realize that despite the unexpected protest against him (or perhaps because of it), the concert was "a brilliant highlight" of his life, though he removed *Prometheus* and *Bull God* from the programs in other cities on the tour itinerary, replacing them with the crowd-pleasing *Ramadan* (1929) and *Mevlevi Dervish* (1924). Shawn then went on to perform his concert in Munich, where he received similarly rave reviews minus the Nazi protest. That is not to say that he did not also have his detractors. One reviewer unfavorably compared Shawn to Jodjhana, a Javanese performer who had been living in Holland for eight years, performing Europeanized versions of Javanese court dances, mostly women's roles in the *wayang* style. Shawn went to see Jodjhana for himself the day after his Bachsaal performance and was unimpressed with the "thin somewhat effeminate Javanese man."[70]

On the heels of Shawn's relative success in Berlin, Wallmann asked Shawn to play the title role in her upcoming production of *Orpheus-Dionysos*, the largest production scheduled for the Third German Dance Congress in June 1930. Wallmann had gathered over thirty solo dancers who would otherwise not have been able to appear at the congress, and formed them into "Tanzer-Collectif-1930." The production was conceived by Dr. Felix Emmel, who was the president of the Tanzgemeinschaft (an organization of the dancers of Germany). Emmel was Wallmann's former lover, and at the time, "her abject slave" according to Shawn, a dynamic that made him hesitate to accept this otherwise exceptional offer. Moreover, it would have been the first time Shawn had performed in a work choreographed by anyone other than himself and with anyone other than his own dancers. He was reluctant to submit himself to someone else's vision on such a high-profile stage as the congress, so he negotiated a plan with Emmel and Wallmann whereby he would compose his own solos and Wallmann would compose the group dances. Wallmann agreed to Shawn's conditions for participating in her dance for the congress. She even wrote to Dreier to ask for additional financial support for Shawn to extend his stay in Germany for the June congress, along with Fred Beckman and Mary Campbell.

Following the Munich performance, Dreier took a sojourn in Paris, leaving time for Shawn to travel once again. He took a brief trip with Beckman, Wheeler, and the Vandeveers to the Bavarian Alps to visit the castles of Ludwig II, "the mad king of Bavaria," to take in their murals depicting scenes from Wagner operas. Mother Vandeveer bought Shawn and Beckman coordinating Bavarian costumes—embroidered short lederhosen, plush hats with *Gamsbärte* (a tuft of hair), suspenders, socks, the whole gambit. They wore them all day, posing for photos of themselves in situ, some walking hand in hand. (See Figure 4.7.)

Back in Berlin, Shawn was anticipating his opportunity to see Wigman perform live, thinking it was the only way to understand the fascination with her. But then, he ran into American dancer Ruth Page, who was en route to Spain from Russia where she had just completed a tour. Her excitement about traveling to Spain during Holy Week convinced Shawn and Beckman to join her, even on their tight budget. Although Shawn did not want to miss Wigman, he really could not refuse the opportunity to revisit Spain with Beckman or the chance to gather new Spanish dance material, so they spontaneously boarded a train for a ten-day trip.

They arrived in Barcelona, meeting up with Page and revisiting Shawn's circle of friends and teachers. Unfortunately, Perfecto Perez, with whom Shawn had studied while in Spain in 1923, was in Naples, but that led him to Savall, another teacher from whom he received seven hours of private lessons, as well as three new dances choreographed especially for Shawn, all for the cost of $12. Savall flattered Shawn by saying that he could likely fool even gypsy dancers with the authenticity of his *cuadros*.

Shawn and Beckman followed Page south to Seville for Holy Week to find a flood of pilgrims. Shawn joined Page at one of her lessons from Realito and then Otero, which he thought was more valuable watching than actually

Figure 4.7. Ted Shawn and Fred Beckman in Weilheim, Germany, March 1930. Ted Shawn Papers, Additions. Courtesy of the Jerome Robbins Dance Division, New York Public Library.

taking. He also demonstrated his new dances for Otero, who was impressed. All remaining time was spent on high-intensity tourism of museums and cafés to see flamenco. Following yet another private class on Easter morning, Shawn and Beckman went to high mass at the cathedral and a *corrida*, both of which were attended by the entire royal family, including the King and Queen of Spain.

It was yet another magical trip with Beckman, but Shawn needed to get back to Germany for his upcoming performances in Dusseldorf (Schauspielhaus, April 25), Cologne (Opera House, April 27), and Hamburg (April 30). They traveled back to Berlin via Paris. Beckman's infatuation with the City of Lights cleansed the otherwise "bad taste" it usually left with Shawn. Upon his return, Shawn received a letter from Dreier who scolded him for taking the trip. She took offense that the money she had given him to extend his stay so he could perform in the congress was instead used for a trip with Beckman. Shawn shot back with a detailed accounting of his finances. Not even Dreier could bring him down. His performances were very well received, especially in Dusseldorf where critics uniformly hailed his performances as "a series of triumphs." (See Figure 4.8.)

Following the solo tour dates, Shawn went back to Berlin to begin rehearsals for *Orpheus-Dionysos*. By mid-June he had learned that Wallmann decided that she would play Euridice to his Orpheus-Dionysos. Shawn interpreted this decision as a sign of Wallmann's sexual attraction to him: "One of the things she wanted was to get into bed with me—but having a will of my own, and not wanting this—I managed to get my way."[71] He was determined to take advantage of this exceptional opportunity to increase his stature abroad, especially within the epicenter of German modern dance, as well as immerse himself in the culture, politics, and aesthetics of modern or "absolute dance." He approached the experience as a chance to get beneath the skin of German modernism—"its real source, direction, values and limitations." To that end, he relocated to a pension closer to the rehearsal studio, which turned out to be a boarding house for patients undergoing psychoanalysis. While there, a visiting psychoanalyst from England diagnosed Shawn with "infantile narcissism."[72] Shawn joked that it was sometimes hard to distinguish between the mental patients and the modern dancers, but what was clear was the value of state sponsorship of the arts. The Third German Dance Congress was funded by the city of Munich. Though the dancers rehearsed and performed without salary, their travel and board was covered by municipal funds. Emphasizing the power of the collective, this particular conference was dedicated to dance

Figure 4.8. Illustration of Ted Shawn and Katherine S. Dreier. Denishawn Scrapbook, vol. 20. Courtesy of the Jerome Robbins Dance Division, New York Public Library.

groups, with the minor exception of a limited program of solo performers. Wallmann put together an ad hoc group of otherwise solo performers to serve as a chorus for the production. The cast was essentially composed of Wigman students and disciples who were reluctant to accept Shawn, though he was determined to win them over. Shawn tried to comport himself to gain their trust and respect, both in and out of the studio: "I put on none of the airs of a star, was simple, unaffected, obviously concentrated on getting the finest possible results for the group; as a whole, as well as showing myself to advantage. And this attitude gradually broke down all barriers, and they took me to their heart."[73]

Shawn was a paragon of discipline, but even he was amazed by the work ethic and commitment of the German dancers. They exhibited a drive and focus during rehearsal that he had never before encountered. "The pre-war military discipline has found a haven in the dance training," he reported back to St. Denis. He marveled at how they would spend up to eight hours daily in rehearsal, sometimes dedicating several hours to perfect a two-and-a-half-minute sequence of choreography. He was stunned how the ensemble of thirty people would rehearse thirty-two measures of choreography more than thirty-two times. Even with its diverse repertories and unrelenting touring schedule, Denishawn's rehearsal practices paled in comparison to those of their German counterparts.

The German dancers were unlike Denishawn socialites in other ways. Once Shawn was able to move beyond the superficial observations, such as their less-disciplined rituals of hygiene, he began to understand deeper differences. He noticed that the eight men in the group were poor, more so than the women. They had little money for cigarettes or travel. Some had to walk miles to get to rehearsal. The one exception among the German dancers was a young Dutch baron who was attractive, quiet, and gentlemanly. One night, Shawn and Beckman did the rounds of the famous nightclubs of Berlin and found the baron at Johnny's Night Club, "a place where men, still in their ordinary masculine street clothes, danced. With each other!"[74]

For all of the respect Shawn gained for the dancers, he never developed any respect for the work itself, not even that of Wigman. Shawn eventually attended one of her solo concerts in Berlin. After the first three numbers, Shawn turned to Wallmann and Emmel in stunned amazement that the dances lacked "design, architectural structure, real content or meaning." Wallmann and Emmel somewhat agreed with Shawn, though they promised that her older dances were better. Shawn also commented on Wigman's looks and her masculine movement, which he found "just as repulsive as feminine movement by a man dancer." He elaborated:

For instance she did a "Whirling Dance" which was created also at a later date than my own "Dervish Dance" although it was heralded in Germany as something never before done. And she tired, traveling aimlessly all over the stage and she did nothing but whirl—there was no theme, significance or idea back of it. Then when she got tired of whirling and couldn't think of a way to end the dance, she just flopped down on the stage, full length. In my "Dervish" the technical stunt of the 4-1/2 minutes of whirling, disciplined by remaining on one spot, is justified by the theme of the Dervish going through an ancient ritual to achieve union with God—and this struggle between the pull of the senses and the spiritual aspirations is taken care of by the movements of the head, arms, and torso; and at the end, instead of exhaustion, I went into a finale of double speed, showing an exaltation and spiritual triumph.[75]

His disappointment with Wigman's performance emboldened him to experiment with modern choreographic ideas. He wrote to St. Denis to describe his approach to choreographing his role in *Orpheus-Dionysos*: "I am hunting for those movements which are truly out of my own soul and yet which are in harmony with the German key. I have all keys within me—they have but few—and so it is easier for me to play that key which they can play."[76] Seeing that the power of the German dance movement came from "not only one German ballet, or group, but many," he acknowledged the criticism that his vision for a singular American ballet, composed of all Americans, was "too limited."[77] Based on the success of the Germans, he became convinced that only with "American solidarity" could American dance progress based on the success of the Germans: "Their whole movement is only ten years old. And already they have a dozen big all-German dance groups many of which have city or government support, and an interest and spiritual support of writers, philosophers, artists and musicians that turns me green with envy. With such concentration of attention the most mediocre talent can go to great lengths here."[78]

Shawn's unexpected embrace of German expressive dance was driven more by commercial opportunity than aesthetic conversion. Throughout his time in Europe, he sought ways to capitalize on the interest in German dance back home. He considered inviting the influential movement theorist and choreographer Rudolf Laban to teach at Denishawn but learned "that he is a great heart, but a poor teacher and very erratic and impractical."[79] Once Shawn learned that impresario Sol Hurok was set to produce a "scratch tour" of Mary Wigman in the United States, he invited Margarete Wallmann to teach at Denishawn on two conditions. First, he required that she secure a letter from Wigman herself declaring Wallmann "the first authorized representative to visit America who could properly teach her method" and permission to publish the letter in all press, advertisements, and brochures. Second, he asked that no one except for Wallmann, not even Wigman herself, to teach the Wigman method in the United States and that all teaching inquiries for lessons be exclusively referred to Wallmann, so as to capture all of the attention and profits from Wigman's great following. He urged St. Denis to write to Wallmann to help recruit her to Denishawn, promising that their affiliation with Wallmann would improve their school's luster: "Wallmann will give John Martin-Doris-Charles-Martha quite a shock when they see how she estimates them in comparison to us."[80] With Wallmann on faculty, Denishawn would essentially become a Wigman franchise that would "out-modern" the American moderns.

The artistic inspiration Shawn took from Germany came not from the stage but from the art studio. Early in the rehearsal period for Orpheus, Wallmann relayed a request to Shawn from the famous sculptor Georg Kolbe (1877–1947) to observe Shawn's rehearsal and sketch him in motion. Shawn agreed, despite the rather unusual condition that Shawn not engage with the sculptor beyond an initial introduction. Plus, Shawn also had to promise not to ask to see any of his sketches. As soon as the session started, Kolbe began to furiously sketch on a 16x20 sketch block, asking Shawn to hold whenever he saw a position or shape that interested him. Shawn was excited to see how his physique inspired Kolbe, and it took every ounce of control for him to refrain from asking to view the results.

Inspired by their first encounter, Kolbe invited Shawn to meet at his studio to embark on a sculpture. The studio was filled with about fifty sculptures, all life-sized figures with a godlike nobility. Shawn felt like he was in "a race of super-men." Shawn went to Kolbe's modern two-storied studio each morning for four hours (with a cigarette break at midday) to pose naked on a stand. Shawn had never stood motionless for such a long period of time. At the end of their time together, Kolbe reportedly told Shawn that if he could he would never seek out another model besides Shawn. Shawn finally saw the results. He was impressed by the life-sized sculpture Kolbe created. Katherine S. Dreier, however, hated it. (See Figure 4.9.) Shawn took the chance to ask whether he could see the sketches. Kolbe immediately agreed, laying out over 300 sketches across the studio floor. He invited Shawn to take as many as he pleased. Shawn knew their value yet limited himself to six, which Kolbe signed. (See Figure 4.10.)

Shawn hit an artistic stride by mid-June. He was in the thick of rehearsals for *Orpheus-Dionysos*, getting along with Beckman, and now in possession of valuable Kolbe sketches that he could sell to finance his next project. Then arrived a twenty-four-page letter from St. Denis, the first he had heard from her or anyone at Denishawn in weeks. St. Denis asked Shawn for a divorce, an entirely predictable response to a letter Shawn had sent to her weeks prior that described his romantic getaways with Beckman. The divorce proposal was likely also a result of mounting pressure from a man named Charles with whom St. Denis had begun a romantic relationship in the fall. In her

Figure 4.9. Sculpture of Ted Shawn by Georg Kolbe, Berlin, 1931. Photograph by Margrit Schwartzkopff. Ted Shawn Collection. Courtesy of the Jerome Robbins Dance Division, New York Public Library.

journals, St. Denis wrote how "C." often brought up the topic of marriage, once prompting her: "Suppose you were not already married. Would you marry me?"

St. Denis begrudgingly answered, "That's a stupid question."[81] But the invitation to imagine a life unmarried to Shawn was hard for her to resist. When Charles presented St. Denis a "love ring" to symbolize their "spiritual marriage," she decided against seeing Charles again until she had a "clearer vision" and in that pursuit, wrote to Shawn to ask for a divorce. In her journal, she wondered: "Teddy, Fred, Charles . . . there must be a divine pattern?"[82]

Shawn knew about Charles. He even sent cordial greetings to him in his letters to St. Denis. Her divorce plea, however, made Shawn very anxious. He responded stoically, telling her that he had read her lengthy letter out on the balcony while sunbathing and waited several days to reflect before forming a response. He arrived at the following:

Figure 4.10. Georg Kolbe Drawing of Ted Shawn (1930). (*In memory of Ted Shawn, from a grateful Georg Kolbe, June 1930.*) Joseph E. Marks Collection. Courtesy of Houghton Library, Harvard University.

> I have tasted a condition of life which I have never known before and which feeds my growth as an artist. I believe that your own real center is in your work and if you can find a condition which feeds, stimulates and strengthens your growth and productivity—you should have it and I want you to have it. If it seems necessary for you to have a legal divorce to clear up something in your own state of mind, I shall of course not fight it—for I truly want you to get to the place where I am.[83]

Decades later, Shawn was cavalier about describing the subtext of his response: "Darling, if that's it, if you want a divorce I will do everything in my power to facilitate it. I'll do anything that's necessary, I'll be caught in 'fragrant delight' as they call it, or I'll go to Reno or anything. I'll even financially pay the bill."[84] St. Denis was furious at his terse response to her soul-baring letter.

Shawn had little choice but to grant her request to divorce, if only to avoid "a very dirty affair," figuring that he would have to "accuse her of adultery or something" to contest her motion. He considered challenging the divorce on grounds of desertion: "Some said, well desertion if she had left my bed and board, which by God she did. She walked right out, and refused to come back." But ultimately, he weighed the damage that a legal proceeding would inflict on his professional career: "I had the feeling—look everybody will say . . . I was the younger man, I'd married her, she was famous and I was unknown. Then I used her to build my reputation."[85] His explanation, of course, elides the consequences that would arise from her likely rebuttal: that he, too, was adulterous, mostly with men.

About the same time Shawn and St. Denis were seriously grappling with the possibility of a divorce, one of his former students and dancing partners Ernestine "Tini" Day arrived in Germany to participate in the Third German Dance Congress, finding herself with a coveted spot on the only program dedicated to solo performers. Shawn shared his anxiety with her about what a divorce would mean for his career and proposed that the two join forces as a dancing partnership. He also proposed marriage, should St. Denis hold him to his promise for a divorce. "Tini" agreed. They made the agreement with no pretense of romance, suggesting that he might have been frank with her about his homosexuality and untraditional arrangement with St. Denis. He worried that people would think that he had left St. Denis for a younger dancer. Though Shawn and Day never married, they did make good on their arrangement to form a successful dance partnership, based in part on their time together at the congress.

During the congress, Shawn rehearsed every day, thus he was unable to attend the lectures and symposia. He regretted missing them when he heard about the intense debates between dancers about art. During one symposium, one critic allegedly attacked another with a razor, and the victimized critic in turn tried to commit suicide with said weapon. But Shawn was focused on making the best possible impression, especially when he had heard that Wigman and her group would have to cancel their appearance at the congress, thus making *Orpheus-Dionysos*—featuring his choreography and performance—the biggest feature.

Orpheus-Dionysos (A Dance-Drama in Four Parts) by Felix Emmel was presented on Sunday, June 22, 1930, at the National Theatre in Munich. In the piece Emmel explored the idea of Orpheus as a possible forerunner to Dionysius, with aspects of Apollo. He set the piece to an arrangement of

Gluck's opera *Orpheus*, that omitted the vocal component, which he justified by citing Gluck's own rearranging of the opera into a one-act drama. He
then arranged the Gluck opera to fit the pattern of the dance interjected with
sections of drumming. It was an hour long.

Shawn had previously created his own version of Orpheus and Eurydice
for the Berkeley pageant—a romanticized version complete with lyre,
sandals, and wreath. This collaboration with Wallmann was markedly different. Orpheus was neither a singer nor a lyre player, but instead a dem-
igod with magical powers. The photos of the performance look like film noir,
with Shawn's striking asymmetrical shapes brooding over Wallmann before
a huge pyramid of stairs that serves as a portal between the underworld,
the Elysian Fields, and the human plane. (See Figure 4.11.) John Martin of
the *New York Times* traveled to Munich to review the congress but entirely
ignored the production and Shawn's presence. His review instead focused on
the festival's disorganization.

After the performance, Shawn was able to see a few other programs, to
which he had a visceral negative reaction. The highlight for him, it turned
out, was attending a movement choir at the Laban School in Essen. There
he watched workers from munitions factories—middle-aged men with
their wives and families—move in intricate kaleidoscopic patterns in time
with a drum, all a result of free classes in "Tanz-Gymnastic." Shawn found
the experience "vital and interesting . . . and saner than anything else in
the whole Congress." He was beside himself that the entire program, and
dance in education, was supported by the German Ministry of Culture.
A choreographer for both vaudeville and pageant circuits, Shawn thought
he had understood the power of mass spectacle, but never before had he
choreographed for a mass of equals. There was a power in the group that he
came to understand not only from Laban's movement choir but also from
Wallmann's *Orpheus*.

Ultimately, the trip did not fulfill Dreier's expectation that Shawn would
adopt the values of her favorite German modern artists though he was grateful
for the artistic and professional relationships he developed on his own with
Wallmann and Kolbe. Shawn left Germany without gaining a new appreciation for German modernism. Unwilling or unable to find value in the formal
experimentation and with a negative view of its core values, he wrote: "Dance
must be 'abstract' 'pure' 'free'—it must have no narrative, racial, dramatic,
literary or other content—but must just be dynamic movement for its own
sake. The result was that in their frantic search for movements which did not

Figure 4.11. Ted Shawn with German dancers' group in *Orpheus-Dionysos* (Choreography by Shawn and Margarete Wallmann) in Berlin, 1930, for the Third German Dance Festival. Ted Shawn Collection. Courtesy of the Jerome Robbins Dance Division, New York Public Library.

look like anything else on earth, they achieved sheer insanity of movement, ugly, grotesque (which is far different from distortion) and clinical movement."[86] Later, he would characterize his relation to German modernism as "the very antithesis of everything I stood for."[87] He did not profit from the tour. In fact, he had to cable home to inquire about borrowing $1,500 from his life insurance account to cover costs.

On their return trip to New York, Shawn and Beckman stopped in London, and there the two once again renegotiated the terms of their relationship. Their relationship was as close to a romance with a man as Shawn had known until that point, but Shawn was sure it had no future: "There was no real happiness or security or any kind of a life with Fred."[88] Beckman stayed involved with Shawn in a strictly business capacity and continued to work business hours at Denishawn House after their return. St. Denis was increasingly frustrated with their ongoing involvement, the depths of which she conveyed in her journals: "I ran away when Ted and Frank were in the house—I could not conquer the pain and limitation that seeing them, hearing their voices, and wondering about them continually bought me."[89] To Shawn's utter perturbation, she began to express her frustration beyond her diaries to mutual friends, threatening to name Beckman as a co-respondent in her divorce complaint, even as she continued to spend time with Charles.

Beckman was gone by Christmas 1930, having left to chaperone some millionaire's alcoholic son on a trip around the world. Beckman later married three times. The second Mrs. Frederic W. Beckman was Hazel Bache, the daughter of Jules Bache, the affluent financier and a major donor to the Metropolitan Museum of Art. His marriage into one of the highest echelons of New York society affirmed Shawn's sense of Beckman's social climbing skills.

Shawn maintained a cordial relationship with Beckman's mother. She always came to see Shawn whenever he performed in Chicago and whenever possible, he visited her at home in Kankakee, Illinois. In early 1935, she wrote Shawn to ask for his prayers as she convalesced from a serious gall bladder infection. Shawn wrote to promise that he would visit her in a few weeks when he was in the Chicago vicinity, and he did so, to hand deliver to her a flowering plant. A weary woman answered the door and told Shawn that Mrs. Beckman had died just two days earlier. Shawn went inside to pay his respects to the grieving family, including Fred Beckman who was upstairs. They went outside to talk, and Shawn noticed how considerably worn down he was. He was disappointed but not surprised to hear that Beckman had not seen his mother in over a year, nor had he visited her while she was ill.[90]

Following their accidental reunion at Mrs. Beckman's funeral, Shawn and Beckman kept in touch, occasionally meeting when Shawn was in town with his men's group. Sometime after 1947, Shawn heard that Beckman had died peacefully, though prematurely, at his home in Scottsdale, Arizona. Though sad, Shawn was grateful for their last visit together at Beckman's home in Princeton, New Jersey, after a benefit for Jacob's Pillow. Seated beside a fireplace, Shawn had finally articulated all the unspoken affection he had withheld during their time together: "Every memory I have of you is positive. You gave me what I needed when I needed it. You gave me a pure undiluted faith in myself. You always said to me, 'Never doubt you are a great artist in your own right.' I believed it, the world believes it, don't you ever disbelieve it. You sustained me through the worst crisis of my life, and I will always be grateful to you, always remember you with love and affection."[91]

Shawn thought: "If I had the craftsmanship to be a good novelist I think the story of his life would be a fascinating one, and today it could be told in more detail than it could have been when we first met him."[92] This is especially true of Shawn's time with Beckman in Germany, about which he noted: "It was a great chapter."

The Price of Pioneering, July 1930–March 1933

On July 5, 1930, Ted Shawn returned from four months in Europe determined to confront the inevitable end of his marriage to Ruth St. Denis and their Denishawn school and company. The confrontation turned out to be more civil than he had imagined it might be. Over a cup of tea, they reached an agreement on the terms of their divorce, then planned a final Denishawn tour. They also decided that the school would remain open one more semester to honor the invitation they extended to German dance teacher Margarete Wallmann to teach at Denishawn. Within a month's time, they met with a lawyer to review their agreement, but stopped short of memorializing the terms, which made it possible for St. Denis to try to renegotiate the terms of their informal divorce plan. From time to time her desire for a legal divorce would surface, keeping Shawn in a constant state of financial, emotional, and artistic vulnerability.

There was little time for Shawn to contemplate the future of his personal and professional life, as he had to attend to immediate obligations, especially the company's commitment to perform at Lewisohn Stadium for the fourth time since 1925. Shawn was eager to present his *Rhapsody*, a group dance for an all-male ensemble, as well as new works such as *Geometric Dance* to music by Max Reger, and *Bavarian Dance*, a frivolous number based on the popular German *laendler* dance that showcased the authentic costumes he had acquired in Germany. St. Denis premiered her Cambodian dance-drama *Angkor Wat*, which she had worked on during Shawn's time in Europe. To please their fans, Shawn and St. Denis agreed to perform the period piece *Josephine and Hippolyte*. Shawn did not think the program was strong but was pleased that it broke attendance records nonetheless.

To gather his thoughts and plot next steps, late in the summer of 1930, Shawn and Beckman spent a weekend with their friend Goddard Dubois and his mother at the family's Forest Farm, a 1,200 acre "gentleman's farm" near Winsted, Connecticut. Shawn was on the lookout for a new property where he could build a school since his Westport studio venture had proved un-successful. Though fond of attending theater, Westport residents were reluc-tant to have their children train for a life on the stage. Plus, Shawn could not tolerate the flies that swarmed the riverfront studio. The Berkshires seemed like the perfect place to relocate. Goddard introduced Shawn to family friend Arthur E. Morgan, president of Antioch College, from which Goddard had just graduated. Morgan owed a farm nestled in the Berkshire Hills that he was eager to sell.

The eighteenth-century homestead lay on 150 acres of wood and meadow that was former Mohican territory. It was situated in Becket, just nine miles east of Lee, Massachusetts, a small town settled after the Revolution by farmers unfazed by the land's inhospitability to agriculture. Indeed, Lee sits on the hardest granite in the country. Jacob Carter and family first settled on the property in 1790 and built the main saltbox farmhouse, which remained in the Carter family for five generations. In the mid-1800s, it served as a stop on the underground railroad for fugitive slaves making their escape to Canada. Around 1909, the Carters sold the property to the Morgans. By the time Shawn arrived, the property was overgrown with waist-high weeds and blackberry brambles were growing up through the rotting floorboards of the patio. The three existing barns were weather-beaten. The main house had not been lived in for five years and had gone unpainted for many more. Inside he came upon a letterhead that read "Jacob's Pillow, A Mountain Farm— Arthur E. Morgan Prop." Shawn inquired about the biblical reference in the property's name, learning that since sometime before the Revolution locals had referred to the main road east of the property (US 20) as "Jacob's Ladder," a reference to the Old Testament vision that Jacob had of a ladder that connected the earth to heaven, thus allowing angels to traverse the terres-trial and celestial realms. In the Berkshires, Jacob's Ladder was an old wagon

Figures 2.7 and 2.8. Ruth St. Denis and Ted Shawn in *Garden of Kama* (1915) from the "Land of the Best" photo-essay in *National Geographic*, April 1916. Autochrome by Franklin Price Knott. Courtesy of the Jerome Robbins Dance Division, New York Public Library, and Byam Shaw illustration from *Garden of Kama and Other Love Lyrics from India* (1901).

Figure 2.12. Ruth St. Denis and Ted Shawn in an Egyptian dance from *A Dance-Pageant of Egypt, Greece, and India* (1916). Photograph by Arnold Genthe. Denishawn Collection, Jerome Robbins Dance Division, New York Public Library.

Figure 3.6. *Denishawn Magazine, A Quarterly Review Devoted to the Art of The Dance*, vol. 1, no. 1 (1924), with illustrations by Bernice Oehler and logo by Rose O'Neill.

Figure 4.4. Katherine S. Dreier's "The Psychological Abstract Portrait of Ted Shawn" (1929), oil on canvas (30" x 25"). Purchased in honor of the Museum's current and former docents, 96.29. Munson-Williams-Proctor Arts Institute. Photo Credit: Munson-Williams-Proctor Arts Institute / Art Resource, New York.

Figure 5.14. Ted Shawn as Montezuma in *O, Libertad!* (1937). Photograph by John Lindquist. John Lindquist Collection. Courtesy of Houghton Library, Harvard University.

Figure 5.21. "Air" from *Dance of the Ages* (1938). Photograph by John Lindquist. Courtesy of Jacob's Pillow Dance Festival Archives.

Figure 6.12. Ted Shawn in *Atomo, the God of Atomic Energy* (1950). Photo © Jack Mitchell. Courtesy of the Jacob's Pillow Dance Festival Archives.

Figure 6.16. Ruth St. Denis and Ted Shawn in a pose from *Siddhas of the Upper Air* (1964) in the tea garden at Jacob's Pillow. Photography by John Lindquist. Courtesy of Jacob's Pillow Dance Festival Archives.

Figure 6.19. Ted Shawn at home in Eustis, Florida. John Christian and Ted Shawn Photographic Collection. Courtesy of the Jacob's Pillow Dance Festival Archives.

Figure 6.21. Ted Shawn and his roses. Ted Shawn Papers, Additions. Courtesy of the Jerome Robbins Dance Division, New York Public Library.

road that zig-zagged up and down the hills, bridging Chester to Pittsfield and towns in between. The farm's name, "Jacob's Pillow," was a reference to the massive boulder outside the farmhouse, which the devout Christians who lived in the area imagined as the spot where Jacob rested his head and experienced his divine vision. A former theology student, Shawn knew that when Jacob awoke from his sleep, he realized that where he lay was the Gate of Heaven and thus consecrated his rocky pillow into an altar, a site for both sacrifice and worship. This farm thus stood on holy ground, with a rock-solid foundation and a revolutionary history. Shawn immediately placed a $500 down payment on the property and soon sold his Westport acre to pay for the rest.[93]

Shawn spent the remainder of the summer at Denishawn House preparing for the arrival of Margarete Wallmann. He threw her a welcome party upon her arrival on September 21, 1930, perfectly timed with the announcement of Mary Wigman's upcoming US tour. He publicly introduced her as "Germany's Newest Genius" in a *Dance Magazine* feature, which profiled Wallmann's discovery of dance as well as her professional relationship to Wigman, emphasizing that she ran the first authorized Wigman school in Germany. Shawn was trying to draw students eager to study German expressionism to Denishawn. This was nearly a year before Hanya Holm established the Mary Wigman School in New York.

Shawn solicited Wallmann's advice on two new and quite different solos: an abstract, "metaphysical" dance and an interpretation of American folk songs. *The Divine Idiot* (1930) was inspired by Plato's "Allegory of the Cave," a philosophical exploration of relationships between truth and freedom. Based on the allegory's central figure of an escaped slave, Shawn's *Divine Idiot* is a charismatic leader who is persecuted for his attempts to convince his fellow man that there exists a higher truth than what he can know from sensory experience alone. Set to four different études by Alexander Scriabin (op.11, nos. 16, 4, 20; op. 65, no. 3), the work is organized in four sections that trace the Idiot's journey from enslavement to sensory knowledge to illumination by reason.

The Divine Idiot was a radical choreographic departure for Shawn. The dance's subtext of a man who risks becoming a social pariah in order to achieve freedom resonated with Shawn's recent separation from St. Denis. It also resonated with his determination to make dance exclusively for men. Either interpretation could be corroborated by Shawn's own explanation that he decided he could no longer make "boy meets girl stories."[94] Whatever Shawn had in mind, his body had a whole new expression. For the first time,

Shawn ventured to dramatize internal conflict rather than outwardly display beauty, project courage, or gesture with some invisible force. Performed shirtless and in pants, Shawn signaled a new direction even in costuming choice. His reliance on pantomime was reserved to a few meaningful gestures, such as his lumbering walk onstage with arms behind his back as if in manacles. In the last section he repeats a wild arm gesture toward the wings of the stage, as if to direct his slaves to turn their heads to the light, to life beyond the cave. Shawn's abiding attention to shape and line, whether the statuary aspect of his poses or his deliberate use of pathways on stage, gave way to the expressive tensions within, whether shuddering, shaking, or throwing around passive weight. Most unusual for a Shawn solo, *Divine Idiot* ends with an exit offstage rather than a dramatic pose onstage, a difference that might mean nothing more than that Shawn at long last had a reasonable expectation that he would perform the dance in traditional theaters with wings.

In a somewhat opposing choreographic vein, *Four Dances Based on American Folk Music* (1933) was a solo vehicle for Shawn to demonstrate the dynamic, rhythmic, and tonal range of American folk music and experience. The dance opened with a jovial heel-toeing jaunt about the stage to an old fiddler's breakdown "Sheep 'n Goat Walking to the Pasture," followed by a somber yet passionate pleading to the negro spiritual "Nobody Knows the Trouble I've Seen." The Methodist revival hymn "Give Me That Old Time Religion" took its choreographic cue from Shawn's dance liturgy, with its euphoric spinning and heaven gazing. To the strains of the "Battle Hymn of the Republic," Shawn mustered the illusion of a one-man army making a slow yet steady march into the battlefield, but there was more hymn than battle in this final dance.

These new solos formed part of the program for "Ted Shawn and the Denishawn Dancers," which toured from October 1930 through February 1931 and garnered Shawn some of his best performance reviews to date. Critics seem to have acclimated to seeing men dancing on the theatrical stage as an art rather than as a novelty act. Shawn's tour in Germany no doubt helped shape the new critical reappraisal of him as an artist, and a modern artist at that. One enthusiastic critic noted:

> There can be no question that his late German tour was, for him, more than an occasion to accept triumph. It was a time of study. The impress of radical German thought and of neighboring Russian art exploration is sharply upon his program. His fresh numbers click with the machine, carry the

clean angular lines of the new modernism. The old familiar dances, picturesque and multicolored, tinged with the romance of twilight and roses,
have been pared in his scheme.[95]

Some critics were inclined to celebrate Shawn in nationalist terms, especially compared to Wigman who was also touring the United States.
Responding to a rather dim box office response, influential music critic
Glenn Dillard Gunn lamented that Shawn had received the "enthusiastic ap-
probation that has been accorded the Germans of today and the Russians
of yesterday."[96] He went on to proclaim Shawn's *Divine Idiot* a revolutionary
work, "as filled with imagination as anything the Germans had presented,
and surely as expert in terms of technique."

Hailed as the "First Master of His Curious Art," Shawn finally received
critical attention for his dancing rather than his mission: "There is nothing
ornamental about the dancing of Ted Shawn, neither is there flourish nor
blowing of trumpets. Rather it displays a seriousness, a regular rhythmical
beat of a spirit absolutely sincere in its interpretation of what has always been
Man's manner in expressing his greatest joys or deepest sorrows—the dance.
He is surging ahead in his goal for the new modernism."[97] However, in true
Shawn style, he found fault even at the avalanche of praise he received, frustrated that he was now identified with modernism. He even "defended" himself against the impression that *Divine Idiot* was a modern dance. Missing
both the point and the opportunity, he insisted that he had created the dance
before he went to Germany, as if a modernist aesthetic could not take root
on American soil. Unwilling to see a relationship between his work and that
of Wigman (an influence he actively sought to absorb while in Germany) he
insisted that his work was entirely of his own creation. In addressing sympathetic critics and producers, he merely repeated what his fans allegedly told
him: "Thank God you are touring—you are our only hope—our only weapon
and answer against this German menace!"

At long last, Shawn received the critical approval that matched the seriousness of his artistic intentions. However, the tour was a financial disaster and
he could no longer pay salaries. At a stop in St. Louis, Shawn held a company
meeting to present his dancers with the option of continuing on with the tour
for living expenses only or to disband the tour. He gave them twenty-four
hours to think about it. Representing the dancers, Lester Shafer told Shawn
they would rather go home. Shawn did not blame them. With a strikingly different attitude toward his dancers, he thought they owed him nothing, least

of all Shafer whose school admirably upheld the Denishawn brand: "On the contrary he was doing me a favor to even come on the tour—underpaid and underappreciated."[98]

In spring 1931, Shawn returned to Germany, this time without Fred Beckman. Instead, he took along his childhood friend Allene Seaman for companionship. Mary Campbell also went as his accompanist, and Katherine S. Dreier met them on the ground. Shawn was happy to reunite with his Orpheus cast at the Wigman Schule. He also went to visit with Kolbe, but found him in a depression, likely because his works had not been selling. Shawn also toured Switzerland with a scaled-down concert that could be performed only with items that could fit in a single trunk—no props, no costumes, no scenery. At Dreier's insistence Shawn added a "happy" dance to lighten the mood of his new serious program to ensure that audiences would go into the *grosse pause* in a good mood for their beer and sausages. Dreier encouraged him to perform a dance based on one of his popular classroom exercises "Spring, Beautiful Spring," which she renamed *Frohsinn*, meaning "the very soul or essence of joy."

Shawn stopped in London on his return to the States. He performed to a drawing room full of royals at the house of Lady Cunard. Shawn also sat for a portrait by the Duchess of Rutland, though he detested the result, as it made him look like an adolescent or as Shawn put it, "a fetus." He rehearsed in ballet star Anton Dolin's studio, then went to see the "prince of British ballet" perform. Shawn was baffled by his poorly conceived concert, including Dolin's performance of classical ballet to the negro spiritual "Nobody Knows the Trouble I've Seen." Shawn's primary goal in London was to meet the composer Ralph Vaughan Williams and discuss plans to use his score to choreograph a dance about the biblical figure Job for Denishawn's fifth and final appearance at the Lewisohn Stadium.

Shawn returned to the United States on the SS *Leviathan* on June 11, 1931. St. Denis reluctantly met him at the dock. While Shawn was abroad, she came to terms with her resentment toward him. One night she dreamed that Shawn told her that he would return to India to perform. In her dream, she snapped back: "Well, I suppose in that case you will do nautch dances."[99]

Also awaiting him at the dock was a young man named Barton Mumaw, a music and dance student Shawn had met in Florida just weeks after first meeting Beckman on the Ziegfeld tour in 1928. At Shawn's invitation, Mumaw came to study at Denishawn in the summer of 1930 and to serve as Shawn's valet. Mumaw accepted the invitation with a note handwritten on the reverse side of music paper, assuring Shawn "Yes, I can drive a car, though New York traffic may present some difficulties."[100] Mumaw was cast in St. Denis's Cambodian fantasy *Angkor Wat* for the Lewisohn Stadium show, but an ankle injury prevented him from making his Denishawn debut. Crushed, he went back home to accept his piano scholarship at Rollins College, and it was there that Shawn and Mumaw reunited when Denishawn played at the Rollins later that year. Shawn invited him to watch the performance from backstage. Later, they met in Shawn's hotel room for dinner and more. In his autobiography, Mumaw offers a tender if not demure recollection of the evening he spent in Shawn's hotel room. Without divulging too many details, he reveals that he reached for Shawn's hand as he approached him with "his white robe open above his naked body," overcome with a feeling of "warmth and understanding" as he had never before known and with "no shame, no fear, no hesitancy."[101] It was a transformative moment for Mumaw, and no doubt for Shawn as well, who subsequently invited Mumaw back to New York, covering all tuition, housing, and meals in exchange for Mumaw to serve as his dresser. Apart from the romantic feelings Shawn felt toward Mumaw, he also recognized his potential as a great artist, so much so that he cast him in the important role of "Lead Comforter" in the production of *Job* for Denishawn's 1931 concert at Lewisohn Stadium.

In the midst of rehearsing the Lewisohn concert, St. Denis announced the impending dissolution of the Denishawn company and school in a "farewell" article she wrote for the July 1931 issue of *Dance Magazine*. Though St. Denis focused her remarks on the company and school, the essay's melodramatic title, "The Denishawns Go Their Separate Ways," suggested that the famous couple at its helm were likewise disbanding. Careful not to expose too many personal details, St. Denis instead made an evasive statement about the couple's need to return to being "private citizens."

The article raised Shawn's defenses, especially as it trivialized the cause and significance of Denishawn's dissolution to a personal decision or worse, an artistic failure. To emend the record, Shawn wrote his own article for the November 1931 issue of *Dance Magazine* titled "The Price of Pioneering," which gives an in-depth exposé of Denishawn's fate in financial terms, essentially reframing the Denishawn dissolution as a symptom of a systemic problem in the state of dance as a performing art in the United States. Shawn's article begins with a heavy-handed, hard-selling narrative about the virtues of the pioneer, counting himself among America's illustrious discoverers and settlers, none of whom ever "profits by his own discoveries." But once he exercises the belabored forefather metaphor, he writes lucidly and candidly, in a way that leaves him far more vulnerable than he had ever before allowed himself to be in print. He lets the world into the financial reality of America's first dance company, revealing that the system under which concert managers operate "is an impossible one for the dance artist." He goes as far as to itemize the company's unsustainable budget to show how its $200,000 gross income left little for St. Denis and Shawn beyond their expenses: concert booking commissions ($40,000); salaries ($44,000); travel ($56,000); printing, photography, and advertising ($24,000); production and sets ($20,000); miscellaneous expenses ($2,000); and actual living expenses for St. Denis and Shawn ($10,000).[102]

Shawn benefited from occasional support from patrons over the years, and thus conceded that concert dance in the United States needed state sponsorship. He pleaded: "We have given the conditions and the opportunity for the large majority of the young worthwhile dancers in America to get their start, but are we, ourselves not entitled to some help, encouragement, and support?" To illustrate the point, he compared Denishawn to the only other peer touring company of similar scale, Diaghilev's Ballet Russes, which he noted came to the United States under heavy subsidy for its lavish scenery, costumes, and big orchestra, even after which the directors of the Metropolitan Opera had to make up a $300,000 deficit. Shawn defensively groused that no one ever subsidized "even three cents" of Denishawn's deficits.

Art and business aside, he also put forth his own personal investment in the Denishawn enterprise: "Everything in my life has been sacrificed to this pioneering work. I have no real home, I have no money, and no domestic life. The schedule . . . has made it impossible to develop friendships, other than with those immediately connected to the work. I have had no vacations, no recreation, no escape from this all-absorbing task of pioneering in the art dance in America."

Though the artistic and personal cost of dismantling Denishawn was incalculable, Shawn was forced into making an arrangement with St. Denis when she unilaterally decided to take Denishawn House off the market so that she could pay its lease and run it as "The Ruth St. Denis School," a plot hatched by Pearl Wheeler. By spring 1932, she fell behind on payments, making him liable for over $3,000 in expenses. Shawn was irate and admonished her for using the Denishawn name in brochures for her own school. After resisting Denishawn in idea and practice since its inception, St. Denis was clinging to it in its demise. He refused to forgive her for squandering the great empire they had built. She wrote to Shawn to justify herself, but he just responded by asking her to no longer call him "Teddy."

"This is indeed the end," she wrote in her journal.[103]

Following the final Lewisohn Stadium appearance in the summer of 1931, Shawn drove up to the Jacob's Pillow farm with secretary Margerie Lyon and dancers Barton Mumaw, John "Jack" Ewing Cole, Don Moreno, and Harry Joyce. For a month, the men performed heavy labor to transform the farm into an artist colony, with help from a local carpenter who was doing basic work to make the home livable. The first order of business was to hoist the foundation of the house and to install a hot air furnace. The dancers worked on converting the barn into a dance studio by resurfacing the floor, installing salvaged ballet barres from the Westport studio, and moving in a grand piano gifted from Mrs. Cox. They discovered a brook on the property, which they dammed to create a small pool. In the process, Shawn suffered numerous mosquito bites, which poisoned him and rendered him bedridden for several days. Once recovered, Shawn traveled back and forth between the city and the farm to check on the progress and to rehearse the group of men and women for an upcoming tour. The men stayed on the farm and the women boarded at the nearby Greenwater Lodge.

The farm's idyllic atmosphere had a productive effect on Shawn's dances. (See Figure 4.12.) One of the first solo dances he created in his new barn-studio was a character study of St. Francis of Assisi, the thirteenth-century patron saint of animals and nature. The son of a wealthy merchant and a lover of troubadours and fabric, Francis experienced a spiritual awakening wherein he renounced his privileged existence to take on a life of poverty and chastity. Shawn was staging his own conversion of sorts and St. Francis's example demonstrated austerity as a religious virtue, especially as Shawn reportedly foraged for berries and greens in the brambles surrounding the farm. Perhaps Shawn understood his commitment to restoring the dilapidated Berkshire barn into a center of artistic creativity as a vocation, just as St. Francis devoted his life to restoring the fallen churches of Christ.

In that regard, St. Francis was a model of modern asceticism for Shawn, who came to understand the religious figure through the writings of another one of Shawn's personal "saints"—Havelock Ellis, who included a psychological portrait of St. Francis and his "double-sided life" in his book *Affirmations* (1915). Ellis's description of St. Francis focuses on the saint's "free play of the individual soul in contact with Nature and men," which was precisely Shawn's

Figure 4.12. Men Dancers in Barn Studio, Jacob's Pillow. Ted Shawn Papers, Additions. Courtesy of the Jerome Robbins Dance Division, New York Public Library for the Performing Arts.

intention. Echoing his eugenic writings, Ellis also interprets the Franciscan approach to nature as a "spiritual Pasteurism" to cleanse and transform.

Shawn called the resulting solo *O Brother Sun and Sister Moon*, a reference to the way St. Francis famously considered all creatures his brother or sister. Set to a suite of three preludes based on Gregorian Chants by Italian composer Ottorino Respighi, the dance takes its cue from Ellis's point that "famous historical persons who have passed through two antithetical phases of character" are remembered only "post-conversion." In this three-minute solo Shawn embodies what he called "dynamic stillness," subtle gestures to convey divine radiance. The solo represents a choreographic departure for Shawn, who attempts to get to the bare essentials of movement in the piece, rejecting his usual applause-provoking displays of technical tricks and virtuosity. In fact, he never took a bow for the dance and even asked audiences to withhold applause in order to maintain an air of austerity and piousness. (See Figure 4.13.)

St. Denis spent fifteen years trying to dismantle the marriage and school that she had created with Shawn, though seemed genuinely surprised when he was no longer a presence in her life. In her diary she wrote about her loneliness at Denishawn House: "Just now I stopped a moment by Teddy's open door—the room is empty—he has sent for all his furniture to take up to his farm. It looked so deserted and I thought again 'What does this cruel and stupid thing mean? We started out to build something—to conceive and raise? Our 'children of the brain'—what happened? Was the whole idea wrong?"[104]

Despite the failure of the Ted Shawn and His Dancers tour in 1930–31, Shawn set out on the road again only to be met with the same result. He turned to Katherine S. Dreier, who at the time was busy completing a book called *Shawn, the Dancer*. Shawn needed new representation, so Dreier put him in touch with J. J. Vincent, a concert promoter who was formerly with Sol Hurok, the most influential producer of dance at the time. Vincent had catapulted the career of successful German opera singer Johanna Gadski who had recently died in an automobile accident. In search of a new star client, Vincent took a meeting with Shawn and Dreier. When they met, Shawn was easily seduced by Vincent's praise for his choreography and dancing. They plotted an international touring production of a modern Don Juan, a stage spectacle that would bring together drama, music, and dance and star Shawn in the leading role. Shawn also floated the possibility of producing an all-man dance group in Europe and returning stateside as a "novelty sensation." He invited Vincent and his wife to the farm to see a rehearsal of a new work set to Brahms's Rhapsody, op. 119, no. 4. Shawn said they were moved to tears.

The encouraging dynamic between Shawn and Vincent changed as soon as the ink dried on their contract. Vincent began to accost Shawn with questions about Dreier's wealth, prying him for information about how she and her sisters managed their $3 million inheritance. Shawn warned Dreier about Vincent's preoccupation with siphoning her money through him. Dreier confronted Vincent about Shawn's accusation, making it clear he

Figure 4.13. Ted Shawn as St. Francis in *O Brother Sun and Sister Moon* at Jacob's Pillow (1930). Photo by Ralph Hawkins. Ted Shawn Collection. Courtesy of the Jerome Robbins Dance Division, New York Public Library for the Performing Arts.

would never see a cent of her fortune. Vincent then turned to Shawn to procure money, going as far as to advise him to prostitute himself to raise funds for the production. Shawn alleged that Vincent told him: "Surely you know some rich old women you can sleep with who'll put up the money. For after all, every artist must consider his body as just one of the tools of his trade, and use it in any way to further his career."[105]

Shawn knew he could not go about "finding, attracting and seducing rich old ladies." However, he was not opposed to seducing them from the stage. He approached Alfred Barton of the Surf Club in Miami Beach, whom he knew well from the Denishawn days, asking if he would book him to present his dances to the club's members, almost all millionaires. Barton invited him to perform for an hour at a special dinner hosted by the president of the Woolworth Company, where leaders of all stripes were sure to be in attendance. Shawn took a gamble and presented his *Brahms Rhapsody*, featuring five nearly naked men to "a room of 400 bald-headed men expecting naked girls." Though Shawn was not successful in raising money at that event, it proved invaluable for him to observe the positive reaction to his new work and recognize that audiences might actually tolerate—perhaps even take pleasure in—his vision of male beauty on stage.

When his partnership with Vincent showed no signs of contracting work, Shawn looked elsewhere. However, Vincent held Shawn to the letter of their contract, which stipulated that Shawn would be obligated to pay Vincent $5,000 to cancel their contract or would owe him a hefty cut of all his future earnings for the three-year period of the contract.[106] At first, Shawn called Vincent's bluff and began to piece together some performances, including a production of *Lysistrata* at the Falmouth Playhouse on Cape Cod and at the Berkshire Playhouse. Vincent pursued a court injunction against Shawn, and, to place pressure on him from all angles, convinced Shawn's printer and major advertiser, *The Musical Courier*, that Shawn was about to go into bankruptcy and would never be able to pay his debts for their services. Vincent convinced the publisher to attach Shawn's receipts in Pittsfield, which led to local authorities seizing Shawn's costumes, trunks, and scenery, effectively making it impossible for him to tour.

Shawn hired experienced theater lawyer Max Chopnick and filed a claim against Vincent, who in turn retaliated by dragging Dreier into the lawsuit, assuring that her ability to throw money at a settlement would be worth more than attaching Shawn's receipts. Vincent alleged that Shawn had confided in him that he was "tired of Miss Dreier because she had given him much less money than she promised." The accusation had an air of truth to it and Dreier knew it. The press devoured the uncorroborated but entirely plausible story that Dreier, the wealthy matron of modernism, exploited the poor modern dancer. The headlines followed: "Devotion to Patroness Hauls Apollo of Dance into Court."[107] Despite the onslaught of press concerning the alleged fallout between Shawn and Dreier, the two artists maintained a

tremendous affection and loyalty to each other. The tabloids put Dreier's reputation into question over Shawn's professional woes. She received her share
of unsolicited letters from her friends and acquaintances with damaging
reports of Shawn's infidelities and homosexuality. Dreier staunchly defended
Shawn's reputation.[108] No doubt the legal debacle strained their professional
relationship, though they remained cordial and deeply connected by their
shared interest in the publication of *Shawn, the Dancer*. Shawn distanced
from Dreier, claiming it was to maintain an air of objectivity surrounding
the sales and marketing of the book, concerned that his active involvement
would diminish whatever luster Dreier's authorship brought to it. Ultimately,
Chopnick won the case for Shawn in the Supreme Court of New York.
Shawn felt vindicated that the judge determined to annul the contract on the
grounds that it was inequitable between manager and artist. Unfortunately,
he was left with legal fees in the amount of $400, which he did not have.

While contending with his legal woes, Shawn continued to create new
dances with his four men at the farm. He was inspired by the intensity of
these men, especially Mumaw whose temperament, fortitude, and work
ethic stood out in the studio. He was also hired to choreograph the Falmouth
Theatre Unit's successful production of *Lysistrata*. Shawn brought dancers
Campbell Griggs and J. Ewing Cole to help work with the seventy locals performing as extras. Among them was a handsome eighteen-year-old with a
chiseled body and a head of glossy black hair named Frank Overlees. Shawn
was intrigued to learn that he was the grandson of a "full-blooded Cherokee
Indian."[109] Shawn detected that he was "somewhat aimless," so he invited
Overlees back to the farm to work on new material.

To circumvent the legalities of his agreement with Vincent, Shawn developed a lecture-demonstration titled "Dancing for Men" as a vehicle to present his growing repertory of dances for men. In the audience at one of those
lecture-demonstrations in September 1932 was Dr. Laurence Doggett, president of Springfield College, the leading physical education school whose
students went on to become directors of physical education programs across
the nation. Convinced that Shawn's revolutionary dances could positively
expand the school's physical education curricula, he invited Shawn to perform for the school's students and faculty. Based on the positive response,
he then invited Shawn to join the Springfield College faculty to teach dance,
assisted by four men dancers. Shawn jumped at the opportunity, not only because the legal battle with Vincent diminished his capacity to book dates and
earn an income as a performer, but also because it allowed him to develop

lectures focused on dance in physical education that would form the basis of a textbook that could be used by physical education instructors across the country. Before accepting his appointment, Shawn insisted on meeting all fourteen "hard boiled men" of the physical education faculty in order to secure their promise to support the experimental venture in dance. He assured them that his goal was not "to turn out Bachelors of the Terpsichorean Art, with diplomas guaranteeing each of them 26 weeks in vaudeville."[110] He won them over. Starting on January 11, 1933, Shawn taught a required dance class for freshmen, as well as an elective to upperclassmen and graduates. His 500 students included the captain of the wrestling team, an intercollegiate swimming champion, and members of the football team.

The *Springfield Leader* dedicated an entire page to the performance and Shawn's appointment, sparking a series of editorials and letters about the relationship between dance and sports.[111] Edward Eddy's *Very Idea* Sunday column suggested that a dance performance may be as worthy of promotion as a wrestling or boxing match. What, Eddy inquired, "is the comparative entertainment value—and news importance—of the two shows? Well box-office records show that the wrestling match cost promoters over $40 with the balance of Convention Hall receipts totaling $183. Shawn's performance at Clare Thompson Hall of Music grossed $472 and earned promoters $60. The audience was larger too."

Eddy's economic rationale for supporting dance in Springfield stirred the ire of several influential Springfielders, including the lead police reporter (the self-proclaimed "Lowest of the Lowbrows") who stepped outside his beat to declare that Shawn's concert was his least entertaining night out since he had gone out on a date with a "deaf and dumb girl." He likened the program notes to an inscrutable French menu and could not get past the fact that the dancers were barefoot, convinced the decision was some sort of publicity stunt. He was similarly outraged at Shawn's costume, which he described as a rhinestone surcingle for a horse that made Gandhi's loincloth look like a deep-sea diver's outfit. He seemed relieved that there was a colonial-era dance where the "dawncers" put on shoes.

Similar vitriolic responses came from the lead sports editor and the lead movie critic, who opined that if left to their druthers, audiences would sooner want to see Middleweight Midget Fischer and Sailor Joe Cook in the wrestling ring over Ted Shawn.

Shawn had plenty of defenders who wrote letters against the impertinent responses, forcing the *Springfield Leader* to run an article about the local controversy itself, quoting one upset citizen who surmised that the negative responses were an affront to the intellect and open mindedness shared by "8 out of 10 Springfieldians."[112]

Though Shawn's concert elicited a range of responses from the Springfield public, his class at Springfield proved to be a unanimous success. Upon submitting final grades at the end of the term, Shawn asked students to write "before and after" essays to candidly explain how their ideas about dancing evolved as a result of studying with him. The students reported developing an overwhelmingly positive relationship toward dance and seemed able to echo Shawn's points about the benefits of dancing to physical, spiritual, and social development. Several confided how dancing opened them up to hitherto unexplored emotional pathways, experiences of pleasure, and the power of expression. One wrestling student explained that he was an erstwhile folk dancer who had grown bored with its "mechanical routine." Seeing Shawn's dancers in concert and attending Shawn's class offered an outlet for his "mental revolt" against popular dancing from which he had lost all pleasure. Upon graduating from Springfield in 1933, this wrestling champion, Wilbur McCormack, joined Shawn's company of men dancers and remained for the entire duration of its seven-year existence.[113]

Shawn made a convincing argument about the virtues of restoring dance to its "rightful place in modern life." His students and audiences alike were persuaded by his argument that dance was not intrinsically a sphere of women's activity but was also a dignified realm for men. The downside to Shawn's influence on this front was that it unleashed an affront on women and effeminacy. Newspaper reporters eager to write about the novel idea of men dancing represented Shawn's cause in ways that either overlooked or discredited the labor and innovation of women in dance or that disreputed male dancers in ballroom, Broadway, and ballet as "daisies," "pansies," "butterflies," or "sissies," offensive terms that Shawn himself did not use to justify his vision.

While facing legal injunction and without a touring company for the first time in over fifteen years, Shawn had developed a considerable amount of work that he was eager to share with the public. Rather than wait for a producer and a legitimate business contract, he agreed to present a week of concerts in March 1933 at the Repertory Theatre in Boston to benefit a local women's charity, the Boston Circle of the Florence Crittenton League, a "big sister" organization of Welcome House, dedicated to "the protection and care of delinquent and wayward girls." Part of the proceeds from the concert were designated to relocate the recently defunct Welcome House from Jamaica Plain to Brighton.

Shawn's concerts had to compete for the attention of Boston audiences with two other prominent theatrical productions that week: pioneer of Italian puppetry Vittorio Podrecca was in town with a marionette show that enjoyed huge success in New York, and "The First Lady of the American Theatre" Ethel Barrymore delivered her starring turn in the play *An Amazing Career*. Moreover, Shawn had to overcome the unforeseen obstacle of a bank holiday that President Franklin Delano Roosevelt declared days after he took office that year, which meant all banking transactions were frozen between March 6 and March 10, just prior to his performances on March 20–25, leaving potential ticket buyers without nickels for fare or food, never mind theater tickets. To incite potential ticket buyers, the Florence Crittenton league published the names of its "exceedingly swanky" patronesses who were sure to be in attendance, as well as the list of out-of-town theatergoers and socialites who had already reserved seats.[114]

During the afternoon of the company's opening night performance at the Repertory Theatre, Shawn, Miriam Winslow, and four other company members performed a benefit recital at the United States Veteran's Hospital in Bedford, along with three members of the Crittenton League who accompanied the troupe and served ice cream. To raise additional funds, at the Friday performance, in the sunroom of the theater a team of debutantes sold flowers, shrubs, and trees all donated from a Newton agriculturalist. A team of debutantes volunteered as ushers. It was a taxing day for Shawn, all the more so due to serious back pain he was enduring, forcing him to tightly brace his torso except when on stage, a solution that left a girdle of blisters.

For the Repertory Theatre appearance, Shawn assembled four different programs for nine concerts over six days. Shawn programmed the concerts with a range of styles and themes so there would be something to please all tastes. Whereas many praised the emotional content of his religious dances, especially the Negro spirituals, others adored character pieces such as *Boston Fancy* or abstract dances like *Divine Idiot*. Most everyone enjoyed the Spanish dances. Margaret Lloyd, dance critic for the *Christian Science Monitor*, applauded Shawn's "warm and winning" dances for their "human glow, vibrant with understanding." Unlike the impulse with modern dance on either side of the Atlantic, all of which aspired to attain levels of abstraction, Shawn's dances, argued Lloyd, expressed the choreographer's "sympathetic imagination," his desire and capacity to commune with the subjects of his dances.[115]

Of the nine concerts at Repertory Theatre, Shawn dedicated the entire Tuesday evening program to his all-man dances featuring a cast of thirteen men, eight of whom were Springfield College students. Billed as "Ted Shawn and His Ensemble of Men Dancers," the concert featured the dances for men he had choreographed for the Berkeley Pageant more than fifteen years earlier as well as the recent works he had completed at the farm. A reviewer for the *Boston Traveler* predicted that the concert marked "the beginning of a Renaissance in the modern American interpretive dance."[116] H. T. Parker, the noted theater and music critic for the *Boston Evening Transcript*, was struck by the "insistent masculinity" of the program, declaring that it brought a refreshing "balance" to the appearance of Mary Wigman and "her attendant damsels" a month earlier at Symphony Hall, just across the street from the Repertory Theatre.[117] Another notice ran in the *Film Review* column of the *Boston Globe*.[118] The uncredited writer claimed that the "rather small but enthusiastic" audience recalled Shawn to the stage multiple times, prompting him to give a closing speech during which he "paid tribute . . . to great women dancers," especially his wife. At the end of his speech, Shawn passionately conveyed his desire to continue making dances for men, saying that he hoped that one day, forty or sixty men would appear in "motion choruses."

It had taken Shawn twenty years to realize his dream of presenting a full program of men dancing on a concert stage. Working around legal, artistic, and financial obstacles, he finally achieved it and in the black at that! Thanks to a check from Brother Dennis, he was able to cover his Boston hotel bill and still have $10 in his wallet, a minor miracle given all the wealth he had lost in missed performances, box office appeal, school earnings, and real estate. Ironically, the very same week in which he realized his vision to produce a concert of all-man dances at the Repertory Theatre in Boston, the dormitory of Greater Denishawn went into foreclosure. It would take just over a year before he and St. Denis had to hand over the deed for Denishawn House to the Railroad Co-operative in exchange for complete release from the bond. Shawn was furious, especially as he never considered Denishawn House personal property but something that he had hoped to leave for dancers.

In retaliation against Shawn's success in Boston, St. Denis once again went to the press with personal matters to garner some publicity, this time in connection with her retrospective concert at the Mansfield Theater in New York during the week of April 23, 1933. As with the announcement of her marriage to Shawn nineteen years before, news of their separation made national headlines when she self-interestedly "leaked" confidential information to a reporter. In this instance, she confirmed rumors of her separation from Shawn. Front page headlines of national newspapers made a mockery of their announcement: "Ruth St. Denis says 'Leave 'Em then Love 'Em'"; "How to Be Happy through Living Apart"; "Shawns Dance Solo but Love Goes On"; "St. Denis Quits Ted in 'New Deal' Love." One reporter somewhat sincerely reported: "Now they love each other more than before, because they are free of restrictions." The explanation was entirely misleading, patently absurd, and also entirely true.

Shawn was traveling to San Antonio, Texas, to participate in a pageant when the news broke in the press that his marriage was officially over. To seek refuge from the humiliation, he retreated to his Jacob's Pillow farm, where the miracle of spring on his new hilltop home offered a welcome distraction. He watched in wonder as the lilac bushes bloomed and rhubarb sprouted beneath the brush of the garden. He also planted twenty-five tomato plants, a generous donation from his spiritual advisor Mrs. Cox who visited the farm one weekend to help him plot his next personal and professional steps. Shawn was convinced that the men's concert at the Repertory Theatre was not only the culmination of a lifelong dream, but also the start of a new creative and professional venture. However, it was unclear to him exactly if or how he could establish a dance company for men.

5

Seven Magic Years

Adventures with Dances, 1933–1936

Ted Shawn's one-time concert of all-man dances at Boston's Repertory Theatre on Tuesday, March 21, 1933, received enthusiastic reviews, nearly eclipsing the coverage of the eight other programs he presented that week. Having read the uniformly positive reviews of the concert, including one that ran in his very own *Boston Globe*, the editorial writer and "Mentor to New England" Lucien Price (1883–1964) attended Shawn's concert the very next night. A former music and theater critic, Price had seen a Denishawn program in 1931, though that hardly prepared him for the transformative experience he was about to have. At the concert, Price saw several of Shawn's all-man dances and was stunned not only by Shawn's innovative treatment of classical music but also by the appearance of men dancing in revealing costumes—or as Price often described them, "naked save for cinctures." That evening, Price wrote over a dozen pages in his journal trying to come to terms with the concert's social significance, convinced that these dances had conveyed a "not impossible but remote future."[1] He was particularly awed by an intense five-minute quintet performed by Shawn and four of his men dancers and set to Brahms's Rhapsody, op. 119, no. 4. A modern exercise in male bonding, the dance is composed of a series of intricate figures and formations that evoke the soldierly maneuvers within a covert mission. They lead and follow one another, shoulder each other's weight, retreat blindly in phalanx, and form human chains that twist and knot yet prove resilient under stress. Price admired the men's commitment to the dance and to each other, a sentiment powerfully conveyed by the dance's final monumental tableau, wherein Shawn stands victorious with his fallen comrades draping from his body. About the dance, he wrote: "I never expected to see anything in my life as beautiful as *Rhapsody* of Brahms. Stranger still, I had imagined such a thing but never dreamed that I should see it." (See Figure 5.1.)

Junius Lucien Price was born in Kent, Ohio, a son of three generations of physicians. After attending Western Reserve Academy, he graduated

Ted Shawn. Paul A. Scolieri, Oxford University Press (2020). © Paul A. Scolieri.
DOI: 10.1093/oso/9780199331062.001.0001

Figure 5.1. Ted Shawn and Men Dancers rehearsing the final pose of a music visualization to Brahms's Rhapsody in E flat major, op. 119, no. 4, outside the barn studio. Photo by John Lindquist. John Lindquist Collection. Courtesy of Houghton Library, Harvard University.

from Harvard University in 1907, then began writing music and theater reviews for the *Boston Transcript*. Between 1914 and his death in 1964, he contributed to "Uncle Dudley," the lead editorial column of the *Sunday Boston Globe*, a post he shared with two other writers. He developed a reputation as "the most superb essayist and penetrating social philosopher in New England journalism."[2] Price maintained personal relationships with several esteemed scholars and artists of his time and wrote about them for leading literary journals. His correspondents included the Finnish composer Jean Sibelius, Oxford classicist Sir Richard Livingstone, Harvard philosopher Alfred North Whitehead, pioneering brain surgeon Harvey Cushing, and Nobel Prize–winning writer Romain Rolland. Gore Vidal dedicated his novel *Julius* to Lucien Price in 1964, the year Price died. He was also a fixture in Boston social circles, dining several times a week at posh eateries such as the Parker House and the Tavern Room. He could also be spotted at Symphony Hall several times a week, usually in his trademark French beret.

A homosexual, Price had to carefully protect his private life so as not to threaten his existence as a public intellectual. During the years that Price wrote on important social, political, and philosophical issues for Boston's largest newspaper, he was also hard at work at writing one of the first *romans-fleuves* to deal with gay male society. *All Souls* was the title of his serial novels, which depict the lives of a network of gay men between 1893 and 1943. Price began working on the novels in 1919 and finished in 1946, though he did not start to publish them until 1951, since no publisher wanted to handle the explicit sexual content. Determined to reach gay readers, Price self-published the books and donated copies to leading university libraries so as to protect his celebration of homosexual lives from obscurity. In the words of one of his *All Souls* characters, a writer like Price himself, he hoped his gay-themed books would explode like "a series of bombs" in the minds of readers: "If one didn't explode, another would. The explosions would keep on coming until they could no longer be ignored."[3]

The Secret Legion was the name of the last four installments of *All Souls*, so named for the elite ancient Greek military regiment made up of 150 pairs of homosexual lovers. As chronicled by the ancient historian Plutarch, the legion was dedicated to a cult of creativity. Defenders of Greece against cultural annihilation, the soldiers were honored throughout Hellas. The Sacred Legion was annihilated in 338 B.C. in the Battle of Chaeronea against the Macedonians, thus leaving ancient Greece susceptible to Christian subjugation. For Price, the Sacred Legion was not merely an ancient legend but a model for a modern homosexual consciousness. A devoted student of classical arts and letters, Price was part of an intellectual movement that gained momentum between the wars, which held that Hellenism was a better political and social model for modern America than Christianity. Price's unique interpretation of Plutarch held that modern homosexuals were descendants of this sacred legion, charged with the responsibility of rescuing American culture from Christian morality, a charge for which homosexuals were best suited.

As Price watched Shawn's men dance to Brahms's "Rhapsody," he realized that a modern Sacred Legion was "not an impossibility." The image of Shawn's loin-clothed dancers performing lyrical duets and marching in phalanxes was a sign of "adroit social poetics."[4] For Price, Shawn and his dancers were the physical embodiments of both the Sacred Legion and the men of Goodale Academy, the fictional Exeter at the center of many plots in *All Souls*. Shawn, "at least from the neck down," reminded Price of Robert Moore, the quasi-autobiographical, central protagonist of his novels. Price was so affected by the Wednesday evening performance that he attended the three subsequent concerts, quickly developing an addiction to the experience of seeing his vision of homosociality manifest in dance. He had to ensure a way for these dances to survive.

Giving himself a full week "to cool off," Price wrote to Shawn.[5] Handwritten on personal stationery, the letter conveyed Price's reaction to the concert. Describing his letter as "an adventure in intellectual sportsmanship," Price suggested that Shawn consider establishing a permanent all-male touring company. He wrote: "Suppose you did succeed in persuading an entire generation of school and college youth that dancing is a fine art, and that they should learn it; you would have given them a personal experience in artistic appreciation by having been active participants, which would reduce the ranks of cultural Philistines in this country by a good many thousands."

Price assured Shawn that American men would be "electrified" to learn dancing. He even offered him practical suggestions for this most abstract goal, promising him connections with headmasters and college administrators and noting that rehearsals could take place in gymnasiums. He even mentioned three grant opportunities to help fund his "missionary work." Certain yet humble, Price went as far as to offer an idea for a dance, a modified dramatization of a war scene similar to that of the Sacred Legion's demise at Charonaea:

> It was, of course, the decisive victory of free democracies that began our political liberties—or such as we have. Also historically the event was danced. For we know that the dancers were led by the poet Sophocles, then a boy sixteen, chosen for his extraordinary physical beauty. It would have been danced on the island of Salamis after the naval victory of the Greeks, because the Athenians had taken refuge there, the Persians having captured and burned Athens. Of course, it could be for men and women, but would it not be more stirring if danced by two choirs—one of boys in their teens, the other of men in their twenties, perhaps armed to the extent of helmet, shield and sword? There is, as you doubtlessly know, a bas relief of this sort of dance by men naked, I think, somewhere in Rome.... I merely mention this as showing that the idea is no mere half-cocked, snap-judgment, but one of long growth and organic development.

Price barely identified himself in the letter, humbly describing himself as a "hard-working journalist" and a Harvard graduate in the postscript. To convey the depth of his sincerity, he mentions that he wrote the letter on his "one free afternoon in the week," time ordinarily reserved for activities other than writing. Price sent the letter via special delivery.

Shawn was astounded by the letter. For two decades he had dealt with manipulative agents, managers, and bookers. Now Price was offering his support and contacts and asking for nothing in return. This was especially refreshing to Shawn, given that he had only recently untangled himself from one of the most pernicious professional agreements he had ever made, a contract with the agent J. J. Vincent who had imposed a legal injunction against him. Shawn said that although he had many friends who were sympathetic to his experiment, Price's was the only unconditional "endorsement of the cultural validity" of the idea for a men's company.

Through a series of letters, Price and Shawn began to sketch the details of their "preliminary campaign" to raise interest in and money for the new venture. Price contacted Mason Hammond, president of Harvard Classical Club as well as the president of Wheaton College. George Judd, the assistant manager of the Boston Symphony Orchestra, made an "avowal of interest" in the venture. Price went to Western Reserve Academy to conduct "a little propaganda." He also "went to bat" with Arthur Landers, the dean and music director at Exeter, who turned out to be interested only in English country dancing.[6]

On Friday, May 26, Shawn and Price finally met in person over dinner at the Tavern Room. Price was taken off guard by Shawn's childlike candor. Apparently, he told Price his life story in "one sitting," including the circumstances surrounding his separation from Ruth St. Denis. Price was moved by how desperately Shawn craved conversation with a peer. In his journal Price described Shawn as "a little boy who had been lost and had had a bad time." With childlike frankness, Shawn told Price that during the past few years he had routinely thought that he had gone insane, freely admitting that he had seriously contemplated suicide over the demise of Denishawn and its collateral damage.

After dinner, they headed back to Price's apartment at 75 Hancock Street. All of his belongings were packed in boxes, as Price was departing for Europe in the morning. They conversed for six hours more, touching upon their shared experiences of losing an older brother during their youth and losing a male lover to a wealthy woman. Mostly, they focused on their shared vision for Ted Shawn and His Men Dancers.

They walked out into the rainy Boston night. As they parted, Shawn told Price, "I am surrounded by people to whom I must give, give, give. What a relief it is, for once, to be given to."

"Well, we have only just begun," Price responded.

"Yes. We have only just begun."

Price left for Europe the next morning, while Shawn went to New York City to secure funding from a list of contacts Price had given him. These included John Hays Hammond, the wealthy mine owner and president of the Rocky Mountain Club, a recently disbanded men's society based in New York City. However, much of the funding for the first tour came from Shawn's own contacts, especially Mary Washington Ball, a dance teacher at the University of Texas, who at the time was teaching at the State Normal School in Cortlandt, New York. He also secured a six-month loan in the amount of $500 from the Amalgamated Bank.

With this seed money, Shawn regrouped some of the dancers from the Repertory Theatre concert at the farm for rehearsal: Barton Mumaw, Frank Overlees, Wilbur McCormack, and John "Jack" Ewing Cole. He also recruited George Gloss, a cast member of Shawn's production of *Job* at Lewisohn Stadium and a recent graduate of the physical education program at Columbia University. One afternoon, F. Cowles Strickland, director of the nearby Berkshire Playhouse at Stockbridge, came to watch a rehearsal. Moved by the experience of seeing the men rehearse in the studio-barn, Strickland urged Shawn to host Friday afternoon "tea dances" for the Berkshire locals, in hopes that he might attract dowagers to invest in the company. The first was held on July 14. The *Berkshire Eagle* advertised the event with information to reserve one of the limited twenty-five guest spots. Fifty-seven people showed up. For 75 cents, guests listened to Shawn lecture about the art of making dances while his dancers demonstrated class exercises. In rehearsal robes of white terry cloth, the men dancers served the audience tea and sandwiches just before they took to the makeshift barn stage to preview four dances, two group works and two solos by Shawn. It was an enormous success. Word of mouth led to progressively larger audiences of sixty, seventy-four, ninety people in subsequent weeks. At the third tea, the barn walls shook for a full ten minutes with applause for Shawn's dance to the Rhapsody, op. 119, no. 4. The boys scrambled to buy more tea cups and find time to add making finger sandwiches to their already tight schedule of chores. Shawn began to accept reservations via mail. At the last tea of the summer, added by popular demand, 200 people crammed into the studio-barn.[7]

Shawn wrote about the success of the teas in his letters to Price, who was in Germany attending a festival commemorating the fiftieth anniversary of Wagner's death. Price read Shawn's letter in a park adjacent to the *festspielhaus*, surrounded by Wagner enthusiasts rereading the libretto in advance of the evening's performance. Shawn also wrote to Price about a new work he had created over the summer, a "plastique" to Bach's sixth prelude in the *Well-Tempered Clavier*. Price was pleased with Shawn's musical choice, one of the most important works in the Western classical repertory. A week earlier, Price had visited Bach's home in Eisenach, Germany, where he examined the manuscript to Bach's Chaconne from the Partita in D minor.: "How these ideas of artists travel and endure," Price wrote to affirm Shawn's discriminating choice.[8]

Shawn broke the news to Price that during the early summer, he had "finally got rid of John Ewing Cole, a standout dancer who had performed in various iterations of Shawn's company since Denishawn. Shawn recognized that "Jack" Cole was a "young genius," an intuition that was duly validated in the decades to come when he emerged as an illustrious performer and Hollywood choreographer. However, Cole's fiery temperament routinely thwarted the camaraderie between men in the intimate setting of the studio-barn, as well as rattled Shawn's confidence as he experimented with new choreographic ideas. Shawn made the difficult decision to ask his finest dancer to leave the company.

Price could barely wait to return stateside to see Shawn's new dances and to share in the excitement of the revolutionary movement he helped to catalyze. In early October 1933, Price made his first trip to Jacob's Pillow. (See Figure 5.2.) It was a critical time at the farm, only a week after the last summer tea dance and two weeks before the company's debut tour. Shawn, Mumaw, and George Horn met Price at the Springfield train station and drove him on the unpaved roads of Jacob's Ladder to the Pillow. Price thought he had stepped into a dream. It was late afternoon, and the sun was setting the Berkshire hills ablaze with caramel colors. But as soon as they arrived at the farm, reverie gave way to action: Shawn hastened Price into the barn-studio and within a quarter hour of his arrival, the company members were assembled and ready to rehearse. Shawn led exercises on the floor, at the barre, and in the center, all the while explaining their significance to Price. That particular morning Shawn led grueling drills to improve balance. He asked the boys to balance on one leg while mirroring his shape-shifting torso. As their bodies warmed, they flung open the southern doors of the studio to the radiant October sun.

Between exercises, Price studied the converted barn-studio. It had a bare hardwood floor, wide windows and doors, a battered Chase grand piano, a phonograph, a stove, and a low bench that rested along a mirrored wall. A shed, serving as a makeshift property room, held stacks of traveling trunks,

Figure 5.2. Lucien Price at Jacob's Pillow. Stanley Davis Scrapbook (1938). Courtesy of Jacob's Pillow Dance Festival Archives.

percussion instruments, and costumes wrapped in wire net to fend off the mice.

After rehearsal, a clearer picture of life on the farm emerged. For example, Price learned that the men did all their own housework, cooking, cleaning, and vegetable gardening. He marveled at the late eighteenth-century farmhouse. He especially appreciated the reconstructed walls of fieldstone that the men had built like "Pharaoh's pyramid slaves." Their water supply came from an outdoor well with an iron pump. There was a shower bath upstairs in the house, but the season was so dry that they conserved water by bathing in a beautiful brook pool in the woods. After rehearsal, Price followed the boys to the pool. It was his first chance to speak to them one on one.

He told them, "If life were easy for you fellows, I could not feel the way about you that I do. If you had plenty of money and could go out and buy anything that you needed, this effort would not be so stirring. It's very difficult. Its very desperation is proof of its vitality. Here is a movement that in fifty years, possibly ten, will be prosperous and institutionalized. But it is in its stage of struggle that it is exciting and vital."

The men understood that Shawn had the highest respect for Price and thus respectfully listened to him romanticize their humble existence. Most of the dancers were content to have meals, lodging, and the opportunity to perform. The company's future impact on art and society was not quite yet on their minds. They were still trying to learn the dances they would have to perform in two weeks' time.

That evening the men dined in a large room in the main farmhouse by the light of a kerosene lamp and a fire on the hearth. They enjoyed a meal of vegetables that they themselves had grown. For dessert, Price brought mulberry jam and coffee. During dinner conversation, Price learned that Havelock Ellis was Shawn's "patron saint" and heard about his life-changing meeting with him. Price regaled the men with an account of meeting Ellis in the Caribbean in 1925. Shawn fetched his volume of *Dance of Life* and read aloud the paragraph that had so influenced his life.

At the table was Wilbur "Mac" McCormack, whom Price distinctly remembered dancing with "fire and imagination" on the all-male Repertory Theatre program, despite the fact that he was "too long in the torso and short in the legs for perfect symmetry." Shawn told Price that Mac had been abandoned by his father when he was an infant and by his mother when he was six years old. Neighbors in nearby Chelmsford, Massachusetts, had raised him. Shawn found him wrestling at Springfield Training College and fast became a father figure to him. He sometimes called Shawn "Papa." Some of the others followed suit. Mac had left college in his senior year to study with Shawn and stayed with the company for its entire seven-year existence.

Frank Overlees also performed in Shawn's inaugural all-male concert and stayed with the company as dancer, driver, and stage manager until its end. At nineteen years old, Overlees was the youngest company member at the time. At dinner that evening, Overlees impressed Price when he offered the Greek word for "moderation" in the context of a discussion about Hellenism.

"How did you know that?" Price asked.

"My mother teaches Greek," Frank responded. "She has brought me up on that word: 'Do what you like, only do it in moderation.'"

Price decided that Overlees was the "sturdy soul" of the bunch.

There were several faces at the farm that Price did not recognize from the Repertory Theatre concert. George Horn had recently joined the group. He left after its first tour, though he returned throughout the years to help Shawn with costumes and props. According to Price, Horn looked older and "a bit sad, as if life had used him unkindly. . . . There is some long story behind him." Horn did initially not stay around long enough for Price to learn that story.

Months earlier, Shawn had stopped in Arkansas City, Arkansas, en route to Texas where he taught a class organized by Ernestine Day. A young man named Dennis "Denny" Landers had taken that class. Shawn invited him to the Pillow to study, an offer he accepted, leaving behind his position as a store manager. He borrowed $500 to pay the tuition and joined Jess Meeker on a bus to New York City. Meeker was a pianist who had accompanied several of Day's local appearances (as well as one of Shawn's several years before). When Shawn returned to the Pillow, he wrote to Meeker, inviting him to join the group as accompanist, as Mary Campbell had recently given notice. Campbell believed that a men's company ought to have a male accompanist. Meeker was by no means a composer, yet he had the right grit for Shawn's group.

"The first thing to do is to create the music and after that to learn how," Meeker told Price.

Price was impressed by all of the men Shawn had assembled, especially the disarming George Gloss. About thirty and thus older than the other dancers, Gloss was a midwesterner who had served a year as a naval officer on the Great Lakes. He had only recently completed a master's degree in physical education at Columbia University when he met Shawn and decided to take a chance with the men's group, a decision that required him to decline an offer to direct a high school physical education program, a position paying an annual salary of $4,000. However, Gloss decided against performing, though he trained with the other men. Instead, he managed the company's bookings, using his contacts in the physical education world to find performance dates and classes. He was instrumental to the company's early success, always arriving at venues days before the company in order to drum up audiences. Although Shawn had spoken to Price about Gloss in glowing terms, Price thought Shawn grossly underestimated his personality, beauty, and intelligence.

> Price recalled that when he and Gloss first met, Gloss exclaimed to
>   Shawn, "He has blue eyes!"
> "So has Jess," Shawn chaffed.
> "Yes, but Jess's aren't blue enough."
> The easily seduced Price found Gloss "uncommonly easy to love."[9]

Price carefully observed the group dynamics around the dinner table, noting that the conversation was interesting, but that the younger men tended to listen but say little. Shawn, on the other hand, spoke ceaselessly and kept the boys in gales of laughter.

Price began to lecture about the impossible standards of Judeo-Christian law, though it fast became clear that he was preaching to the choir. Price felt that he was merely confirming their own beliefs. Mastering an art, Price thought, was so strenuous that it generated its own morality. He had the feeling that it was possible to speak much more freely with these young men than with his peers and was somehow more clearly understood.

At 11:00 P.M., the men left for bed. Price stayed in Mumaw's room in the farmhouse. Eager to impress their guest, Mumaw left on the nightstand a vase of orange and blue delphiniums, Price's favorite flowers, and on the dresser, a henna-colored dressing gown. Price marveled at how Mumaw decorated the room with East Indian fabrics Shawn had purchased during his tour in the Far East. The shelves were lined with books, including a worn copy of Price's travelogue *Winged Sandals*. Mumaw was too shy to ask Price to inscribe the book to him, so Shawn asked on his behalf. Price also appreciated a strategically placed copy of a book by John Addington Symonds, the homosexual British poet and literary critic. Price noted that it was a rare "privately printed" edition, which even he had only been able to read at the Boston Athenaeum. Its very presence made Price wonder: "Was it left there on purpose knowing that I would understand? Or was it so unself-conscious that it was left there without a thought of removing it? Either way was dignified and fitting. I had the feeling of any tact and good breeding having been trusted in a most honoring manner. People who have matured to a certain stature do not need to have been taught to behave in a given novel situation. They know by the instinct of good breeding, I was not ever being tested. They knew I would know how."[10]

The next morning Price bathed on the lawn by dumping a bucket of cold water over himself. Mumaw applauded his rite of passage. He then joined the others for breakfast. Shawn usually had his coffee and toast in bed, "To save these boys from the possibility of a sometimes grouchy presence at breakfast." Later they entered the studio to run through the first program. Shawn began with his *Invocation to the Thunderbird*, a solo offering that Price recalled seeing at the Boston Opera House in February 1931, just two months after Ben, his former lover, had left him to marry the daughter of a wealthy land baron. The painful memory subsided as the "splendor of Shawn's body" executing the same dance, as if for him alone, made Price feel as if he and Shawn were brought together by some "spiritual law." The informal recital lasted until one o'clock, at which point the men posed for photographs that Price took and would later share with his friends in Boston, as if he needed evidence to prove to both himself and his friends that this otherwise unimaginable weekend had transpired.

After the rehearsal, Shawn, Mumaw, Gloss, Meeker, and Price gathered in the studio to listen to the recording of the Brahms Piano Quintet that Price had loaned Shawn in May. As the music began, Price thought of how often he had listened to it at his seaside home in Nahant, Massachusetts, imagining Robert Moore, his main character from *Sacred Legion*. There, in the darkened studio, he seemed to be with them both. He wondered: "Had that intense thought externalized? It was a company in which I felt utterly at ease and contented. Why did I feel so? They were comparative strangers. I felt I was understood and accepted and welcome for exactly what I am and that is an unusual feeling for me."

When the scherzo began, he gathered the courage to share his "imaginary choreography" for this music. "If not to them, then to whom?" he reasoned.

He asked, "Do you know what the Sacred Legion was?"

"I understand something about it," replied Shawn.[11]

Price proceeded to give an encyclopedic explanation of the elite homosexual militia and how he thought this company was its modern-day equivalent. He also shared his idea for a dance based on the Battle of Charonaea. Price was obsessed with memorializing this tragic loss and was convinced Shawn and His Men Dancers were his way of doing justice to the sacrifice of these ancient lovers.

Before leaving for the train station the next day, Price joined Shawn on the marble terrace in front of the farmhouse. They passed most of the time in silence, looking westward into the valley and picking the delicate blue flowers of the fringed gentian. Price wrote: "I felt myself understood and accepted without a word of explanation having been uttered." He knew that he and Shawn felt similarly, especially after the previous night's conversation about the Sacred Legion. It was as if Shawn's vision for his company had exponentially expanded.

During the car ride to the train station, Gloss admitted that Shawn safeguarded Price's letters at his bedside, as it was his letters that convinced Shawn to pursue his idea for the men's group. He lost so much money on the Repertory Theatre concert that he had considered signing a vaudeville contract.

"Then your letter came. It was out of the blue. You weren't a henchman. You didn't even know him. He had never seen you. It was completely disinterested. It gave him heart."[12]

Price decided to memorialize his extraordinary weekend at the farm in one of his *Sacred Legion* novels. In the meantime, he went to work on an article about the company for the *Boston Sunday Globe* in which he extolled Shawn's mission to transform American ideas about the male dancer. Price described Shawn as a quintessential American Romantic, the "frontiersman of an art-form" who labors in solitude to "restore the art of the dance for men to its rightful place in modern life." Dance, he says, is for "men of action." He went to excessive lengths to familiarize his reader with the idea of dance as art by likening Shawn's process to those of a composer, a painter, a writer, and an athlete. "I think Father Brahms himself, rough, true-hearted Teutonic bear that he was would have been electrified by Shawn's *Rhapsody.*" The article appeared in print a day before the company's very first performance. Shawn could not have imagined better or more timely press. He requested 15,000 reprints of the article to publicize the company's first tour, which began on October 23, 1933.[13]

Price insisted that Shawn take on the road with him a copy of the influential mathematician and philosopher Alfred North Whitehead's *Adventures of Ideas* (1933). Price met the Harvard professor in 1932 and fast became his Boswell, transcribing their discussions on art, democracy, education, and science. Decades later, Price achieved his greatest critical and popular success as an author when he edited and published these transcriptions as *Dialogues of Alfred North Whitehead* (1954). Price started to address Shawn as his "Fellow Athenian" and peppered his letters with fragments of his ongoing conversations with Whitehead, especially affirmations that the Midwest of the United States was destined to be the stage of a Periclean age.

Price assured Shawn: "You are living an adventure of an idea!"[14]

One of the most consistent topics in their correspondence during the company's first tour was Shawn's solo dance *John Brown Sees the Glory: An American Epic*. When Meeker joined the group in 1933, he and Shawn collaborated to create a dance and musical composition about the legendary abolitionist, inspired by Stephen Vincent Benét's 1928 Pulitzer Prize–winning poem. The work premiered during one of the teas at the farm that summer and was added to the first touring program. As described in the program, the dance's subject was ripped from the "torso of mid-19th century history." At seventeen minutes long, the composition was of an unparalleled duration for a solo dance:

> John Brown, as a young man, walks out alone on the plains. There the spirit of God descends upon him. In a vision he sees a procession of all the slaves of the world, and accepts his destiny as being appointed of God to be the instrument for setting them free. There is revealed to him the whole drama yet to come: his calling of the little band of volunteers; the Battle of Harper's Ferry (even to the moments when he gazes into the faces of his two dead sons); his defeat, imprisonment, hanging and funeral. Then he sees his soul rise from the grave to lead the forces of freedom to victory—and knows that though his body will lie mouldering in the grave, his soul will go marching on.[15]

The dance became a lightning rod of racial controversy, provoking divergent responses among audiences wherever Shawn performed it. He found that liberal audiences such as those in Oberlin, where abolitionist sympathies were strong, brought on more bows, whereas it was met with lukewarm reception in mid-Atlantic cities. Though Shawn received praise for *John Brown* in several quarters, he was taken aback by the glowing reception the work received at Hampton College, a historically black college in Virginia. Shawn had previously performed at Hampton on Denishawn tours, but nothing had prepared him for the excitement *John Brown* generated, including a review in the *New Journal and Guide* that hailed the solo as Shawn's "newest and greatest work."[16]

In his letters to Price, Shawn emphasized the "electric" performance at Hampton College, which he characterized as a "highlight" of the tour until that point. He made special note of performing the dance to a packed house of 2,000, "about three fourths negro."[17] The crowd gave Shawn an ovation, and many waited for an hour after the concert for him to autograph their programs.

Shawn's time at Hampton gave him the opportunity to reestablish his relationship with Charles H. Williams (1886–1978), the physical education director at the college whom Shawn had met in 1925 while touring with Denishawn. A graduate of Springfield College and the author of *Cotton Needs Pickin'* (1928), a book about Negro folk dances, Shawn invited Williams to study at the Pillow the following summer with the hope that Williams might stage similar all-male dances with his own students. Shawn had an idea for a dance for Williams that would complement his *John Brown* based on the life of Henri Christophe, the legendary Haitian slave revolutionary: "What a dance drama *Black Majesty* would make!" He told Price that "they feel I have started something real at Hampton."[18] That coming year, on the occasion of the Hampton's Anniversary, Williams established the Hampton Institute Creative Dance Group, a touring group for the black college circuit. On the program was a suite of dances *Labor Rhythms* that included Shawn's own *Cutting the Sugar Cane* paired with an original dance set to the work song "Dis Ole Hammer."

John Brown may have inspired "something real" at Hampton, but elsewhere in the South it elicited intolerance and anxiety. The first unpleasant reaction occurred at the Mississippi State College for Women in Columbus, where Shawn had grown accustomed to being received with great fanfare by its female physical education director, Miss Emma Ody Pohl. Instead, a college administrator prohibited Shawn from performing *John Brown*. Of course, the ban only made audiences want to see it more. Shawn performed another solo instead, using the *John Brown* score as accompaniment. The finale included the "Glory, Glory, Hallelujah!" melody from "Battle Hymn of the Republic," an anthem for the North during the Civil War. Shawn noted the melodic strains had on an old stagehand, who "tilted back on the two hind legs of the chair back stage, sat forward, shoved his hat back off his eyes, like an old war horse scenting powder smoke—but settled back again when the theme disappeared again." When the college president brought the treasurer backstage to write the check to Shawn, he refused to shake his hand and glared at Shawn with a "venomous hatred." Shawn recognized that the president was "a professional Southerner who still fights the Civil War who thinks of John Brown only as a rascal who came down to incite the negroes to rise up and murder the whites."

When Shawn recounted the incident to the Forbes family in Athens, Georgia, Stanton, the family's twenty-year-old son, responded: "And that's all he was, too!" Shawn was dismayed by Stanton's response, especially as he had just offered the boy a position in the company.

Price responded to Shawn's account in most encouraging terms: "What a fight your life is! Union highway robbery in Charleston, sectional prejudice at Williams and Mary where at least it might be supposed to have been outgrown—is there any time limit to the evil of military violence? They need St. Francis as much as John Brown."[19]

Shawn's hope that *John Brown*'s "universality" would compensate for any "local impingements" were often disappointed. In Tallahassee, Florida, a theater manager refused even to print the name "John Brown" in the program. He came across similar resistance in Meeker's hometown of Arkansas City, Kansas, prompting Shawn to declare to Price that it is the "dumbest city" in the "dumbest state" and "could be obliterated as far as [he was] concerned, without any loss save the sentimental loss of John Brown's first battleground."[20]

Matters were not much better in Kent, Ohio, where Shawn assumed that the former home of both John Brown and Price would receive the dance positively. Before the company's appearance there, Price wrote to Shawn about his many trips to John Brown's house in Kent: "In my boyhood he was already a legendary figure."[21] (Though Price imagined what life could have been if instead Shawn and his dancers were his boyhood heroes: "What a dream of delight it would have been for me as a little boy to have seen you big boys in your splendor as you are today.")[22]

Alas, the highly anticipated Kent performance was an abysmal failure, though not because of the racial content of the work. The high school audience that filled the front rows of the theater talked, laughed, and heckled. "The quiet moments of John Brown were ruined by the noise of those embryo racketeers!" Shawn wrote to Price.[23] Following the performance, he delivered what he characterized as a composed curtain speech to express his disappointment at the audience:

> My company and I have just completed a tremendously successful tour. We've played before hillbillies of the Carolinas and cowboys of Texas but you are the most ill-bred and ill-mannered audience to which we've ever been subjected. Nothing could bribe us to come back, although after you've heard what I think of you, you will not want us.[24]

An offended local reporter, however, described his speech as a "rip snortin' verbal lashing" in an article titled "Ted Shawn, Apostle of Dance in Natural, Razzes Kent Audience for 'Bad Manners.'" The review returned the insult, declaring that the dancers were "attired to make Mr. Gandhi look overdressed." Shawn's interpretation of John Brown, the writer continues, tested the audience's patience but bought a "sigh or two of relief as the nimble Shawn enacted what was supposed to have been a hanging scene at Harper's Ferry." Price claimed the reporter's negative response as a victory for Shawn and "the voltage of rebellion" that he had generated in Kent."[25]

In Somerset, Kentucky, the company played a theater that had been abandoned for over eight years. The producer had to hire a band of convicts to spruce it up for Shawn's performance. During *John Brown*, just at the point when Brown rouses the audience to join his crusade, the stage lights went out. Shawn stood in the dark and had Jess play the music as he, Shawn, narrated the rest of the dance to the crowd. When the lights went back on, he resumed the dance, though he was never sure whether the blackout was caused by a fuse or an intolerant patron, especially since the company truck was shot at as it made its way through the mountain country. "Moonshiners, miners, or just social?!" Shawn wondered.[26]

During the summer following the company's first tour, Shawn sent Price a clipping from the *Berkshire Eagle* that uncovered the Pillow's history as a station on the underground railroad, the secret network of paths by which slaves escaped to free states or Canada in the nineteenth century. Stephen Carter, a descendent of the original owners of the farm, was an active abolitionist. Price saw this connection as a divine sign: "That Jacob's Pillow, *John Brown*, and the fugitive slave station on the underground may be coincidence to people not in rhythms but to anyone with a knowledge of spiritual law is a startling verification. To think that your John Brown dance-saga should have steamed up into being on such ground! You should find the anniversary to the anti-slavery movement, one of Brown's dates, or Lloyd Garrison or Abraham Lincoln's and dance it in the studio on the midnight with sacrifices and libation to the *manes* and *genius loci* with only initiates present. (I'm not joking, I think that would be worth doing.)"[27] Price's readiness to claim this information as socially and spiritually meaningful may have had something to do with his own family history. He was a descendant of Philadelphia Quakers who were leaders in the abolitionist movement and whose own home was also a station on the underground railroad. When Shawn and Price later discussed the explosion at Kent, they agreed that it was not as much an accident as it seemed.

The program for first tour of Ted Shawn and His Men Dancers balanced Shawn's controversial religious solo with more popular and physical dances based in the radically transforming principles and practices of modern labor. Though Shawn upheld dancing's spiritual dimension as an antidote to the encroaching mechanization of the modern world, he presented his Men Dancers as ideal embodiments of Taylorism—efficient, reliable, durable laborers. Programs for the Men Dancers' first tour included two spectacles of labor: *Cutting the Sugar Cane* (1933), a study in the choreography

of agricultural work, and *Japanese Rickshaw Coolies* (1933). Shawn's fascination with the intersection between labor and dance received its fullest
exploration a year later with *Labor Symphony* (1934), a four-part dance that
explored the choreography of physical labor—in the fields, forest, sea, and
factory. The final section featured a stunning "machine dance" wherein the
dancers perform elaborate sequences patterned after automated pistons,
cogs, and gears. (See Figure 5.3.) In one section, the dancers formed a
living telegraph: their lower bodies create the machine's pulsing rhythm
with stringent sideways strides as their sleeve-covered arms slide across
their bare chests, creating the illusion of the dots and dashes of Morse code
on a ticker tape.

Following the last leg of the tour in the Northeast in June and a week's respite at Shawn's Jacob's Pillow farm, Shawn and the company visited Price at
Harvest House, the Williamstown residence of a close friend. Shawn brought
Price a copy of his book *The American Ballet*. Price could hardly wait to
hear in greater detail about the triumphs and tribulations that Shawn had

Figure 5.3. "Mechanized Labor" from *Labor Symphony* (1934). Photograph by
Shapiro Studio. Ted Shawn Collection. Courtesy of the Jerome Robbins Dance
Division, New York Public Library.

written about. Before dinner, Price entertained the men on the lawn with his recordings of Brahms's "Ballade in G Minor" and Bach's "Jesu, Joy of Man's Desiring." He reveled in introducing the boys to these masterpieces and in their astonished delight at the free fantasia section of the Brahms first movement. Overlees shared his idea for a dance based on the music involving a man on his knees struggling to free himself from manacles. Price was awed that this twenty-year-old's extemporaneous idea for a dance scenario was nearly identical to that which had first prompted Brahms to compose the piece.

Price ended the listening session with Beethoven's *Diabelli Variations*, then rode back with the men to the Pillow where he spent the next few days. He immediately noticed changes that had taken place in the nine months since he had been there last. Most noticeably, there were new faces, as Shawn had decided to expand the company from six to eight. (See Figure 5.4.) Fred Hearn from Asheville, North Carolina, had joined the company mid-tour as a replacement for Willard Van Simons. A recent graduate of business school, Hearn had eagerly traveled to Florida to learn the company's repertory during its two-week break at Christmas. Foster Fitz-Simons from Atlanta, Georgia, came to replace George Horn. A graduate of the University of North Carolina, Fitz-Simons was a poet and athlete who had not only written plays at college but also competed as a swimmer and fencer. Moreover, he had studied dancing with Phoebe Barr, one of Shawn's former pupils. Price called him "an aristocrat." Another newcomer was William Howell, a dark-haired, dark-eyed young man scarcely out of adolescence, who had studied with one of Shawn's former pupils at Denishawn House in New York.

At breakfast, Price met one of the nineteen young men whom Shawn had recruited from tour stops to study alongside his company at the Pillow. This particular student was the youngest Price had ever seen on the farm. He sauntered into breakfast wearing a jersey and blue swimming tights, sandaled, but bare legged from his ankles almost to the groin. In his southern drawl, he introduced himself to Price: "I am Ned Coupland." He then sat on the floor by the hearth, stretched his legs, and uttered wistfully, "I wish my legs were straight."[28]

Coupland's legs were not quite straight, nor was his left eye. He had only recently arrived at the Pillow after five days and four nights on the bus from Texas. Shawn had provisionally offered him a position in the company, though promised nothing until he saw Coupland in the studio. He told Price

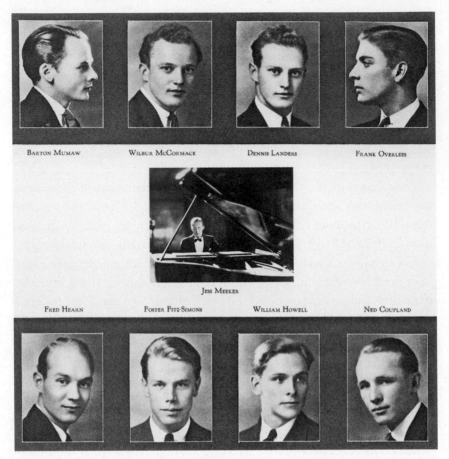

BARTON MUMAW   WILBUR MCCORMACK   DENNIS LANDERS   FRANK OVERLEES

JESS MEEKER

FRED HEARN   FOSTER FITZ-SIMONS   WILLIAM HOWELL   NED COUPLAND

Figure 5.4. Men Dancers from Ted Shawn and His Men Dancers Souvenir Program, 1934–35.

that he hoped Shawn would offer him a place in the company. Otherwise, he said, "I must find a job up here in the winter and pay back the money I borrowed to come."

The other men objected to Coupland, telling Shawn during a company meeting that he was "fresh and uppity" and that when Shawn turned his back, he tried to "ruin things." Shawn had a serious talk with Coupland, telling him that he could join the company but that he had to "mind his step." The young Texan was worth the trouble. In addition to his passion, he had five years of dance training from a former member of the Russian ballet, which posed both advantages and disadvantages to Shawn's purpose. Shawn told

Price: "Ned is still our tight little bud waiting to open. The thing I will say for him: once in the studio nothing else exists for him but the dance. I wish I could say as much for Denny."

That evening Coupland led Price by kerosene lamp to one of the cabins. He showed Price around the interior and then led Price to his bedroom. Price was touched that he wanted him to see it. They developed a special friendship, and Price began to refer to him as "my little brother." The other boys became aware of the special bond that had formed between them, especially as they spoke together in French. Price asked Shawn to keep him apprised of Coupland's progress, vowing to take responsibility for him if he were ever dismissed from the company.

Not all of the nineteen young hopefuls were as promising in Price's estimation. For example, one of the new pupils at the farm that summer was a boy who had followed the company's tour everywhere within a sweeping radius of his hometown. He was desperate to be admitted as a student. Though he lost forty pounds during the winter in anticipation of coming to study at the farm, he was still "something of a baby whale." Eventually, the men dancers convinced Shawn to accept him. One argued, "Oh, let him in. He won't bother us, and we can't stand seeing him outside looking so hungry." Shawn obliged as he believed that he was uniquely eager and determined: "Who knows what my ugly duckling may bring forth?" Shawn's instincts were right, for although "ugly duckling" Walter Terry never performed with the group, he would play an enormous role in the life of the company as a dance critic.[29]

Price observed how in addition to new faces, the farm also had new features. Just before the new students arrived on the farm, the men decided to surprise Shawn by building a stone dining room while he was away on a three-week teaching stint. Upon his return, Shawn was shocked with delight, especially at the stone fireplace they built at one end of the dining room. The men were also in the process of enlarging the barn-studio by twenty-four feet for additional dancing space, so class was conducted against the sound of hammering and sawing. The dancers created a cozy loft in the barn adjacent to the studio to use as a dormitory. Denny Landers stored a weaving loom there, as well as all the rugs and scarves he had woven. One afternoon, Price watched as Mac and a few of the new students erected a stone wall around the premises to keep casual automobilists from intruding. Others lived in the Red House, an old homestead a quarter mile from the studio, originally called "el Bethel," a reference from the biblical story of Jacob's Ladder meaning "place of God."

Shawn also implemented a strict regimen for training and working. He taught a company class at 8:00 A.M., first barre exercises, then floor sequences, then short études. (See Figure 5.5.) Price noticed how disciplined the class had become. Shawn was an exacting teacher. He was blunt about telling students what they were not doing well. Sometimes instead of teaching by word, he would leap up and demonstrate a phrase adding a bit of bravura. The men would stand or kneel watching, often spontaneously bursting with

Figure 5.5. Shawn teaching class at Jacob's Pillow. Photograph by Richard Merrill. Courtesy of Jacob's Pillow Dance Festival Archives.

delighted laughter at the pleasure of seeing what he had wanted them to do but what was for them clearly too difficult to emulate.

Following a cigarette break, Mac took over teaching duty at 11 A.M. He was serious about teaching, as he aspired to be the first from the group to teach dancing to men in college. He began to develop his own eclectic dance terminology. Once Price caught Mumaw laughing as he stood outside the studio listening to Mac gave fanciful instructions to the boys: "Now, fellows, chisel! Now, *pas de basque!*"

At noon everyone joined Shawn on the platform outside the studio. The men ate tray lunches and sunbathed naked on straw mats or bath towels while Shawn read aloud from Plato, Havelock Ellis, Oupensky, or Whitman. "If this isn't Hellenic *palaestra*, then what is it?" Price wondered. (See Figures 5.6, 5.7, 5.8.)

In the afternoons, Shawn gave private lessons to five girl pupils while the men scattered to perform their duties—gardening, woodcutting, stonework. Shawn had recently hired a cook, a pleasant German woman from a fraternity house at the University of Chicago, who lived in a little cottage in the dooryard. Between 4 and 5 P.M., the dancers rehearsed on their own and had

Figure 5.6. Frank Overlees (*left*) and Ted Shawn (*right*) at lunch hour on the patio. Stanley Davis Scrapbook (1938). Courtesy of Jacob's Pillow Dance Festival Archives.

Figure 5.7. "Palaestra" of the Berkshires (Lunch hour with Shawn and men dancers on the patio). Courtesy of Jacob's Pillow Dance Festival Archives.

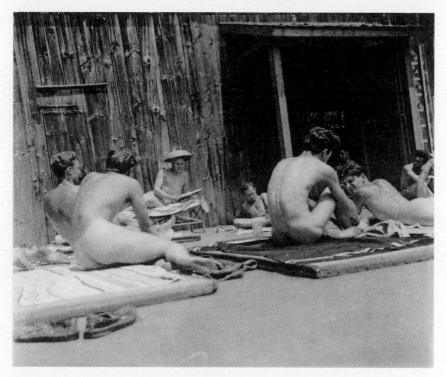

Figure 5.8. "Lunch buns" and "Food in the nude!" Dale Lefler Scrapbook.
Courtesy of Jacob's Pillow Dance Festival Archives.

a light snack of crackers and milk. Then for two hours, Shawn and Meeker
worked in the studio on musical arrangements. Dinner was at 7:30 P.M. sharp.
Shawn sat at one end of a long table, Mumaw at the other. The neophytes sat
at two smaller tables.

After a day of strenuous physical and mental labor, the boys retired early to
their rooms. Once again Price stayed in Mumaw's room next door to Shawn's
on the second floor of the main house. He delighted in the fact that Mumaw's
walls were now covered with cleverly mounted prints and photographs collected during the company's tour.

The next morning, Price went into the studio to watch Shawn rehearse
a music visualization to Bach's "Three-Part Invention," no. 12. Shawn had
originally choreographed the dance for a "mixed" group of Denishawn
dancers, but was adapting it for his men's company. Under Shawn's direction,
Mumaw, Mac, and Landers worked for over an hour, teaching the intricate
phrases of the ninety-second composition. Shawn created the dance so that

each of the three groups of dancers corresponded to one of the three lines of counterpoint in the music. Throughout, the men remain relentlessly vertical, with arms crossed at the chest and hands resting on shoulders as if in a self-embrace. Maintaining the integrity of the lines, the dancers advance and retreat, cross and change direction, all the while pulsing up and down in strict correspondence to the counterpoint, as if they were the keys on a player piano.

Price was left breathless from the way the choreography captured the "intellectual and impersonal note" of the music, a quality he believed made it pleasurable for the dancers to perform: "Their eyes were intense and serious: nine men thinking, and dancing as they thought. Thoughtful dancing!"[30]

Shawn's response was quite different from Price's. He expressed his frustration that the dancers were wearing trunks of different colors and textures—and others nothing at all. Because he sought uniformity and precision, Shawn suggested that the group rehearse entirely nude. The boys complied.

Initially, Price had voiced the opinion that nudity would detract from the dance's elegance but came around once the men were naked before him: "Why is it that stripped they look so much taller, nobler and more chaste?" He reasoned that when a dancer performed nude, "the whole being is permitted to speak, and no false and artificial horizontal lines to cut the harmonious vertical lines of the erect human body." Price was stunned by the affect of "nine Ionic columns moving in stately rhythms, shifting position without ceasing in their function to uphold the elements of their portico." (See Figure 5.9.) Price was especially bewildered to learn that Shawn had no intention of programming the dance: "We have a right to do a piece now and then simply for our own satisfaction."

"And for mine," Price thought to himself.

After rehearsal, Price and Mumaw walked back to the farmhouse to enjoy one last dinner before Price left for Boston. He took the opportunity to convey his appreciation for writing to Shawn throughout the tour.

"It seems as if your letters are 'timed' to just where and when they were most needed." Mumaw told Price. "Shawn is happier than he has ever been in his life."

Price believed him. "He is at last expressing his own individuality and I smile to see how hard the youthful aspirant and the Methodist

Figure 5.9. Shawn and Dancers in Bach's "Three Part Invention, no. 12." Photograph by Shapiro Studio. Ted Shawn Collection. Courtesy of the Jerome Robbins Dance Division, New York Public Library.

Ministry in him dies, for on the sun-platform after lunch, he talks to these youngsters with the earnestness of a preacher, and his artistic zeal is at one with a passion for souls."

Mumaw added, "This work spoils one for anything else. Not one of the boys, once in, can ever get out."

"Why?"

"Because without it life seems meaningless."[31]

Price agreed, but only after being away from the farm did he realize how spoiled he truly was for the opportunity to see Shawn and dancers at work. He could barely wait to return. Shawn invited him back in the fall of 1934, just three days before the company set out on their second tour. Shawn was anxious to give Price a preview of his latest composition, a dance set to Beethoven's *Diabelli Variations*, which Price had suggested to Shawn at Harvest House the previous summer. Shawn took his choreographic inspiration from a Roman frieze of a pyrrhic dance. *Variations on a Theme of Diabelli* consists of six of Beethoven's thirty-three variations and had them filmed in 1935.

In the first variation, Shawn enters the stage wide-eyed and smiling, then establishes the dance's theme—the virtuosity of swordsmanship.

To the "muscular" chords in the Beethoven score, he lunges forward like a fencer on attack, his arms becoming foils. In the next variation, "Alla Marcia," the dancers march in lines, then peel off into four pairs and spar with one other until, in unison and in profile, one in each pair suffers a fatal blow and collapses to the floor. Price's favorite variation was a lovely duet for Mumaw and Fitz-Simons, in which they trotted and pranced across the stage as if in some spectacular joust. The final variation literally reverses the dance's theme of running, marching, advancing, and riding as it had all eight men retreating and withdrawing, literally leaping and skipping backward, as if these modern warriors were returning to their ancient frieze.

Shawn also presented Price with *The Hound of Heaven*, a seven-minute solo based on the poem by Francis Thompson (1859–1907) set to original music by Jess Meeker. (See Figure 5.10.) The dance loosely follows the structure of the 182-line poem about God's relentless pursuit

Figure 5.10. Ted Shawn in *Hound of Heaven* (1934). Photograph by Shapiro Studio. Ted Shawn Collection. Courtesy of the Jerome Robbins Dance Division, The New York Public Library.

of the human soul. Shawn appears on stage with a cloak, which he uses to hide, shield, and protect his soul. He then uses it as a cape or wings with which he attempts to stray away from the path of righteousness. The cloak becomes leaden and weighs him down with guilt. He peels it off, slowly revealing the soul within. He seeks the support of a stepped platform—an altar of sorts—upon which he leans, pulls himself across, and climbs. He then stands and slowly raises his arms to his sides, as if crucified.

Nobody applauded. The silence lingered until Price rose to his feet and cheered. He walked over to Shawn and quietly told him that the dance surpassed even his *John Brown*: "That theme was factional in a certain sense. This includes everybody. And it has romantic beauty."[32] Shawn was grateful for Price's reaction, explaining that he had conceived of the dance over twenty years ago but waited for the right opportunity and the right composer to take on the subject of religious mysticism.

"This dance took a lot of praying!" Shawn told Price. He could not render Thompson's literary portrayal of the slow succumbing to faith until he had first lived the experience himself.

Price looked deep into Shawn's eyes as he wiped the perspiration from his haggard face and thought: "How little you suspect, Shawn, that the same is true of me with my *All Souls*, and that perhaps you and I in this very spot are first living our Secret Legion." After rehearsal, the group returned to the farmhouse for a special dinner prepared by Lillian Cox, Shawn's spiritual advisor, and Mrs. Huston, the keeper of a nearby lodge beside Greenwater Pond where Shawn received his telephone and telegraph messages. Shawn himself was on a strict diet of eggs and orange juice, so initially resisted his urge to devour the roast leg of lamb. The men enthusiastically urged him to eat, except for Mumaw, who castigated him: "What is the use of dieting if you don't diet?" Shawn ignored the question and ate the lamb.

After dinner, the men gathered to hear Price talk about the tensions between Hellenism and Christianity based on a recent lecture of Sir Richard Livingstone, the Oxford classicist. The men listened as they made finishing touches on costumes and props, enthralled to realize that philosophy and theater were affined means for advancing culture. Price remarked that the war clubs they were carving looked like canoe paddles. Mac replied, "We not only paddle our own canoe, but we make our own paddles!" That statement became the company's unofficial motto.

Shawn, Mumaw, and Price settled by the fire for a quiet talk over a bottle of orange wine made by Mumaw's parents in Florida. Price went to Mumaw's room to go to bed, when "something quite happy occurred," as he wrote. Ned Coupland had come upstairs to talk with Shawn. As he emerged from Shawn's bedroom, Price beckoned him into his room. The two looked into each other's eyes. "He seems to crave it," Price wrote, "and I like the look of him into me full as well." Price recounted their exchange in his journal.

"I want you to stay with the company this season and do well," Price whispered.

"I want to," he replied.

"Do it for my sake. I am very fond of you. Be a credit to me. You are my little brother."

"Do me a favor?" Coupland asked. "Do you have a picture of yourself? May I have one?"

"No, but I will get one made."[33]

Price and Coupland embraced for the briefest instant, as they heard someone open the nearby door to Meeker's room. Price wrote: "With the instinctive delicacy which one comes to expect in that household, the steps drew back into the chamber and waited."

"I shall shake hands with you downstairs as with the others, when I leave," Price said, "but this hug is for you alone."

The next morning, Price said his goodbyes and got into the waiting car that swept through the valley into the October mist. Aboard the train for Boston, he nodded off while envisioning the men acting out his scenario for Greek heroes such as Cheiron, the Argonauts, Theseus, and finally, the Sacred Legion's Battle at Charonaea. He awoke, realizing that his dream had already come to pass: "I have seen the Sacred Legion dancing in the Berkshires," he scribbled in his journal.[34]

In the final stretch of the second tour of Ted Shawn and His Men Dancers in 1934–35, the famed producer Daniel Mayer, who had catapulted Denishawn to international acclaim, invited the company to perform its successful program in London. For two weeks in June 1935, during the height of the Silver Jubilee festivities for King George V, the "He-Man Dancers" or "The First Male Dance Team" as the British press called the company, attracted respectable crowds to its three matinee concerts at His

Majesty's Theater, making it possible to book an additional week at the Apollo Theater. Unfortunately, large audiences did not result in a financial windfall owing to Shawn's misunderstanding of the contract structure. More disappointing to Shawn, the company received a few damaging reviews, which limited the possibility of a more extensive Europe tour. He cut his losses by bonding with his dancers who were enjoying their first time abroad, then headed back to the farm where much was awaiting him. (See Figures 5.11 and 5.12.)

Not long after returning to Jacob's Pillow, Shawn made the radical decision to incorporate the troupe, making each dancer an equal shareholder in the newly formed enterprise Shawn Dancers, Inc. One of the first collective decisions the company made was to purchase 55 acres of land that abutted the 150 that formed the Pillow. The buildings on the new parcel would be used as dormitories for students during the summer.[35] That fall, the company members voted to increase their salaries, a decision Shawn opposed in favor of saving the company's modest earnings for the off-season. He was unanimously outvoted. During the first tour, George Gloss had tried to convince the boys that they were underpaid. It was a hard argument to make given that Shawn himself was earning the same amount as his dancers. Meeker was the only one to receive more. At the beginning of the 1936–37 tour, the boys voted that Shawn would earn the same amount as Meeker, $20 a performance but no more than $100 week. The vote was cast on Shawn's birthday. Taking note of this uncommon operating structure, one reporter began to refer to the company as "Shawn's Communist ballet."

The company's third tour in 1935–36 took the men to the West Coast. As had become customary, Price went to the Pillow to serve as a test audience for the new programs. Frank Overlees met Price at the train station and took a circuitous route back to the farm giving them time to catch up. Price reflected on how their relationship had grown since they had first met. Though he remained the "sturdy soul" of the group, Overlees also seemed more willing to participate in group conversations. He even tried to convey to Price the absurd predicament of a dancer who comes to know a dance from the inside out:

"You never see anything, you don't know how it looks. I've never seen the *Rhapsody* though I have performed it hundreds of times. When I look up all I see are dirty canvas drops and lights glaring in my eyes. Sometimes in the studio I catch a glimpse of a formation in the mirror and see that it is really

Figure 5.11. Ted Shawn and His Men Dancers in London, 1935. Ted Shawn Collection. Courtesy of the Jerome Robbins Dance Division, New York Public Library.

beautiful, but in performance, you have to think to the music, think with the rhythm, think in your own body."[36]

It is not surprising to learn that Overlees was thinking about dancing as a way of understanding the world. It was the very subject of a new dance that Shawn had created for the coming tour, and as with other of Shawn's dance for his men's group, it was based on an idea Price had suggested. In July 1935, Price had sent Shawn a copy of *The Classical Tradition in Poetry*

Figure 5.12. Men's group in "Dance of the Dynamo" from *Labor Symphony* (1934) taken in a London power plant, 1935. Ted Shawn Collection. Courtesy of the Jerome Robbins Dance Division, New York Public Library.

(1927) by the Australian classicist, translator, and dramatist Gilbert Murray. Shawn read the book and discovered a chapter that discussed the Greek concept of *molpai*. A predecessor to the ancient Greek dithyramb, molpai were embodied expressions of meaning for which there are no linguistic equivalents. In ancient Greece molpai were performed on mountain tops, threshing floors, and altars. It was a word that Shawn would have had to coin had it not already existed, though he readily admitted that before reading the book, he likely would have thought that "molpai" referred to a new brand of toothpaste or a brand of breakfast food.

Eager to share his latest choreographic effort with Price, Shawn welcomed him to a seat beside the stove in the barn-studio and handed him a glass of rum to take the edge off the October chill in the air. The men then took their places to debut *Kinetic Molpai*. The twenty-minute dance is organized by a series of eleven studies of physical and kinetic forces: oppositions, falls, successions, foldings and unfoldings, and surges. Set to a score by Meeker, the dance grew organically out of Delsartean exercises and "abstract movement problems" the dancers had identified in class. Abandoning his usual approach of organizing a dance around a specific narrative or character, Shawn developed original movement and group formations, relying less heavily on his usually limited palette of balletic jumps and turns. He made virtually no use of pantomime. Price considered the dance one of Shawn's best. Walter Terry, too, claimed it was the "greatest piece of abstract choreography."[37]

About the dance's most distinctive section, "Surge," Price wrote: "There is a discharge of physical energy from it into the beholder. I felt an actual physical invigoration."[38] Wearing wide-legged trousers and wrist cuffs, the men, summoning the ferocity of the breaking surf, rose, fell, and rolled to the rhythm of rushing arpeggios. It was a showstopper on tour as well. Yet despite the celebration of physical power, the dance conjured a sense of mourning— or as Price says, the "masculinity of grief." (See Figure 5.13.)

That evening, Shawn read aloud from *God and My Father* (1932), Clarence Day's humorous memoir. This was a primer for a serious lecture by Price on world history. Price intended for the lecture to inspire a discussion among the men about their individual artistic identities in relation to the group. After having made a series of points about developing self-respect, peace of mind, and good conscience, Price asked if he had made himself clear. Frank Overlees spoke up in his deep voice, "Yes. And you have said a lot, Mr.!"

The boys left for bed. Ned Coupland stayed behind with Shawn and Price. He went to Price, smiling and holding out his arms like a child. He laid his cheek against Price's and said "Thank you for a wonderful evening." When he left, Shawn shared his suspicion with Price that Coupland's obvious child-like tendencies resulted from his relationship with his unmarried mother, "a stormy soul," and that his immaturity was interfering with his dancing. Taking Price's hands into his own, Shawn said "It seems as though you were sent here to help me." Price was happy to help, especially with Coupland, but

Figure 5.13. *Kinetic Molpai* (1935). Photograph by John Lindquist. John Lindquist Collection. Courtesy of Houghton Library, Harvard University.

left Shawn with the sinking feeling that his affection would not be enough to save him.

The next morning, everyone gathered in the studio. Price sat in an armchair beside an open door, drenched in a rectangular ray of sunshine. Wrapped in a steamer rug and a Bavarian hunting jacket, he watched the company rehearse *Kinetic Molpai* once again. At a point in the dance when Overlees was not dancing, he stood behind Price's chair and rested his hands on his shoulders. Price reached around and took Overlees's hand. He pressed the back of his hand briefly to his lips, quivering with emotion. Overlees knew that he was loved and was in good hands. Though not a single word was said about the exchange, Price noticed that when they next spoke, Overlees's voice was somehow more gentle.

In his journal, Price wrote: "Everything was understood. What was understood? Nothing for which any words exist." Their exchange was the very meaning of *molpai*, embodied acts that words cannot sufficiently represent.

June 1936 was a pivotal moment for Shawn and the Pillow. He had mailed brochures, and for the first time, men officially came to the farm to study dance. Moreover, the company was working on a new dance to be performed that August at the Robin Hood Dell in Philadelphia with the Philadelphia Orchestra. For this high-profile performance, Shawn planned on creating a dance to the Finale of Antonín Dvořák's *New World Symphony* (1893), a work based on "negro" and Native American melodies that the Czech composer had encountered in the United States during the 1890s.

Price spent mornings in the studio watching the work progress. He noticed how efficiently Shawn worked with the senior company members. He also observed that Shawn, who lacked the technical language to express his rhythmic needs to Meeker during rehearsal, often raised his voice, shouting at him as though he were deaf. Shawn proudly told Price that he went all summer without having raised his voice.

Frank rejoined, "Not because Shawn has improved, but because Jess has."

Shawn looked at Price plaintively and asked, "You see how they treat me?"[39]

Together they listened to a record of the Dvořák symphony, as Price led a discussion about its structure. He divided the music into four sections and charted the development of the choreography. Shawn selected the work because it evoked the theme of pioneers on the frontier, but left room for him to create scenarios and movements that were "understandable but not too realistic."[40] Price left the men to do their work. Later that afternoon, Price was called to the studio to see a sketch of the result. It was more literal than he had hoped. It dramatized the life of a band of frontiersmen braving the elements—animals, hunger, boredom, and Indians. As leader, Shawn scanned the horizon, then directed the men through pantomime, pointing them toward an ever-receding frontier.

Price noticed one of the newest dancers, Fred Hearn, who like Foster Fitz-Simons was a graduate of the University of North Carolina and had been a student of former Denishawn dancer Phoebe Barr. The other newcomer was Horace Jones, a wrestler from Oklahoma A&M College who had studied with a former Denishawn student Mary Tree. Jones was hired to replace "little brother" Ned Coupland, whom Shawn ultimately asked to leave the company on account of his immaturity. Horace became known as Horace "Beautiful Body" Jones. "A magnificent specimen of young manhood in every sense," according to Price, Horace had the physique that sculptors seek in models. Price reveled in describing every detail of his physique: his powerful torso, slender hips, broad shoulders, heavily muscled arms and legs, extraordinary phallus, rugged head, powerful jaw, broad forehead, wide blue eyes full of candor and friendliness, strong white teeth, and wavy brown hair. Despite his physical perfection, Price thought that Horace's movements were "heavy."[41]

Horace took to life at the Pillow like a duck to water. He pulled pranks that were playful yet offensive. His antics were a symptom of the fact that he was not entirely sure what all the dancing was about. One afternoon in a discussion about nakedness in dance, he drawled: "The first time I saw these fellows in a public performance I thought 'what do these guys think they are doing dancing naked?'"

It was a legitimate question. Among the men, the topic of nudity in Shawn's dances came up persistently in conversations both practical and philosophical. Price recalled an episode in the studio during a costume fitting the previous spring. Shawn was finalizing decisions about costumes for a Maori war dance when Mac suddenly exploded with anger. He refused to wear yet another revealing costume. When Mac saw that Shawn was humiliated by his outburst, he immediately apologized. In Mac's defense, Price assured him that the matter was worthy of discussion.

"How complicated the question of costume can be even in as simple a matter as trunks," said Price.

"Simple? It is the simple costumes that are the hardest. We have never yet found a design that satisfied us," Mac complained.[42] He was especially frustrated with wearing loincloths or "cinctures" as Price insisted on calling them. Mac's objection to them was based as much on mechanics as modesty. To make his case, he took Price to the side of the studio and demonstrated the difficulty of strapping a loincloth over his genitals and the limits it placed on his movement.

"It's still too small for public performance!" Mac protested.

The topic of nudity led to several awkward conversations, many instigated by Price, who took pleasure in memorializing the exchanges in his journals. Despite the fact that the company's displays of exposed flesh were virtually unprecedented in American theater, critics rarely commented on the men's scanty costumes. Those who did were shocked more by the fact that they danced barefooted than bare-chested. In fact, writers would more often criticize the men's elaborate costumes than their lack thereof.

"It's a dilemma," Landers added. "If we overemphasize the trunks, they say, 'We know you've got 'em, so why cover them up?' If you underemphasize them, then it is as if you are dancing naked, so why wear anything? What would happen if we sprang nakedness on a studio audience?"

"We'd all be pinched!" said Mac.

"Very well, then, let's go to court, give an exhibition and let the judge decide."

"He'd decide to never let any of us dance again," Mac said.[43]

The controversy surrounding public nudity had been recently fueled by the 1933 trial of fan dancer Sally Rand (1904–1979). A star attraction of the Chicago World's Fair that year, Rand titillated audiences by dancing with oversized ostrich feather fans to conceal her otherwise naked body. Chicago Mayor Edward J. Kelly repeatedly threatened legal action against the Fair's organizers who turned a blind eye to Rand's indecent exposure. Eventually she was arrested (multiple times in one day, according to some reports), then tried in the Women's Court of Chicago, only to be released after paying a $25 fine. The following month, she was arrested once again, though this time, if the local papers are to be trusted, Rand was ordered to perform her fan dance before a jury charged with determining whether her dance was immoral. Found guilty of indecency, Rand was sentenced to a year in jail and a $200 fine, though she was released on a $2,000 cash bond. She returned to the "Streets of Paris" exhibition at the World's Fair the very next day. The harsh sentence only served to increase Rand's star status. The lesson was not lost on other burlesque and novelty dancers, who began to picket outside courthouses demanding that they be arrested as well, at least according to one cynical reporter.[44]

As male "artist-athletes," Shawn's dancers were not subjected to the same level of scrutiny as female popular entertainers of the day, even if they had a reputation as "God's gift to the women's colleges of America" and "the only male striptease act in captivity."[45] In 1934, a year after Shawn established his company, Hollywood film producers began to enforce the Motion Picture Production Code of 1930 (or the "Hays Code"), a set of guidelines by which the film industry agreed to censor what was considered immoral and indecent content in Hollywood films. The code outlined specific restrictions concerning both dance and costuming in film. For example, the code forbade "obscene" dancing, defined as any movement that suggests or represents a sexual act or "indecent passion."[46] It also stipulated that dancing costumes intended to permit "undue exposure or indecent movements in the dance" be censored. Under the Hays Code, nudity was permitted only in documentary films that depicted "ethnographic" realities. A similar logic applied to Shawn's repertory in that his dancers tended to show more flesh in dances based on primitive themes. Moreover, like female dancers, Shawn's men transformed their bodies into "art" by depilitating then powdering their bodies so that they appeared to be sculpted from marble. In other instances, they painted their faces and bodies to approximate the complexions of the Native Americans, Asians, and North Africans they portrayed in their dances.

Price asked the dancers if they thought audiences would ever be sufficiently ready to experience nudity as an aesthetic rather than a sexual experience. The dancers said that they were inured to nudity and thought they could watch nude dancing as art without sexual distraction. Price insisted that he, too, watched them dance without a thought about sex, though the dancers knew that the near-naked display of their bodies was an essential aspect of the experience of Shawn's dances for members of the audience, including Price. This much was clear when they realized that among their most ardent fans at the Friday teas were members of the Burgoyne Trail, a nudist colony located eight miles from the farm and founded at the same time the company formed.

Next to dancing and nudity, sex was the most common topic of discussion between Price and the dancers. Shawn encouraged his dancers to speak frankly about sexuality and to accept it as a natural rather than shameful aspect of their lives. He understood that his dancers were virile young men "in the pink of condition," as Price put it, and thus established a very liberal policy regarding their sexual lives: "What you do behind chamber doors is no affair of mine and won't be inquired into."[47] It was a self-serving policy for sure. To dignify the topic of human sexuality, Shawn once asked Price to give the dancers a "sex talk." All the men attended. Some even brought friends. Price lectured on the history of sex, beginning with the sexual freedom of the ancient Greeks, the "excessive preoccupation with chastity" of Christianity, and finally the "sexual revolution," which for Price meant the ideas of Havelock Ellis and Sigmund Freud. Price's "sex talk" was more intellectual than technical, and thus not quite what the young men had expected, but they were compelled by his message that the Greek ideal of human sexuality was a viable alternative to the confining values of modern American sexuality.

The Men Dancers were sex symbols of the sorority circuit. Price once encouraged Shawn to sell posters of his buff dancers, promising that he would become rich from selling them to college girls who would no doubt cover their dorm walls with them. The men conveyed some surprise at how routinely young women would make sexual and romantic overtures. "They know we are here today and gone tomorrow," explained one. "Plus, they have had a whole evening to look us over practically naked and pick out the one they want. They identify us from the program knowing we must be sound, for otherwise we couldn't do what they have just seen us do!"[48]

Rumor had it that Landers had a girlfriend in every city. His uncontrollable libido often landed himself in trouble, danger even. During a rare tour layover in Ford City, Pennsylvania, he went for a drive in the company truck with a girl named Julie, who, as it turned out was already involved with a married man. During their joyride, Julie's married paramour drove alongside them, forcing Landers to drive off the road. He went to punch the guy, but instead, the man beat Landers senseless and threatened Julie. Landers called Shawn and the men who immediately drove to the scene. Only later, when police arrested the man, did Landers learn that he was carrying a gun.

Shawn was distressed by Landers's erratic behavior. His philandering had taken a toll on his dancing, too. One night while sleeping in the spare cot in Landers's cabin, Price learned that Landers was convinced he would never become a great dancer, so he planned to leave the company to start a business venture with Alfred Barton, a wealthy friend of Shawn's. Barton was the manager of the Miami Beach Club in Florida during the winter and the Montauk Hotel in summer. He was also a frequent visitor to the farm. Price warned Landers against being beholden to a wealthy patron and pointed out that Alfred Barton himself was "owned" by his "40 million dollar wife."[49] Having lost his lover Ben to the wealthy daughter of a land baron, Price was particularly sensitive to men who traded their love for men for the security offered by wealthy wives.

Denny Landers was not the only one planning to leave the company. Wilbur "Mac" McCormack wanted to finish his senior year at Springfield College. Foster Fitz-Simons planned to create his very own company. Jess Meeker was aware that the dancers were plotting exit strategies. It concerned him enough that he approached Price to help mitigate the dissent brewing within the ranks. The problem, according to Meeker, was Shawn's choreography, especially the sequences of his dances that were "too personal" and thereby "too embarrassing to watch." Shawn received many bad reviews on account of his intense and personal portrayal of grief. Meeker reminded Price of the most devastating: "Shawn Dies Four Times in First Third of Program."

"Why complain? Shawn dies so beautifully! Just let him die four times," Price replied, even though he understood Meeker perfectly well. To help company morale, he advised Shawn to mellow the melodrama in *New World*.[50]

Jess Meeker warned Price that the group would likely disband within two years if Shawn did not give his dancers the opportunity to choreograph their own dances, arguing that no conservatory of music would prohibit its students from composing. Meeker also worried about the "lack of scope" in both Shawn's choreography and his teaching, pointing out that the boys were "put through the precisely same technical drills as in summer of 1933." Adding to this dangerous mix was the fact that Shawn was too overworked even to notice the restlessness within the company. Agreeing with Meeker and determined to keep the company together, Price promised to speak with Shawn that evening at a "housewarming" party at Denny Landers's recently built cabin, an extraordinary structure the men called "Landerbilt."

That evening at Landerbilt, the men gathered around a fire. Frank Overlees and Denny Landers resting on one cot, Mumaw and Jess on another. Foster perched on the straight-back chair, Shawn on the bench. Mac's collie and Foster's black Scottie named Gil romped together on the floor, pulling at the rag rug. At an appropriate turn in the conversation, Price diplomatically raised the suggestion that the boys be required to choreograph for themselves. Their faces lit up at the mere suggestion. Price told Shawn their reaction to the subject. At first Shawn was defensive, but he ultimately conceded. He needed to hear it from Price. Sensing that the channels of communication had been opened, Price also addressed Meeker's concern about Shawn's melodramatic solos by relaying an important lesson he had learned from studying Michelangelo's preliminary sketches for the frescoes of the Sistine Chapel: "The artist knows that merely personal grief is not very important. It becomes significant only when generalized." The men were not certain whether Shawn made the connection to his own choreography, but they were pleased that Price had at least broached the topic. "How often hereafter I shall call the magic of this evening out of these boards!" Landers told Price.

Over the course of the first three of the "seven magic" years of Ted Shawn and His Men Dancers, Price's commitment to the company and its "adroit social poetics" strengthened. He conveyed as much to Shawn in a 1935 New Year's letter: "I think we are now on our way to one of the goals of human liberation, and even if I were not so interested in you as a human being and artist, I would be as a social force. Believe in yourself and your work, for I believe in them and I know."[51] Price was convinced that through their beauty, Shawn's dances would "liberate" American attitudes toward sexuality. However, this goal was continually threatened by the company's troubled finances, which kept the group on the brink of collapse. Price was always willing to mediate the inevitable artistic and personal tensions that developed between Shawn and his dancers, usually by expressing his unconditional belief in the company's cultural significance. However, unbeknownst to most of the dancers, Price was devoting significant time and counsel to help Shawn confront threats to the company's existence that lay beyond the Pillow, namely, the growing influence of modern dance in America.

Modernism on Main Street, 1936–1939

In fall 1936, Ted Shawn and His Men Dancers were rehearsing in their remote farm in the Berkshire Hills for the fourth national tour of small cities and towns, preparing to bring their unique brand of homespun modernism to Main Street, USA. Though the company performed in several metropolitan areas, it never quite achieved critical and commercial success in New York City, the epicenter of the modern dance movement. In Shawn's justified estimation, this predicament had everything to do with *New York Times* dance critic John Martin's deliberate attempts to exclude him from the modern dance enterprise. Shawn's sense of estrangement from the modern dance world grew, as did his "rage" toward Martin, so much so that between 1936 and the company's end in 1940, Shawn's writings and choreography embodied two opposing impulses: a desire for recognition within the modern dance movement and an effort to undermine its legitimacy altogether.

In 1927, John Martin was appointed as the first dance critic at the *New York Times*. In that role, he helped to establish the burgeoning modern dance movement, including the careers of former Denishawn dancers Martha Graham, Doris Humphrey, and Charles Weidman. In 1931–32, Martin joined the faculty of the New School in Manhattan's Greenwich

Village and delivered lectures about modern dance, often inviting Graham and Humphrey to demonstrate some of his key ideas. In 1936, Martin joined the faculty of the Bennington School of the Dance, to proselytize the virtues of modern dance at the experimental summer dance program established by dancer and teacher Martha Hill at Bennington College in 1934, just months following the first tour of Shawn and the Men Dancers. Conceived as "a center for the study of modern dance in America," the program's faculty included Graham, Humphrey, Weidman, and German dancer and teacher Hanya Holm. Louis Horst taught composition and served as musical director at Bennington. Also in that year, Horst created *Dance Observer*, a magazine dedicated to the art of modern dance. A modern-day version of the Denishawn School, Bennington shared aspects of Denishawn's approach to dance education, not to mention some of Denishawn's finest teachers. Bennington was a threat to Shawn's vision for establishing his own school at Jacob's Pillow, just forty-five miles south.

During the Men Dancers' first tour, Shawn received a copy of Martin's book *The Modern Dance* (1933). Shawn was irate that Martin wrote in most glowing terms about his "disloyal students" (a Christian Science designation) Humphrey and Graham, yet mentioned Isadora Duncan only twice, St. Denis once, and Shawn not at all. Shawn unfairly characterized the premise of Martin's book thus: "imitate the methods of Mary Wigman both as to dance and use of music."[52] Martin did write his first notice about Ted Shawn and His Men Dancers during its first tour in 1934. He called Shawn an "ardent crusader" for establishing the presence of men in dance and unequivocally recognized the remarkable fact that "no other dance in the country can boast of . . . a tour" such as his, with a route list of more than a hundred cities.[53] Though Martin mentioned news items and listing information concerning Shawn and his company, he rarely ever actually reviewed the company again until its farewell performances. Shawn was incensed by the omission.

Shawn grew increasingly resentful that Martin's influence had eclipsed his own in matters regarding American dance. In the spring of 1936, Shawn had the opportunity to publicly redress the oversight. At the request of *Boston Herald* owner Sidney Winslow Jr. (the father of Miriam Winslow, a former Denishawn pupil), the newspaper's editor Robert Choate offered Shawn the opportunity to write a series of twenty-seven dance editorials, three a week for nine weeks beginning on April 7. Shawn jumped at the chance to confront Martin in his own arena of the printed page and to reestablish himself as America's leading dance ambassador. Though many of his editorials retreaded familiar ground that Shawn had covered in previous publications and lectures—such as dance as religious expression, the value of physical education, and the "scourge" of tap dancing on the dance world—with these editorials, Shawn seized the opportunity to challenge Martin's definitions of dance modernism.

In one editorial, Shawn dismisses the very term "modern dance" on existential grounds. He first points out that he has yet to meet a dancer who could explain what "modern dance" means. He then tries to delegitimize the significance of the term "modern dance" on the basis that it could only be defined through negative differentiation: "It is not the scarf flutterings of Isadora, not the incense laden orientalism of Ruth St. Denis, not the spectacular stage shows of the Russian ballet (thus dismissing in supercilious words three of the greatest contributions of the dance of our times.)"[54] Of course, Martin also conceded that the term "modern dance" was "obviously an inadequate one."[55]

In a related editorial on the rise of expressionism in Germany and its influence on American modern dance, Shawn reminds his readers that in 1931 he brought Margarete Wallmann, director of the Berlin-Wigman Schule to America to teach at the Denishawn School.[56] He contends that German modern dance was firmly based on the teachings of Rudolf Laban, which he claims are "pure Delsarte," a philosophy and practice he himself had studied. Thus Denishawn had been operating for several years under the Delsartean influence before Wigman presented her first solos in 1919. In essence, he argues that Denishawn was modern before there was German expressionism. He then minimizes the contributions of German expressionists, noting that their single contribution to theatrical dance was amplifying the "emotional attack" of movement. Shawn disparaged the aesthetics of the modern choreographers, most especially Martha Graham's dark, psychological dances. American youth, he insisted, are not interested in such "abnormal psychology." He contended that apart from a brief interest in the "neurotic and the perverse" during the post-war years, American audiences had returned to the "normal business of living" and deserved a dance reflective of that spirit. "A system of dance based on pathology" ran counter to the "wholesome, normal, balanced, and clear-visioned" character of American youth. Indeed, Shawn believed that modern dance was a passing fad, subject to a statute of limitations of six years, though he begrudgingly admitted that the moderns had left "some nugget of eternal value" in American dance.

Shawn also rejected the term "modern dance" on semantic grounds: "If you are interested in dynamics of movement, rather than lyric beauty; if you are concerned with movement coming from an inner kinetic impulse, rather than clean cut design and clarity of bodily line; if you prefer spontaneous improvisation rather than learning already created routines of dance steps; if you feel that learning of the accepted alphabet, grammar and rhetoric of the dance would cramp your individual style—then say so! But do not call it 'modern' for there have been dancers who have felt this way in every generation of human history."[57] Shawn's offense to the term is significant, for it demonstrates his awareness of the defining formal and compositional aspects of modern dance and even justifies a rationale for distinguishing it from other forms of theatrical dancing, thus making it evident that Shawn's real concern was with the authority Martin had established to designate it as such.

Apart from the philosophical, historical, and sematic factors contributing to his resistance to the term "modern dance," Shawn differentiated himself from modern choreographers in political terms. Foremost, he refuted the characterization of modern dance as a "gesture of revolt." Since the ballet profession in the United States had not yet been established, Shawn reasoned that American dancers had neither an artistic nor a labor basis against which to revolt, unlike their German counterparts who had to contend with a state theater system. Widening his target beyond Martin and the "big four," Shawn aimed his criticism at the New Dance Group, a radical left-wing company and school founded in 1932 dedicated to the principle that "Dance is a Weapon of the Class Struggle" (or as Shawn minimized: "using dance itself as a political pamphlet").[58] The New Dance Group established alliances with other left-wing groups in cities across the country, thus forming the Workers Dance League (and later New Dance League). Shawn denounced this vital network of artists, claiming, "These dancers living in big cities have a very limited vision of America." Moreover, Shawn felt he had to defend himself against the leftist dance groups, which threatened to render his populist approach to creating and presenting dance outdated or otherwise insignificant:

There are various dance leagues and dance groups in all our largest American cities who are definitely radical, communist, Marxian, what-you-will, in their political beliefs. They say that the one great problem of modern times is the class struggle—the battle between capital and labor, between fascism and democracy, between the proletariat and the dictator—and the dance which does not deal with these problems (assuming of course that the dancer be on the side of labor and the proletariat) is old-fashioned, anemic or sterile.[59]

Shawn blamed these "amateurish radical groups," as well as the ad hoc groups of Martha Graham and Doris Humphrey, for forfeiting many of the gains he had made toward establishing dance as a professional art during his Denishawn days. He responded to the criticisms of the left-wing modern dancers by using their own socialist ideals against them. He defended his work by emphasizing its mode of production: rather than create work about collectivity and labor, Shawn managed his men's group as a social "collective" wherein all members owned everything in common—real estate, scenery, costumes, motor vehicles, as well as income from their teaching and performances. Shawn was proud that each member of his group received year-round living expenses, including housing and food, clothes, medical and dental care. As star, teacher, producer, and director of the men's group, Shawn arguably deserved a greater share in the profits, but accepted the same salary as his dancers.

Shawn's defense of his "Communist ballet" was in response not only to the New York moderns but also to the Federal Dance Project, a New Deal program that had only formed months earlier. "The first national program dedicated to the financial support of dance and dancers," the Federal Dance Project was established to mitigate the negative impact of the Depression on the arts and artists by creating performance and teaching opportunities for unemployed dancers in major cities such as New York, Chicago, Los Angeles, Portland, and beyond.[60] Shawn would spend the later years of his career lamenting that he never received federal and foundation support. However, at this particular breakthrough moment in federal arts funding, Shawn dismissed the groups and projects receiving state support as amateur. To Shawn's mind, professionalism meant commercial success (or at least financial solvency), a holdover view from his Denishawn days, and a goal of his Men Dancers company, despite his claim that it functioned as a collective and thus embodied socialist ideals more fully than the left-wing modern dance groups. Shawn would later explicitly criticize the Works Progress Administration (WPA): "Anything in an art way that the federal government is mixed up with is not inclined to be of any great value as a work of art."[61]

In his *Boston Herald* editorials, Shawn attempts to undermine the modern project even as he establishes himself at its center. Nowhere in his writings does he seem to understand why dancers and audiences alike found the idea of "modern dance" so vital, demonstrating the very close-mindedness toward dance that he had decried for decades. His growing sense of estrangement from the broader modern dance community, and his obsession with Martin's refusal to recognize him in particular, saturated his correspondence with Price. Shawn relied heavily on Price in all matters modern as it was not a topic of conversation that necessarily interested his dancers who cared little about Martin and his opinions. Shawn explained that he would have "spit out bile" in his editorials were it not for Price's "benign spirit guiding [his] fingers."[62] However, Price was also guilty of fanning the flames of Shawn's paranoia. Price characterized the dismissal among New York critics and dancers as a "serious situation," a "boycott," and a form of "sabotage." He unconditionally defended Shawn against Martin, going as far as to dispatch his peers in the press—his "secret service agents"—to spy on Martin so as to determine whether he actually attended any of Shawn's performances. The plausible yet unfounded suspicion fueling Price's elaborate espionage plot was that Martin was guilty of internalized homophobia, secretly enjoying Shawn's Men Dancers, but distancing himself from the project altogether.

As a young man, Shawn seemed to thrive on his ability to achieve what others thought impossible. However, the resistance and rejection he experienced from Martin and the moderns bordered on acrimonious and made him despondent, perhaps unnecessarily so. Had he read Martin's reviews more carefully, he would have known that Martin also harshly judged Graham for her superficial treatment of social protest themes and Humphrey for betraying the modern project with bouts of romanticism. Instead, Shawn experienced the rejection of his work from the modern dance "clique" as a personal attack. Indeed, it sometimes was. Shawn once wrote to Price about a hurtful statement Graham made to a *Providence Bulletin* reporter: "Ted Shawn is not at all a great dancer, even though he has got a [great] group of men."[63] Horst, too, was willing to malign Shawn in print. Shawn explained to Price:

I realize more and more how truly Hellenistic I am through and through—and also how at war with much in this age the Greek spirit is. In New York I was battered at by the clique, which is out to discredit me root, trunk, and branch. That magazine called the *Dance Observer* published by the Humphrey–Weidman–Graham–Horst crowd, had reviewed our performance, and it was literally foul. It was only a hair's breadth outside the range of a libel suit—using words like "hokum," "vaudeville," "trivial," "superfi-cial," "outmoded," etc. etc. Then they announced that I would be the subject of a portrait interview in their next issue![64]

Price responded: "If the modern spirit is the kind of stench from the pages of *Dance Observer* I congratulate you on not being in it."[65] Price counseled Shawn to conserve his energy for the stage, promising him: "You will con-quer [New York] from the outside." By that, Price meant to encourage Shawn to value his own success with audiences beyond New York, to places the moderns did not dare go: "If those dance modernists in New York had ven-tured any farther away than Baltimore or Philadelphia, they would have had to walk home on the railway ties."[66] Shawn was touring the United States, Canada, Mexico, and England and always coming back with enough money to live on until the next September."

Price was ever so eager to assist Shawn in his campaign to take New York. In November 1936, Price finally published an essay about Shawn and his company that he had intended to write since his very first visit to the farm in 1933. "All Man Performance" appeared in the *Atlantic Monthly*, the first time a dancer was the subject of an essay in an American learned journal.[67] In the months leading up to the essay's publication, Price sent drafts to Shawn, on the condition that Shawn keep it a secret so that it might serve as a "surprise attack" against Martin and the moderns.[68] Shawn made a Trappist vow of se-crecy, which nearly killed him, since he was beyond moved by the validation Price's essay brought to his art. "I don't want to return the carbon copy. . . . I want to sleep with it under my pillow," he wrote Price.[69] As with the ar-ticle Price wrote in 1933 just a day before the company's first tour, "All Man Performance" had an immeasurable impact on Shawn's company, including the right dose of publicity to secure some hard-won bookings, including three nights Havana, Cuba, in January 1937.

Price's article avoided discussion of the New York modern dance scene al-together. Instead, Price addressed his largely academic audience about the merits of bridging physical and philosophical education through dance. To orient his readers, he likened Shawn's company to the successful all-male Harvard Glee Club under the direction of Dr. Archibald Davison. His goal was to precipitate "the reversing of a national habit of thought" that otherwise stigmatized young men from dancing—and audiences from appreciating male dancers. To that end, he parroted many of Shawn's central arguments that dancing is "the most masculine of the arts." Price perhaps overstated the case that the company had ignited a national movement that college deans ought not ignore.

He offered a thumbnail history of the company's hardscrabble existence at the Pillow, their travails on the road, and above all, the rigor of their training. In his concluding paragraph, he mentioned Shawn's failed applications to endowed foundations for funding. (He bemoaned the fact that those monies were instead awarded to a Norwegian scientist who studied the sex life of the evening primrose!) Price wanted to ensure that Shawn could use the article in future applications as a means to pressure future award panels. Shawn was eternally indebted to Price for the article, of which he made thousands of reprints to use in his press campaigns. Inspired, he even began to plot his very own "secret attack" against Martin by writing a chapter about modern dance for his book *Dance We Must* (1938), a collection of lectures he had given over the years. However, at the advice of both Dreier and Price, he ultimately decided to drop it, though he somewhat delusionally "thought it would be funny if the only immortality of this little group" of modern dancers were to come from writing about them in his book.[70]

Even as he sought to distinguish himself from the moderns, Shawn could not help trying to beat them at their own game. Taking a cue from their choreography, he also began to devise dances that engaged political and social ideas, though he was careful not to court controversy that would alienate his rural audiences. He also decided to focus on choreographing full-length or "symphonic" dances organized around a central idea rather than solo and "chamber" dances. In late August 1936, Shawn started work on what he conceived of as the first full-length modern dance. At Price's suggestion, Shawn titled the dance *O, Libertad!* after the Walt Whitman poem. He conceived of the dance as a "rhythmic biography of America." Structured in three acts— the past, present, and future—the dance dramatized moments in the history of the Americas from Montezuma to modernism.

The dance begins with a defining moment in the continent's history. Shawn, as the Aztec emperor Montezuma, wears a headdress ("bigger than Mae West's" noted one critic) and dances to a dirge upon learning about the arrival of Spanish conquistadors.[71] (See Insert Figure 5.14.) Subsequent scenes portray the rituals of flagellation and crucifixion performed by *los penitentes*, the "secret" religious order of the Southwestern United States, and the square dances of Forty-Niners at a Gold Rush camp.

To portray times that were current, Shawn created "The Present," a dance inspired by World War I—victory dances, college marches, war dances. A dance called "No Man's Land" conveys the trauma of "modern warfare" as experienced by the soldier. "March of the Veterans of Future Wars" for which a local American Legion expressed its outrage bears a striking similarity to Kurt Jooss's political dance *Green Table*, a dance Shawn admired.

The most curious moment in *O, Libertad!* comes at the end of its middle section, a two-part solo called "Modernism and Credo." In "Modernism," Shawn appears as a masked hag wearing a cloak emblazoned with a graph of the 1929 stock market crash. A disturbing convergence of Mary Wigman's *Witch Dance* (1926) and Martha Graham's *Lamentation* (1930), the dance is the choreographic expression of Shawn's views against modernism in general and his criticism of Wigman and Graham specifically, both of whom publicly disparaged him and his work. In the program notes, Shawn remarked, "Depression was coincident with the peak of 'modernism in the dance,' " forcing an association between the economic crisis, on the one hand, and, on the other, his sense of the aesthetic impoverishment of dance modernism. Throughout the two-minute solo, he indulges in expressive gestures, stomps on the floor, and strikes gnarled poses. It is hard to know what Shawn intended to convey with this mockery of modernism; there is no way he could have expected most of his audiences to have understood the choreographic or visual references. However, the only resolution Shawn offers to the disturbing ambiguity of modernism is his own body and self. At the end of "Modernism," Shawn unmasks himself and disrobes, revealing himself in a one-shouldered leotard with arm and leg cuffs performing a sequence of poses, twirls, and militaristic gestures, as if portraying a messianic figure leading the masses to its future. Indeed, in this, one of the last solos he created for himself during his Men Dancers years, Shawn became one of the Theban warriors in the Battle of Chaeronea, though his conflict was not with the ancient Athenian army but with John Martin and his "clique" of moderns. Shawn once described "Credo" as his autobiography in movement in that it conveyed his personal belief in dance's capacity "to lead humanity into continually higher and greater dimensions of existence."[72] From a certain perspective, Shawn's solo comes across as a self-righteous criticism of two groundbreaking women artists who were leading the vital social and aesthetic modern dance movement; from another perspective, Shawn's ambiguous final solo was a defense, figured in the imagery of the ancient Greek sacred legion, against the censure of homosexuality he had experienced from the modern dance establishment. In effect, with "Credo" Shawn intended to position himself either above or beyond "modernism."[73] (See Figure 5.15.)

When he reviewed *O, Libertad!* in 1938, Owen Burke, dance critic for the leftist magazine the *New Masses*, conveys that he appreciated the possible homosexual subtext. He was pleasantly surprised at Shawn's conscious attempt to avoid the "sentimental victorianisms and narcissus-like glorifications" of his Denishawn days and instead to explore "moral persuasion as a prime force for good."[74] He wrote: "Shawn is concerned for first time with the liberty of men; not as the democratic Whitman was concerned, surely, but as one who is for the first time discovering undemocratic repressions."

"Credo" was the source of the only documented contretemps between Shawn and Price. During a rehearsal of the work, Price warned Shawn that although its intentions were clear to him, the solo was "not publicly intelligible." Always a diplomat, Price said the dance was not his "best work." Shawn responded adversely, making Meeker and the other dancers uncomfortable to witness even a hint of discord between Shawn and Price. They told

Figure 5.15. Ted Shawn in "Credo" from *O, Libertad!* (1937). Photograph by John Lindquist. Joseph E. Marks Collection. Courtesy of Houghton Library, Harvard University.

Shawn as much and Shawn later wrote Price to apologize for his outburst and affirming that Price's constructive criticism was always welcomed.[75]

The final section of *O, Libertad!* was a suite of dances based on sports called "Olympiad." (See Figure 5.16.) The men developed the choreography themselves, which Shawn stitched together into a twelve-minute finale. A spectacle of male strength and vitality, the dance was a perfect way to cleanse the audience's palate of the work's earlier references to politics, history, and art. However, even the seemingly innocuous "Olympiad" was a point of political comparison between Shawn and Graham.

Shawn originally conceived of the idea of choreographing a dance based on Olympic sports in December 1935, when former dancer and visual artist Hubert Stowitts (1892–1953) invited Shawn and his dancers to pose nude for a series of paintings called "The American Champions." (See Figure 5.17.) Commissioned by the US Olympic Committee, the fifty-five 4x8-foot painted panels of nude American athletes were to be displayed at the Berlin

Figure 5.16. "Olympiad" from *O, Libertad!* (1937). Photograph by John Lindquist. Joseph E. Marks Collection. Courtesy of Houghton Library, Harvard University.

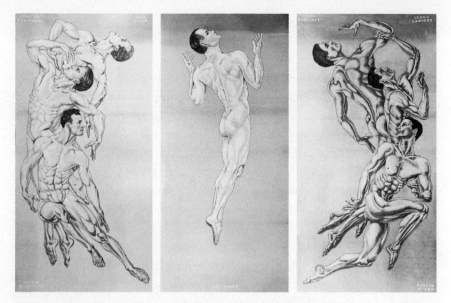

Figure 5.17. Ted Shawn and His Men Dancers from "The American Champions" (1935) by Hubert Stowitts.

Olympics that summer. Stowitts thought that Shawn's dancers ought to be included in his tribute to American athletes.

The US Olympic Committee ultimately determined that the vibrantly colored, larger-than-life panels were undignified and refused to display them in any official capacity. Instead, Stowitts planned to exhibit them in a private gallery, but the Nazi Ministry of Culture prohibited him from displaying the images of black and Jewish athletes. The panels caught the eye of Stowitts's friend, a former dancer and filmmaker named Leni Riefenstahl, the controversial director of *The Triumph of the Will* (*Triumph des Willens*, 1935), a documentary commissioned by Adolf Hitler to celebrate the Nationalist Socialist Party's 1934 convention at Nürnberg which helped to galvanize Nazi sympathy among Germans. Riefenstahl was filming events connected to the Berlin Olympics for her next documentary project, *Olympia* (*Olympische Spiele*, 1938), a two-part film that idealized the Aryan body. She wanted to use Stowitts's paintings in the opening sequence of her film. Instead, she filmed an elaborate prologue that envisioned ancient Greece, including sculptures of classic athletes that "came to life" through the spectacle of double exposure. Stowitts helped Riefenstahl with the post-production of these films.

Shawn's *Olympiad* premiered in October 1936, well before Riefenstahl's films were finished and Riefenstahl never saw Shawn's dance. However, Shawn's dancers, as seen through the prism of Stowitts's painting, helped to inform Riefenstahl's vision. Shawn, Stowitts, and Riefenstahl shared a similar sensibility in glorifying athletic bodies, that at least in Riefenstahl's case had fascist implications. Shawn was by no means a Nazi sympathizer. However, his association with the "American Champions" placed him far out of line with leftist American artists. In fact, the very same week that Shawn and his dancers posed for Stowitts, in a gesture of solidarity with German artists who had been persecuted under the Nazi regime, Martha Graham declined an invitation from Rudolf von Laban to participate in the 1936 Olympic Games festival in Berlin.[76]

Shawn perpetually felt misunderstood and needed someone to help communicate his message. When he finished writing his editorials for the *Boston Herald* in 1936, the paper's managing editor, Robert Choate, invited Shawn to write a weekly article for the paper. As much as Shawn would have loved to use the newspaper as his personal soap box, he begrudgingly declined the offer. There was no way he could write a weekly column while running the company and school. However, Shawn convinced Choate to offer the position to a former devoted student named Walter Terry. Shawn knew of Terry's ambition to become a dance writer, and since he thought Terry was too "cherubic" to join the Men Dancers, he wholeheartedly recommended him to Choate for the job. With Terry writing for the *Herald*, Shawn thought he would have another "secret weapon" in his arsenal against Martin and the moderns. In an apparent swipe at Martin, Shawn wrote an editorial about the state of dance criticism, insisting that "the true dance critic, when he emerges on the scene, will be a man or woman who has worked some years physically and actually in dance studios."[77] Terry fit the bill, though Shawn was evidently unaware that Martin, like Terry, had studied and performed theater before becoming a writer. Shawn assured Terry that Choate was apprised of the "John Martin situation" and the paper "needed a real dance critic."[78] An adoring and impressionable student, Terry, then twenty-three years old, was in a position to do some of Shawn's own press and fight some of Shawn's battles. Terry admitted that at times he was Shawn's spokesperson, though denied he was ever Shawn's "tool."[79]

Shawn began to read Terry's reviews to the men dancers while on tour, just as he had with Price's letters. However, Shawn scrupulously kept his correspondence with Terry a secret, even from his company members, so as to avoid the perception of impropriety. Though laced with praise and encouragement, Shawn's letters to Terry were laden with criticism. In several instances, Shawn lashed out against him, especially whenever Terry "slipped into a hidden trap" set by Martin and the Bennington "clique" to disparage Shawn. For instance, Shawn once castigated Terry for having lavished praise on St. Denis who had appeared on a program with Graham and Humphrey for the Dance International Festival in New York, a five-week festival celebrating folk dance. In the review, Terry lionized St. Denis's contributions to the development of modern dance without ever mentioning Shawn's. Shawn backfired that he was the rightful "father of modern dance" for having brought American and contemporary themes and pure movement to the dance stage. Shawn advised him to rectify his omission: "This, I think you can straighten out sometime."[80]

Terry made matters worse when later that year he made a sincere effort to do damage control. In his negative review of Graham's *American Document* (1938), Terry suggested, "Perhaps Miss Graham should look in on her former teacher and see what he is doing, for like him or not, Ted Shawn is an American dancer." He underscored the suggestion: "make us wish that such talented moderns would run back to the mother and father of the American dance (Ruth St. Denis and Ted Shawn) for some good sound advice."[81] Shawn was terribly embarrassed by Terry's overzealous proposition and made him wonder whether Terry was exploiting Shawn's vulnerable position for his own recognition. Terry exacerbated the tension when he publicly responded to a spate of letters from readers who accused Terry of "pro-Shawn" bias: "Why drag him by the hair into a review about Graham?" one reader asked.[82] Terry used his column to explain that he wasn't "pro-Shawn" but "pro-dance."

Critics routinely pit Graham and Shawn against each other. (See Figure 5.18.) However, there were similarities between Shawn and Graham's dances of the 1930s. They similarly staged American folk material as well as modern takes on primitive rituals and myths. Their works also shared formal concerns. Most were either solos or group works organized around a leading figure with his or her acolytes: Graham's female dancers, Shawn's men dancers. In their dancing, both dramatized an overwhelming need to communicate that could only be satisfied by moving. That said, there were deep differences between the two performer-choreographers. Graham developed a highly stylized movement vocabulary that dramatized the clash of the psychic and the physical. She approached modern themes with primitive instincts, transforming the dance stage into a theater of the senses. Her

Figure 5.18. "Ted Shawn vs. Martha Graham." Illustration by Don Freeman in the *New York Herald Tribune* (April 1929). Courtesy of Roy Freeman.

dancing eschewed some of Shawn's most deeply held values about dance—balance, symmetry, line. For Shawn, virtuosity meant complying with the codes of classical ballet vocabulary and the rules of Delsartean gesture; for Graham, virtuosity was the pursuit of revealing the body's three dimensionality through new shapes and new pathways of space. Whereas Shawn searched for new ways of achieving new physical heights—bigger jumps, longer balances, greater lifts—Graham fell, repeatedly, and turned the act of recovery into an art of its own.

Though there are formal bases upon which to compare the artists, Martin had it right when he said that modern dance ultimately was as much an approach as it was a technique. Shawn's dances were spectacles of transcendence, enlightenment, or victory whereas Graham's lingered in ambiguity, sustaining experiences of grief, terror, or pleasure. While watching Shawn's dances, one never doubts that the moral universe will remain intact. Dancing was often a means to display man's ability to control nature, psychology, and history. Graham's dancing showed that power as well, but also gave glimpses of the body's own vulnerability, the human psyche's subordination to a nervous reflex, a flash of memory, or the flow of blood. For Shawn, dancing was the exertion of muscle; for Graham, the contraction of the conscious.

Several months after his review of *American Document*, Terry tried to make amends with Shawn by writing an article that secured his place in the dance scene: "Ted Shawn, After 25 Years, Still Is at Helm of American Dance." The article begins with a series of leading questions: "Is Ted Shawn truly great? Is he a profound artist or a super showman? Is he still a leader in the dance, or should he be rated as an old-timer?" Of course, Terry opines that the secret of Shawn's longevity and "great popularity" is that he is equal parts "master showman" and "great artist."[83]

In January 1938, the company had several dates in Florida, including in Barton Mumaw's hometown of Eustis, where Shawn had purchased property abutting Mumaw's parents' home with the intent of building a winter studio, and which his company of men eventually helped to build. When the company returned to New England later that month, Price could hardly stay away. He joined the men at Brown University in Providence, Rhode Island, pleased to see their sunburned faces and to receive gifts of citrus fruit. He crammed into one of the trucks, the only way the company traveled, and headed to the Shubert Theater in New Haven where they were to perform. (See Figure 5.19.) At long last, Price got a taste of what it was like to tour with the company. It was an especially gratifying journey since Price was going to escort his dear friend, pioneering brain surgeon Dr. Harvey Cushing, to that evening's performance. As they drove along the sun-glittered Long Island Sound, Shawn read aloud and led a discussion and debate, this time about capitalism, social revolution, and its effects on the company's programs and personnel. The conversation was fodder for a new idea for a dance provisionally titled *Beyond Democracy*.

Price was somewhat surprised by Shawn's political turn, especially as Shawn's reluctance to delve deeply into social and political matters had become something of a joke between them. Price once wrote to Shawn: "What will he be at work on next? Obviously not Fascism or Communism!"[84] Price had spent many a long session at the *Boston Globe* offices wading through news reports coming from Europe. In fact, during this time Price wrote to Shawn about an all-nighter he spent at the office over a speech by Hitler and the unexpected resignation of British Foreign Secretary Robert Anthony Eden after Benito Mussolini's violation of an agreement. Shawn took his cue from Price about the seriousness the European political landscape. He also

Figure 5.19. Men Dancers on Tour, 1934. From left to right: Shawn (standing), Landers, Meeker, Hearn, Horn, Mumaw, McCormack. (Overlees not pictured). Joseph E. Marks Collection. Courtesy of Houghton Library, Harvard University.

apparently figured that to keep up with the moderns, he would have to confront the political realities of the day. War was imminent.

Price pointed out to Shawn the similarity between his chosen title *Beyond Democracy* and Edward Carpenter's *Towards Democracy* (1883), the gay writer's prose poem that celebrates society's march toward a cosmic "freedom." Shawn was intrigued by the suggestion and later mined Carpenter's poem as a choreographic source, though he changed the title of the dance to *Dance of the Ages* so as "not to be so controversial."[85]

Onstage, the Men Dancers appeared as a well-oiled, cohesive unit, embodying Shawn's ideals about art, democracy, and fraternity; offstage, the company was showing signs of distress. Both Denny Landers and Foster Fitz-Simons notified Shawn that they were going to leave the company at the season's end. Though four main dancers remained for nearly the entirety of the company's seven-year existence, most dancers stayed for only two years, creating serious pressure on Shawn to continually rehearse and cast new dancers in the repertory. Now he had to contend with losing two of his most important dancers. Price had little sympathy: "It is the price he pays for youth and worth what it costs."[86] He knew Landers had planned his departure for over a year, when one night the two had a tête-a-tête over breakfast at the Parker House. According to Price, Landers spent a few nights at his Hancock apartment about a month prior to his departure from the company. Price attempted to mentor him on seemingly routine matters such as organizing his time, keeping up with exercise and reading, and maintaining contact with his fellow dancers. The conversation delved into deeper matters Price described as "everything from the soles of our feet to the crowns of our heads, including entrails and genitals."

Price was disarmed by the candor of the conversation: "We are conversing on such a plane as few mortals that I have known of ever reach. In fact we were speaking of a stage of civilization which may be decades, even centuries ahead of where these states now live." He warned Landers "about the responsibilities of persons having beauty the temptation to trade on it and exploit those who were touchingly grateful to anyone having it." He was speaking about Landers's newfound friendship with Alfred Barton for whom Landers had finally decided to work upon leaving the company. Price was proud to see that Landers had matured as a result of his mentorship. Landers noticed, too, and was quick to credit Price for inspiring many changes in his disposition and behavior. Landers recalled the immediate impact Price made when he once came to the farm at Shawn's request to give the men a sex talk.

Landers explained, "When it was decided that you should come and give 'the talk' . . . that evening at the farm by the living room fire I listened while you went over the subject century by century. Everything was reasonable. At last I understood myself for the first time. After I had a while to think it over the whole problem straightened out and I was at peace with myself."[87]

Price responded, "It is extremely generous of you to tell me this for it is important for me to know probably explains the frame of mind of most young men. This is really all of us. It has been denied, repressed and outlawed for centuries until we have long since forgotten that it is a perfectly normal, perhaps necessary, phase of human development—for some, as I said to you at the farm last autumn, a halfway house, or others of terminal station. But how are we to know that under this present system of religious veto?"[88] Shawn appreciated that Price had positively counseled some of the company members regarding sex, as it was never a topic he could broach with them and vice-versa. Landers had once told Price: "I will always love Shawn—always—I could never tell him this. We just can't do those things correctly."[89] Price also had the luxury of titillating himself with sexually charged conversations, then leaving for long periods of time. Shawn, on the other hand, had to contend with the day-to-day negotiations of his dancers, careful to protect the genuine fraternity among the men despite their differences in their sexual orientations and experiences.

Decades after the Men Dancers era, Frank Overlees described the situation with characteristic bluntness: "There was no prejudice, no idea that you had to have a certain sexual preference and the result was that we all got along very well. We all knew each other's proclivities but so what? So what? You know? You're free to do what the hell you want, and it's your own damn business and that's all there was to it. And we all had a beautiful time."[90]

Fitz-Simons, on the other hand, departed under slightly different circumstances. He was determined to follow Shawn's example and pursue his own choreographic ambitions. He joined forces with Miriam Winslow, Shawn's former Denishawn student whose family had financially supported Shawn's choreographic endeavors. Shawn regretted that he would unlikely benefit from that support moving forward. According to Terry, Fern Helscher, the company manager, undermined several of the Fitz-Simons–Winslow engagements with bookers, and substituted the Men Dancers instead.

With the impending departure of Landers and Fitz-Simons, Shawn developed a "four year plan" that involved touring in the United States (1938–39); Australia, Java, India, and Egypt (1939–40); and South America, Cuba, and Mexico (1940–41). Mac embraced his seniority within the group by rallying the men to support Shawn's plan. Backstage after a performance, he announced that for him there would be "no more late hours, gay parties, or liquor or cigarettes" and that he already felt the emotional and physical effects of his newly disciplined lifestyle.[91]

"You have arrived at the morality of an artist," Price told him. "It is more fun to excel than to pleasure."[92]

Despite their best efforts, the international touring never came to pass as events showed clearly that the nation was headed to war. As early as spring 1934, Price had begun to make references in his letters to Hitler and the fascist campaigns of the National Socialist Party. (Price was surprised that his friend Romain Rolland's book escaped the Nazi book burning campaigns in Leipzig.) By early 1938, despite signs to the contrary, Price consistently tried to assure Shawn that it would be impossible for them to experience another world war in their lifetime. War was on Shawn's mind and led him to develop his apolitical dance about politics, *Dances of the Ages*.

Shawn completed *Dance of the Ages* in a single week before Price's arrival on May 25, 1938. For the next three days, Price was at the Pillow alone with the company—no audiences, no guests, no students. He noticed that without Landers, there was more harmony than usual among the men, several of whom Price had met for the first time that weekend. Among the new members were John and Frank or the "Delmar Twins." The brothers had appeared in Broadway musicals and at Radio City Music Hall. During a summer hiatus, they applied to Shawn's training camp to develop their technique. Their acrobatic skills appealed to Shawn; their humor appealed to everyone else. The dissonance between their innocent boyish faces and their raunchy humor kept the rest of the men in stitches. Shawn asked Frank to join the company in February. That summer, John rose from understudy to an official company member.

Price also met Johnny Schubert. A German from Montana, Schubert had black hair, blue eyes, and a classic profile. Like Ned Coupland, Schubert had a wounded soul and gravitated toward Price who willingly offered himself as a father figure. In his journal, Price once again reflected on how many of the dancers shared a similar story of one parent who stands by them and another who rejects them. Schubert put this dynamic into high relief when he confided in Price: "I want to win back my mother's love. Father understands but mother doesn't."[93] With Landers gone, Price took on Johnny Schubert as a mentee, and in time, a lover.

Price's main reason for visiting, however, was to serve as test audience for *Dance of the Ages: An Elemental Rhythmus in Four Movements*, wherein each movement refers to one of the natural elements (fire, water, earth, air), and correlates with a different "stage of social development" (tribal, city-state, democratic state, and post-democratic utopia) as represented by different types of leaders (the primitive shaman, the poet-philosopher, the democratic statesman, and finally, the creative artist as healer of the utopian post-democracy).

As with Shawn's very first full-scale dance *Dances of the Ages*, a film he created for the Thomas A. Edison Company, the similarly titled *Dance of the Ages* and the thematically similar *Labor Symphony* demonstrate Shawn's long-standing fascination with evolution as a choreographic structure. Building on the success of *O, Libertad!*, he wanted to create another full-length work, like a "symphony," he would often explain. A "curious compound of mysticism and muscle," *Dance of the Ages* positions dancing as the expression of science, politics, and art.[94] The first section "Fire" is an amalgam of scenarios that demonstrate men's primitivism—hunting and gathering scenes, a shaman's ecstatic dance, and a final ritual of initiation. The men, completely covered in black robes taunt a nearly naked initiate who stands writhing at the center of this menacing brotherhood. To convey his successful passage, the men open their cloaks to reveal their own naked bodies against vibrant red lining of the cloaks, then drape them across their outstretched muscled arms as they process in a stately manner.

The second part, "Water," features the men bare-chested and in tight seafoam colored bottoms and what resemble stylized swim caps. (See Figure 5.20.) The dance dramatizes the many manifestations of water—from fierce waves to steam—and man's movements through, against, and beneath the ocean surfaces. Shawn associates water and its dynamics to the city-state and its leader, the poet-philosopher, which he himself depicts in a bright blue and seafoam striped leotard and a silvery wig to suggest the crest of a wave.

Figure 5.20. "Water" from *Dance of the Ages* (1938). Photograph by John Lindquist. Ted Shawn Collection. Courtesy of the Jerome Robbins Dance Division, New York Public Library.

The third section, "Earth," explores various geological and agricultural patterns—continental drift, glacial formation, afforestation, wind patterns, as well as animal movements and human interactions with the soil: plowing, hoisting, digging. But soon the terrestrial imagery gives way to a political landscape. Shawn explores the idea of democracy as if it were little more than a game of emotions. In one scene the dancers form a metaphorical war machine that Shawn, as demagogue, stokes with empty gestures. The machine combusts with the politician's insincerity, leading to annihilation. The section ends with the dancers strewn across the stage as if war carnage. In the program notes, Shawn says "Neither Fascism nor Communism is the answer and that something beyond democracy is indicated." Shawn's original working title for the dance had been "Beyond Democracy." Fittingly, he explores what might there be "beyond democracy," in the final section. Unsurprisingly, for Shawn, what exists "beyond democracy" is not a political order but a religious state.

"Air," the final section, begins where the previous section ended, with the corpses now covered with black fabric, suggesting a mass grave. Shawn rises from the ashes, and stands. Somehow unburdened by death or misery, he begins to fly in freedom, a transformation he refers to as the "birth-struggle of the creative artist." He pulls at the fabric covering his men and twists it around his body, revealing a row of near naked men in fetal positions. As he twists, turning his body into a human pulley, the young men begin to walk hesitatingly, like young chicks venturing from their nests. Gusts of wind propel them into moments of flight and thus begins a long section that dramatizes man's desire for flight—the soaring eagle and the military plane, and spiritual transcendence. (See Insert Figure 5.21.)

Dances of the Ages was the centerpiece of the company's penultimate tour, as well as Shawn's most daring attempt to convey his vision of a political and social order in which love between men could thrive, a vision informed by social reformer Edward Carpenter who coined the term "homogenic," thus providing a young Shawn with a means by which to name his same-sex desire. The dance embodies Carpenter's ideals of social progress espoused in *Towards Democracy*, albeit enshrouded in a complex plot about the evolving relationship between the natural and political order. Still, Shawn's intentions are discernible in his choreographic choices. Throughout the dance, Shawn literally "conducts" his dancers onstage, motioning to directions toward which they flock or manipulate their dynamics through sympathetic gesture. Though audiences might have understood Shawn's relationship to his younger dancers within the dance in a variety of different ways (as a father figure, a military commander, a musical conductor, a teacher, a spiritual leader), Shawn described his own relation to the action as leading his men into "a whole new life, a greater dimension of existence."[95]

In *Dance of the Ages*, Shawn employed one of his favorite choreographic devices since his pageant days: tableaux. Summoning the silhouette and solemnity of a war monument, Shawn's tableaux are moments of arrested action that evoke heightened states of male bonding. Apart from these tableaux, Shawn's choreography rarely requires for his dancers to make physical contact with one another. The conceit of these tableaux was that they allowed the men to physically connect, albeit without making eye contact with each other. Instead they deliberately look away, as if to deflect the gaze of the audience from the physical intimacy staged before it. Even though the tableaux deny the dancers a visual awareness of each other, they convey a heightened sense of intimacy through touch, weight, and time. These means of physical and sensory connection did not elude the audience. Consider a caricature by German-born, San Francisco-based illustrator Wolo, that lampoons an otherwise serious moment in Shawn's *Polonaise* (1933), a music visualization featuring a cast of six men in flesh-colored barely there briefs, by depicting one of the dancer's tickling another's foot. (See Figure 5.22.) Shawn republished Wolo's caricature in the Men Dancers souvenir book the following season, ostensibly to take the edge off the intense audience reaction to the dance's opening illusion of naked men on stage. When the curtain rose on *Polonaise* in London, audiences let out a horrified gasp. With US audiences, however, the men were met with "more swoon than shock."[96] No matter the response, audiences easily perceived the implied intimacy between Shawn's men dancers even when they barely ever touched or even looked at one another.

Though Price praised Shawn and the dancers for their effort, in his journals, he expressed a growing frustration with Shawn's choreography, particularly Shawn's reluctance to critically engage with the historical or philosophical subject matter of the scenarios he created, preferring instead to engage audiences more through the emotions than through the intellect:

Intellectually, the content of his choreography is slight, and all my efforts in six years to increase that content have had little effect. I have bombarded

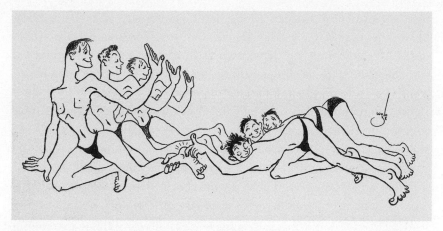

Figure 5.22. Cartoon by Wolo (Baron Wolf von Falkenstein) based on Ted Shawn's *Polonaise* (1933), Ted Shawn and His Men Dancers Souvenir Program, 1938–39.

him with ideas and books, each year the repetitive elements in the new program are so evident as to be almost glaring. His religious mysticism is largely emotional, when it comes to the tough thinking of grasping large political or philosophical concepts, he either will not or cannot make the effort. His dislike of the proletariat is an aesthetic disrelish and a sense that they annoy and trouble the leisured, agreeable people who usually patronize his art.[97]

Price's frustration intensified as the curtain slowly began to lower on the men's company without Shawn ever having fully realized his vision of staging "the rebirth of homosexual love in the modern world as a creative and civilizing force."[98] His feelings about Shawn's choreography began to unsettle his otherwise steadfast devotion to the Men Dancers enterprise. About his weekend visit, he wrote: "One is disarmed there and for days afterward, but it is a bit like champagne. It sparkles, bubbles, and intoxicates, but next morning leaves a dry throat and a query what the excitement was about."[99] His lukewarm response to the dance might also have been function of the fact that Price seemed only to enjoy Shawn's "musical visualizations" or "pure" dances. With the exception of *John Brown*, Price barely mentions Shawn's religious dances or ethnic dances, such as *Cutting the Sugar Cane* or *Primitive Rhythms*.

Dance of the Ages premiered at the final tea dance on September 22, 1938. It received its share of favorable reviews, especially from Terry, whose treatment of the dance formed the centerpiece of an article about Shawn's legacy: "A Great Man Dances On." In Terry's estimation, *Dance of the Ages* demonstrated that Shawn was "America's most important and valuable dancer for the simple reason that he is bringing the most understandable art to the greatest number of people."[100] Even leftist critic Owen Burke commended Shawn for avoiding "the mess of modernism" in order to return to dancing that is "instinctive . . . elemental . . . unified."[101] This statement points to the tension between Shawn's populist appeal and the narrower modern aesthetics of the Bennington group. *Christian Science Monitor* writer Margaret Lloyd, an otherwise dependable supporter of Shawn's dances, praised the work's ambition, but pointed out the absurdity of trying to tell a world history—"in Lizstian grandeloquence"—without even as much as a single reference to women![102]

Over the course of the sixth tour, Shawn sent Price clippings of the company's reviews. When Price read the praise Shawn's dances elicited, he considered tearing out the pages of his previous journal entries that cast doubt on Shawn's talent and intelligence. Instead, he wrote an extensive *mea culpa* and took inspiration from Shawn's example, writing affirmations about his own capacity to express emotion. At times, Price envied the artistic success of his "younger brother." For over a year, he had sought a publisher for his four novels, all part of the *Sacred Legion* series. No editor was willing to publish his homoerotic fiction. Price sent drafts of his manuscript to Shawn while on tour. He offered Price his unconditional support of the project.

"Your work has not ever been heard," Shawn consoled Price, convinced that the editors who read *All Souls* were not capable of understanding it. Shawn assured Price that he was a "surgeon of the emotions" and that his literary greatness would soon be recognized.[103]

Price's reconsideration of *Dance of the Ages* was also prompted by a letter from Johnny Schubert, the newest and youngest member of the company, written from the farm just hours before its premiere. With great excitement, he wrote: "Some will disagree but when we prove our point and can tell our story to the majority, I don't think we can fail. I only wish you could be with us to reap some of the benefits that will be ours after tonight's performance."[104] Schubert's optimism and ambition restored Price's faith that Ted Shawn and His Men Dancers might still fulfill its promise to rescue the nation from American morality and modernism.

Farewell, Sacred Legion, 1939–1940

With the undeniable encroachment of the war, the Horner-Moyer Bureau had a hard time booking Ted Shawn and His Men Dancers. The company members were understandably concerned about its fate. Shawn could no longer feign confidence either. He had a difficult time concealing his frustration when his dancers plotted their next career moves aloud. "If they think that they are necessary to me, they are mistaken. They ride on my reputation."[105]

Shawn considered a number of options, including taking a year's hiatus or accepting an offer to retire from the stage with a professorship at Peabody College. He also flirted with the idea of bringing women into the company. He sketched a scenario for "Morte d'Arthur" starring three "women stars," but soon realized that integrating women into the company would require time and expense he did not have. There was a humorous newspaper article about a twenty-two-year-old "strip" dancer named Jade Rhodora who longed to join the Men Dancers, an option Shawn jokingly shared with the men. Shawn never did invite women into the company, although he did begin a serious collaboration with a woman that summer.

Eva Palmer-Sikelianos (1874–1952) was an American-born archaeologist and artist. She moved to Greece, where she met and married the nation's beloved poet and playwright Angelos Sikelianos. The couple famously revived the ancient Delphic Festival in both 1927 and 1930. Without state sponsorship, they staged elaborate productions of ancient Greek plays, folk festivals, and Olympic contests in hopes of inspiring the "Delphic idea" in the modern world. In the early 1930s, she received an invitation to join the Federal Theater Project in the United States, a New Deal program that created work for unemployed stage artists. Sikelianos was determined to stage a version of Aeschylus's *The Persians* for a chorus of fifty men. After several unsuccessful attempts with colleges and theater collectives, she was introduced to Shawn by Katherine Dreier. They were mutually impressed with each other's vision. Sikelianos thought Shawn came closer to the classic ideal than any other dance artist, including Isadora Duncan. Shawn invited her to the Pillow to train his male students, thinking Sikelianos might be the ticket to taking the Men Dancers abroad to Delphi, thus sidestepping the company's bleak prospects in the States.

Sikelianos spent long hours in the studio training the men to sing in Greek so that she could realize her dream of recreating the all-male choral form, a combination of song and dance in modal music. She also brought her loom to the Pillow and made all sorts of classic wool robes and capes for the men, as well as taught them how to make leather sandals. Sikelianos's presence was felt everywhere that summer. When Price came to visit to the Pillow in June, his last visit during the Men Dancers era, he was somewhat shocked by how fully everyone accepted Sikelianos's artistic vision, which he considered to be questionable. He was even less impressed with her personal style. She had abandoned modern dress altogether in favor of homespun traditional Greek garments. Price's vision of ancient Greek had nothing to do with peasants. He was, however, bemused at the sight of students wandering around Jacob's Pillow in Delphic lace-up sandals and chitons. The Pillow had truly become the "The Acropolis of the Berkshires," but not quite the way he had envisioned.

The weekend was anything but ordinary for Price, for Shawn was teaching at Peabody College and it was the first time he had visited during Shawn's absence. Mumaw arranged to stay behind to host Price. That evening, he invited Price to join him in the studio. They talked about the Sikelianos number, which Mumaw apparently enjoyed performing. He showed Price a wine-colored chlamys that she had woven for his role as Dionysius. Mumaw stripped naked and put on the loose garment and began to move about, demonstrating for Price how free his movements could be. Price was mesmerized by how much Mumaw looked like the Greek warriors painted on vases. He agreed with Mumaw that the choreography was best served by these costumes, which allow the whole body to be seen, genitals and all. Mumaw began a private performance of his own solos for Price. He danced *Pierrot and the Dead City*, a short work about the sad clown figure in the *commedia dell'arte*, performed in a loose-fitting costume with ruffled neck collar, like the Pierrot figure. It was the first solo Shawn created for Mumaw in 1931, inspired by the aria in Erich Wolfgang Korngold's wildly successful 1920 opera *Die tote Stadt* (*Dead City*) that Shawn had heard during his time in Germany.

In his journal Price wrote, "Pierrot naked is more affecting than clad. You will never see anything more beautiful than this—you never expected to see anything as beautiful. How did this happen, that you came here, and are seeing something so utterly unique in the modern world?"[106]

His admiration was reciprocated. Mumaw told Price, "I never so enjoy dancing as when I dance for you. In public performances I am always thinking of perfection and technique. That detracts from my own pleasure and makes it mostly hard work. But I know that you know I can do it correctly if I want to, so if I make mistakes dancing for you, or it is a little ragged in spots, that doesn't matter, so I can let myself go."[107]

Price thought of the shy young man he had met seven years before—the vase of flowers and silk robe he had left for him in his farmhouse chamber, his nervous laughter when he performed yard work, and of course, the first time he saw him dance at the Repertory Theater. Over the years they had developed a quiet fraternal affection that seemed both nurtured and hampered by Shawn's presence. They walked arm-in-arm from the studio, when one of the Delmar twins asked: "What are you doing there?"

"We are Hamlet and Horatio on the platform waiting for the ghost," answered Price. When Shawn returned from Peabody, his working relationship with Sikelianos began to unravel over the direction of the play. Shawn insisted that the songs be sung in English and not, as she wholeheartedly insisted, in Greek. Instead, they set the movement to verses from the Book of Isaiah, Whitman, and Shelley's "Prometheus Unbound." They presented some of the studies at a tea dance. John Martin caught wind of the collaboration and wrote about his "keen interest" in it. He considered Shawn's dancers "ideal material" for Sikelianos's experiment with dance and choral music, which he considered "vital and contemporary, and may well bring about significant clarifications in the practice of modern dance."[108]

Neither Shawn nor Sikelianos was pleased with the results of their collaboration. However, Shawn was in no position to scrap the many hours the company poured into the project, nor was he willing to dismiss the opportunity to impress Martin. Thus, Shawn effectively buried it within a much larger full-evening work, which turned out to be Shawn's last for the Men Dancers. *The Dome* takes its name from a verse from Percy Bysshe Shelley's elegy "Adonaïs": "Life, like a dome of many-coloured glass/Stains the white radiance of Eternity." Shawn found the poem's lament for the death of Adonis, the embodiment of classical masculine beauty, the ideal inspiration for composing his last dance for his Men Dancers.

The first section of *The Dome* was a revival and reinvention of some of his most successful music visualizations set to the music of Bach. These

included the "Two-Part" and "Three-Part" inventions Shawn had created in 1917 for Denishawn. The second section, titled "Remembrance
of Things Past," included a mix of "primitive," romantic and folk
divertissements, as well as some of the company's most popular solos, such
as Mumaw's *Pierrot* and McCormack's *Turkey in the Straw*, a humorous
dance he performed in chaps and a cowboy hat. Other highlights included
Fred Hearn's *Bamboula*, a Cajun-inspired drum dance that featured
Hearn's "legginess" and Sam Steen's *The Green Imp*, a spritely number with
a cartoonish edge.

The Delmar Twins created a dance called "Remembrance of Charonaea."
(See Figure 5.23.) Finally, Price's long-standing wish to see the Men Dancers
embody his vision of the Sacred Legion had been fulfilled, albeit brought
to life by a duo of twin brothers rather than an army of homosexual lover-
warriors. That difference did not change the significance of the dance for
Price, who fictionalized the dance in one of his *Sacred Legion* books.

Without ever mentioning Ted Shawn and His Men Dancers specifically,
Price has his central characters Bob and Adrian drive two hours to the
Berkshires to see a men's dance company rehearse in their studio, then catch
a performance of the Delmar Twins' "The Theban Brothers: Memories of
Charonaea," thus leaving a description of the dance in literary form:

So? And what would they be doing with this theme? Two young fellows
about twenty, almost identical, classical profiles and facial oval, the Dorian
type, blue eyes and fair hair, bodied tanned to the buff of Pentelic marble,
"The Twins" had been known on Broadway since they were adolescents,
but it had remained for this company to subtilize them.

Martial music. The pair attired only in the loin pleats of Greek hoplites
enter at a brisk marching step, one slightly in advance of the other and just
off profile, suggesting a bas-relief from which a long rank of warriors may
be imagined, beginning with the two foregrounded figures. . . . They sight
the enemy, the Macedonian phalanx of Philip at Charonaea where that
corps d'élite of Thebes, the Sacred Legion, the immortal three hundred,
perished on the field to the last man, and with them the liberties of Hellas.

The battle starts. Flights of arrows, shaft after shaft being plucked from
quivers borne on shoulder to be sent winging; then they close at hand-to-
hand combat with their short sword, cut and thrust. The whirling, dusty,
clangorous melee is seen and heard in those two superb bodies as they flash
in combat.

Figure 5.23. Frank and John Delmar in "Remembrance of Charonaea" from *The Dome* (1940). Photograph by John Lindquist. Ted Shawn Collection. Courtesy of the Jerome Robbins Dance Division, New York Public Library.

One is struck down mortally. The other fights on, not knowing His enemy flees, he pursues and conquers. In his moment of victory he turns to his comrade, sword uplifted in triumph. Then only does he see the prone body. He stands motionless as one frozen. Not in facial muscles, only in his eyes can be seen the bitterness of death in that moment of triumph. The eyes dilate, the proud body stiffens; but the hand which holds aloft the sword does not tremble. Love is gone. There remains victory.[109]

Following a rehearsal of *The Dome*, a group of the boys went to the theater in nearby Stockbridge. Price, Shawn, and Mumaw stayed behind to catch up. Shawn lay on his mahogany four-poster bed, Price in a roomy wicker chair. Mumaw brought ice, whiskey, and soda, which they drank as Price tested out the plot of his next installment of the *Sacred Legion*. Shawn advised Price to try to publish all volumes of the series simultaneously so as to avoid the possibility that a "premature explosion could prevent the publication of the complete work." Shawn thought highly of excerpts he had read over the years: "This can restore the dignity of human love. It is free, between equals, untainted by economic dependence or exclusive ownership."[110]

Conversation drifted from Price's novel to Ruth St. Denis's autobiography, especially as she was expected to arrive at the Pillow the next day. Shawn had the wearing experience of reading swaths of the manuscript and reliving several traumatizing events. She arrived at the farm with Jack Cole, both of whom had begun teaching at Adelphi College on Long Island. Cole was also performing at the Rainbow Room in New York City. Shawn thought he had sobered considerably in the intervening six years, as he spoke thoughtfully about the limits imposed on artists by academic institutions. Price, once impressed by Cole's dancing, was turned off by the man before him, perhaps in deference to Shawn's upset over Cole's disloyalty to him.

Price welcomed St. Denis on the platform outside the house and engaged in an hour's profitable conversation. He was immediately impressed. He also spent time practicing his German with Katherine S. Dreier who also was visiting.

That night, Price slept in the guest chamber with Mumaw. (There was no way that Shawn and Mumaw would share a room while Shawn's wife was on the premises.) With the diverse range of personalities at the Pillow and the tour just weeks away, Shawn was overwhelmed. With hopes of recharging his battery, Price invited Shawn and Mumaw to spend a weekend with him in Nahant. Price made special arrangements for them to stay at an oceanfront inn, anxious to return the hospitality that Shawn had shown him over the years. They spent a day cruising the bay under a gray sky. Price pointed out historical and literary landmarks that dotted the coastline. Shawn took it all in, his eyes like those of a young boy enjoying himself to the utmost. Price was pleased that he could grant Shawn a moment's peace and happiness before setting out on the road one last time.

The quiet gave Shawn the opportunity to hear a "small voice" inside him telling him that the great experiment of the Men Dancers had run its course.

When he returned to the farm, Shawn met privately with each member of the company, in the order of their seniority, to convince them to put the company's dissolution to a vote, which they did. The company nearly unanimously voted to make its upcoming tour its final one. Thirty minutes after casting the vote, Shawn wrote to Price, the company's honorary member, with the unsurprising news. Price supported Shawn's decision completely, though throughout the years he had often warned Shawn that he would be devastated were the company ever to disband: "If anything happened to you or your company, it would be a major disaster to my spiritual husbandry."[111] Price was a stalwart for Shawn and helped him to craft a press release. He even helped to procure a possible buyer for the farm, which Shawn could no longer financially sustain. Martin announced the news in the *Times*, describing the dissolution of "one of the most successful dance companies of the day" as "rather astonishing" and "a surprise."[112]

By January, Shawn agreed to lease the Pillow to Mary Washington Ball, one of the earliest champions of the company. The *Christian Science Monitor* announced that Ball would run a six-week summer dance training program at the Pillow with Miriam Winslow and Foster Fitz-Simons as teachers and Harry Coble as assistant. Shawn planned to be a guest teacher. Overlees signed on as superintendent. Though it was not the most profitable arrangement for Shawn, who had hoped to sell the farm, he was relieved to have the temporary financial stability. He knew he was going to end the tour in debt, figuring he had lost about $20,000 over the course of the seven years. Lincoln Kirstein laughed when Shawn once tried to elicit sympathy from the ballet impresario over that figure: "You only lost $20,000 in the whole seven years? Why I lost $50,000 a year on Ballet Caravan!"

Shawn shot back: "Yes, Lincoln, but I don't have a Papa who owns a department store and will meet my losses."[113]

In addition to financial freedom, Shawn sought to be unburdened by the huge responsibility that the farm had become. He wrote to Dreier: "It seems wisest to close up this whole place, and offer it for sale. Then I will be freed from the associations of past endeavors and can make a new nest for the new things to be born in a fresh place. It is now too big and complicated for me to live in alone, poor to work in without a staff."[114]

Audiences for the company's final tour were the largest and most enthusiastic that the Men Dancers had ever attracted. Even Shawn enjoyed himself immensely, except for a sudden kidney stone attack at the University of Minnesota. After hours on the X-ray table and a dose of intravenous medication, he drove back to the theater to perform. On the road, the boys openly discussed plans for life after the company. Shawn avoided these conversations, as he did not want to interfere in their plans, nor did the men solicit his advice.

There was one exception. Johnny Schubert, the youngest and newest member of the company, tried to convince Shawn to keep the company going. He wrote to Price, hoping he could somehow persuade Shawn to change his mind about what seemed inevitable: "I want to get back to the farm and talk with you. I feel that if we get together and talk we can come to some conclusion as to how to keep the company intact."[115] Indeed, they did talk things over one evening at the Parker House. They talked until 4 A.M. and then had breakfast before returning back to the Pillow.

During the winter break, Shawn created one last dance for the Men Dancers, a fourth section for *The Dome*. With this final movement, he staged his own remarkable story without any pretense of a literary, political, or social scenario. He called the dance "Jacob's Pillow Concerto," and it was a choreographic paean to the first all-male dance company. (See Figure 5.24.) The dance gives the audience a fly-on-the-wall perspective into Shawn's barn-studio. With the stage set with a piano and a small bench, audiences watched

Figure 5.24. "Jacob's Pillow Concerto" from *The Dome* (1940). Photograph by John Lindquist. Courtesy of Jacob's Pillow Dance Festival Archives.

a simulation of the inner workings of one of the most revolutionary artistic collectives of the twentieth century. As if guests who joined for tea or one of the privileged few invited to watch Shawn create with his dancers, the audiences were invited into the choreographic process.

The dance began with Shawn on stage. One by one, the dancers entered, each wearing the signature white terry robes that they had customarily worn at the teas between dances and after the performances. Each dancer was given a turn to display his virtuosity, most referencing or sampling sections from the company's repertoire. Then they danced together, with Shawn orchestrating the men as they moved into and out of their signature cluster formations, then one by one they dispersed from the stage, leaving Shawn center stage as took his final bow to an unresolved chord.

In February 1940, Ted Shawn and His Men Dancers performed a unique program on each of its final three nights at Carnegie Hall. Shawn was determined to make a lasting impression in New York. He avoided solid food for weeks before the performance to get in shape. He even took advice from Walter Terry about scaling back on his excessive costumes and makeup, which Terry confided some audiences laughed at. Shawn had hoped that Martin, who attended each night, would have made some conciliatory gesture in his final reviews. However, Martin was not impressed with the performances. In fact, his three terse reviews of the programs convey his unconditional disapproval of Shawn's choreography. About *O, Libertad!*, Martin wrote that it was "at its best when it concerned with vigorous, athletic movement and at its least effective when it deals with poetic imagery and symbolism." He thought even less of *Dance of the Ages*, asserting that "Perhaps there are choreographers living who could translate [its] pretentious theme into dance, but Shawn has not proved himself to be one of them." Of the three dances, Martin thought *The Dome* excelled the most as it was "freest of cosmic purpose."[116] Even though Martin eviscerated Shawn's choreography, he recognized the talents of the Men Dancers, especially Mumaw, whom he described as "a first-rate ballet dancer if he cared to turn his mind in that direction." He also noted the loss of both Landers and Fitz-Simons, a curious admission that he had followed the company more closely than his limited record of published reviews suggest. He singled out McCormack, Hearn, and company newcomer Sam Steen, "who succeeded in stopping the show."

The road for the Men Dancers ended where it all began. On May 6 and 7, 1940, the company performed its final concerts for sold-out crowds at Symphony Hall, just across the street from the Repertory Theatre in Boston, home to Shawn's first all-male program in 1933. The company performed *Dance of the Ages* and *The Dome*. Friends, fans, and students came to witness the end of an era. Of course, Price was there, and so, too, was Terry whose review focused on the enthusiasm of the crowd—the whistling, stamping, and standing ovations—and the significance of the company itself, but also mentioned "a few flaws" in the choreography.[117]

After the final curtain, the men greeted their fans. Price said he could not pry Shawn free until one o'clock in the morning, at which time he escorted him, Mumaw, and Fern Helscher to his favorite Greek restaurant for an intimate meal. He arranged it so that they had a dining room all to themselves to commiserate to their heart's content, which they did. The next morning, Price memorialized his feelings about the Men Dancers experiment in a letter to Shawn:

> I am more than ever struck by the similarity of our function in the cultural life of our land and times. By those who know, it is understood and loved whole-heartedly; by those who do not, it is often met with indifference if not actual dislike. That is to be expected. We need not complain. Both of us live anywhere from four to ten times as much and as vividly as the average mortal, which is why so few of them can take the current at top voltage, and this voltage has increased in us so gradually and by a process so organic that we ourselves are scarcely aware of its force.[118]

With these words, Price acknowledged the significance of the "cultural work" Shawn's company performed on behalf of "those who know." Elsewhere he noted that Shawn's profound influence on him as an artist "simply had to do with the telling of the truth, first to oneself and then to one another, and then discussing everything openly. It was a remarkable experience and was a determinant one for me. I have written several books since, and they've all been deeply influenced by the candor of life and speech that took place in that company and which I knew perfectly . . . well, I doubted that it existed outside of military life . . . since 4th century BC."[119] Indeed, Price's only publication that deals explicitly with homosexual relationships is *All Souls*, the novels written during "the seven magic years" he spent with the Shawn and the Men Dancers.

Some of the men bade farewell to Shawn at the theater. Others went back to the farm to collect their belongings. Shawn prepared the premises for Mary Washington Ball who was soon to assume the tenancy. He also had to reconcile financial matters. To cover his financial deficit, Shawn borrowed money against his life insurance. He divided what little remained after covering expenses among the dancers as "bonuses"—$50 for each year a dancer was a member of his company. He hoped this money would help tide them over as they went on to their next chapters. Shawn was proud that the "bonuses" exceeded the base minimum that the union would have required him to pay them, not to mention their medical and dental bills. But even with that level of support, Shawn lamented that "none of them had saved a cent, and I could not send them forth in the world penniless. So I borrowed to the limit and paid them these bonuses, and also the outstanding unpaid bills against Shawn Dancers, Inc."[120]

In the weeks following the final concert, Shawn took care of maintenance in the studio and prepared costumes and sets for deep storage, which kept him occupied as the remaining few dancers prepared to move on to new projects. Frank Overlees accepted an offer to dance with Maria Gambarelli, a dancer with the Metropolitan Opera whose concert tour he considered managing. Harry Coble eventually taught with German dance teacher Hans Weiner (later known as Jan Veen) in Boston. The Delmar twins returned to the world of musical theater. Fred Hearn went home to Asheville to perform in a rhododendron festival, though promised to return to the farm for a few weeks in late summer. Wilbur "Mac" MacCormack landed right where Shawn had discovered him in 1933, at Springfield College, where he accepted a fellowship to complete his bachelor's degree and pursue his master's. Barton Mumaw went to Florida to spend time with his parents, though he planned to come back to the farm to prepare his own solo concert.

The men went on to their next endeavors with the increasing expectation that they would be drafted into military service over the ensuing years. Nearly all were. Shawn was exceptionally proud of his dancers, as if he had truly achieved his own Sacred Legion. Dennis Landers went into the US Navy. Wilbur McCormack, Jess Meeker, and Ned Coupland joined the US Army. Following their New York appearance in Irving Berlin's wartime musical *This Is the Army*, Fred Hearn and William Howell were drafted into the army and placed in a special service outfit that allowed them to perform in hospitals. Frank and John Delmar performed in the Broadway production of *Johnny Belinda*, until Frank was finally drafted and spent four-and-a-half years overseas. Henry Coble went into the Air Force. Foster Fitz-Simons had a university appointment so was not obliged to enlist. Overlees stayed in nearby Pittsfield to work as an electrician at the General Electric Company, though he later went into the Peace Corps. Shawn worried deeply for their lives. In his letters to Price after the "seven magic years" he outlined his plans to erect a building for the men for when they came home from war, hoping to create conditions for fulfill the fantasies they shared about living permanently on the farm, even raising their families there. (See Figure 5.25.)

On the eve of Barton Mumaw's departure for Camp Kearny Air Force Base in 1944, Price consoled Shawn: "I am terribly sorry for you. He is your inheritor, and both as a man and as an artist you made him. Comforters have had a bad name ever since the *Book of Job*, but if I, Old Friend, may offer the comfort of fellow feeling from having lost a comrade artist in 1918 by war, I hope you will accept some solace from the thought that thus far at least your comrade artist is still alive."[121] The "comrade artist" to whom Price referred was Fred Demmler, a beloved friend who was killed in battle in Belgium during the final days of World War I, on All Soul's Day to be precise. Losing Demmler on All Saint's Day forever imbued the Christian festival of the dead with special meaning for Price. From that day forward, he observed All Saint's Day every

Figure 5.25. "Farewell, Sacred Legion," Ted Shawn's Men Dancers, 1935. Ted Shawn Collection. Courtesy of the Jerome Robbins Dance Division, New York Public Library.

year, as a modern version of the ancient Greek Anthesteria, a spring festival to Dionysius that celebrated the power of resurrection and rebirth. In one of his first letters to Shawn, Price explained: "All Soul's is my central day of the year. Share it with me."[122]

The theme of loss suffused Price's literary imagination, and more than ever before, he wrote to ease an unrelenting burden to render visible the lives and loves of gay men that went unrecognized. He wrote a proper memoir of Demmler, *Immortal Youth: A Study in the Will to Create* (1919), in which he eulogizes Demmler and his love, possibly unrequited, for him. Every year after Demmler's death in 1918, Price dedicated his *Boston Globe* editorial on All Soul's Day to commemorate his loss. He eventually compiled and published these writings in *Litany for All Souls* (1945). And finally, Demmler's death inspired what Price considered his greatest literary achievement, *All Souls*, the four-volume novel cycle that included *The Sacred Legion*. During his "seven magic years" with Ted Shawn and His Men Dancers, Price found a respite from his sense of loss. For Price, the vital and virile bodies of Shawn's Men Dancers, embodying gods, warriors, and socially progressive ideals, conjured the spirit of Price's deceased artist-soldier-lover. In Shawn's dances, Price rediscovered "the creative force of homosexuality in the 20th century."[123]

At the end of the "seven magic years" and the start of yet a new world war, Price found himself again in a state of unspeakable pain, with the loss of another artist-soldier to the ravages of war. Defying all odds, Shawn's dancers survived the war, but for one. On July 20, 1943, Shawn wrote a terse letter to Price, relaying information from a wire he had just received from the parents of Johnny Schubert, the youngest of the Men Dancers and Price's lover: "War Department has informed us Johnny is missing in action—no details."[124]

In his journal on the evening he first saw Ted Shawn and His Men Dancers program at the Repertory Theater in 1933, Price wrote that Shawn's dances limned a "not impossible but remote future."[125] Price and Shawn shared the vision of that future, one modeled in spirit on the ancient Sacred Legion, wherein male lovers were recognized as vital members of the social order. Through his choreography, Shawn attempted to body forth that future, and in fleeting moments he sensed how its power fueled a political imagination beyond the theater. However, he and Price also tacitly recognized that the Men Dancers company was as much an elaborate thought experiment conducted in their correspondence and conversations as it was a radical social experiment they endeavored to test on the stage.

6

Jacob's Pillar

I.
This is the place they came upon long years
Ago and marked the granite and the pine
With careful, hungry eyes: and saw supine
Across unviolated places the seasons' fears
Where careful hands of God had filled the tears,
The wounds of glacier, with the gentle line
Of hill on hill—made suddenly divine
For them in hardness and in heavy cares.

If I should take you up the road and say:
"Look!—Now do you see just what I mean
About the way that rock . . . those shadows lean
Half tenderly across this summer day . . . ?"
But then I'd stop—knowing well you could
Receive your answer from the wood.
—"Jacob's Pillow: A Testament from the Hills,"
A Sonnet Sequence by Foster Fitz-Simons (1935–37)

War and the Artist, 1940–1945

"What Can Art Say of War?" asked dance critic Margaret Lloyd as if to rouse choreographers to do their part in the war effort.[1] She listed dances that she considered to express the appropriate urgency for the political land-scape of an America on the brink of World War II: Martha Graham's anti-war suite *Steps in the Street* (1936) and *Chronicle* (1936), José Limón's *Danza de la Muerta* (1937), and Ted Shawn's memorable sketch of a returned sol-dier in his American saga *O, Libertad!* (1938). "What have these dancers

Ted Shawn. Paul A. Scolieri, Oxford University Press (2020). © Paul A. Scolieri.
DOI: 10.1093/oso/9780199331062.001.0001

accomplished? What can dancers effectually say of war? What can dancers effectively do for peace?"

Shawn ruminated on these questions, though he did not choreograph during the war years. Instead, he focused his energy on transforming Jacob's Pillow from a secluded farm collective into a viable arts institution. Whereas many businesses and cultural institutions languished under the economic pressures of the war years, Jacob's Pillow endured, strengthened even, given the construction of the Ted Shawn Theatre in 1942, the first US theater dedicated to the presentation of dance. Shawn's extraordinary efforts to sustain the "Pillow" were not only a way for him to ensure his legacy—and to keep himself employed—but also a means to honor a commitment he had made to his Men Dancers, nearly all of whom were drafted in the war, that he would keep the Pillow's operations and reputation afloat to ensure they would have a place to return.

In May 1940, following the final performance of Ted Shawn and His Men Dancers, Shawn made his time-honored trip to the Peabody Institute in Nashville to lead a two-week workshop for young dance educators. Whereas he had once relished the opportunity to work with new crops of dance teachers, he began to feel frustrated that he no longer held a position of influence without an operating dance company. He agreed to return to Peabody for one last session, a meaningful decision, seeing that Shawn had rarely ever turned down a teaching opportunity, let alone one that paid a fee. To mark the end of this chapter, he compiled his notes from lectures he had given throughout his Peabody years into a privately published book called *Dance We Must* (1940).

He went back to Jacob's Pillow to serve as a guest teacher at the summer program now under the direction of Mary Washington Ball, though he could barely tolerate watching her helm the enterprise that he himself created. He wrote to Mumaw who was spending time at his parents' home in Florida, about his agony being at "that place," wandering around "like a disembodied ghost." "No one pays any attention to me—Mary Ball never introduces me to any one and while I am not egotistic (or am I?) I am a little hurt that no deference is shown to me whatever in that place, either by former students or Mary Ball. Well—this too shall pass."[2]

He suffered through Ball's direction of the school, criticizing her faculty (including his own "children" Foster Fitz-Simons and Miriam Winslow), as well as her transformation of the beloved tea dances into "The Berkshire Hills Dance Festival." Though he admired her approach to programming weekly concerts that integrated different forms of dance—classical ballet, modern, ballroom, and Oriental—an approach he emulated when he regained the artistic reins of the festival, he grew infuriated at seeing audience sizes dwindle from the heydays with the Men Dancers, to a total of twenty-six (not including students). When Shawn learned that Ball had intended to conclude the festival by August, just when audiences were usually at their largest, he decided to rent the studio to produce his own series of concerts for the remainder of the summer, including a concert of the Men Dancers that was billed as both a "Farewell Performance" and a "Homecoming Program." A local ad emphasized the draft age of the dancers, thus noting the company "certainly may never be reassembled fully again."[3] The result was four jam-packed audiences. At the end of the summer, Ball rescinded her offer to buy the Pillow, having lost the financial backing of both her uncle and the bank. That left Shawn with the unforeseen burden of finding another buyer, preferably one who valued the dance audience that he had cultivated over the years.

That winter he and Mumaw moved temporarily to New York, renting an apartment at the Sevilla Hotel on West 58th Street. The two-bedroom unit had a spacious living room that they converted into a studio. As Shawn traveled between the city and the farm to meet potential buyers, he tried to forge a path for Mumaw's professional future. There were moments of downtime, too. Shawn rekindled a friendship with a former student who convinced him to study ice dancing. That summer, she also hosted him at the nudist colony Burgoye Trail, an experience that uplifted Shawn. With an unconditional recommendation of Ruth St. Denis, that winter Shawn went to the "body-conditioning gym" of the German gymnast and bodybuilder Joseph Pilates at the Van Dyke Studio, the same location where Shawn had taught his first New York classes in 1914. Impressed with Pilates's "contrology" system of training, Shawn invited him to teach at the Pillow the following year. Pilates was a full-time faculty member in 1942 and 1943, teaching his mat classes to students and visiting performers. Shawn did not invite him back after the summer of 1943 owing to their personality conflict. Pilates thought dance was trivial and that the Pillow should be turned into a health farm. Pilates would later return to teaching at the Pillow and even purchase land nearby with the intent of developing a health and fitness colony of his own.

British ballet dancer and choreographer Anton Dolin, then star and resident choreographer of Ballet Theatre (now American Ballet Theatre), advised Mumaw to go into classical ballet and offered to waive tuition to his classes at Carnegie Hall, the same studio where Shawn had taught during the Denishawn days. When the men's group toured England in 1935, Dolin was very supportive. Shawn tended to reciprocate the respect. Dolin even talked to Shawn about creating works for Ballet Theatre. While studying for a possible defection to ballet, Mumaw auditioned for Broadway shows, but before he landed a role, Shawn booked dates for Mumaw's debut solo concert at Carnegie Hall, financed with money Shawn borrowed against the Pillow. They began to rehearse a program of Mumaw's most successful works from the Men Dancers repertory and also created new ones.

Billed as the "American Nijinsky," Mumaw presented his debut solo concerts at Carnegie Hall on April 16–19, 1941, the same week that Martha Graham presented a concert at the Guild Theater on 52nd Street featuring the premieres of *Letter to the World* and *El Penitente*. That very same week Doris Humphrey and Charles Weidman presented children's dance matinees, including *Square Dances, Life of the Bee*, and *The Shakers* at their intimate studio-theatre at 108 West 16th Street, where earlier in the month they had presented their first repertory programs of Humphrey-Weidman works. Two days before Mumaw's first performance, the Kamin Dance Book shop hosted a reception and preview for an exhibition of drawings and photographs of Mumaw by the theatrical photographer Marcus Blechman, male physique photographer Earle Forbes, and "official" Jacob's Pillow photographer John Lindquist, among others. One of the highlights was a Malvina Hoffman sculpture that served as inspiration for Shawn's dance *The Mongolian Archer* (1941), which was on the Carnegie program.

Mumaw included one of his own choreographic efforts on the program, a solo dance titled *War and the Artist* (1941) set to Franz Liszt's piano piece "Funérailles." Mumaw described *War and the Artist* as his choreographic response to the foreboding news that England had entered the war. Channeling his sense of dread into creativity, he went to work in the studio and the result was a dance "about two soldiers lost in battle and the effect of their death on an artist (me)."[4] Following the premiere of the dance at Carnegie Hall, Walter Terry described the dance as "the bewilderment of a youth trained in processes of art creation yet forced into processes of war."[5] Terry watched the dance cognizant that Mumaw could and likely would be drafted. Indeed, Mumaw received a draft notice ten days before the Carnegie concert, but applied for and received a temporary postponement so that he could keep his professional commitment. Terry claimed that the concert "placed him head and shoulders above his contemporaries in the field of modern dance in America." Others disagreed. Some critics found *War and the Artist* too "pretentious" and rife with "banal heroics."[6] John Martin conveyed his respect for Mumaw as a dancer, paying the compliment that he could even be a ballet dancer were he not committed to the "barefoot-ballet style, so novel twenty-five years ago." Ultimately, he found the program to be "neither fish nor fowl nor good pink fleshings."[7]

Following the Carnegie Hall performance, ballet dancer Lisa Parnova went to see Shawn about the possibility of engaging Mumaw to replace her dancing partner who had been drafted into the army. At first Shawn and Mumaw hesitated, but they were sold by Parnova's argument that Mumaw would likely get a year's deferment from the draft if he had a formal contractual obligation. Parnova was born in Kansas but spoke with a contrived Russian accent, one of her many acting skills that she used to convince the draft board to grant Mumaw another deferment so he could tour with her for a year.

After considering several buyers for Jacob's Pillow, including Lincoln Kirstein who was interested in the site as a home for Ballet Caravan, Shawn entered an arrangement with Anton Dolin to lease the property for a summer, backed by English balletomane Reginald Wright. Wright was essentially a sponsor of ballerina Alicia Markova, who used his considerable wealth to fund her vacations and draw her away from the Ballet Russe de Monte Carlo and toward Ballet Theatre. Wright sold her on the idea of forming a school with Dolin at the Pillow. They agreed. Wright relocated to the posh Red Lion Inn that summer to be near the Pillow—and Markova—and financed most of Dolin's operating expenses.

One of the highlights of the newly named "International Dance Festival and School" at Jacob's Pillow that summer was the appearance of Ruth St. Denis in a revival of her signature 1906 dance *Radha: The Mystic Dance of the Five Senses,* which she had not performed since 1915. Consequently, none of St. Denis's former Denishawn students had ever seen the dance. Needless to say, they were eager to see the legend perform the role that had launched her career—and in turn their own. Former Denishawn dancers Doris Humphrey, Charles Weidman, and Pauline Lawrence—all of whom were established artists in their own right by 1941—drove from Bennington, Vermont, to Jacob's Pillow to see the performance. (Martha Graham had seen a dress rehearsal of *Radha* a few weeks prior.) Not to be upstaged by St. Denis on his own turf, two weeks later Shawn performed a solo concert on July 25, featuring *Cosmic Dance of Siva,* which he had not performed in over thirteen years.

Ballet Theatre also performed at the farm that summer, with guest appearances by Markova, Dolin, and Agnes de Mille. Mumaw and Parnova performed selections from their touring program, but their personality clashes translated to the stage and audiences took note. Though there were certainly high-quality performances at the farm under Dolin's direction, the overall atmosphere and conditions made it seem like "a madhouse" to Shawn. The cabins were overcrowded, with dancers and guest artists sleeping in the hallways. The forced retrofit of the barn into a theater with a complete lighting system seriously obstructed sight lines for anyone seated behind the front row; plus, the installation of blackout curtains overheated the theater. Then there were the interpersonal conflicts. Shawn and Dolin had a dust-up over contractual issues, especially concerning the number of weeks Shawn would teach. Dolin promised to keep Shawn on faculty for four weeks if he attracted at least ten students, an agreement he was reluctant to honor, even though Shawn's classes attracted over thirty students. The overall mismanagement was upsetting to many, above all Wright who had financed the venture.

Given the marginal success of Dolin's festival, Wright encouraged Shawn to take over the management of the farm. Already $20,000 in debt, Shawn needed financial support. Wright agreed to underwrite a portion of the expenses, as did Shawn's long-time friend Mabel Busey, a board director of the Lee National Bank. Realizing the dire prospects for the Pillow's future, Wright, Busey, and fellow Berkshire supporters proposed a plan that would resolve Shawn's financial liability and assure a future for what had become a beloved local attraction. The plan was for Shawn to sell his Jacob's Pillow property to a new artistic and educational nonprofit entity called Jacob's Pillow Dance Festival, Inc., whereby a board of directors performs the executive functions of the corporation, and Ted Shawn, in the capacity of managing director, oversees all artistic and educational matters. The idea for the structure came from the Berkshire Symphonic Festival, the precursor to the Tanglewood Music Center in nearby Lenox, Massachusetts.

On October 9, 1941, a committee of local supporters gathered at Busey's home to charter Jacob's Pillow Dance Festival, Inc. as a nonprofit art and education corporation and to form the first board of directors. Judge Frederick Myers of Pittsfield drew articles of incorporation, a statement on aims and purposes, and the by-laws. With Reginald Wright serving as president, the board of Berkshire locals voted to raise $25,000 to purchase the property and appoint Shawn as managing director. It also resolved to raise an additional

$25,000 to fund the design and construction of a theater on the site, with hopes of transforming the farm into an arts center the likes of Tanglewood. In fact, among the locals appointed to the board was Joseph Franz, the architect-engineer who built the Music Shed at Tanglewood and who was ultimately charged with designing and constructing the theater at the Pillow. Shawn agreed to defer his payment toward the mortgage so that the monies raised could immediately be put toward theater construction. The rest of the board consisted of Frank Diamond (then cashier of the Lee National Bank), treasurer; Mrs. Eric Joslin, secretary; Miss Annabelle Terrell; and Mrs. Henry Wilds Smith. The Commonwealth of Massachusetts approved the application to charter the Pillow as an educational, artistic, and nonprofit institution. The board met several times in the coming months about the fundraising campaign. Within that year, the US Treasury established the institution's capacity to receive tax-deductible contributions.

As the board plotted the fledgling arts institution's financial future, Shawn retreated to his winter home in Eustis, Florida, to program its artistic future as well as to develop the "University of the Dance," his name for the Pillow's education curricula. He also nurtured his new interest in woodcarving. He bought a set of chisels, but without a sculptor's bench, he resorted to holding the wood in his left hand and chiseling with his right. The inevitable happened. He cut the tip of his finger, which required five stitches. "Why don't you model in clay?" Mumaw asked. Modeling did not interest him. Shawn explained his urge was to carve in wood. Perhaps the slabs of wood reminded him of the heavily forested Berkshire Hills or perhaps carving gave him a sense of control over nature. The new hobby was a welcome distraction to the loneliness he felt during the time Mumaw was on tour with Lisa Parnova. The distance was hard on their relationship. Shawn sent Mumaw a Christian Science pamphlet that had comforted him when he was at Camp Kearny in 1918. It was a peace offering of sorts. Just weeks earlier Shawn had written Mumaw on the road to accuse him of a sexual liaison with a boy in Texas, an assumption he made based on the glowing tones Mumaw conveyed to describe someone he had only just met.

Shawn was woodworking when he received news of the attack on Pearl Harbor on December 7, 1941. For months, he wrote to the draft-age Mumaw with concern about his future. Months later, Shawn heard the welcome news that a recently instituted military ruling meant that men over the age of twenty-eight were indefinitely deferred from the war draft. Mumaw, then twenty-nine, was no longer obligated to tour with Parnova to avoid the draft, so he dissolved the partnership. However, by June 1942, that ruling was reversed and Mumaw was notified to report to the Keesler Field Air Force Base in Biloxi, Mississippi. A unit of the Air Corps Technical Command, Keesler Field had the largest airplane mechanics school in the country next to Pearl Harbor. Mumaw was enlisted as a lowly private and initially enrolled in a thirteen-week mechanics course that ran twenty-four hours a day in three 8-hour shifts. Soon thereafter he was placed in the Special Services unit where, to Mumaw's utter relief, his assignment included entertaining the troops.

Mumaw was grateful to see a number of familiar faces among the ranks at Keesler, including former students of Mary Washington Ball. Dancer Daniel Nagrin was also at Keesler. Mumaw gravitated toward Nagrin, despite Nagrin's admirable yet constant attempts to go through Mumaw to get work for his wife, choreographer Helen Tamiris, at the Pillow during the lean war years. Paul Magriel, Lincoln Kirstein's assistant and the curator of the Dance Archives at the Museum of Modern Art was also at Keesler. He had married a woman whose family owned the *Times-Picayune*. "Isn't that a surprise?" Mumaw asked Shawn. Mumaw thought Magriel looked "despondent" and physically unfit, stressed by the rumor that Kirstein would soon be drafted.

Mumaw became involved in the great level of activity among the many artists of all stripes at Keesler. He found a recreation hall with a 2x4-foot platform stage and a broken-down upright piano, as well as a "boy" pianist named Wayne Kirkland who happened to have played for Ruth St. Denis years earlier. Kirkland recognized Mumaw's name and offered to accompany his upcoming performances at the base. Mumaw then met Del Arden (Delbert Fradenburg), a lyric tenor from New York, who had performed several seasons with the Ziegfeld Follies and in the Broadway musical *Show Boat*. Mumaw and Arden became fast friends and immediately started to collaborate on a revue. They began to perform wherever asked—at local hospitals, squadron platforms, chapels, and the theater at Keesler. They even sometimes held performances at 9 A.M. to accommodate soldiers who worked the night shift at the mechanic shop.

Their program alternated between Arden's songs and Mumaw's dances, but always closed with Mumaw's *War and the Artist*, which he renamed yet again at Keesler, this time to *A Tribute to the American Soldier*. He also experimented with the dance by placing Arden on stage to represent an American soldier and changed the costume—from a "Malibu Beach number" to a tattered mechanic's jumper—thus recontextualizing the dance's original

Figure 6.1. Barton Mumaw in *Funerailles* or *War and the Artist*. Courtesy of Jacob's Pillow Dance Festival Archives.

Figure 6.2. Barton Mumaw in *A Tribute to the American Soldier*. Courtesy of Jacob's Pillow Dance Festival Archives.

ancient Greek scenario to the contemporary United States. (See Figures 6.1 and 6.2.) To Mumaw's surprise, it was an instant success among his outfit: "I can't understand how *War and the Artist* is so impressive—seems too simple and obvious to me + to make it just about as corny, I've changed the end to a salute, which goes over big."[8] Mumaw unexpectedly found a devoted following at Keesler, and not only among fellow artists. Julia L. Foulkes succinctly captures the reality of "dancing in the army" in general and Mumaw's own sense of his newfound fan base in particular: "The enthusiastic reaction to dance—even modern dance—in the armed forces probably had more to do with the boredom and stress of military life than with a new passion for dance."[9] Foulkes also concedes that a "sexual attraction to men" might have fueled the interest in dance. Mumaw's own reaction and response to his military audiences also suggest that the "heroic masculinity" embodied in his choreography and performance might have had a reassuring yet unspoken effect on the trainees at Keesler who were intensively involved in preparing for a war from which they were physically removed. His dancing gave a mythical luster to the grueling and dehumanizing labor in the mechanical plant.

Like Shawn's letters to St. Denis during his time at Camp Kearney during World War I, Mumaw's letters from Keesler Field to Shawn are expressions of love and fear told through descriptions of dancing in the military. In his letters to Mumaw, Shawn narrates the transformation of his beloved farm into Jacob's Pillow Dance Festival, Inc. In the month leading up to breaking ground for the new theater, he announced his ideas for a summer festival centered on the idea of American Dance. He also shared a preliminary roster of teachers including Bronislava Nijinska and Argentinita, as well as performers Martha Graham, Irene Castle, Helen Tamiris, Agnes de Mille, Sybil Shearer, and Seiko Sarina.[10] However, on May 22, just as announcements of the concert program and festival faculty were advertised, a gasoline ration was imposed, which severely restricted audiences who reached the remote farm by automobile. Shawn called an emergency meeting of the board, proposing to cancel the contracts under the "act of God" clause or to go forward with the risk of running a $3,000 deficit. The board encouraged Shawn to proceed as planned, assuring him that board members would make up the deficit. The board, however, came up with only $1,000, leaving Shawn strapped with bills throughout the year.[11]

To alleviate the financial burden, in the summer of 1942, Shawn began to write *How Beautiful Upon the Mountain: A History of Jacob's Pillow*, a self-published booklet. He used the net proceeds from its sales to help underwrite scholarships at the Pillow for returning dancer-soldiers. Shawn described his mission as follows: "I want Jacob's Pillow to be here, waiting, and in full operation so that any American solder, sailor or marine, who gave up his career as a dancer to fight for a better world for all of us, can come here for his rehabilitation. The artist of any kind cannot be rehabilitated in a veteran's hospital."[12] Shawn used his vast network of former students and fans to distribute the publication to servicemen across the globe in an effort to recruit them after the war. A former Pillow student, Corporal William Miller, who was eventually awarded a bronze star for bravery in the army, wrote to Shawn to share his gratitude for *How Beautiful Upon the Mountain*:

> Today I received the history of Jacob's Pillow. I cannot tell you in mere words what a present it was. For me, as long as I've been in the army—not the war itself—but the fear that I might not be able to return to dancing again, has been the greatest depressing factor. You know how easily you lose your strength and technique when you are not able to practice regularly. It has been over two years now since I have performed, and if it has to be years longer, I still want to dance, If I survive this war I hope to be able to take advantage of your rehabilitation program.[13]

No doubt Shawn's many initiatives to raise funds to support scholarships for returning soldiers was a sincere act of patriotism, yet it is also true that the Pillow was in dire financial straits, and Shawn was counting on the plight of the artist-soldier to encourage would-be donors to make a financial contribution. Just months before Shawn mailed *How Beautiful*, in April 1942, they had broken ground for the construction of the theater at Jacob's Pillow.

The building was designed and closely supervised by Joseph Franz. He even designed the three-foot weathervane in the form of Mumaw in his signature dance *Bourrée* (1939). Mumaw's absence seemed even more real to Shawn once the weathervane was placed on top of the theater's cupola. He tried to describe the weathervane to Mumaw: "You are with me, invisibly by my side, through the day and night. Each morning when I shave I look out of the bathroom window and see you dancing, so free and so glorious, against the sky on top of the theater, so I begin the day joyously stimulated by your beauty."[14]

In addition to his personal grief over Mumaw's absence, Shawn was also experiencing a low-grade "nightmare of activity" from the chaos surrounding the premiere program in the new theater. He had difficulty managing the complex personalities of those most directly involved in the production, including some of the biggest names in the dance world, such as Bronislava Nijinska and Agnes de Mille, on top of all the remaining tasks yet to be completed for the building itself. Amidst the chaos, just days before the theater's official opening night, Shawn invited faculty, students, and staff into the new theater to experience a moment of calm and shared purpose. He "dedicated" the stage by performing his dance liturgy *The Doxology*, and, in keeping with the season's theme of "American Dance," his signature *Four Dances Based on American Folk Music*. It helped galvanize the Pillow community. In the remaining days leading to opening night, everyone pitched in. Students wheelbarrowed heaps of debris and tucked them away just out of the view of visitors. Fern Helscher collected stray pieces of lumber that had been strewn across the lawn. Dancer Sammy Steen prepared a bazaar.

During the evening of opening night, Thursday, July 9, 1942, Shawn ran into John Martin who arrived with Walter Terry to participate in this extraordinary event. Martin shocked Shawn with his presence and praise. Shawn claimed Martin called the theater "the most beautiful thing he ever saw."[15] In print, Martin's enthusiasm was slightly more nuanced. He described it as "an up-to-date theatre, innocent of any taint of quaintness or self-conscious rusticity."[16] He went on to say it was the embodiment of New England

frugalism ("Not a wasted nail or an unnecessary board anywhere") and especially praised the ingenuity of the raked audience seating, an innovation
for a dance, allowing the entire stage to be visible from any of the 525 seats in
the auditorium. A little after five o'clock the asbestos curtain went up. Mary
Campbell performed the "Star Spangled Banner" on the piano. Then, board
president Reginald Wright stepped from behind the brown curtain to introduce Shawn, who read a tribute to Mumaw and the Men Dancers whose effort and artistry made the theater a possibility and whose absence due to the
war was deeply felt.

When the curtain finally opened it exposed the natural wood of the
theater's back wall, an ideal backdrop for a program of decidedly American
fare or, as Martin put it, "so unpretensious that it seemed to have grown out
of the surroundings." Indeed, the theater was designed so that the rear wall
of the stage was composed of two large sliding doors that when opened,
revealed the scenic Berkshire hills as the backdrop. The debut program
was a perfect way to introduce the first season's "Survey of the American
Dance." First came a suite of square dances performed by local residents and
choreographed by Sammy Spring, a resident of nearby Otis who had a reputation as an outstanding square dance caller. A series of concert dances derived from American folk dances followed.

Closing the program was Agnes de Mille's new *Hell on Wheels*, about the
lighthearted shenanigans caused by the unlikely crossing of a troupe of actors and a railroad gang in 1864, all set against a life-sized replica of a locomotive and an enormous American flag as the backdrop. The dance began
with Shawn, in a theater-within-a-theater situation, drawing open the stage
curtain while barking to the audience: "Come in ladies and gentlemen, come
in—there's room for all." He was playing the role of J. Emerson Fitzgomery,
a walrus-mustachioed stage manager who helmed the troupe of traveling
thespians. It could not have been a more fitting role for Shawn that evening,
the ultimate emcee and host who makes theater happen. De Mille might have
even tailored the stage action for the occasion of the theater's opening night
and perhaps to accommodate Shawn's acting abilities. (She said he could not
even convincingly perform the role of a bad actor!) Shawn wrote Mumaw
to express his anxiety about playing a character so beyond his comfort zone
while having to clog, sing, and recite lines.[17] He worried that such a character
role compromised his reputation as an artist especially among the students.
However, de Mille also made an appearance in the dance as a champion
floorwalker who almost succeeds in dancing down a set of husky boys. The

dance sections had the high energy of a rodeo, with reels and crossing lines, slapping and two-stepping, flag waving and skirt swirling. In fact, from the Pillow, de Mille went directly to work with the Ballet Russe de Monte Carlo, a booking that meant Shawn had to release her from her obligations at the Pillow. She integrated some of the *Hell on Wheels* material into what became one of her signature works, *Rodeo* (1942).[18]

Shawn played the role of stage manager both onstage and off. After his bit as J. Emerson Fitzgomery, he was responsible for bringing down the final curtain. Though he had not yet learned to operate the tricky counterweights or the safety rope, he had little option as all of the other male stagehands were recruited to perform on stage for the final section of the dance.

After the performance, Shawn joined de Mille, Wright, Terry, and Martin on the porch of the main house to toast the extraordinary achievement of opening night. The box office took in nearly $140. All told, de Mille earned only $58 for her week's work, which also covered the wages for the two dancers she brought with her, but Shawn was pleased to say that she was a good sport about it. Plus, he later reasoned she left the Pillow with choreographic material that defined her career.

The next day, Aaron Copland came to the performance, after which he whisked away de Mille into the studio so she could get her first listen to his score for *Rodeo*. Shawn overheard what he later described as Copland "banging out jazz on the stage piano," claiming to have yelled "Stop that dreadful noise," but neither Copland nor de Mille heard him. Later he admitted to telling de Mille he thought Copland represented the "anti-Christ in music." He even told her that "This kind of music is the very reason we are having a world war. . . . I will welcome Mr. Copland and his page turner (Leonard Bernstein) as guests, but I will not salute them as artists." Copland and Bernstein laughed when they heard about Shawn's reaction to their presence.[19]

At Keesler Field, Mumaw read about the theater from a steady stream of letters, many including clippings of newspaper reviews of the opening night program. He was pleased to read John Martin's cautiously optimistic prediction about the future of Jacob's Pillow: "What the future may hold only a bold prophet would dare to predict in these stormy days, but certainly the beginning has been propitious. The audiences have been a good size, in spite of the general inaccessibility of the place in times of gas and tire problems, and the school is overflowing."[20] In August, Mumaw wrote Shawn to share the news that he had received a leave and was able to make it to the Pillow later that summer to surprise audiences with a few dances in the new theater that was crowned by a weathervane with his likeness. Jess Meeker, too, arranged a leave. The local press clamored about the reunion of Private Barton Mumaw and Private Jess Meeker, both back at the Pillow for a brief furlough. Mumaw shared a "mixed program" with West African dancer Asadata Dafora and the dance team of Arthur Mahoney and his wife ballet dancer Thalia Mara, who would later play a vital role in the Pillow's history. In the *Christian Science Monitor*, Margaret Lloyd commended the patriotic tones of the summer's programming and the presence of the dancer-soldiers in particular. Above all, she celebrated Shawn's "feat of sustaining a dance festival in war time."[21] The debut series of concerts of Jacob's Pillow Dance Festival was precisely the response she had in mind when she asked "What Can Art Say of War?"

The new theater in the remote Berkshire Hills farm attracted over 5,000 people that first summer, an impressive number considering the nationwide gas rationing. The dormitories were at capacity with eighty students, all of whom benefited from dance classes with Shawn and Bronislava Nijinska and conditioning with Joseph Pilates. German modern dancer Steffi Nossen taught free dance classes to the community. The "magnetic exponent of 'ethnic' dance" La Meri (Russell Meriwether Hughes, 1899–1988), was a constant presence on the Pillow faculty roster. La Argentinita taught Spanish dancing and taught a course on religious dancing. All told, there were forty lectures on dance and forty performances. Though a magnificent critical success, the first season of the Jacob's Pillow Dance Festival and University of the Dance resulted in a deficit of over $3,000.[22] Shawn went unpaid for his first season as managing director. To remedy the default on his payment, the board voted to pay Shawn 25 percent of all future contributions up to $1,000 and only after the $6,000 deficit had been met.

In the fall of 1942, the Athletics and Recreation Division at Keesler Field, a camp of a strikingly different kind than the Pillow, began to work on its own theatrical production. *High Flight* was a two-act musical conceived and written by members of the Special Services at the field based on a poem by "poet-flyer" John Gillespie Magee Jr. Eager to participate in the production, Mumaw requested a transfer to Special Services. He had met a fellow soldier at Keesler who offered to help with the transfer by pulling his family's ties to the War Department and to US Army General Henry H. Arnold. His name was Edbert K. Ruhl. His wife was the companion and nurse to the wealthy socialite Mrs. Evalyn Walsh McLean and mother-in-law to US Senator

Robert Rice Reynolds from North Carolina, chairman of the Military Affairs Committee of the US Senate. Because of that connection, Ruhl and his wife had special permission to live off base, among other entitlements. A trained singer, Ruhl tried to connect with Mumaw as a fellow artist, telling him that he was the only performer to have ever made him "feel inside."[23] Mumaw wrote Shawn: "He's a bitch but being very useful and kind to me."[24] It was at this point in his time at Keesler that Mumaw realized that censors had been reading his correspondence, thus advising Shawn to wait until they were together in person for the details.

As the production for *High Flight* got under way in early October 1942, Shawn arrived in Biloxi for a three-month respite and to be near Mumaw. That first month Shawn mostly rested in his hotel room at nearby Hotel Biloxi on the Gulf of Mexico. (See Figure 6.3.) The resort was a haven and refuge for Mumaw, too, who worked out an arrangement that allowed him to stay with Shawn whenever he was not on assigned duty, about six nights a week. The living arrangement came about thanks in large part to the immediate rapport Shawn established with Keesler's Colonel Robert E. M. Goolrick. The colonel's philosophy was that a happy military unit was a successful one, so he supported the many artists within his troops. He even wrote an introduction to *Art and the Soldier*, a book featuring the art of the soldiers at Keesler Field compiled by Paul Magriel. Goolrick's wife Marjorie was a sophisticated woman who was similarly eager to support art at the base. The Goolricks enjoyed hosting a celebrity like Shawn. They took him on a personal tour of the field, entertained him with dinners and cocktail parties, and joined him at the theater. The colonel and his wife took Mumaw under their wing as a result of their fondness for Shawn.

Colonel Goolrick made Shawn feel like part of the unit, putting him to work where he could be most useful. He authorized Shawn to perform benefit concerts to raise funds for a "Reception Cottage"—a place where soldiers could "receive" their wives and girlfriends when they came to visit. (See Figure 6.4.) Shawn also made a woodcarving to adorn the mantel of the cottage's fireplace.[25] He carved into the sculpture the Latin phrase *Sustineo Alas* or "I sustain the wings"—a phrase drawn from Lucien Price's *Winged Sandals*, ensuring that the specter of homosexual love was somehow represented in this cottage designed for heterosexual conjugality.

The Goolricks were not unaware of the love between Shawn and Mumaw, no matter how well Shawn and Mumaw thought they had concealed it. One

Figure 6.3. Barton Mumaw (*left*) and Ted Shawn (*right*) at the Hotel Biloxi. Jacob's Pillow Scrapbook, vol. 2. Courtesy of the Jerome Robbins Dance Division, New York Public Library.

night at a cocktail party, Mrs. Beeman, a local woman who was actively involved with members of the recreation department, pried a bit into Mumaw's relationship with Shawn. Mumaw explained to Shawn: "She told everybody there how much you loved me and some said 'I suppose you feel the same way about Shawn' and without thinking I said 'I do' in such a tone of sincerity or force or something that Mrs. B. repeated it. 'Of course this was as a father-son basis. But don't let Walter Winchell get a hold of it.' "[26]

Figure 6.4. Souvenir Program of Ted Shawn and Corp. Barton Mumaw Benefit Concert at Keesler Field, 1942. Joseph E. Marks Collection. Courtesy of Houghton Library, Harvard University.

The intensity around *High Flight* peaked in May 1943, when it was announced that playwright and director Moss Hart was planning to make Keelser his first stop on a tour of military bases to scout for talent to cast in an all-soldier revue, *This Is the Army* by Irving Berlin. Goolrick authorized Shawn to take charge of directing *High Flight*, an otherwise all-soldier production. For the production, Mumaw created a mechanical ballet, an adaptation of the "Machine" section from Shawn's *Labor Symphony* for himself and five fellow soldiers, including Larry Leonard (a former student of Men Dancer Dennis Landers), Howle Fisher (a former Denishawn dancer in 1923), and two other men with some modern dance training. (See Figure 6.5.)

Shawn approached his directorial debut with utmost seriousness, especially given the possibility of having Hart see his choreography. "Army plus show business" is how Shawn described his new routine in Biloxi. "We sleep these days until ten—then I get Barton off to the Field for a twelve o'clock matinee, and I do Pilates and mail and woodcarving—until when I meet him downtown for his one main meal of the day. Then we come home, and he bathes brown makeup off, and gets a nap, and off for the night show, and I go with either Mrs. Beeman or the G[oolrick]'s—then food, bath and to bed. Isn't it wonderful, doing eight shows a week in the army!"[27] *High Flight* was a success. They had to turn away civilians from the first six performances. Goolrick was pleased with the results.

Shawn returned to the Pillow to oversee the 1943 summer season. Although all other Berkshire cultural ventures had closed their doors to wait out the war, Shawn's indomitable spirit would not allow such a forfeit. The board advised Shawn that it could not fund another season of school and festival activity after two years of deficits, so Shawn decided to assume all financial responsibility through the Operating Fund which he controlled. According to Shawn, the season ended in the black, offset by the sale of blueberries and the profits from a recently installed Coca-Cola machine. Critic Edwin Denby reported otherwise, claiming that the 1943 season accrued a $3,000 deficit, though he profusely praised Shawn for keeping the Pillow going during wartime.[28]

During summer 1943, Barton Mumaw once again returned to the Pillow to perform on a brief furlough. Immediately following the end of the season, Shawn went back to Keesler. Sensing Shawn's excitement to be at Keesler, Goolrick made the perplexing suggestion that Shawn, a few days shy of his fifty-second birthday, apply to enlist in the Special Services. Flattered, Shawn followed Goolrick's suggestion. He even went as far as to take the entrance physical exam. His application was ultimately rejected. To make amends, Goolrick put Shawn in charge of another venture. The colonel had recently authorized the installation of a $25,000 carillon at Keesler Field. Goolrick charged Shawn with creating a musical revue called *Let Freedom Ring* that would feature the bells piped into the theater. Shawn knew that the success of the show required that he placate Edbert Ruhl, who increasingly enjoyed

Figure 6.5. "Corp. Barton Mumaw and His Men Dancers" in an adaptation of Ted Shawn's *Labor Symphony*, with fellow soldiers at Keesler Field. "High Flight" Souvenir of the Technical Schools and Basic Training Center Army Air Forces Technical Training Command of Keesler Field. Barton Mumaw Scrapbook vol. 5. Courtesy of the Jerome Robbins Dance Division, New York Public Library.

special benefits and privileges due to his family's influence. Shawn offered him the lead in the show, hoping to keep Ruhl on his good side, as it was evident that Ruhl was increasingly envious of Shawn's influence at Keesler, to say nothing of his relationship with Mumaw.

Then, out of the blue, on Monday, February 7, 1944, an order came via phone (then in a written document delivered via special plane) that Mumaw be processed for overseas shipment to join a combat unit. Out of 40,000 troops, Mumaw was singled out for this deployment, an assignment which he was entirely untrained to fulfill. Not only was the order unprecedented, but the routine furlough that every soldier was granted before overseas deployment was denied before Mumaw even had a chance to request it. The order baffled everyone at Keesler, including Goolrick, who promoted Mumaw to staff sergeant before he left Keesler with hopes that the higher ranking would ease his way wherever he landed. It was a sign of how ominous the order was. He was restationed within three days.

What followed was an ordeal that lasted several months and was one of the most distressing times in Shawn's life. In his autobiography, Mumaw only briefly glosses over the nightmarish period of his service between February and April of 1944 wherein he was essentially "disappeared" by the US military, then shipped to England without a word to his family or an opportunity for a farewell visit. His letters to Shawn and family were withheld, and for two weeks, no one even knew his whereabouts. Shawn said the experience caused him the "greatest mental anguish" he had ever endured. Desperate to locate Mumaw, he pulled at every possible string that had an attachment to Washington. Katherine S. Dreier and Lucien Price used their considerable influence to reach elected officials and the War Department with pleas to investigate this order and to bring the untrained Mumaw off the front lines. Dreier's sister Mary Dreier promised to raise the issue directly with President Franklin Delano Roosevelt.

When contact with Mumaw was eventually reestablished, it became obvious, though unmentionable in correspondence that was routinely censored, that Edbert Ruhl—referred to only as "Robbie" in Mumaw's autobiography—had leveled an accusation of homosexuality against Mumaw to his connections in the War Department that resulted in Mumaw's terrifying experience. It also became clear that Ruhl had not only leveled charges against Mumaw but had also alleged that Goolrick was under Shawn's influence and that Shawn was actually running Keesler Field. He also claimed that the Goolricks and Shawn took an army bomber to New York City to see

Broadway shows and that Shawn was drawing a military salary. Damaging as these allegations were, they were entirely plausible given the remarkable liberties Goolrick had given Shawn at the base. The accusations greatly limited Goolrick's ability to help Shawn in his pursuit to locate and bring Mumaw back home.

By May 1944, letters from Mumaw began to reach home, bringing some solace to his family and friends. In them he reported that he was in England, trapped in a daily ordeal to find an assignment. Defying military prohibitions on carrying personal effects overseas, Mumaw stitched sheet music and concert programs into his military uniform, instinctively knowing he needed a way to establish his identity as well as a means to perform. To his great relief, he found several opportunities to entertain troops throughout western England, opportunities that on several occasions spared him from heading to the front lines. *War and the Artist* was always the centerpiece of his programs.

The summers of 1944 and 1945 were grueling on Shawn as he had made an agreement with the board of Jacob's Pillow to assume all deficits and to perform all duties, from the artistic to the janitorial, in order to save the Pillow from going into receivership or shuttering altogether. To raise funds, in April 1945, he produced gala concerts at Carnegie Hall in New York City, and Symphony Hall in Boston and Baltimore. In the press he explained that the benefit concerts were to raise scholarship funds for a free season of instruction to returning soldiers—to "recondition themselves for their profession."[29] For the concert, Shawn assembled twenty performers and a dozen accompanists. Staff Sergeant Walter Terry served as emcee. Ruth St. Denis headlined, and following her appearance, delivered an impassioned curtain speech about how she and Shawn were "battling for beauty."[30] Other performers included dancer La Meri; Natya dancers, Kurt and Grace Graff; and West African dancer Asadata Dafora. The lackluster size of the audience disappointed Shawn; he blamed it on the rainy weather and the recent death of President Roosevelt just days earlier on April 12, 1945. Though pleased that Truman was sworn in as president, he was disappointed by the dismal box office intake of about $4,300, roughly the cost to produce the gala. To help raise additional funds to support Pillow activities, Shawn also delivered lectures in New York and four other cities, accompanied by showings of John Lindquist's Kodachrome slides. Those combined efforts raised only $1,000.

By the summer of 1945, Shawn and Mumaw resumed regular correspondence. Addressing him as "B.B." ("Best Beloved") Shawn tried to circumvent the military censors to express his ongoing devotion to Mumaw and his latest efforts in his campaign to bring him back from England. To keep morale high, Shawn shared details about the festival as if any day Mumaw would return to routine: "Oh, come home soon, my associate director, so you can resuscitate fallen privy's, move garbage dumps, and clean cesspools, too! I'm very sick of this whole job. It's not any of it any fun anymore. And it definitely won't be until you are here to carry it on in full partnership."[31]

In addition to serving as managing director, Shawn officially joined the Jacob's Pillow Board of Directors in the summer of 1945, and in that new capacity, reasserted his directorial authority over the Pillow in a written statement that criticized the board's plans to institute an advisory committee to oversee the Pillow's education and artistic policy. Shawn bristled at the board's inability to raise sufficient funds for him to hire faculty and build dorms necessary to fulfill his vision to establish an accredited University of the Dance. More to Shawn's point, the board had not raised sufficient funds to pay Shawn his $2,500 salary, a modest figure that was meant to cover all his work during the festival, as well as the year-round preparation of recruiting students, programming the festival, and managing publicity. To Shawn's credit, the income from school tuition ($7,800) was approximately four times that from ticket sales ($1,800). Shawn finally made an ultimatum: "Unless money in some considerable quantity is paid on my mortgage (to enable me to meet principal and interest of my life insurance liens) I must keep myself open and available for paid jobs during the fall."[32] He pleaded with the board: "I was to direct, teach and perform, but was not expected to scrub, dig, be carpenter, mason, painter, roof mender and sewer man. However, up to now, it was a choice of doing it myself or not opening the place. I made the decision myself and therefore have no one but myself to blame for the grueling two months I have put in each year for the past four wartime seasons." The summer of 1945 was the last wartime season, but it was the most difficult and rainiest summer on record since 1814, making it nearly impossible to overcome leaking roofs and flooded studios.

At 6:45 A.M. on August 14, 1945, Fern Helscher awoke Shawn with the news that Japan had surrendered and that the war was over. From that moment on, Shawn counted the days until Mumaw would arrive home, arriving at a meaningful calculation: "It just came to me . . . that Jesus began his ministry at 30 and was crucified at 33—the same three years in his life that you have spent in the army."[33] However, it took an unanticipated six months before Shawn would see him again.

Upon his return stateside on January 25, 1946 (and reunited with Shawn in New York on January 29), Mumaw immersed himself in the dance world, taking classes with Agnes de Mille, seeing Jerome Robbins's wartime ballet *Fancy Free*, and training with Joseph Pilates. He stopped regularly at the Kamin Dance Book Shop, a specialty store in the theater district, where he befriended proprietor Sally Kamin, who offered to help Mumaw get on his feet by offering to sell souvenir photographs of him at the shop.

Shawn and Mumaw went to Eustis to train and then toured with La Meri for a Jacob's Pillow benefit performance program. Even Shawn was astounded to see that his protégé was dancing more magnificently than ever. Mumaw spent that summer at the Pillow in charge of the men students, including a class of seventeen returning soldiers who were studying dance under the GI Bill of the Veterans Administration. Choreographer José Limón was also at the Pillow during the final weeks of the summer at the suggestion of Doris Humphrey.

Shawn referred to the 1946 festival as his first "peace summer." By many standards, the summer festival was a success, with weekly attendance up to 1,000 and the first sold-out performances since before the war. Enrollment was at near capacity, including the seventeen veterans.[34] Despite those achievements, in a letter to St. Denis, Shawn jokingly wrote: "All I can say is if this is Peace, give me War!"[35] He was referring to his struggle to meet the impossible demands that returning audiences placed on the Pillow's infrastructure. For example, full houses meant inadequate parking and an undependable supply of water. The stress took its toll on Shawn's body, too: "That summer nearly killed me. I lost 30 pounds, had low hemoglobin, low blood pressure, and very low morale."[36] Most physical demands of the Pillow took their toll on Mumaw, as well.

After closing up the Pillow for the 1946 season, Mumaw went to New York to reunite with his Keesler pal Del Arden to present a concert at Carnegie Hall, then reunited with Shawn and his family in Eustis to celebrate Christmas, the first they had shared in five years. It was not a festive event. Without the distraction of the war, a tour, or the Pillow, Mumaw sat down with Shawn to end their relationship. Of course, Shawn tried to convince Mumaw otherwise, but, according to Mumaw, he ultimately acknowledged that a great rift had grown between them. Mumaw went back to New York and settled into a Lower East Side apartment with John Stoakley, a former Pillow student. He soon joined the national touring company of the Broadway musical *Annie Get Your Gun* at the invitation of choreographer Helen Tamiris, taking on the role of "Wild Horse," which was originated by another of his former Keesler pals, Daniel Nagrin.

Shawn was devastated by Mumaw's decision to end their relationship. He was at the end of his five-year contract as managing director of Jacob's Pillow and decided he needed a break. He told the board of directors they would need to grant him a leave of absence or accept his resignation. The Jacob's Pillow board granted Shawn his requested time off, as well as a $2,000 bonus, on the condition that he return as managing director.

During his break from the Pillow, Shawn accepted an invitation to teach and perform in Australia for an extended period. His decision to accept the invitation did not go unnoticed. An article in the *New Republic* noted that Shawn went to Australia "under circumstances mystifying to anyone who knew his hopes and dreams for Jacob's Pillow."[37] Shawn thought it was the only way to escape the pain of losing Mumaw. Before he departed for Australia, Barton Mumaw Sr., who had the utmost respect for Shawn and his relationship with his son, wrote: "I pray for you and Barton at least three times a day. I always have a prayer each time I go by the Catholic church between nine and ten in the morning and one and two in the afternoon and always at night."[38]

Between March and August, Shawn spent what he called a "sabbatical year" in Australia. Not quite a year and certainly no sabbatical, Shawn's trip consisted of forty solo programs, each lasting two hours, in all major Aussie cities, seventy-eight radio broadcasts, six lecture-lunches, and forty public lectures. It included more than 300 hours of teaching. While planning for the trip, Shawn leveraged every favor possible to find a way to see aboriginal dancing. After months of organizing, he finally secured written approval from an Australian official. The Department of Native Affairs assigned the "Walt Whitman of Australia," W. E. Harney, author of several books about the aboriginal culture, as the patrol officer to accompany Shawn's excursion to the Northern Territory to see a *corroboree*, an aboriginal ritual that involves dancing.

The writer J. K. Ewers and his wife went backstage to meet Shawn after one of his performances in Perth. Shawn gloated about his clearance to see a corroboree. Ewers offered to join the journey to take motion pictures and notes while Shawn immersed himself in the experience.[39] Together they gathered in the bush city of Delissaville Aboriginal Reserve, home of the Wargaitj tribe, to participate in a five-day corroboree in Shawn's honor, a privilege only once before extended to King George VI. Shawn called the experience "one of the richest choreographic experiences" of his life.

During Shawn's sabbatical, the Pillow was under the direction of Arthur Mahoney and his wife Thalia Mara, New York dancers and teachers. The Pillow missed Shawn's "posturing spirituality"; Mahoney had a "businesslike air" and lacked artistic sensibilities, favoring what one critic called a "set of musical-comedy bromides."[40] Audiences were upset by the replacement of Shawn's "free tea" with "nickel pop" (at 15 cents per bottle!). Shawn was relieved to receive a cable from the Jacob's Pillow board asking him about his plans to return.

Shawn and Mumaw corresponded with each other throughout Shawn's sabbatical in Australia. Mumaw described the effect of reading Shawn's angry letters as tremors from a "distant earthquake." No matter how sincerely Mumaw ingratiated himself to Shawn, there was no way to defuse his anger and sense of betrayal. Battered by Shawn's onslaught of accusations, Mumaw finally admitted to having an affair, though he explained that it was with one of Shawn's fans, someone who had read all of Shawn's books and wanted to study with him, somehow sensing that only flattery could mitigate Shawn's wrath or to make his act of betrayal seem reasonable. Still, Shawn was desperate to see Mumaw.

Shawn spent his fifty-seventh birthday making a stop on his journey home from Australia in Kansas City, Missouri, to see Mumaw's critically praised turn as "Wild Horse" in *Annie Get Your Gun*. They had not seen each other in many months. They reunited in Mumaw's room at the Muehlbach Hotel, where the Men Dancers had stayed, a fact that brought Mumaw a false sense of comfort and familiarity as he prepared to affirm the rumor that he had fallen in love with a man named John Christian. Shawn, fifty-seven, learned that Mumaw, thirty-four, was in love with John "Chris" Christian, twenty-four. More concerned that Shawn would feel humiliated rather than heartbroken by the news of his love for a younger man, Mumaw conceded: "I'll have to pay the full price—what it is, I don't know yet." The price was steep. Shawn could not control his anger and physically assaulted Mumaw over the news.[41]

The letters between Shawn and Mumaw following the altercation echoed the words and spirit of those between Ruth St. Denis and Shawn decades earlier. Mumaw pleaded for independence, a feeling that Shawn could only experience as alienation or betrayal: "You have been an individual, an entity for your entire career. Don't be furious I'm in the process of being on my own for the first time in my entire life." For months, Mumaw pleaded for Shawn's understanding: "I'm in love with Christian and ask your blessing."[42] Indeed,

Mumaw even wrote about his "engagement" to Christian and intention to marry him, whatever that might have meant to him in 1947. Shawn eventually made a paternalistic gesture by offering his "blessing" on the condition that he and Christian conduct their relationship in a certain way. (Mumaw registers Shawn's infantilization in the title of the chapter in his memoir about the episode: "The Bough Breaks.") Mumaw refused Shawn's condition (though he never specified what Shawn had required). In all probability, Shawn asked Mumaw and Christian to keep their relationship a secret, presumably to protect Mumaw's "disguise" and conceal the truth about Shawn and Mumaw's own romantic relationship by extension.

Mumaw even tried to convince Shawn that the anger and upset he felt was tied not only to the dissolution of their relationship, but to the oppression experienced by all homosexuals: "Ted, I believe that much unrest and unhappiness in our consciousness is due to the world situation—there are things, awful sinful things battering at us night and day and I think if we realize this and ask for protection and for the knowledge to help fight it it will help us."[43]

When Shawn reached New York, he arranged a meeting with John Christian through John Stoakley, Mumaw's roommate and a former student of Shawn's. Christian was a talented set designer and costumer. His talent, combined with his good looks, made it difficult for Shawn to resist. He invited Christian to serve as his stage manager for his upcoming tour. Mumaw was delighted with the development, believing, perhaps naïvely, that meeting Christian was Shawn's way of extending an olive branch: "I'm so glad you and Chris really hit it off—he writes beautifully about you and I know you must really hit it off for you to go and stay overnight."[44] Mumaw was under the impression that by taking Christian under his wing, Shawn was helping Christian establish himself in the theater world and in the process, making it possible for Mumaw and Christian to build a life together. Shawn offered Christian a position at the Pillow, which he accepted. At the final week of the 1948 festival, Mumaw joined them at the Pillow during a week's vacation from *Annie Get Your Gun*. It was the first time the three men had come face to face. Mumaw learned that during the intervening year while he was on tour, Shawn and Christian had developed a romantic relationship between them. Mumaw was devastated by the betrayal.

In his autobiography, Mumaw relates that decades after the war, he spotted Edbert Ruhl on the streets of New York City and decided to confront the man who made allegations that wrought havoc on his life during the war. Concealing his "murderous rage," Mumaw tried to explain the incalculable distress he caused. Ruhl readily admitted that his actions were borne out of his jealousy of Mumaw, as well as a response to his own deep "unfocused anger" concerning the death of a soldier whom Ruhl had loved.[45]

Mumaw expressed a similar rage toward Shawn and Christian. Though in time Mumaw was able to accept their relationship, one that endured until Shawn's death, he never fully recovered from the pain and loss caused by the three men—Ruhl, Shawn, and Christian—in pursuit of loving him.

Dancing for Kinsey, 1945–1948

On November 3, 1945, just two months after the official surrender of Japan to the Allies, Indiana University professor of zoology Alfred C. Kinsey mailed Ted Shawn a check in the amount of $34.10 with a request that he send copies of all of his publications, as well as a series of nude photographs of himself and his Men Dancers. In reply, Shawn sent him three issues of *Denishawn Magazine* and a copy of his book *The American Ballet*, but no nude photographs. In his typed response, Shawn whetted the zoologist's appetite with a list of dancers whose exclusive photographs he could provide—Alicia Markova, Anton Dolin, Helen Tamiris, La Meri, among others. He also offered an officious explanation about his reluctance to send nude photographs:

> Unfortunately, there is a rigid federal law which prevents sending through the mail, or by express, any photograph of a male nude which shows the generative organ, or <u>even the pubic hair</u>! Various physique photographers who have disregarded this law have recently got into serious trouble. One in New York a few months ago had his studio raided, all his negatives, cameras, equipment seized and confiscated, himself put in jail plus having to pay a heavy fine. And I had reports on another in California who has just gone through the same ordeal.
>
> Personally I think the law is ridiculous and stupid. But from the way the Law regards the penis you would think it was the atomic bomb itself. Will you <u>ever</u> grow up and face the facts of life as they are, and say "So what." You and I can—but apparently General Public can't, or isn't allowed yet. We are not yet an adult nation.[46]

Instead, Shawn sent Kinsey two pages of photo proofs of Barton Mumaw from a photo shoot with physique photographer and former Denishawn dancer, Earle Forbes. The proofs were doctored by an artist who hand-painted a g-string on the negatives to conceal Mumaw's "atomic bomb." (See Figure 6.6.) Kinsey sympathized with Shawn's refusal, acknowledging that he, too, knew the jailed photographers to whom Shawn referred in his response. Still, Kinsey was apparently unsatisfied with the mediated proofs, so when the following year he came across an advertisement Shawn had placed for limited edition photographs of Mumaw, Kinsey sent Shawn a handwritten letter to inquire: "Are these complete nudes or draped figures? I will order the whole set if they are complete nudes and unretouched."[47]

Shawn was reasonably suspicious of Kinsey, perplexed by the zoologist's interest in nude photographs of his Men Dancers. Shawn would soon learn, however, that Kinsey's interest had to do with his research into human sexuality, which included what he called "the sexual element in the dance."[48] Kinsey expressed his interest in meeting Shawn to discuss in person what could not safely be communicated in letters. He also invited Shawn to take part in his research. Shawn obliged, unknowingly participating in what

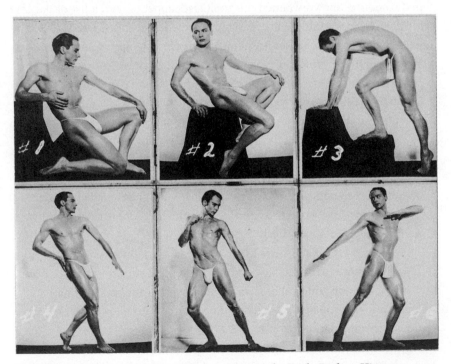

Figure 6.6. Censored photos of Barton Mumaw by Earle Forbes. Kinsey Institute. Courtesy of Houghton Library, Harvard University.

would become one of the most controversial yet influential scientific research projects on twentieth-century American culture—the Kinsey Reports.

Kinsey published his groundbreaking research into American sexual activities, behaviors, and attitudes in two volumes: *Sexual Behavior in the Human Male* (1948) and *Sexual Behavior in the Human Female* (1953). Together they became popularly known as the Kinsey Reports and immediate bestsellers. The objective of the research was to capture data about sexual practices and proclivities unmediated by social, moral, or political ideology. To that end, Kinsey's methodology involved training a team of scientists to identify and enlist Americans from all social strata to take surveys about their "sexual life histories." The responses to these specially designed questions were recorded in highly impenetrable code so as to guarantee confidentiality. The Kinsey team collected over 18,000 interviews, the majority of which were collected by Kinsey himself.

The key findings in the reports shattered ideas about American sexual norms. Most especially, the reports confirmed the prevalence of masturbation, extramarital sex, and homosexuality in the sexual lives of Americans. It also introduced the "Kinsey scale," a seven-point scale that scientists used to measure an interviewee's sexual behavior or attraction on a continuum between exclusively heterosexual and exclusively homosexual. A biologist by training, one facet of Kinsey's research focused on a possible link between human physiology and sexuality. To ascertain potential links, the Kinsey scientists inquired about characteristics of male interviewee's genitalia—about structure, curvature, direction of erection, and circumcision. To gather data about length and circumference, each male subject was asked to self-measure his penis and report the results on a postcard that he was to return. Kinsey used these data to debunk several pathologizing ideas, including the theory that *hypospadia* (the congenital growth of the urethra beneath the tip of the penis) is linked to an intersexed subjectivity or otherwise represents some form of nonconforming gender expression. Thus, Shawn finally came to understand why Kinsey was so interested in nude photographs of his dancers. Kinsey also sent Shawn a penis survey, though Shawn evidently declined to submit his results, as an incomplete "penis survey" remains with his archived correspondence with Kinsey.

Dancing was a topic covered by the Kinsey survey. The team inquired whether interviewees participated in dancing as a recreational activity. They also asked about affective responses to burlesque shows, dancing, and physical contact. The underlying premise of this line of inquiry is that dancing or watching dance activates a sexual experience. For that reason, Kinsey was keenly interested in interviewing dancers, especially gay male dancers, so as to study a possible correlation or to refute the association between dancing and effeminacy.

Kinsey studied the relationship between dancing and sexuality through means other than the surveys. With support of the Rockefeller Foundation, in 1947, Kinsey established the Institute for Sex Research at Indiana University to study and archive the massive volumes of re-search materials he had amassed to study human sexuality. This collec-tion includes a hitherto unpublished cache of George Platt Lynes's nude photographs of prominent ballet and modern dancers, such as Nicholas Magallanes, Talley Beatty, Erick Hawkins, and John Butler. Kinsey also accumulated an extensive collection of nineteenth- and twentieth-century anti-dance literature from homemade pamphlets against the scourge of the ballroom to add to his sociological studies of public dance halls. The collection also includes *realia* that blur the boundaries between dance and pornography, such as a bronze figurine of a can-can dancer with exposed genitalia (a variation on upskirt photography) and a titillating cartoon flip book titled "A Flying Fuck" featuring Ginger Rogers taking a spin on Fred Astaire's penis.

It took more than two years to synchronize their busy travel schedules, but during the week of November 1, 1948, Ted Shawn and Alfred C. Kinsey finally met in person at the Kamin Book Shop, "the first book-shop in America devoted to all phases of the art of dance." (See Figure 6.7.) Opened in 1926, the shop was located on 59th Street and Sixth Avenue in Manhattan and owned by Martin Kamin and his wife Sally. It was Mrs. Kamin, a former dancer, who suggested that they focus their business on books and prints related to dance and art, which they did starting in the 1930s. Though the shop had two browsing rooms and a garden, most of its business was through mail order. The Kamins were famous in the dance world for their highly specialized and perpetually updated bibliographies on various themes: ballroom and social dance, African American dance, Oriental dance, Spanish dance. The Kamins were also known in the an-tiquarian world. When Martin Kamin was in North Africa during World War II he went into a bookstore in Casablanca and asked for a particular book about dance. The owner advised him to contact Kamin in New York City. The Kamins went to Europe each summer to acquire private libraries

Figure 6.7. Kamin Dance Book Shop in New York City.

and collect original manuscripts, souvenir programs, costume designs, and autographs.[49]

The Kamin Book Shop was also an important outlet for Shawn's self-publishing ventures. It was the major distribution center for his books, second only to his home office. The Kamins also hosted lectures, launch parties, and an exhibit in Shawn's honor. A bibliophile, Shawn would visit the Kamins regularly when in the city, always ending his visits with a friendly plea for them to forfeit at least part of their summer vacations abroad to visit the Pillow. Wherever he traveled, Shawn procured rare books and souvenir programs for the Kamins. In return, they imported homoerotic books and magazines from Europe for Shawn. The Kamins and Shawn similarly identified and collected research materials for the Kinsey Institute.

In many respects, the Kamin Book Shop was the ideal location for Shawn and Kinsey to meet, especially as part of their discussion centered on developing a list of homosexual dancers who might participate in the study. They also discussed Shawn's own research into sexuality, an essay titled "Sex and the Modern Art of the Dance," which he published in an edited volume *Sex in the Arts: A Symposium* (1932). In his introductory essay to the volume, Floyd Dell observed that experts across the arts observed a type of "comparative sexlessness" within the modern arts. Shawn, for example, claimed that the modern art of the dance, relative to modern drama or fiction, exhibited "far more freedom, fearlessness and variety in dealing with the sex themes," though Shawn pointed out that "the suggestion or symbolism through movement is more difficult to apprehend than are definite spoken words."[50] It was precisely this idea that interested Kinsey in Shawn and his dances.

Kinsey was grateful for the "splendid help" that Shawn and John Christian had given to his research by participating in the survey. Along with many thousands of Americans who contributed sexual histories to Kinsey scientists, Shawn felt liberated by the experience of talking candidly and to a nonjudgmental ear about his homosexuality. Finally, Shawn understood the possible liberating benefits of complying with Kinsey's request for photographs of nude male dancers. At their meeting, Shawn expressed his gratitude by giving Kinsey a nude photographic portrait of himself, wherein an oiled Shawn stands on a rock framed by wildflowers, a depiction that evokes the homoerotic watercolor paintings of Andrey Avinoff. (See Figure 6.8.)

Andrey Avinoff (1884–1949) was a Russian-born lepidopterist (butterfly collector) and artist. He emigrated to the United States during the Russian Revolution and between 1926 and 1946 served as director of the Carnegie Museum in Pittsburgh, home to one of the most distinguished collections of natural history.[51] He was also a well-known painter of orchids, landscapes, and of course, butterflies and moths. However, Shawn knew Avinoff primarily as the creator of exquisitely detailed homoerotic watercolors that provocatively merged the arts of pornography with natural history illustration. Nijinsky, too, was a perennial subject of Avinoff. Throughout various stages

Figure 6.8. Autographed Photograph of Ted Shawn ("To Alfred Kinsey, With all good wishes from Ted Shawn"). Photograph by John Lindquist. Kinsey Institute for Sexual Research.

of his life Avinoff worked on new studies of Nijinsky in his various stage personas, as if each time coming to a more precise representation of his sexual attraction to the ballet star. Shawn had met Avinoff in Pittsburgh in 1937, at which time he painted a portrait of Barton Mumaw. Shawn immediately wrote to Lucien Price about his encounter with the "shy, bird-like, sixtyish" man with a "real feeling for the beauty of the male body." Shawn was confused as to how this great talent, "a gentleman-in-waiting to the last czar, a renowned scientist and a painter," should also be a "pathetic, hungry, frustrated soul—and it shouldn't be!"[52] There was more to the story; Shawn promised to tell Price in person.

Avinoff made line drawings based on Shawn's choreography for the Men Dancers, which were prominently featured in the company's 1938–39 souvenir tour program. Avinoff focused on the male ensemble in tableaux, nearly all resembling a metamorphosis in action, as with his beloved butterflies. The linear equivalent to the amorphous Rorschach inkblot, the drawings invite multiple perceptions and associations—a dance, a butterfly, an orgy. (See Figure 6.9.)

Kinsey and Avinoff shared an interest in science and entomology, sexuality, and art. They met, possibly through Shawn, in 1947, two years before Avinoff's sudden death at the age of sixty-five. Together they had begun to collaborate on a history of erotic art. In one of his last substantive letters to Shawn, a deeply saddened Kinsey wrote to commiserate over the news of Avinoff's death: "He was a very remarkable man and had done a great deal for us." Kinsey also wrote that Avinoff's sister had gifted the Kinsey Institute several hundred of Avinoff's sketches and dozens of his finished drawings. Kinsey offered to house Shawn's own collection of original drawings by Avinoff. There is no record of his response, but Shawn held onto the drawings. In one of his last letters to Shawn, Avinoff expressed how satisfying it was to know that Shawn had them in his possession.

Although scientists have rightly discredited many of Kinsey's methods and findings, the Kinsey Reports made an irrefutable and enduring impact on American perceptions about sexual behavior, particularly regarding the prevalence of homosexuality. Knowing that his "sexual history," especially his "homosexual history," helped to fuel the sexual revolution and the nascent gay rights movement was profoundly meaningful to Shawn, so much that he wanted to maintain a connection to Kinsey. Shawn sent Kinsey films of his choreography as well as the documentary footage of aboriginal dancing he had taken in Australia. Kinsey acknowledged that he had seen the films but made no suggestion about what impression they made on him or the impact they had, if any, on his research. Shawn and Christian both wrote Kinsey to inquire about visiting the Sex Institute to see for themselves the archive of materials related to dance and sexuality that Kinsey had amassed. They also tried to persuade Kinsey to visit the Pillow, but Kinsey always was away on research trips. Shawn even proposed to him the idea of dedicating an entire

Figure 6.9. (*left*) Andrey Avinoff's Studies of Ted Shawn and His Men Dancers and (*top*) a variation from "Sixth Prelude from the Well-Tempered Clavichord" (1933), Ted Shawn Papers, Additions; (*center*) "Earth" section from *Dance of the Ages* (1938). Photography by Shapiro Studio, Ted Shawn Collection; and (*bottom*) "Toccata and Fugue in D Minor" from *The Dome* (1940), Photography by Shapiro Studio, Ted Shawn Collection. Courtesy of the Jerome Robbins Dance Division, New York Public Library.

summer's program at Jacob's Pillow to Kinsey's work: "8 Weeks of complete dance study and interview with Dr. Kinsey."[53] Although the Kinsey program was never realized, arguably, the following summer festivals at Jacob's Pillow were an experiment in the new ideas and attitudes about sexuality that the Kinsey Report unleashed.

Pillow of Stone, 1947–1971

Ted Shawn left no milestone unturned. Throughout his years as director of the Jacob's Pillow Dance Festival and University of the Dance, he often identified an anniversary of some sort around which to organize a special program, a curtain speech, a fundraising effort, or a publicity campaign. Most of the celebrations had to do with Shawn himself or one of his many "firsts," though many were also related to landmark dates in the Pillow's own exceptional history. Commemorating the past was part of the Pillow ethos from its inception. For example, for the opening night of the theater in 1942, Shawn curated and installed an exhibition in the lobby to commemorate the first informal public tea dances held in 1933 with his Men Dancers, a gesture that was meant to mark the significance of the tea dances to the realization of the theater, as well as to honor the men themselves, nearly all of whom were enlisted in the military by that point. Foremost on Shawn's mind in the early years of transforming his Men Dancers training camp into a school and festival was to ensure that his dancers had a place to return to and work after the war.

"Shawn's Anniversaries," as Walter Terry had come to refer to the never-ending string of celebrations, were part of the work of building a legacy and inculcating institutional memory.[54] For Shawn, they created a context for shared experiences among Pillow students, performers, and audiences; they even oriented tourists and other dance novitiates into a history, introducing countless thousands to the notion that dance actually had a history. Plus, Shawn was hopelessly sentimental, a personality trait that imbued his lifetime of dances and writings. Shawn's intense nostalgia for the Pillow's past was fueled by anxiety about his legacy. He celebrated his own personal and institutional achievements with urgency and intensity, knowing that recognition and adulation would come from nowhere else, at least not for quite some time. The Pillow's future was never assured, so he assiduously documented its milestones in articles, interviews, and the self-published souvenir booklet *How Beautiful Upon the Mountain* that was at the center of many fundraising campaigns.

The Pillow was the ultimate expression of Shawn's life's work as a performer, choreographer, teacher, scholar, and producer. He described the University of the Dance as a continuation and expansion of the Denishawn idea, especially in terms of its inclusiveness. Modeled on the liberal arts college, the University of the Dance embodied an idea that was advertised in the very first pamphlet for Denishawn: "We believe that the art of the dance is too big to be encompassed by any one system or style; on the contrary, dance includes every way that people of every race and nationality, and in every period of the world's history have moved rhythmically to express themselves."[55] Based on that idea, Shawn developed a curriculum that trained students in ballet, modern, and ethnic dance ("an all-embracing term covering racial, primitive, national and folk dance"), as well as courses in pantomime, ballroom, social dance history, stagecraft, media, notation, and countless other topics.

The Pillow developed into a modern-day Denishawn, but it also—and sometimes more so—reflected what Shawn found most inspiring about other utopic art communities that he had encountered throughout his life: the entrepreneurialism of Roycrofters, the ritualism of Bohemian Grove, the artistry of Mariarden. He also set standards of behavior and community at the Pillow that he had learned from the progressive dance union in Germany, as well as his military forays at Camp Kearny and later at Keesler Field. His shock and awe tours of the national and royal courts throughout Asia where dance was treated as sacrosanct also shaped his vision for the Pillow. The biblical reference in the "Jacob's Pillow" name was always much more than a coincidence; the Pillow became a way for Shawn to finally bridge the spiritual and artistic impulses that animated his dances. The Pillow was a school, a theater, and a sanctuary. Moreover, it was Shawn's home, the only place he lived consistently for more than a few years, apart from his winter cottage in Eustis, Florida.

During the summer of 1971, Shawn's last at the Pillow, he celebrated several milestones: his eightieth birthday, his sixtieth year as a dancer, the fortieth year of Jacob's Pillow as a Festival, and the thirtieth year of the groundbreaking for the theater. Shawn had every reason to celebrate his impact on the cultural, artistic, and physical landscape of the Pillow—and American dance by extension. Shawn's resolve—as solid as his granite "Pillow"—is the single reason that the festival survived the war years. Through his physical labor, artistry, innovative programming, and organizational savvy, he nurtured the festival into an internationally renowned arts institution and tourist destination, one that he celebrated at every opportunity, knowing that the financial, cultural, and even physical odds were against its success. Shawn took enormous pride in his position as a pillar of the institution and the Berkshire arts community more broadly. (See Figure 6.10.) However, for every milestone in transforming his men's training camp into an international school and festival, there were Pillow fights.

Figure 6.10. Jacob's Pillar—Ted Shawn on the terrace of the theater at Jacob's Pillow. Photograph by John Lindquist. Ted Shawn Collection. Courtesy of the Jerome Robbins Dance Division, New York Public Library.

In October 1947, Shawn returned to the United States from his sabbatical in Australia. Following his visit with Barton Mumaw in Kansas City, an encounter that ended in fisticuffs, he headed to New York City to attend an emergency meeting of the Jacob's Pillow board with the goal of regaining his role as director of the Festival and University of the Dance that he had founded. Shawn had set into motion his plan to regain leadership months earlier while he was in Australia by sending a letter to the board that he asked be read aloud at the annual meeting on September 27, 1947.

In the letter Shawn expressed his interest in returning as director under the condition that the board unanimously agree to grant him complete control over the Pillow's artistic programming, which for Shawn meant ensuring that the school and festival focus exclusively on dance, the institution's original raison d'être. Current board president Russell Chapin had begun to "diversify" the festival programming with opera, much of which featured his wife, soprano Rosamond Chapin. Chapin's plan to increase the theater and opera offerings on the Pillow stage was a factor that led to Shawn's decision to take his 1947 sabbatical. Anticipating that several influential board members would resist his overture to return to the Pillow, Shawn enlisted the help of "latent" board members who had long since been inactive in board affairs but who nonetheless could exercise a vote. Shawn wrote to his long-time supporters, rousing solidarity among them by voicing his concern that Chapin was intentionally running Jacob's Pillow into foreclosure, so that he could purchase it "for a penny" and then transform it into a theater for "an opera singer." From Australia, Shawn essentially choreographed a coup, sending La Meri, Fern Helscher, Earle Garrett, and former board president Edward T. Clark to the meeting to support the proposal and conditions outlined in his letter.

The board was taken off guard by the presence of Shawn's closest allies at the meeting and bristled at their support of his return, assuming that his sabbatical was actually a resignation and the $2,000 bonus they granted him a severance offer.[56] Moreover, the board was reluctant to renege on its commitment to Arthur Mahoney and Thalia Mara, the couple who had taken over the school in Shawn's absence. The board had promised to renew their contract on the condition of a successful season. Though the board paid the couple $1,000 more than they had paid Shawn, nearly 40 percent more, the duo reportedly closed the 1947 season with an impressive gross income of $35,000 with expenses coming in $7,000 under budget. Plus, they received great press, including a feature photo-essay in *Life Magazine* that hailed the Pillow as "the dance capital of America."[57] Under their leadership, the Pillow continued to produce critically acclaimed concerts with Ballet Theatre, including programs featuring Jerome Robbins's *Fancy Free* and *Interplay*. Mahoney and Mara attended the meeting fully expecting a celebration of their success. Instead, they were entirely blindsided by Shawn's tactic to replace them.

Ultimately, Shawn's united bloc voted in favor of reappointing him as managing director under his desired conditions. Board president Chapin and treasurer Joseph Franz resigned on the spot. Secretary Alfreda Joslin resigned in the days following the meeting.[58] Though powerless against Shawn's influence, Chapin and the Mahoneys sought some revenge in the press by disclosing sensitive financial information about the Pillow, including a tax action by the Town of Becket over the Pillow's tax-free status as an educational institution. Someone also leaked the allegation that a $20,000 promotional fund was depleted around the same time that Shawn took a "good will tour of the South in interest of Jacob's Pillow," an allegation designed to unsettle the Pillow's trusting base of donors.

Upon his return to the United States from Australia, Shawn attended an emergency board meeting on October 31, 1947, convened to elect a new slate of officers. Clark was appointed board president and Shawn was elected treasurer. The new board granted Shawn's request for support to relieve him of the enormous administrative burden of directing the school and festival. They approved the appointment of Jackson Parker, an Air Force veteran who had managed theaters and events at Keesler Field and with whom Shawn had previously worked, in the new role of business manager. John Christian joined as stage manager. With a revitalized board and staff, Clark seized the moment to refocus the Jacob's Pillow mission for the post-war era and to deliver on the promise that the "University of the Dance" would have "profound import on national culture."[59]

It was a tall order, given that the Pillow was in serious disrepair following the war years. Even with the nation at peace there were limited resources. During the war years, performances were held only once a week, with Shawn featured in about a third of these and faculty members doubling as performers. Audiences fell to about twenty-five people a night on account of the Pillow's remote location. Many locals had cars, but even when gas was available, there was limited parking on the premises. Most dedicated fans came via bus, walking nearly a mile from the nearby bus stop on US Route 20. Some came on horseback. It was not uncommon to see horses tied up outside the theater, resting between round trips.

Shawn spent the next decades determined to rebuild and expand the Pillow's physical premises and artistic landscape. As Shawn aspired to develop audiences from the local Berkshire communities, he was also hopeful that he could transform his rural farm into an international center for dance world. One of the first steps in that direction was to attract high-caliber talent, such as Martha Graham, José Limón, Jane Dudley, and Sophie Maslow, all of whom presented concerts in the opening performance series of the American Dance Festival at Connecticut College (NYU-Connecticut College School of the Dance), which opened in 1948. To compete at that level, Shawn had to reverse his pernicious habit, born out of the austerity of the war years, of requiring artists to pay their own transportation to and from the Pillow and to perform without compensation.

Inasmuch as opportunity and logistics would allow, Shawn followed a "something for everyone" approach to programming concerts by making sure that ballet, modern dance, and ethnic dance were represented at each concert. He was always scouting for performers, but he would start the actual work of programming in early spring. He described how he initiated the planning cycle for the festival each year:

On April 1 (fittingly) each year, I take a big piece of cardboard and with a ruler draw lines which make a set of thirty oblong spaces—three wide by ten deep (for the [ten] weeks of performance.) No jigsaw picture, no crossword puzzle or double crosstic is as difficult to solve as to fill in those thirty blank spaces with the names of solo, duet, group, company—ballet, modern, ethnic, and what-have-you dancers, so that the schedule of Jacob's Pillow Dance Festival can be in the printer's hands six weeks later.[60]

Programming the festival involved days of writing and responding to letters, telegrams, and cables, as well as long-distance phone calls. (Negotiations with St. Denis, who appeared in the first three summers before the war and then again after the war nearly every season until her death, could take all year and even once settled could change at a moment's notice.) For weeks at a time, Shawn would camp out at the Hotel Dauphin in Manhattan on 67th and Broadway, making it his temporary home and holding court with aspiring artists, the press, and friends. Once he arrived at a final roster he printed 10,000 flyers with the schedule in nearly the exact block schema that it appeared on his drawing board, which he and his small staff would fold into "serpentines" and mail. He would then take time in his Eustis studio for rest and relaxation before returning to the Pillow in May to begin readying the campus and welcoming the first of the scholarship students to help with the preparations.

For the first few years after he regained the artistic helm of the Festival, Shawn began to choreograph once again, not only to keep his artistic signature on the Pillow programming, but also to create opportunities to collaborate with his lover John Christian, who designed and created elaborate sets and costumes. Together they embarked on a number of ambitious dance-dramas that recalled the heydays of Denishawn. In 1948, he created *Minuet for Drums*, a forty-five-minute work for twenty-five dancers, inspired by Stefan Lorent's book *The New World: The First Pictures of America* (Duell, Sloan & Pearce, 1946), a volume that chronicles a 1564 French expedition to conquer Florida, sponsored by Catherine de Medici. The book contains reproductions of the iconic sixteenth-century engravings of Theodor de Bry depicting indigenous life through the lens of European conquerors. Rather than attempt to recreate authentic native dancing from these images, Shawn choreographed a dance that Catherine de Medici might have conjured upon hearing accounts of the indigenous war, fertility, and celebration dances that her conquistadors encountered in the New World. Shawn performed in the dance, taking on the lead role of the Indian chief Saturiba. In a lengthy solo, Shawn performed a series of arrow-slinging jumps, as if to convince audiences that he was as physically fit as ever and back for good. Though the dance was largely pantomimic, there is one exceptional group dance of Indian maidens, each holding a pair of two short sticks that transform, as if kaleidoscopically into deer hooves, then antlers, then fire-starting sticks.[61]

The following year, Shawn created a dance called *The Dreams of Jacob* (1949) based on the Book of Genesis story, featuring "Papa" Shawn, the patriarch of American dance, in the role of Jacob, the patriarch of the Israelites. He chose the subject matter not only for the biblical figure's association with the name of his farm but also as a way to honor the formation of the Israeli state in May 1948, an event professed by the life of Jacob.[62] Shawn created a dance in five movements, each dedicated to a passage in the Bible concerned with Jacob's life, focusing on Jacob's dream, when he places his head on a rock to sleep, then dreams of angels ascending and descending a ladder to Heaven. In the dance this scene was realized with an actual ladder that led into the wings of the theater, which dancer-angels walked up and down, blessing Shawn, as Jacob, who was resting on his "pillow." (See Figure 6.11.)

The highpoint of the dance is the dramatization of the moment in the Genesis story when Jacob wrestles with an angel. Shawn insisted on including this section as it represents the first time in the Bible that Jacob is referred to as "Israel." In Shawn's version, a "Dark Angel" appears mysteriously to Jacob, then attempts to physically dominate and restrain him. (Joseph Pilates, who had by then returned to the Pillow, reportedly coached the wrestling section.)

Figure 6.11. Ted Shawn and company in *The Dreams of Jacob* (1949). Photograph by John Lindquist. John Lindquist Collection. Courtesy of Houghton Library, Harvard University.

Though there are many possible interpretations of the physical struggle and the wound that the angel inflicts upon Jacob, Shawn saw the episode as a rite of passage that every person must endure in order to establish a relationship with God. Following the tussle, the Dark Angel brings Jacob a princely robe. Jacob wears it, and limps upstage as the lights dim, accepting his destiny as the founder of Israel.[63]

Shawn's treatment of the subject resonated with Ruth St. Denis, who attended the world premiere of *The Dreams of Jacob* and wrote a poem titled "Dreams of Jacob" inspired by the dance, especially the scene with angels ascending and descending the heavenly and material realms, as well as the final image of Jacob's victory over the "Dark Angel," as if it somehow vindicated her own lifelong struggle with religion:

> My own spirit is renewed by these bright angels
> Ascending and descending the stairways of God.
> My heart is confronted by this victory of Jacob
> And his final standing in the Light.

> For these mighty rhythms and wrestlings
> These mighty gestures of strength
> Are symbols of the soul
> Revealing the vast, ceaseless powers of man![64]

During the off-season months, Shawn toured and accepted commissions for special appearances. In 1950, he created a solo representing "Atomo, the God of Atomic Energy," for the finale of the 150th annual costume ball of the Bal Boheme Arts Club, an extravagant social event attended by prominent members of Washington's social, government, and military orbits.[65] Local dance schools in the capital city created futuristic dances to celebrate the theme "2100 A.D." To portray "Atomo," Shawn wore a fishnet bodysuit cinched at the waist with tassels dangling over each thigh, a broad shouldered cape, and a headpiece depicting a nuclear explosion. (See Insert Figure 6.12.) Shawn wanted the dance to convey "the beneficent aspects of what atomic energy can do for mankind." He set the piece to the "Uranus" section of Gustav Holst's *The Planets*, a short yet relentlessly propulsive section of blazing brass and crashing cymbals. "A fee is a fee" is how Christian later rationalized Shawn's participation in the ball.

That same year, presumably governed by the "a fee is a fee" logic, Shawn agreed to choreograph an eagle ballet for an ensemble of men to perform at a halftime show during a football game in the Polo Grounds in New York City. Contracted to pay for costumes from his fee, Shawn decided to design and construct them himself. He ordered turkey feathers from a farm in New Hampshire to create wings. However, the feathers arrived freshly picked from the turkeys, encrusted with mud and filled with worms, which Shawn proceeded to clean in his New York City rental apartment.

By 1950, Shawn confidently asserted Jacob's Pillow's status as the "most famous summertime dance center."[66] With the success of the Pillow outpacing his own artistic achievement, Shawn decided to mount several revivals. He was already thinking retrospectively, for that summer, the main branch of the New York Public Library on 42nd and Fifth Avenue held an exhibit called "Ted Shawn, American Dancer" in the Music Division Room, with photographs, posters, programs, and costumes that limned the highlights of his career.[67] Shawn revived *Prometheus Bound* at Jacob's Pillow, but during a dress rehearsal, the manacles meant to keep Shawn bound to the rock snapped, sending him flying off the set and into a momentary state of unconsciousness. John Martin mentioned the accident in the *New York Times*, and, as if to prove his resiliency, Shawn performed *Prometheus* several weeks later during an unscheduled but entirely welcome visit to the Pillow by St. Denis and La Meri.

He also revived *The Mountain Whippoorwill*, a large group dance based on the 1925 ballad by Stephen Vincent Benét and set to folk tunes by Dorothy Jenkins. The plot of *Whippoorwill* is summed up in the ballad's subtitle: "How Hill-Billy Jim Won the Great Fiddler's Prize, A Georgia Romance." Shawn played Whippoorwill, the young champion fiddler who incited the couples of "mountain folk" in square dance formations. Shawn originally choreographed the dance in 1944 (following Benét's death in 1943) when there were only two male scholarship students, George Horn, and himself to cover the male roles, so he revived the dance in 1946 with equal numbers of boys and girls.[68]

In 1951, Shawn created another full-length work with a biblical theme. *Song of Songs* was based on the Old Testament love triangle between King Solomon, played by Shawn, his thousandth wife, the Shulamite Maid, played by La Meri, and her shepherd lover, played by Peter di Falco. The dance was set to an original score by Manuel Galea. Once again, Christian created the sets and costumes, this time inspired by Gustave Moreau's symbolist watercolor painting of an exotic Shulamite maid holding flowers and wearing a glittering sheath that barely covers her breasts. The set design featured an upstage screen flanked by columns, upon which Solomon appeals to his maiden as a man rather than as king. The choreography requires more partnering than any other of Shawn's dances, with him and La Meri interconnecting arms and sharing weight throughout. Shawn had originally planned to compose the dance for him and St. Denis during the Denishawn days, a representation of a more balanced and equal partnership on stage than St. Denis ever allowed in their marriage. Shawn shared the history of *Song of Songs* with La Meri, making her somewhat trepidatious to take on the role as St. Denis's surrogate. To celebrate the new work, Shawn threw an extravagant post-show party complete with champagne and lobster, during which he presented each cast member with a gift related to his or her role in the dance.[69] He was proud of his effort and thus was taken aback when the reviews deemed the dance "old fashioned" in the style of Denishawn. Shawn's greatest claim to artistic achievement had become an artistic liability. Even Walter Terry, Shawn's most ardent champion, expressed disappointment with the dance, writing that "the glowing, tantalizing, and fantastic" images evoked by the Bible were not realized in the choreography, which rarely rose above "elementary pantomime."[70] Shawn retaliated by explaining that the dance was meant to be nostalgic—"in the style of Denishawn"—a wink and nod to the elaborate groundbreaking spectacles of the Daniel Mayer days. Even as an homage or pastiche, the dance was weighed down by its elaborate costumes, set, and plot on the one hand and the unremarkable design of movement on the other. *Song of Songs* ended up being Shawn's swan song, at least in terms of his post-war choreographic aspirations.

All three of Shawn's post-war dances, even his performance as "Atomo," were period pieces that relied heavily on (or more nearly, created opportunities for) the talents and interests of John Christian, Shawn's lover and collaborator. All three pieces featured Christian's set designs—a throne, a ladder, a screen—devices meant to stage multiple locales, plots, and eras within Shawn's dance-dramas, yet they ultimately obfuscated the strength of Shawn's choreography: its attention to emotion and character.

"A new life begins at 60!" Shawn proclaimed as summer turned to fall and he reached another milestone. For Shawn, part of that new life involved performing roles that were suitable to his "age and state of madness," which turned out to be deranged fathers and harbingers of death. In 1953, Shawn returned to the Pillow stage in *El Amor Brujo*, a dance-drama by La Meri. In this work, Shawn was once again cast as a specter, this time as a lover who haunts his beautiful wife (played by La Meri) who tries in vain to avoid the attention of a young gypsy lover (Peter di Falco). One remarkable aspect of his appearance in this production was that it marked Shawn's first steps on the stage of the theater that had officially been renamed the Ted Shawn Theatre. Shawn accepted the honor with uncharacteristic modesty. In fact, he shared the news in his annual newsletter, buried within a parenthetical statement.[71]

When Shawn sought to perform in his later years, he turned to Myra Kinch who created featured roles for him that were "tailored to his increasing physical limitation," as Walter Terry put it.[72] Myra Kinch (1904–81) had an enduring and influential presence at the Pillow. A dancer from California with a background in television, movies, and the stage, Kinch directed the Los Angeles unit of the Federal Dance Project, a New Deal initiative that supported the development of modern dance in its nascent years. Shawn called her "the pioneer modern dancer of the West" and in Kinch's dances found a compelling humanity, especially the way she brought together comedy and tragedy, the silly and the sublime. A former student of La Meri, Kinch directed the modern program at the Pillow for over twenty-five years, starting in 1948, and presented several premieres in the Ted Shawn Theatre, including her most famous *Giselle's Revenge*, a humorous take on the conceits and conventions of the Romantic ballet.

In 1955, Shawn appeared in Myra Kinch's *The Bajour*, a dance about a gypsy family living in a modern city. "Bajour" is the Serbian term for "beautiful flower" as well as the confidence game played by gypsies, which forms the dance's dramatic center. Shawn played the role of the patriarch of a family who fleeces an old woman of nearly all her worldly possessions. She realizes the trick and summons the police and the gypsies wind up behind bars, but only until they devise another con.

Later that year, in December 1955, Shawn was a "guest star" in Kinch's production of *Sundered Majesty* at the Brooklyn Academy of Music, a dance based on *King Lear* that was presented at the Pillow the following summer. Critic Richard V. Happel noted that Shawn seemed to do justice to the "madness, and withal the dignity of the old king comes clear and sharp." Doris Hering applauded his "heroic mime." The always faithful Terry called Shawn's performance the highlight of the program, which included the highly anticipated appearance of the Russian American ballerina Alexandra Danilova and her partner, the South African dancer Michael Maule (who had performed at the Pillow previously, as a partner to Maria Tallchief).[73]

In 1958, Kinch cast Shawn as yet another disturbed and blind father, this time in a dance set in medieval Italy. *Sound of Darkness* was a dance-drama based on the play *The Love of Three Kings* by Sem Benelli. Convinced of his daughter-in-law's infidelity, the blind father hatches a plot that results in the death of his son, his wife, and her lover. Taking a deliberate turn away from drama, in 1960, Shawn appeared in Kinch's *A Waltz Is a Waltz Is a Waltz*, a light and frothy dance that cleansed the palette of old kings he had portrayed in years past. In fact, Kinch was inspired to create the dance by a statement that had followed Shawn since his early years as a dancer: "Shawn's heart beats to three-quarter time." Shawn loved this quote and Kinch transformed it into a slapstick routine for two couples set to a few Strauss tunes. It was a fitting way for Shawn to conclude his regular appearances on stage in full-scale premieres, though he continued to perform at the Pillow's many special anniversary events and benefits. Indeed, Shawn was sixty-nine years old at the premiere of *A Waltz Is a Waltz Is a Waltz*, which was meant to mark the silver jubilee of his uninterrupted fifty years as a dance artist, dating back to his appearance as a nineteen-year-old in a ballroom exhibition with Norma Gould.

Throughout the years, Shawn took advantage of his breaks from the Pillow stage to exercise his acting muscles. He performed in a series of plays by a local amateur theater company in Eustis, Florida, figuring that acting was a good way to express himself or at least was an easier way to carry around his "180 pound, sixty-year-old body across the stage." In 1949, in Mt. Dora, a town near his home in Eustis, he first performed as an actor in a benefit to help finance a new community troupe known as the Ice House Players. Shawn took on the titular role in *Death Takes a Holiday*. He reprised the role that summer during the opening weekend of the Berkshire Playhouse in Stockbridge, Massachusetts, proud to work alongside a Broadway-caliber cast. In 1954, he appeared in a farce, W. Somerset Maugham's *The Circle* in the "cut-to-order" role of the clever father. Christian played the role of Shawn's son, in addition to assuming many stage management responsibilities that he took on to ensure that the production was up to Shawn's standards. In 1955, Shawn had a role in the comedy *My Three Angels*, for which he received his best acting reviews. Shawn was equally delighted and surprised, seeing that he had always considered himself entertaining but never funny.

By 1952, Jacob's Pillow had established itself as a known quantity well beyond the worlds of the Berkshires and the dance community. In that year, banking on his inclusive programming formula to translate into dollars on the road, Shawn created a touring program with a group of dancers he called the "Jacob's Pillow Dance Festival Company." (See Figure 6.13.) Though the troupe bore the festival name for publicity purposes, Shawn took personal financial liability for the venture. Billing it as the "Most Important Dance Attraction," Shawn arranged an eight-week tour that aspired to bring the magic from the remote hills of the Berkshires across America, though, in reality, it stayed within the New England and Mid-Atlantic states. The touring company was a practical way for Shawn to earn money—for his dancers and himself—during the Pillow's lean fall months. However, he described its existence in broader and more philanthropic terms as being inspired by an exchange he witnessed between Helen Tamiris and producer Sol Hurok at the Dance Archives exhibit at the Museum of Modern Art in 1940. Tamiris, allegedly approaching Hurok in a "vital whirlwind," backed him against a wall and interrogated him as to why he had never given the same level of support to American artists that he had given to European ones. Shawn recalled Hurok's response, which made for an unconvincing answer but a terrific idea: "Well, if you American dancers would get together, and form me a company as big and with as many stars in it as the Russian ballet—I would certainly be interested in promoting it."[74] Thus, Shawn conceived the tour as a way for individual artists to come together to advance the dance field in the United States.

Figure 6.13. Jacob's Pillow Dance Festival Company featuring Ted Shawn (*seated at center*) and counterclockwise: John Christian, Mary Campbell, Vanya, Richard Stuart, La Meri, Myra Kinch, Nicholas Polajenko, Tatiana Grantzeva, and Ralph McWilliams. Photo © Jack Mitchell. Courtesy of the Jerome Robbins Dance Division, New York Public Library.

Under contract with Columbia Artists Management, Shawn assembled Pillow faculty and guest artists as a touring company with La Meri and Kinch as headliners. The roster also included ballroom dancers Richard Stuart and Vanya. Shawn emphasized that the pair worked in the style of Vernon and Irene Castle, though their "theatrical" ballroom style was quite distinctive. One adagio they performed required Vanya to wear an oversized cape that she manipulated while partnering Stuart, à la Loïe Fuller. However, Shawn struggled to book the right ballet couple for the tour. He was looking for the youngest, best looking—and, ideally, cheapest—duo but ultimately settled on three dancers.[75] Shawn's next task was to find an existing classical *pas de trois* for his three booked ballet dancers. He soon learned there were none, so he commissioned Antony Tudor to create a work, a lovely trio in the classic tradition called *Trio con Brio*, set to music from Glinka's *Russlan and Ludmilla*.

The tour was a worthy gamble given the Pillow's enormous popularity but did not yield the financial win Shawn had hoped for, so the company's first tour was also its last. Shawn shifted his focus back to attracting audiences to the Pillow by developing it as an institution that was part local theater (in harmony with the tastes and values of the Berkshire community) and part international tourist destination, a "mecca for dance-lovers" as he liked to claim.

The secret to the Pillow's sustainability was Shawn's inclusive, diverse, or otherwise "eclectic" programming philosophy. Nearly every concert Shawn produced at the festival was a mixed bill of classical ballet, modern dance, and "ethnic" dance, plus a mime or specialty performer that effectively expanded the definition of dance beyond ballet and modern dance. His goal was to curate "a sweeping all-inclusive picture of dance achievement."[76] The eclecticism was also a reflection of Shawn's training philosophy: like Denishawn, the Pillow uniquely offered an inclusive dance training curriculum, which distinguished it from other dance schools, such as American Dance Festival at Connecticut College where modern dance reigned. About Shawn's approach to programming at the Pillow, Charles Weidman once said, "He's so used to vaudeville he always has to have several attractions on his program."[77] Weidman was right in the sense that a vaudeville program had to appeal to a wide variety of tastes. From his years in vaudeville, Shawn understood that for the festival to last, it must satisfy the high artistic expectations of dance aficionados and also appeal to the educational, cultural, or entertainment interests of locals, tourists, and dance novitiates: "Critics have hurled the words 'eclectic' and 'hybrid' at me as if they were critical bombs. . . . [O]n the contrary I have always gloried in the word 'eclectic.'"[78] One of those critics was John Martin, who at least once used the term "random" to refer to Shawn's programming choices.[79] Noting that Shawn's "formula" worked well for many years at Jacob's Pillow "with summer and tourists and education in the air," he scoffed at replicating the model in the "concentrated, big-pressure city . . . which is broadminded but certainly decentralized. These programs might be considered as having something for everybody. But the reverse is also true; they are guaranteed also to have something that everybody will dislike."[80] This diatribe against Shawn's programming philosophy opened Martin's 1954 review of a Pillow performance where he observed that a quarter of the audience left after the main attraction of ballerina Alexandra Danilova, leaving the house thinner for Inesita, a "Spanish dancer," whose performance Martin actually quite enjoyed.

Shawn's commitment to "ethnic dance" was part of Pillow programming from the very start. In his lifetime, he saw ethnic dance ("the step-child" of the dance world) develop into an established area of performance and research.[81] To develop this aspect of the program, he had a trusted teacher and advisor in La Meri, an accomplished Spanish and Indian dancer who had studied and performed around the world before the war kept her grounded in New York, where she met Ruth St. Denis and with her founded the School of Natya dedicated to Indian dance in 1940. They occupied a studio at 66 Fifth Avenue in the same building where Martha Graham had established hers. St. Denis lived on the ground floor. When St. Denis moved to Los Angeles in 1945, the studio became La Meri's own venture, the Ethnological Dance Center, and moved to 110 East 59th Street. In 1947, La Meri inaugurated a Young Artists series at her Center, which became a font of talent for the Pillow.

As much as ethnic dance was part of Shawn's artistic signature from the beginning of his career and a thread that carried through Denishawn and the Men Dancers, he also took his cue from the new discourse and policy of internationalism that surrounded post-war art and culture. Jacob's Pillow developed at the same time as the United Nations, which was founded in 1945, and similarly envisioned itself as an institute of cultural diplomacy, though exchanged ideas in the "international language of dance." Indeed, over the years Shawn referred to the Pillow as the "United Nations of Dance."[82] Shawn took another cue from a special program produced by Hazel Lockwood Muller at the American Museum of Natural History between 1943 and 1952: "Around the World with Dance and Song."[83] La Meri was involved with the program, and Shawn and St. Denis performed in it in 1950 and 1951. According to Shawn, the "Around the World" series fostered ethnic dance, helping it "get into its stride" in the post-war years.[84]

In 1950, Ballet Theatre, New York City Ballet, and Martha Graham all toured abroad. In 1954, José Limón became the first artist to be sponsored to travel overseas under the aegis of an "international exchange" program sponsored by the US State Department. To remain competitive in this new and rapidly evolving international, intercultural dance landscape, Shawn and the Pillow had to increase their involvement. Indeed, the Pillow hosted two of the earliest international artists sponsored by the State Department's exchange program. By 1954, the festival garnered notable national media coverage for its internationalism, especially Shawn's " 'world's eye view' to programming."[85] The list of notable ethnic dancers from abroad who performed at the Pillow is extensive and impressive, including Hadassah from Israel, Geoffrey Holder from the West Indies, Ram Gopal from Bangalore, India, and Mexican dance artists Josefina Garcia and Alonzo Rivera. (Rivera, who was also gay, became a personal friend of Shawn and someone Shawn helped to become an American citizen to support his promising career as a dancer and, more important, to escape the persecution of gays in Mexico.) In 1955, the Pillow hosted Xenia Zarina, the "dancing teacher to the Shah of Iran" and "danseuse etoile" at the Iranian court who had been teaching Oriental Dance in Mexico City for the Mexican Department of Fine Arts since 1953.[86]

Despite the success he had in developing the Pillow's international profile, in 1954, Shawn tried to realign the programming and faculty more closely with the Pillow's mission to become a University of the Dance and thus aspired to program new artists on the Pillow stage and appoint new faculty, those more sympathetic to his focus on teacher education rather than training professional dancers. This meant that many familiar faces who helped the Pillow achieve its many successes, most notably La Meri, were no longer invited back under Shawn's "fresh faces" policy. Shawn said he had suffered a "seven-year itch" since 1947, when he regained the reins of the Pillow. He could easily implement such a policy since he had amassed the lion's share of proxy votes on the board.

The opening event of the 1957 Silver Jubilee season featured Native American dancer, musician, and craftsman Tom Two Arrows (Thomas Dorsey) of the Onandaga Indian Reservation in New York.[87] Two Arrows had recently returned from an extensive tour of India, Indonesia, Japan, and other areas of the Far East in 1956 and 1957. Sponsored by the State Department (through ANTA, the American National Theater Academy), the tour had a mission to rehabilitate Cold War perceptions of the United States abroad, a mission that Two Arrows might have taken too far. He reportedly explained to audiences in India that US colonists did not "segregate" Native Americans in the United States and that they were "very much loved and respected," raising questions about how Two Arrows might represent the history of indigenous genocide to audiences in the Berkshires, many of whom owned vacation properties on former Mohican territory.[88] At the Pillow, Two Arrows performed three ceremonial dances and the next day participated in a panel discussion on men in dance.

Months before Two Arrows appeared at the Pillow, US representative John J. Rooney of New York wrote a racist piece about the dancer, expressing the pride he felt when the Native American's name no longer appeared on the State Department budget, lamenting the "high priced talent we are sending all over the earth at the expense of the tax payer." In a violent racist fantasy about his disappearance, the representative wondered: "Maybe Two Arrows was shot?"[89] He soon learned that Two Arrows appeared on the budget under his given name Thomas Dorsey. It was this type of racism that Shawn, the Museum of Natural History, and the State Department were working against through the soft power of dance.

Shawn considered one of the Pillow's greatest legacies its ability to create conditions for racial and ethnic inclusivity through dance and education. In 1957, the Music Division at the New York Public Library curated an exhibit to honor the Pillow's silver anniversary. One of the highlights of the "25 Years at Jacob's Pillow" exhibit was "a map showing the dance forms of various nations and indicating their place and date of origin."[90] To see all paths across the globe converge on his farm gave Shawn a great sense of pride. He was especially proud of the many black dance artists that he invited to teach and perform at the Pillow, which led to some distinctive moments in the histories of ethnic dance, modern dance, and ballet. The first festival programmed by Shawn in 1942 featured West African dancer-choreographer Asadata Dafora from Sierra Leone. Dafora presented his acclaimed dance-dramas on a program with Shawn and Mumaw.[91] Much of the press coverage for Dafora's first appearance focused on his pet panther Kaboo, who arrived at the Pillow on a leash and was deemed a "sissy" for his inability to tolerate the cool overnight temperatures in the Berkshire Hills.[92] In 1945, Dafora appeared at Carnegie Hall in a Jacob's Pillow benefit with St. Denis, but never returned to the Pillow.

On the eve of the civil rights movement, Haitian dancer and drummer Jean Léon Destiné became the first person of color to join the Pillow faculty in 1949. He taught and performed at the Pillow with his dance partner Jeanne Ramon and percussionist Alphonse Cimber.[93] That same year, ballet dancer Janet Collins performed at the Pillow and Carmen de Lavallade would later appear with Lester Horton's company and several times thereafter.

African American choreographer Talley Beatty, a former dancer with Katherine Dunham, debuted at the Pillow in 1948. The day after the program's close, Beatty wrote a letter to Shawn, accusing him of racial discrimination owing to Shawn's apparent reaction to an altercation that involved Beatty's dancers and the staff at the Greenwater Lodge where the company stayed during performance week: "All because of a bottle of whiskey in the living quarters." Beatty says Shawn's response, or lack thereof, was "one of the most insulting and degrading we have had as dancers."[94] Beatty lambasted Shawn for referring to his dancers as "you people" and "children," widening his criticism as "a slap in the face to all Negro dancers." Beatty threatened Shawn that he would go public with his accusation.

Shawn responded that he was "much disturbed and hurt" by Beatty's accusation, writing to him as a "sincere friend"—though he carbon copied his letter to his publicists, Isadora Bennett and Richard Pleasant—to maintain his record, which he described as "100% clean." Shawn defended himself by explaining the lengths he went to make the group's appearance possible, even pulling strings with his neighbor Mrs. Hodge, the proprietor at Greenwater Lodge, to arrange their stay. (Notably, African Americans were not welcome in most Berkshire hotels and motels until the 1960s, thus requiring Shawn to make special arrangements for any black artists he engaged.) "She is a New England woman, with typical New England standards," Shawn pointed out before enumerating all the instances of Beatty's unprofessionalism, including his failure to confirm the company's reservations, missing dress rehearsal, and, above all, bringing candles on stage, a serious threat to Shawn's wood temple. Shawn had reason to be frustrated with Beatty, which unfortunately clouded his ability or willingness to acknowledge Beatty's serious upset over the racist humiliation he and his dancers experienced.

At some point after the debacle, Beatty wrote Shawn an apology: "my conduct at the Pillow that summer though from nervous fatigue, frustration, fear, was appalling." From the basis of his previous letter, Beatty was entirely justified to defend himself and his dancers from "racial implications," though he later expressed contrition over threatening Shawn. "Over the past four years I have come to realize a good many things about myself and people and life itself—this has aided me I believe and made for a certain point of view in my work and I think that I have attained a great deal of maturity. I must say were it not for you Mr. Shawn and a few others who helped me so generously at the very beginning it might be a different story."[95] In the summer of 1952, Beatty shared a program at the Pillow with works by Roland Petit, Doris Humphrey, and José Limón, and again in 1960.

Another remarkable appearance at the Pillow came in 1954 when the Lester Horton Dance Theater performed for its second consecutive season, less than a year after Horton's death in November 1953. In his absence, a relatively new dancer to the company named Alvin Ailey stepped forward to fill the program and premiered his *According to St. Francis*. Ailey would later return to the Pillow with his own company, most notably in 1961 to present his signature work *Revelations* for the first time in its present form. Shawn thought highly of Ailey as a performer, choreographer, and person, especially when Ailey spontaneously interrupted a television interview with

Shawn to sing "Papa's" praises. Shawn was deeply flattered and thought he and Ailey "make a terrific sister act!"[96]

The same year Ailey debuted at the Pillow with Lester Horton, so too did the Negro Dance Theater, the first black men's ballet ensemble, an experimental group that Shawn played a crucial role in helping to form. The idea for a company of black men performing classical ballet came from Aubrey Hitchins, the British dance teacher and former partner of Anna Pavlova and ballet master at the Metropolitan Opera. His vision was to feature a cast of black men as a classical ballet ensemble that specialized in the style of the Italian Renaissance. In December 1953, Hitchins tested the idea with an eight-week trial period of free "closed" classes for black dancers. Put another way, the dancers, all of whom possessed established Broadway and television credentials, agreed to participate in unpaid rehearsals. Hitchins was able to raise interest but not funding with his idea, so he turned to Shawn. Hitchins explained that "Shawn came to see what we had to show him: an incomplete cast and two boys holding two coat hangers to represent candelabra! His comment was 'This is an evolution in Negro dance.' And he signed the company for four performances in August 1954. Thus was born the Negro Dance Theater."[97]

The Negro Dance Theater's first appearance at Jacob's Pillow featured Hitchins's choreography for Bach's *Italian Concerto*. The critics tried admirably to engage the company in artistic terms rather than as a novelty act: "Hitchins has not entirely solved the problem of using Bach and at times the movement becomes 'busy' or too unified. There are no women dancers in the troupe as yet, which added to the monotony of movement. Mr. Hitchins has on occasion fitted such feminine movements to the music that he must be accused of destroying the essential virility of the dancers."[98] The company returned for a two-week engagement in 1955, the same year that Arthur Mitchell became the first African American principal dancer in the New York City Ballet. The company presented another world premiere, *Gotham Suite*, inspired by the five boroughs of New York City, choreographed by former Jacob's Pillow student Tony Charmoli, who by then had become a television choreographer. *Our World* magazine ran a feature on the company, accompanied by images, including one of Danish ballerina Inge Sand posing with black dancer Charles Queenan, that captured—and even celebrated—racial integration at the Pillow.[99]

Though Shawn supported modern dance and ethnic dance from the Pillow's inception, the festival's commercial success relied heavily on the presence of ballet on every program. To that end, Shawn developed relationships with ballet companies large and small, as well as with established and emerging ballet choreographers. Some of the greatest names in twentieth-century ballet danced on the Pillow stage. Shawn knew how to leverage each dancer's fame to generate box office income.

Perhaps one of the most significant ballet programming coups at the Pillow came in 1949 when Shawn made an arrangement for Ballet Theatre (then a young ballet company just shy of a decade old, now American Ballet Theatre) to become the official resident ballet company of the school and festival.[100] After their closing night at the Metropolitan Opera, members of the Ballet Theatre company rushed north to the Pillow for a season of summer work. They presented a combination of classic variations pared down to piano (*Les Sylphides, Black Swan*, and *Sleeping Beauty*) and new works, such as Antony Tudor's *Jardin aux Lilas* and Jerome Robbins's *Interplay*. In the studio, Tudor served as principal ballet teacher for the school. After the company departed two weeks shy of the festival's end, ballet dancer and choreographer Ruth Page appeared on two programs that included her own *Harlequinade, or Love Is Not Too Simple*.

Shawn supported full-fledged ballet companies such as Ballet Theatre and the San Francisco Ballet, which had its three-week East Coast debut engagement in 1956 at the Pillow. He also programmed the US debuts of the National Ballet of Canada in 1953, the Ballet Rambert in 1959, and Nederlands Dans Theater in 1965. However, Shawn was equally interested in civic and regional ballet troupes, which grew in number and popularity throughout the 1950s and 1960s. Eager to have a front row seat to "a movement of great magnitude in its early stages," Shawn regularly lent his time and celebrity to support local civic companies by serving as an adjudicator at regional ballet festivals. Between 1958 and 1968 he attended over a dozen festivals as adjudicator or guest speaker. His involvement was a time-consuming endeavor, often requiring him to travel to small towns for weeks at a time to select companies to compete at the regional festivals designed to build solidarity between local companies as well as to foster artistic excellence through competition. Shawn was impressed by the seriousness of the aspiring professional dancers he encountered: "I had seen the grass roots of American dance as it is today. And it's pretty encouraging. I had seen invariably a serious, professional approach by directors and dancers."[101] Shawn made clear that he preferred the civic ballet movement, led by "true American youth" and "upstanding Americans," to the counterculture hippie movement sweeping the nation, a statement that resonated with his rhetoric from his early days when he placed his wholesome Denishawn dancers above the youth obsessed with jazz music and dance.

Working closely with Dorothy Alexander, "the mother of the regional ballet movement," Shawn was committed to inviting regional ballet companies to the Pillow. In 1958, he booked the Atlanta Civic Ballet. In 1960, he invited the Washington Ballet (on a bill with Patricia Wilde as guest star), and he presented the Boston Ballet for the first of many engagements in 1962. In 1971, Shawn's last season, the festival kicked off by hosting the Northeast Regional Ballet Festival.

Perhaps Shawn's greatest programming coup was booking an engagement of ten stars from the Royal Danish Ballet, then a 200-year-old company and the world's oldest next to the Paris Opera. The series of events that led to this three-week festival initiated in 1954, when the press agent for the Danish prima ballerina Inge Sand called Shawn to see if it would be possible to arrange for her US debut at the Pillow before her impending return to Denmark. Sand had received a fellowship to study in New York with George Balanchine. Shawn managed to juggle some programs around to accommodate her request. She appeared with her partner Vladimir Dokoudovsky performing variations from August Bournonville's *Konservatoriet* (1849) and Emilie Walbom's *Dream Pictures* (1915) as well as a pas de deux by Dokoudovsky. Their debut shared a program with Aubrey Hitchins's Negro Dance Theater. The success of the premiere led to conversations about future appearances at the Pillow between Sand, Shawn, and Erik Bruhn, the Danish ballet star who had been dancing for Ballet Theatre and happened to live in the Hotel Dauphin, Shawn's winter headquarters in the Big Apple. They developed a program of pas de deux and small-scale ensemble work showing a range of 100 years of Danish ballet and Bournonville style, the likes of which US audiences had never experienced. Even scaled down, the production was prohibitively expensive, so Shawn had to cobble together performances beyond the Pillow to make it financially feasible for the engagement to happen. He secured a night for the program at Lewisohn Stadium and elsewhere. What was a busman's holiday for the Danes turned out to be what Shawn himself called "the apex of our achievement in presenting dancers at Jacob's Pillow," acknowledging the significant consequences that the rare performances had for the festival, for the US dance world more broadly, and for Shawn's life in particular.[102] The event was so important that John Martin cut short his vacation to attend a performance (a fact he mentioned in his review). *Dance Magazine* delayed its printing in order to include Jack Mitchell's photographs of the performance in that month's issue. Shawn said he had never heard such ovation in the Ted Shawn Theatre.

The following year, during the 1957 Silver Jubilee season, and just a few months after Shawn had traveled to Denmark to see the company perform in a full-scale production (and to visit with some of the dancers who had performed at the Pillow), he received perhaps one of the highest and most unexpected honors of his life. Mr. Johannes Laursen of the Danish Information Office offered his congratulations to a confused Shawn prior to a Pillow performance of the "Eight Soloists of the Royal Danish Ballet." When Shawn claimed not to know what the official was referring to, Laursen produced a carbon copy of a letter from the Danish Ambassador explaining that Shawn had been awarded the Cross of Dannebrog, the highest award the Danish king can bestow on a private citizen. His Majesty Frederick VIII of Denmark wished to recognize Shawn as a "Balletens Ridder" or "Ballet Knight" for the wave of good press that the Royal Danish Ballet received as a result of Shawn's invitation. Moreover, the Royal Danish Ballet was important to the king, "a perceptive balletomane," who routinely attended performances with his three daughters, who would visit dancers like Sand backstage and invite them to the palace for parties.[103]

Shawn traveled to Europe for the knighting ceremony. On the morning of November 17, 1958, Christian helped Shawn dress in his formalwear at the Palace Hotel in Copenhagen. Shawn was rightfully anxious, though justifiably disappointed that Christian would not be able to join him at this most special moment. Shawn was driven to the Christiansborg Palace, where he was led to a waiting room with seven others awaiting a private audience. Shawn was brought in first to meet His Majesty Frederick VIII, who presented him with the Cross of Dannebrog. Conversation centered on their shared regard for Erik Bruhn.

Following the knighthood ceremony, Shawn and Christian went on a whirlwind tour of Europe, which included meetings with possible guest artists for the Pillow. Upon his return stateside, he learned that Doris Humphrey had died just days earlier on December 28, 1958, finally having succumbed to a battle with cancer. Though Humphrey neither performed nor taught at the Pillow, her choreography was represented on programs featuring her protégé José Limón. Shawn did not hold back in expressing his opinion that Limón's *The Moor's Pavane* (1949), first presented at the Pillow in 1951, surpassed any choreography his deceased mentor had created for him. The legacy of modern dance at the Pillow was a fraught subject for Shawn, given his own complicated relationship to "modern dance." Though he increasingly claimed to be the "father of modern dance," he never fully acknowledged modernism in dance as an actual artistic movement in the United States. Even as late as 1959, when he wrote *Thirty-Three Years of American Dance*, he still resisted the idea of "modern dance," instead calling it "American dance." He continued to harbor resentment that the birth of modernism seemed to require annihilistic criticisms of him and his work. Shawn sounded the death knell of modernism in return: "Modern dance has arrived at a sort of Sargasso Sea, going around in circles and getting nowhere."[104] Though the Pillow School and Festival used the term "modern dance," in his writings and lectures, Shawn would insist on another classification system and genealogy, referring to Isadora Duncan, Ruth St. Denis, and himself as the "First Generation of American Dancers." He classified Humphrey, Graham, and Charles Weidman as the "Second Generation of American Dancers." Of these three Second Generation dancers, only Weidman ever performed at the Pillow, first in 1947, while Shawn was on sabbatical, and again in 1954.

Shawn invited Graham several times to perform at Jacob's Pillow to no avail, though she did visit. In 1956, Shawn heard through the grapevine that Graham and her patron Baroness Bethsabée de Rothschild were staying at the posh Red Lion Inn in nearby Stockbridge, so he sent a message encouraging her to come to see him in a solo concert, featuring *Invocation to the Thunderbird*, a dance he first created when Graham was still a Denishawn student. According to Shawn, Graham returned the call and in a voice "just as simple and sweet and unaffected as possible" said she regretted that she could not make the concert but asked whether she could visit a class the following morning, which she did. Shawn treated her a tour, a spaghetti lunch, and an earful of warm reminiscences. Graham also watched Myra Kinch teach a modern class. Later that evening Shawn accompanied her to a performance at the Pillow of the San Francisco Ballet. By that time, photographers Jack Mitchell and Rad Bascombe were on the scene, tipped off by Shawn himself. Shawn and Graham were photographed coming and going, fore and aft, outside the theater and in their seats. (See Figure 6.14.) Graham went backstage to greet San Francisco Ballet choreographer Lew Christensen and the dancers. Shawn called it a "red letter day" for the Pillow. Plus, the visit provided the basis for a new relationship between him and Graham. More than a year afterward, on New Year's Eve, December 31, 1957, Shawn had a long visit with Graham in her Manhattan apartment and left feeling "the

Figure 6.14. Martha Graham (*left*), Bethsabée de Rothschild (*center*), and Ted Shawn at Jacob's Pillow, 1956. Photo © Jack Mitchell. Ted Shawn Papers, Additions. Jerome Robbins Dance Division, New York Public Library.

final healing of the long breach" between them. He also left with Graham's promise that her company would appear at the Pillow the following summer, which did not come to pass.[105]

There is something to be learned from Shawn's ideas about programming and audiences from one of the most regularly produced yet least discussed artists in the first two decades at the Pillow: Iva Kitchell (1908–83). The "Mistress of Dance Satire," Kitchell performed dance parodies (backed by her "Invisible Dance Company") that took aim at all dance forms: classic ballet, modern, and scarf and garland dances. The comedy rested not only in her impeccable sense of humor but also in her serious dance training. At 5'1", Kitchell was a member of the Chicago Civic Opera Ballet who knew she would never be a prima ballerina, so she set off on her own solo concert tour of the United States and Europe in the mid-1940s. One of the hallmarks of her routines was planting a makeup table on stage, to which she would return between acts to minimally add or subtract costumes or accessories (which, according to one reviewer, "looked as though they had been run up on an old sewing machine by a wounded seamstress").[106] One never knew which of the fifteen numbers in her repertory she would perform. Program notes would offer possibilities but make no promises. Thus there was an aura of surprise in her appearances. Among her most popular routines were *Soul in Search*, about the self-consciousness of modern dance, *Pseudo Voodoo*, about ethnic dance, and *Variation on a Variation*, a sendup on *The Nutcracker*. Her performances helped to release any artistic or cultural tensions that could arise as result of the many different dance styles on Shawn's mixed bills. By exaggerating the conceits, conventions, and aspirations of every dance style, she humored not only well-informed insiders but also the many uninitiated audience members who attended the Pillow, to embrace the numerous ambiguities and incongruities between artists. Her appearances helped blunt the sharp edge between artists on shared programs, say, for example, one in which she appeared on a program with Sonia Arova in the *Black Swan* pas de deux and Jean Léon Destiné's carnival and slave dances. Kitchell performed regularly at the Pillow between the mid-1940s and late-1950s before retiring in 1958 at age fifty.[107]

The excitement around the Pillow's artistic achievements made it a desirable tourist destination in the Berkshires. By 1950, Jacob's Pillow had begun to appear on tourist maps alongside other star attractions such as the Elm Court Vanderbilt Estate, the Berkshire Museum in Pittsfield, the Mission House in Stockbridge (the former home of missionary John Sergeant), and the Berkshire Playhouse. The Pillow benefited from significant glare from the spotlight on Tanglewood, the music festival and school in nearby Lenox, which served as a summer home to the Boston Symphony Orchestra. The Pillow, and other cultural centers, became part of the "Bach and brook trout" subscription series, which included overnight accommodations at one of the new mid-century modern motels that sprang up to accommodate the uptick in tourism. Shawn sought to attract visitors from the city, but also to develop audiences within the Berkshires, sometimes quite cantankerously. He once implored: "Every single year-round resident of the Berkshire area should attend at least one performance at Jacob's Pillow before deciding that they 'don't like dancing.'"[108] He also scolded local homeowners for not supporting the Pillow during its quieter weeks when it remained open beyond the Tanglewood season.

One of Shawn's proudest moments came in May 1951 when the editors of *National Geographic* recognized the Pillow as one of the great natural and human resources of the New England mountains.[109] The map ran alongside a photo of him teaching at the Pillow, as well as the Franklin Price Knott autochrome of him and St. Denis posing in *The Garden of Kama* that first appeared in the April 1916 issue, in which they went unidentified. He was even more proud fifteen years later when the December 1966 issue of *National Geographic* published a feature on the state of Massachusetts with a map that singled out Jacob's Pillow as a Berkshire landmarks, prompting Shawn to reflect on its underdog status, especially compared to Tanglewood: "The Boston Symphony, backed by all the social, political and financial power of Boston and ancient in its prestige, and me a poor boy out of Kansas City, backed by none of these—but I have created a cultural institution that is world famous and now 'on the map.'"[110]

Though the Pillow's location was fixed on the map, its physical grounds were constantly shifting. As the institution grew artistically and organization-ally, Shawn supervised a steady stream of infrastructure projects to support his growing ambitions. The first major improvement came in May 1946 when Shawn installed a 15,000-gallon water tank on the premises with a blueprint from Joseph Franz and the muscle of scholarship boys who helped to cut into bedrock to install the eighteen-foot wooden tower. In the Ted Shawn Theatre programs, Shawn would outline the campus improvements each year, often with a fundraising plea. In 1950, the parking lot was considerably expanded, welcoming more guests to the campus. In 1952, he extended the box office. In 1953, he oversaw the building of the first new faculty cabin (and the first with a tub!), as well as the first public bathroom, to keep unticketed visitors from using student bathrooms. The following year brought improvements to the theater (installing showers, dressing rooms, and a new scenery shed) and upgrades to pedestrian pathways, for which Shawn poured the concrete himself. The 1954 season welcomed the 100th premiere at the Pillow, John Butler's *Three Promenades with the Lord*; it was also the year that electricity was provided to all buildings on campus.

Among the perennial physical constraints at the Pillow were inadequate housing for students and parking for audiences. On Shawn's sixty-fifth birthday in 1956, local papers ran a picture of the birthday boy in the driver's seat of a bulldozer breaking ground on a six-unit dormitory and recreation hall, ushering in a "new era at Jacob's Pillow." This made way for Ballet Plaza, a mini "campus" of cabins that served as student dorms, each named for a ballet dancer who had made a lasting impression on Shawn or the festival. In 1958, eight female students moved into Cia Fornaroli Toscanini House, named for the La Scala dancer with whom Shawn studied in New York. In 1959, addi-tional cabins were built, each named in honor of a famous ballerina, such as

Alicia Markova, Alexandra Danilova, and Inge Sand. In 1960, the Nora Kaye House was added, and, in 1969, two others, named for Maria Tallchief and Violette Verdy. The male students resided in cabins named for Men Dancer John Schubert, who died in World War II, and John Christian.

With increased space for more students, Shawn decided there ought to be more room at the dining room table, figuratively and literally, so, also in 1957, he added a "nook" on the student dining room. Students were not the only ones eating in the dining room; porcupines had eaten away at the wooden floor, so Shawn replaced the floor originally laid by the Men Dancers in 1935 by resurfacing it with concrete. Joseph Pilates helped.

In addition to the physical improvements, there were curricular developments. Shawn's idea for the "University of the Dance" came closer to fruition in 1950 when Springfield College began to award credit at the undergraduate and graduate levels to teachers attending the school. Shawn's insistence on including ethnic dance in the curriculum was to give dance teachers a more capacious understanding of dance than one would receive at a local dance school or even at a university, where dance was taught predominantly in the context of physical education. The teachers' program with Springfield was a small step in the right direction, though only three students were registered in the first cohort. Shawn had to hire three faculty to administer the required courses while denying registration to a good number of high school students to comply with the agreement that all students would have a high school diploma. The school suffered its greatest financial loss to date.

One of the highlights of the 1957 Silver Jubilee Season was the "homecoming" of the original lineup of Men Dancers, except for Dennis Landers. (See Figure 6.15.) The men came reasonably unsure what to expect after so much time had passed, though Shawn later reported, "It was a wonderful week in every way, for again we seemed to have demolished time, and the boys and I fell into the old, easy familiarity as if it were still 1940."[111] Mumaw performed that week with Meeker at the piano. After the show, the dancers all reunited in the dining room for a private party.

Part of building the Pillow institution and its legacy meant ensuring its publicity and preserving its archives. Shawn had at least two formidable champions on that front. John Lindquist (1890–1980) was a Boston photographer who had begun capturing the Men Dancers on film in 1938. Lindquist had photographed nearly all of the artists who performed at the Pillow and his images helped shape the Pillow's brand—especially his photos of dancers against the open Berkshire sky. Shawn actually exerted tremendous

Figure 6.15. Ted Shawn and His Men Dancers reunite at Jacob's Pillow on Friday, August 2, 1957 (*left to right*: Meeker, Overlees, Mumaw, Shawn, Fitz-Simons, Horn, Coble) Jacob's Pillow Dance Festival Photographs (v. 11, 1957, photo 211). Photograph by John Lindquist. Courtesy of Jacob's Pillow Dance Festival Archives.

control over the circulation of Lindquist's images. In one instance, he directed Lindquist to destroy the negatives and prints of a photograph of a male dancer in drag, concerned that parents would never send their students to study at the Pillow should the image circulate widely. Shawn subsequently required Lindquist to first show Shawn all of the photos he had taken at the

Pillow before sharing them with anyone else, including photos of artists and staff. To a somewhat lesser extent, local photographer John Van Lund also documented Pillow artists beginning in 1946. Notably, Shawn managed to employ the services of both Lindquist and Van Lund at little direct expense, paying them only a nominal amount for finished prints.

Another pillar of the Pillow was Carol Lynn (1893–1987), who administered the school from 1936 to 1960. During a portion of that time she also served as chair of the dance department at the Peabody Conservatory in Baltimore, Maryland, where she ran her own dance school and presented recitals of dances she had learned as a student at Denishawn in New York City in 1922. In her twenty-three years at Peabody, she trained hundreds of dancers including the influential choreographer Martha Clarke, and her contributions to life at the Pillow were many. It was Lynn who convinced Shawn to open the school to women. In the 1950s, she made an arrangement with Shawn to film many of the performers who were presented on the Pillow stage, leaving behind an unparalleled archive of mid-century American dance. Based on her early forays in dance on film, she taught Pillow students a course on audiovisual aids for dance, a proto-dance technology course.

The 1957 Silver Jubilee year was a turning point. With twenty-five years of the Pillow behind him, Shawn needed support to ensure its future. Shawn was simply no longer able to manage the minutiae of the festival and school by himself. In 1958, Shawn's dentist, Dr. Ira Colby (who became a long-time Pillow board member), introduced him to Grace Badorek, a capable career woman who was recently widowed and seeking a steady job and more income. Shawn hired Badorek, who had previously worked as an Avon salesperson among other jobs, as a business manager, and she moved to a new home in nearby Lee so she could run the Pillow operation year-round. Badorek became Shawn's eyes and ears, a trusted friend, and a staunch defender of all Pillow matters.[112]

Shawn consistently said that the greatest obstacle to the Pillow's success was the "autocratic ruling" of the local Becket township that would not grant the Jacob's Pillow school not-for-profit status for tax filing purposes. "While the Pillow is chartered by the Commonwealth of Massachusetts as an educational institution that is recognized by the state and federal government, and even the admissions for programs given at the theater are exempt from an amusement tax, the Town of Becket continues to levy a confiscatory real estate tax on the property and buildings. This year Becket made an arbitrary raise in the assessed value of the property of nearly 20 percent."[113] The "Pillow

Case" was scheduled to go before the Supreme Court.[114] Shawn relentlessly pressured the Town of Becket to reverse its decision. Once he wrote an editorial for the *Berkshire Eagle*, taking the opportunity to weigh in on the matter of the tax issue as a plight of all summer residents who pay taxes but have no vote in local affairs. He explained his then ten-year tax battle with the local government and how the Pillow, the second-largest taxpayer in the township, received "no service whatsoever for these taxes—no police protection, no fire protection, and our dirt road is dragged only once each year."[115] When Shawn could win favor neither in the Supreme Court nor in the court of public opinion, he sought out a resolution whereby the board would transfer the title of the Pillow's property to Springfield College in order to benefit from its tax-exempt status. The plan was never instituted.

In 1966, yet another threat to the festival's survival entered the scene: the Saratoga Performing Arts Center opened a theater in Saratoga Springs, New York, just ninety minutes away from the Pillow, that would compete for potential audiences. The threat became reality when the New York City Ballet launched its three-week summer residency at the new Saratoga theater, causing attendance at the Pillow to drop 15 percent from the previous year. Shawn envied Saratoga's $3 million endowment, continuing to boast that the Pillow had never received federal funding nor a private endowment large enough for institutional impact. The irony was underscored by Shawn's recent appointment to the US State Department's "Panel of Dance Experts" for Cultural Presentations in 1965–66, which allowed him to participate in decisions regarding the awarding of federal grants. "At nearly 74, I finally made it!" he quipped at the appointment.[116]

The largest external force on the Pillow's development came in 1970, when the National Endowment for the Arts (NEA) required that dance companies receiving federal grants must collect from producers a minimum fee set by the NEA. In order to pay dance companies this minimum fee, Shawn would have had to dedicate an entire program to a single modern dance company, which Shawn was convinced would never work for Pillow audiences: "NO modern dance company will draw at the box office."[117] The NEA policy made it impossible for Shawn to program any dance companies receiving federal funds, thus excluding some of the most exciting companies, many of whose eligibility for funding, in part, was based on their previous success at the Pillow. The irony was not lost on Shawn that as a dancer he had always advocated for federal support of dance, yet as an arts presenter and producer, federal funding worked against him.

On Shawn's sixty-ninth birthday in 1960, his long-awaited autobiography, *One Thousand and One Night Stands*, was finally published. Shawn was displeased with the final result to say nothing of its reception, so to redeem his effort to celebrate his legacy on the page, he decided to mount a revival of his most successful work on the stage. In 1962, the thirtieth anniversary of the festival, dancer and choreographer Norman Walker recreated Shawn's 1935 *Kinetic Molpai*, a work Shawn had grown to accept as his greatest. Writing for the *Springfield Union*, Wayne C. Smith described the rousing ovation it received: "In the 16 years that we have been reviewing the programs at Jacob's Pillow we have never seen such an ovation given to a performance and to a choreographer, as that which Ted Shawn and Norman Walker and his group of men dancers received."[118]

Despite his upset with his autobiography, Shawn pursued yet another publishing venture: an edited volume of his correspondence with Lucien Price. The two friends reunited at the Pillow in the fall of 1963 to review their correspondence, which they planned to publish in a book tentatively titled *Seven Magic Years*. They shared memories and suggestions for revisions, but the project never came to fruition. Price died that spring. Shawn eulogized his friend in an essay "The Greatest Man I Ever Knew" for the *Boston Globe* (April 4, 1964). In addition to extolling his many personal attributes, Shawn claimed that Price's life and art inspired his own: "Through his books he has guided, illumined, and ennobled the lives of countless thousands. In this lies his immortality. He will never be forgotten. The sum of his contributions to his time and humanity will not be fully realized for a hundred years." [119] He shared a more personal reaction to Price's death with a friend, the dance writer and performer Lillian Moore: "At 72, I suddenly feel like an orphan."[120]

That same year, 1963, Shawn suffered another personal loss: Aunt Kate died. Only eight years older than Shawn, Kate was the only member of his family who had been a constant presence throughout his adult life. She visited often when Shawn was in high school and accompanied him on dates and dances. He called her "my girl." Kate lived with St. Denis and Shawn at Denishawn at the beginning of World War I.[121] She also loaned money to Shawn when he most needed the help, a favor that truly made his career, and Martha Graham's, as Shawn was fond of pointing out.

The Golden Wedding anniversary of Ted Shawn and Ruth St. Denis in 1964 was the most elaborate celebration ever hosted at the Pillow. As the couple had been separated for more than thirty years, the event commemorated what came forth from the marriage rather than the relationship itself. The celebration took place on the actual date of their wedding, August 13.

Their anniversary received attention from every major news outlet and, of course, they performed. Before an invitation-only audience at the Ted Shawn Theatre, St. Denis took the stage with *The Incense*, and Shawn performed his *O Brother Sun and Sister Moon*. To a commissioned score by Jess Meeker, Shawn choreographed a modest and final duet for him and St. Denis based on a poem St. Denis had written called "Siddhas of the Upper Air":

> In the blue spaces between the stars
> The Siddhas stand together.
> Blown by the lifting winds of the whirling worlds
> They move side by side with the effortless motion of the
> Divine Dance.
>
> Gazing ahead their hearts beat to the
> Unearthly rhythm of perfected love.
>
> They are moving towards the light of the unimaginable sun.
> And their garments are blown behind them.
> Like a comet's saffron tail.[122]

St. Denis's poem about "siddhas," or those who have achieved religious enlightenment, had special resonance for St. Denis and Shawn, who valiantly tried to resolve their personal and professional rifts by relating to each other on a spiritual plane. In fact, Shawn ended one of his most memorable letters to St. Denis during their protracted separation with an image of themselves as two siddhas in the upper air, sharing a love unfettered by obligation or custom: "Meet me daily in the Upper Air, my lovely and Beloved Siddha—there is nothing lost but the dross which would have kept us down."[123] For the celebration of their fifty-year union, St. Denis and Shawn presented a restrained dramatization of St. Denis's poem, also titled *Siddhas of the Upper Air*, which featured the couple in a loose embrace while gliding across the stage "towards the light of the unimaginable sun."[124] (See Insert Figure 6.16.) The regal procession across the stage poignantly evoked the very first dance they ever performed together, *Ourieda, A Romance of a Desert Dancing Girl* (1914), a similitude rendered all the more poignant by the fact that *Siddhas of the Upper Air* was the last dance Shawn and St. Denis ever performed together. (See Figure 2.1.)

Ruth St. Denis died on July 21, 1968, just four years after their Golden Wedding anniversary. She was perhaps the Pillow's greatest star attraction, having made an appearance nearly every year since the end of World War II. During the summer that Shawn had to contend with the loss of his wife and his biggest star, the foundation of the Ted Shawn Theatre crumbled. It was a devastating setback but also a form of poetry: on St. Denis's death, Shawn's theater sank.

The Pillow had just celebrated the twenty-fifth anniversary of the Ted Shawn Theatre in 1967. To mark the occasion, Shawn delivered an hour-long curtain speech, in which he also celebrated his twentieth anniversary with Christian. When Shawn introduced Christian and tried to describe what he had meant to the festival, Shawn choked up. In some measure, Shawn's tribute to Christian was a way to publicly acknowledge their personal relationship. On the topic of their personal relationship, Shawn claimed Christian as his family and his heir.[125]

Of course, Shawn's health was also steadily declining. In his 1967 newsletter, Shawn announced his "enforced slowing down," a response to grave health issues he faced in 1966. Shawn was sick and conspicuously absent from the last weeks of the festival with a bronchial infection, a worsening condition that led to action by the Pillow Board of Directors during its annual fall meeting. The directors designated Shawn as "Founder and Artistic Director" ("to advise and consent") and John Christian as "Executive Director." In a related decision, the board approved hiring Barton Mumaw to help with the transition. Shawn shared the news with his "family" via newsletter, assuring that he would still be "Papa" and that there was no talk of his retirement. The change in appointments reflected how things had been operating for at least the past year.

Christian handled most of the logistics of a particularly high-profile venture in 1969, a two-hour television documentary on Jacob's Pillow that was broadcast by the Corporation for Public Broadcasting, later known as PBS. Incorporating characteristically diverse dance footage of Donald McKayle, Lotte Goslar, Maria Alba, Nala Najan, Norman Walker, Toni Lander, and Bruce Marks, the program was also conceived to include four scenes with Shawn himself. Although he was hospitalized for ten days leading up to the scheduled taping, Shawn managed to rally himself for several hours in front of the camera, then returned to the hospital immediately afterward where he was confined for five more days. Shawn considered the national exposure well worth the effort, and he was heartened to hear favorable comments from viewers as far away as Vancouver and Hawaii.

In addition to his knighthood from the King of Denmark, Shawn accepted many honors and awards in his later years. On March 19, 1957, he had been awarded the Capezio Award, from the maker of dance shoes and apparel, for "service to the dance" by way of Jacob's Pillow as "an institution of international recognition." He attended the luncheon reception at the St. Regis Hotel to receive his citation and the modest cash prize of $500. Shawn figured the press was more valuable than the purse, especially as the ceremony coincided with the twenty-fifth anniversary of the festival, breaking its own record with 22,000 people in attendance by the sixth week. On that special occasion, John Martin suggested that the dance world bestow upon him the honorary title "Almus pater" ("Great Father"). "That the American dance owes him some such recognition is incontestable."[126]

In 1970, Shawn was one of the recipients of the annual *Dance Magazine* Award, along with Carolyn Brown (the inspiring Merce Cunningham dancer and daughter of one of Shawn's former students, Marion Rice) and Sir Frederick Ashton (the renowned British ballet dancer and choreographer). It was a particularly validating moment even if long overdue. He had attended the ceremony a decade earlier when the award was given to Martha Graham, though he harbored no hard feelings, since Shawn felt vindicated from her acceptance speech wherein she acknowledged Shawn and Louis Horst for their support during the earliest stage of her career.

There were several causes for celebration in 1971: Shawn's eightieth birthday, his sixtieth year as a dancer, the fortieth year of Jacob's Pillow (as a festival). He maintained a presence at the Pillow throughout the summer, appearing during his ritual curtain speeches before performances. "I am, from now on, strictly *emeritus*!" he would tell audiences, always wearing a splash of lime green—a pocket square, a cravat—to match the color of the season's souvenir program book. Later that fall, on his eightieth birthday, Genevieve "Gegi" Oswald hosted a celebration at the Dance Collection at the New York Public Library for the Performing Arts, to which Shawn had bequeathed most of his papers and archives. The ceremony was observed on October 18, 1971, a Monday, when the dance world tended to be dark, thus allowing working dancers to attend and pay their respects to Papa Shawn. In his final years, Shawn himself would personally tend to his massive collection of letters, scrapbooks, and photographs. Whenever he was in the city he would go to the Dance Collection to view a film or hunt down a photograph for a lecture. Because of the significance of his personal archive, as well as the donation of 150 reels of film and audio cassettes of his lectures from Jacob's

Pillow, his name was inscribed on the marble Benefactors' Column at the Main Library on Fifth Avenue in 1969. Of the many honors he received, this was one of the most meaningful to Shawn. His journey into adulthood began in a library, surrounded by books that sparked his interest in dance, religion, and sexuality. He was deeply proud that his life's work expanded an understanding of each and their points of convergence.

No doubt, Shawn would have written at length in his annual newsletter about the eightieth birthday party at the New York Public Library. He would have especially enjoyed sharing the names of the illustrious friends and associates from every phase of his life who came to wish him well and the types of tributes that were shared about his life and legacy. He would also have written about the milestones he was planning to celebrate in the summer of 1972, his sixtieth year as a dancer, and the thirtieth anniversary of the Ted Shawn Theatre. However, Shawn died weeks before President's Day, the date he set aside each year to write his newsletter. Instead, that year Christian wrote a letter to Shawn's "family" of newsletter readers about Papa's death. He shared information about Shawn's final days. More important, he reminded readers that Shawn considered Jacob's Pillow his "living memorial." The letter was informative though respectfully reserved, true to the relatively officious tone of Shawn's own newsletters, which rarely veered too deeply into personal affairs. Shawn was always conscious of being "Papa," a term of affection he would almost always write in quotes, so as to acknowledge the distinction between his public personae and the private man.

In 1972, Christian led the fortieth annual Jacob's Pillow Dance Festival in its celebration of the thirtieth anniversary of the Ted Shawn Theatre and the life of "Papa" Ted Shawn. Had Shawn been around to edit the souvenir book and press release, he no doubt would have insisted on adding another milestone: the first Jacob's Pillow Festival without its beloved founder. It was his last first in a lifetime of many.

Death of Adonis, 1972

In January 1969, Shawn had invited his former student and dance writer John Dougherty to his winter home in Eustis, Florida, for a month to conduct extended interview sessions. Shawn was committed to retelling the story of his life, a version that he had previously been reluctant to disclose, particularly regarding all matters sexual. With the death of his estranged wife Ruth St.

Denis about six months earlier, Shawn finally felt at liberty to reminisce about the relationship between his dances and his sexuality. However, two weeks into the interview process, Shawn suffered an embolism. He was rushed to the hospital and stabilized but forced into a period of convalescence that led him even deeper into reflection about his legacy, now with an urgency intensified by newly prescribed daily doses of nitroglycerin, which prevented him from ever again feeling like himself. His need to narrate a more authentic version of his life and legacy was even more pressing.

Shawn was discharged from the hospital in February 1969 to his Florida home, where he, one of the most well-traveled men of his era, lived proudly "as a hermit," storing energy reserves which he would need for the summer months to survive the festival. He kept a consistent routine in his final years: coffee in bed, ablutions (a term he used to elevate basic acts of hygiene into religious ritual), reading mail. He would then spend several hours at his typewriter, keeping up with correspondence and working on lectures, often with his Maltese cat Beau Nash by his side. He generally spent his afternoons on his patio engaged in "active sunbathing" ("I just hate lying doing nothing to get sun on my body"), which ordinarily meant gardening in the nude, showing off his "20-acre shave" (his code term for a full-body depilation, one of the rare rituals he retained from his performing days). Then, he would take his lunch, a pureed meal served in a drinking glass. After a nap, he would spend time woodcarving in his studio, then early drinks (a snifter of Christian Brothers brandy), and early to bed.

Following his hospitalization, he kept meetings and obligations to a minimum, though he accepted an enticing invitation from an editor at *Esquire* to write a 200-word reflection for the magazine's "end-of-the-decade" issue. As pitched by the editor, the article was to feature forecasts from luminaries in various fields of arts and science, all of whom were born in the nineteenth century, to predict the trends in their respective fields of expertise by the end of the twentieth century. Shawn wrote a paean to the dance, celebrating its tremendous development in stature within the art world. He wrote, "Dance has an audience so great that one night not long ago in New York there were more people watching dancers perform than the total of all audiences in every other theater." He predicted that the new century would usher in dance masterpieces "equal to *Hamlet*, the Sistine Chapel ceiling, and the 'Ninth Symphony.'"[127] His contribution was published in the December 1969 issue of *Esquire*, alongside reflections from cultural giants such as Lillian Gish, Maurice Chevalier, Louis Armstrong, Norman Rockwell, and Buckminster

Fuller. However, to Shawn's utter dismay, the editor titled the article "Good-bye to You All!" A death knell of sorts, the article promised its younger readers "advice from distinguished, nineteenth-century citizens, while we could get it." Shawn rightfully decried the "sadistic treatment" he had received.

Even more dispiriting, that particular issue of *Esquire* also ran another ageist feature called "The New Homosexuality," a probing exposé of life among young "radical" homosexuals who sought deviation from rather than complicity within social and sexual norms. Journalist Tom Burke opens the article with yet another death knell that resonated with Shawn: "Pity: just when Middle America finally discovered the homosexual, he died," essentially declaring that politicized homosexual youth had upended the uneasy tolerance the American public had mustered for "homosexual senior citizens—anybody over twenty-nine." According to Burke and the many young men he interviewed at parties and bars in Greenwich Village, these "hopelessly outdated figures" exhibit stereotypical qualities ("Soft, weak, sensitive!") similar to the characters in Mart Crowley's successful Broadway play *The Boys in the Band* (1968), a production that had riveted Shawn. Burke went on to describe the "type" in a patronizing tone: "a curio-shop proprietor with an uncertain mouth, wet basset eyes, and a Coppertone tan and a miniature Yorkshire, who lives in a white and silver Jean Harlow apartment, drinks pink gin, cooks *boeuf Bourguignon*, mourns Judy, makes timid liaisons on Forty-second Street."[128] Shawn's heart sank reading this character assassination, sensing the acrimony directed at him, even though he did not own a curio-shop (but a dance school) nor a miniature Yorkie (Beau Nash was a Maltese cat) and lost no love on Judy (though he was married to Ruth St. Denis, whose gay fan base rivaled Judy Garland's in her day). That said, Shawn was perennially suntanned and would not refuse pink gin if brandy were not available.

Shawn confided in Walter Terry that the article made him feel "as old fashioned as a lace valentine."[129] Perhaps worse, it burdened him with guilt. Toward the end of the article, Burke blames the older generation of homosexuals for their complicity within the status quo, making it necessary for "new sexual deviants" to escalate resistance, such as the violent riots between police and gays, lesbians, and transgendered people at the Stonewall Inn that took place earlier that June. To further shame the politically neutered older generation of queers, Burke suggests the new radical homosexuals chose the early morning of Sunday, June 28, to launch its rebellion, a gesture aimed at "scorning elder traditionalists who flew the flags on their Cherry Grove cottages at half-mast and sat home in decorous seclusion, mourning."

Shawn was never one for Fire Island nor overt flag-waving, but from the relatively remote reaches of the Berkshires and central Florida, he closely watched the opening of a growing field of modern gay male representation in 1960s literature, television, and film. His main source of information about the urban gay world came from his consistent correspondence and occasional visits with friend Richard "Dick" Stuart, a former ballroom dancer and a company member of the Jacob's Pillow Dance Festival Tour. As if he were Shawn's personal roving reporter, Stuart diligently wrote letters about gay life in New York, everything from breakthroughs on Broadway and at the ballet to police raids at the Continental baths. He wrote about his harrowing experiences cruising for sex on 42nd Street as well as his joy at attending the "first" wedding between two men at the "gay church" (Church of the Beloved Disciple in Chelsea, New York). He also reported to Shawn about the activism within homophile organizations or "Gay Power" groups such as the Mattachine Society, the Westside Discussion Group, and the Gay Active Alliance, of which he was an active member. In return, Shawn warmly hosted Stuart's "caravan" of gay friends who made pilgrimages to Jacob's Pillow, which within certain circles of gay men had achieved status as a tourist destination to rival Fire Island, New Hope, and Provincetown. It was also Stuart who first broke the news to Shawn about the Stonewall riots as well as the march from Christopher Street to the Sheep Meadow in Central Park to commemorate its first anniversary.

Unwilling to have his reputation or existence annihilated by two *Esquire* writers he had never even met, Shawn sought to affirm that his life and his dances formed part of the impetus that gave the gay rights movement its momentum. He understandably wanted to avoid seeing his life and work be forgotten or, perhaps worse, dismissed as camp. The topic of "camp" figured prominently in Stuart's letters to Shawn, especially in Stuart's diatribes about the new *Batman* television series. Like superhero comics, Shawn's dances stage a clearly delineated moral universe led by mythical figures determined to save the world—the "protector from modernism" in *Credo*, the explosive "Atomo, the God of Atomic Energy," the torch-wielding "Artist Soul" crusader of "An American Ballet."

Shawn wanted to avoid the circumstances that befell the legacy of Paul Swan, the dancer-sculptor-painter once known as the "Most Beautiful Man in the World." In some respects, Swan's fame made Ted Shawn's entire career possible, if not because in 1914 a newspaper reporter confused Shawn for Swan, never imagining there might be two male expressive dancers on the scene, then because Swan was actually the first professional male interpretive dancer, though unlike Shawn, he was never invested in challenging anyone to claim that distinction. Though Shawn tried to distance himself from the unabashedly eccentric Swan, the two were inextricably linked by reputation as modern Adonises. Fittingly, the *Death of Adonis* was a signature routine in the repertory of both artists. (See Figure 6.17.)

Swan's status as a camp icon was cemented by Andy Warhol in two experimental films. A documentary of sorts, *Paul Swan* (1965) immortalizes the private performances Swan presented to audiences of dedicated fans and curious onlookers at his Carnegie Hall studio throughout the 1940s and decades later at his apartment in the Van Dyke public housing residence. Warhol's camera captures the then eighty-two-year-old Swan as he moved through the paces of the solo performances that had brought him fame fifty years earlier. The occasional chords of a piano accompany Swan as he marks his dance of Adonis, delivers his monologue from Julius Caesar, and recites original poems. There are few edits to the seventy-minute film. Warhol's static camera keeps rolling as Swan transitions between scenes, exposing him as he undresses down to his dance belt, and at a few points when he altogether disappears for uncomfortably long periods of time from the makeshift stage at Warhol's Factory where the film was shot. By transforming his camera into a tool for surveillance and arguably exploitation, Warhol exposes Swan's performance as theatricality and artifice, the hallmarks of camp.

Inspired by Susan Sontag's recently published essay "Notes on Camp" (1964), Warhol cast Swan in his film *Camp*, also from 1965. Interestingly, Sontag identifies Martha Graham as a camp icon: "In every move the aging Martha Graham makes she's becoming Martha Graham." For Warhol, "Swan had become the embodiment of camp."[130] In Warhol's care, Swan's aging body, his prosthetically enhanced bulge, his caked-on stage makeup, his physical and mental feebleness contribute to a morbid study in the death of a modern gay male sensibility, a prospect enlivened by a scene in his film *Camp*, when Swan performs his own choreographed death at the end of *To Heroes Slain*, a dance he performed in honor of soldiers killed in World War I. Warhol, and perhaps *Esquire* reporter Tom Burke also, exhibited a morbid fascination with the aging gay male body and its demise, transforming his fixation on youth as social pathology. In some respect, Warhol's film is a postmodernist reversal of the classical myth of Adonis, whose tragic death is most often associated with the promise of rebirth.

Shawn documented his own aging process, with one of Warhol's favorite mediums: the snapshot. "I have always had a birthday picture taken every year as a record of how the instrument stands up under increasing years." Indeed, Shawn would send his closest friends snapshots of himself posing in various stages of undress among the plants he lovingly tended on his patio in Eustis. Though he made many prints of each shoot, he personalized most with a brief handwritten message: "Not bad for 72!" or "How do you like my roses?" referring to a strategically placed bouquet over his groin. Some snapshots proudly record his weight. In his later years, Shawn finally dipped below 172 pounds, the absolute minimum he could ever attain, even during his most active years of diet and daily Pilates workouts. He took pride in the weight loss, though it was not as much an achievement as a symptom.

Shawn's snapshots again call to mind *Death of Adonis* (1923). (See Figures 6.17 and 6.18.) Inspired by his visits to Italian museums, he created this "sculpture solo" to display his nude body. With the exception of a g-string, he was entirely nude and covered in white paint, giving the impression that he was an alabaster sculpture. Poised on a plinth, he moved through a series of sumptuous poses to the strains of Godard's "Adagio Pathétique." In some

Figure 6.17. Ted Shawn in *Death of Adonis* (1923). Photograph by James Walter Collinge (Courtesy of Thomas Schmidt). Ted Shawn Papers, Additions. Jerome Robbins Dance Division, New York Public Library.

Figure 6.18. Ted Shawn on the patio at his home in Eustis, Florida, 1969. Ted Shawn Papers, Additions. Jerome Robbins Dance Division, New York Public Library.

measure, the dance is the pinnacle of Shawn's choreography as it embodies his fascination with Greek myth, beauty, and Delsartean posture, bringing him as close as possible to dancing nude on stage—one of his life's goals. Shawn sometimes included it on a program knowing it would cause a stir, just as it did when he premiered it at Mariarden. In an article he wrote for *Theater Magazine* to coincide with the premiere of *Adonis* on tour, Shawn tried to convince the American public that looking at his nude body was not only a suitable national pastime but also good for democracy: "Our progress depends upon ideals of beauty."[131] In his lifetime of dances, Shawn delivered exquisite displays of beauty as politics or aesthetics as social critique.

Inasmuch as Shawn chronicled the story of his body from his rehabilitation after paralysis to his status as "America's Most Handsome Man," he detailed his body's decline, though with the same intent to find beauty. He acknowledged his strange preoccupation with his medical history, going as far as to include detailed medical information in his annual newsletters, with the following disclaimer: "Nothing is so dull as reading about other people's illnesses—no matter how close the friends or relatives—a person's illnesses are interesting to the person who is ill—*my* back, *my* headache, *my* operation, *my* arthritis—*ad nauseum*, ad infinitum! So, relax, I will give the clinical report as briefly and as concisely as possible."[132]

Of course, the details of his later medical conditions were just a footnote to a far longer story Shawn recounted about his body. He endured lifelong dental problems stemming from bad dental work he received as a child. He had teeth pulled on three different continents. Eventually, he had every tooth in his upper jaw removed for dentures. "Thank Heaven the new teeth won't affect my diction on the typewriter," he joked.[133]

Then there were the injuries related to performing and manual labor: every imaginable foot injury, including broken toes and infected skin from dancing barefoot on every manner of surface, a dislocated sacroiliac that landed him in a corset brace, and several cracked ribs. He suffered a host of travel-related ailments and diseases: ptomaine poisoning, dengue fever, Asian flu. He also endured age-related illnesses: bursitis from decades of flexing his joints, an enlarged prostate for which he had surgery, and a cataract that blinded him in his right eye in 1970, a loss that made it nearly impossible for him to read. In his final years, John Christian read books to him over cocktails.

A chronic cigarette smoker, Shawn had several bronchial infections and bouts with pneumonia and was eventually diagnosed with emphysema, a disease that progressively debilitated him and eventually led to heart disease.

When he suffered his first heart attack in 1961 at the age of sixty-nine, he was in the process of being treated for hip pain caused by his trochanter. Grace Badorek had driven him to the hospital for routine blood work and on the drive home he turned gray. She stopped at Shawn's dentist's office to ask for medical advice. He instructed her to take him back to the emergency room where he was diagnosed with angina pectoris and put in an oxygen tent, which he loved, as it allowed him to breathe without distress. By that time, Shawn was prone to spasmodic coughing spells that sometimes lasted up to thirty-six hours. He asked if he could take the tent home.

In fact, once stabilized, Shawn had a tape recorder brought to him in his hospital room so that he could document all the details of his hospitalization. As if delivering one of his curtain speeches, he shared pleasantries about the hospital staff to an audience of nurses whose laughter can faintly be heard in the background. He also made a promise for a full recovery: "If there's any medicine good for a busted heart, it's love."[134] Shawn's words were optimistic, but his voice was strained by fear. He must have thought he was delivering his final words. Those closest to Shawn said that he never talked about death or the afterlife. He wanted his death to be like his life: meaningful and well chronicled, so he devoted most of his final years at his typewriter trying to manage his legacy. He also grabbed his camera, taking photographs for his friends and fans, but also for himself. Shawn began to experiment by bringing a mirror into his garden to shoot provocative photos of his body's reflection, most without his face, as if it would give away an age that his physique could easily deny. (See Insert Figure 6.19.)

In 1971, Shawn was hospitalized four times for a total of forty-two days. On New Year's Day in 1972, he had a tracheotomy to help him breathe more easily. Just over a week later, at 9 P.M. on Sunday, January 9, 1972, Shawn died alone at Florida Hospital in Orlando.

Shawn thought funerals were barbaric, so John Christian and Fern Helscher organized a private service at Jacob's Pillow that May. A minister from neighboring Springfield who did not personally know Shawn opened the ceremony with a reading of "How Beautiful upon the Mountain" (Isaiah 52:7), a verse Shawn chose as the title of his volume about the history of Jacob's Pillow. Everyone in attendance felt goosebumps, knowing how Shawn would have delighted in that coincidence. Shawn's remains were scattered at the "Pillow" boulder in the yard beside the house where he lived, wrote, and danced. His beloved Pillow is now, in essence, a headstone. (See Figure 6.20.)

Figure 6.20. Ted Shawn on the "Pillow." Photo by Eric Sanford. Courtesy of Jacob's Pillow Dance Festival Archives.

One version of the Adonis myth posits that when the god of beauty died, his lover, the goddess of love Aphrodite ran to his side and along the way scratched herself on a thicket of thorny white rose bushes. As she ran, her blood stained them red. On his patio in Eustis, Shawn raised red roses. They appear in many of the photos he snapped and shared, including a portrait of him taken on his patio, a sturdy slab of concrete he poured himself. Wearing a crisp white romper, he stands at attention, presenting one of his prized rose bushes placed on a chair. On the border of the snapshot the date is stamped "Sept. 72," eight months after he had died. It is likely the last time Ted Shawn posed for a photograph. (See Insert Figure 6.21.)

Notes

Introduction

1. Arthur Myers, "Shawn and the Pillow: A Look Forward," *The Eagle*, July 21, 1962, 7A.
2. O. B. Keeler, "Ted Shawn," *Atlanta Journal*, December 11, 1933.
3. Letter, Ted Shawn to Lucien Price, December 25, 1933, JEMC (Joseph E. Marks Collection Relating to Ted Shawn and Jacob's Pillow, 1913–1979, *2004MT-31, Harvard Theater Collection, Harvard University), box 10.
4. Letters, Shawn to Ruth St. Denis, June 22, 1936 (RSDL, fol. 183) and August 28, 1938 (RSDL, fol. 185).
5. Ruth St. Denis, *Ruth St. Denis: An Unfinished Life: An Autobiography* (New York: Harper & Brothers, 1939 [Brooklyn, NY: Dance Horizons, 1969]), 156.
6. Letter, Shawn to Fern Helscher, February 18, 1936, Fern Helscher Papers, box 1, fol. 8, Jerome Robbins Dance Division, New York Public Library. Shawn is referring to Elizabeth Selden's *The Dancer's Quest: Essays on the Aesthetic of the Contemporary Dance* (Berkeley: University of California Press, 1935), and Virginia Stewart's edited volume *Modern Dance* (New York: E. Weyhe, 1935).
7. Ted Shawn, *One Thousand and One Night Stands, Unpublished Manuscript of Ted Shawn's Autobiography* (hereafter UNPUB) II, 12, Jerome Robbins Dance Division, New York Public Library.
8. UNPUB I, 12.
9. Baird Hastings, "The Denishawn Era (1914–1931)," *Dance Index* (June 1942): 225–37.
10. John Martin, "The Dance: Valued Events," *New York Times*, July 12, 1942.
11. Letter, Shawn to Barton Mumaw, January 17, 1945, JPA, box 167.
12. UNPUB VIII, 546.
13. Letter, Shawn to Lucien Price, August 2, 1962, LPN, fol. 4 (Shawn, Ted, Letters to Lucien Price; 1943–1963).
14. Letter, Shawn to Walter Terry, December 1, 1969, TSC, fol. 544.
15. Newsletter, 1961.
16. For sound recording and transcript of these interviews, see *Reminiscences: From Childhood to the Dissolution of Denishawn*, Ted Shawn, interview by John Dougherty, January 11–30, 1969, *MGZTL 4-69, Jerome Robbins Dance Division, New York Public Library. See also the John Dougherty Papers, especially box 1, fol. 13, MS-P 3, Special Collections and Archives, UCI Libraries, Irvine, California.
17. Thomas Dixon, "Ivan Crozier (Ed.), *Sexual Inversion: A Critical Edition: Havelock Ellis and John Addington Symonds (1897)*, Basingstoke, Palgrave Macmillan, 2008," *Medical History* 54, no. 4 (2010): 558.

18. See Jeffrey Weeks, "Havelock Ellis and the Politics of Sex Reform," in *Socialism and the New Life: The Personal and Sexual Politics of Edward Carpenter and Havelock Ellis*, ed. Sheila Rowbotham and Jeffrey Weeks (London: Pluto, 1977).

19. *Reminiscences*, 211.

20. In Havelock Ellis's *The Dance of Life* (Boston: Houghton Mifflin, 1923). The title of the chapter, based on Ellis's *Atlantic Monthly* article, "The Philosophy of Dancing," was changed to "The Art of Dancing."

21. Ted Shawn, "The Dancer's Bible: An Appreciation of Havelock Ellis's *The Dance of Life*," *Denishawn Magazine* 1, no. 1 (1924): 12.

22. Letter, Shawn to Terry, November 29, 1968, TSC, fol. 542.

23. Letter, Shawn to Terry, January 30, 1938, TSC, fol. 517.

24. Walter Terry, *Ted Shawn, Father of American Dance: A Biography* (New York: Dial Press, 1976), 179.

25. Gerry Franklin and Walter Terry, *Conversation with Gerry Franklin*, 1975, *MGZTCO 3-833, Jerome Robbins Dance Division, New York Public Library.

26. Terry, *Ted Shawn, Father of American Dance: A Biography*, 4.

27. Terry, *Ted Shawn, Father of American Dance: A Biography*, 84.

28. John Dougherty, "*Ted Shawn: Father of American Dance* by Walter Terry" (Book review), *Dance News*, December 1976.

29. Letter, Barton Mumaw to Jane Sherman, August 17, 1977, JSP, box 9, fol. 2.

30. The costumes now form "The Killinger Collection: Costumes of Denishawn and Ted Shawn and His Men Dancers" at the Florida State University in Tallahassee, Florida. For more, see Tricia Henry Young's catalog.

31. De Mille in "Early Drafts and Papers Relating to Martha: The Life and Work of Martha Graham," (S) *MGZMD 80, box 2, 69, Jerome Robbins Dance Division, New York Public Library.

32. Martha Graham, *Blood Memory* (New York: Doubleday, 1991), 70. For an inquiry into the book's authorship, see Victoria Phillips, "Martha Graham's Gilded Cage: *Blood Memory: An Autobiography* (1991)," *Dance Research Journal* 45, no. 2 (October 24, 2013): 63–84.

33. Graham, *Blood Memory*, 70.

34. Agnes de Mille, *Martha: The Life and Work of Martha Graham* (New York: Random House, 1991), 61.

35. *Music and Ballet: Interview with Ted Shawn and Jess Meeker on O, Libertad!* (1938), conducted by Irving Deakin, sound recording, March 10, 1938, *MGZTL 4-1, no. 57, Jerome Robbins Dance Division, New York Public Library.

36. Iris M. Fanger, "Ruth St. Denis and Ted Shawn—The Breakup," *Dance Magazine*, February 1976.

37. See especially Ramsay Burt, *The Male Dancer: Bodies, Spectacle, Sexualities* (London: Routledge, 1995); Julia L. Foulkes, "Dancing Is for American Men: Ted Shawn and the Intersection of Gender Sexuality, and Nationalism in the 1930s," in *Dancing Desires: Choreographing Sexualities On and Off the Stage*, ed. Jane C. Desmond (Madison: University of Wisconsin Press, 2001), and *Modern Bodies: Dance and American Modernism from Martha Graham to Alvin Ailey* (Chapel Hill: University

of North Carolina Press, 2002); Susan Leigh Foster, "Closets Full of Dances: Modern Dance's Performance of Masculinity and Sexuality," in *Dancing Desires*; and Susan Manning, "Coding the Message," *Dance Theatre Journal* 14, no. 1 (Winter 1998): 34–37, and "Looking from a Different Place: Gay Spectatorship of American Modern Dance," also in *Dancing Desires*.

38. John "Chris" Christian Ammann (1921–1982) assumed the leadership of the Pillow in Shawn's later years and for less than a year after Shawn's death owing to his own health problems.

39. UNPUB VIII, 118.

40. Stephen Gottschalk, *The Emergence of Christian Science in American Religious Life* (Berkeley: University of California Press, 1973), 234.

Chapter 1

1. *Reminiscences: From Childhood to the Dissolution of Denishawn*. Ted Shawn, interview by John Dougherty, January 11–30, 1969, sound recording and transcript, *MGZTL 4-69, Jerome Robbins Dance Division, New York Public Library (hereafter *Reminiscences*), 113 and 115.

2. *Reminiscences*, 120.

3. *Reminiscences*, 131.

4. *Reminiscences*, 117.

5. Ted Shawn, *One Thousand and One Night Stands* (New York: Da Capo, [1960] 1979), 39.

6. UNPUB I, 2.

7. *Reminiscences*, 208.

8. *One Thousand and One Night Stands*, 40.

9. *Reminiscences*, 125.

10. *Reminiscences*, 131.

11. *Reminiscences*, 125.

12. *Reminiscences*, 132.

13. *Reminiscences*, 132.

14. *Reminiscences*, 216.

15. *Reminiscences*, 35.

16. In 1913, Christian Ficthorne Reisner published a book about his area of expertise: *Church Publicity: The Modern Way to Compel Them to Come In* (New York: The Methodist Book Concern, 1913). Shawn proofread the first draft of the book, which describes many of the more direct techniques Reisner deployed in developing his ministry in Denver, such as using billboards and electric signs in front of the church and distributing handbills.

17. UNPUB I, 4.

18. *Reminiscences*, 138.

19. *Reminiscences*, 26.

20. Ted Shawn's Report Card, University of Denver, Penrose Library, University of Denver.

21. UNPUB IV, 276.

22. *Reminiscences*, 53.

23. *Reminiscences*, 54–60.

24. Lynn Garafola, *Diaghilev's Ballets Russes* (New York: Oxford University Press, 1989), 36.

25. "Pavlova and Mordkin, Famous Russian Dancers Appear at Denver Auditorium Friday," *Gazette-Telegraph*, November 6, 1910, 21.

26. For more on Kolsoff's appearances on the vaudeville stage, see Suzanne Carbonneau Levy, "The Russians Are Coming: Russian Dancers in the United States, 1910–1933," PhD dissertation, New York University, 1990.

27. Ted Shawn, *Ruth St. Denis: Pioneer and Prophet, Being a History of Her Cycle of Oriental Dances*, vol. 1 (San Francisco: John Henry Nash, 1920), 34.

28. *Reminiscences*, 137.

29. "Two Farces Given by the Women of St. Mark's Church—'Sunbonnets' and 'A Box of Monkeys,'" *Denver Post*, May 17, 1911. Also Betty Poindexter, "Ted Shawn: His Personal Life, His Professional Career, and His Contributions to the Development of Dance in the United States of America from 1891 to 1963," Thesis, Texas Women's University, 1963, 113 and ff. The review was based on a performance on May 16, 1911.

30. UNPUB I, 9. "The Black Crook," the "progenitor of the musical comedy," opened on September 12, 1866, at Niblo's Garden in New York City ("Black Crook," in *International Encyclopedia of Dance*, ed. Selma Jeanne Cohen and Dance Perspectives Foundation [New York: Oxford University Press, 1998]). Bonfanti appeared in the ballet interludes in the four-act spectacle. Agnes de Mille later performed the Bonfanti role ("Musical Theater," in *International Encyclopedia of Dance*).

31. "Reminiscences, 1977," Hazel Wallack Papers, box 1, fol. 3, Jerome Robbins Dance Division, New York Public Library.

32. The production was held at Elitch's on June 18, 1911. The play *The Man Who Lied to Himself* was written by and starred Mann Page in the title role. Mann Page was married to the playwright Izola Forrester, the daughter of vaudeville performer Ogarita Booth Henderson, who alleged to be the daughter of the actor John Wilkes Booth, Abraham Lincoln's assassin. Forrester and her mother received great notoriety for their allegation and years later Forrester wrote a book to substantiate the claim, *This One Mad Act: The Unknown Story of John Wilkes Booth and His Family by His Granddaughter* (1937). It is curious that Shawn never mentioned Forrester's alleged relation to Booth, since Shawn, too, had claimed to be a distant relative of Booth's on several occasions.

33. *The Female of the Species* (typescript of motion picture scenario), TSC, fol. 625.

34. Letter, Allene Seaman to Shawn, February 27, 1912, TSC, fol. 2.

35. "Hazel Wallack and Ted Shawn to Interpret 'La Danse d'Amour,'" DS, vol. 2.

36. *Reminiscences*, 48.

37. *Reminiscences*, 26.

38. "Reminiscences, 1977," Hazel Wallack Papers, box 1, fol. 3, Jerome Robbins Dance Division, New York Public Library.

39. Letter, Shawn to Gray Poole, April 2, 1960, TSC, fol. 584.

40. UNPUB I, 10.

41. The original English and German publications of *Sexual Inversion* were attributed to Havelock Ellis and John Addington Symonds (1840–1893), a historian of homosexuality who contributed case studies to Ellis's research but died before the volume was completed. Publishers removed Symonds's name from subsequent editions at the request of Symonds's family. Ellis distinguishes between "inversion" as an innate desire and "homosexuality" as behavior. He defines inversion as "a sexual instinct turned by inborn constitutional abnormality toward persons of the same sex." Havelock Ellis, *Studies in the Psychology of Sex*, vol. 2, 3rd. ed. (Philadelphia: F.A. Davis Company, 1921), 1.

42. Ellis, *Studies*, vol. 2, 44. In the third edition of the book, Ellis included a lengthy discussion of Oscar Wilde, who was serving a prison sentence for "gross indecency" at the time Ellis wrote the book. No doubt Ellis's tolerance and sympathy were a response to the hypocrisy and cruelty with which Wilde was publicly treated under the Criminal Law Amendment Act of 1885.

43. "Elmer E. Shawn Dies in Denver," *Kansas City Star*, March 25, 1912, 4.

44. The Angelus Hotel, once the tallest building in Los Angeles, opened on December 28, 1901, at Spring and Fourth Streets. It was owned by C. C. Loomis, whose daughter Margaret later studied at the Los Angeles Denishawn school before becoming a film star. The Angelus was not only a high-end luxury hotel noted for its design amenities but also the site of a local Elks chapter. For more on the Angelus Hotel, see "Entertaining Elks," *The American Globe*, July, 1909, 11. Built in 1906, the Alexandria Hotel is located at 501 S. Spring Street in Los Angeles. Once a playground for Hollywood celebrities, the building has since been renovated and is now a building for low-income residents.

45. UNPUB II, 12.

46. *When the World Was Young* (motion picture scenario), TSC, fol. 625. Nijinsky's *L'Après-midi d'un faune* was planned by autumn of 1910, but did not premiere until May 29, 1912. See Garafola, *Diaghilev's Ballets Russes*, 56 and 404.

47. *Reminiscences*, 76.

48. Shawn, Letter to the Editor, *Variety*, February 7, 1916.

49. Julie Stone Peters, "Drama, Primitive Ritual, Ethnographic Spectacle: Genealogies of World Performance (ca. 1890–1910)," *Modern Language Quarterly* 70, no. 1 (March 2009).

50. After writing their respective books, Frazer and Grove married on April 22, 1896. In 1911, about or before the time Shawn conceived of *Dances of the Ages*, London publishers John Bale, Sons & Danielsson, Ltd., published *The Dance: Historic Illustrations of Dancing from 3300 B.C. to 1911 A.D.* The lavishly illustrated book charts the iconography of dance from ancient Egypt and Greece to medieval Europe. The book was clearly inspired by Grove's (and in fact references Grove in its final pages) and quite possibly served as an inspiration for Shawn to stage the history of dance in *Dances of the Ages*.

51. James George Frazer's theories of magic profoundly shaped twentieth-century perceptions of "primitive dance." In his influential comparative study of ancient

rites and myths *The Golden Bough* (London: Macmillan, 1890), he puts forth his theory about the role of "imitative magic" in primitive worlds, including its role in dance. Frazer contends that primitive dances can be classified in two types of magic. The first form he calls "sympathetic magic" to describe when "the magician infers that he can produce any effect he desires merely by imitating it" ("like produces like" or "effect resembles its cause"). The second he calls "contagious magic," which is when "the magician infers whatever he does to a material object will affect equally the person with whom the object was once in contact, whether it formed part of his body or not."

Lee J. Vance, a forgotten figure in the history of folklore, expressed a similar sentiment on scientific grounds. He argues, "Dancing, as an art, has been of gradual growth, and subject to the law of evolution." Vance concludes that modern dances are "survivals of a primitive impulse" calibrated by man's mental evolution ("The Evolution of Dancing," *Popular Science Monthly, 1872–1895* [October 1, 1892]: 61.)

52. Years later, Shawn encountered Frazer and Grove's ideas in the writings Havelock Ellis, who cites both writers in developing his theory that dancing is a form of "unconscious eugenics." See *Ellis, The Dance of Life*, 43.

53. T. A. Faulkner, *From the Ball-Room to Hell* (Chicago: Henry Publishing, 1892).

54. Beryl and Associates, eds. *Immorality of Modern Dances* (New York: Henry Publishing, 1904).

55. H.W. Lytle and John Dillon, *From Dance Hall to White Slavery* (Chicago: Charles C. Thompson, 1912).

56. Bliss Carman, *The Making of Personality* (Boston: L.C. Page, 1908), 213.

57. Before that, for seven years they rented a cottage at Twilight Park, a colony near Haines Falls in the Catskills, from which they ran a winter school called "Moonshine."

58. Letter, Bliss Carman to Ted Shawn, November 13, 1912, JPA, box 194, fol. 13.

59. *Reminiscences*, 218.

60. UNPUB I, 16.

61. The itinerary included Barstow, California; Needles, California; Williams, Arizona; Gallup, New Mexico; Albuquerque, New Mexico; Amarillo, Texas; Wellington, Kansas; Newton, Kansas; Chillicothe, Ohio; and unspecified stops in Illinois. Decades after the tour, Betty Poindexter tried to recreate the exact itinerary. She contacted the railroad's administrative offices but could not locate any additional information. See Poindexter, "Ted Shawn: His Personal Life, His Professional Career, and His Contributions to the Development of Dance in the United States of America from 1891 to 1963."

62. Receipt from Mary Perry King (January 24 until February 10, 1914), JPA, box 192, fol. 65.

63. UNPUB I, 18.

64. Ruth St. Denis, *Ruth St. Denis: An Unfinished Life: An Autobiography* (New York: Harper & Brothers, 1939 [Brooklyn, NY: Dance Horizons, 1969]), 158.

65. Carman, *The Making of Personality*, 218–19.

Chapter 2

1. Ted Shawn, *One Thousand and One Night Stands* (*hereafter* OTONS), 21.
2. Suzanne Shelton, "Ruth St. Denis," in *International Encyclopedia of Dance: A Project of Dance Perspectives Foundation, Inc.*, ed. Selma Jeanne Cohen and Dance Perspectives Foundation (New York: Oxford University Press, 1998).
3. Suzanne Shelton, *Ruth St. Denis: A Biography of the Divine Dancer* (Austin: University of Texas Press, 1990 [1981]), 107.
4. St. Denis, *Ruth St. Denis: An Unfinished Life*, 157.
5. UNPUB I, 31.
6. *Reminiscences*, 160.
7. "Ruth St. Denis and Her Company Pleased Audience (However, No One Raved over Her Classical Dances," *Logansport Pharos–Reporter*, September 26, 1914, 2.
8. Schlundt says *Garden of Kama* was the first joint work and premiered in San Francisco on February 22, 1915 (*The Professional Appearances of Ruth St. Denis & Ted Shawn: A Chronology and an Index of Dances, 1906–1932*, 21), though *Ourieda* premiered the summer prior in Ravinia (according to Schlundt) and even earlier according to Shawn ("Interview with Ted Shawn, 1965," Jerome Robbins Dance Division, New York Public Library).
9. Untitled clipping, *Kansas City Times*, November 7, 1914, DS, vol. 3.
10. Letter, St. Denis to Shawn, 1915, RSDL, fol. 2.
11. Letter, St. Denis to Shawn, 1915, RSDL, fol. 2.
12. OTONS, 37.
13. St. Denis, *Ruth St. Denis: An Unfinished Life*, 167.
14. Letter, St. Denis to Shawn, February 6–9, 1922, RSDL, fol. 23.
15. St. Denis, *Ruth St. Denis: An Unfinished Life*, 156.
16. *Daily Colonist*, January 29, 1915 (hand copied by Shawn) and untitled clipping, DS, vol. 3.
17. "Dancing as a Manly Sport," clipping, August 31, 1914, DS, vol. 3.
18. "You Can Never Tell," clipping, March 20, 1916, DS, vol. 3.
19. *Toledo Times*, December 11, 1916, quoted in Nesta Macdonald, *Diaghilev Observed by Critics in England and the United States, 1911–1929* (New York: Dance Horizons, 1975), 200.
20. "No Contest Here," clipping, November 11, 1914, DS, vol. 3.
21. Untitled clipping, *Kansas City Times*, November 7, 1914, DS, vol. 3.
22. "When Is Art Art?" *Chicago Herald*, October 3, 1914, DS, vol. 3.
23. Untitled clipping, *Evansville Press*, November 4–14, 1914, DS, vol. 3.
24. *Reminiscences*, 168.
25. Untitled clipping, *St. Louis Post-Dispatch*, October 30, 1914, DS, vol. 3.
26. Aaron Gillette, *Eugenics and the Nature-Nurture Debate in the Twentieth Century* (New York: Palgrave Macmillan, 2007), 2.
27. Marouf Arif Hasian Jr., *The Rhetoric of Eugenics in Anglo-American Thought* (Athens: University of Georgia Press, 1996), 1.

28. Ted Shawn, *Fundamentals of Dance Education* (Girard, KS: Haldeman-Julius, 1937), 11–12.

29. Galton in Hasian, *The Rhetoric of Eugenics in Anglo-American Thought*, 1.

30. Christine Rosen, *Preaching Eugenics: Religious Leaders and the American Eugenics Movement* (New York: Oxford University Press, 2004), 85.

31. For an overview of prominent eugenicists and research centers in the United States, see Richard Lynn, *Eugenics: A Reassessment* (Westport, CT: Greenwood, 2001), 24–27.

32. The article is largely a critique of the argument that war negatively affects race betterment because the "best men" go to war and are killed.

33. Hasian, *The Rhetoric of Eugenics in Anglo-American Thought*, 43.

34. For a discussion of the Eugenics Record Office and the relation between eugenics and twentieth-century US drama, see Tamsen Wolff, *Mendel's Theatre: Heredity, Eugenics, and Early Twentieth-Century American Drama* (New York: Palgrave Macmillan, 2009).

35. Rosen, *Preaching Eugenics*, 53–84.

36. "Eugenics in Love Stage Match," *San Francisco Examiner*, December 5, 1914, DS, vol. 3.

37. Letter, St. Denis to Shawn (undated, 1915), RSDL, fol. 1.

38. "Denishawn Dance Film" (*MGZIDVD 5-3572), Jerome Robbins Dance Division, New York Public Library. (Accessible online through the New York Public Library Digital Collections.)

39. "The Education of the Dancer," *Vogue*, April 1, 1917, 62–64, 134, 136.

40. Ted Shawn, "A Defence of the Male Dancer," *New York Dramatic Mirror*, May 13, 1916, 19.

41. "Town Talk," clipping, September 27, 1917, DS, vol. 4.

42. *Reminiscences*, 247.

43. Henry Christeen Warnack, untitled clipping, *Times*, September 1916, DS, vol. 4.

44. While Denishawn performed at the Shrine Auditorium, the home of Shawn and St. Denis was robbed of cash and jewelry valued at $1,000, about a year's salary. While the robbery received serious coverage on the front page of the *Los Angeles Morning Tribune* (September 16, 1916, DS, vol. 4), other reporters made light of the matter by conjuring the image of the unknowing dancers blissfully performing while a team of looters ransacked their home, as if the true crime were that dancers like St. Denis and Shawn could even afford a house and a few modest prized possessions.

45. *Los Angeles Express*, August 21, 1917, DS, vol. 4.

46. Michael S. Kimmel, *Manhood in America: A Cultural History* (New York: Free Press, 1996), 130–31.

47. "Letter to the Editor: Defend Ted Shawn," *Enterprise*, DS, vol. 8.

48. "Shawn Makes Hit with Church Dance," *Enterprise*, September 16, 1921, DS, vol. 8.

49. UNPUB I, 79.

50. "Music Visualization," *Denishawn Magazine* 1, no. 3 (Spring 1925): 3.

51. Letter, Shawn to St. Denis, [February 1918], RSDL, fol. 95.

52. Letter, Shawn to St. Denis, March 7, 1918, RSDL, fol. 102.

53. Schoepflin, *Christian Science on Trial*, 36.

54. Letter, Shawn to St. Denis, February 26, 1918, RSDL, fol. 99.

55. Letter, Shawn to St. Denis, March 11, 1918, RSDL, fol. 103.

56. Letter, Shawn to St. Denis, February 17, 1918, RSDL, fol. 97.

57. "Denishawn Dancers," DS, vol. 2.

58. The Denishawn name has been attached to a variety of early silent films, though in many cases the connections are impossible to verify if not because many of the films are no longer in existence then because those that have been preserved credit neither dancers nor choreographers. The impressive list of film stars who studied at Denishawn includes Lillian and Dorothy Gish, Seena Owen, Mary Alden, Rosczika Dolly, Ina Claire, Julanne Johnston, Mabel Normand, Enid Markey, Louise Glaum, and Bessie Eyton. Films that featured Denishawn students include *Lily and the Rose* (1915), which is preserved by the Motion Picture, Broadcasting, and Recorded Sound Division, Library of Congress. The film stars Lillian Gish as a recently married woman who loses her husband to a cabaret dancer named Rose (played by Roszika Dolly), whose performs a dance with a striking similarity to St. Denis's *Incense* (1906). *Sex* (1920) stars Louise Glaum as Adrienne Renault, the queen of the Follies, who performs an exotic "spider dance" at the film's fictional Frivolity Theater alongside Denishawn dancers. ("Vamp Deluxe Is Glaum in Sex," *LA Examiner*, April 12, 1920, DS, vol. 7). Denishawn dancers appear in a ballroom scene in the Metro feature *Legion of Death* (1918), a film about the Russian Revolution that was released while Shawn was at Camp Kearny. Another wartime film that was actually shot at Camp Kearny, according to cameraman Maurice "Maury" Kains, who at the time was an enlisted soldier and a drum major in the camp's band, is *Pettigrew's Girl* (1919), a silent film about the unexpected love that blossoms between a lonely soldier about to be shipped overseas and a chorus girl betrothed to a millionaire. One of the scenes features the film's dancing heroine Daisy Heath (portrayed by Ethel Clayton) performing a routine alongside a chorus of dairy maidens, Martha Graham among them. (See Richard Koszarski, "Down Memory Lane with Lillian and Dorothy Gish, Billy Bitzer, George William Hill, and D.W. Griffith," *Film History* 24, no. 3 [2012]: 350–53). Shawn and Graham would later embark on a related theater-film project with Samuel "Roxy" Rothafel (1882–1936), the broadcasting and theater entrepreneur who transformed the entertainment industry through his innovative integrations of live performance and motion picture exhibition. The name "Roxy" is most closely associated with the countless movie theaters he established, especially the Roxy Theater near Times Square. In 1932, he became managing director of the new Radio City Music Hall at Rockefeller Center in New York, home to "The Rockettes," the world-famous precision dance company, which had been previously though briefly known as the "The Roxyettes" owing to Roxy's "discovery" of them. In January 1920, twelve years prior to the opening of the Radio City Music Hall and the revolution it sparked in crossing theatrical, broadcast, and motion picture industries, Roxy was working on producing "presentations" or live components that were thematically linked to films. For the premiere of the Goldwyn Film feature *Cup of Fury* (1920) on January 8, 1920, Shawn created the *Flame Dance* to be performed at the Roxy Theater. The live component of the film exhibition "featured an atmospheric prelude, six additional presentations

of live and recorded entertainment, and an interpretative dance [the *Flame Dance*] by a then little-known member of the Denishawn dance company, Martha Graham." (Ross Melnick, *American Showman: Samuel "Roxy" Rothafel and the Birth of the Entertainment Industry, 1908–1935*, New York: Columbia University Press, 2012, 183). Later that year (according to *Film Daily Magazine*), Graham appeared in the *South Sea Savage Dance* performed as part of a bill at the Rialto.

59. Less than three months before he died, Shawn wrote to Terry imploring him to "squash" the rumor and fix the historical record on that front: "Hundreds of times both Ruth and I have vehemently denied ANY connection with *Intolerance* at all!" (Shawn to Terry, November 6, 1971, TSC, fol. 542.) The rumor likely started with the fact that Griffith sent actresses to Denishawn that first summer of the school who were subsequently cast in *Intolerance*. Also, Griffith purportedly had a relationship with one of the Denishawn students ("Denishawn Dancers," clipping, DS, vol. 2).

60. Letter, St. Denis to Shawn, June 1918, RSDL, fol. 23.

61. "Ted Shawn Wants Army of Dancers," *Daily News*, June 2, 1918, DS, vol. 6.

62. Untitled clipping, *Detroit News*, December 14, 1918, DS, vol. 6.

63. UNPUB I, 96

64. "Afternoon of a Shawn" *The Sun*, October 10, 1922, DS, vol. 7.

65. Some of the notable theatrical adventures he pursued during this period include directing six former Denishawn dancers in *Victims*, a satirical play that opened at the Mason Opera House in Los Angeles on September 15, 1919 (*New York Clipper*, September 17, 1919). On May 28, 1921, he appeared as "The Spirit of Dance" in *A Woodland Fantasy*, a play written by Paul Wisener for the dedication ceremony for the Uplifters Ranch, a Prohibition-era social club in the Pacific Palisades (Uplifters Ranch Program, DS, vol. 8). On June 4, 1921, he participated in a one-day benefit event for the Actors' Fund at the Los Angeles Speedway called *The Eternal Feminine, a Vision of the Adornment of Woman*, and the *Awakening of Romance* that featured tableaux and live performances of upcoming motion picture releases. The event featured motion picture star Mary Pickford as well as Gloria Swanson, Douglas Fairbanks, and Will Rogers. Shawn contributed his drama *Egypt* with Margaret Loomis and Betty May ("Plays and Players" by Cal York, *Photoplay* 20, no. 4 [September 1921], DS, vol. 8.) In the summer of 1920, he assumed the lead role of Bacchus in *Les Mystères Dionysiaques*, a ballet he created for vaudeville, set to the *Bacchus* opera by Jules Massenet.

66. *Reminiscences*, 190.

67. *San Francisco Examiner*, July 20 and 21, 1919, DS, vol. 7.

68. "Shimmy a Part of Dramatic Art in Biblical Play," clipping, DS, vol. 7.

69. UNPUB I, 98.

70. "Huge Crowd at Performance at 'Sister of Moses,'" *Oakland Inquirer*, August 2, 1919, DS, vol. 7.

71. Helen Bishop, "Miss Margaret Severn Tells How She Originated Mask Dance," *Boston Herald*, 1921, DS, vol. 8. In addition to training with St. Denis, Severn studied ballet with Luigi Albertieri in New York and had several lessons from Michel Fokine.

72. In a similar vein, "Little Lillian" Guenther entertained cooking classes with performances of the "Nubian Slave" and "Vogue" dances.

73. "List to the Problem of Ruth and Ted," *Cincinnati Commercial Tribune*, August 12, 1923, DS, vol. 12.

74. "Letter to the Editor," *Variety*, DS, vol. 4.

75. "Letter to the Editor," *Variety*, February 26, 1917, DS, vol. 4.

76. "Prosecution by Better Business Bureau of Ad Club Attracted Unusual Crowd to Court Room" and "Jury Decides Ivan de Marcel Deserves Mercy," clippings, DS, vol. 5.

77. "Home Brew Dance by the Denishawns," *Genius* (Uniontown, PA), November 28, 1923, DS, vol. 12.

78. "Aztec Theme," *Los Angeles Express*, October 5, 1920, DS, vol. 7.

79. For a persuasive account of Cornejo's role in *Xochitl*, see Mitch K. Snow's "Emperadores Aztecas y Princesas Toltecas: Ted Shawn, Martha Graham y Los Albores de la Danza Moderns, *Interdanza* (April 2015). Coordinacíon Nacional de Danza (México). Shawn chronicles his visit to the library in a letter to St. Denis, November 7, 1921, RSDL 32, fol. 132. In his 1965 interview with Don McDonagh, Shawn finally credited Cornejo for the scenario.

80. Letter, Shawn to St. Denis, September 20, 1920, RSD, box 32, fol. 124.

81. Untitled clipping, October 2, 1920, DS, vol. 7.

82. Bruno David Ussher, "Homer Grunn Writes Fine Music for Shawn Dance in LA," *Pacific Coast Musical Review*, October 10, 1920, DS, vol. 7.

83. "'More in Love than Ever,' Says Dancer after Six Years of Marriage," *Boston Post*, September 12, 1920, and "Ruth St. Denis Denies Schism," *Los Angeles Times*, April 3, 1920, DS, vol. 7.

84. Letter, Shawn to St. Denis, Tuesday noon, RSDL, fol. 107.

85. Letter, Shawn to St. Denis [January 31, 1920], RSD, fol. 107. This letter is incorrectly dated. It was written on December 31, 1920.

86. Letter, Shawn to St. Denis, [January 31, 1920], RSD, fol. 107. This letter is incorrectly dated. It was written on December 31, 1920.

87. Letter, Shawn to St. Denis, August 1920, RSD, fol. 114.

88. Letter, Shawn to St. Denis, August 28, 1920, RSD, fol. 112.

89. Charles Caldwell Dobie sponsored Shawn's official membership to the Bohemian Grove (UNPUB I, 112).

90. "Ted Shawn; Denishawn Dancers; Ruth St. Denis" (Moving Image) (Identifier 0.266), Jacob's Pillow Dance Festival Archives.

91. The play opened on April 25, 1921, at the Players Theater on Bush Street in San Francisco.

92. Don Ryan, "Should Men Be Graceful" *Physical Culture*, June 1921.

93. "Ways of the World," clipping, DS, vol. 8.

94. Letter, St. Denis to Shawn, October 26, 1921, TSC, fol. 8.

95. Letter, Shawn to St. Denis, November 15, 1921, RSDL, fol. 134.

96. UNPUB I, 133.

97. *Reminiscences*, 221.

98. *Musical America* 34, no. 2 (May 7, 1921).

99. Commentary, *MGZTL 4–45, Jerome Robbins Dance Division, New York Public Library. See Carrie Preston, *Learning to Kneel: Noh, Modernism, and Journeys in Teaching* (New York: Columbia University Press, 2016), 282, fn. 63.

100. Untitled clipping, *World-Herald* (Omaha, NE), October 25, 1921.

101. Gilbert Brown, "Church Service in Dance Startles Shawn Audience," *Los Angeles Record*, September 9, 1921, Louis Horst Scrapbooks, Jerome Robbins Dance Division, New York Public Library.

102. "Ted Shawn Delights with Artistic Dances," *World-Herald* (Omaha, NE) October 25, 1921, Louis Horst Scrapbooks, Jerome Robbins Dance Division, New York Public Library.

103. "Dance Service Is Condemned" and "Shawn Replies to Critics of Dance," *Shreveport Journal*, DS, vol. 8.

104. Letter, Shawn to St. Denis, November 5, 1921, RSDL, fol. 132.

105. Letter, Shawn to St. Denis, December 2, 1921, RSDL, fol. 138.

106. *Musical Courier*, December 8, 1921.

107. Letter, Shawn to St. Denis, December 3, 1921, RSDL, fol. 138.

108. Letter, St. Denis to Shawn, December 30, 1921, TSC, fol. 15.

109. Letter, Shawn to St. Denis, December 28, 1921, RSDL, fol. 140.

110. Letter, Shawn to St. Denis, January 1, 1922, RSDL, fol. 142.

111. Letter, Shawn to St. Denis, January 8, 1922, RSDL, fol. 144.

112. Letter, Shawn to St. Denis, January 9, 1922, RSDL, fol. 144.

113. Letter, St. Denis to Shawn, December 30, 1921, TSC, fol. 15.

114. Letter, St. Denis to Shawn, March 1, 1922b, RSDL, fol. 62.

115. St. Denis, *Ruth St. Denis: An Unfinished Life*, 223.

116. "Ted Shawn Opens Dancing School Here," *Evening Telegram* (New York), March 6, 1922, DS, vol. 9.

117. Letter, Shawn to St. Denis, November 7, 1921, RSDL, fol. 132.

118. *Reminiscences*, 276.

119. "Reel Chatter by the Chatter Box James W. Dean," clipping, May 15, 1922, DS, vol. 9.

120. "Screen: Pictures of 1922," *New York Times*, July 2, 1922. Following the experiment, they were approached to work on a related film venture. Thomas Wilfred, the inventor of the Clavilux, went to Mariarden where St. Denis and Shawn were teaching to explore possibilities for finding "a new field in the terpsichorean art" by "synchronizing the movements of the dance with figures from a color organ," thus bridging color and movement ("Denishawns Experiment with Color Organ as Dance Accompaniment," *Musical America*, September 1, 1923, 29).

121. Wieczorek had previously created two portraits of Shawn—one in his army uniform and another in costume as "Young Moses" from the previous year's pageant ("Picture of Shawn Exhibited in New York," DS, vol. 9).

122. "Loving Cup for Pavlowa," *New York Times*, April 26, 1922, DS, vol. 9. "Pavlova Honored," *Evening Globe* (New York), April 26, 1922, DS, vol. 9. See also Keith Money, *Anna Pavlova, Her Life and Art* (New York: Random House, 1982), 305.

Other committee members included fellow sculptor Malvina Hoffman, ballet dancer Adolf Bolm, Anglo-Indian dancer Roshanara, and visual artist Troy Kinney.

123. For a detailed explanation as to how Ellis's medical explanations were adopted by campaigners for homosexual rights, see Weeks, "Havelock Ellis and the Politics of Sex Reform."

124. See Angélique Richardson, *Love and Eugenics in the Late Nineteenth Century: Rational Reproduction and the New Woman* (Oxford: Oxford University Press, 2003), 216.

125. Ellis, quoted in Richardson, *Love and Eugenics in the Late Nineteenth Century: Rational Reproduction and the New Woman*, 93.

126. Ellis, *The Task of Social Hygiene*, viii–ix.

127. Ellis, *The Dance of Life*, 36.

128. Ellis, *The Dance of Life*, 45. Also quoted in Ted Shawn, *The American Ballet* (New York: Henry Holt, 1926), 114. For more on Ellis's ideas about sexuality and dance in relation to Shawn, see Foster, "Closets Full of Dances."

129. Judith B. Alter, "Ellis's Essay 'The Art of Dancing': A Reconsideration," *Dance Research Journal* 24, no. 1 (Spring 1992): 27.

130. Shawn, "The Dancer's Bible," 12, and *Reminiscences*, 281.

131. *Reminiscences*, 192.

132. The paper was included in a letter from Ellis to Shawn, November 17, 1921, TSC, box 39, fol. 4.

133. *Reminiscences*, 281.

134. *Reminiscences*, 283.

135. In 1967, Shawn wrote a letter to one of his former students and dancers, John Dougherty, wherein he ruminates about St. Denis's lesbian relationship with one of their young Denishawn dancers, Pearl Wheeler:

> She had a doglike devotion to Miss Ruth personally. Between you and me, privately, it was apparent to me that it was inherently Lesbian, although so far as I know there was no overt expression of this. However, Miss Ruth used Pearl, and trading on this attraction, tossed bits and scraps of physical caresses at times when Pearl needed coaxing or was about to blow up. Pearl often came to me when Miss Ruth was especially "ruthless" and cried on my shoulder, but when there was any real question of choice, she belonged to Ruth body and soul—as maid, companion, general errand girl, as well as costumer, wardrobe mistress, costume designer, dancer—anything Miss R needed, Pearl tried to be that. (Letter, Ted Shawn to John Dougherty, December 20, 1967, John Dougherty Collection, UCLA)

136. Attributed to Ellis in *Reminiscences*, 281.

137. *Reminiscences*, 288.

138. *Reminiscences*, 289.

139. Letter, Havelock Ellis to Shawn, June 9, 1922, TSC, box 39, fol. 4.

140. Attributed to Ellis in Dougherty, *Reminiscences*, 289.

Chapter 3

1. "Police Ponder Censorship for Dancing Team to Appear Here: Spurred by Isadora Duncan's Exhibition, Women of City Demand Official Supervision of Steps," *Courier-Journal* (Louisville, KY), December 2, 1922, DS, vol. 10.

2. "Dancer Deplores Comparison of Her Art with Isadora Duncan's: Ruth St. Denis Declares Her Work Is a Real Contribution to Cause of Education," *Courier-Journal* (Louisville, KY), December 6, 1922, DS, vol. 10.

3. Untitled clipping, *Courier-Journal*, December 7, 1922, DS, vol. 10.

4. "Pavlova Gives Her View on US Women," *Los Angeles Herald*, January 26, 1922, DS, vol. 9.

5. "Dress Degrees," *Bulletin* (San Francisco, CA), April 10, 1923, DS, vol. 11.

6. *Courier-Journal*, December 6, 1922, and *Star Journal*, October 5, 1922, DS, vol. 10.

7. "A Denishawn Dance Suggesting King Tut," *Journal of Lewiston*, Maine, October 18, 1923, DS, vol. 12. "King Tut Will Meet Cleopatra at Ritz in Egyptian Ball," *New York American*, April 15, 1923, DS, vol. 11.

8. *Musical Courier*, November 1, 1922, DS, vol. 10.

9. Young Boswell Interview, *New York Tribune*, April 23, 1923, DS, vol. 11.

10. Ted Shawn, "Dancing Cures Nerves," *Physical Culture*, November 1922, DS, vol. 10.

11. Untitled clipping, *Journal* (Pottsville, PA), DS, vol. 10.

12. Shawn previously used the term "music visualization" to categorize dances in his 1921 solo tour.

13. Ruth St. Denis, "Music Visualization," *Denishawn Magazine* 1, no. 3 (Spring 1925).

14. Interview with Louis Horst conducted by Jeanette Schlottmann Roosevelt, 1959, transcript, 46, *MGZMT 3-2261, Jerome Robbins Dance Division, New York Public Library.

15. "The Denishawns Dance," *Post Express* (Rochester, NY), November 1922, DS, vol. 10.

16. "Ancient Races Live Again in Modern Dances: Ruth St. Denis and Ted Shawn Re-Create Peoples of the Past in Oriental Dances," *Sun* (Baltimore, MD), October 22, 1922, DS, vol. 10.

17. "What We Think of Things Theatrical," *Post Express* (Rochester, NY), November 2, 1922, DS, vol. 10.

18. For example, "Denishawn Dancers," *Musical America*, April 21, 1923, DS, vol. 11.

19. S.D., "American Dancers for the American Public," *Musical Courier*, April 5, 1923, DS, vol. 11.

20. Letter, Martha Graham to Shawn, "Monday Night" (April 23, 1923), JPA, 192 (Poindexter), "Letters from Famous People." For more on this letter, see Norton Owen and Jane Sherman, "Martha Graham & Ted Shawn," *Dance Magazine*, July 1995.

21. "Spanish Dancers Top the Palace Bill: Fascinating Members of Late 'Land of Joy' Co. in Songs and Dances," *New York Tribune*, May 14, 1918; "A Breath of Spain," *New York Times*, 1917; "'The Land of Joy' with 'L'Argentina,'" *New York Times*, November 2, 1917.

22. Carl Van Vechten, *The Music of Spain* (New York: Alfred A. Knopf, 1918), 99.

23. Van Vechten, *The Music of Spain*, 100.

24. "Denishawn Dancers Fascinate Audiences," *North American* (Philadelphia), April 8, 1923, DS vol. 11. Shawn's earlier choreographic efforts in Spanish dance included *Seguidilla* (1921), a flamenco solo that allowed him to show off his *zapateo* (or rhythmic footwork). For Graham, he choreographed another shawl dance, *Valse Aragonaise* (1921). He later choreographed *Shawl Plastique* (1922) for St. Denis, which she performed to music by Enrique Granados, wearing a white satin shawl covered in red flowers, a gift from the famous opera singer Amelita Galli-Curci.

25. Ballets Russes, Mikhail Fedorovich Larionov, and Pablo Picasso, eds. [Souvenir Program], *Théâtre de La Gaîté-Lyrique, Mai 1921*. Paris: M. de Brunoff, 1921.

26. Havelock Ellis, *The Soul of Spain* (London: Constable, 1908), 189.

27. UNPUB II, 30.

28. Letter, Shawn to St. Denis, Saturday, May 5, 1923, TSC, fol. 28 ("Third Letter from Spain").

29. Ted Shawn, "Fundmentalism in the Dance: *The Dance; Its Place in Art and Life* by Troy and Margaret Kinney," *Denishawn Magazine* 1, no. 3 (Spring 1925): 12–16.

30. Letter, Shawn to St. Denis, May 18, TSC, 31, fol. 28.

31. The quotes in this section are drawn from three related yet distinct sources, each containing unique information: Shawn's original letters to St. Denis ("Tales of Teddy the Terpsichorean Traveler"), Letters, Shawn to St. Denis, April 25–June 19, 1923, TSC, fols. 26–35; his compilation of these letters with redactions and additions for his memoir (UNPUB IV, 29–125); and the edited and published selections of the above in *Gods Who Dance* (New York: E. P. Dutton, 1929), chap. 15, "Dancing in North Africa," 178–93.

32. Floyd Gibbons, "Algeria: Where East Meets West," *Chicago Daily Tribune*, April 15, 1923.

33. Frank Edward Johnson, "Here and Now in North Africa," *National Geographic* 25, no. 1, 1–132.

34. John M. Lord, "Mariarden: A Commemorative Tribute to What May Have Been the First Outdoor Theatre in America" (Hancock, NH: Macmillan, 1990).

35. Ted Shawn, "Is Nudity Salacious?" *Theater Magazine*, November 1924, 12.

36. Shawn paid $1,200 for the score (UNPUB II, 128).

37. Shawn, *The American Ballet*, 19. In his unedited autobiography, Shawn describes a number of experiences seeing native dancing in the early days of 1925 while on tour in the Southwest with Denishawn. He mentions that "a group of Indians" came to perform for the company in Phoenix, Arizona, and that he traveled to pueblos and missions throughout New Mexico, such as Isleta Pueblo on Monday, January 12, 1925, and the San Felipe Pueblo the very next day (UNPUB II, 155–60). However, it is uncertain when he visited the Walpi Pueblo prior to 1923, when he choreographed *Feather of the Dawn*.

38. Shawn, *The American Ballet*, 18.

39. For more on the bans, see Jacqueline Shea Murphy, *The People Have Never Stopped Dancing* (Minneapolis: University of Minnesota Press, 2007), esp. 84; and Sharyn R. Udall, "The Irresistible Other: Hopi Ritual Drama and Euro-American Audiences," *Drama Review* 36, no. 2 (Summer 1992): 23–43.

40. *Interview with Ted Shawn, 1965,* conducted by John Dougherty. Sound recording, February 25, 1965, *MGZTL 4–2965, Jerome Robbins Dance Division, New York Public Library.

41. Charles W. Schoffstall, "Ted Shawn–Dance King," *Sigma Phi Epsilon Journal,* 1921: 485–86.

42. For more on the Braggiotti Denishawn School, see chapter 4 in Jody Weber's *The Evolution of Aesthetic and Expressive Dance in Boston* (Amherst, NY: Cambria Press, 2009).

43. Contracts for 1922 and 1923 in RSDP, fol. 379 and Ruth St. Denis Papers and Addenda (1904–2007), vol. 2, Huntington Library.

44. Marian Chace Scrapbook (1896–1970), Jerome Robbins Dance Division, New York Public Library.

45. The Carol Lynn Studio in Baltimore, Maryland, offered Denishawn classes and staged adaptations of Denishawn dances. After the dissolution of Denishawn, St. Denis adapted Lynn's model to franchise her own schools. She entered a contract with Jane Sels in March 30, 1934, in which Sels guaranteed a minimum of $300, $100/year for three years plus the gross income of 10 percent–25 percent on every additional $100. The agreement stipulated earnings on any and all tuition over school breaks and provided for incentives to teachers who recommended students to the main Denishawn School.

46. Shawn, *The American Ballet,* 135.

47. Hubbard eventually wrote "Getting a Start in Vaudeville" in his other publication, *FRA: Exponent of American Philosophy* 7, no. 3 (June 1911).

48. Shawn, *The American Ballet,* 43. For original passage, see Ellis, *The Dance of Life,* 46.

49. Havelock Ellis, "Introduction," *The American Ballet,* ix–xii.

50. Shawn, *The American Ballet,* 52 (*italics added*).

51. Shawn, "The History of the Art of Dancing in Four Parts: Part III," *Denishawn Magazine* 1, no. 3 (1924): 11.

52. Isadora Duncan, *My Life, Isadora Duncan* (New York: Liveright, 1955), 244.

53. "Jazz Hounds Are Mental Infants," clipping, March 20, 1923, DS, vol. 11.

54. See Edna Nahshon, ed., *From the Ghetto to the Melting Pot: Israel Zangwill's Jewish Plays: Three Playscripts* (Detroit, MI: Wayne State University Press, 2006), 211.

55. Shawn, *The American Ballet,* 51–52.

56. Shawn, *The American Ballet,* 40.

57. Adolph Bolm, "The Future of the Dance in America," *Shadowland* (April 1923): 14–15, 71.

58. "Outline and First Scenario for 'An American Ballet' in Three Acts," JPA, box 194. The scenario is six pages. The first three pages outline the three acts of the dance with sparse descriptions of their individual sections. The other three pages are written as "Notes to the Composer" and give a more detailed explanation of the dance.

59. Shawn, *The American Ballet*, 77.

60. St. Denis had performed a solo, *Spirit of the Sea*, since 1915. They adapted the solo to a group work for the second Daniel Mayer tour in 1923–24.

61. Walt Whitman, *Leaves of Grass* (Boston: Small, Maynard, [1855] 1904), 99.

62. Shawn, *The American Ballet*, 8.

63. Walt Whitman, *Leaves of Grass* (Boston: Small, Maynard, [1855] 1904), 293.

64. "Outline and First Scenario for 'An American Ballet' in Three Acts," JPA, box 194.

65. Shawn, *The American Ballet*, 14.

66. Shawn, *The American Ballet*, 45.

67. Clifford Vaughan Papers, Huntington Library.

68. The concert was produced by Sol Hurok. Theodore Stier, "Around the World with Anna Pavlova," *New York Times*, September 9, 1923.

69. Isamu Susno, "Western Classical Dancing: A Tribute to the Denishawn Dancers," *Japan Times*, September 13, 1925, Suzanne Shelton Buckley Papers on Ruth St. Denis, The Carson-Brierly Giffin Dance Library, Penrose Library, University of Denver.

70. It was Baroness Ishimoto's husband, the writer Baron Ishimoto, who ran an open letter in the *Japan Advertiser* (September 22, 1925) to welcome Denishawn to Japan.

71. St. Denis, *Ruth St. Denis: An Unfinished Life*, 273.

72. Jane Sherman, *Soaring: The Diary and Letters of a Denishawn Dancer in the Far East, 1925–1926* (Middletown, CT: Wesleyan University Press, 1976), 57.

73. "Art of the Dance Personified by Denishawn Company," *Shanghai Times*, November 18, 1925.

74. Shawn, *Gods Who Dance*, 56.

75. Shawn crossed out this information in his notes. TSP Additions, box 15, fol. 4 (Writings—Shawn, Ted—Notes, 1920s–1960s).

76. UNPUB III, 47.

77. Shawn, *Gods Who Dance*, 85. (See also, "Nautch Dancers of Old India," *Dance Magazine*, July 1926).

78. Nadia Lavrova, "What Ruth St. Denis Learned about Dancing in Orient," *San Francisco Examiner*, December 5, 1926.

79. UNPUB III, 63–64.

80. For more on St. Denis's role in the renaissance of Indian dance, see especially Uttara Asha Coorlawala, "Ruth St. Denis and India's Dance Renaissance," *Dance Chronicle* 15, no. 2 (1992):123–52.

81. Sherman, *Soaring*, 91.

82. UNPUB III, 82.

83. See Peter H. Hansen, "The Dancing Lamas of Everest: Cinema, Orientalism, and Anglo-Tibetan Relations in the 1920s," *American Historical Review* 101, no. 3 (1996): 712–47.

84. For film of their lessons, see "Ceylon, Singapore and Darjeeling dances," *MGZHB 4–275, Jerome Robbins Dance Division, New York Public Library.

85. Shawn, *The American Ballet*, 26. This striking statement inverts a related idea espoused by Havelock Ellis in *Soul of Spain*, a book Shawn had read before his 1922 trip to Spain: "A nation that is alive must needs borrow from other nations. The

process is vital and altogether beneficial so long as the borrowed elements are duly subordinated to the development of the national genius. A nation that in its anxiety to reach the level of other more prosperous peoples molds itself servilely on their ways and lets go the hold of its own traditions condemns itself to hopeless mediocrity" (p. 10).

86. Shawn, *Gods Who Dance*, 164.
87. Doris Humphrey, *Doris Humphrey: An Artist First. An Autobiography* (Middletown, CT: Wesleyan University Press, 1972), 60; Sherman, *Soaring*, 44.
88. UNPUB III, 137.
89. Baron Ishimoto, *Japan Advertiser*, September 22, 1925. Suzanne Shelton Buckley Papers on Ruth St. Denis, The Carson-Brierly Giffin Dance Library, Penrose Library, University of Denver.
90. "Journals," RSD, box 1.

Chapter 4

1. James Doering, *The Great Orchestrator: Arthur Judson and American Arts Management* (Urbana: University of Illinois Press, 2013), 2.
2. St. Denis, *Ruth St. Denis: An Unfinished Life*, 308.
3. M(ary) W(atkins), "Denishawn Dancers in Attractive Program: Performance Considered Best in New York This Season," *New York Herald Tribune*, April 5, 1927.
4. "Denishawn in Pantomime: Performance Inspired by Native Dances Seen in Orient," *New York Times*, April 5, 1927.
5. Ted Shawn, *Thirty-Three Years of American Dance (1927–1959)* (Pittsfield, MA: Eagle, 1959), 7.
6. UNPUB IV, 211.
7. St. Denis, *Ruth St. Denis: An Unfinished Life*, 309.
8. "Proposal," TSPA, box 13, fol. 1.
9. Sherman, *Soaring*, 256–57.
10. UNPUB IV, 170.
11. When they met, Beckman told Shawn he was twenty-nine, though Shawn later learned from Beckman's mother that he was born in 1898 and thus two years older than Beckman had claimed (Letter, Shawn to Katherine S. Dreier, TSPA, box 10, fol. 4).
12. *Reminiscences*, 232
13. UNPUB IV, 170.
14. Letter, St. Denis to Fred Beckman, November 28, 1927, RSDL, fol. 338.
15. St. Denis, Journal, December 8, 1927 ("Journals – Autumn 1924 – January 4, 1928"), RSD, box 2.
16. UNPUB IV, 174.
17. Shawn, Diary 661 (Monday, January 30), TSC.
18. Humphrey, *An Artist First*, 62–63.
19. St. Denis, Diary (May 5, 1935), RSD, box 25.

20. UNPUB IV, 184.

21. Letter, Shawn to Katherine S. Dreier, November 2, 1929, TSPA, box 10, fol. 4.

22. *Reminiscences*, 235.

23. Letter, St. Denis to Beckman (undated), RSDL, fol. 362.

24. Letter, St. Denis to Beckman (undated), RSDL, fol. 362.

25. Letter, St. Denis to Beckman (undated), RSDL, fol. 362.

26. Letter, St. Denis to Beckman (undated), RSDL, fol. 362.

27. St. Denis, Diary, February 16, 1929, RSD, box 2.

28. Letter, Shawn to John Dougherty, December 20, 1967, John Dougherty Papers, 1922–1988 (MS-P003), UCLA.

29. Ruth St. Denis, *Ruth St. Denis: An Unfinished Life*, 323–25.

30. Rodney Dutcher, "Coolidges Live Just Like Million of Other Small Town Folks," *States* (New Orleans, LA), April 5, 1929, DS, vol. 7.

31. Letter, Shawn to St. Denis, March 10, 1929, RSDL, fol. 166.

32. Letter, Shawn to St. Denis, March 10, 1929, RSDL, fol. 166.

33. Letter, Shawn to St. Denis, March 28, 1929, RSDL, fol. 166.

34. *Reminiscences*, 233.

35. *Reminiscences*, 239–40.

36. John Martin, "A Man's Art: Three Careers Which Have Triumphed over Old Opposition," *New York Times*, December 2, 1928.

37. John Martin, "Folk Forms: Ted Shawn in Recital," *New York Times*, April 14, 1929; the unattributed review, "Ted Shawn Welcomed in Solo Dancing: Indomitable Vitality and Prodigious Technical Equipment in Evidence," *New York Times,* April 16, 1929; John Martin, "The Dance: An Era Ends: Increased Opposition to the Romantic Domination," *New York Times*, April 28, 1929.

38. Mary F. Watkins, "Ted Shawn Scores with Old Favorites in Solo Recital," *New York Tribune*, April 16, 1929, 20.

39. John Martin, "Doris Humphrey Gives An Effective Dance," *New York Times*, April 1, 1929.

40. John Martin, "Achievement: The Unique Success of Doris Humphrey in Ensemble Building," *New York Times*, April 7, 1929.

41. James A. Pegolotti, *Deems Taylor: A Biography,* Boston: Northeastern University Press, 2003.

42. Charles D. Isaacson, *New York Telegraph*, August 10, 1929.

43. John Martin, "The Dance: Its New Approach," *New York Times*, August 11, 1929.

44. Letter, Shawn to St. Denis, May 6, 1929, RSDL, fol. 170.

45. Letter, Shawn to St. Denis, May 8, 1929, RSDL, fol. 170.

46. UNPUB IV, 186.

47. Letter, Shawn to St. Denis, Christmas 1928, RSDL, fol. 164.

48. Letter, Shawn to Dreier, November 19, 1928, KSDP, box 32, fol. 942.

49. Ruth L. Bohan, *Société Anonyme's Brooklyn Exhibition: Katherine Dreier and Modernism in America* (Ann Arbor, MI: UMI Research Press, 1982), 7.

50. Letter, Dreier to Shawn, January 25, 1929, KSD, box 32, fol. 942.

51. Robin Veder, *The Living Line: Modern Art and the Economy of Energy* (Hanover, NH: Dartmouth College Press, 2015), 231.
52. Letter, Dreier to Shawn, February 28, 1932, TSPA, box 12, fol. 2.
53. Letter, Dreier to Shawn, February 16, 1931, TSPA, box 11, fol. 3.
54. Veder, *The Living Line*, 277.
55. Shawn wrote an article, "The White Magic of the Dance," which was rejected by the *Atlantic*, TSPS, box 10, fol. 4.
56. Katherine Sophie Dreier, *Shawn, the Dancer* (New York: Société Anonyme, Museum of Modern Art, 1933).
57. Letter, Dreier to Mary E. Dreier, March 21, 1930, Mary Elisabeth Dreier Papers, 1797–1968. MC 309, fol. 254, Schlesinger Library, Radcliffe Institute, Harvard University, Cambridge, MA.
58. UNPUB IV, 238.
59. Letter, Shawn to St. Denis, March 5, 1930, RSDL, fol. 173.
60. In a 1933 letter to Shawn, Dreier wrote: "I am terribly excited about Hitler. I wonder whether I shall be as right in my prognostication as I was with Hoover. I don't know whether I mentioned it but to me he is not the Mussolini of Germany but rather the Abraham Lincoln. I wonder" (Letter, Dreier to Shawn, March 6, 1933, TSPA, box 12, fol. 1).
61. UNPUB IV, 242.
62. Letter, Shawn to St. Denis, March 27, 1930, RSDL, fol. 173.
63. Letter, Shawn to St. Denis, March 27, 1930, RSDL, fol. 173.
64. UNPUB IV, 240.
65. Letter, Shawn to St. Denis, March 27, 1930, RSDL, fol. 173.
66. Letter, Katherine S. Dreier to Mary Dreier, March 21, 1930, Mary Elisabeth Dreier Papers, 1797–1968, MC 309, fol. 254, Schlesinger Library, Radcliffe Institute, Harvard University, Cambridge, MA.
67. Letter, Katherine S. Dreier to Mary Dreier, March 21, 1930, Mary Elisabeth Dreier Papers, 1797–1968, MC 309, box 18, fol. 254, Schlesinger Library, Radcliffe Institute, Harvard University, Cambridge, MA.
68. Letter, Shawn to St. Denis, March 27, 1930, RSDL, fol. 173.
69. Letter, Shawn to St. Denis, March 27, 1930, RSDL, fol. 173.
70. Letter, Shawn to St. Denis, March 27, 1930, RSDL, fol. 173.
71. UNPUB IV, 260.
72. UNPUB IV, 251.
73. UNPUB IV, 256.
74. UNPUB IV, 258.
75. UNPUB IV, 261.
76. Letter, Shawn to St. Denis, May 11, 1930, RSDL, fol. 173.
77. Letter, Shawn to St. Denis, April 29, 1930, RSDL, fol. 173.
78. Letter, Shawn to St. Denis, April 29, 1930, RSDL, fol. 173.
79. Letter, Shawn to St. Denis, March 27, 1930, RSDL, fol. 173.
80. Letter, Shawn to St. Denis, May 11, 1930, RSDL, fol. 174.
81. Journals February 3–April 14, 1930, RSD, box 4.

82. Journals February 3–April 14, 1930, RSD, box. 4.
83. Letter, Shawn to St. Denis, June 14, 1930, RSDL, fol. 174.
84. *Reminiscences*, 242.
85. *Reminiscences*, 246.
86. UNPUB IV, 264.
87. UNPUB IV, 279.
88. *Reminiscences*, 243.
89. Journal (Sunday, September 11, [1930]) RSD, box 5 ("RSD Journal Complete and Unedited as Written").
90. Letter, Shawn to St. Denis, March 31, 1935, RSDL, fol. 182.
91. *Reminiscences*, 244.
92. *Reminiscences*, 230.
93. Barbara Bartle, "The Harlem Renaissance," in *African American Heritage in the Upper Housatonic Valley*, ed. David Levinson (Great Barrington, MA: Berkshire Publishing Group, 2006), 129.
94. "Ted Shawn's solos, no. 3, *The Divine Idiot* commentary [sound recording]" (195-?), Jerome Robbins Dance Division, New York Public Library.
95. Untitled clipping, *Providence Journal*, January 9, 1931, DS, vol. 20.
96. "Ted Shawn Proves Himself as Able a Dancer as Any European," *Chicago Herald and Examiner*, January 19, 1931, TSPA, box 11, fol. 3.
97. Untitled clipping, *Providence Journal*, January 9, 1931, DS, vol. 20.
98. Letter, Shawn to St. Denis, January 24, 1932, RSDL, fol. 176.
99. Journal (Sunday, April 19, 1931) RSD, box 5 ("RSD Journal Complete and Unedited as Written").
100. Letter, Barton Mumaw to Shawn, April 9, 1931, TSP 133, box 25, fol. 4.
101. Barton Mumaw and Jane Sherman, *Barton Mumaw, Dancer: From Denishawn to Jacob's Pillow and Beyond* (New York: Dance Horizons, 1986), 36.
102. Two years earlier, Shawn shared a more favorable portrait of the company's finances, with a payroll of $25,000, leaving a greater share of the $200,000 gross for St. Denis and Shawn. See Joseph Arnold, "Does Classical Dancing Pay? A Rebuttal," *Dance Magazine*, July 1929, 21.
103. Journal (March 20, 1932), RSD, box 5 ("Ruth St. Denis Journal, Complete and Unedited as Written").
104. St. Denis, Journal, September 5, 1931, RSD, box 5.
105. UNPUB IV, 299.
106. Shawn said $2,000 in a letter to Ruth St. Denis, August 11, 1932, RSDL, fol. 176.
107. "Devotion to Patroness Hauls Apollo of Dance into Court," *Daily News*, September 29, 1932, DS, vol. 20.
108. See letters between Katherine S. Dreier and Mrs. Mortimer L. Erle, for example, TSPA, fol. 1.
109. "Trained Athletes as Dancers," *News-Chronicle* (London), DS, vol. 24.
110. Untitled clipping, *Telegram* (Worcester, MA), November 11, 1932, DS, vol. 20.
111. "Highbrow and Lowbrow Report Shawn's Dance," *Springfield Leader*, DS, vol. 20.

112. "Criticize Shawn Stories: Some Springfieldians Consider Lowbrow Review of Dance Recital Affront to Art and Intelligence," *Springfield Leader*, February 18, 1932, DS, vol. 20.

113. "Before and After Papers, Extracts," TSP 133, box 69, fol. 27.

114. "Out-of-Town Guests for Shawn Programs," *Transcript* (Boston, MA), March 18, 1933, DS, vol. 21.

115. Margaret Lloyd, "Under the Comic Mask," *Christian Science Monitor*, April 17, 1933.

116. W. T. C. Jr. "Male Dancers Only Are on Program," *Boston Traveler*, March 21, 1933, DS, vol. 21.

117. Olive Holmes, ed., *Motion Arrested: Dance Reviews of H. T. Parker* (Middletown, CT: Wesleyan University Press: 1982), 162–64.

118. "Repertory Theatre: Ted Shawn and His Men Dancers," *Boston Globe*, March 22, 1933, in Wilbur McCormack Scrapbook (box 165.1), Jacob's Pillow Archive.

Chapter 5

1. Lucien Price Notebooks (LPN), vol. 110 (March 26, 1933), Houghton Library, Harvard University.

2. Louis M. Lyons, *Newspaper Story: One Hundred Years of the* Boston Globe (Cambridge, MA: Belknap Press, 1971), 175.

3. Lucien Price, *Sacred Legion*, v. 3 (*Lion of Charonaea*), 109. See also Michael Dunn, "Lucien Price," Unpublished Report, Personal Collection of Jonathan Ned Katz.

4. LPN, vol. 110 (March 26, 1933).

5. Letter, Lucien Price to Shawn, April 2, 1933, TSC, fol. 616. (Original in JEMC, box 9.)

6. Letter, Price to Shawn, April 19, 1933, TSC, fol. 616.

7. "90 at Shawn's See Premiere of Dance: Dance Group Interprets Music of Bach at Weekly Tea," *Berkshire Eagle*, July 30, 1933, in Wilbur McCormack Scrapbook, box 165.1, Jacob's Pillow Archive. See also "First of Ted Shawn Teas Tomorrow: Leading Male Exponent of Dance Opening His Camp in West Becket," *Berkshire Eagle*, July 13, 1933.

8. Letter, Price to Shawn, July 29, 1933, TSC, fol. 616.

9. LPN, vol. 110 (October 7, 1933).

10. LPN, vol. 110 (October 7, 1933).

11. LPN, vol. 110 (October 7, 1933).

12. LPN, vol. 110 (October 7, 1933).

13. "Mountain Farm a Studio of Dancers' Art," *Boston Sunday Globe*, October 22, 1933. Price helped to arrange the reprinting, though politely asked that Shawn remove his name from future reprints that were to appear in programs. Shawn redacted the byline so it instead read "L.P." (Letter, Price to Shawn, October 27, 1933, TSC, fol. 616.)

14. Letter, Price to Shawn, December 7, 1933, TSC, fol. 616.

15. Ted Shawn and His Men Dancers Souvenir Program, 1934–35, JPA.

16. George Kuyper, "Variety Marks Shawn Program at Hampton," *New Journal and Guide*, December 9, 1933.

17. Letters, Shawn to Price, December 3, 1933 (TSC, fol. 616) and December 24, 1933 (JEMC, box 10). Portions of the latter letter, including cited matter, was redacted from the edited correspondence.

18. Letter, Shawn to Price, December 3, 1933, TSC, fol. 616.

19. Letter, Price to Shawn, January 16, 1934, TSC, fol. 616.

20. Letter, Shawn to Price, March 31, 1934, TSC, fol. 616.

21. Letter, Price to Shawn, October 10, 1933, TSC, fol. 616.

22. Letter, Price to Shawn, April 18, 1934, TSC, fol. 616.

23. Letter, Shawn to Price, April 21, 1934, TSC, fol. 616.

24. Quoted in "Dancer au Naturel Delivers Scathing Rap at Audience," *Signal* (Middletown, OH), April 2, 1934, DS, vol. 22.

25. Letter, Price to Shawn, April 24, 1934, TSC, fol. 616.

26. Letter, Shawn to Price, February 1, 1935, TSC, fol. 617.

27. Letter, Price to Shawn, August 14, 1934, TSC, fol. 617.

28. LPN, vol. 111 (July 9, 1934).

29. LPN, vol. 112 (July 9–13, 1934).

30. LPN, vol. 112 (July 9–13, 1934).

31. LPN, vol. 112 (July 9–13, 1934).

32. LPN, vol. 112 (October 1, 1934).

33. LPN, vol. 112 (October 1, 1934).

34. LPN, vol. 112 (October 1, 1934).

35. The property, complete with an open-air studio, was previously owned by a dance teacher, Ralph McKernan, whose students included Eleanor Powell and Robert Alton.

36. LPN, vol. 114 (October 8, 1935).

37. "Kinetic Molpai Commentary" (Shawn's curtain speech, recorded July 3, 1962, in the Ted Shawn Theatre at Jacob's Pillow), *MGZTL 4-2005B, Jerome Robbins Dance Division, New York Public Library.

38. LPN, vol. 114 (October 8, 1935).

39. LPN, vol. 114 (October 8, 1935).

40. Ted Shawn, "Finale from the New World Commentary" (sound recording) 1951, *MGZTL 4–39, pt. 3, Jerome Robbins Dance Division, New York Library.

41. LPN, vol. 116 (June 17, 1936, and September 15, 1936).

42. LPN, vol. 114 (October 8, 1935).

43. LPN, vol. 114 (October 8, 1935).

44. For early yet seemingly unreliable reports on Sally Rand's arrest, see "Nude Dance Shows Ordered Closed at World's Fair," *Atlanta Constitution*, August 2, 1933; and Virginia Gardner, "Sally Rand Has Day in Court with Cops; Judge Fines Her $25 Just as a Persuade," *Chicago Daily Tribune*, August 9, 1933. See also H. I. Phillips, "The Once Over: World's Fair Nudity Trial," *Washington Post*, July 3, 1939.

45. Letter, Shawn to Gray Poole, April 2, 1960, TSC, fol. 584.

46. "A Code to Govern the Making of Motion and Talking Pictures" by the Motion Picture Producers and Distributors of America, Inc., 1934. In 1956, the articles regulating dance were entirely stricken from the code.

47. Lucien Price Audiotapes, JEMC, box 1.

48. LPN, vol. 114 (October 8, 1935).

49. Letter, Shawn to Price, January 14, 1940, TSC, fol. 75.

50. Lucien Price Audiotapes, JEMC, box 1.

51. Letter, Price to Shawn, January 3, 1935, JEMC, box 10.

52. Letter, Shawn to Price, December 24, 1933, JEMC, box 10.

53. John Martin, "The Dance: Male Artists," *New York Times*, February 11, 1934.

54. Ted Shawn, "Self-Styled 'Modern' Dancers Discussed by Ted Shawn Today," *Boston Herald*, April 23, 1936.

55. John Martin, *The Modern Dance* (New York: A.S. Barnes and Co., 1933), 3.

56. Ted Shawn, "The Influence of Germany upon the American Dance," *Boston Herald*, May 10, 1936.

57. Ted Shawn, "Self-Styled 'Modern' Dancers Discussed by Ted Shawn Today," *Boston Herald*, April 23, 1936.

58. Ted Shawn, "Shawn Refuses to Use Propaganda to Advance Cause of Communists," *Boston Herald*, May 28, 1936.

59. Shawn, "Shawn Refuses to Use Propaganda to Advance Cause of Communists," *Boston Herald*, May 28, 1936.

60. Ann Dils, "The Federal Dance Project (FDP 1936–1939)." Dance Heritage Coalition website: http://new.danceheritage.org/html/treasures/fdp_essay_dils.pdf.

61. Frederick H. Kimball, "Shawn Scoffs at W.P.A. Art Value," *Watertown Times* (New York), October 21, 1938.

62. Letter, Shawn to Price, May 2, 1936, JEMC, box 10.

63. Letter, Shawn to Price, February 24, 1936, JEMC, box 10.

64. Letter, Shawn to Price, January 20, 1935, JEMC, box 10.

65. Letter, Price to Shawn, January 20, 1935, JEMC, box 10.

66. Lucien Price Audiotapes, JEMC, box 1.

67. "All-Man Performance," *Atlantic Monthly* 158, no. 5 (November 1936): 602–6. This issue featured essays about painting and conducting, including an interview with the famous Russian conductor Serge Koussevitzky.

68. Letter, Price to Shawn, July 29, 1936, TSC, fol. 617.

69. Letter, Shawn to Price, July 31, 1936, TSC, fol. 617.

70. Letter, Shawn to Price, October 21, 1938, TSC, fol. 71.

71. R.L.F.M., "Athletics and Dancing Combined in a Performance of Shawn Group," *Columbus Citizen*, Wednesday, March 1938. In McCormack Scrapbook, JPA.

72. Ted Shawn, *Credo*, a pamphlet that shares the name with the "Credo" solo, JPA.

73. Years later, when Shawn's attitude toward modernism eased, he renamed the pair of solos "Depression and Credo."

74. Owen Burke, "Ted Shawn: A New Trend," *New Masses*, March 22, 1938, 30–32.

75. Letter, Price to Shawn, October 3, 1937, UNPUB V.

76. Letter, Shawn to Price, December 23, 1935, TSC, fol. 617. The session was in Los Angeles on December 17, 1935.
77. Ted Shawn, "Shawn Says Dance Criticism Still in Its Infancy in America," *Boston Herald*, May 21, 1936.
78. Letter, Shawn to Terry, April 10, 1936, TSC, fol. 516.
79. Walter Terry, *Ted Shawn: Father of American Dance* (New York: Dial Press, 1976), 12.
80. Letter, Shawn to Terry, January 30, 1938, TSC, fol. 516.
81. Terry, "Birth Struggle of American Dance Discussed," *Boston Herald*, October 16, 1938.
82. Walter Terry, "Present Career and Future of Martha Graham," *Boston Herald*, October 30, 1938.
83. Walter Terry, "Ted Shawn, After 25 Years, Still Is at Helm of American Dance," *Boston Herald*, March 11, 1938.
84. Letter, Price to Shawn, January 9, 1938, TSC, fol. 67.
85. Letter, Shawn to Price, April 17 (Easter Sunday), 1938, TSC, fol. 68. He also considered naming the work *The Voice Prophetic*.
86. LPN, vol. 118 (March 11, 1938).
87. LPN, vol. 118 (March 11, 1938).
88. LPN, vol. 118 (March 11, 1938).
89. Letter, Dennis Landers to Price, October 23, 1936, JEMC, box 9.
90. "Frank Overlees Interview," with Ron Honsa, August 7, 1982 (Video, Identifier 0.287), JPA.
91. LPN, vol. 118 (March 11, 1938).
92. LPN, vol. 118 (March 11, 1938).
93. LPN, vol. 119 (May 25, 1938).
94. Harry R. Burke, "Shawn Attains American Ballet," *St. Louis Daily Globe*, November 15, 1938.
95. *Dance of the Ages: Commentary*, sound recording, 1953, *MGZTL 4–44, Jerome Robbins Dance Division, New York Public Library.
96. OTONS, 263. Susan Manning has discussed the homosexual subtext in *Polonaise* in "Coding the Message," *Dance Theatre Journal* 14, no. 1 (Winter 1998): 34–37.
97. LPN, vol. 120 (September 28, 1938).
98. Michael Dunn, "Lucien Price," Unpublished Report, Personal Collection of Jonathan Ned Katz, 18.
99. LPN, vol. 120 (September 28, 1938).
100. Walter Terry, "A Great Man Dances On: Ted Shawn," *Boston Herald*, February 26, 1939, Terry Scrapbook, New York Public Library.
101. Owen Burke, "Ted Shawn: A New Trend," *New Masses*, March 22, 1938, 30–32.
102. Margaret Lloyd, "Shawn's Elemental Rhythmus Makes Its Boston Debut," *Christian Science Monitor*, March 2, 1939.
103. Letter, Shawn to Price, October 15, 1938, TSC, fol. 71.
104. Letter, Johnny Schubert to Lucien Price, September 22, 1938, JEMC, box 9.
105. Letter, Shawn to Price, April 23, 1939, TSC, fol. 71.

106. LPN, vol. 121 (June 3, 1939).

107. LPN, vol. 121 (June 3, 1939).

108. John Martin, "Visible Song," *New York Times*, August 6, 1939.

109. Lucien Price, *All Souls: The Sacred Legion, Davencliffe, Book II* (Cambridge, MA: University Press, Inc. 1955), 179.

110. Letter, Shawn to Price, September 4, 1939, TSC, fol. 74.

111. Letter, Price to Shawn, September 11, 1937, TSC, fol. 65.

112. John Martin, "The Dance: Miscellany, Shawn Group to Disband," *New York Times*, October 29, 1939.

113. UNPUB VII, 3.

114. Letter, Shawn to Dreier, October 14, 1939, KSD, box 32, fol. 947.

115. Letter, Johnny Schubert to Price, Tuesday [April or July] 25, 1939, JEMC, box 9 ("Letters to Lucien Price from Dancers, etc.").

116. John Martin, "Ted Shawn Group Opens Dance Here," *New York Times*, February 21, 1940; "Shawn Group in New Work," *New York Times*, February 22, 1940; and "Ted Shawn's Final Performance," *New York Times*, February 24, 1940.

117. Walter Terry, "Ted Shawn," *Boston Herald*, May 7, 1940 and May 8, 1940. Margaret Lloyd similarly wanted to register a final appraisal about Shawn's choreography, offering him advice for future choreographic projects, such as infusing more counterpoint, asymmetry, and abstraction. ("Men Dancers Are Cheered in Dance of the Ages," *Christian Science Monitor*, May 7, 1940).

118. Letter, Price to Shawn, May 9, 1940, TSC, fol. 76.

119. Lucien Price Audiotapes, JEMC, box 1.

120. UNPUB VII, 2.

121. Letter, Price to Shawn, February 26, 1944, JEMC, box 9 ("Price to Shawn 1963").

122. Letter, Price to Shawn, November 12, 1933, TSC, fol. 616.

123. Letter, Shawn to Price, August 2, 1962, LPN, fol. 4 (Shawn, Ted, 1891–78, Letters to Lucien Price; 1943–1963).

124. Letter, Shawn to Price, July 20, 1943, JEMC, box 9 ("Letters to Lucien Price from Dancers, etc.").

125. LPN, vol. 110 (March 26, 1933).

Chapter 6

1. Margaret Lloyd, "What Can Art Say of War?" *Christian Science Monitor*, September 9, 1939.

2. Letter, Shawn to Barton Mumaw, July 20, 1940, JPA, box 167, fol. 1.

3. The four programs featured solo concerts of Ted Shawn (August 10), Ruth St. Denis (August 17), and Barton Mumaw (August 24). The Men Dancers concert (August 31) included all members of the company except for the Delmar twins who were rehearsing for a show in New York. One notable "substitute" was Tony Charmoli, who went on to become a prominent Hollywood film and television choreographer. The concert also featured women dancers in the Denishawn number *Boston Fancy*,

including Miriam Winslow. See "Farewell of Shawn and Men Is Just That," clipping, JPS (Jacob's Pillow Dance Festival Scrapbooks), vol. 1.

4. Barton Mumaw and Jane Sherman, *Barton Mumaw, Dancer: From Denishawn to Jacob's Pillow and Beyond* (New York: Dance Horizons, 1986), 295.

5. Terry, "Barton Mumaw Makes Debut as Dance Soloist," *New York Herald Tribune*, April 17, 1941.

6. I.K. (initials only), "Mumaw Dances," *New York Sun*, April 17, 1941, DS, vol. 20.

7. John Martin, "The Dance: Barton Mumaw Gives Recital," *New York Times*, April 17, 1941.

8. Letter, Mumaw to Shawn, May 26, 1943, JPA, box 167.

9. Julia L. Foulkes, *Modern Bodies*, 138.

10. "Festival to Depict Dance in America," *New York Times*, March 11, 1942.

11. "Report of the Managing Director," November 1, 1953, Jacob's Pillow Board of Directors Records, 1941–2007, Jacob's Pillow Dance Festival Archives.

12. Ted Shawn, *How Beautiful upon the Mountain: A History of Jacob's Pillow* (Lee, MA: Jacob's Pillow Dance Festival, 1943), chapter 8.

13. Quoted in letter, Shawn to Nancy Burncoat, August 3, 1944, JPA, box 98, fol. 3.

14. Letter, Shawn to Mumaw, July 6, 1942, JPA, box 167.

15. Letter, Shawn to Mumaw, July 10, 1942, JPA, box 167.

16. John Martin, "The Dance at Jacob's Pillow," *New York Times*, July 19, 1942.

17. Letter, Shawn to Mumaw, June 10, 1942, JPA, box 167.

18. A video of the final section of the 1954 revival of *Hell on Wheels* is at the Jerome Robbins Dance Division, New York Public Library. See also Anthony Fay's "The Festival of '42" in *Dance Magazine*, July 1976.

19. Agnes de Mille, "Early Drafts and Papers," (S) *MGZMD 80, box 2, fol. 21c, 67, Jerome Robbins Dance Division, New York Public Library.

20. John Martin, "Jacob's Pillow," *New York Times*, July 19, 1942.

21. Margaret Lloyd, "Dance Festival in War Time," *Christian Science Monitor*, August 8, 1942.

22. Edwin Denby, "Dancing at Jacob's Pillow," *New York Herald Tribune*, September 12, 1943.

23. Letter, Mumaw to Shawn, August 22, 1942, JPA, box 209.

24. Letter, Mumaw to TS, June 15, 1942, JPA, box 209.

25. The concerts were held on November 3 and 4 at the Post War Department Theater No. 1. See Sgt. Jack Kreismer, "Ted Shawn, Barton Mumaw Will Give Dance Recitals Next Week," *The Keesler Field News*, October 28, 1942.

26. Letter, Mumaw to Shawn, July 2, 1942, JPA, box 205.

27. Letter, Shawn to Fern Helscher (undated), FHP, box 11, fol. 10.

28. Edwin Denby, "Dancing at the Pillow," *New York Herald Tribune*, September 12, 1943, DS, vol. 29. Denby claimed the 1943 season accrued a $3,000 deficit.

29. John Martin, "20 Dancers Seen in Gala Festival: Jacob's Pillow Group Presents First Local Program, with Ruth St. Denis as Star," *New York Times*, April 18, 1945.

30. Letter, Shawn to Mumaw, May 11, 1945, JPA, box 167.

31. Letter, Shawn to Mumaw, June 28, 1945, JPA, box 167.

32. Shawn, "Reply to Report of Edward T. Clark," July 22, 1945, Jacob's Pillow Board of Directors Records, 1941–2007, Jacob's Pillow Dance Festival Archives. Per the board meeting minutes following his death, Shawn earned $5,000 a year in his final years.

33. Letter, Shawn to Mumaw, August 20, 1945, JPA, box 167.

34. Walter Terry, "Jacob's Pillow Dance Institute Offers Festival," *New York Herald Tribune*, August 18, 1946.

35. Letter, Shawn to St. Denis, July 24, 1946, RSDL, fol. 189.

36. Shawn, "Pillow Was a Stone: Some Rocky Reminiscences," *Dance Magazine*, July 1970.

37. "Jacob's Pillow," *New Republic*, July 21, 1947, 35–36.

38. Letter, Barton Mumaw Sr. to Shawn, March 18, 1947, JPA, box 5.

39. See "The Aboriginal Ballet" by John Keith Ewers in TSP, box 65, fol. 3. See also Ewers, "Aboriginal Ballet" in *Walkabout*, December 1, 1947, 29–34; and *With the Sun on My Back* (Sydney: Angus and Robertson, 1953).

40. Mahoney appeared in Pillow concerts and also taught on the faculty as early as 1943. In a school brochure Shawn described him as "an authority on eighteenth-century dance and a faculty member at the Juilliard School."

41. Letter, Barton Mumaw to Shawn, "Friday Night after the Show" [1947], JPA, box 206, fol. 17. His given name was John Christian Ammann.

42. Letter, Barton Mumaw to Shawn, "Friday Night after the Show" [1947], JPA, box 206, fol. 17.

43. Letter, Mumaw to Shawn, Wednesday 1947, JPA, box 206, fol. 17.

44. Letter, Mumaw to Shawn, Monday 1947, JP, box 206, fol. 17.

45. Barton Mumaw and Jane Sherman, *Barton Mumaw, Dancer: From Denishawn to Jacob's Pillow and Beyond* (New York: Dance Horizons, 1986), 174–75.

46. Letter, Shawn to Alfred C. Kinsey, undated, Alfred C. Kinsey Correspondence Collection, Kinsey Institute.

47. Letter, Kinsey to Shawn, February 27, 1946, TSP, box 19, fol. 7.

48. Letter, Kinsey to Mr. and Mrs. Kamin, November 7, 1948, Alfred C. Kinsey Correspondence Collection, Kinsey Institute.

49. The shop moved to 50 W. 53rd in 1960. "Kamin Dance Bookshop Thrives in a Specialized Field," *Publishers Weekly*, April 10, 1961, 44.

50. Ted Shawn, *Sex in the Arts: A Symposium* (London: Harper & Brothers, 1932), 118.

51. Geoffrey T. Hellman, "Black Tie and Cyanide Jar," *New Yorker*, August 21, 1948, 32–33.

52. Letter, Shawn to Price, November 13, 1937, TSC, fol. 66.

53. Letter, John Christian to Alfred C. Kinsey, November 10, 1948, Alfred Kinsey Correspondence, Kinsey Institute.

54. Walter Terry, "The Anniversaries of Ted Shawn," *Dance Magazine*, November 1971.

55. Quoted in *Dance We Must*, 108. See also Ted Shawn, "ALL GOOD: Ideal of Jacob's Pillow Is a True Eclecticism Academic Precedent Inclusive Dance," *New York Times*, July 16, 1950.

56. In *Thirty-Three Years of American Dance*, Shawn wrote that he "resigned" from the Pillow, then uses the term "sabbatical" in scare quotes, suggesting that he had intended to make his time away from the festival more permanent than he had suggested at the time of his return (p. 28).

57. "Jacob's Pillow," *Life Magazine*, August 11, 1947.
58. "Jacob's Pillow Fight Brings Resignations," *Berkshire Eagle*, October 10, 1947, DS, vol. 31.
59. "Jacob's Pillow Mission Statement" (Rough Draft by Mary H. Howry), TSPA, box 4, fol. 1.
60. Shawn, "The Secret Life of a Summer Impresario," *Dance Magazine*, August 1953, 20–22.
61. Following the Pillow premiere on August 27 and 28, Shawn was in talks with the Jacksonville Historical Society to present the dance in Florida, near the first white settlement in the region.
62. *Dreams of Jacob* Commentary (sound recording) with Ted Shawn, *MGZTL 4–39, track 2, Jerome Robbins Dance Division, New York Public Library.
63. *Dreams of Jacob* was set to a score by French composer Darius Milhaud that was commissioned by the Elizabeth Sprague Coolidge Foundation of the Library of Congress, a foundation dedicated to supporting chamber music in the United States and that had previously commissioned Igor Stravinsky's *Apollon Musagète* (1928) for Adolph Bolm as well as Aaron Copland's *Appalachian Spring* (1944) for Martha Graham. Coolidge also had roots in Berkshire County, having founded South Mountain Concerts in 1918. She donated $1,500 for *Dreams of Jacob*, with $500 going to Milhaud and the remainder paid to musicians and the recording session ("Dreams of Jacob" [Coolidge, Milhaud], 1949, JPA, box 31). Coolidge provided additional financial support of the Pillow, which Shawn said at one point rescued it from shuttering. She also donated a new sound system to the theater at Jacob's Pillow.
64. In "Current Biography by Ruth St. Denis" (1963), typescript, 5, *MGYB (St. Denis) 15-6998, Jerome Robbins Dance Division, New York Public Library.
65. The ball took place at the Statler Hotel on April 17.
66. "The Dance: Jacob's Pillow Flourishing," *New York Herald Tribune*, July 31, 1949, JPS vol. 4.
67. Walter Terry, "THE DANCE WORLD: Shawn: Forty Years of Dancing Covered by Library Exhibition," *New York Herald Tribune*, July 2, 1950.
68. Shawn revived "The Mountain Whippoorwill" twice more, in 1950 and again in 1964.
69. La Meri, "Shawn's Love for a Woman of Magic," *Boston Globe*, May 21, 1972.
70. Walter Terry, "THE DANCE WORLD: Ted Shawn and Myra Kinch Provide Festival with Modern Dance Works," *New York Herald Tribune*, August 26, 1951.
71. Newsletter, February 22, 1953. The dedication was proposed by Carol Lynn at the board meeting.
72. Terry, *Ted Shawn, Father of American Dance*, 170.
73. Richard V. Happel, "Shawn Stars in Program," *Berkshire Evening Eagle*, September 3, 1955; Doris Hering, "Reviews: Myra Kinch and Company with Ted Shawn," *Dance Magazine*, February 1956; Walter Terry, "Jacob's Pillow," *New York Herald Tribune*, September 3, 1955.
74. UNPUB VII, 13.
75. The dancers were Tatiana Grantzeva from the Ballet Russe de Monte Carlo and the Metropolitan Opera company, Nicholas Polajenko ("his real name," Shawn affirms

in the press release) from the Ballets des Champs-Élysées and Roland Petit's Ballet de Paris, and Ralph McWilliams from Ballet Theatre, who also performed in modern dances.

76. Wayne C. Smith, "American Modern Dance at Connecticut College," *Republican*, August 22, 1954.

77. Letter, Weidman to John Dougherty, April 16, 1964, JDC, box 5, fol. 4.

78. Shawn, "THE DANCE: ALL GOOD: Ideal of Jacob's Pillow Is a True Eclecticism Academic Precedent Inclusive Dance," *New York Times*, July 16, 1950.

79. John Martin, "DANCE: SUMMER: Opening of Jacob's Pillow Festival—Random Items from Coast to Coast Westward More or Less Hereabouts," *New York Times*, June 30, 1957.

80. John Martin, "The Dance: In Town," *New York Times*, July 11, 1954.

81. Shawn, *Thirty-Three Years of American Dance*, 28.

82. "Shawn Refers to His Creation as the United Nations of Dance," *Transcript-Telegram*, June 30, 1962, JPS, vol. 23.

83. See Walter Terry, "The World Dances through Manhattan: Dancers of Exotic Lands Lure the Pent-Up New Yorker," *New York Herald Tribune*, May 18, 1952; and Rebecca J. Kowal, "Choreographing Interculturalism," in *The Oxford Handbook of Dance and Ethnicity*, ed. Anthony Shay and Barbara Sellers-Young (New York: Oxford University Press, 2016).

84. Shawn, *Thirty-Three Years of American Dance*, 30.

85. Margaret Lloyd, "Danish Ballet Dancers in U.S. Debut," *Christian Science Monitor*, July 16, 1955.

86. In 1954, Celtic Ballet, "the first indigenous dance company of Scotland," made its American debut at the Pillow, helmed by Margaret Morris, a dancer, educator, notator, and all-around impresario whom Shawn met during his tour to London in 1923. Shawn wrote a profile piece for the *New York Times* about Morris that celebrated her as his counterpart in terms of ingenuity in the dance world. Shawn, "The Dance: Margaret Morris," *New York Times*, July 18, 1954.

87. Walter Terry, "Dance Limon. Two Arrows," *New York Herald Tribune*, December 30, 1956. For more on Tom Two Arrows as a performing artist working with US termination-era policy in the1950s, see Shea Murphy, *The People Have Never Stopped Dancing*, esp. chap. 6, "Held in Reserve: José Limón, Tom Two Arrows, and American Indian Dance in the 1950s."

88. "NO 'SEGREGATION' LAWS IN U.S.: American Indians," *Times of India* (1861–Current), Mumbai, India, March 7, 1956.

89. George Dixon, "Washington Scene: Rep. Rooney Solves Mystery of Mr. Two Arrows." *Washington Post and Times Herald*, March 22, 1957.

90. "Exhibition on Dance to Open at Library," *New York Times*, July 8, 1957.

91. Robert Lawrence, "Dance Lush and Lean," *New York Herald Tribune*, August 16, 1942.

92. "Panther Turns Sissy in Wilds of Berkshire Hills," JPS, vol. 1.

93. For more on Jean Leon Destiné and his history on the Pillow, see Pillow Interactive by John Perpener: https://danceinteractive.jacobspillow.org/themes-essays/african-diaspora/jean-leon-destine/.

94. Letters, Beatty to Shawn (July 13, 1952), and Shawn to Beatty (July 21, 1952), JPA, box 55.

95. Letter, Beatty to Shawn (undated), JPA, box 55.

96. Letter, Shawn to Dougherty, February 15, 1964. Collection of Ted Shawn typed and autograph letters to John Dougherty, and the carbon responses of Dougherty, 1956–1971, UCLA Special Collections.

97. Aubrey Hitchins, "Creating the Negro Dance Theatre," *Dance and Dancers*, April 1956; see Zita Allen, "Blacks and Ballet," *Dance Magazine*, July 1976.

98. Gladys Lasky, "Jacob's Pillow Festival," *Dancing Times*, October 1954, 24.

99. "Dancing at the Pillow," *Our World*, 1954, 8–10, Jacob's Pillow Dance Festival, Inc., clippings, *MGZR, Jerome Robbins Dance Division, New York Public Library.

100. The company had appeared at the Pillow in 1941 as part of a summer-long residency, with a program of Fokine's *Les Sylphides* and three contemporary ballets by de Mille, Antony Tudor, and Laing.

101. Ted Shawn, "The Care and Feeding of Lions: Or the Adventures of a Regional Ballet Festival Adjudicator," *Dance Magazine*, August 1959.

102. "On Jacob's Pillow," *Time Magazine*, July 25, 1955, 67.

103. OTONS, 281.

104. Shawn, *Thirty-Three Years of American Dance*, 29.

105. Letter, Shawn to St. Denis, January 8, 1958, RSDL, fol. 196. Though Shawn would have eagerly welcomed Graham's company at the Pillow, his priority—out of necessity if not commitment—was to present emerging modern dance artists that represented the "Third Generation of American Dancers." This included many current and former dancers of Graham's company, most especially John Butler and Pearl Lang whom he presented several times. The Mississippi-raised Butler came to New York to train with Graham and Balanchine and eventually danced in Graham's company from 1943 to 1955, when he started his own company. During that time, he also successfully choreographed for television and opera. Shawn was fond of Butler's choreography but also must have also sensed a kinship with him over their shared relationship with Alfred Kinsey and invited him to perform at the Pillow. (Kinsey had also reached out to Butler and made arrangements to see his company rehearse.)

Pearl Lang from Chicago was a soloist in the Martha Graham Company between 1942 and 1952. In 1947, she became the first woman to take over Graham's leading roles. In 1952, she founded her own company and began creating her own dances, many with Jewish themes. Lang appeared several times at the Pillow (1954, 1959, and 1970) and also taught in the school. Another Graham dancer, Paul Taylor, performed at the Pillow as a dancer and then, in 1964, appeared for the first time with his company, which included the professional debut of Twyla Tharp. Merce Cunningham danced with Graham between 1939 and 1945, and presented at the Pillow in 1955 in *Septet* with Carolyn Brown, Viola Farber, and Remy Charlip, with John Cage and David Tudor at the piano. He shared the program with flamenco dancer La Marquita and Cuban ballet star Alicia Alonso.

106. Harold C. Schonberg, "Iva Kitchell, 75, Solo Dancer; Presented Parodies of Ballets [Obituary]," *New York Times*, November 21, 1983.

107. Kitchell was not the only satirist. Lotte Goslar, a protégé of Mary Wigman and Grete Palucca, performed seriocomic "dramas without words," testing boundaries of what constituted dance. Her frequent Pillow appearances began in 1954 and continued through the 1980s.

108. "Letter to the Editor," *Berkshire Eagle*, JPS, vol. 12.

109. F. Barrows Colton and Robert F. Sisson, "Mountains Top Off New England," *National Geographic* 99, no. 5 (May 1951).

110. Newsletter, 1967.

111. Newsletter, 1958.

112. Richard V. Happel, "Grace Badorek: She Keeps Things Dancing," *Berkshire Eagle*, Summer 1966, JPS, vol. 29.

113. Rosalyn Krokover, "Jacob's Pillow Marks Twenty-first Season," *Musical Courier*, August 1953, JPS, vol. 9.

114. Katherine S. Cunningham, "Christian's Progress from This World . . . to That Which Is to Come," *Berkshire Week*, JPS, vol. 40.

115. "Unfair Tax," Letter by Ted Shawn in *Berkshire Eagle*, August 14, 1953, JPS, vol. 10.

116. Newsletter, 1966.

117. Newsletter, 1971.

118. Smith, "Shawn Dance Gets Ovation from Crowd," *Springfield Union*, July 5, 1962, JPS, vol. 24.

119. "The Greatest Man I Ever Knew," *Boston Globe*, April 4, 1964.

120. Letter, Shawn to Lillian Moore, April 22, 1964, Lillian Moore Papers, fol. 426, Jerome Robbins Dance Division, New York Public Library.

121. Newsletter, 1964.

122. Ruth St. Denis, "Poems" (pamphlet) from her series "Poetic Biography," 1955, 35, Louis Horst Collection, Jerome Robbins Dance Division, New York Public Library.

123. Letter, Shawn to St. Denis, March 10, 1929, RSDL, fol. 166.

124. Edmund Penney filmed a rehearsal of *Siddhas of the Upper Air*, leaving what has become the last motion picture of "America's first couple of dance" performing together. For a brief clip of that motion picture, see *The Dancing Prophet* (produced by Mentor-St. Ives; filmed by Sven Walnum and David Harrington; and directed by Edmund Penney, 1972).

125. "Twenty-fifth Anniversary of the Ted Shawn Theatre: Lecture" (sound recording), *MGZTL 4–52, Jerome Robbins Dance Division, New York Public Library.

126. John Martin, "The Dance: Sixth Annual Capezio Award," *New York Times*, March 17, 1957.

127. "Good-bye to All of You," *Esquire*, December 1969, 159.

128. Tom Burke, "The New Homosexuality," *Esquire*, December 1969, 178.

129. Letter, Shawn to Walter Terry, December 1, 1969, TSC, fol. 544.

130. Callie Angell, *The Films of Andy Warhol* (New York: Whitney Museum of Art, 1994), 23.

131. Ted Shawn, "Is Nudity Salacious?" *Theater Magazine*, November 1924, 12.
132. Newsletter, 1967.
133. UNPUB IV, 130 and 159.
134. "Ted Shawn Speaks," Sound recording, 1961, *MGZT0 7–1411, Jerome Robbins Dance Division, New York Public Library.

Bibliography

"Afternoon of a Shawn." *New York Sun*, October 10, 1922.

Allen, Zita D. "Blacks and Ballet." *Dance Magazine*, July 1976, 65–70.

Alter, Judith B. "Ellis's Essay 'The Art of Dancing': A Reconsideration." *Dance Research Journal* 24, no. 1 (Spring 1992): 27–35.

"Ancient Races Live Again in Modern Dances: Ruth St. Denis and Ted Shawn Re-Create Peoples of the Past in Oriental Dances." *The Sun* (Baltimore, MD), October 22, 1922.

Anderson, Jack, and Tom Borek. "Jacob's Pillow Sampler, No. 2, Ted Shawn Theatre, Lee, Mass., Aug. 9 & 23, 1969." *Dance Magazine*, October 1969, 30.

Angeline, John. "Dreier the Painter." *Art in America* 94, no. 6 (June/July 2006): 101–7.

Angell, Callie. *The Films of Andy Warhol: Part II*. New York: Whitney Museum of Art, 1994.

Arnold, Joseph. "Does Classical Dancing Pay? A Rebuttal." *Dance Magazine*, July 1929, 21.

"Around the World with Anna Pavlova." *New York Times*, September 9, 1923.

"Art of the Dance Personified by Denishawn Company." *Shanghai Times*, November 18, 1925.

"Aztec Theme." *Los Angles Express*. October 5, 1920.

Ballets Russes. Souvenir Program: *Théâtre de La Gaîté-Lyrique, Mai 1921*. Paris: M. de Brunoff, 1921.

Barnes, Clive. "Men in Modern Dance." *Dance Magazine*, October 1991, 106.

Bartle, Barbara. "The Harlem Renaissance." In *African American Heritage in the Upper Housatonic Valley*, ed. David Levinson. Great Barrington, MA: Berkshire Publishing Group, 2006.

Beaumont, Cyril W. *Michel Fokine & His Ballets*. London: Dance Books, 1996.

Bénét, Stephen Vincent. *John Brown's Body, a Poem*. New York: Ltd. Editions Club, 1948.

The Berkshire Hills. Compiled and written by members of the Federal Writers' Project of the Works Progress Administration for Massachusetts; sponsored by the Berkshire Hills Conference Inc. New York: Funk & Wagnalls, 1939.

Bérubé, Allan. *Coming Out under Fire: The History of Gay Men and Women in World War Two*. New York: Free Press, 1990.

Beryl and Associates, eds. *Immorality of Modern Dances*. New York: Henry Publishing, 1904.

Bishop, Helen, "Miss Margaret Severn Tells How She Originated Mask Dance," *Boston Herald*, 1921.

Bohan, Ruth L. *The Société Anonyme's Brooklyn Exhibition: Katherine Dreier and Modernism in America*. Ann Arbor, MI: UMI Research Press, 1982.

Bolm, Adolph. "The Future of the Dance in America." *Shadowland*, April 1923, 14–15, 71.

Brady, Susan, ed. *After the Dance: Documents of Ruth St. Denis and Ted Shawn. Performing Arts Resources* 20. New York: Theatre Library Association, 1996.

"A Breath of Spain." *New York Times*, November 11, 1917.

Brown, Gilbert. "Church Service in Dance Startles Shawn Audience." *Los Angeles Record*, September 9, 1921.

Bruhm, Steven. *Reflecting Narcissus: A Queer Aesthetic*. Minneapolis: University of Minnesota Press, 2001.

Burke, Harry R. "Shawn Attains American Ballet." *St. Louis Daily Globe*, November 15, 1938.

Burke, Owen. "Ted Shawn: A New Trend." *New Masses*, March 22, 1938.

Burke, Tom. "The New Homosexuality." *Esquire*, December 1969, 178, 304.

Burt, Ramsay. *Alien Bodies: Representations of Modernity, "Race" and Nation in Early Modern Dance*. London: Routledge, 1998.

Burt, Ramsay. *The Male Dancer: Bodies, Spectacle, Sexualities*. London: Routledge, 1995.

Caffin, Caroline. *Dancing and Dancers of Today: The Modern Revival of Dancing as an Art*. New York: Dodd, Mead, 1912.

Caldwell-O'Keefe, Jennifer Riley. "Whose Nation Is It Anyway? Performing 'GI American' through World War II Soldier Shows." PhD dissertation, University of California, Santa Barbara, 2011.

Callahan, Daniel. "The Dancer from the Music: Choreomusicalities in Twentieth-Century American Modern Dance." PhD dissertation, Columbia University, 2012.

Carbonneau Levy, Suzanne. "The Russians Are Coming: Russian Dancers in the United States, 1910–1933." PhD dissertation, New York University, 1990.

Carman, Bliss. *Daughters of Dawn: A Lyrical Pageant or Series of Historic Scenes for Presentation with Music and Dancing: By Bliss Carman and Mary Perry King*. N.p.: Mitchell Kennerley, 1913.

Carman, Bliss. *The Making of Personality*. Boston: L. C. Page, 1908.

Carpenter, Edward. *Homogenic Love: An Essay*. From the collections of Sheffield Archives. [1894].

Carpenter, Edward. *Towards Democracy*. London: S. Sonnenschein, 1905.

Chauncey, George. *Gay New York: Gender, Urban Culture, and the Makings of the Gay Male World, 1890–1940*. New York: BasicBooks, 1994.

"A Code to Govern the Making of Motion and Talking Pictures." [Washington, D.C.]: Motion Picture Producers and Distributors of America, Inc., 1934.

Cohen, Barbara. "The Franchising of Denishawn." *Dance Data* 4 (1979): 2–47.

Cohen, Selma Jeanne, and Dance Perspectives Foundation, eds. *International Encyclopedia of Dance: A Project of Dance Perspectives Foundation, Inc*. New York: Oxford University Press, 1998.

Cohen-Stratyner, Barbara. "Denishawn Dances Notated for Purchase." *Performing Arts Resources* 20 (1997): 75–92.

Colton, F. Barrows, and Robert F. Sisson. "Mountains Top Off New England." *National Geographic* 49, no. 5 (May 1951).

Conner, Lynne. *Spreading the Gospel of the Modern Dance: Newspaper Dance Criticism in the United States, 1850–1934*. Pittsburgh, PA: University of Pittsburgh Press, 1997.

Coorlawala, Uttara Asha. "Ruth St. Denis and India's Dance Renaissance." *Dance Chronicle* 15, no. 2 (1992): 123–52.

Crimp, Douglas. *"Our Kind of Movie": The Films of Andy Warhol*. Cambridge, MA: MIT Press, 2012.

"The Dance." *Baltimore Sun*, January 26, 1935.

The Dance; Historic Illustrations of Dancing from 3300 B.C. to 1911 A.D. London: John Bale, Sons & Danielsson, Ltd., 1911.

"Dance Magazine Awards: Recognition of a World Community." *Dance Magazine*, August 1970, 60–62.

"Dancer Deplores Comparison of Her Art with Isadora Duncan's: Ruth St. Denis Declares Her Work Is a Real Contribution to Cause of Education." *Courier-Journal,* December 6, 1922.

De Mille, Agnes. *Martha: The Life and Work of Martha Graham.* New York: Random House, 1991.

Denby, Edwin. "Dancing at Jacob's Pillow." *New York Herald Tribune,* September 12, 1943.

"Denishawn: An Institution of National Importance." *Los Angeles Herald,* July 12, 1915.

"The Denishawns Dance." *Post Express* (Rochester, NY), November 1922.

"A Denishawn Dance Suggesting King Tut." *Journal of Lewiston,* October 18, 1923.

"Denishawn Dancers Fascinate Audiences." *North American* (Philadelphia), April 8, 1923.

"Denishawn Dancers." *Musical America,* April 21, 1923.

"Denishawn in Pantomime: Performance Inspired by Native Dances Seen in Orient." *New York Times,* April 5, 1927.

Dils, Ann. "The Federal Dance Project (FDP 1936–1939)." Dance Heritage Coalition Website: http://new.danceheritage.org/html/treasures/fdp_essay_dils.pdf.

Dixon, George. "Washington Scene: Rep. Rooney Solves Mystery of Mr. Two Arrows." *Washington Post and Times Herald,* March 22, 1957.

Dixon, Thomas. "Ivan Crozier (Ed.), *Sexual Inversion: A Critical Edition: Havelock Ellis and John Addington Symonds* (1897), Basingstoke, Palgrave Macmillan, 2008." *Medical History* 54, no. 4 (2010): 557–59.

Doering, James M. *The Great Orchestrator: Arthur Judson and American Arts Management.* Urbana: University of Illinois Press, 2013.

Domhoff, G. William. *The Bohemian Grove and Other Retreats: A Study in Ruling-Class Cohesiveness.* New York: Harper & Row, 1974.

Dougherty, John. "Ted Shawn: Father of American Dance by Walter Terry" (Book Review), *Dance News,* December 1976.

Dowling, Linda C. *Hellenism and Homosexuality in Victorian Oxford.* Ithaca, NY: Cornell University Press, 1994.

Dreier, Katherine Sophie. *Shawn, the Dancer.* New York: Société Anonyme, Museum of Modern Art, 1933.

"Dress Degrees." *Bulletin* (San Francisco, CA), April 10, 1923.

Duncan, Isadora. *My Life, Isadora Duncan.* New York: Liveright, 1955.

Dunn, Michael. "Lucien Price." Unpublished Report. Personal Collection, Jonathan Ned Katz.

Dutcher, Rodney. "Coolidges Live Just Like Millions of Other Small Town Folks." *States* (New Orleans, LA), April 5, 1929.

Eddy, Mary Baker. *Science and Health with Key to the Scriptures,* 144th ed. Boston, J. Armstrong, [1875] 1898.

Ellis, Havelock. *Affirmations.* New York: Houghton Mifflin, 1915.

Ellis, Havelock. *The Dance of Life.* Boston: Houghton Mifflin, 1923.

Ellis, Havelock. "The Philosophy of Dancing." *Atlantic Monthly* 113 (February 1914): 197–207.

Ellis, Havelock. *The Soul of Spain.* London: Constable, 1908.

Ellis, Havelock. *Studies in the Psychology of Sex,* vol. 2, 3rd. ed. Philadelphia: F.A. Davis, 1921.

Ellis, Havelock, and John Addington Symonds. *Sexual Inversion (1897): A Critical Edition.* Edited by Ivan Crozier. New York: Palgrave Macmillan, 2008.

"Elmer E. Shawn Dies in Denver." *Kansas City Star,* March 25, 1912.

"Eugenics in Love Stage Match." *San Francisco Examiner*, December 5, 1914.

Ewers, John Keith. "Aboriginal Ballet." *Walkabout*, December 1, 1947.

Ewers, John Keith. *With the Sun on My Back*. Sydney: Angus and Robertson, 1953.

"Exhibition on Dance to Open at Library." *New York Times*, July 8, 1957.

Fanger, Iris. "Ruth St. Denis and Ted Shawn—The Breakup." *Dance Magazine*, February 1976, 51–58.

Fass, Paula S. *The Damned and the Beautiful: American Youth in the 1920's*. New York: Oxford University Press, 1979.

Faulkner, T. A. *From the Ball-Room to Hell*. Chicago: Henry Publishing, 1892.

Fay, Anthony. "The Festival of '42: A History Making Summer at Jacob's Pillow." *Dance Magazine*, July 1976, 61–65.

"Festival to Depict Dance in America." *New York Times*, March 11, 1942.

"First of Ted Shawn Teas Tomorrow: Leading Male Exponent of Dance Opening His Camp in West Becket." *Berkshire Eagle*, July 13, 1933.

Fitz-Simons, Foster. "Jacob's Pillow: A Testament from the Hills, a Sonnet Sequence." Unpublished Manuscript. Ted Shawn Papers, Jerome Robbins Dance Division, New York Public Library, box 67.

Fokine, Michel, Vitale Fokine, and Anatole Chujoy. *Fokine: Memoirs of a Ballet Master*. Boston: Little, Brown, 1961.

Forrester, Izola L. *This One Mad Act; the Unknown Story of John Wilkes Booth and His Family by His Granddaughter*. Boston: Hale, Cushman & Flint, 1937.

Foster, Susan Leigh. "Closets Full of Dances: Modern Dance's Performance of Masculinity and Sexuality." In *Dancing Desires: Choreographing Sexualities On and Off the Stage*, ed. Jane C. Desmond. Madison: University of Wisconsin Press, 2001.

Foulkes, Julia L. "Dancing Is for American Men: Ted Shawn and the Intersection of Gender, Sexuality, and Nationalism in the 1930s." In *Dancing Desires: Choreographing Sexualities On and Off the Stage*, ed. Jane C. Desmond. Madison: University of Wisconsin Press, 2001.

Foulkes, Julia L. *Modern Bodies: Dance and American Modernism from Martha Graham to Alvin Ailey*. Chapel Hill: University of North Carolina Press, 2002.

Franko, Mark. *The Work of Dance: Labor, Movement, and Identity in the 1930s*. Middletown, CT: Wesleyan University Press, 2002.

Frazer, James George. *The Golden Bough; a Study in Comparative Religion*. London: Macmillan, 1890.

Garafola, Lynn. *Diaghilev's Ballets Russes*. New York: Oxford University Press, 1989.

Gardner, Virginia. "Sally Rand Has Day in Court with Cops; Judge Fines Her $25 Just as a Persuade." *Chicago Daily Tribune*, August 9, 1933.

Gibbons, Floyd. "Algeria: Where East Meets West." *Chicago Daily Tribune*, April 15, 1923.

Gillette, Aaron. *Eugenics and the Nature-Nurture Debate in the Twentieth Century*. New York: Palgrave Macmillan, 2007.

Gish, Lillian. *Lillian Gish: The Movies, Mr. Griffith, and Me*. Englewood Cliffs, NJ: Prentice-Hall, 1969.

"Good-bye to All of You." *Esquire*, December 1969, 158–162, 130.

Gordon, Rae Beth. *Dances with Darwin, 1875–1910: Vernacular Modernity in France*. Farnham, Surrey, England: Ashgate, 2009.

Gottlieb, Beatrice. "Walter Terry's 'Dance Laboratory': 1: Maria Tallchief and Ted Shawn." *Dance Observer*, December 1951, 152–53.

Gottschalk, Stephen. *The Emergence of Christian Science in American Religious Life.* Berkeley: University of California Press, 1973.

Graham, Martha. *Blood Memory.* New York: Doubleday, 1991.

Greenberg, J. A. "If You Teach Children." *Dance Magazine,* June 1930.

Grosvenor, Gilbert H. "The Land of the Best." *National Geographic* 29, no. 4 (April 1916).

Grove, Lilly. *Dancing: A Handbook for the Terpsichorean Arts in Diverse Places and Times, Savage and Civilized.* London: Longmans, Green, and Co., 1895.

Guest, Ann Hutchinson. "Ted Shawn: An Appreciation." *Dancing Times,* March 1972, 309.

Haines, Aubrey B. "Ted Shawn Proved Dancing Is a Man's Business." *Dancing Digest,* March 1957, 103–10.

Hansen, Peter H. "The Dancing Lamas of Everest: Cinema, Orientalism, and Anglo-Tibetan Relations in the 1920s." *American Historical Review* 101, no. 3 (1996): 712–47.

Happel, Richard V. "Grace Badorek: She Keeps Things Dancing." *Berkshire Eagle,* Summer 1966.

Happel, Richard V. "Ted Shawn's Home Undergoes Extensive Restoring." *Berkshire Eagle,* July 1, 1967.

Harris, Walter. *Christian Science and the Ordinary Man: A Discussion of Some of the Teachings of Mary Baker Eddy, Discoverer and Founder of Christian Science.* New York: G.P. Putnam's Sons, 1917.

Hasian, Marouf Arif Jr. *The Rhetoric of Eugenics in Anglo-American Thought.* Athens: University of Georgia Press, 1996.

Hastings, Baird. "The Denishawn Era (1914–1931)." *Dance Index* (June 1942): 225–37.

"Heard at the Stage Door." *New York,* November 2, 1919.

Hellman, Geoffrey T. "Black Tie and Cyanide Jar." *New Yorker,* August, 21, 1948, 32–33.

Hering, Doris. "Reviews: Myra Kinch and Company with Ted Shawn, Guest Artist (December 10, 1955)." *Dance Magazine,* February 1956.

Hitchins, Aubrey. "Creating the Negro Dance Theater." *Dance and Dancers,* April 1956, 12–13.

"Home Brew Dance by the Denishawns." *Genius* (Uniontown, PA), November 28, 1923.

Hope, Laurence. *The Garden of Kama and Other Love Lyrics from India.* Illustrated by Byam Shaw. London: William Heinemann, 1901; reprint, New York: John Lane Company, 1914.

"Huge Crowd at Performance at 'Sister of Moses.'" *Oakland Inquirer,* August 2, 1919.

Hubbard, Elbert. "Getting a Start in Vaudeville." *FRA: Exponent of American Philosophy* 7, no. 3 (June 1911).

Humphrey, Doris. *Doris Humphrey: An Artist First. An Autobiography.* Middletown, CT: Wesleyan University Press, 1972.

"Invasions of Ballet." *New York Times,* April 3, 1927.

Jackson, Paul. *One of the Boys: Homosexuality in the Military during World War II.* London: McGill-Queen's University Press, 2004.

"Jacob's Pillow." *Life,* August 11, 1947, 63–64.

"Jacob's Pillow." *New Republic,* July 21, 1947, 35–36.

"Jacob's Pillow Fight Brings Resignations." *Berkshire Eagle,* October 10, 1947.

Jewell, James E., ed. *The Visual Arts in Bohemia: 125 Years of Artistic Creativity in the Bohemian Club.* The Annals of the Bohemian Club, vol. 8. San Francisco: Bohemian Club, 1997.

Johnson, Frank Edward. "Here and Now in North Africa." *National Geographic* 25, no. 1 (January 1914): 1–132.

Jowitt, Deborah. *Time and the Dancing Image.* New York: W. Morrow, 1988.

"Kamin Dance Bookshop Thrives in a Specialized Field." *Publishers Weekly,* April 10, 1961, 44–45.

Keeler, O. B. "Ted Shawn." *Atlanta Journal,* December 11, 1933.

Kendall, Elizabeth. *Where She Danced: The Birth of American Art-Dance.* Berkeley: University of California Press, 1979.

Kimball, Frederick H. "Shawn Scoffs at W.P.A. Art Value." *Watertown Times* (New York), October 21, 1938.

Kimmel, Michael S. *Manhood in America: A Cultural History.* New York: Free Press, 1996.

"King Tut Will Meet Cleopatra at Ritz in Egyptian Ball." *New York American,* April 15, 1923.

Kinsey, Alfred C., Wardell B. Pomeroy, and Clyde E. Martin. *Sexual Behavior in the Human Male.* Philadelphia: W. B. Saunders, 1948.

Kirstein, Lincoln. *Dance: A Short History of Classical Theatrical Dancing.* New York: G.P. Putnam's Sons, 1935.

Koshy, Susan. "American Nationhood as Eugenic Romance." *Differences* 12, no. 1 (May 1, 2001): 50–78.

Koszarski, Richard. "Down Memory Lane with Lillian and Dorothy Gish, Billy Bitzer, George William Hill, and D.W. Griffith." *Film History* 24, no. 3 (2012): 350–53.

Kowal, Rebekah J. "Choreographing Interculturalism: International Dance Performance at the American Museum of Natural History, 1943–1952." In *The Oxford Handbook of Dance and Ethnicity,* ed. Anthony Shay and Barbara Sellers-Young. New York: Oxford University Press, 2016.

Kracauer, Siegfried. *The Mass Ornament: Weimar Essays.* Cambridge, MA: Harvard University Press, 1995.

Kreismer, Sgt. Jack. "Ted Shawn, Barton Mumaw Will Give Dance Recitals Next Week." *Keesler Field News,* October 28, 1942.

Krokover, Rosalyn. "Jacob's Pillow Marks Twenty-first Season." *Musical Courier,* August 1953.

Kuyper, George. "Variety Marks Shawn Program at Hampton." *New Journal and Guide,* December 9, 1933.

La Meri. "Shawn's Love for a Woman of Magic." *Boston Globe,* May 21, 1972.

"'The Land of Joy' with L'Argentina." *New York Times,* November 2, 1917.

Lasky, Gladys. "Jacob's Pillow Festival." *Dancing Times,* 24.

Laverty, Mary Ann. *Finding a Way Out: Charles H. Williams and the Hampton Institute Creative Dance Group.* Saarbrücken, Germany: Lambert Academic Publishing, 2012.

Lavrova, Nadia. "What Ruth St. Denis Learned about Dancing in Orient." *San Francisco Examiner,* December 5, 1926.

Lawrence, Robert. "Dance Lush and Lean." *New York Herald Tribune,* August 16, 1942.

Leddick, David. *Intimate Companions: A Triography of George Platt Lynes, Paul Cadmus, Lincoln Kirstein, and Their Circle.* New York: St. Martin's Press, 2000.

Lippincott, Louise, and Andrey Avinoff. *Andrey Avinoff: In Pursuit of Beauty.* Pittsburgh, PA: Carnegie Museum of Art, 2011.

"List to the Problem of Ruth and Ted." *Cincinnati Commercial Tribune,* August 12, 1923.

Lloyd, Margaret. "African Dances, American Plan." *Christian Science Monitor,* May 17, 1938.

Lloyd, Margaret. "Dance Festival in War Time." *Christian Science Monitor,* August 8, 1942.

Lloyd, Margaret. "Danish Ballet Dancers in U.S. Debut." *Christian Science Monitor*, July 16, 1955.

Lloyd, Margaret. "Festival: The Dancer's Holiday." *Christian Science Monitor*, September 13, 1941.

Lloyd, Margaret. "The Personal Equation: Ted Shawn's Un-Christmas Greeting." *Christian Science Monitor,* December 27, 1952.

Lloyd, Margaret. "Shawn's Elemental Rhythmus Makes Its Boston Debut." *Christian Science Monitor,* March 2, 1939.

Lloyd, Margaret. "The Summer Dance Season." *Christian Science Monitor,* June 2, 1941.

Lloyd, Margaret. "Under the Comic Mask." *Christian Science Monitor,* April 17, 1933.

Lloyd, Margaret. "What Can Art Say of War?" *Christian Science Monitor,* September 9, 1939.

Lord, John M. "Mariarden: A Commemorative Tribute to What May Have Been the First Outdoor Theatre in America." Hancock, NH: MacMillan, 1990.

"Loving Cup for Pavlowa." *New York Times,* April 26, 1922.

Lynn, Richard. *Eugenics: A Reassessment.* Westport, CT: Greenwood, 2001.

Lyon, Luke. "History of Prohibition of Photography of Southwestern Indian Ceremonies." In *Reflections: Papers on Southwestern Culture History, in Honor of Charles H. Lange,* ed. Anne V. Poore. Santa Fe: Papers of the Archaeological Society of New Mexico, 1988, 238–72.

Lyons, Louis M. *Newspaper Story: One Hundred Years of the* Boston Globe. Cambridge, MA: Belknap Press, 1971.

Lytle, H.W., and John Dillon. *From Dance Hall to White Slavery.* Chicago: Charles C. Thompson, 1912.

Macdonald, Nesta. *Diaghilev Observed by Critics in England and the United States, 1911–1929.* New York: Dance Horizons, 1975.

Macintosh, Fiona. *The Ancient Dancer in the Modern World: Responses to Greek and Roman Dance.* Oxford: Oxford University Press, 2010.

McClure, W. Raymond. *Prometheus: A Memoir of Lucien Price.* Boston, MA: University Press of Cambridge, 1965.

Magriel, Paul David. *Art and the Soldier.* Biloxi, MS: Special Service, Keesler Field, 1943.

Magriel, Paul David. *Chronicles of the American Dance.* New York: H. Holt, 1948.

Manning, Susan. "Coding the Message." *Dance Theatre Journal* 14, no. 1 (Winter 1998): 34–37.

Manning, Susan. "Looking from a Different Place: Gay Spectatorship of American Modern Dance." In *Dancing Desires: Choreographing Sexualities On and Off the Stage,* ed. Jane C. Desmond. Madison: University of Wisconsin Press, 2001.

Manning, Susan. *Modern Dance/Negro Dance: Race in Motion.* Minneapolis: University of Minnesota Press, 2004.

Martin, John. "Achievement: The Unique Success of Doris Humphrey in Ensemble Building." *New York Times,* April 7, 1929.

Martin John. "The Dance: Barton Mumaw Gives Recital." *New York Times,* April 17, 1941.

Martin, John. "The Dance: An Exhibition: Records of Two Centuries at Museum of City of New York." *New York Times,* February 15, 1942.

Martin, John. "The Dance: In Town." *New York Times,* July 11, 1954.

Martin John. "The Dance: Its New Approach to Music." *New York Times,* August 11, 1929.

Martin, John. "The Dance: Male Artists." *New York Times,* February 11, 1934.

Martin, John. "The Dance: Miscellany, Shawn Group to Disband." *New York Times*, October 29, 1939.

Martin, John. "The Dance: Sixth Annual Capezio Award." *New York Times*, March 17, 1957.

Martin, John. "The Dance: SUMMER: Opening of Jacob's Pillow Festival—Random Items from Coast to Coast Westward More or Less Hereabouts." *New York Times*, June 30, 1957.

Martin, John, "The Dance: Valued Events." *New York Times*, July 12, 1942.

Martin, John. "Doris Humphrey Gives an Effective Dance." *New York Times*, April 1, 1929.

Martin, John. "An Era Ends: Increased Opposition to the Romantic Domination." *New York Times*, April 28, 1929.

Martin, John. "Evening of Dances by Ruth St. Denis." *New York Times*, September 30, 1950.

Martin, John. "Folk Forms: Ted Shawn in Recital." *New York Times*, April 14, 1929.

Martin, John. "Jacob's Pillow." *New York Times*, July 19, 1942.

Martin, John. "A Man's Art: Three Careers Which Have Triumphed over Old Opposition." *New York Times*, December 2, 1928.

Martin, John. *The Modern Dance*. New York: A.S. Barnes and Co., 1933.

Martin, John. "100 Years of Dance Depicted in Show." *New York Times*, October 23, 1940.

Martin, John. "Revival of 'Radha' by Ruth St. Denis." *New York Times*, July 12, 1941.

Martin, John. "Shawn Group in New Work." *New York Times*, February 22, 1940.

Martin, John. "Ted Shawn Group Opens Dance Here: Male Company Starts Series of Three Recitals as Their Farewell Engagement." *New York Times*, February 21, 1940.

Martin, John. "Ted Shawn's Final Performance." *New York Times*, February 24, 1940.

Martin, John. "Ted Shawn Welcomed in Solo Dancing: Indomitable Vitality and Prodigious Technical Equipment in Evidence." *New York Times*, April 16, 1929.

Martin, John. "20 Dancers Seen in Gala Festival: Jacob's Pillow Group Presents First Local Program, with Ruth St. Denis as Star." *New York Times*, April 18, 1945.

Martin, John. "Visible Song: Eva Sikelianos Conducts Experiment with Ted Shawn." *New York Times*, August 6, 1939.

Marvin, Courtenay D. "The House That Dancing Built." *The Dance*, June 1928.

Matheson, Katherine [Katy]. "Ted Shawn and Margarete Wallmann: An American-German Dance Encounter." Unpublished paper, Jacob's Pillow Archives, July 1979.

Matheson, Katy. "The Treasures of Eustis, Florida: The Denishawn Collection." *Dance Magazine*, July 1990, 38–39.

Maynard, Olga. "In Homage to François Delsarte: 1811–1871." *Dance Magazine*, August 1971, 64–65.

Mead, Margaret. *Coming of Age in Samoa: A Psychological Study of Primitive Youth for Western Civilisation*. New York: W. Morrow, 1928.

Melnick, Ross. *American Showman: Samuel "Roxy" Rothafel and the Birth of the Entertainment Industry, 1908–1935*. New York: Columbia University Press, 2012.

"Men Dancers Are Cheered in Dance of the Ages." *Christian Science Monitor*, May 7, 1940.

Myers, Arthur. "Shawn and the Pillow: A Look Forward." *The Eagle*, July 21, 1962.

Money, Keith. *Anna Pavlova, Her Life and Art*. New York: Random House, 1982.

Moore, Lillian. "Horizons of the Royal Danish Ballet." *Dance Magazine*, September 1955, 32–33, 52, 58.

"Mordkin on Turkey Trot: Russia Won't Stand for It and He Curls His Lips in Scorn—Did It Once in San Francisco." *St. Alban's Daily Messenger* (VT), February 1, 1912, 3.

"'More in Love than Ever,' Says Dancer after Six Years of Marriage." *Boston Post*, September 12, 1920.

Mouvet, Maurice. *Maurice's Art of Dancing*. New York: G. Schirmer, 1915.

Mumaw, Barton, and Jane Sherman. *Barton Mumaw, Dancer: From Denishawn to Jacob's Pillow and Beyond*. New York: Dance Horizons, 1986. (Reprint with new foreword by David Gere, Hanover, NH: Wesleyan University Press/University Press of New England, 2000).

Myers, Arthur. "Shawn and the Pillow: A Look Forward." *The Eagle*, July 21, 1962.

Nahshon, Edna, ed. *From the Ghetto to the Melting Pot: Israel Zangwill's Jewish Plays: Three Playscripts*. Detroit, MI: Wayne State University Press, 2006.

Narodny, Ivan. *The Dance*. New York: National Society of Music, 1916.

"New Feather Dance." *Los Angeles Express*, December 10, 1919.

"90 at Shawn's See Premiere of Dance: Dance Group Interprets Music of Bach at Weekly Tea." *Berkshire Eagle*, July 30, 1933.

"NO 'SEGREGATION' LAWS IN U.S.: American Indians." *Times of India* (Mumbai), March 7, 1956.

"Nude Dance Shows Ordered Closed at World's Fair." *Atlanta Constitution*, August 2, 1933.

"Numerous Artists for 1926–27 Listed by Four Managers." *New York Herald*, May 16, 1926.

"On Jacob's Pillow." *Time Magazine*, July 25, 1955, 67.

Ordover, Nancy. *American Eugenics: Race, Queer Anatomy, and the Science of Nationalism*. Minneapolis: University of Minnesota Press, 2003.

Owen, Norton. *A Certain Place: The Jacob's Pillow Story*. Becket, MA: Jacob's Pillow Dance Festival, 2002.

Owen, Norton. "The Jacob's Pillow Archives: Creating and Nurturing an Indispensable Resource." In *Many Happy Returns: Advocacy and the Development of Archives*, ed. Larry J. Hackman and Society of American Archivists. Chicago: Society of American Archivists, 2011, 215–31.

Owen, Norton. "Ted Shawn's Moving Images." In *Envisioning Dance on Film and Video*, ed. Judy Mitoma, Elizabeth Zimmer, and Dale Ann Stieber. London: Routledge, 2013.

Owen, Norton. "The Untold Story of Jacob's Pillow." *The Gay & Lesbian Review Worldwide* 13 (November 2006): 12–14.

Owen, Norton, and Jane Sherman. "Martha Graham & Ted Shawn." *Dance Magazine*, July 1995.

"Pavlova and Mordkin, Famous Russian Dancers Appear at Denver Auditorium Friday." *Gazette-Telegraph*, November 6, 1910, 21.

"Pavlova Gives Her View on US Women." *Los Angeles Herald*, January 26, 1922.

Pegolotti, James A. *Deems Taylor: A Biography*. Boston: Northeastern University Press, 2003.

Perkins, Ray. "The Music Mart: A Discussion of Reproducing Piano Rolls as Aids in Teaching and Rehearsing—New Dance Records." *Dance Magazine*, July 1928, 41.

Perpener, John O. *African-American Concert Dance: The Harlem Renaissance and Beyond*. Urbana: University of Illinois Press, 2001.

Peters, Julie Stone. "Drama, Primitive Ritual, Ethnographic Spectacle: Genealogies of World Performance (ca. 1890–1910)." *Modern Language Quarterly* 70, no. 1 (March 2009).

Phillips, H. I. "The Once Over: World's Fair Nudity Trial." *Washington Post*, July 3, 1939.

Phillips, Victoria. "Martha Graham's Gilded Cage: *Blood Memory: An Autobiography* (1991)." *Dance Research Journal* 45, no. 2 (October 24, 2013): 63–84.

Poindexter, Betty. "Ted Shawn: His Personal Life, His Professional Career, and His Contributions to the Development of Dance in the United States of America from 1891 to 1963." PhD dissertation, Texas Women's University, 1963.

"Police Ponder Censorship for Dancing Team to Appear Here: Spurred by Isadora Duncan's Exhibition, Women of City Demand Official Supervision of Steps." *Courier-Journal* (Louisville, KY), December 2, 1922.

Pouillaude, Frédéric. *Unworking Choreography: The Notion of the Work in Dance.* New York: Oxford University Press, 2017.

Preston, Carrie J. *Learning to Kneel: Noh, Modernism, and Journeys in Teaching.* New York: Columbia University Press, 2016.

Preston, Carrie J. "Michio Ito's Shadow: Searching for the Transnational in Solo Dance." In *On Stage Alone: Soloists and the Modern Dance Canon*, ed. Claudia Gitelman and Barbara Palfy. Gainesville: University Press of Florida, 2013.

Preston, Carrie J. *Modernism's Mythic Pose: Gender, Genre, Solo Performance.* New York: Oxford University Press, 2011.

Prevots, Naima. *Dancing in the Sun: Hollywood Choreographers, 1915–1937.* Ann Arbor, MI: UMI Research Press, 1987.

Price, Lucien. *All Souls.* Boston: Printed at University Press, 1951–88.

Price, Lucien. *Immortal Youth; A Study in the Will to Create.* Boston: McGrath-Sherrill Press, 1919.

Price, Lucien. *Litany for All Souls.* Boston: Beacon Press, 1945.

Price, Lucien. "The Man Who Ate 15-Cent Lunches 'On the Road' Receives a Surprise Honor from Denmark's King: Paralyzed at 18, Ted Shawn's Dancing Has Won Him Knighthood." *Boston Globe,* August 4, 1957.

Price, Lucien. "Mountain Farm: A Studio of Dancers' Art." *Boston Sunday Globe*, October 22, 1933.

Price, Lucien. *The Sacred Legion.* Cambridge, MA: University Press, 1955.

Price, Lucien. "Ted Shawn: All-Man Performance." *Atlantic Monthly*, November 1936.

Putney, Clifford. *Muscular Christianity: Manhood and Sports in Protestant America, 1880–1920.* Cambridge, MA: Harvard University Press, 2001.

Reisner, Christian Ficthorne. *Church Publicity: The Modern Way to Compel Them to Come In.* New York: Methodist Book Concern, 1913.

"Repertory Theatre: Ted Shawn and His Men Dancers." *Daily Boston Globe*, March 22, 1933.

Richardson, Angélique. *Love and Eugenics in the Late Nineteenth Century: Rational Reproduction and the New Woman.* Oxford: Oxford University Press, 2003.

Roof, Judith. "Kinsey, Alfred C. 1894–1956." *Encyclopedia of Sex and Gender* 3, ed. Fedwa Malti-Douglas. Detroit: Thomson Gale, 2007, 837–41.

Roosevelt, Theodore. "Twisted Eugenics." *The Outlook*, 106, 30–34.

Rosen, Christine. *Preaching Eugenics: Religious Leaders and the American Eugenics Movement.* New York: Oxford University Press, 2004.

Rowbotham, Sheila. *Edward Carpenter: A Life of Liberty and Love.* New York: Verso, 2008.

"Ruth St. Denis Denies Schism." *Los Angeles Times*, April 3, 1920.

Ruyter, Nancy Lee Chalfa. *The Cultivation of Body and Mind in Nineteenth-Century American Delsartism.* Westport, CT: Greenwood Press, 1999.

Ryan, Don. "Should Men Be Graceful?" *Physical Culture*, June 1921.

St. Denis, Ruth. "The Denishawns Go Their Separate Ways—Along the Same Road." *Dance Magazine*, July 1931.

St. Denis, Ruth. "The Education of the Dancer." *Vogue*, April 1, 1917, 62–64, 134, 136.

St. Denis, Ruth. "Music Visualization." *Denishawn Magazine* 1, no. 3 (Spring 1925): 1–7.

St. Denis, Ruth. *Ruth St. Denis: An Unfinished Life; An Autobiography*. New York: Harper & Brothers, 1939; reprint Brooklyn: Dance Horizons, 1969.

St. Denis, Ruth. "THEATRE: USA: A Half-Century." *Theatre Arts* 34, no. 9 (1950): 46.

St. Denis, Ruth, and Ted Shawn. "Dancing Real Factor in Developing Strong and Virile Race of Men." *Mercury* [1915].

Sargent, John Singer, and John Esten. *John Singer Sargent: The Male Nudes*. New York: Universe, 1999.

Schlundt, Christena L. *The Professional Appearances of Ruth St. Denis & Ted Shawn: A Chronology and an Index of Dances, 1906–1932*. New York: New York Public Library, 1962.

Schlundt, Christena L. *The Professional Appearances of Ted Shawn & His Men Dancers: A Chronology and an Index of Dances, 1933–1940*. New York: New York Public Library, 1967.

Schlundt, Christena L. "Ted Shawn: His Centennial." *Ballett International* 14, no. 12 (December 1991): 27–29.

Schoepflin, Rennie B. *Christian Science on Trial: Religious Healing in America*. Baltimore/London: Johns Hopkins University Press, 2003.

Schoffstall, Charles W. "Ted Shawn—Dance King." *Sigma Phi Epsilon Journal* (1921): 485–86.

Schonberg, Harold C. "Iva Kitchell, 75, Solo Dancer; Presented Parodies of Ballets." *New York Times*, November 21, 1983.

Schulman, Jennie. "Ruth St. Denis and Ted Shawn; Museum of Natural History, October 27, 1951." *Dance Observer* (December 1951): 155–156.

S.D. "American Dancers for the American Public." *Musical Courier*, April 5, 1923.

Selden, Elizabeth. *The Dancer's Quest: Essays on the Aesthetic of the Contemporary Dance*. Berkeley: University of California Press, 1935.

"Shawn Makes Hit with Church Dance." *Enterprise*, September 16, 1921.

Shawn, Ted. "All Good: Ideal of Jacob's Pillow Is a True Eclecticism." *New York Times*, July 16, 1950.

Shawn, Ted. *The American Ballet*. New York: Henry Holt, 1926.

Shawn, Ted. "The Care and Feeding of 'Lions' or 'The Adventures of a Regional Ballet Festival Adjudicator.'" *Dance Magazine*, October 1959, 50–53.

Shawn, Ted. "The Changes I've Seen: The Basic Virtues No Longer Seem Necessary." *Dance Magazine*, June 1963, 26–27.

Shawn, Ted. "The Dance: Margaret Morris." *New York Times*, July 18, 1954.

Shawn, Ted. "The Dancer's Bible: An Appreciation of Havelock Ellis's *The Dance of Life*." *Denishawn Magazine* 1, no. 1 (1924): 12–14.

Shawn, Ted. *Dance We Must: The Peabody Lectures (1938)*. Pittsfield, MA: Eagle Printing and Binding, 1940.

Shawn, Ted. "Dancing Cures Nerves." *Physical Culture*, November 1922.

Shawn, Ted. "A Defence of the Male Dancer." *New York Dramatic Mirror*, May 13, 1916, 19.

Shawn, Ted. *Every Little Movement: A Book about François Delsarte, the Man and His Philosophy, His Science and Applied Aesthetics, the Application of This Science to the Art of the Dance, the Influence of Delsarte on American Dance.* Pittsfield, MA: Eagle, 1954; 2nd ed., rev. and enl., 1963.

Shawn, Ted. "Fundamentalism in the Dance: *The Dance; Its Place in Art and Life* by Troy and Margaret Kinney." *Denishawn Magazine* 1, no. 3 (Spring 1925): 12–16.

Shawn, Ted. *Fundamentals of Dance Education.* Girard, KS: Haldeman-Julius, 1937.

Shawn, Ted. "Germany's Contribution to the Art of the Dance." *Foreword* 18, no. 2 (November 1930).

Shawn, Ted. "Germany's Newest Genius." *Dance Magazine,* August 1930, 15, 54–55.

Shawn, Ted. *Gods Who Dance.* New York: E. P. Dutton, 1929.

Shawn, Ted. "The Greatest Man I Ever Knew." *Boston Globe,* April 4, 1964.

Shawn, Ted. "The History of the Art of Dancing in Four Parts: Part III." *Denishawn Magazine* 1, no. 3 (1924): 11.

Shawn, Ted. *How Beautiful upon the Mountain: A History of Jacob's Pillow.* Lee, MA: Jacob's Pillow Dance Festival, 1943.

Shawn, Ted. "The Influence of Germany upon the American Dance." *Boston Herald,* May 10, 1936.

Shawn, Ted. "Is Nudity Salacious?" *Theater Magazine,* November 1924, 12–14.

Shawn, Ted. "Jacob's Pillow Was a Stone: Some Rocky Reminiscences." *Dance Magazine,* July 1970, 49–61.

Shawn, Ted. "Letter to the Editor." *Variety,* February 7, 1916.

Shawn, Ted. "Masculine American Dancing." *Educational Dance,* February 1941, 2–3.

Shawn, Ted. "The Price of Pioneering: What It Costs in Effort and Money to Beat Out a New Path on the Dance Highway." *Dance Magazine,* November 1931, 24–25, 55–57.

Shawn, Ted. *Ruth St. Denis: Pioneer & Prophet; Being a History of Her Cycle of Oriental Dances.* San Francisco: Printed for J. Howell by J. H. Nash, 1920.

Shawn, Ted. "The Secret Life of a Summer Impresario." *Dance Magazine,* August 1953, 20–22.

Shawn, Ted. "Self-Styled 'Modern' Dancers Discussed by Ted Shawn Today." *Boston Herald,* April 23, 1936.

Shawn, Ted. "Sex and the Modern Art of the Dance." In *Sex in the Arts: A Symposium.* ed. John Francis McDermott. London: Harper & Brothers, 1932.

Shawn, Ted. "Shawn Refuses to Use Propaganda to Advance Cause of Communists." *Boston Herald,* May 28, 1936.

Shawn, Ted. "Shawn Says Dance Criticism Still in Its Infancy in America." *Boston Herald,* May 21, 1936.

Shawn, Ted. "The Story of Jacob's Pillow" [pamphlet]. Lee, MA, 1969.

Shawn, Ted. "Ted Shawn Wants Army of Dancers." *Daily News,* June 2, 1918.

Shawn, Ted. *Thirty-Three Years of American Dance (1927–1959).* Pittsfield, MA: Eagle, 1959.

Shawn, Ted. "Unfair Tax." *Berkshire Eagle,* August 14, 1953.

Shawn, Ted, and Ann Hutchinson Guest, eds. *Shawn's Fundamentals of Dance.* New York: Gordon and Breach, 1988.

Shawn, Ted, with Gray Poole. *One Thousand and One Night Stands.* Garden City, NY: Doubleday, 1960.

Shea Murphy, Jacqueline. *The People Have Never Stopped Dancing: Native American Modern Dance Histories.* Minneapolis: University of Minnesota Press, 2007.

Shelton, Suzanne. *Ruth St. Denis: A Biography of the Divine Dancer.* Austin: University of Texas Press, 1990; originally published 1981.

Shelton, Suzanne. "Ruth St. Denis." In *International Encyclopedia of Dance: A Project of Dance Perspectives Foundation, Inc.*, ed. Selma Jeanne Cohen and Dance Perspectives Foundation. New York: Oxford University Press, 1998.

Shepherd, William G. *Great Preachers as Seen by a Journalist*. New York: Fleming H. Revell, 1924.

Sherman, Jane. "The American Indian Imagery of Ted Shawn." *Attitude* 9, no. 1 (Winter 1993): 17–21.

Sherman, Jane. *Denishawn, the Enduring Influence*. Boston, Mass.: Twayne Publishers, 1983.

Sherman, Jane. *The Drama of Denishawn Dance*. Middletown, CT: Wesleyan University Press, 1979.

Sherman, Jane. *Soaring: The Diary and Letters of a Denishawn Dancer in the Far East, 1925–1926*. Middletown, CT: Wesleyan University Press, 1976.

Sherman, Jane, and Barton Mumaw. "How It All Began: Ted Shawn's First Modern All-Male Dance Concert." *Dance Magazine*, July 1982, 42–46.

Smith, Wayne C. "American Modern Dance at Connecticut College." *Republican*, August 22, 1954.

Smith, Wayne C. "Shawn Dance Gets Ovation from Crowd." *Springfield Union*, July 5, 1962.

Snow, K. Mitchell. "Emperadores Aztecas y Princesas Toltecas: Ted Shawn, Martha Graham y Los Albores de la Danza Moderns." *Interdanza* (Coordinacíon Nacional de Danza, México), April 2015.

Sontag, Susan. "Notes on 'Camp.'" *Partisan Review* 31, no. 4 (Fall 1964): 515–30.

"Spanish Dancers Top the Palace Bill: Fascinating Members of Late 'Land of Joy' Co. in Songs and Dances." *New York Tribune*, May 14, 1918.

Spring, Justin. *Paul Cadmus: The Male Nude*. New York: Universe, 2002.

Stebbins, Genevieve. *Delsarte System of Expression*, 2nd ed. New York: E. S. Werner, 1887.

Stewart, Virginia, ed. *Modern Dance*. New York: E. Weyhe, 1935.

"Students of Eugenics Closely Watching this Marriage: Union of the Splendidly Developed Dancer Ruth St. Denis and Edwin Shawn, 'the Handsomest Man in America,' May Produce Results of Great Value to the Science of Race Betterment." *Washington Post*, November 22, 1914.

Susno, Isamu. "Western Classical Dancing: A Tribute to the Denishawn Dancers." *Japan Times*, September 13, 1925.

Sutherland, Eugene W. "An Answer to Ted Shawn from a Dancer's Father." *Dance Magazine*, August 1963, 28–29.

"Ted Shawn Delights with Artistic Dances." *World-Herald* (Omaha), October 25, 1921.

"Ted Shawn Opens Dancing School Here." *Evening Telegram* (New York), March 6, 1922.

"Ted Shawn Proves Himself as Able a Dancer as Any European." *Chicago Herald and Examiner*, January 19, 1931.

Tenneriello, Susan. "The Divine Spaces of Metaphysical Spectacle: Ruth St. Denis and Denishawn Dance Theatre at Lewisohn Stadium, the Esoteric Model in American Performance." *Performance Research—A Journal of Performing Arts* 13, no. 3 (2008): 124–38.

Tepsic, M. Jean. "Bread and Tickets: An Historical Study of the Dance Events at Lewisohn Stadium, 1925–1945." PhD dissertation, New York University, 1994.

Terry, Walter. "The Anniversaries of Ted Shawn." *Dance Magazine*, November 1971, 26–29.

Terry, Walter. "Barton Mumaw Makes Debut as Dance Soloist." *New York Herald Tribune*, April 17, 1941.

Terry, Walter. "Birth Struggle of American Dance Discussed." *Boston Herald*, October 16, 1938.

Terry, Walter. "The Early Years at Jacob's Pillow." *Afterdark*, August 1975.

Terry, Walter. "A Great Man Dances On: Ted Shawn." *Boston Herald*, February 26, 1939.

Terry, Walter. "Jacob's Pillow Dance Institute Offers Festival." *New York Herald Tribune*, August 18, 1946.

Terry, Walter. "Leader of the Dance: Ted Shawn." *New York Scrapbook*, 1940.

Terry, Walter. *Miss Ruth: The "More Living Life" of Ruth St. Denis*. New York: Dodd, Mead, 1969.

Terry, Walter. "Present Career and Future of Martha Graham." *Boston Herald*, October 30, 1938.

Terry, Walter. "Shawn: Forty Years of Dancing Covered by Library Exhibition." *New York Herald Tribune*, July 2, 1950.

Terry, Walter. "Ted Shawn, after 25 Years, Still Is at Helm of American Dance." *Boston Herald*, March 11, 1938.

Terry, Walter. "Ted Shawn and Myra Kinch Provide Festival with Modern Dance Works." *New York Herald Tribune*, August 26, 1951.

Terry, Walter. "Ted Shawn: A New Appraisal of a Historic-Modern Dancer." *Dance Scrapbook*, August 1, 1948.

Terry, Walter. *Ted Shawn, Father of American Dance: A Biography*. New York: Dial Press, 1976.

Terry, Walter. "The World Dances through Manhattan: Dancers of Exotic Lands Lure the Pent-Up New Yorker." *New York Herald Tribune*, May 18, 1952.

Tian, Min. *Mei Lanfang and the Twentieth-Century International Stage: Chinese Theatre Placed and Displaced*. New York: Palgrave Macmillan, 2012.

"A Timeline of History—1790 to 2007." *Berkshire Eagle,"* June 15, 2007.

Todd, Arthur. "Jacob's Pillow: America's Summer Dance Capital." *Ballet Today* 3, no. 26 (August 1950): 13–17.

"Two Farces Given by the Women of St. Mark's Church—'Sunbonnets' and 'A Box of Monkeys.'" *Denver Post*, May 17, 1911.

Udall, Sharyn R. "The Irresistible Other: Hopi Ritual Drama and Euro-American Audiences." *Drama Review* 36, no. 2 (1992): 23–43.

Ussher, Bruno David. "Homer Grunn Writes Fine Music for Shawn Dance in LA." *Pacific Coast Musical Review*, October 10, 1920.

"Vamp Deluxe Is Glaum in Sex." *Los Angeles Examiner*, April 12, 1920.

Van Vechten, Carl. *The Music of Spain*. New York: Alfred A. Knopf, 1918.

Vance, Lee J. "The Evolution of Dancing." *Popular Science Monthly, 1872–1895* (October 1, 1892).

Veder, Robin. *The Living Line: Modern Art and the Economy of Energy*. Hanover, NH: Dartmouth College Press, 2015.

Watkins, Mary F. "Ted Shawn Scores with Old Favorites in Solo Recital." *New York Herald Tribune*, April 16, 1929.

[Watkins, Mary] M.W. "Denishawn Dancers in Attractive Program: Performance Considered Best in New York This Season." *New York Herald Tribune*, April 5, 1927.

Weber, Jody. *The Evolution of Aesthetic and Expressive Dance in Boston*. Amherst, NY: Cambria Press, 2009.

Weeks, Jeffrey. "Havelock Ellis and the Politics of Sex Reform." In *Socialism and the New Life: The Personal and Sexual Politics of Edward Carpenter and Havelock Ellis*, ed. Sheila Rowbotham and Jeffrey Weeks. London: Pluto, 1977.

Wentink, Andrew Mark. "Being an Idealist: Doris Humphrey's Letters Regarding Her Break with Ruth St. Denis and Ted Shawn." *Dance Magazine*, February 1976, 48–50.

Wentink, Andrew Mark. "From the Orient . . . Oceans of love, Doris: The Denishawn Tour of the Orient as Seen through the Letters of Doris Humphrey." *Dance Chronicle* 1, no. 1 (1977): 22–45.

West, Martha Ullman. "The Development of American Dance Criticism: Book review of *Spreading the Gospel of Modern Dance: Newspaper Dance Criticism in the United States, 1850–1934*, by Lynne Conner (Pittsburgh: University of Pittsburgh Press, 1997); and *First We Take Manhattan: Four American Women and the New York School of Dance Criticism*, by Diana Theodores (Amsterdam: Harwood Academic Publishers, 1996). *Dance Chronicle* 21, no. 2 (1998): 331–38.

"What We Think of Things Theatrical." *Post Express* (Rochester, NY), November 2, 1922.

"When Is Art Art?" *Chicago Herald*, October 3, 1914.

Whitehead, Alfred North. *Adventures of Ideas*. New York: Macmillan, 1933.

Whitehead, Alfred North. *Dialogues of Alfred North Whitehead, as Recorded by Lucien Price*. London: M. Reinhardt, 1954.

Whitman, Walt. *Leaves of Grass*. Boston: Small, Maynard, 1904; originally published 1855.

Whitworth, Geoffrey. *The Art of Nijinsky*. New York: McBride, Nast, 1914.

Williams, Charles H. *Cotton Needs Pickin': Characteristic Negro Folk Dances*. Norfolk, VA: Guide, 1928.

Wolff, Tamsen. *Mendel's Theatre: Heredity, Eugenics, and Early Twentieth-Century American Drama*. New York: Palgrave Macmillan, 2009.

Young, Tricia Henry. *The Killinger Collection: Costumes of Denishawn and Ted Shawn and His Men Dancers*. Tallahassee: Florida State University Department of Dance, 1999.

Yu, Arlene. "The Jerome Robbins Dance Division of The New York Public Library: A History of Innovation and Advocacy for Dance." *Dance Chronicle* 39, no. 2 (August 2016): 218–33.

Select Interviews and Sound Recordings

Badorek, Grace, and Genevieve Oswald. *Interview with Grace Badorek*. Sound recording, 1978. *MGZTCO 3–553. Jerome Robbins Dance Division, New York Public Library.

Franklin, Gerry, and Walter Terry. *Conversation with Gerry Franklin*. Sound recording, September 17, 1975. *MGZTCO 3–833. Jerome Robbins Dance Division, New York Public Library.

Horst, Louis, Ruth Lloyd, Norman Lloyd, Theodora Wiesner, and Jeanette Schlottmann. *Interview with Louis Horst*. Sound recording, 1959. *MGZMT 3–2261. Jerome Robbins Dance Division, New York Public Library.

Price, Lucien. Audiotapes, box 1, Joseph E. Marks Collection Relating to Ted Shawn and Jacob's Pillow, 1913–1979, Houghton Library, Harvard University.

Shawn, Ted. *Dance of the Ages* Commentary. Sound recording, 1953 at the Jacob's Pillow Dance Festival, in Lee, MA. *MGZTL 4–44. Jerome Robbins Dance Division, New York Public Library.

Shawn, Ted. *Dreams of Jacob* Commentary. Sound recording, 1951. *MGZTL 4–39, track 2. Jerome Robbins Dance Division, New York Public Library.

Shawn, Ted. *Finale from the New World* Commentary. Sound recording, 1951. *MGZTL 4–39. Jerome Robbins Dance Division, New York Public Library.

Shawn, Ted. *Interview with Ted Shawn*, conducted by Don McDonagh. Sound recording, September 7, 1971. *MGZTL 4–2533. Jerome Robbins Dance Division, New York Public Library.

Shawn, Ted. *Interview with Ted Shawn, 1965,* conducted by John Dougherty. Sound recording, February 25, 1965. *MGZTL 4–2965. Jerome Robbins Dance Division, New York Public Library.

Shawn, Ted. *Kinetic Molpai* Commentary. Sound recording, July 3, 1962. Shawn's curtain speech in the Ted Shawn Theatre at Jacob's Pillow. *MGZTL 4–2005B. Jerome Robbins Dance Division, New York Public Library.

Shawn, Ted. *Ted Shawn Speaks.* Sound recording, 1961. *MGZTL 4–1411. Jerome Robbins Dance Division, New York Public Library.

Shawn, Ted. *Twenty-Fifth Anniversary of the Ted Shawn Theater: Lecture.* Sound recording, 1967. *MGZTL 4–52. Jerome Robbins Dance Division, New York Public Library.

Shawn, Ted and Jess Meeker. *Music and Ballet: Interview with Ted Shawn and Jess Meeker on O, Libertad!* (1938), conducted by Irving Deakin. Sound recording, March 10, 1938. *MGZTL 4–1, no. 57. Jerome Robbins Dance Division, New York Public Library.

Index

An italicized *f* or *n* following a page number refers to a figure or an endnote respectively. "TS" refers to Ted Shawn.